NORTHWEST BEST PLACES

Restaurants, Lodgings, and Touring
in Oregon, Washington, and British Columbia

Stephanie Irving

SASQUATCH BOOKS
SEATTLE

Copyright ©1998 by Sasquatch Books
All rights reserved. No portion of this book may be reproduced or utilized in any form, or by any electronic, mechanical, or other means, without the prior written permission of the publisher.

Printed in the United States
Distributed in Canada by Raincoast Books Ltd.

Twelfth edition.

00 99 98   6 5 4 3 2

Library of Congress Catalog Card Number LC88-655110

Proofreaders: Kris Fulsaas and Miriam Bulmer
Interior design: Lynne Faulk
Cover design & interior composition: Kate Basart
Maps: Karen Schober

Special Sales
Best Places® guidebooks are available at special discounts on bulk purchases for corporate, club, or organization sales promotions, premiums, and gifts. Special editions, including personalized covers, excerpts of existing guides, and corporate imprints, can be created in large quantities for specific needs. For more information, contact your local bookseller or Special Sales, Best Places Guidebooks, 615 Second Avenue, Suite 260, Seattle, Washington 98104; (800)775-0817.

Best Places®. Reach for it first.

SASQUATCH BOOKS
615 Second Avenue, Suite 260
Seattle, WA 98104
(206)467-4300
books@sasquatchbooks.com
www.sasquatchbooks.com

CONTENTS

Introduction and Acknowledgments

It's always amusing to me when friends take me aside and ask, "Do I *really* need to buy another edition of Best Places?" as if I'll confide to them some secret truth. But the truth is that every edition is new. A number of places do indeed maintain consistency year after year, but there is always change—owners sell, chefs come and go, closings disappoint, and new openings excite. For instance, this 12th edition finds a stunning new resort on Desolation Sound, an impeccable sun-drenched bed and breakfast in Leavenworth, and a top-notch hotel in Portland where you can bring your own pooch. (Or how about that ranch in Mazama that only allows animals *over* 1,000 pounds!) As the Pacific Northwest continues to thrive and evolve, so will the list of places we recommend.

And *Northwest Best Places* is a guidebook with history and integrity: For over two decades, we've chronicled the region, monitoring the quality and range of places we'd all like to visit. Every edition, we pull no punches, accepting no advertisements, no favors, no payments. Every edition, our reviewers scour the region, ferreting out not only the good from the bad, but the best from the good. When there are only 52 weekends in a year, but tens of thousands of possible destinations, you need an inside perspective. We've narrowed down the choices for you, reasoning that more than 1,200 best places will leave you plenty of options each weekend, and then some.

That said, I'd like to thank everyone who helped me to make the final selection. There are people who think I've got the best job in the city (and, frankly, it is a pretty good one), but credit really goes to those who do the bulk of the work—my team of reviewers out there on the front line. It's a tough job but someone's got to do it. So thanks to all those someones: Angela Allen, Kim Carlson, Corbet Clark, Sheri Doyle, Susan English, Richard Fencsak, Carrie Floyd, Jan Halliday, Lauren Kessler, Nancy Leson, Gary Luke, Rosemary Neering, Kathryn Robinson, Clare Sakal, David Sarasohn, Cleve Twitchell, and Kasey Wilson.

Thanks also to fact-checkers Pat Andrews, Meg Lee, and Stephanie Viele, who vicariously traveled across the Pacific Northwest with a little help from US West; copyeditor Alice Copp Smith, who knows her food and wine; and Sasquatch Books' in-house editor Kate Rogers, who took my place when I stepped out to new horizons . . . and then somehow convinced me to continue editing *Northwest Best Places*. It's been wonderful working with the entire Sasquatch staff again, this time from the outside looking in.

—Stephanie Irving
Editor

ABOUT BEST PLACES® GUIDEBOOKS

Best Places® guidebooks, which have been published continuously since 1975, represent one of the most respected regional travel series in the country. Each guide is completely independent: no advertisers, no sponsors, no favors. Our reviewers know their territory, work incognito, and seek out the very best a region has to offer. Because we accept no free meals, accommodations, or other complimentary services, we are free to provide tough, candid reports about places that have rested too long on their laurels and to delight in new places whose efforts have paid off. We describe the true strengths, foibles, and unique characteristics of each establishment listed.

Northwest Best Places is written by and for locals, and is therefore coveted by travelers. It's written for people who live here and who enjoy exploring the region's bounty and its out-of-the-way places. Paradoxically, these very characteristics make *Northwest Best Places* ideal for tourists, too. The best places in the region are the ones that denizens favor: independently owned establishments of good value, touched with local history, run by lively individuals, and graced with natural beauty. With this latest edition of *Northwest Best Places*, travelers will find the information they need: where to go and when, what to order, which rooms to request (and which to avoid).

We're so sure you'll be satisfied with our guide, we guarantee it.

Note: Readers are advised that places listed in previous editions may have closed or changed management, or may no longer be recommended by this series. The reviews in this edition are based on information available at press time and are subject to change. The editors welcome information conveyed by users of this book, as long as they have no financial connection with the establishment concerned. A report form is provided at the end of the book, and feedback is also welcome via email: books@sasquatchbooks.com.

HOW TO USE THIS BOOK

This book is arranged by regions within Oregon, Washington, and British Columbia. All evaluations are based on numerous reports from local and traveling inspectors. Best Places® reporters do not identify themselves when they review an establishment, and they accept no free meals, accommodations, or any other services. Final judgments are made by the editors. Every place featured in this book is recommended.

Stars Restaurants and hotels are rated on a scale of zero to four stars, based on uniqueness, loyalty of local clientele, performance measured against goals, excellence of cooking, value, and professionalism of service. Reviews are listed alphabetically within each star rating.

 ★★★★ The very best in the region

  ★★★ Distinguished; many outstanding features

   ★★ Excellent; some wonderful qualities

    ★ A good place

 (no stars) Worth knowing about, if nearby

[*unrated*]   New or undergoing major changes

    ♿   Appears after listings which have wheelchair-accessible facilities

Price Range Prices are based on high-season rates (off-season, rate changes vary—call ahead). Prices throughout the British Columbia section are in Canadian dollars.

$$$ Expensive (more than $80 for dinner for two; more than $100 for lodgings for two)

$$ Moderate (between expensive and inexpensive)

$ Inexpensive (less than $30 for dinner for two; less than $70 for lodgings for two)

Email and Web site addresses With the understanding that more people are using email and the World Wide Web to access information and to plan trips, Best Places® has added email and Web site addresses of establishments, where available. Please note that the Internet is a fluid and evolving medium, and that Web sites can be "under construction" or, as with all time-sensitive information in a guidebook such as this, may no longer be valid.

Checks and credit cards Most establishments that accept checks also require a major credit card for identification. Credit cards are abbreviated in this book as follows: American Express (AE); Diners Club (DC); Discover (DIS); MasterCard (MC); Visa (V). In British Columbia there are two more cards which are often used: Enroute (E) and a Japanese credit card (JCB).

Maps and Directions Each section in this book begins with a regional map that shows the areas being covered. Throughout the book, basic directions are provided with each entry (in Canada, distances are given both in kilometers and in miles). Whenever possible, call ahead to confirm hours and location.

Bed and Breakfasts Many B&Bs have a two-night minimum-stay requirement during the peak season, and several do not welcome children. Ask about a B&B's policies before you make your reservation.

Smoking Assume a no smoking (or outdoors only) policy, but call ahead to confirm.

Pets Assume that no pets are allowed, unless otherwise specified in the review.

Index All restaurants, lodgings, city and town names are listed alphabetically at the back of the book.

Reader Reports At the end of the book is a report form. We receive hundreds of reports from readers suggesting new places or agreeing or disagreeing with our assessments. They greatly help in our evaluations. We encourage you to respond.

Money-Back Guarantee Please see page 600.

OREGON

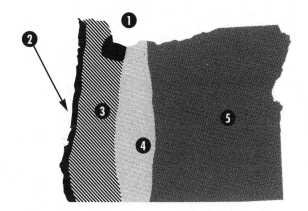

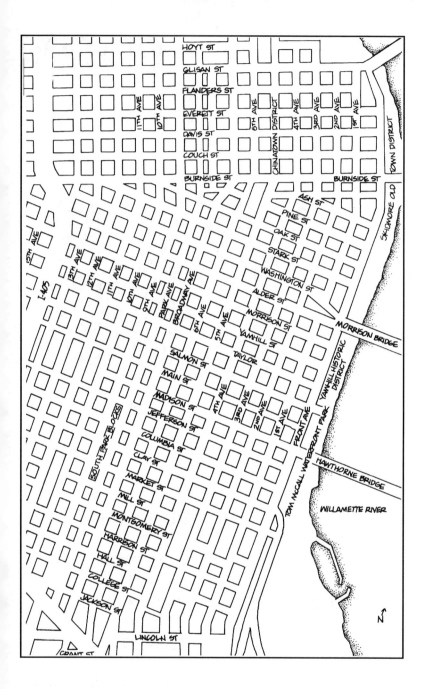

Portland and Environs

Including outlying areas: Forest Grove, Beaverton, Hillsboro, and Tigard to the west, Lake Oswego and West Linn to the south, Milwaukie to the southeast, Gresham to the east.

PORTLAND

For decades, Portlanders worked hard to make the Rose City a great place to live, and by almost every measure they've succeeded. With its plethora of parks, its charming downtown core, its splendid westside riverfront, and its proximity to so many of Oregon's finest diversions, Portland is a gem. Now the secret's out, and Portlanders are experiencing dramatic population growth. Still, there's every reason to think that this city can hold on to those ideals that have made it such a sought-after place.

It has a nationally noted light-rail service, which goes to Gresham and soon to Beaverton; a small jewel of a downtown performing arts center and an art museum within a few blocks of one another; a downtown shopping complex starring Saks Fifth Avenue; a major convention center; and stunning digs for its science museum, the Oregon Museum of Science and Industry, (503)797-OMSI. The development along on the west side of the riverfront continues apace, with construction of new housing and office buildings to the north and south of Tom McCall Waterfront Park.

Below is a glimpse of Portland (followed by reviews of its top restaurants and lodgings); for a more comprehensive city guide, see our series companion, *Portland Best Places*.

THE ARTS

Music. Portlanders pack the city's beloved Arlene Schnitzer Concert Hall, at 1000 Broadway, 52 weeks a year. A variety of performers—classical, jazz, and rock—play the "Schnitz" each season; the essential house "given" is the Oregon Symphony Orchestra, under conductor James DePreist; (503)228-1353.

Chamber Music Northwest presents a five-week-long summer festival spanning four centuries of music; (503)223-3202.

Theater. Neighboring the Schnitz is the Center for Performing Arts, which contains two performance spaces. Its full-time resident company, Portland Center Stage, (503)274-6588, began as an offshoot of the acclaimed Shakespeare festival in Ashland, but is now wholly independent. PCS offers excellent production values, whatever the play (light comedies seem to play best). You can always be assured of work by Shakespeare with productions by Tygres Heart, (503)222-9220, housed in the same facility. The Portland Repertory Theater, (503)224-4491, puts on critically acclaimed productions in a theater just off Front Street. Musicals of any caliber land at Civic Auditorium (222 SW Clay Street)—also home of the Portland Opera; (503)241-1802.

Visual Arts. Gallery walks once a month (on "First Thursdays") encourage Portlanders to visit their corner of the art world: The Portland Art Museum (1219 SW Park Avenue, (503)226-2811); and the Augen, (503)224-8182; Blue Sky and Nine, (503)225-0210; Quartersaw, (503)223-2264; Blackfish, (503)224-2634; Elizabeth Leach, (503)224-0521; Pulliam Deffenbaugh, (503)228-6665; and Laura Russo, (503)226-2754; are among the hot showcases of both local and national work. The city is popping with public art, too; just watch for it—or pick up the *Public Art: Walking Tour* booklet, free at the **Regional Arts & Culture Council** (309 SW Sixth Avenue, Suite 100; (503)823-5111) to hunt down these treasures. Pioneer Courthouse Square, off of Broadway and Yamhill Streets, is a good place to begin your search, and the stunningly renovated Central Library, on SW 10th Avenue, is a great place to end it; (503)248-5123.

Dance. The Oregon Ballet Theater enlists youth and daring to serve the needs of Portland's ballet fans; (503)227-6867.

Literature. Powell's, the superpower of bookstores (1005 W Burnside, (800)878-7323 out-of-state or (503)228-4651 in-state), presides over literary Portland. It and many other excellent local bookstores, as well as local churches and colleges, present readings by local and visiting writers. Literary Arts produces a series of lectures by nationally known literary figures—the Portland Arts and Lectures Series—and although tickets are scarce, you might get lucky; (503)227-2583.

OTHER THINGS TO DO

Nightlife. Check local newspapers' calendar listings for what's happening in the jazz world *(Willamette Week* is out each Wednesday; the *Oregonian*'s entertainment section is in Friday's paper). One gig you can depend on is at the Portland Art Museum: its After Hours programs on Wednesdays at 5:30pm are still going strong after a decade (see phone in Visual Arts). Rock fans get their licks at Berbati's Pan or LaLuna, while folkies hang at the Aladdin. If you feel like dancing, head to the refurbished Crystal Ballroom on West Burnside, where the music—from reggae to ballroom—starts at 9.

Sports. The town's big-league action can be found at the shiny new Rose Garden Arena, home of the Portland Trail Blazers men's basketball team. The Trail Blazers usually manage to make the playoffs, although they haven't won the championship since 1977; call Ticketmaster, (503)224-4400. Portland also has one of nine professional women's teams in the new American

Basketball League: the Portland Power went 15-25 in their first season (the wins came after a coaching switch midseason); call Ticketmaster. The Portland Winter Hawks, a member of the Western Hockey League, hit the ice 36 times a season at home; for tickets, call Ticketmaster. Individual sports thrive in the region: runners have access to over 50 manicured miles of trail in the 5,000-acre Forest Park, (503)823-4492; rowers are guaranteed miles of flat water on the Willamette; and bicyclists use more than 100 miles of off-street paved bike paths in the greater Portland area.

Parks and Gardens. Besides the sprawling and primitive Forest Park (see phone in Sports), there are nearly 150 other parks in the city. The Hoyt Arboretum, close to the Washington Park Zoo, has an impressive collection of native and exotic flora, as well as the best-kept trails; (503)228-8733. More formalized grounds are the International Rose Test Garden, (503)823-3636; the Japanese Garden, (503)223-1321; and, across town, the Crystal Springs Rhododendron Garden, (503)823-3640. Also in Washington Park is the largest memorial of its kind in the nation, the Vietnam Veterans' Living Memorial, an inspiring outdoor cathedral commemorating the Oregon victims of that conflict.

Shopping. Crafts can be found weekends at Saturday Market under the Burnside Bridge; upscale specialty shops and eateries are found at Pioneer Place, the Water Tower at John's Landing, and Lloyd Center—or at suburban malls Clackamas Town Center and Washington Square. Northwest Portland's 23rd Avenue and SE Hawthorne Boulevard between 20th and 45th feature great neighborhood merchants; NE Broadway and Multnomah (in southwest Portland) are also bright spots in the neighborhood shopping scene. Antiques are found in Sellwood, in the city's southeast corner.

Transportation. The city's public transportation system, Tri-Met, runs throughout the metropolitan area and is free in the downtown core area; (503)238-7433. The light-rail system, MAX, is a speedy conduit east to Gresham now, and in late 1998 will go west to Beaverton as well; (call Tri-Met). Amtrak heads north, south, and east from the handsome Union Station; (800)872-7245. The airport (PDX) is a $25 cab ride (or pay less than half that for airport shuttle buses from major downtown hotels); (503)335-1234. Parking meters must be fed even on Saturdays in Portland. For the best parking deals downtown, look to the Smart Park garages (75 cents an hour/$3 max on weekends).

RESTAURANTS

Genoa ★★★★ For 25 years, the elaborate, minuetlike seven-course meals (with a fewer-course option on weekdays) at Genoa have provided Portland with special interludes of elegance and artistry—and they seem to be getting even better. Cathy Whims, the current chef and co-owner, has been enlivening the kitchen with newer Italian inspirations, without losing the distinctive Genoa grace notes.

The pasta course can still stop you in your tracks. Changing constantly, like the rest of the menu, it might be ravioli di zucca, thin sheets enfolding squash, sweet potato, and biscotti crumbs. Preceded by an antipasto that might include marinated goat cheese and exquisite crostini, the pasta course is followed by the set entree of the evening, which might be Muscovy duck with honey and grapes, something deft with fish, or a successful effort to make a steak more interesting—and Italian. That just gets you to a powerhouse dessert tray, with a double-digit range of choices from homemade pear ice cream with caramel to a creation that mixes fruit and chocolate into a result as intricate as a palazzo.

The remarkable part is that the extravagant meal and the three hours still pass leaving one seduced rather than overwhelmed. The famously dark dining room has lightened a bit, and the full experience is now balanced with a shorter option, offered on weekdays and early and late on weekends. Not every course will be spectacular, but a couple will certainly be, and the rest will be very good. Knowledgeable staff carefully describe the food and know the wine list. ■ *2832 SE Belmont St (NE 29th and Belmont), Portland; (503) 238-1464; $$$; beer, wine, and aperitifs; AE, DC, MC, V; checks OK; dinner Mon–Sat.* &

The Heathman Restaurant and Bar ★★★★ There's only one place in Portland—and perhaps not a lot of places anywhere— where you could start with a napoleon of grilled apple and St. André cheese and move on to roast suckling pig. Philippe Boulot, brought to the Heathman from Paris's three-star Jamin restaurant by way of The Mark Hotel in New York, has brilliantly put his own mark on the hotel's restaurant, with the collaboration of his wife, Susan, Portlander and pâtissier. (Entrees and appetizers come and go, driven by the seasons and Philippe's inspirations, but Susan's warm chocolate gourmandise cake endures—joined, in season, by fresh berry napoleons.) Boulot doesn't exactly merge classic French cuisine with Pacific Northwest trends; rather, he expands the classics to absorb local ingredients, producing, maybe, a pasta tossed with Pacific prawns and buttery nuggets of foie gras or a stunning salmon in a pesto crust with a shard of crisp salmon skin planted on top—although he might treat the salmon to a Thai barbecue. Boulot has been creating new wine events for the Heathman, and diving deep into local produce—surfacing with fiddlehead ferns, organic baby greens and radishes, or a tart dried-cherry jus for a roasted pheasant. The king salmon hash prevails at breakfast, and lunch produces its own creations, including rich soups, pungent salads, and heartening stews. Evenings bring jazz, and brandy from upstairs and downstairs bars. ■ *1009 SW Broad-*

way (Salmon and SW Broadway), Portland; (503) 241-4100; www.holog.com/heathman; $$$; full bar; AE, DC, MC, V; checks OK; breakfast, lunch, dinner every day. &

Zefiro ★★★★ After starting—and dazzling—with a Mediterranean menu, the restaurant that many consider Portland's most exciting has been migrating steadily toward Asia. Chef/proprietor Chris Israel, after his own Asian interludes, has brought back Eastern inspirations—although the creativity is still all his, with nightly offerings ranging from a Vietnamese quail salad to clams sautéed in black bean sauce. But the menu never forgets its Riviera roots; diners may still encounter an intense Tuscan beef stew, a Moroccan lamb mixed grill, or a vibrant Spanish seafood-and-squid-ink risotto. Signature dishes include a crisp, perfect Caesar salad for two—crunchy canoes of romaine. Desserts never disappoint. The food is set off by one of the city's liveliest atmospheres, and the feeling that there might be someone rather famous at the next table. Zefiro's bar area (a good bet if you arrive without a reservation) is prime territory for scoping out Portlanders, and also for cool and trendy martinis. (In a different direction, the atmosphere is now balanced by Zefiro's own ice-cream parlor, the hazelnut-gelati-toned Zero's, next door.) Zefiro's has even managed to do something about the noise level, but its buzz is louder than ever. ■ *500 NW 21st (corner of Glisan), Portland; (503) 226-3394; zefiro@teleport.com; $$$; full bar; AE, DC, MC, V; local checks only; lunch Mon–Fri, dinner Mon–Sat.* &

Atwater's ★★★ Taking over Portland's showcase restaurant—30 floors up and looking Mount Hood in the eye—Bay Area chef Joe Nouhan has kept the emphasis on local ingredients and pumped them into a spirited continental-inspired menu. It switches around seasonally, and each month Nouhan offers a lively regional four-course prix-fixe dinner, which might hail from Paris or Morocco or the American South. The menus cover a lot of ground, but Nouhan has the range to follow them, from a deep bouillabaisse to juicy, pungent herb-crusted lamb. The flavors of Northwest fruits explode in Deborah Putnam's American-themed desserts; peach shortcake is a terrific argument for summer, and pecan sweet potato tart seems like a natural for fall. Because Nouhan's arrival is relatively recent, his range of possibilities is as wide as the view; cooking classes and wine dinners are already more visible. More casual—but hardly pedestrian—options are available in the glossy bar, with live jazz on weekends. Either menu offers access to the literally voluminous wine list, in the huge, etched-glass wine cellar in the middle of the dining room. ■ *111 SW 5th Ave (off W Burnside), Portland; (503) 275-3600; $$$; full bar; AE, DC, MC, V; no checks; dinner every day.* &

Avalon Grill ★★★ Since its splashy, flashy opening three years ago, the Avalon, with its dramatic, angular design and dazzling riverside location, has been rising like the Willamette in winter. Chef Matthew Lasof seems steadily more surefooted, matching signature dishes, such as spicy crab cakes or goat cheese ravioli with walnuts and crabmeat, with lively innovations such as beef and veal tenderloins with truffles and red wine sauce. He can still go occasionally overboard—a smoked salmon and fried oyster napoleon?—but the average level is high, and rising. Up in the high-tech, postmodern bar, one of Portland's more animated places to be seen, there's live jazz, cigars, and 25 different wines by the glass. ■ *4630 SW Macadam Ave (near Johns Landing), Portland; (503) 227-4630; $$; full bar; AE, DC, MC, V; checks OK; lunch Mon–Fri, dinner every day, brunch Sun.* ᧒

Briggs and Crampton's Table for Two ★★★ It's been years now since the meal that defines "intimate"—one table, one seating, one lunch—burst into the *Wall Street Journal* and *People* magazine. And still, at 8:30am sharp on the first business day of the quarter, people leap for their phones to try to snag a day in the following quarter. (Be quick; you can linger at the table, but not on the phone.) For $75, not counting wine or tip, a couple gets a four-course lunch designed to order: the week before, you send over a list of what you like, what you can't stand, what makes you break out. Then you show up, and encounter something like halibut steaks with a red pepper salsa or roasted rack of lamb in a saffron-tomato demiglace, and an orange mascarpone torte. And you linger; people have been known to make lunch last until dinner. The intricate presentation of each course dazzles, as do the pretty china and the intimate setting. ■ *1902 NW 24th Ave (near Montgomery Park between Thurman and Vaughn), Portland; (503) 223-8690; $$$; beer and wine; MC, V; checks OK; lunch Tues–Fri (by appointment only).*

Cafe des Amis ★★★ Dennis Baker knows exactly what he's doing, and a generation of diners know exactly what they want him to do. Baker's specialties have become landmarks: delicate, briny Dungeness crab cakes; rich, intense soups ranging from cream of mussel to carrot with a hint of lemongrass and wasabi; a buttery, 2-inch-thick filet of beef in a port and garlic sauce; cobblers and fruit tarts that look like they've just been glazed in a Boulevard St. Germain pâtisserie. Of course, you might just skip the entree and make a light, satisfying meal of soup and salad and some pâté. But before you do, at least consider the moist salmon, or the duck in blackberry sauce. For true bistro status, this cozy, intimate cafe tucked onto a northwest Portland residential street would need only outdoor tables—and a climate change that not even Baker could cook up. ■ *1987 NW Kearney St (corner of 20th), Portland; (503) 295-6487; $$; full bar; AE, MC, V; checks OK; dinner Mon–Sat.* ᧒

Couvron ★★★ This tiny, elaborate restaurant is named after hostess Maura Demes's French hometown, but it could also be called the "Oklahoma" restaurant—each dish is as high as an elephant's eye. Chef Tony Demes, adding another dimension to presentation, stacks up his dishes into napoleons or small hillocks, and sends stalks or sprays of herbs towering up from them. It takes a lot of cooking skill to match this architecture, and Demes tends to be equal to the challenge: roasting monkfish or rabbit, or constructing condominums of beef and garlic potatoes, or scallops and herb ravioli. Desserts include soufflés, tarte Tatin, and chocolate arrangements with the complexity of a microchip. You can also waive all decisions by going for the six-course tasting menu, for $45, but even with the regular menu, you won't have any problem filling up your evening. The dining rooms may feel a bit small and crowded, but the location is striking—Couvron is directly on the new Westside light-rail line. It deserves its own station. ■ *1126 SW 18th Ave (2 blocks from Civic Stadium), Portland; (503)225-1844; $$$; beer and wine; AE, MC, V; local checks only; dinner Tues–Sat.*

Esparza's Tex-Mex Cafe ★★★ This rollicking down-home hangout is no longer just the best Tex-Mex restaurant in Portland—with loads of atmosphere, from The King on the jukebox to the marionettes dancing over the bar to nifty posters for Gene Autry Westerns in the back room. It's now, according to the neon sign on the bar, also the "Esparza's Tequila Shrine," with a wide array of curiously shaped bottles. This way, you can decide just which tequila goes with the Cowboy Tacos, filled with thick slabs of smoked sirloin, barbecue sauce, guacamole, and pico de gallo, or the Uvalde, a smoked lamb enchilada, or some nopalitos—the best cactus appetizer around. The menu and specials have the reach of Texas—from red snapper to smoked pork loin stuffed with spiced buffalo and ostrich to calves'-brains tacos. It's all hand-smoked and hand-designed by Joe Esparza—who, perched at the bar, keeps as watchful an eye on the food as he does on the proceedings. ■ *2725 SE Ankeny St (1 block south of E Burnside, on the corner of SE 28th and Ankeny), Portland; (503)234-7909; $$; full bar; AE, MC, V; no checks; lunch, dinner Tues–Sat.*

Fiddleheads ★★★ Fernando Divina's vision of Western regional cuisine runs deep; it runs to a memory that there was a regional cuisine before anybody called it the West. That can mean Shoshone corn dumplings or Zuni-style succotash and fry bread, but it also means a dazzlingly skilled hand with all kinds of local fare, from a vibrant chowder of Dungeness, steelhead, and crawfish to a huckleberry sorbet that seems just off the mountain. Divina's vision of the West reaches down to masa-fried oyster tacos and posole, and he offers inspiring five-course special vegetarian dinners. In Portland's laid-back (but rapidly gentrifying) Westmoreland neighborhood, Fiddleheads may be the most exciting of Portland's newer restaurants, in a compact but elegant space adorned with Northwest Indian art. And just so you don't have to ask, "tatonka" means buffalo—braised with woodland mushrooms, mild chiles, and wild boar bacon. ■ *6716 SE Milwaukie (in Westmoreland, near corner of Bybee), Portland; (503)233-1547; $$; full bar; AE, MC, V; checks OK; lunch Mon–Fri, dinner every day, brunch Sat–Sun.* &

Higgins ★★★ When he first headed a few blocks south from the Heathman Hotel, where he'd been a pioneer of Pacific Northwest cuisine, chef Greg Higgins's dishes sometimes seemed to have a few extra ingredients thrown in without thought. But Higgins—the chef and the restaurant—is now increasingly sure-handed and consistent. That means a deeply, deftly seasonal Northwest menu, strong on local meats, poultry, and especially seafood—perhaps a saffron bourride of regional shellfish, or a delicate special of grilled Columbia sturgeon in a fish stock laced with anchovy. (This restaurant has a particular allure for people who like their fish cooked gently.) Spectacular presentation endures, especially in desserts, which might be a roasted pear in filo or a chocolate-almond-apricot tart. Thinner wallets will appreciate Higgins's bar next door, which serves bistro fare after 2pm every day—and opens for cigars after 10pm. This may be the only fine restaurant in the city that goes out of its way to welcome young children. ■ *1239 SW Broadway (corner of SW Jefferson), Portland; (503)222-9070; $$$; full bar; AE, DC, MC, V; checks OK; lunch Mon–Fri, dinner every day.* &

L'Auberge ★★★ This warm, three-level, dual-personality establishment has always been among Portland's most notable restaurants. Now, French-born chef Nicolas Adam is making L'Auberge une auberge, with a menu nearly as French as its name. Actually, he's producing several menus—a four-course fixed-price special; à la carte offerings, with wider latitude; a French provincial special, drawn each month from a different province; and the more laid-back but never laid-off bar menu. This allows for skipping around from the trademark L'Auberge chicken, veal, and spinach pâté to a rich Les Halles onion soup to a monkfish pot au feu, or to more elaborately presented marinated quails in a crisp crêpe or a sautéed duck breast with rhubarb chutney ravioli. Just be sure to end up with the desserts, from the classic lemon cheesecake to something more intricate and Parisian.

Up a few steps from the relaxed, restrained elegance of the dining room, the bar is a softly lit den of upscale hipness with a well-stoked hearth in winter and, in all seasons, a witty, personable staff. Instead of the onion soup, the muscular bar menu, and the desserts, you could just get some cheese and brandy and a view of the fire—and, in summer, a deck that is all the outdoor activity some Portlanders need. ■ *2601 NW Vaughn St (at 26th), Portland; (503) 223-3302; $$$; full bar; AE, DC, MC, V; local checks only; dinner every day (Sunday, dinner in bar only).* ⅅ

Lemongrass ★★★ Just as Srichan Miller rose from a storefront into the larger Bangkok Kitchen, her daughter Shelley Siripatrapa has moved from the same storefront into an elegant old Portland Victorian, where she dispenses dazzling curries and seafood. The menu is limited, but the focus is powerful. Tastes here are bright and sharp, sweet and hot and tangy, from emerald pools of green curry to snap-your-eyes-open shrimp with garlic and basil. Even fried rice, a cliché in other places, here pulses with chile paste. There's a choice of heat intensity, but getting much past mild takes you into a place of pain. There are no reservations, and nothing is cooked ahead of time; you'll wait for a table, and then wait again at your table. But after you do, you'll come back and wait again. ■ *1705 NE Couch (turn on NE 17th off Burnside), Portland; (503) 231-5780; $$; beer and wine; no credit cards; checks OK; lunch Mon–Tues and Thurs–Fri, dinner Thurs–Tues.*

McCormick & Schmick's Seafood Restaurant ★★★ With an array of vast new McCormick & Schmick seafood palaces extending from Los Angeles to Washington, D.C., the original M&S still holds its excitement and liveliness, and a kitchen that skillfully handles its extensive fresh list. The fresh dragnet reaches from Alaska to Florida to Chile, and the fish caught in it can end up in roasted garlic vinaigrette, tandoori glaze, or fresh raspberry beurre rouge. Still headlining, however, is grilled alder-smoked salmon, and the smoke aroma announces the restaurant a block away. The place is frequently jammed, offering a lively bar scene, complete with a pianist and an extraordinary selection of single-malt Scotches. Call early for reservations for monthly Cigar Nights, which could smoke a salmon right in the dining room. ■ *235 SW 1st Ave (at Oak St), Portland; (503) 224-7522; $$; full bar; AE, DC, MC, V; checks OK; lunch Mon–Fri, dinner every day.* ⅅ

Murata ★★★ At Murata's tiny sushi bar, the specials are listed in Japanese, with a "translation" underneath: Japanese names spelled out in English. Compromise is limited at a restaurant that often seems directly aimed at visiting Japanese businessmen; it's perhaps the only serious restaurant closed on weekends because the core clientele is on the Delta nonstop back to Tokyo. But Murata is the best Japanese restaurant in Portland. Once someone has translated the specials, they're often worth the culinary gamble—crisp grilled sardines, mackerel necks, layers of deep purple tuna. If there's kasu cod, by all means order it, and if you've got some friends along, try one of the nabe—huge bowls of stewlike soups, thick with seafood. Those with time, money, and nerve should order (in advance) an elaborate Japanese multicourse banquet, kaiseki, starting at $35 per person and running as high as your wallet allows. Murata has recently branched out with its own bento parlor; it's not like other Portland bento parlors, either. ■ *200 SW Market (downtown, between 2nd and 3rd), Portland; (503)227-0080; murata@teleport.com; $$; beer and wine; AE, DC, MC, V; no checks; lunch, dinner Mon–Fri.*

Paley's Place ★★★ In a constant culinary orbit, Kimberly Paley circles the intimate, thoughtfully designed dining room, closely watching everything that her husband, Vitaly, sends out from the kitchen—and how it's received. Invariably, the reception is warm. The food here is best described as exquisite, with Northwestern freshness married to an artistic sensibility that the Paleys brought from the dance and art world—as well as the kitchens—of New York. A bisque of spring asparagus, broccoli, and spinach offers a dazzling texture, a green essence with a tangy undertone of chive; a tart of caramelized onion with fresh goat cheese provides the same sure sense of balance. Confit of duck distills the bird to a crisp richness, and steelhead is set off by a smoked seafood sausage. Menus change with the harvests, but a lemon buttermilk tart, with a blueberry sauce and an artful meltingness, should always be in season. In just a few years, Paley's Place has established itself as a premier Portland restaurant. ■ *1204 NW 21st Ave (corner of Northrup), Portland; (503)243-2403; www.teleport.com/~paleys; $$$; beer and wine; AE, MC, V; local checks only; lunch Tues–Fri, dinner Tues–Sat.*

Papa Haydn ★★★ In both locations—northwest and southeast Portland—the dessert list is literally musical: it trills from Autumn Meringue (layers of chocolate mousse and meringue, festooned with chocolate slabs) to Georgia Peanut Butter Mousse Torte to Boccone Dolce (a mountain of whipped cream, chocolate, meringue, and fresh berries) to White Chocolate Mousse Charlotte. People who think that pastry is a branch of architecture would want to study construction here. At the northwest branch, the rest of the menu runs to pastas and pâtés, with a few elaborate choices such as smoked chicken or seasoned prime rib. The place has come a long way since the days when it served up lunchy items so people wouldn't feel guilty about just eating dessert. The southeast location (on Milwaukie Avenue) is more low-key, but both have lines stretching out the door. ■ *701 NW 23rd Ave (at Irving), Portland; (503)228-7317; full bar.* ■ *5829 SE Milwaukie Ave (between Bybee and Holgate, in Sellwood district), Portland; (503)232-9440; $$; beer and wine; AE, MC, V; local checks only; lunch, dinner Tues–Sat, brunch Sun.* ♿

Pazzo Ristorante ★★★ The wood-grill aroma reaches out into the entryway, and the shrewd diner will follow it. At Pazzo, now established as one of Portland's most beloved restaurants, executive chef David Machado oversees a dazzling menu ranging from thick veal chops to daily fish specials, which might be an ethereal sea bass or a succulent king salmon. Pasta offerings include a trademark smoked salmon ravioli in lemon asparagus cream, or you might find a skillfully executed risotto with woodsy wild mushrooms. Pazzo's dining options: the brick dining room perfumed by the grill, the bar with hanging garlic, or one of the glass-enclosed private rooms. (Lately, there's also Pazzoria, a pizza, panini, and pastry hangout next door.) On Friday and Saturday nights, there's reserved seating in the romantic downstairs wine cellar. Knowledgeable and engaging servers recite the day's specials, in reverent detail. Listen closely to the entire description; Machado lavishes particular care on side dishes, and your entree decision may hang on whether the accompaniment is silken garlic mashed potatoes, a forceful risotto, an enlivened bed of spinach, or an aggressive Tuscan bread salad. ■ *627 SW Washington St (in Vintage Plaza Hotel, corner of SW Broadway), Portland; (503) 228-1515; info@pazzo. com; www.pazzo.com; $$; full bar; AE, DC, MC, V; checks OK; breakfast, dinner every day, lunch Mon–Sat.* ⛐

3 Doors Down ★★★ In just a few years, this austere storefront has made a real impact on the Hawthorne neighborhood—first because its deft mingling of Northwest seafood and Italian instincts offers a lively, inviting local option, and second because its no-reservations policy often leaves a line out on the street. The line is for the bountiful seafood Fra Diavolo, shrewdly grilled salmon on polenta, and a half-dozen firm and flavorful pastas. The small, spare storefront, three doors down from Hawthorne Boulevard (hence the name), has a warm atmosphere, if a considerable noise level, and a way with garlicky steamed clams. There are occasional slips, but the odds are in your favor, especially if you start with the outsized antipasto of tender marinated eggplant and finish with an intense chocolate mousse cake or the walnut torte with a zinfandel sabayon. Pace yourself—you can always come back, and you probably will. ■ *1429 SE 37th Ave (north of Hawthorne), Portland; (503) 236-6886; $$; beer and wine; AE, DC, MC, V; checks OK; dinner Tues–Sat.* ⛐

Wildwood ★★★ Wildwood goes from strength to strength, as chef/owner Cory Schreiber hones his skills and goes deeper into Northwest cuisine. Schreiber, who found fame as a chef in San Francisco, returned to his hometown to open Wildwood (named after a trail in Forest Park) and to fill his huge, wood-fired oven with regional ingredients and his own imagination. Lately, that could mean Muscovy duck breast with sweet onion potato cake and huckleberries, or grilled Columbia River sturgeon with leek and smoky bacon risotto. Regular oven specialties include skillet-roasted mussels, designer pizzas such as duck confit and apple, and seductive, elegantly presented desserts like banana bread pudding with caramel sauce. In its open, boisterous style, Wildwood feels a bit like San Francisco, but it tastes like Oregon—and usually the best of Oregon. If there's a salad on the menu that features fried oysters and pancetta on an herbed crêpe, make it your starter. Free parking in the lot next to the building. ■ *1221 NW 21st Ave (corner of Overton), Portland; (503) 248-9663; cory@wildwoodpdx.com; www.wildwoodpdx.com; $$$; full bar; AE, MC, V; checks OK; lunch, dinner every day, brunch Sun.* ⅃

Al-Amir ★★ The elaborately crenellated Bishop's House has hosted multiple restaurants in its time; this elegant, skillful Lebanese outpost has now outlasted them all. Starring here are the smoky, intense baba ghanouj and the creamy hummus, but the kitchen's reach is extensive. The shish kabob, lamb vibrant with spices and juices, highlights a menu that stretches to kharouf muammar, a huge pile of moist, faintly sweet lamb chunks; and dujaj musahab, a charcoal-grilled chicken breast in lemon and olive oil. Don't depart without trying the grape leaves. A little Lebanese beer makes the light through the stained-glass windows shine even more brightly. ■ *223 SW Stark St (downtown between 2nd and 3rd), Portland; (503) 274-0010; $$; full bar; AE, MC, V; local checks only; lunch Mon–Fri, dinner every day.* ⅃

Alexis ★★ Most restaurants offer a meal; Alexis is a party. The welcome here is warmer than the flaming saganaki (Greek cheese ignited with ouzo). From the first course of chewy squid to the last of seriously sweet baklava, the food here is authentic and memorable. Plump grape-leaf packets are available meatless or with lamb; the little pillows of filo and feta known as tiropitas are worth the 15-minute wait. In fact, regulars often order these and other appetizers and call it dinner. Baskets of warm house bread come with the meal—and if you like what you taste, take heart: Alexis sells it by the loaf. The Alexis Bakourous family and their loyal staff attentively patrol the premises, and on weekends they're joined by Aurelia, the region's hottest Middle Eastern dancer. ■ *215 W Burnside (between 2nd and 3rd), Portland; (503) 224-8577; $$; full bar; AE, DC, MC, V; local checks only; lunch Mon–Fri, dinner every day.* ⅃

American Palate ★★ The food at this Northwest hideaway is as direct as its name: creative American cuisine solidly prepared, and usually successful. Pan-seared monkfish here actually shows why the fish is called "poor man's lobster"; it's sweet and tender and holds its texture. Grilled pork tenderloin with an apple-scallion fritter treats a delicate meat equally respectfully. Desserts change, but a chocolate mousse cake chases cocoa through an exploration of tones and textures, and cinnamon bread pudding can bolster your patriotism. The service and the cozy dining room are equally direct—which doesn't keep them from being comfortable and successful, either. ■ *1937 NW 23rd Pl (corner of Vaughn), Portland; (503) 223-6994; $$; beer and wine; MC, V; checks OK; lunch Mon–Fri, dinner Mon–Sat.* &

Assaggio ★★ This is the place for carbo-loading. For $10 a person, Assaggio will serve you three courses of pasta—maybe a spicy spaghetti alla puttanesca, followed by a carbonara and perhaps some penne dense with woodsy wild mushrooms and leeks. You can skip their picks and explore the 20 pasta choices by yourself, and it's hard to go wrong. Take a deep breath and start out with three different kinds of polenta with three different toppings—notably smoky grilled artichokes with Parmesan shavings. Try to fit in another combination of bruschettas—maybe wild mushrooms on one, Tuscan bean salad on the other. The rooms where this all happens (now expanded to include a wine bar) are as carefully decorated as the pasta. And those who take up long-distance running or rowing, or something, will want to come back. ■ *7742 SE 13th Ave (in Sellwood, at 13th and Lambert), Portland; (503) 232-6151; $$; beer and wine; AE, MC, V; local checks only; dinner Tues–Sat.* &

B. Moloch/The Heathman Bakery and Pub ★★ After going through more formats than Windows 95, the Heathman's casual cousin across the South Park Blocks has found a new one. This time it's less casual and more hearty, as Mark Bernetich takes over the menu. It's still a brewpub, but now it's also a place with sweeps of tiles, rich wood, and table service. All this is set off by walls of windows, high ceilings hung with artful banners, and Second Empire caricatures. The food is now more meaty, less delicate, with smoked pork chops, smoked sausages, and rib-eye steaks. There are still salads, pastas, and serious sandwiches, such as smoked lamb on focaccia and a Reuben with house-cured pastrami. B. Moloch continues to serve one of the city's better breakfasts, with such dishes as an open-faced smoked salmon and crème fraîche omelet. And the place always provides some of Portland's best people-watching—inside and outside. ■ *901 SW Salmon St (at the north end of the South Park Blocks), Portland; (503) 227-5700; $$; beer and wine; AE, DC, MC, V; checks OK; breakfast, lunch, dinner every day.* &

Bangkok Kitchen ★★ Portland's Thai restaurant market may have drawn some newer, more elaborate contenders, but crowds still stream here for the unadorned basics of Southeast Asian cooking: hot and sour soups, curries, salads of fresh shrimp and lime, and noodles. The funky, informal atmosphere—with waiters in jeans and T-shirts and a no-frills decor—has attracted a

▼

Portland

Restaurants

▲

faithful following of neighborhood locals and cross-river pilgrims who come for the family feeling and the famous whole crisp sea bass in chile sauce. Kids are more than welcome—the staff members wear their sense of humor like name tags. ■ *2534 SE Belmont St (at 25th Ave), Portland; (503)236-7349; $; beer and wine; no credit cards; checks OK; lunch Tues–Fri, dinner Tues–Sat.* &

Berbati ★★ Skip the noisy atmospherics and concentrate on the consistently good Greek food. Order a tableful of appetizers and expect to be perfectly satisfied (and possibly full) before you get any further. Sautéed prawns are a signature dish, but the menu runs wide. The chicken souvlaki is served alongside a wedge of buttery, mustard-kissed potato. The tiropita—a hot, cheese-filled pastry—is so smooth it cries out for an accompanying glass of pine-scented retsina. And the calamari is simply the best fried squid in town. At the other side of the building is Berbati's Pan, with live music and a bustling scene. If anything, Berbati has just become more of a hangout—but we've been hanging out here all along. ■ *19 SW 2nd Ave (1 block south of W Burnside), Portland; (503)226-2122; berbati@teleport.com; www.teleport.com/~berbati/; $$; full bar; MC, V; local checks only; dinner Tues–Sun.* &

BJ's Brazilian Restaurant ★★ Portland's only Brazilian restaurant is a boisterously colored place of blues and yellows and purples, with a huge mural of Rio de Janeiro sweeping across one wall. But its most dramatic element is its version of *feijoada*, Brazil's national dish, a deep stew of black beans, pork, and sausage. Chicken dishes, including one baked in dark beer and red palm oil, are also admirable, as are the small, deep-fried meat pies called pastels. Everything comes with rice, a grain dish called farofa, and a mixture of chopped cilantro and red pepper that should be spooned on everything in sight. A dark Brazilian beer called Xingu is served up in huge bottles, or try the potent cacha, a sugarcane liquor. ■ *7019 SE Milwaukie Ave (½ block off Bybee), Portland; (503)236-9629; $$; beer and wine; MC, V; checks OK; lunch Mon–Fri, dinner Mon–Sat.* &

Brasserie Montmartre ★★ There are several places to eat in Portland after midnight, but there's only one real restaurant at that hour. Until 2am weekdays and 3am on weekends, Brasserie offers everything from veal with mushrooms to eggs Benedict to beluga caviar. The major ingredient, however, may be the scene—Doc Martens and suits, nightly local jazz, an occasional strolling magician, and dancing—all happening behind a glass and wood exterior as flashy as the black-and-white-checked floor. But the food deserves notice, too. Whatever the hour, it's surprising how consistent it is—and it's always a good time for the sweetly succulent crab cakes or the roast lamb sandwich on focaccia. Dining at more traditional times, you might notice the petrale sole in a caper-butter sauce—and the framed crayoned illustrations on the walls. ■ *626 SW Park Ave (between Alder and Morrison), Portland; (503) 224-5552; $$; full bar; AE, DC, MC, V; checks OK; lunch, dinner every day, brunch Sat–Sun.* &

Bread and Ink Cafe ★★ In this lofty, well-lit bistro in the heart of the Hawthorne neighborhood, there have been changes in both the ownership and the kitchen, leaving some things warmly recognizable and some a bit more ambitious. Longtime fans will still find impressive baked desserts (including a poppyseed cake that will ensnare people who didn't think they liked poppyseed cake), rugged black bean chili, a Sunday-warming three-course Yiddish brunch, and a serious hamburger, with homemade condiments that do it justice. Dinner now seems to aim a bit higher, with roast steelhead and duck cooked two ways, and the results may be more solid than soaring. But Bread and Ink, with its wall drawings and huge windows onto Hawthorne, still draws its loyal crowd—along with a few more adventurous diners. ■ *3610 SE Hawthorne Blvd (corner of SE 36th), Portland; (503) 239-4756; $$; beer and wine; AE, MC, V; checks OK; breakfast, lunch, dinner Mon–Sat, brunch Sun.* &

Bush Garden ★★ There's an extensive Japanese menu here, with several unexpected offerings such as scallop batayaki and different views of tofu—along with the widest choice of tatami rooms in Portland. But the most interesting options come through the sushi bar, where you can quickly rattle off words like uni, ama ebi, and toro; point and look hopeful; or just ask the chef to surprise you. Chefs here turn out versions of sushi and sashimi not found elsewhere—Alaskan roll with surimi and smoked salmon, fiery spicy tuna maki, pungent pickled plums. They also like to show off; ask for a translation of the day's specials. Or just leave it to the chef's inspiration, and end up with something like a deliciously crunchy, sweet soft-shell spider crab roll. ■ *900 SW Morrison St (9th and Morrison, near Nordstrom), Portland; (503) 226-7181; $$; full bar; AE, DC, MC, V; no checks; lunch Mon–Fri, dinner every day.* &

Caffe Mingo ★★ This resolutely casual new trattoria, on a stretch of NW 21st that's becoming to restaurants what NW 23rd is to shopping, rejects both reservations and high prices. Instead, it maintains a solid, inviting version of Italian cafe cuisine, from vivid shrimp spiedini to pillowy gnocchi to a headliner of Northwest mushrooms roasted in parchment. The menu is limited but handled well, and a wide sampling won't get you a hefty bill. As you work slowly through your lemon tart, relax and enjoy the moment—and just ignore all those people clustered on the street waiting for your table. ■ *807 NW 21st (between Johnson and Kearney), Portland; (503) 226-4646; $$; beer and wine; AE, MC, V; local checks only; dinner Mon–Sat.* &

Campbell's Barbecue ★★ People come into this little house along Powell Boulevard and just inhale, and get more of a barbecue hit than some places can provide in a rack of ribs. The dining area is quaint, the servers cheerful and efficient, and side dishes—especially the potato salad and the corn bread—are inviting. But what packs the place is an exuberant vision of barbecue. Pork ribs are messy and satisfying, slathered with the smoky brown-sugar sauce, but there are plenty of other options: smoked turkey, chicken, beef, or sausages. A space is available for parties, though some people claim any meal here is a party, and the party's never over until they've run out of peach cobbler. ■ *8701 SE Powell St (exit off I-205, corner SE 85th), Portland; (503) 777-9795; $; no alcohol; MC, V; no checks; lunch, dinner Tues–Sat.* &

Caprial's Bistro and Wine ★★ As hot regional chef Caprial Pence has been raising her own profile, with a weekly Oregon Public Broadcasting cooking show and more cookbooks, her neighborhood bistro has taken her name and acquired an additional chef, Mark Dowers. The result has been no loss of imagination and a bit more consistency, and the place fills up for lunches and dinners. Vivid flavors go shooting around the storefront, from Hot as Hell Chicken at lunch (grilled chicken with chile sauce over pungent peanut-sauced pasta) to dinner entrees such as steelhead with lemongrass aioli. There are also creative sandwiches and salads, and an intense array of desserts: a chocolate turtle cake can make you forget that the name originally belonged to a candy. The menus shift around but never stray too far from the Northwest; dishes just get here in a different way. The walls are lined with a sizable retail wine supply; a $2 corkage fee gets any bottle from the shelf to your table. ■ *7015 SE Milwaukie Ave (just south of Bybee), Portland; (503) 236-6457; $$; beer and wine; MC, V; checks OK; lunch, dinner Tues–Sat.*

Delfina's ★★ On a restaurant row that's a faster and faster track, Delfina's has kept its traditional popularity while reaching for some more ambitious menu efforts. What was a popular pizza-and-pasta place has followed the trend toward greater Italian authenticity. Its menu is now smaller and oft-changing, and the results are pleasing. The offerings now extend to Dungeness crab and pasta in a lemon cream sauce, seafood stew, rack of lamb, and specials like beef braised in espresso. Meanwhile, the pastas are a lot more interesting than they once were. Delfina's is building its own popular ambience with low lighting, fresh-baked rustic breads that require manual disassembly, and Italian language lessons broadcast in the restaurant. ■ *2112 NW Kearney St (corner of NW 21st), Portland; (503) 221-1195; $$; full bar; AE, DC, MC, V; no checks; lunch Mon–Fri, dinner every day.* &

Esplanade at RiverPlace (RiverPlace Hotel) ★★ Esplanade is a visually stunning place with picture windows that front the RiverPlace marina. Executive chef John Zenger has carefully designed a menu that might be described as Northwest nouvelle with continental input. The menu sings of grilled steelhead with apple salsa and blackberry catsup, and pan-roasted sturgeon with huckleberry honey and mustard butter; and if execution sometimes seems wobbly, ingredients are always strong. Lunchers can light into a Northwest salmon club sandwich or fish and chips in microbrew beer batter. The deeply rich (and equally expensive) lobster bisque has endured, and elaborate salads run to choices such as grilled Bombay chicken with mango chutney dressing. The admirable and scenic sit-down brunch, with a fantasy of a breadbasket, is an excellent reason to gather at the river. ■ *1510 SW Harbor Way (off SW Front), Portland; (503) 295-6166; $$$; full bar; AE, DC, MC, V; checks OK; breakfast, lunch Mon–Sat, dinner every day, brunch Sun.* &

Fong Chong ★★ Just because Fong Chong has been Portland's brightest dim sum place for a long time, don't think the offerings are just the same old chicken feet. Along with vibrant humbao buns and addictive sticky rice in a lotus leaf, you might find something surprising, such as shallot dumplings. This is where Portland's dim sum devotees put the cart before each course. The much larger House of Louie, under the same ownership, is across the street. But whether it's the Chinese grocery next door, or because the place is crowded and loud, or because watching the carts maneuver through the tables is like watching the Super Mario Brothers, we like Fong Chong better. It's fun, inexpensive, and impressively tasty. At night, Fong Chong is transformed into a quiet Cantonese eatery, with average preparations and a few surprises. ■ *301 NW 4th Ave (at Everett), Portland; (503) 220-0235; $; full bar; MC, V; no checks; lunch, dinner every day.* &

Il Fornaio ★★ Il Fornaio is, inescapably, a California chain. But once you forgive it that, you'll notice that the skill of its grills and ovens is undeniable, from a wide range of crusty breads to a substantial menu of pastas and entrees. Lobster ravioli is lovely and briny, and if "chicken under a hot brick" sounds like fowl abuse, it somehow produces something meaty and pungent. The room is huge and at dinnertime is often filled with both diners and aromas; the aromas are rich, but one of the attractions here is that the diners don't have to be. A mellower time is in the mornings, when smaller groups toy with cappuccino and whatever the bakers have just brought from the ovens (there are fresh pastries every morning). The menu goes on an annual tour of Italy; any particular month will find full offerings—from the breads to the wines—of any place from Sicily to the Veneto. ■ *115 NW 22nd Ave (just north of Burnside),*

Portland; (503) 248-9400; www.ilfornaio.com; $$; full bar; AE, MC, V; local checks only; lunch, dinner every day, brunch Sat–Sun. &

Indigine ★★ Chef/owner Millie Howe's restaurant has followed its pattern for years now, and it's got the fans to keep it flying. Weekdays, Northwest ingredients are blended with Eastern spices and other inspirations, producing crisp-skinned pesto roast chicken or thick crab cakes at hearteningly reasonable prices. Saturdays are reserved for the blowout East Indian feast, an extravaganza that might start with something like tandoori chicken wings and apricot chutney, followed by a fresh seafood salad, and then lead into a searing shrimp-and-sausage vindaloo or chicken with saffron butter. Not everything bursts with fire and flavor, but the handcrafted items on the crowded dessert tray—from pecan pie to saffron-laced yogurt to boccone dolce—send diners away purring. When the weather allows, dinner on the back deck is delightful. ■ *3725 SE Division St (a few blocks east of Nature's), Portland; (503) 238-1470; $$; beer and wine; MC, V; checks OK; dinner Tues–Sat.* &

Jake's Famous Crawfish ★★ In a restaurant over 100 years old, you should take some time to read the menu. That's a particularly good idea here, because the menu goes on for a while—from the 30-to-40-item fresh list through the day's inspirations to the long list of Jake's standards. It's a restaurant strong on tradition, from the polished wooden fixtures to the waiters' white jackets, but the menu runs to constant experimentation—you might find spearfish and prawn brochettes with habanero barbecue sauce, or stuffed prawns with Jamaican spices. More familiarly, there are bouillabaisse, Maine lobster, various terrific smoked seafood and, at least at the right time of year, crawfish. The combination of old tradition and new ideas applied to very fresh seafood could keep Jake's going for another century. Those without reservations might wait an hour, knowing their patience will be rewarded with some of the better seafood in the city and some of the best service anywhere. Jake's was an early fan of Oregon wines, and it has also assembled a powerful dessert tray—starting with the trademark truffle cake and three-berry cobbler and ending (where you should) with the huckleberry crème brûlée. ■ *401 SW 12th Ave (Stark and SW 12th), Portland; (503) 226-1419; $$; full bar; AE, DC, MC, V; checks OK; lunch Mon–Fri, dinner every day.* &

Jarra's Ethiopian Restaurant ★★ Several Ethiopian restaurants have appeared in Portland over the years, but Jarra's is still the place to get into an explosive, sweat-inducing Abyssinian stew. This is the restaurant to teach you what's wat: made with chicken, lamb, or beef, the wat (stews) are deep red, oily, and packed with peppery after-kicks. Full dinners come with assorted stewed meats and vegetables, all permeated with vibrant spices and mounded on injera—the spongy Ethiopian bread that doubles as plate and fork. Stashed into the bottom of an old Portland home, this is the neighborhood's unequaled heat champ. ■ *1435 SE Hawthorne Blvd (at SE 14th), Portland; (503)230-8990; $; beer and wine; MC, V; local checks only; dinner Tues–Sat.* &

London Grill (Benson Hotel) ★★ In the hearts of many Portlanders and power lunchers, the London Grill occupies a permanent position. While Trader Vic's, its fellow Benson restaurant, has been replaced by a middling California Italian chain eatery, the London Grill remains steady. The tableside cooking carts still glide across the room, the ingredients are still of highest quality, the flambé flames reach for the ceiling, and the strains of the harpist still wash over the deep, comfortable armchairs at each table. (Comfortable is good; you may be waiting a while.) Waiters, practiced in the art of tableside service, produce endearing versions of steak Diane and crêpes Suzette, and the crab cakes are thick with crabmeat. But in many cases, both innovation and flavoring seem to be restrained (okay, subtle menu changes reflect an interest in heart-healthy cuisine). The longest wine list in town is especially strong on French bottlings. ■ *309 SW Broadway (at Oak St), Portland; (503)295-4110; www.holog.com/~benson; $$$; full bar; AE, DC, MC, V; checks OK; breakfast, lunch, dinner every day, brunch Sun.* &

Montage ★★ Portland's definitively hip late-night hangout is now open for lunch; you won't get the 2am energy, but you'll get the same unexpectedly good Southern/Cajun cuisine. If you join the later group, you may have to wait for a spot at the long tables for such Cajun specialties as Spicy Mac (glorified macaroni with Cajun gravy, jalapeños, tomatoes, and Parmesan), blackened snapper, or jambalaya topped with crab, rabbit sausage, or alligator meat. Dinners are both ambitious and unique—from spicy frogs' legs to alligator pâté to green eggs and Spam. (When Montage says spicy, it's not kidding.) Round out your meal with a slice of pecan pie. The loud hum of conversation and music—and we're not talking Top 40—is punctuated with waiters' shouts to the open kitchen announcing an order of an oyster shooter single. Lots of wines are offered by the glass, promptly refilled with a nod in the right direction. The topnotch waiters manage to look as if they're having as good a time as most of the guests. Open late every night. ■ *301 SE Morrison St (underneath the Morrison St Bridge), Portland; (503)234-1324; $; full bar; no credit cards; checks OK; lunch Mon–Fri, dinner every day.* &

Opus Too ★★ Fortunately, the cooks at the mesquite-fed grill are as deft with the fish as with the great hunks of red meat that are still available. And while the fish tends to appear in austere simplicity, the béarnaise and beurre rouge sauces prevail, along with Cajun and barbecue possibilities, daily specials, and a range of lunchtime sandwiches. The decor is urban cool—tile floor, dark-wood booths, and a long swivel-chair bar overlooking the open kitchen and grills. A terrific sourdough bread is part of the deal, as is the live jazz that floats in from Jazz de Opus next door. Opus Too has a respectable wine list, fine desserts, and piles of fettuccine. ■ *33 NW 2nd Ave (NW Couch and 2nd, Old Town district), Portland; (503) 222-6077; $$; full bar; AE, DC, MC, V; no checks; lunch Mon–Sat, dinner every day.* &

The Original Pancake House ★★ Lots of things may change in Portland, but the people waiting patiently outside this landmark restaurant seem to have been there since 1955. This place hums from the time it opens at 7am practically until it closes in midafternoon. The sourdough flapjacks—from wine-spiked cherry to wheat germ to a behemoth apple pancake with a sticky cinnamon glaze—are made from scratch. A good bet is the egg-rich Dutch baby, which arrives looking like a huge, sunken birthday cake, dusted with powdered sugar and served with fresh lemon. Omelets big enough for two (made from a half-dozen eggs) arrive with a short stack. The service is cheerful and efficient; after all, there are people waiting for your table. ■ *8600 SW Barbur Blvd (Barbur Blvd exit from I-5 south; at SW 24th), Portland; (503) 246-9007; $; no alcohol; no credit cards; checks OK; breakfast, lunch Wed–Sun.* &

Red Star Tavern & Roast House ★★ The folks who came up from San Francisco to open the Fifth Avenue Suites Hotel (in the old downtown Frederick & Nelson department store) started with a shrewd idea: hiring Mark Gould, one of the most creative young chefs around. Gould, in turn, showed them a whole different side of his creativity—instead of the upscale Asian Rim elegance of his previous work at Atwater's, he's doing remarkable things with a wood grill, perfuming the air and the tables. He serves up huge, family-sized platters of pork loin, duck, and other meats, and everything from oysters and mussels to heavily laden flatbreads passes through the oven. The smokiness can be a bit too pervasive, but portions are sizable, the atmosphere is entertaining—the tone reflects giant workingman murals of the restaurant's bounty—and Gould is highly talented, a point reinforced from salads to corn bread to desserts. A great place for breakfasts too. ■ *503 SW Alder (just north of Meier & Frank), Portland; (503) 222-0005; $$; full bar; AE, DC, MC, V; local checks only; breakfast, lunch, dinner every day.* &

The Ringside ★★ Sure, lots of people speak well of the fried chicken or the fish, and there really is a mean seafood caesar. But after more than 50 years, the only real question for most fans of the Ringside is which cut—the New York, the filet mignon, the prime rib. People come here for beef, and that's what they get—in large, juicy slabs. In this territory these steaks are hard to beat; for texture, color, flavor, and character, they're everything you could want from a hunk of steer. Still, it's the plump, light, slightly salty onion rings, made with Walla Walla sweets, that single-handedly made the Ringside famous; an order is essential. The dignified black-jacketed and bow-tied waiters are eminently professional, and the wine list is substantial—especially if you're looking for something to go with beef. ■ *2165 W Burnside (2 blocks west of Civic Stadium), Portland; (503) 223-1513; $$; full bar; AE, DC, MC, V; checks OK; dinner every day.* ♿

Ron Paul Catering and Charcuterie ★★ In some ways, ambitions are growing with the number of addresses (the latest of which is a take-out spot downtown); the restaurants are reaching out into wine dinners and upscale cooking classes. But the core here stays the same: a range of distinctive dishes such as barbecued chicken, spinach-mushroom lasagne, pan-fried oysters, Sichuan noodle salad, and some of the best specialty breads in town (try the rich, dark walnut wheat). The ever-changing dinner menus now get considerably more advanced, from elaborately prepared chops and fish to cassoulet. Desserts, from the rhubarb pie with filo crust to the ultrarich Black Angus Cookies to the carrot cake with ricotta and raisins, rank high. Quality control here is an obvious priority: the kitchen smokes the sausages, mixes the pâtés, and cures the salmon—which, on the homemade bagels, brightens up one of Portland's more inviting weekend brunches. A take-out only branch (507 SW Broadway, (503) 221-0052) has a slightly different menu. ■ *1441 NE Broadway (corner of 15th), Portland; (503) 284-5347* ■ *6141 SW Macadam Ave (at Carolina), Portland; (503) 977-0313; $$; beer and wine; AE, MC, V; checks OK; continental breakfast Mon–Fri, lunch, dinner every day, brunch Sat–Sun.* ♿

Saucebox ★★ When Chris Israel, proprietor of Zefiro, opened up this sleek, small, slacker-black place, he seemed to be thinking in terms of a hangout—somewhere for Portland's more gilded youth to drink deep into the night. But somewhere along the way, it turned into one of the city's most alluring restaurants. The small, carefully assembled pan-Asian menu runs to noodles, chicken dumplings, and a Thai curry, with a few more substantial elements such as steamed fish in a banana leaf and an intense, fragrant grilled salmon fillet, crisped in soy, garlic, and ginger. Hardly anything costs more than $10—and it's still a good place for that drink. ■ *214 SW Broadway (diagonally across Broadway from the Benson), Portland; (503) 241-3393; $; full bar, AE, MC, V; local checks only; lunch Tues–Fri, dinner Tues–Sat.* ♿

▼

Sweetwater's Jam House ★★ After starting out in a tiny out-post in the Hollywood district, this lively Caribbean spot has moved to larger (and unquestionably cooler) digs in the ice-cool Belmont area. In the process, it's lost none of its fire—peppered shrimp and goat curry could cauterize your taste buds—or its fun, with terrific barbecued ribs and jerk chicken and zippy, fruity chicken skewers. Sides are stunning, from dark, molasses-infused corn bread to ethereal coconut rice, and three of them, such as not-for-Thanksgiving curried pumpkin, come together for the veggie-flashy Rastafarian plate. There is also an extensive list of Caribbean rums, and a wicked list of things the bar does with them. ■ *3350 SE Morrison (one block west of Belmont, in the renovated Belmont Dairy), Portland; (503) 233-0333; $; beer and wine; AE, MC, V; no checks; dinner every day, brunch Sun.*

Tapeo ★★ Northwest Portland may be a bit drizzly for a com-parison to Spain, but the menu and atmosphere here can get you close. Thirty different tapas—small plates designed for ca-sual munching—and a list of 20 different sherries can make you feel trans-Iberian, especially in a place with small tables and a general sense of no hurry at all. The idea is to start by com-bining a few cold tapas—maybe some marinated trout, or ham and cheese on thick toasted bread—with some hot items, such as a white bean stew or a zarzuelita, seafood in brandy, almonds, and cinnamon. Then, after some sipping and some conversa-tion, and some wiping off the empty plates with crusty bread, retrieve the menu and explore a bit further. As in a sushi bar, the bill can mount up, but it will record some striking flavors. Come summer, tables outside make NW Thurman seem even more Southwest European. ■ *2764 NW Thurman (corner of NW 27th), Portland; (503) 226-0409; $$; beer and wine; MC, V; lo-cal checks only; dinner Mon–Sat.* &

Toulouse ★★ If the only appeal of Toulouse was as Portland's only steady source of the southern French bean stew known as cassoulet, it would be a gain for the city. But the place also of-fers impressive items out of its fiery wood oven, such as rich pork chops, vividly moist chicken, and a dazzling veal chop with a Madeira sauce. The menu makes successful forays into other parts of the European continent for dishes such as gravlax and pasta with wild mushrooms. Desserts, such as tarte Tatin and silken vanilla crème brûlée, are memorable. The big warm room, with an almost equally outsized bar next door, is rapidly becoming a downtown hangout, and warm weather promises a backyard cigar patio. ■ *71 SW 2nd Ave (just south of Burnside), Portland; (503) 241-4343; $$; full bar; AE, MC, V; no checks; lunch, dinner every day, brunch Sun.* &

Typhoon ★★ Bo Kline does a Thai cuisine with more colors than curry. From openers of Miang Kam (spinach leaves which you can fill with a half-dozen ingredients) and beggar's purses of lively shrimp, the menu ranges into a kaleidoscope of curries, inspired seafood dishes, and pungent Thai noodle dishes. (The King's Noodles, with chicken and most spices you can think of, has fanatic devotees.) Scored into a checkerboard grid, a fried fish blossoms into a pinecone. Kline has a particularly deft hand with shrimp and fish, allowing the delicate flavors to surmount ginger, garlic, basil, and some spices that could cook a flounder by themselves. Typhoon also offers 50 different Asian teas— but with these chiles, you might stick to beer. ■ *2310 NW Everett (in Everett Market, just off NW 23rd Ave), Portland; (503) 243-7557; $; beer and wine; AE, DC, MC, V; no checks; lunch Mon–Sat, dinner every day.*

Zell's: An American Cafe ★★ If you're truly inconsolable about founder Tom Zell's departure, you can comfort yourself with a Bloody Mary—one of the few noticeable menu changes. Otherwise, you can once again pile into one of the best breakfasts in this time zone: fresh fruit waffles, a range of pancakes (try the ginger if they're available) and inspired eggs. To the trademark chorizo-and-peppers omelet has now been added a Brie-and-tomato effort and, if you're lucky, scrambled eggs with smoked salmon, Gruyère, and green onions. Expect a warm welcome here, even on chilly weekend mornings when you may be forced to wait outside for a table: the awning is outfitted with heating elements, and you can get a hot cup of coffee and a heartening view of the feathery scones. Of course there is a lunch menu, with thick burgers, vegetarian sandwiches, and fresh fish specialties, but the breakfasts are tough to beat. ■ *1300 SE Morrison St (13 blocks east of the Morrison Bridge), Portland; (503) 239-0196; $; beer and wine; AE, MC, V; checks OK; breakfast, lunch every day.* ᕦ

Bima ★ The question, really, is whether the food is the point here at all. Sure, among fans of the vaguely Caribbean menu, there are those who speak well of the elaborate tacos; and the grilled fish dishes and lunchtime skewers—from porcini mushrooms to squid—can be lively and inviting. An oozy tres leches cake can also be refreshing. But the star here is the scene, architecturally and socially. Once you pass through the nondescript industrial-area door, Bima has one of Portland's most dramatic spaces, concrete warehouse walls towering up to a layered bare wood ceiling, the room splashed with color and asymmetrical furniture. Nights, the bar is lit up by a Pearl District art crowd—and sometimes they even eat something. ■ *1338 NW Hoyt (between NW 13th and 14th), Portland; (503) 241-3465; $$; full bar; AE, MC, V; no checks; lunch, dinner Mon–Sat.* ᕦ

▼

Portland

Restaurants

▲

The Brazen Bean ★ Generation X comes here to smoke cigars and to sample the wide, creative range of beverages—from Armagnac to chai to Scotch older than some of the customers—that can go with them. The place also features other legal smokables and a few pasta and salad entrees, together with some enthralling desserts. This offbeat place is charming and fun, even if the lighting can be as black as the customers' wardrobe. Of course, if you're something beyond twentysomething, the dim lighting helps. ▪ *2075 NW Glisan (just east of NW 21st), Portland; (503)294-0636; $; full bar; AE, MC, V; local checks only; dinner Mon–Sat.*

Casablanca ★ Among Portland's many new restaurants, this Moroccan hot spot spellbinds diners with elaborate atmosphere and decoration, and food that provides its own richness. Dinner begins with enticing appetizers, such as filo pastries enfolding seafood or chicken. Entrees run to couscous, kebabs, and tagines (intense Moroccan stews). Baklava is as rich, sweet, and flaky as you'd expect from a place that specializes in filo. And if, in this crazy world, the problems of two little people don't amount to a hill of beans, at least it's worth finding out what Casablanca does with beans, notably lentils and garbanzos. ▪ *2221 SE Hawthorne (at 22nd Ave), Portland; (503)233-4400; $$; beer and wine; AE, MC, V; local checks only; lunch Mon–Fri, dinner every day.* ♿

Doris' Cafe ★ Just because the first sign of the restaurant is the barbecue smoker outside, don't overlook the rest of the menu here. Doris' is a full-scale soul food restaurant from oxtails to fried fish to greens, and the fried chicken wings could put Buffalo out of business. Doris' has become a meeting place in inner northeast Portland, and now other development, including a jazz-and-coffee bar next door, seems to be rising around it. The cool, attractive space with wood floors and high ceilings is also one of the few places around where Portlanders of all races regularly mingle, and a pile of rib tips isn't the worst accompaniment for it. The smoky barbecue comes in a sauce more sweet than angry, the fried chicken is lovely, fresh, and gently complex, and lunchtime means a run on the fried fish. Desserts vary, but the buttery pound cake and the mousselike sweet-potato pie should not be missed. ▪ *325 NE Russell (near Kirby exit off I-5 northbound), Portland; (503)287-9249; $; beer and wine; AE, MC, V; local checks only; lunch, dinner Mon–Sat.* ♿

Formosa Harbor ★ At lunch this skillful, reasonably priced Chinese restaurant is jammed; at dinner the crush is easier. But at both meals, the flavors are vivid and clean, from General Tso's chicken to brimming bowls of soup or noodles. Try to get there when asparagus is in season; Formosa Harbor stir-fries it quickly with a choice of meats, and produces something that tastes like spring on a chopstick. Lunch specials are highly satisfying, from twice-cooked pork to shrimp with cashews. Weekend nights, there is activity around the enormous two-story bar, but the more interesting events are in the kitchen. ■ *915 SW 2nd Ave (diagonally across 2nd from Yamhill Market), Portland; (503) 228-4144; $; full bar; MC, V; no checks; lunch Mon–Fri, dinner Mon–Sat.*

Hunan ★ If all the portions of chicken in tangy sauce that have been served here were laid out in a row—which would be a great waste—they might rival the Great Fowl of China. The specialties here have been on the menu from the beginning, and there must be a reason for that. After nearly two decades, Hunan still produces some of Portland's most consistently good Chinese cooking—at a more reasonable cost than many of the city's Peking palaces. Favorites such as Lake T'ung T'ing Shrimp, dumplings in hot oil, and beef with orange flavor grace the menu. And the restaurant's versions of the spicy standards—General Tso's chicken, twice-cooked pork, dry-sautéed string beans—are pungent and massively popular. ■ *515 SW Broadway (between Washington and Alder), Portland; (503) 224-8063; $$; full bar; MC, V; no checks; lunch, dinner every day.*

Jake's Grill ★ Sure, this is McCormick & Schmick, so there is some fresh seafood. But it's also a three-meal-a-day Governor Hotel dining room, and a steak house feels right in this grandly restored building. Choose from eight kinds of juicy steak and fist-thick double lamb chops. But the range is wide, with a comfort-food section of meat loaf and macaroni (almost too pedestrian) and more interesting sandwiches and salads, such as blackened rockfish and spinach, Dungeness crab roll, and smoked salmon club. Appetizers and desserts are familiar from the other M&S outposts, along with the high-ceilinged, turn-of-the-century saloon decor. The styles shift during the day: lunch is casual, while the dinner mood gets more flashy. You really should dress for that huge wood-and-glass bar—and the lamb chops. ■ *611 SW 10th St (at Alder in the Governor Hotel), Portland; (503) 241-2100; $$; full bar; AE, DC, MC, V; checks OK; breakfast, lunch, dinner every day.* &

Kornblatt's ★ Kornblatt's may have added a fancy downtown branch in an architecturally striking building, but the core menu here is still chewy, determined bagels, pungent corned beef, and forceful chopped liver. The bagels come in mind-bending varieties—blueberry cinnamon?—but the super onion warms to the excellent smoked fish, just as the cold cuts are bolstered by a pickle bowl on the table. Cabbage borscht, blintzes, and kugel are inspiring, and there is even a shot at a pot roast—with latkes. If you have a choice, stay with the original branch; the downtown location (on NW 23rd) doesn't know from service. ■ *628 NW 23rd Ave (near Glisan), Portland; (503) 242-0055* ■ *1000 SW Broadway (across from the Performing Arts Center),*

Portland; (503) 242-2435; $; beer and wine; MC, V; checks OK; breakfast, lunch, dinner every day. &

Yen Ha ★ With 160 items, Portland's most extensive Vietnamese menu (and one of its oldest) offers a range of possibilities that invite intricate exploration. One shortcut—which isn't that short—is Yen Ha's signature specialty, seven courses of beef, including soup, meatballs, skewers, and a delicate wrapping (with vegetables and spices) in rice paper. You might also try a messy, tangy whole Dungeness crab, game hen with coconut rice, or one of the remarkable preparations of frogs' legs. Some local Vietnamese have been heard to mutter that the menu (and the spicing) has become a bit Americanized, but the crowd is consistently multicultural. The ambience is Formica and Budweiser; concentrate on your beef. ■ 6820 NE Sandy Blvd (at 68th Ave), Portland; (503) 287-3698; $; beer and wine; AE, MC, V; local checks only; lunch, dinner every day.

LODGINGS

The Heathman Hotel ★★★★ The intimate, elegant Heathman has long been hailed as the best place to stay in Portland. While its appeal is broad—excellent business services, a central downtown location, and fine artistic details—guests especially appreciate the meticulously courteous staff. This landmark hotel provides exceptional but low-key service from checkin to checkout. The common rooms are handsomely appointed with Burmese teak paneling, and the elegant lobby lounge is a great place to enjoy afternoon tea or evening jazz performances. Depending on your interests, you might be impressed by the video collection, the library (with author-signed volumes), or the fitness suite (personal trainer available). A strong supporter of the arts, the hotel itself features an impressive display of original artwork, from Andy Warhol prints to the fanciful Henk Pander mural on the east wall of the Arlene Schnitzer Concert Hall (of which 80 guest rooms have an exclusive view). And, finally, you're just steps (or room service) away from one of the Northwest's few four-star restaurants (see review for the Heathman Restaurant and Bar). ■ 1001 SW Broadway (downtown, at Salmon), Portland, OR 97205; (503) 241-4100 or (800) 551-0011; www.preferredhotels.com/preferred.html; $$$; AE, DC, DIS, JCB, MC, V; checks OK. &

Hotel Vintage Plaza ★★★★ This refined, smart hotel in the heart of the city is run by the Kimpton Group, and like many of the other Kimpton hotels, it is elegant but not opulent. We like the intimate scale of the Vintage Plaza (107 rooms), the inviting lobby, and the gracious staff. Among the standard niceties here are attentive bellhops who don't let you lift a thing and the complimentary Oregon wines and classical piano in the early evening. Rooms are named after Oregon wineries, and others after NBA players (this is their stomping ground when in town). Attention shows in details: hidden televisions, plush towels, and lots of convenient hideaways to stow your belongings. Best rooms are the spacious bi-level suites or the top-floor starlight rooms with greenhouse-style windows (ask for one of the larger corner rooms). All rooms come with complimentary shoe shine, nightly turn-down service, morning coffee and baked goods in the lobby, and the newspaper delivered to your door. Pazzo Ristorante on the main floor serves excellent Northern Italian cuisine in a variety of settings (see review). Pazzoria Cafe, next door to the restaurant, sells pastries, crusty Italian breads, and panini sandwiches to take out or eat in. ■ *422 SW Broadway (downtown, at Washington), Portland, OR 97205; (503) 228-1212 or (800) 243-0555; www.holog.com/vintage; $$$; AE, DC, DIS, JCB, MC, V; checks OK.* &

The Benson ★★★ Still the first choice for politicos and film stars, the Benson was for many years the only classy lodging in town. A $20 million restoration almost 80 years after lumber tycoon Simon Benson built the 1912 hotel was a gallant attempt to return it to its original stature. The palatial lobby features a stamped-tin ceiling, mammoth chandeliers, stately columns, and a generous fireplace, surrounded by panels of carved Circassian walnut imported from Russia. Owned by WestCoast Grand Hotels, the 286-room Benson distinguishes itself with stunning architecture and an opulent interior. The guest rooms lack the grandeur of the public areas, with modern furnishings in shades of maroon and beige. Characterized by service that's completely competent, though sometimes impersonal, the Benson is, literally and figuratively, really quite corporate. The London Grill (see review), with its white linens, upholstered chairs, tableside steak Diane, and formal service, caters to an old-fashioned dining crowd. The hotel's streetside casual restaurant, formerly Trader Vic's, has traded Polynesian kitsch for Italian rustica and is now Piatti. ■ *309 SW Broadway (downtown, at Washington), Portland, OR 97205; (503) 228-2000 or (800) 426-0670; www.holog.com//benson; $$$; AE, DC, DIS, JCB, MC, V; checks OK.* &

5th Avenue Suites ★★★ The Kimpton Group has done it again. This time they revamped the Lipman, Wolfe & Company department store (two blocks from the Vintage) and turned it into one of the most pleasant stays in the city—for business travelers, yes, but excellent for well-to-do families too. Although most of the 221 rooms are spacious suites, they all have a sense of grandeur (and plenty of room for a crib, if requested). They even have extra strollers on hand to assist young families. Each suite has three phones (with personalized voice mail and data ports) and a couple of televisions, and some even have their own fax machines; all rooms are equipped with such traveler-choice details as pull-down ironing boards and irons, plush cotton robes, and hair dryers. The staff is gracious and the bellhops are extremely attentive (and unlike any other hotel of this caliber, they even welcome the occasional dog). Kimpton has covered its bases: everything from indoor parking with an unloading area to protect you from the (high) chance of rain to the stunning but welcoming lobby with its large corner fireplace, where you'll find complimentary coffee and newspapers in the morning, and wine-tastings come evening. The Red Star Tavern & Roast House (see review) is an excellent open-spaced bistro. ■ *506 SW Washington (5th and Washington), Portland, OR 97205; (503) 241-4100 or (800) 551-0011; www.preferredhotels.com/ preferred.html; $$$; AE, DC, DIS, JCB, MC, V; checks OK.* &

The Governor Hotel ★★★ If the Heathman Hotel embraces art and the Hotel Vintage Plaza celebrates wine, the Governor honors history. Nowhere is that more apparent than in the hotel's clubby lobby, which features a long and dramatic mural depicting scenes from the Lewis and Clark journey, Arts and Crafts–style furniture, yards of mahogany, and a true wood-burning fireplace. Welcome to Wild West grandeur. The rooms are a departure from the lobby: done in Northwest earth-tone pastels with a faint oak-leaf pattern wallpaper, they feature standard hotel furnishings (although there is an irritating lack of places to set things). Some rooms have whirlpool tubs; suites feature fireplaces, wet bars, and balconies. Almost all the rooms have big windows, but the upper-floor rooms on the northeast corner of the adjacent Princeton Building sport the best city views (we like guest room 5013). The list of amenities is long; among them are access to the Princeton Athletic Club ($8 fee) and to the business center, as well as 24-hour maid service. The restaurant downstairs, Jake's Grill (see review), also provides the ultimate room service fare. ■ *611 SW 10th Ave (downtown, at Alder), Portland, OR 97205; (503) 224-3400 or (800) 554-3456; governor@transport.com; www.govhotel.com; $$$; AE, DC, JCB, MC, V; checks OK.*

The Lion and the Rose ★★★ Housed in a 1906 Queen Anne mansion in the Irvington district, the Lion and the Rose represents Portland's most elegant B&B. The three hosts let few details go unchecked—from the candles in the baths to beverages in the refrigerator to the extra blankets upon request. Magazines are current, cookies are fresh, the hosts are gracious. Depending on your particular room, the interior might seem rather masculine (the Starina, with its high-back bed and linens of rust and gold, exemplifies the Ralph Lauren look) or particularly feminine (the lavender-and-white Lavonna room, with window seats in the cupola, evokes Laura Ashley), but it all feels indisputably decorated. Breakfast is lavish (available in the formal dining room or in your room), and a lovely tea is offered from 4 until 6pm. ■ *1810 NE 15th Ave (1 block north of NE Broadway), Portland,*

OR 97212; (503)287-9245 or (800)955-1647; lionrose@ix.netcom.
com; www.lionrose.com; $$$; AE, MC, V; checks OK.

RiverPlace Hotel ★★★ If you're looking for a room with a view, look no further than RiverPlace. The only downtown luxury hotel that fronts the busy Willamette River—and the boat show that comes with it—the pink-hued RiverPlace (run by West-Coast Grand Hotels) is lovely to look at and glorious to look out from. The better rooms among the 84—doubles, suites, and condominiums—face the water or look north across park lawns to the downtown cityscape. Inside are plush furnishings, TVs concealed in armoires, and generously sized bathrooms. Complimentary continental breakfast can be brought to your room, along with the *New York Times*; massage and spa treatments are available by apppointment. Use of the adjacent RiverPlace Athletic Club is extra ($8 a day), but there's also plenty of opportunity for exercise right outside: wide, paved paths lead from the hotel through the fountains and monuments of Tom McCall Waterfront Park. (At night, you can watch Rollerbladers whiz by.) Downstairs, the Esplanade restaurant makes a stunning location for a meal (see review). ■ *1510 SW Harbor Way (off Front Ave), Portland, OR 97201; (503)228-3233 or (800)227-1333; $$$; AE, DC, MC, V; checks OK.* &

Heron Haus B&B ★★ Set in the exclusive hills overlooking the city, Heron Haus is just blocks away from Portland's trendiest restaurants and hippest boutiques. The common areas in this 10,000-square-foot English Tudor home include a bright living room with a cushy sectional sofa, a mahogany-paneled library punctuated by an inviting window seat, and a wicker-furnished sun room that overlooks the outdoor swimming pool. Five guest rooms, each with a private bath (one bathroom has a seven-nozzle shower), are comfortably furnished in pastels, with large brass beds, sitting areas, telephones, and TVs. The extraordinary bath in the Kulia Room features an elevated spa tub with a city view and all the deluxe bathing accoutrements one could want—from his-and-her robes to a rubber ducky. Don't expect a lot of fussing-over; innkeeper Julie Keppler caters to the business crowd (hence the reduced corporate rate, phone hookups, and no-frills continental breakfast served at individual tables in the dining room). And don't get your heart set on a particular room; requests are only sometimes honored. ■ *2545 NW Westover Rd (NW 25th and Johnson), Portland, OR 97210; (503)274-1846; heronhai@aol.com; www.innbook.com/heron.html; $$$; MC, V; checks OK.*

MacMaster House ★★ Everything here—from the florid furnishings and eclectic art to the mismatched, albeit lovely, china—reflects the personality of the amiable host, Cecilia Murphy. The massive portico flanked by Doric columns makes for an imposing exterior, but the interior of this mansion feels more like Dr. Doolittle's library. Seven rooms range from small and bookish to large and fanciful; all of them house antiques, four boast fireplaces, two have private baths. Our favorite, the Artist's Studio on the third floor, has the feel of a Parisan garret apartment, complete with a claw-footed tub. Lavish breakfasts—pear clafouti, gingerbread, maybe salmon cakes—are served communally in the stately dining room. And the location couldn't be better, two blocks from the entrance to Washington Park (which incorporates the Rose Gardens, the Japanese Garden, and Hoyt Arboretum) and a straight shot down to 23rd Avenue, renowned for its boutiques, galleries, and restaurants. ■ *1041 SW Vista Ave (4 blocks south of W Burnside), Portland, OR 97205; (503) 223-7362; $$; AE, MC, V; checks OK.*

Portland Guest House ★★ Owner Susan Gisvold has created an urban retreat just off NE Broadway. White carpets and antique linens lend the classiness of an intimate hotel, and comfortable mattresses ease the separation from home. Gisvold doesn't live here, but she's usually around long enough to advise you on Portland doings and make sure the flowers in the window boxes are watered. In the morning, she'll drop in to serve a fine breakfast of fresh fruit, scones, and an omelet. Each of the seven rooms—five have private baths—has its own phone and clock (items not standard in many B&Bs), making this a good place for business travelers, too. When the weather's warm, the garden brick patio is the spot to be; when it's not, relax in the simple parlor or set out to explore the many shops along Broadway. ■ *1720 NE 15th Ave (in Northeast Portland, off Broadway), Portland, OR 97212; (503) 282-1402; pgh@teleport.com; www. teleport.com/~pgh/; $$; AE, DC, MC, V; checks preferred.*

Portland's White House ★★ This place looks a bit like its Washington, D.C., namesake, complete with fountains, carriage house, and circular driveway. It was built of solid Honduras mahogany by a local timber baron, Robert F. Lytle; the Japanese maples flanking the Greek columns at the entrance soften the mansion's imposing stature. Inside are six exquisite guest rooms, each with its own bath. The Canopy Room is especially inviting, with its large canopied bed and bright bath. The Garden Room's private terrace is nice in summertime, and if you like you can have your breakfast here. Tea is served in late afternoon; evenings, wander down to the formal parlor for a glass of sherry or a game of chess. New owners Lanning Blanks and Steve Holden have converted the carriage house into two new guest rooms (and we expect to see a few more welcome surprises, as well). ■ *1914 NE 22nd Ave (2 blocks north of NE Broadway), Portland, OR 97212; (503) 287-7131; $$$; DIS, MC, V; checks OK.*

Sheraton Portland Airport Hotel ★★ For the traveling businessperson, the airport's Sheraton tops the list. For one thing, it's located—literally—on the airport grounds (FedEx planes load up next door, and arrival and departure times are broadcast at the hotel's main entrance). Inside, amenities abound: everything from meeting rooms and a complete, complimentary business center (IBMs, printers, fax machine, and secretarial services) and on-site travel agency to an indoor swimming pool, sauna, and workout room. The executive suites consider the personal needs of the businessperson, providing two phones, sitting areas, jacks for computer hookup, and pullout makeup mirrors in the bathrooms. Mount Hood stands tall to the east, but you'd never know it from the airport-facing rooms. ■ *8235 NE Airport Way (just before the terminal), Portland, OR 97220; (503) 281-2500; www.sheraton.com; $$$; AE, DC, JCB, MC, V; checks OK.* ⑤

Mallory Motor Hotel ★ Located just west of the downtown core, a 15-minute stroll to Pioneer Square, the beloved Mallory remains the favorite lodging of many regular visitors to the City of Roses—and has been since they were kids. It's an older establishment in every sense, from the massive hunks of ornate wooden lobby furniture to the senior staff. It's also one of the best bargains in town, starting at $70 for a double and topping out at $110 for a suite—so it's a good idea to reserve a room far in advance. The Mallory sits in a quiet area of town where its new four-story parking garage makes parking a breeze. Have breakfast in the restaurant—simple, charming touches and almost motherly service—and dinner downtown. The quirky cocktail lounge draws in denizens from both the older and retro crowds for the reasonably priced well drinks and bowls of cheesy popcorn. ■ *729 SW 15th Ave (at SW Yamhill), Portland, OR 97205; (503) 223-6311 or (800) 228-8657; $$; AE, DC, DIS, MC, V; checks OK.* ⑤

Marriott Residence Inn/Lloyd Center ★ This hotel near the Lloyd Center Cinema has 168 rooms that you might mistake, from the outside at least, for apartments. It's geared toward longer stays (four to seven days) and rates drop accordingly. Each suite has a full kitchen, as well as a sitting area with a couch and a desk, and most have wood-burning fireplaces. Extra conveniences include dry cleaning and grocery-shopping services. There isn't much of a view and there's no restaurant, but a complimentary continental breakfast and afternoon hors d'oeuvres are served in the lobby. Three Jacuzzis and a heated outdoor pool are on premises for guest use. An extra $4 a day gains you access to the Lloyd Center Athletic Club seven blocks away. ■ *1710 NE Multnomah (2 blocks east of Lloyd Center), Portland, OR 97232; (503) 288-1400; $$$; AE, DC, DIS, MC, V; checks OK.* ⑤

Red Lion at Lloyd Center ★ Its daunting size (a map in the lobby directs you to the three restaurants) and proximity to the Lloyd Center, Memorial Coliseum, and the Convention Center make this a good choice for eastside conventions or seminars. With 476 guest rooms, it's Oregon's second-largest hotel (the Portland Marriott is slightly bigger), outfitted with a number of well-organized meeting rooms, an exhibit hall, an outdoor pool, a workout room, and a courtesy airport van. Reserve an east-facing room above the fifth floor for a view of Mount Hood. The service at times seems as worn as the decor, which could be characterized as corporate hotel chic. The hotel's restaurant, Maxi's, turns out better-than-average Northwest cuisine; on Sundays families cozy into the pink clamshell booths for the bounteous brunch and bottomless champagne. ■ *1000 NE Multnomah St (Lloyd Center/Weidler exit from I-5), Portland, OR 97232; (503)281-6111 or (800)547-8010; www.teleport.com/-~peekpa/rlion.htm/; $$$; AE, DC, MC, V; checks OK.* &

FOREST GROVE

Pacific University is why most people come here, and the towering firs on the small campus do justice to the town's name. But there's also quite a collection of local **wineries**, making the area worth exploring, perhaps on your way to the ocean. South of town on Highway 47 is the huge Montinore Vineyards, (503)359-5012, which has a fancy tasting room and wines that are improving with each vintage. In nearby Gaston, Elk Cove Vineyards, (503)985-7760, has a spectacular site for a tasting room perched on a forested ridge, and Kramer Vineyards, (503)662-4545, is a tiny place in the woods with tasty pinot noir and excellent raspberry wine. West of Forest Grove on Highway 8, on the site of a historic Oregon winery, Laurel Ridge Winery, (503)359-5436, specializes in sparkling wines and also makes good sauvignon blanc. Shafer Vineyards, (503)357-6604, has produced some fine, ageable chardonnays, and Tualatin Vineyards, (503)357-5005, produces exquisite chardonnay, as well as an excellent Müller Thurgau. Finally, just outside of town you can sample sake from Momokawe Sake, (503)357-7056, a new Oregon sake brewery.

RESTAURANTS

El Torero ★ You may have a tough time getting past the terrific, light, crisp chips, but if you do, you'll probably end up devouring all your excellent homemade-tasting frijoles refritos. For the main course, stick with the specialty beef items—the massive serving of carnitas de res is super. The decor is college hangout, but the service is very friendly and the English (authentically) limited. ■ *2009 Main (just off Hwy 8 on Main), Forest Grove; (503)359-8471; $; full bar; MC, V; checks OK; lunch, dinner every day.* &

RESTAURANTS

Ikenohana ★★ The suburban strip mall storefront opens into a modest space (with a tiny sushi bar in one corner) where Japanese paper screens and lanterns give a private and charming feel, and even when things are busy it's not noisy. The menu allows a wide range of options, from sushi and sashimi to tempura, katsu dishes, teriyaki, and noodles. You can't go wrong here: the sashimi is elegantly presented and very fresh and firm. A plentiful plate of sushi includes wonderful mackerel and eel. Even the simple yakisoba noodles are spicy and cooked just right. If you look like you don't know how to mix the wasabi sauce for the sushi, the waitress will show you. ■ *14308 SW Allen Blvd (in the shopping center at Murray and Allen), Beaverton; (503) 646-1267; $; beer and wine; MC, V; no checks; lunch Tues–Fri, dinner Tues–Sun.* &

McCormick's Fish House and Bar ★★ Chef Jon Wirtis has maintained this suburban outpost of the M&S empire as a solid seafood house, with few nonmaritime options. With the same fresh list—and the same knowing, professional service—as the other links in the chain, McCormick's Fish House produces solid, skillful food that sometimes surprises. The mood and the feeling are more casual than downtown, but don't take that as a sign that you can confidently walk in without a reservation on weekends, on Thursday nights, or for Sunday brunch. ■ *9945 SW Beaverton-Hillsdale Hwy (about a mile east on Hwy 10 from Hwy 217), Beaverton; (503) 643-1322; $$; full bar; AE, DC, MC, V; checks OK; lunch Mon–Fri, dinner every day, brunch Sun.* &

Swagat ★★ This Beaverton tract house across from Target looks like it should produce Rice Krispies Treats—not great Indian food. But somehow, people enter the door and (at least spiritually) never leave. Starting from pillowy dosas, giant pancakes stuffed with curry or lentils, diners slip eagerly into tandoori dishes with a barbecue bite, spinach paneer laced with cheese cubes and fire, or a spicy, buttery Chicken Makhani. It's hard to spend much money here even at dinner, but the lunch buffet is the best deal. The vindaloos may be vibrant, but the atmosphere is low-key; the feeling is Beaverton, not Bengal. Proprietors have four restaurants in the Bay Area, and Swagat's success has stirred rumors of another one here. ■ *4325 SW 109th Ave (just off Beaverton-Hillsdale Hwy, across from Target), Beaverton; (503) 626-3000; $; beer and wine; AE, DC, MC, V; checks OK; lunch, dinner every day.*

Hall Street Bar & Grill ★ With high, vaulted ceilings and oak floors, Hall Street looks like a typical fern bar. But the kitchen offers some skillful surprises. Burning under the grill are local vineyard cuttings, giving salmon and seafood specials an inviting, tangy undertone. Off the grill, fish meets ingredients like lime, ginger, basil, hazelnuts, and avocado salsa. The rock salt–roasted prime rib is a permanent menu fixture—a favorite that has been known to sell out quickly—and the grilled steaks are terrific. A superb burnt cream with a hard sugar crust leads the strong list of desserts; the wine list emphasizes California and Northwest wines. ■ *3775 SW Hall Blvd (take Cedar Hills Blvd exit off Hwy 26, turn left at Hall, 1 block), Beaverton; (503)641-6161; $$; full bar; AE, DC, MC, V; checks OK; lunch Mon–Fri, dinner every day.* &

LODGINGS

Greenwood Inn ★ Billed as a city hotel with resort-style comfort, the 253-room complex delivers, for the most part, on its promises. The primary draw for businessfolk is the hotel's location—just off Highway 217, a few exits away from the high-tech offices of the Silicon Forest. Given the crowd it caters to, it's disappointing that the service is not better, and doubly disappointing considering that the inn is overseen by the Heathman Management Group. That aside, there are good things to be found here: the eight suites have Jacuzzis and kitchens, there are two outdoor swimming pools in the verdant courtyard, and then there's the Pavillion Bar and Grill. In the last couple of years chef Kevin Kennedy has changed the image of the restaurant, featuring fresh and local ingredients (the herbs are grown in the private garden of the inn). All in all, if you're going to stay in Beaverton, this is the best place. ■ *10700 SW Allen Blvd (Hwy 217 and Allen Blvd), Beaverton, OR 97005; (503)643-7444 or (800)289-1300; $$; full bar; AE, DC, MC, V; checks OK; breakfast, lunch, dinner every day, brunch Sun.* &

LAKE OSWEGO

RESTAURANTS

Thai Villa ★★ The hot thermometer here ranges from "calm" to "volcano" (with little in between). A popular Lake Oswego restaurant, Thai Villa specializes in pungent soups served swirling in a moat around a pillar of flame, and a wide range of seafood dishes. The chef is handy with basil, garlic, and subtle hints of sweetness, and the prices are reasonable, especially on a cost-per-tingle basis. It's a good thing this place sits near the Lake Oswego fire department because someday someone is going to take an innocent bite of volcano gang galee (chicken curry with potatoes) and self-combust. ■ *340 N 1st St (downtown), Lake Oswego; (503)635-6164; $; beer and wine; MC, V; no checks; lunch Mon–Fri, dinner every day.*

Riccardo's Restaurant & Espresso Bar ★ Owner Richard Spaccarelli is a serious enophile, as the over 300 bottles of Italian-only wine (and Riccardo's own wine shop across the way) attest. That list benefits from some of the most knowledgeable wine discussion around. The kitchen produces intriguing pastas and an impressively meaty veal chop, although dishes can sometimes be a bit uneven and service less than perfect. This is one of the few places around where you can chase your pasta with a glass of grappa—or a selection of them. The outside dining area blossoms in nice weather. ■ *16035 SW Boones Ferry Rd (south of Cruise Way in Lake Grove), Lake Oswego; (503) 636-4104; $$; full bar; AE, DC, MC, V; checks OK; lunch Mon–Fri, dinner Mon–Sat.* ♿

Wu's Open Kitchen ★ The flames leaping high behind the windows in the back of the restaurant are firing the large woks in the kitchen, and you can watch the cooks deftly preparing dishes while you wait for dinner. Chef Jimmy Wu's extended family helps run this place, serving a variety of spicy and not-so-spicy dishes from all over China (but the cooks reckon on the American palate—the hot dishes won't wilt too many taste buds). Seafood is fresh, vegetables are crisp, sauces are light, service is speedy and attentive. Kids will feel right at home, and parents will appreciate the modest prices. Prepare for a wait on weekends—Wu's is popular with locals. There is a second restaurant in Tigard. ■ *17773 SW Boones Ferry Rd (shopping center off Boone's Ferry Rd, just east of I-5), Lake Oswego; (503) 636-8899 ■ 12180 SW Scholls Ferry Rd (on Scholls and 121st), Tigard; (503) 579-8899; $; full bar; MC, V; checks OK; lunch, dinner every day.* ♿

WEST LINN

RESTAURANTS

Bugatti's Ristorante ★★ Lydia Bugatti and John Cress's endearing Italian neighborhood restaurant features seasonal foods and a menu that changes every few weeks. Anytime, keep watch for rigatoni carbonara and spaghetti frutti di mare. There's a nice olive oil spiked with garlic for bread-dipping, but save room for dazzling desserts like the cloudlike tiramisu. The place has picked up a strong endorsement from Trail Blazer coach and New Jersey Italian food aficionado P. J. Carlesimo, who hangs out here frequently. ■ *18740 Willamette Dr (south of Lake Oswego on Hwy 43, ½ mile past Marylhurst College), West Linn; (503) 636-9555; $$; beer and wine; MC, V; local checks only; dinner Tues–Sun.*

RESTAURANTS

Thai Restaurant ★★ If you look quickly, you might think it's still a fast-food restaurant. But when you connect with Emerald Pork and its spinach and peanut sauce; with Panang Nuea, beef in a blast of fiery red curry; or with a sizzling salad of grilled shrimp with chile and lemongrass, you may be transported, culinarily speaking, far away from this fast-food strip location. ■ *14211 SE McLoughlin Blvd (across from Fred Meyer), Milwaukie; (503) 786-0410; $; beer and wine; MC, V; no checks; lunch, dinner Tues–Sun.*

Buster's Smokehouse Texas-Style Bar-Be-Que ★ Take a deep whiff. The wood-smoke ovens leave their mark on both the meat and the atmosphere. Brisket, links, chicken, beef, and pork ribs all pass through the cooker and come out estimably smoky and juicy. The barbecue sauces have a sweet brown-sugar base and come in three temps. Have a beer with the hottest. Accompaniments are simple: fries, slaw, beans, and stuffed jalapeño peppers—for devils only. Equal emphasis on barbecue essentials at both the original Milwaukie location and the Gresham branch (1355 E Burnside, Gresham; (503) 667-4811). The Buster's in Tigard (11419 SW Pacific Hwy, Tigard; (503) 452-8384) features a mesquite broiler, for those of fainter disposition. ■ *17883 SE McLoughlin Blvd (2 miles north of I-205, take Oregon City exit), Milwaukie; (503) 652-1076; $; beer and wine; DIS, MC, V; local checks only; lunch, dinner every day. &*

▼

Milwaukie
_____

Restaurants

▲

Mediterranean Grill ★ Joe Wisher spent years traveling the Mediterranean and returned to open a restaurant overlooking a 7-Eleven in Milwaukie. The results? A tangy orange-cured salmon fillet or a chickpea pancake in a veal-stock sauce, and you might get as far from the Mediterranean as a pork Normande. With luck, the baked apple with caramel and mascarpone will be available at the finish. And despite the Slurpees down the hill, this is a very comfortable restaurant, with the feel of a seaside villa enhanced by the stucco walls and an extensive display of Mediterranean artwork. Apparently, Wisher didn't pick up just recipes. ■ *2818 SE Park Ave (between McLoughlin and Oatfield), Milwaukie; (503) 654-7039; $$; full bar; AE, MC, V; local checks only; lunch Wed–Fri, dinner Wed–Thurs, brunch Sun. &*

RESTAURANTS

Roland's ★★ The best reason to go to Gresham since MAX. Roland Blasi's traditional continental cuisine—sizable portions and strong flavors, gathered from his cooking odyssey through four continents—has taken root in Gresham. Roland's is a very personal restaurant in feel and menu; Blasi draws ideas from the full range of European cooking, and comes up with some of his own. So you're offered not only a pungent gypsy chicken, but also a heartwarming pasta Angelo made with Italian sausage, and a deep, fragrant onion soup. ■ *155 SE Vista (right off Powell (Hwy 26), 2 blocks from downtown), Gresham; (503) 665-7215; $$; beer and wine; MC, V; local checks only; dinner Tues–Sat.* ♿

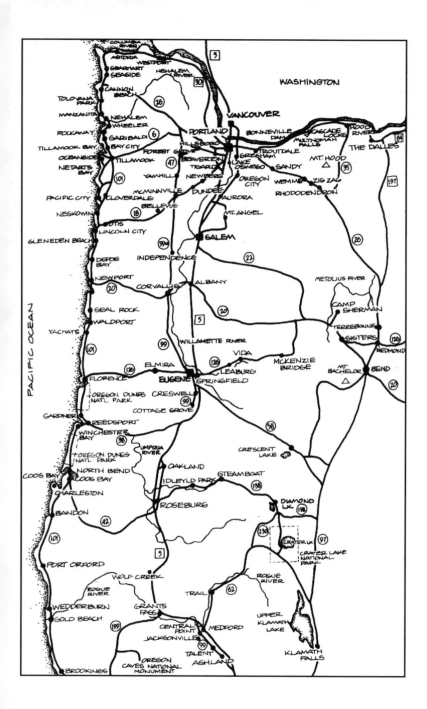

Oregon Coast

From Astoria (at the mouth of the Columbia River), a southward route down the coast to the California border.

ASTORIA

Astoria likes to tout its history. The bustling waterfront—once the locale of canneries and river steamers—is now an active port for oceangoing vessels and fishing boats. The **Columbia River Maritime Museum** (1792 Marine Drive, (503)325-2323) is the finest of its kind in the Northwest. Restored small craft are displayed in the Great Hall, and seven thematic galleries depict different aspects of the region's maritime history. The lightship *Columbia*, the last of its kind on the Pacific Coast, is moored outside (there's a self-guided tour). Named for a prominent 19th-century businessman and Columbia River bar pilot, the **Captain George Flavel House** (8th and Duane Streets, (503)325-2563) is the city's best example of ornate Queen Anne architecture. Both it and the restored **Heritage Museum** (8 blocks away at 1618 Exchange Street, (503)325-2203) feature local history. Six miles southwest of Astoria, off Highway 101, Lewis and Clark's 1805–6 winter encampment is re-created at the **Fort Clatsop National Memorial**, (503)861-2471. Besides audiovisuals and exhibits in the visitors center, there are living history demonstrations (musket-firing, candle-making) during the summer.

For a breathtaking panorama of the Columbia River estuary, the Pacific Ocean, and more, climb the 160 steps of the **Astoria Column**, which sits atop the city's highest point, Coxcomb Hill. To get there, drive to the top of 16th Street and follow the signs.

Fort Stevens State Park, 20 minutes northwest of Astoria off Highway 101, (503)861-1671, is a 3,500-acre outdoor wonderland of paved bike paths, forest trails, a freshwater lake, and uncrowded beaches—including the permanent resting spot of the hulk of the *Peter Iredale*, wrecked in 1906. The 604 campsites make Fort Stevens Oregon's largest publicly owned campground. Within the park, the South Jetty lookout tower, perched at Oregon's northwesternmost point, is a supreme storm-watching spot. It also marks the start of the Oregon Coast Trail, which traverses sandy beaches and forested headlands all the way to the California border. Yurts—roomy wood and canvas structures fitted with electricity, space heaters, bunk beds and skylights—are inexpensive alternatives ($25-$30) to tent or RV camping. They can be found here, and in eight other coastal state parks.

Approximately 50 eagles feed and roost at **Twilight Eagle Sanctuary**, 8 miles east of Astoria (off Highway 30 on Old Highway

30). The **Jewell Elk Refuge** is an area of rolling meadows, at times populated by hundreds of elk; 26 miles east of town on Highway 202, (503)755-2264. Salmon-fishing, bottom-fishing, and river-viewing trips leave from the West End mooring basin, just west of the interstate bridge.

RESTAURANTS

Columbian Cafe ★★ The more publicity the Columbian gets (and it gets plenty), the more crowded it becomes. But this small, vegetarian-oriented cafe continues to be Astoria's best bet for good grub. The wait can still be long, but the interior has been redone and is considerably less cramped. From salmon chowder to vegetable bisque, the soups are satisfying and come with hearty slabs of grill-toasted garlic bread. The seafood and pasta dinners—sturgeon piccata, grilled halibut bathed in Thai nut sauce, rock shrimp spiked with cilantro and black beans— are perhaps the finest on the Oregon Coast. If you're feeling frisky, order the Chef's Mercy, a surprise potpourri of the day's best (and freshest) ingredients. Every Thursday evening in summer, the cafe features a sidewalk fish barbecue showcasing locally caught salmon, sturgeon, and tuna. ■ *1114 Marine Dr (at 11th St, next to the movie theater), Astoria; (503)325-2233; $; beer and wine; no credit cards; checks OK; breakfast, lunch Mon–Sat, dinner Wed–Sat.* &

Ira's ★★ With a storefront setting on bustling Commercial Street, Ira's is part luncheonette, part dinner house. Bagel sandwiches, salmon-and-pepper pastas, and 10-green salads dressed with feta, walnuts, and sun-dried-tomato vinaigrette are excellent noon options. Dinners include locally caught tuna grilled with a peach barbecue sauce and salmon baked in parchment with mango chutney. Star-shaped grit cakes and wild-mushroom polenta are innovative side dishes, while chocolate–peanut butter pie in a graham-cracker crust and decorated with syrupy swirls is an inviting dessert. ■ *915 Commercial St (between 9th and 10th), Astoria; (503)338-6192; $$; beer and wine; MC, V; checks OK; lunch Mon–Sat, dinner Tuesday–Sat.* &

Cannery Cafe ★ Even if you're not hungry, drop by this airy, attractive waterfront cafe specializing in scrumptious baked goods, lunch fare, and a bevy of dinner choices (oyster stew to a rigatoni meat roulade). The building sits on pilings right over the water, and the Columbia River panoramas are superb— every table a scone's throw from the ship traffic and a plethora of finny, furry, and feathery critters. The sandwich selections include a turkey-meatloaf and a panini du jour built around thick focaccia slices, while salads are colorful and creative (look for the black bean gazpacho salad, a thick, stewlike concoction). Breakfast is continental, but Sunday brunch (not your traditional buffet style) is the best in town, with such unusual choices as a mushroom roulade and pan-fried Dungeness crab cakes. ■ *1 6th St (foot of 6th St), Astoria; (503)325-8642; $$; full bar; MC, V; checks OK; breakfast, lunch, dinner Tues–Sat, brunch Sun.* &

Rio Cafe ★ The Mexican-food pipeline has finally reached Astoria, but instead of the usual Tex-Mex fare, this gaily decorated cantina offers inspired south-of-the-border cuisine. Salads feature assorted fruits and veggies, tiny shrimp, and a zingy jalapeño dressing. Three snappy salsas are a perfect match for the huge, handcrafted, crisp chips called totopos. And the Pescado Rojo—fresh sole or cod—is lightly breaded and grilled with a hot-and-sassy red chile and garlic sauce. ■ *125 9th St (a block from the Columbia River), Astoria; (503)325-2409; $; beer and wine; MC, V; checks OK; lunch Mon–Sat, dinner Thurs–Sat.* &

LODGINGS

Rosebriar Hotel ★★ At the turn of the century, the Rosebriar was a private residence. Next it became a convent, and then a halfway house for the mentally disabled. Now, in its finest reincarnation, the place is a rambling 11-room inn. Guest rooms, though generally small, are beautifully furnished and have private baths. A full breakfast is included in the reasonable rates (which begin at $69). The common rooms are spacious and homey, while the outside grounds provide a gardenlike setting, including a porch and front-yard benches affording Columbia River views. All this is within easy walking distance of downtown. ■ *636 14th St (at Franklin), Astoria, OR 97103; (503)325-7427 or (800)487-0224; $; MC, V; checks OK.*

Columbia River Inn ★ Astoria has more bed and breakfasts than any other town on the coast, so it's often difficult to pick the best here; however, this restored turn-of-the-century Victorian, painted in a lovely blue with red and yellow trim, offers four guest rooms (all with private baths), spacious living and dining areas, and elegant furnishings. The Victorian Rose Room features a fireplace, canopy bed, and small spa. Gracious hostess Karen Nelson serves a full breakfast with just the right amount of conversation. Outside, amidst a neighborhood brimming with Victorian residences, there's a terraced garden, with a gazebo, benches, and Columbia River vistas. ■ *1681 Franklin Ave (corner of 17th), Astoria, OR 97103; (503)325-5044 or (800)953-5044; $$; MC, V; checks OK.*

Crest Motel With 40 rooms sited on a forested bluff overlooking the Columbia River on Astoria's east edge, the Crest offers the best motel view in town. When it's foggy, the foghorns bellow up the hillside from the ship traffic below. In the large backyard, you can recline in lawn chairs and enjoy a bird's-eye view of the in- and outgoing tankers and freighters, or unwind in a gazebo-enclosed whirlpool. Pets are welcome; so is smoking in one section. All in all, this is the best alternative to B&B lodging in town. ■ *5366 Leif Erickson Dr (2 miles east of downtown), Astoria, OR 97103; (503)325-3141; $$; AE, DC, DIS, MC, V; no checks.*

Franklin Street Station This is one of Astoria's oldest B&Bs, with a less-than-stellar location two blocks from downtown on a rather ordinary street lacking greenery. But the house itself has style and elegance. The interior is exquisitely appointed with Victorian furnishings, while frilly drapes frame the windows. There are six guest rooms. Two look out to the river and have their own decks. An attic room, the Captain's Quarters, has the best view and its own living room. Unfortunately, the owner does not live on-site and, therefore, is not always available. ■ *1140 Franklin St (between 11th and 12th), Astoria, OR 97103; (503)325-4314 or (800)448-1098; $$; AE, MC, V; checks OK.*

GEARHART

Surely Gearhart, with its assortment of weathered-wood beach-front homes in shades of gray and white, is the town with the most (and the best) examples of Oregon Coast architecture. Fashionable Portlanders put their summer cottages here—some of which are substantial dwellings—when the coast was first "discovered." Unlike other coastal towns, Gearhart is mostly residential. Razor-clam digging is popular, and many gas stations (located along Highway 101) rent shovels. The wide beach is backed by lovely dunes. Gearhart Golf Course, which opened in 1892, is the second-oldest course in the West—a 6,089-yard layout with sandy soil that dries quickly; open to the public, (503)738-3538.

RESTAURANTS

Pacific Way Bakery and Cafe ★★ This airy cafe, with hardwood floors, lots of windows, hip service, cool sounds, and plenty of espresso, is the only restaurant in downtown (such as it is) Gearhart. It continues to thrive on a mix of suspender-and-clam-shovel locals and out-of-town "gearheads"—the BMW-and-summer-beachfront-home crowd who come to hang out, hobnob, and sample the best pastries and breads on the northern Oregon coast. Breakfast is strictly continental-style, and the Greek sandwich and the curried chicken salad are savory lunch possibilities. Crunchy-crust pizzas—available with unorthodox toppings (apple-chicken sausage or dill-ricotta pesto, for instance) if you prefer—and nightly specials, such as flank steak with garlic-mashed potatoes, fiery-hot curry, and cioppino, round out the appealing menu. Save room for baker Lisa Allen's luscious cheesecakes. ■ *601 Pacific Way (downtown, corner of Cottage), Gearhart; (503)738-0245; $$; beer and wine; MC, V; checks OK; breakfast, lunch, dinner Wed–Sun.* ♿

Gearhart Ocean Inn With a New England–style architecture and a quiet, homey feel, these 11 attached cottages on the edge of downtown are low-cost charmers. All units are nonsmoking, and most (except 3, 4, 5, and 6) come with kitchens; some are suites with separate bedrooms, suitable for families. The interiors are appointed with beachy wicker furniture, throw rugs, and colorful comforters. Unit 11 is the biggest, with two bedrooms (sleeps as many as seven). ■ *67 N Cottage (across from the Pacific Way Cafe), Gearhart; (503)738-7373; PO Box 2161, Gearhart, OR 97138; $; MC, V; checks OK.*

SEASIDE

Seaside, the Oregon Coast's first resort town, has become quite crowded (its snarly summer traffic is second only to Lincoln City's). The hordes mill along Broadway, eyeing the entertainment parlors, taffy concessions, and bumper cars, and then emerge at **the Prom**, the 2-mile-long cement "boardwalk" that's ideal for strolling. Lately, they also head for the newly constructed outlet mall along Highway 101 on the town's north end. To escape the bustle, browse the shelves at Charlie's Turnaround Books (111 Broadway, (503)738-3211) or sip something soothing at Cafe Espresso (600 Broadway, (503)738-6169), a cozy coffeehouse overlooking the Necanicum River.

▼

Seaside

Restaurants

▲

Activities. Surf fishing is popular, particularly at the south end of town in the cove area. Steelhead and salmon can be taken (in season) from the Necanicum River, which flows through town. Occasional minus tides provide good razor clamming along the wide, flat beach. Sunset Empire Park and Recreation District, headquartered at Sunset Pool, 1140 E Broadway, (503)738-3311, offers $3 lap swims and information about activities from biathlons to seasonal outdoor concerts. Quatat Marine Park, downtown on the Necanicum River, is a relaxing picnic spot and the setting for free summer concerts. Surfers head for "the Point" at the south edge of town to catch the finest left-handed waves on the Northwest coast.

South of Seaside, a 7-mile trail begins at the end of Sunset Boulevard, winds over **Tillamook Head**, high above the water—part of Ecola State Park (primitive camping facilities only)—and ends at Indian Beach and (farther still) Ecola Point and Cannon Beach.

RESTAURANTS

Breakers ★ Part of a large ocean-front motel complex, this place is far from an afterthought, even though it occupies a windowless basement location. An attractive seashore motif—sand-castle sculptures, colorful kites, and beach umbrellas—substitutes for ocean views. Seafood choices include a pearly white halibut fillet kissed with lime-cilantro butter, salmon simply braised in white wine, and sautéed Dungeness crab legs. And you'll have no beef with the way the kitchen prepares its New York and rib-eye steaks, which are marinated in herbs and balsamic vinegar and then broiled to order. Sunday brunch is a winner. ■ *414 N Prom (part of the Ocean View Resort), Seaside; (503)738-3334 or (800)234-8439; $$; full bar; AE, DC, DIS, MC, V; checks OK; dinner every day, brunch Sun.* &

Dooger's As the line outside all summer will attest, this place is popular. Inside, it's a clean, smokeless, unkitschy, family place with friendly service. Stick with the simpler offerings, like the mighty fine chowder, the halibut, scallops, or the 2-pound bucket of steamers. Most fish can be prepared a number of ways. The Dooger's empire includes a larger version in Cannon Beach at 1371 S Hemlock, (503)436-2225; another on 900 S Pacific in Long Beach, Washington, (360)642-4224; and (as we go to press) one to come on the Astoria waterfront at the foot of 5th Street. ■ *505 Broadway (at Franklin), Seaside; (503)738-3773; $$; beer and wine; MC, V; local checks only; lunch, dinner every day.* &

The Stand Small, tidy, and austerely decorated—with 10 tables and meals served in paper baskets with plastic forks—the Stand serves some seriously satisfying Tex-Mex chow. The place is patronized by a young skate-surf crowd, who appreciate the low prices and no-hassle service. You'll like the fresh—every day—corn tortillas and salsas. Not to mention the many burrito options, including a potent chile verde version packed with pork, Jack cheese, and a tango of green salsa. Veggie burritos and quesadillas are plump with zucchini, mushrooms, myriad peppers, cheese, and all manner of goodies. Our advice? When you're hungry, take to the Stand. ■ *220 Ave U (1 block from the beach), Seaside; (503)738-6592; $; no alcohol; no credit cards; checks OK; lunch, dinner Mon–Sat.* &

LODGINGS

Anderson's Boarding House ★ Fir tongue-and-groove walls, beamed ceilings, and wood paneling recall traditional boardinghouse decor at this solid, turn-of-the-century, blue Victorian. There's even a working Victrola in the parlor. The house fronts Seaside's busy Holladay Drive, but the backyard slopes gently to the Necanicum River—convenient and close to the beach. All six guest rooms have private baths and a wicker-and-wood beachy feeling. There's also a riverfront, miniature Victorian cottage (with a full kitchen) that sleeps up to six people. Full breakfasts are included. ■ *208 N Holladay Dr (at 3rd), Seaside, OR 97138; (503)738-9055 or (800)995-4013; $$; MC, V; checks OK.* &

Beachwood Bed and Breakfast ★ Beachwood, just a block east of the beach, is nicely ensconced in a quiet residential neighborhood, nestled among coastal pines and an easy walk from downtown. The 1900 Craftsman-style lodging offers four guest rooms with private baths. The Astor Room is outfitted with an unusual sleigh-shaped bed and a comfy window seat with a peek of the Pacific. The first-floor Holladay Suite has a frilly canopy bed, a gas fireplace, and a spa. Full breakfasts are provided, but no children or pets are allowed. ■ *671 Beach Dr (at Ave G), Seaside, OR 97138; (503)738-9585; $$; MC, V; checks OK (closed mid-Nov to mid-Feb).*

Gilbert Inn ★ Built in 1892, this Queen Anne–style Victorian located a block off the Prom presents a refreshing visual antidote to the nearby high rises, espresso concessions, and surrey rentals. There are 10 guest rooms within the sprawling, light-yellow structure, all with period furnishings (as well as color TVs), private baths, and a full breakfast. Richly finished tongue-and-groove fir covers the walls and ceilings throughout the inn, and a large fireplace highlights the downstairs parlor, decorated with lush green carpeting and cushy couches. The second-floor Turret Room shows off an ocean view and a four-poster bed, while the Garret, a third-story suite with hand-hewn log beds (one queen, two twins), is great for families. ■ *341 Beach Dr (1*

block off the Prom), Seaside, OR 97138; (503)738-9770 or (800)410-9770; $$; AE, DIS, MC, V; checks OK.

CANNON BEACH

Cannon Beach is the Carmel of the Northwest, an artsy community with a hip ambience and strict building codes that ensure only aesthetically pleasing structures are built, usually of cedar and weathered wood. Still, the town is tourist-oriented, and during the summer (and most winter weekends as well) it explodes with visitors who come to browse the galleries and crafts shops or rub shoulders with coastal intelligentsia on crowded Hemlock Street.

The main draw continues to be the wide-open, white-sand beach, dominated by **Haystack Rock**, one of the world's largest coastal monoliths. At low tide you can observe rich marine life in the tidal pools. Less crowded stretches of sand are located at Chapman Point, at the north end of town (although parking is limited), and at Tolovana Park Wayside, at the south end. The Cannon Beach Energy-Conservation Project operates a natural gas–powered free shuttle in the Cannon Beach–Tolovana Park area year-round.

Arts. Galleries abound, most clustered on Hemlock Street, the main drag. Four especially good ones are the White Bird (251 N Hemlock, (503)436-2681), which has a variety of arts and crafts; the Haystack Gallery (183 N Hemlock, (503)436-2547), with a wide range of prints and photography; Jeffrey Hull Watercolors, Sandpiper Square (178 N Hemlock, (503)436-2600), a collection of delicately brushed seascapes; and Greaver Gallery (739 S Hemlock, (503)436-1185), featuring beachy paintings and prints.

Shops. The Cannon Beach Bakery (144 N Hemlock, (503)436-2592) has one of the few remaining brick oil-fired hearth ovens on the West Coast. Visit Osburn's Ice Creamery & Deli (240 N Hemlock, (503)436-2234) for picnic fixings. Pizza 'a Fetta (231 N Hemlock, (503)436-0333) offers handcrafted pizza by the slice. Hane's Bakerie (1064 S Hemlock, (503)436-0120) features the town's best breads, muffins, and croissants. For take-out or eat-on-premises fish, try Ecola Seafood Market (208 N Spruce, (503)436-9130). Discover a surprisingly extensive selection of books at Cannon Beach Book Company (132 N Hemlock, (503)436-1301).

Hiking. Ecola State Park (on the town's north end) has fabulous views, quiet picnic areas, and fantastic hiking trails. Head up the trail from Indian Beach and catch a glimpse of the former Tillamook Rock Light Station, a lighthouse built offshore more than 100 years ago and abandoned in 1957. Today it's a columbarium (a place where cremated remains are stored) named Eternity at Sea. Camping is permitted at primitive campsites atop Tillamook Head.

RESTAURANTS

Cafe de la Mer ★★ This post-'60s coffeehouse, which became Cannon Beach's first fine-dining establishment 20 years ago, has won a considerable following. The atmosphere inside is warm, and the food is conscientiously sourced and lovingly purveyed by owners Pat Noonan and Ron Schiffman. Seafood, simply and perfectly prepared, is this cafe's raison d'être, manifest in appetizers such as Dungeness crab legs Dijon, scallop ceviche redolent of lime and cilantro, or the choicest steamed clams and mussels in town. Entrees can be as unorthodox as scallops and shrimp sautéed with filberts or as traditional as a lusty bouillabaisse. Salmon delicately broiled with lemon and capers, oysters tarragon, and (in a gesture to carnivores) rosemary-kissed rack of lamb accompanied by blueberry chutney, or grilled antelope topped with an Oregon blue cheese sauce — it's all good, and at times outstanding. However, we've withheld a star because consistency has slipped a bit lately, with some dishes arriving improperly cooked. Arrive early before the best choices are 86'ed, and be ready to pay a high price for relatively small portions. Desserts can be sensational, particularly the white-chocolate torte bursting with marionberries. ■ *1287 S Hemlock (at Dawes), Cannon Beach; (503)436-1179; $$$; beer and wine; AE, MC, V; checks OK; dinner every day (call for winter hours).*

Midtown Cafe ★★ The secret's out about their favorite hang-out, and Cannon Beachers don't like it one bit (sorry, we were just doing our job, ma'am). There are not enough stools at the Midtown Cafe for everyone, so be one of the first to get there. The breakfast lineup here is legendary, with poppyseed waffles, corn-cheddar pancakes, oat scones, and the kosher salami and eggs. Midday at the Midtown means fabulous soups, such as Thai peanut, and unorthodox concoctions such as tuna burri-tos. Be sure to grab a bagel, some gingerbread cookies, or some Haystack apple muffins, if the locals haven't gotten them all before you. ■ *1235 S Hemlock (8 blocks south of downtown, on the east side of Hemlock, the main drag), Cannon Beach; (503)436-1016; $; beer and wine; no credit cards; local checks only; breakfast, lunch Wed–Sat, brunch Sun (closed Jan).* ♿

The Bistro ★ Located in an alley off Hemlock Street, the Bistro is hard to find. But once inside, you'll enjoy its intimate interior, with hanging plants, open-beamed ceiling, and whitewashed walls. You'll also appreciate the emphasis on fresh and simply prepared seafood. Dinners begin with a colorful antipasto plate (unusual at the beach), then move on to soup (perhaps Greek lemon, robust black bean, or mushroom) or a simple salad. Salmon, which may be grilled with leeks and garnished with an understated garlic sauce, or coated with herbs and baked with sun-dried tomatoes, is top-notch. Consider also the farfalle pasta with shiitakes, cheese, and herbs. Service is on the slow side of casual, and lately some of the specials seem less than in-spired, but the adjoining bar is a relaxing venue to catch a brew and order some garlic bread (with pizza sauce, Parmesan, and parsley) or grilled crab cakes finished with a sake-lemon but-ter. Occasional acoustic music, too. ■ *263 N Hemlock (opposite Spruce, downtown), Cannon Beach; (503)436-2661; $$; full bar; MC, V; local checks only; dinner every day (closed Tues–Wed in winter).*

Lazy Susan Cafe ★ Everyone in town seems to gather at this airy, sunny, double-deck restaurant in a courtyard opposite the Coaster Theater. The interior is bright with natural wood, plants hanging from the balcony, and local art on the walls. The tunes are New Age and the service mellow. Breakfast is the best time here, when you can order sumptuous omelets (with egg whites only, if you want), oatmeal, waffles smothered with fresh fruit and yogurt, and excellent coffee to prolong your stay. Lunch (and occasionally dinner) options include quiche and some choice salads, including curried chicken with abundant fruit and a tangy mango chutney. Always worth catching is the Mediter-ranean stew, a cioppinolike mixture of bay scallops, shrimp, and clams, blended with veggies and topped with melted cheese. Expect long waits on sunny weekends. ■ *126 N Hemlock (down-town at Coaster Square), Cannon Beach; (503)436-2816; $; beer* *and wine; no credit cards; checks OK; breakfast, lunch every day, dinner Thurs–Sun.*

LODGINGS

The Argonauta Inn ★ In downtown Cannon Beach, between bustling Hemlock Street and the beach, there are a confusing number of lodging options. The Argonauta, not really an inn but rather a cluster of five well-situated residences, is the best of the bunch. All units are nonsmoking and come equipped with comfy beds, pleasant furnishings, gas fireplaces, and color TVs. All but one have complete kitchens. The Lower Lighthouse, a cozy retreat for two, is the best deal, while the Chartroom offers a full kitchen and will sleep four. The ocean-front Beach House, though expensive, is more like a miniature lodge (with a gas-fired river-rock fireplace, a spacious living room, two sun porches, three bedrooms, and two baths) and can accommodate 10 overnighters. Two suites within the Beach House, perfect for couples, are available at select times during the year. If the Argonauta is full, inquire about the Waves or the White Heron Lodge, nearby and under the same management. ▪ *188 W 2nd (corner of Larch), Cannon Beach; (503)436-2601 or (800)822-2468; PO Box 3, Cannon Beach, OR 97110; waves@seasurf.com; $$; DIS, MC, V; checks OK.*

Cannon Beach Hotel ★ Originally a boardinghouse, the Cannon Beach Hotel is a tidy, nine-room operation with a decidedly European flavor, including a cheery lobby (with lovely bunches of flowers, fresh fruit, hot beverages, and a fireplace) that's just right for lounging or light reading after a stroll on the nearby beach. The rooms are all designated as nonsmoking and vary from a nicely decorated, one-bed arrangement to a one-bedroom suite with a gas fireplace, spa, and ocean view. A newspaper and a light breakfast are brought to your door come morning. The more spendy Courtyard, a jointly managed lodging, offers more seclusion (with its out-of-the-wind brick courtyard) and is situated a tad closer to the ocean. J. P.'s (1116 S Hemlock, (503)436-0908), the restaurant adjacent to the Cannon Beach hotel, is worth a visit regardless of where you're staying. It sports a hip attitude, with an open kitchen that features a theatrical chef (who manhandles fry pans awash with sherry), and serves up a nice selection of tantalizing preparations, including super salads and first-rate halibut and pastas. ▪ *1116 S Hemlock (corner of Gower), Cannon Beach; (503)436-1392; PO Box 943, Cannon Beach, OR 97110; $$; beer and wine; MC, V; checks OK; lunch, dinner every day (restaurant closed Sun in winter except holidays).*

Surfsand Resort An attractive beachfront complex, the Surfsand sits a short distance from Haystack Rock and the town's most crowded stretch of sand. Choose among an array of lodgings, including sleeping rooms, hyper-spendy suites (which sleep 6), and separate houses (which can accommodate up to 10 persons) located on the premises or sited around town. Most units have fireplaces; some sport kitchens and spas. All guests can soak in the indoor pool and spa and also receive complimentary use of the Cannon Beach Athletic Club facilities (located a couple of blocks away). The adjacent Wayfarer Restaurant, with lots of ocean-front windows, a cozy lounge, and so-so chow, is under the same management. Pets are okay in some of the units. ■ *Ocean-front at Grover (turn west at Hemlock and Grover), Cannon Beach; (503)436-2274 or (800)547-6100; PO Box 219, Cannon Beach, OR 97110; surfsand@seasurf.com; www.seasurf.com/~smmc; $$$; AE, MC, V; checks OK.* ♿

TOLOVANA PARK

Nestled on Cannon Beach's south side, Tolovana Park is laid back and less crowded than its northern neighbor, with a more residential character. Leave your vehicle at the Tolovana Park Wayside (with parking and rest rooms) and stroll a quiet beach, especially in the off season. At low tide you can walk all the way to Arch Cape, some five miles south, where you can pick up the Oregon Coast Trail. (But check your tidebook in case the incoming tide might block your return.)

RESTAURANTS

Homegrown Cafe ★ Hip, nutritious, and delicious, the Homegrown Cafe is reminiscent of a '60s-style healthnik eatery, but with a spiffed-up atmosphere and chow with pizzazz. There's a green-chile stew, breakfast burritos, English muffins topped with hot spiced apples, "veg-head" barley soup, and "tease loaf," a meatloaf lookalike concocted from brown rice, mushrooms, nuts, and herbs. ■ *3301 S Hemlock (across the street from Tolovana Wayside Park), Tolovana Park; (503)436-1803; $; no alcohol; no credit cards; checks OK; breakfast, lunch Fri–Tues, dinner Frid–Mon.*

LODGINGS

Stephanie Inn ★★ This gorgeous ocean-front lodging radiates the elegance of a New England country inn. Situated amid other motels and residences, it's not isolated but feels exclusive. Inside, the emphasis is on pampered and purposeful service. Most of the 46 rooms include gas fireplaces, Jacuzzis (or smaller, one-person spas), VCRs, and stunning furnishings; the deck rooms on the third floor are the sunniest and most private. A full complimentary, buffet-style breakfast is served in the dining room. Come evening, Northwest wines are featured in the library. Watch the ocean, play the piano, or cozy up to the fireplace in the hotel's Chart Room. They've got all the pieces to a three-star puzzle and are on their way toward earning the extra star. Prix-fixe dinners are available to guests on a daily basis. There's a two-night minimum stay on Saturdays (and during the month of August). ■ *2740 S Pacific (on the beach, at Matanuska and Pacific), Tolovana Park; (503)436-2221 or (800)633-3466; PO Box 219, Cannon Beach, OR 97110; stephinn@seasurf.com; www.seasurf.com~smmc; $$$; AE, DC, MC, V; checks OK.* ⅄

Sea Sprite Guest Lodgings ★ This cute, always-popular ocean-front motel is a good getaway choice for couples or the family (but not for pets). Each of the five small but homey attached units includes a kitchen, color TV, and VCR. Most have wood stoves. A separate two-bedroom cottage with full kitchen sleeps eight. There's a picnic area and grill, as well as a washer and dryer on the premises. Firewood (well, a presto log), beach towels, and beach blankets are provided upon request. ■ *280 Nebesna St (at Oceanfront), Tolovana Park; (503)436-2266; PO Box 933, Cannon Beach, OR 97110; $$; MC, V; checks OK.*

ARCH CAPE

This collection of shoreside residences between Hug Point and Cape Falcon offers an uncluttered beach. The **Oregon Coast Trail** winds up and over Arch Cape (beginning on the east side of Highway 101, just north of the tunnel; ask for directions at the post office/grocery store) and into Oswald West State Park.

LODGINGS

St. Bernards ★ Is it an English castle or a French chateau? You decide, but proprietors Don and Deanna Bernard roamed Europe for the furnishings gracing their palatial-looking lodging on the east side of Highway 101. You might discover French provincial tables and lounge chairs (the Bernards spent their summers in Provence before moving here) or a 130-year-old Austrian bed (in the Ginger Room). All seven rooms have private baths, gas fireplaces, VCRs, and refrigerators. The top-floor Tower includes a spa and has the best view. Admire the handsome woodwork and wrought-iron lighting and door fixtures throughout the structure, or explore its numerous nooks and crannies and winding, castlelike stairways. Outside, there are trees on most sides, a sizable deck, and a windless courtyard. ■ *3 E Ocean Rd (turn east off Hwy 101, across from the post office/grocery), Arch Cape; (503)436-2800 or (800)436-2848; PO Box 102, Arch Cape, OR 97102; $$$; AE, MC, V; checks OK.*

MANZANITA

Resting mostly on a sandy peninsula with undulating dunes covered in beach grass, shore pine, and Scotch broom, Manzanita is a lazy but growing community gaining popularity as a coastal getaway for in-the-know urbanites. The adjacent beach and nearby

Nehalem Bay have become windsurfing hot spots. **Nehalem Bay State Park**, just south of town, offers hiking and biking trails as well as miles of little-used beaches. There's beachcombing galore on either the ocean side or the Nehalem Bay side of the Manzanita peninsula, and resident sea lions bask on the sand near the mouth of the Nehalem River. Overlooking it all is nearby **Neahkahnie Mountain**, with a steep, switchbacked trail leading to its 1,600-foot summit—the best viewpoint on the northern Oregon coast. Just north of town, **Oswald West State Park** has one of the finest campgrounds on any coast in the world. You walk a half mile from the parking lot (where wheelbarrows are available to carry your gear) to tent sites among old-growth trees; the ocean, with a massive cove and tide pools, is just beyond. Surfing and kayaking are favorite year-round activities. No reservations are taken, and even though the walk cuts down on the crowds, the place is packed in summer. Be sure to secure all of your valuables out of sight in your car, or take them with you. Call (503)731-3411 for advance word on availability.

For sweet treats and espresso, visit Manzanita News and Espresso at 500 Laneda Avenue, (503)368-7450, or enjoy high tea and all the trimmings at Queen Bess Tea Room (411 Laneda Avenue, (503)368-4255). South of town, in Nehalem, the Hill House Deli offers more substantial fare (12870 Highway 101 N, (503)368-7933). Boats and tackle to explore or fish Nehalem Bay can be rented at the Wheeler Marina, 278 Marine Drive, Wheeler, (503)368-5780.

RESTAURANTS

Blue Sky Cafe ★★★ The Blue Sky purveys a blend of cutting-edge Northwest, Southwest, Mediterranean, and Asian cuisines. Think Thai peanut chicken, smoked-duck quesadillas, and black-bean hummus. Also consider baked salmon in a mustard-seed vinaigrette, spinach spaghetti with sautéed pancetta and wild mushrooms, or succulent Gulf shrimp rolled in rice papers with pickled cucumber and spicy soy-roasted peanuts. For dessert, test the sugar-charged "thermonuclear chocolate device," a chocolate truffle cake with brownie crust, caramel sauce, and whipped cream. Even the decor is eclectic. Salt 'n' pepper shakers ranging from miniature bowling pins to cow-driven tractors grace every table, while tiny, lime-green-lighted skeletons line the wine rack and dried peppers hang from the bar. The extensive wine list has an all-Oregon reserve pinot noir section but, alas, lists no vintages. This place is as far away from pretentious as you can get but has incredibly inventive food. ■ *154 Laneda Ave (at 2nd), Manzanita; (503)368-5712; $$$; full bar; no credit cards; checks OK; dinner Wed–Sun.* ♿

Jarboe's ★★★ Outside, Jarboe's resembles a cute but humble beach bungalow. Inside, the decor is unassuming, with unobtrusive lighting and eight tables dressed with crisp white linens and small vases of flowers. Nothing whatsoever is allowed to upstage chef Klaus Monberg's French-inspired cuisine. Along with his wife, Suzanne Lange, the Danish-born, classically trained Monberg purveys a limited à la carte menu that changes—in some cases daily—depending on what foodstuffs are available. Look for intricate colors, textures, and flavors, and expect lots of mesquite-grilled meats and seafood. Appetizers range from a mussel terrine highlighted by basil and saffron to a crisp-crusted pizzetta topped with roasted peppers and a mellow pecorino Romano. Crayfish complement a grilled salmon fillet enhanced with fennel, spinach, and dill, while sea scallops arrive skewered with mussels on a bed of red chard and slow-baked tomato confit. Desserts, such as Grand Marnier custard laced with raspberry sauce or a warm apple charlotte with crème Anglaise, are tantalizing. The exceptional wine list includes some stellar Oregon pinot noir choices. ■ *137 Laneda Ave (at Carmel), Manzanita; (503)368-5113; $$$; beer and wine; MC, V; checks OK; dinner Thurs–Mon (Thurs–Sun in winter).*

Cassandra's ★★ Under the direction of transplanted New Yorker Fawn de Turk, Cassandra's has evolved from a cool place to catch some hot pizza to an overall exceptional eatery (and the finest pizzeria on the Oregon coast). Fawn chooses organic produce for her salads and toppings, and uses only meats and flour without preservatives for her hand-spun pizzas. The colorful digs, just a block off the Manzanita ocean front, are a shrine to ocean play, decorated with vintage surfboards, saltwater paraphernalia, and imprints of water creatures. Pizzas range from traditional to way-different; the primavera pizza is outstanding. ■ *60 Laneda Ave (1 block off the beach), Manzanita; (503)368-5593; $; beer and wine; no credit cards; checks OK; dinner every day.* &

LODGINGS

The Inn at Manzanita ★★ One block off the beach, occupying a multilevel, woodsy setting similar to a Japanese garden, the Inn at Manzanita is a quiet, tranquil retreat. Each of the 13 spacious, nonsmoking units is finished in pine or cedar, with panels of stained glass here and there. Every room has a gas fireplace, a good-sized spa, a TV with VCR, a down comforter on the queen-size bed, and (except for the Hummingbird unit) a treetop ocean view. The Windrider features a vaulted ceiling and a paneled captain's bed (kind of like sleeping in an elegant sea chest). The newer and more modern-looking Cottage and Laneda units come with full kitchens and separate bedrooms. Extra touches include fresh flowers daily, terrycloth robes, and the morning paper at your doorstep. Two-night reservations are required in summer. ■ *67 Laneda Ave (1 block from the beach), Manzanita, OR 97130; (503)368-6754; $$$; MC, V; checks OK.*

Ocean Inn ★★ You'd have to sleep on the beach to get any closer than this to Manzanita's ocean waves. Remodeled (with six additional rooms) and ultra-attractive, the Ocean Inn offers 10 one-bedroom units, all nonsmoking. The cottagelike older units (1 is nicest, with a beachfront living room and sheltered deck) are nearer the ocean and feature knotty pine interiors, good-sized kitchens (with microwaves), wood stoves or fireplaces, and foldout futons. The spacious—and gorgeous—newer lodgings (9 is our favorite) boast vaulted ceilings with stained-glass chandeliers, sound-resistant walls, vertical-grain fir woodwork, and beautiful craftsmanship throughout. Most have full kitchens and wood heaters. Number 10 is fully equipped for persons with disabilities. Covered parking is provided for all guests. One-week minimum stay is required in July and August.
■ *20 Laneda Ave (on the beach), Manzanita; (503)368-6797 or (800)579-9801; PO Box 162, Manzanita, OR 97130; $$$; MC, V; checks OK.*

BAY CITY/GARIBALDI

Tillamook Bay is one of the homes for the summer salmon-fishing fleet, and these two burgs on Highway 101 are good places to find fresh seafood. Drive out on the pier at Bay City's Pacific Oyster Company (on the west side of Highway 101, (503)377-2323), for 'sters and a view. In Garibaldi, stop by Miller Seafood (on Highway 101, (503)322-0355) or Smith's Pacific Shrimp Co. (608 Commercial Drive, (503)322-3316) and ask what's fresh.

If you'd rather catch your own, head for Siggi-G Ocean Charters in Garibaldi (611 Commercial Drive, (503)322-3285). Or try your luck in the bay or nearby rivers. Anglers routinely haul in 30-pound-plus chinooks from the Ghost's Hole section of Tillamook Bay, and the Kilchis, Wilson, Tillamook, and Trask Rivers are superb salmon and steelhead streams.

RESTAURANTS

ArtSpace Gallery Cafe ★ Here's a novel idea: Combine an avant-garde art gallery exhibiting wooden carvings, marble sculptures, and wild-colored, multimedia paintings with an irresistible eatery. Gallery steps lead down to an intimate, bistro-like setting where a young and attentive waitstaff brings meals on octagonal glass tableware. Succulent Tillamook Bay oysters, lightly breaded, garlicked, and grilled or baked Italian-style with herbs and cheeses, are the limited menu's star attractions. But you'll also find a trio of fettuccines, baked chicken lightly bathed in lemon, and a couple of fresh-fish choices (and a tempting shrimp cocktail). Soups (such as the nectar-sweet carrot porridge) and even simple salads are as enlightening as the artwork. An outside deck provides an opportunity for sunny-day sipping and supping. ■ *9120 5th (Hwy 101 and 5th), Bay*

City; (503)377-2782; $; beer and wine; no credit cards; checks OK; lunch every day, dinner Thurs–Sat, brunch Sun. &

TILLAMOOK

A broad, flat expanse of bottomland created by the confluence of three rivers (Tillamook, Trask, and Wilson), Tillamook is best known as dairy country. On the north end of town along Highway 101 sits the home of Tillamook cheese, the **Tillamook County Creamery Association** plant and visitors center (4175 Highway 101 N, (503)842-4481). The tour is self-guided, but interesting. Afterward, nibble the free cheese samples, buy a scoop of Tillamook ice cream, or visit the restaurant and gift shop. Be prepared for hordes of tourists year-round. **Bear Creek Artichokes** (in Hemlock, 11½ miles south of Tillamook, and closed in winter, (503)398-5411), features a first-class selection of fruits, veggies, and herbs.

OCEANSIDE

A tiny seaside resort that defines "quaint," Oceanside lies 8 miles west of Tillamook along the 22-mile **Three Capes Scenic Drive**. Tracing one of Oregon's most beautiful stretches of coastline, the narrow, winding Three Capes road skirts the outline of Tillamook Bay, climbs over Cape Meares (where you can walk up to, and inside, the Cape Meares lighthouse), then traverses the shores of Netarts Bay before reaching **Cape Lookout State Park**, (503)842-3182, another jewel in Oregon's park system. The park offers 250 campsites (and yurts), along with headland-hugging trails and a huge stretch of little-used beach. The scenic drive scales Cape Lookout, the westernmost headland on the northern Oregon coast. Back at sea level lies a desertlike landscape of thousands of acres of sandy dunes, a favorite area for off-road recreational vehicles (which are required to stay in designated areas). The road to Pacific City and the route's third cape, Kiwanda, runs through lush, green dairy country.

▼
Tillamook
▲

RESTAURANTS

Roseanna's Oceanside Cafe ★ Thank goodness there's a worthwhile restaurant in pretty, pint-size (and noncommercialized) Oceanside. Outside, Roseanna's is a converted country grocery fronted by wooden walkways and a funky facade. But inside, pastel tones, polished service, and an upscale menu lend an urbane air. Order tiger prawns or Tillamook Bay oysters with one of three sauces, including a zippy sesame oil, ginger, and jalapeño concoction. Halibut or salmon (cod and snapper, too) might be finished with an apricot-ginger or a Dijon-citrus glaze, while the "big salad" is a cornucopia of vegetables and greens blended with crab, cod, shrimp, or chicken. Steaks, pasta, quiche (try the veggie, herb, and Swiss) and some top-drawer clam chowder are menu stalwarts. Look for warm Toll House pie topped with Tillamook ice cream for dessert. Dining-room views of the ocean and nearby Three Arch Rocks make meals more memorable. ■ *1490 Pacific St (on Oceanside's main drag), Oceanside; (503)842-7351; $$; full bar; MC, V; checks OK; breakfast Sat–Sun, lunch, dinner every day.* &

LODGINGS

House on the Hill Bring your binoculars. The setting, on a 250-foot-high bluff overlooking Three Arch Rocks (a bird, seal, and sea lion sanctuary) and the blue Pacific, is unbeatable. The "house" is actually a collection of buildings, with 16 units (all with refrigerators and ocean vistas) and a honeymoon suite. Nothing fancy, but the views are tops. Choose a unit with a kitchen and stock up on groceries in Tillamook. The Rock Room, with telescopes to spy on the wildlife and scan the horizon for whales, is open to all guests. Kids are fine for some units (but call ahead). ■ *1816 Maxwell Mountain Rd (at Maxwell Point), Oceanside; (503)842-6030; PO Box 187, Oceanside, OR 97134; $$; MC, V; no checks.*

CLOVERDALE

This is lush, green Tillamook County dairy country. The town of Cloverdale, with its high-arched bridge, raised wooden sidewalks, and stately church steeples, bills itself as "Oregon's Best Kept Secret," and that must be because we still haven't discovered anything but cows.

▼

Pacific City

▲

LODGINGS

Hudson House Bed & Breakfast ★★ Perched on a bluff in the middle of nowhere, the picturesque Hudson House, built in 1906 and on the National Register of Historic Places, evokes memories of a country weekend at Grandma's. The entire restored Victorian farmhouse is dedicated to the guests; your hosts, Richard and Judy Shinton, reside next door. The four guest rooms are decorated in an early-20th-century country style (brass beds, claw-footed tubs, and gabled ceilings) and look out on forested hillsides surrounding the pastoral Nestucca River valley, prime dairy country. Breakfasts are exceptional, including unusual treats such as cheese casseroles, apple-filled puff pancakes, and homemade Wholly Cow cereal. Pacific City, Cape Kiwanda, and the ocean are 3 miles away. ■ *37700 Hwy 101 S (2½ miles south of Cloverdale and east of Pacific City), Cloverdale, OR 97112; (503)392-3533; $$; AE, MC, V; checks OK.*

PACIFIC CITY

Pacific City is the home of the dory fleet, Oregon's classic fishing boats. The vessels enter the ocean in the south lee of Cape Kiwanda, sometimes competing with sea lions, surfers, and kayakers for water space. Up above, hang gliders swoop off the slopes of the cape and land on the sandy expanses below. The region's second Haystack Rock (Cannon Beach has the other) sits a half mile offshore.

Robert Straub State Park is situated at the south end of town and occupies most of the Nestucca beach sand spit. Fishing enthusiasts flock to the Pacific City area—the Nestucca and Little Nestucca Rivers are known as two of the finest salmon and steelhead streams in the state.

RESTAURANTS

Grateful Bread Bakery ★ Transplanted New Yorkers Laura and Gary Seide tempt you with robust breads, muffins, and a scrumptious array of sweets—carrot cake and gargantuan cinnamon rolls, to name a couple—in a cheerful, beachy setting. There are extensive breakfast and lunch menus, listing gingerbread pancakes, a hangtown fry bursting with oysters, and some very cheesy New York–style pizza. Other options include veggie lasagne, a few hearty soups, and an array of imaginative sandwiches (try the untraditional ham or turkey "Reuben"). Enjoy your coffee and cake out on the deck, and grab a loaf of bread or a baguette for the road. ■ *34805 Brooten Rd (on the Pacific City loop road), Pacific City; (503)965-7337; $; no alcohol; MC, V; checks OK; breakfast, lunch every day (closed in Jan and Wed–Thurs in other winter months).* &

Pelican Pub & Brewery The best spot for soaking up Cape Kiwanda's geographical splendor is this bright and airy beachfront pub. In-house craft brews include Kiwanda cream ale, Doryman's dark ale, Tsunami stout, and an unfiltered wheat brew called "Heiferweizen" (remember, this is cow country). Finger foods range from warm, garlicky bread sticks to deepfried clam strips. Beefy chili, a tempting sandwich lineup (try the charbroiled chicken), and a selection of thin-crusted pizzas coated with gobs of mozzarella and Tillamook cheeses round out the fare. ■ *33180 Cape Kiwanda Dr (on the beach at Cape Kiwanda), Pacific City; (503)965-7007; $; beer and wine; AE, DC, MC, V; checks OK; lunch, dinner every day.*&

Riverhouse Restaurant You might see a great blue heron perched on a log on the Nestucca River, which flows idly to the sea right outside the window. The Riverhouse is a calming stop, 3 miles off Highway 101, and far removed from the typical tourist trappings. It's small—10 or so tables—with hanging plants and a piano in the corner for local musicians who perform on weekends. The sizable menu (especially for such a diminutive place) ranges from hot tuna or broiled asparagus (with Jack and Parmesan cheeses) sandwiches to crêpes Florentine or a bucket of steamers. Don't miss the apple pie or the frosty ice-cream floats. ■ *34450 Brooten Rd (¼ mile north of the* *stoplight on Brooten Rd), Pacific City; (503)965-6722; $$; full bar; MC, V; checks OK; lunch, dinner every day (days vary in winter).* &

LODGINGS

Eagle's View Bed & Breakfast Eagles may perch here; it's certainly high enough, overlooking Nestucca Bay and the surrounding dairy and forest lands. More than likely, though, one of Mike and Kathy Lewis's dachsunds or Siamese cats will offer a polite greeting after you ascend the steep driveway and multileveled staircase to this secluded B&B. Five guest rooms, furnished with comfy chairs and cheery, handcrafted (by Kathy) quilts, are available. All have private baths, three enjoy spas, and one is wheelchair-accessible. Full breakfasts are served in the sizable downstairs dining area or out on the porch and decks, where the panoramas are grand. ■ *37975 Brooten Rd (½ mile east of Hwy 101), Pacific City; (503)965-7600 or (888)846-3292; PO Box 901, Pacific City, OR 97135; www.moriah.com/inns; $$; DIS, MC, V; checks OK.* &

NESKOWIN

A diminutive, mostly residential community lying in the lee of Cascade Head—a steeply sloped and forested promontory—Neskowin is the final port of refuge before the touristy "20 Miracle Miles" (as the stretch from Lincoln City to Newport used to be called). The beach here is narrower but less crowded than other locales. Proposal Rock, an offshore island, can be reached at very low tides.

Cascade Head has miles of little-used hiking trails that traverse rain forests and meadows, then skirt rocky cliffs. The trails begin at a marked trailhead about two miles south of Neskowin (visible from Highway 101). The old Neskowin Road, a narrow route that winds through horse farms and old-growth forests, is an enchanting side trip.

The **Sitka Center for Art and Ecology** operates on the south side of Cascade Head and offers seasonal classes on many subjects, plus numerous talks and exhibits; (503)994-5485. The Hawk Creek Cafe (4505 Salem, (503)392-3838) is a good bet for enjoying a beer or snack on an outdoor view deck.

LODGINGS

The Chelan ★ This attractive white-and-blue adobe structure encompasses nine condominium units, all with lovely ocean views. Private homes are nearby, but this place feels like a getaway retreat. There's a manicured front lawn, lush gardens, and a secluded atmosphere. Every condo has a well-equipped kitchen, a large living room with a picture window, and a brick fireplace. Most have two bedrooms. Ground-floor units have a private

▼

Neskowin

Lodgings

▲

entrance to a small backyard, with the ocean just beyond. Upstairs accommodations (off-limits to children) enjoy private balconies. ▪ *48750 Breakers Blvd (just off Salem Blvd), Neskowin, OR 97149; (503)392-3270; $$$; MC, V; checks OK.*

Pacific Sands A stone's throw from breaking waves, this well-maintained condo-motel with an average, bland exterior enjoys a super setting, although development is encroaching on either side. Only 10 of the condos are for rent; each has a fireplace, kitchen, and more than enough room to stretch out and get comfortable. Opt for a beachfront unit (if available), and step out to miles of untrampled sand. ▪ *48250 Breakers Blvd (at Amity), Neskowin; (503)392-3101; PO Box 356, Neskowin, OR 97149; $$; MC, V; checks OK.* &

OTIS

RESTAURANTS

Otis Cafe ★ The sole reason to visit Otis, a blacktop blink 2 miles east of Highway 101, is to dine at the Otis Cafe, a hugely popular, retro eatery with no-frills food at old-fashioned prices. Contented diners (no one leaves here hungry) nosh on beefy burgers, thick 'n' chunky soups, filling breakfasts (including plate-sized portions of hashbrowns, onions, peppers, and melted cheese), and huge malts and milk shakes. Dinner offerings include fish, pork chops, and chicken-fried steak. The buttery black bread is sold to go, in case you can't get enough of it while you're there; other baked items, especially the pies, are delish. ▪ *Hwy 18, Otis Junction (2 miles east of Hwy 101), Otis; (541)994-2813; $; beer and wine; AE, MC, V; checks OK; breakfast, lunch every day, dinner Fri–Sun.*

▼
Neskowin

Lodgings

▲

LINCOLN CITY

There is no off season here. Every weekend is crowded, and traffic can be the pits. A slew of factory outlets located halfway through town and gaming casinos (to the north and east) have added to the gridlock. The good news is that the restaurant, lodging, and activity choices have never been so favorable. You can seek some solitude on the 7 miles of continuous sandy beach that begin at Roads End (at the north end of town) and continue south all the way to Siletz Bay.

   Barnacle Bill's seafood store (2174 NE Highway 101, (541)994-3022) is well known (and open daily) for fresh and smoked seafood: salmon, sturgeon, albacore tuna, black cod, crab, and shrimp. On the north end of town, **Lighthouse Brewpub** (4157 N Highway 101, (541)994-7238) handcrafts some alluring ales (and offers 25 beers on tap). Right in the midst of all the hubbub, **Catch the Wind Kite Shop** (266 SE Highway 101,

(541)994-9500) is the headquarters for a successful kite manufacturing company, with eight outlets along the coast from Seaside to Florence. **Ryan Gallery**, north of town at 4270 Highway 101, (541)994-5391), exhibits mixed media, including fine Northwest watercolors and oils. **Mossy Creek Pottery** in Kernville, just south of Lincoln City, a half mile up Immonen Road, (541)996-2415, sells some of the area's best locally made, high-fired stoneware and porcelain.

RESTAURANTS

Bay House ★★★ Shoreside restaurants with spectacular views can often get away with serving overpriced, mediocre food. Happily, this is not the case at the Bay House, located on the banks of Siletz Bay, just out of reach of the glitzy Lincoln City tourist trade. The ambience is traditional—crisp tablecloths and lots of richly finished wood and brass. The seasonal menu features mostly seafood, sometimes in imaginative preparations such as a grilled catch of the day with shiitake and oyster mushrooms in a Bordeaux sauce, along with a blue-cheese potato pancake. Salmon might be highlighted by a hazelnut crust, while halibut could be brushed with Parmesan, baked, and served on a lily white béchamel sauce. Oysters, scallops, Dungeness crab legs (served with angel hair pasta)—they're all afforded reverential treatment. So, too, is rack of lamb roasted in an herb crust with port demiglace. Alongside the grilled pork loin stuffed with andouille sausage (accompanied by apple-currant compote) and the portobello mushrooms bathed in a pomegranate vinaigrette are splendidly simple dishes such as penne pasta tossed with seasonal veggies and herb-infused olive oil. Desserts (lemon-almond cheesecake or tiramisu, for instance) are ethereal. Time your reservations with sunset and experience the solace of Siletz Bay. ■ *5911 SW Hwy 101 (at the south edge of town), Lincoln City; (541)996-3222; $$$; full bar; AE, MC, V; checks OK; dinner every day (Wed–Sun only in winter).* ♿

Chameleon Cafe ★ This small storefront cafe packs one heck of a culinary punch, with plenty of variety. Reggae or Caribbean tunes emanate from the sound system, and the interior is sparsely decorated with outrageous art and patrolled by hip waitresses. The intriguing menu features dishes such as salmon cakes with aioli and red onions and hot artichoke pâté. Brie quesadillas and spicy fish tacos accompanied by black beans, rice, and a scintillating salsa highlight the south-of-the-border selections. Mediterranean cuisine is also in evidence, including various pasta dishes (try the penne with smoked salmon and pine nuts), a super-garlicky hummus served with pita crisps, and marinated eggplant sandwiches. ■ *2145 NW Hwy*

101 (on the west side of Hwy 101), Lincoln City; (541) 994-8422; $; beer and wine; MC, V; checks OK; lunch, dinner Mon–Sat. &

Salmon River Cafe ★ Part deli, part bistro, this is the place for picnic fixings and quality fast food. A large glass case displays unusual salads, pastas, and desserts, including bread pudding and chocolate pots de crème. Pastries, such as buttermilk scones and some mighty fine cinnamon rolls, adorn the counter. Sit-down diners will prize the cheerful service and the tempting aromas wafting from the open kitchen, presided over by Barbara Lowry (who formerly headed the kitchen at the Bay House). Breakfast features smoked salmon and scrambled eggs served with rosemary-and-garlic-kissed potatoes; lunch offerings include Italian-inspired sandwiches and Lincoln City's finest cheeseburgers; dinner (oysters with risotto, for example) will make you want to return the next morning. Browse the Italian and Northwest wine selection while waiting for your meal. ■ *40798 NW Logan Rd (at the north end of town, next to Safeway), Lincoln City; (541) 996-3663; $; beer and wine; no credit cards; checks OK; breakfast, lunch every day, dinner Wed–Sun.* &

Dory Cove Appreciative crowds continue to flock to this place, rain or shine. Hearty American fare, Oregon Coast–style, is the theme here: lots of seafood, steak, tasty chowder, and 20-plus kinds of burgers (including a half-pound monster). Dessert centers around homemade pie à la mode. Road's End Wayside, a small state park with good clamming, is right next door. ■ *5819 Logan Rd (next to state park), Lincoln City; (541) 994-5180; $; beer and wine; AE, DIS, MC, V; checks OK; lunch, dinner every day.* &

LODGINGS

Inlet Garden Oceanview Bed & Breakfast ★ Nestled on a steep hillside amidst shore pines and dense shrubbery, Inlet Garden is an ideal alternative to Lincoln City's glitzy ocean-front lodgings. The house, originally belonging to John Gray (the developer of Salishan, a few miles to the south), is built in the Northwest regional style, with lots of windows and exposed wood and a sizable ocean-view deck (where Oregon wines and hot cider are served). Both bright and airy guest suites have private baths and fireplaces. The Azalea enjoys an engaging ocean view; the Manzanita features a private garden patio. Three-course breakfasts are memorable, and the beach is less than a quarter mile away. ■ *646 NW Inlet (¼ mile north of the D River Wayside), Lincoln City, OR 97367; (541) 994-7932; inlet@newportnet.com; www.newportnet.com/inlet; $$; AE, MC, V; checks OK.*

Across the highway from Salishan, a cluster of shops includes the Gallery at Salishan, (800)764-2318, which exhibits superlative paintings, sculpture, and pottery. Farther south along Highway 101, stop at the Lincoln Beach Bagel Company (3930 Highway 101, (541)764-3882) for a snack.

RESTAURANTS

Chez Jeannette ★★★ Windows with flower boxes, white-washed brick walls, and an intimate woodsy setting (as well as two fireplaces, usually blazing away in winter) give this establishment the appearance of a French country inn. The food is French—traditionally so: butter and cream are used in abundance, and most entrees are carefully sauced. And, bucking the seafood tradition seen up and down the coast, veal (sautéed medallions with a Dijon mustard sauce), roasted rack of lamb (with an Oregon pinot noir sauce), and pork (garnished with garlic, red wine, and juniper berries) make appearances on the menu. There's also a superb filet mignon and a nightly game selection (venison or, perhaps, duckling). But Chez Jeannette is by no means a slouch when it comes to seafood: witness the baked Umpqua oysters, local mussels in a sumptuous saffron-cream sauce, and salmon poached in Triple Sec and served with a rhubarb compote. The escargots are the coast's finest. ■ *7150 Old Hwy 101 (¼ mile south of Salishan Lodge on the old highway), Gleneden Beach; (541)764-3434; $$$; full bar; AE, MC, V; checks OK; dinner every day.* &

LODGINGS

Salishan Lodge ★★★ Salishan aficionados, and there are plenty, were worried when the place was sold (in 1996), but needlessly, because the Oregon Coast's preeminent resort has lost none of its allure. Sprawled over a lush, green, 350-acre landscape, Salishan includes 205 guest rooms, arranged in eight-plex units which are nicely dispersed on a hillside rising from the main entrance. There's an 18-hole (par 72) golf course, plus driving range, 18-hole putting course, pro shop, and resident PGA professional. You can swim in a covered pool, play indoor or outdoor tennis, work out in the sizable fitness center, sweat in a sauna, or jog and hike the forested trails. Kids have their own game room and play area. The huge wooden lodge, with vaulted ceilings and exposed beams, houses restaurants, a nightclub, a library, meeting rooms, and a gift shop. The guest units are spacious and tastefully furnished but not extravagant, with gas-fired fireplaces, view balconies (overlooking the forest, the links, or Siletz Bay), splashes of regional art, and individual carports. Forest, Sandpiper, and Overlook clusters, as well as both Chieftain Houses, benefit from secluded settings. Many unit clusters (including Tournament, Five Greens, Fairway, and the Sunset Suite) overlook the links; Tennis House is nearest the courts. As you'd expect, Northwest cuisine—alder-planked salmon, rack of lamb with a rhubarb-currant chutney, grilled abalone—dominates the menu in the main dining room, with its Siletz Bay views. The voluminous wine list represents a cellar stocked with 15,000 bottles, perhaps the region's foremost selection. Service throughout the resort is refined and purposeful (and less formal than previously). ■ *On Hwy 101 in Gleneden Beach; (541) 764-3600 or (800) 452-2300; PO Box 118, Gleneden Beach, OR 97388; salishan@salishan.com; www.-salishan.com; $$$; full bar; AE, DC, DIS, MC, V; checks OK; breakfast, lunch, dinner every day.* &

DEPOE BAY

Once a charming coastal community, Depoe Bay is today mostly an extension of Lincoln City's strip development. Fortunately, some of the original town, including its picturesque and tiny harbor (surely one of the smallest anywhere), remains intact. Depoe Bay bills itself as a **whale-watching mecca**, and during the gray whale migratory season (December through April) the leviathans may cruise within hailing distance of headlands. Tradewind Charters, (541) 765-2345, and Deep Sea Trollers, (541) 765-2248, are two of several operations offering whale-watching cruises.

The Channel Bookstore (Highway 101, one block south of the bridge, (541) 765-2352) is a used-book paradise. The O'Connell Gallery (42 N Highway 101, (541) 765-3331) features environmental art and a great water-level view.

RESTAURANTS

Tidal Raves ★ Indeed, diners rave about the imaginatively prepared seafood served in this enticing cliffside restaurant. Look for charbroiled Thai prawns, cornmeal-grilled snapper garnished with tomato relish, and penne pasta blended with sautéed scallops, feta, and sun-dried tomatoes. The extensive menu also lists lemon-rosemary chicken with polenta, oyster-spinach bisque, and broiled shrimp or crab sandwiches. Every table in the attractive interior overlooks sculpted cliffs, rock reefs, and crashing waves. Sunset raves too. ■ *279 NW Hwy 101 (on the west side of the highway), Depoe Bay; (541) 765-2995; $$; beer and wine; MC, V; checks OK; lunch, dinner every day.*

LODGINGS

Channel House ★ Intimate seaside inns (generally larger than B&Bs) with great settings and gracious service are gaining favor in the Northwest, and the Channel House was among the first. Spectacularly situated on a cliff overlooking the ocean and the Depoe Bay channel (literally right above the water, since there's no beach below), this place has 12 rooms, all with private baths, ocean views, and, come morning, a hearty breakfast.

Ten units are truly special accommodations, outfitted with private decks, gas fireplaces, and spas (the seven roomier, and spendier, suites feature ocean-front spas on a private deck). Two additional (and similarly appointed) suites are available in the owner's house, a few doors away. Be sure to bring your binoculars, especially during whale-watching season. ■ *35 Ellingson St (at the end of Ellingson St, above the ocean), Depoe Bay; (541) 765-2140 or (800) 447-2140; PO Box 56, Depoe Bay, OR 97341; cfinseth@newportnet.com; www.channelhouse.com; $$$; DIS, MC, V; checks OK.*

Inn at Otter Crest ★ This rambling destination resort perched on 35 acres at Cape Foulweather is lushly landscaped with evergreens, coastal shrubs, and every color of rhododendron imaginable. Upon arrival, you leave your car and hop a shuttle van to your room, where traffic noise is nonexistent. Breathtaking views abound, but Cape Foulweather is aptly named: summer fog often enshrouds the headland, though sunny skies may prevail just north and south. Still, most of the 280-plus units (not all are rentable, as some are privately owned) enjoy fireplaces, full kitchens, and superlative ocean vistas; all have private decks and refrigerators. Other amenities include an outdoor pool (with a sauna and spa) and tennis courts, along with volleyball, horseshoe, and shuffleboard areas. An isolated low-tide beach awaits 50 or so feet below, and nature trails lead to nearby Devil's Punch Bowl and additional beach access. ■ *301 Otter Crest Loop (2 miles south of Depoe Bay), Otter Rock; (541) 765-2111 or (800) 452-2101; PO Box 50, Otter Rock, OR 97369; $$$; AE, DC, MC, V; no checks.* ᕪ

▼

Newport

▲

NEWPORT

The most popular tourist destination on the Oregon Coast, Newport blends tasteful development (the Performing Arts Center, for example) with unending shopping-center sprawl. Lately, the furor over Keiko (the famous "Free Willy" killer whale residing at the Oregon Coast Aquarium) has engulfed Newport like the wind and sideways rain of a winter sou'wester, and the tourist season is unending. To discover all that Newport has to offer, steer away from Highway 101's commercial chaos. Head for the bay front, a working harbor going full tilt, where fishing boats of all types—trollers, trawlers, shrimpers, and crabbers—berth year-round. Many **charter boat** operators have initiated whale-watching excursions, in addition to their half- and full-day fishing trips. Sea Gull Charters (343 SW Bay Boulevard, (541) 265-7441) and Newport Sport Fishing (1000 SE Bay Boulevard, (541) 265-7558 or (800) 828-8777) are two popular operators. Also check out Marine Discovery Tours (345 SW Bay Boulevard, (541) 265-6200 or (800) 903-2628) for unusual saltwater adventures. Rent clam shovels and crabbing gear, as well as boats and bicycles, at the Embarcadero Dock (1000 SE Bay Boulevard, (541)265-5435). Afterward, quaff a native beer at the **Rogue Ales Public House** (748 SW Bay Boulevard, (541)265-3188), home of the local microbrewery. Or sample the fresh catch at the Taste of Newport (837 SW Bay Boulevard, (541)574-9450), which offers indoor and outdoor dining (and is a great stop for kids).

Oceanic Arts Center (444 SW Bay Boulevard, (541)265-5963) and the **Wood Gallery** (818 SW Bay Boulevard, (541)265-6843), both on the bay front, are galleries worth visiting. The former offers mostly jewelry, paintings, pottery, and sculpture; the latter, functional sculpture, woodwork, pottery, and weaving.

The Nye Beach area, on the ocean side of the highway, has fewer tourists and more of an arts-community feel, housing a potpourri of tourists, writers, artists, and fishermen. The **Newport Performing Arts Center** (777 S Olive, (541)265-ARTS) is an attractive wooden structure that hosts music, theater, and other events, some of national caliber. The **Visual Arts Center** at 839 NW Beach, (541)265-5133, offers an ocean-front setting for exhibits and classes. For a bird's-eye perspective of boats, bay, and ocean, take a drive through **Yaquina Bay State Park**, which wraps around the south end of town.

On the southeast side of the Yaquina Bay Bridge, Oregon State University's **Hatfield Marine Science Center** (2030 S Marine Science Drive, (541)867-0100) offers displays, a facsimile tide pool, and a full range of free nature walks, field trips (including whale-watching excursions, which have an admission charge), and films. Nearby, the pride of Newport, the **Oregon Coast Aquarium** (2820 SE Ferry Slip Road, (541)867-3474), features furry, finny, and feathery creatures cavorting in re-created tide pools, cliffs, and caves—and, of course, that famous orca whale. The exhibits are first-class. A drive out South Jetty Road affords sea-level views of harbor ship traffic. A couple of miles farther south is the area's best, and most extensive, camping site, **South Beach State Park**; (541)867-4715. Find yurts here, too.

North of town, above Agate Beach, **Yaquina Head Outstanding Natural Area** features the restored Yaquina Lighthouse (circa 1873 and open to the public), hiking trails, and fantastic cliff-front panoramas. Visit the intertidal area for viewing marine birds, fish, and mammals; it's accessible for persons with disabilities and safe for kids. Check out the new **Yaquina Head Interpretive Center** here.

RESTAURANTS

Canyon Way Restaurant and Bookstore ★★ Canyon Way is as much an emporium as an eatery, with a bookstore, gift shop, deli, and restaurant on the premises. You could easily get sidetracked on the way to your table, or decide to forgo a sit-down meal in favor of the many take-out munchies available. If you stay, you'll find a pleasingly diverse menu loaded with seafood and fresh pasta plates. A Cajun turkey sandwich, grilled lingcod 'n' chips, and Dungeness crab cakes with angel-hair onion rings, along with a variety of salads, are good noontime options. For dinner, there's a different baked oyster preparation daily, and choices as diverse as chicken curry and prawns Provençal. On sunny days, request an outdoor table overlooking the bay. ■ *1216 SW Canyon Way (between Hurbert St and Bay Blvd), Newport; (541)265-8319; $$; full bar; AE, MC, V; checks OK; lunch Mon–Sat, dinner Tues–Sat (bookstore and deli open every day).* &

Whale's Tale ★ In tourist-oriented Newport, where mediocre restaurants come and go, the Whale's Tale has been serving up good food for more than 20 years. Unfortunately, the cavelike whale-motif interior looks ragged around the ribs, er, edges. Customers remain a healthy mix of fishermen, aging hippies, Newport yuppies, and adventuresome tourists. Breakfasts can be outstanding, with fresh jalapeño omelets, scrumptious poppy-seed pancakes, and home-fried potatoes with onions and green chiles smothered in cheese. Lunches include good-sized sandwiches and a lusty fisherman's stew. A plate of grilled Yaquina oysters is a dinnertime favorite, along with lasagne, German sausage, ham and sauerkraut, and excellent black bread. ■ *452 SW Bay Blvd (at Hurbert), Newport; (541)265-8660; $$; beer and wine; AE, DC, MC, V; checks OK; breakfast, lunch, dinner every day (closed Wed in winter).*

Cosmos Cafe & Gallery A step inside this casually hip eatery is akin to a small step into outer space: ceilings are painted deep blue and highlighted by heavenly bodies. You order from a serving counter, cafeteria-style, and then wait for your name to be called. The choices of salads, sandwiches, pastas, omelets, and Tex-Mex concoctions are legion. Try the Hawaiian ham-pineapple-and-onion sandwich wrapped in pita, the sassy Cajun-chicken burrito, or a hot pastrami on rye (a rarity for the coast). The adjacent gallery is also otherworldly and fun. ■ *740 W Olive St (across from the Performing Arts Center), Newport; (541)265-7511; $; beer and wine; DIS, MC, V; local checks only; breakfast, lunch, dinner every day (closed Sun in winter).* &

LODGINGS

Sylvia Beach Hotel ★★ Owners Goody Cable and Sally Ford have dedicated their pleasantly funky bluff-top hotel to book-worms and their literary heroes and heroines. They gave several like-minded friends the task of decorating each of the 20 rooms, and the results are rich in whimsy and fresh, distinct personality—a true beach place, endearingly worn. Best way to do this hotel is to book (well in advance) one of the three "classics." The Agatha Christie Suite, for instance, is decorated in a lush green English chintz, with a tiled fireplace, a large deck facing out over the sea cliff below, and—best of all—clues from the writer's many murders. The "bestsellers" (views) and the "novels" (nonviews) are quite small, not as impressive, but equally imaginative. Books and comfortable chairs abound in the library, where hot wine is served nightly at 10pm. Prepare for a stay sans phones, radios, TVs, and stress. Breakfast is included in the price of the room. Dinners in the hotel's Tables of Content restaurant are prix-fixe, reservation-only affairs. The main attraction is the company; the food (although it's noteworthy) gets secondary billing. ■ *267 NW Cliff St (west on NW 3rd off Hwy 101, 6 blocks to NW Cliff), Newport, OR 97365; (541)265-5428; $$; beer and wine; AE, MC, V; checks OK; breakfast, dinner every day.* &

Nye Beach Hotel & Cafe ★ There are so many lodging choices in Newport, it's fortuitous that two of the finest, and the most unusual, are virtually next door to each other. Just south of the Sylvia Beach Hotel, the newer Nye Beach Hotel & Cafe has a funky, '50s feel. Green metal railings lead to second and third floors, with narrow carpeted hallways sporting wildly shaped mirrors and myriad succulents. All 18 tidy guest rooms feature private baths, fireplaces, willow love seats, balconies, and ocean views. Six units have spas. The hotel's lobby, awash in eclectic tunes, has a piano and a tiny bar. Steps lead down to a bistro-like setting where a suave waitstaff serves shrimp enchiladas, oyster stew, chicken satays, and a scrumptious chocolate sponge pudding dessert. Outside, there's a large and heated deck for ocean-front dining. ■ *219 NW Cliff St (just south of the Sylvia Beach Hotel), Newport, OR 97365; (541)265-3334; www.teleport.com/~nyebeach/hotel.html; $$; full bar; AE, DIS, MC, V; checks OK; breakfast, lunch, dinner every day.* &

Ocean House ★ Roomier and slightly less quaint than its former incarnation, the Ocean House affords some privacy in the Oregon Coast's most bustling area. Host Bob Garrard is the epitome of congeniality, and the setting remains picture-perfect—overlooking the surf at Agate Beach, with Yaquina Head and its lighthouse towering nearby. The five guest rooms, all with private baths and ocean views (and some with spas), are homey and comfortable—neither elegant nor luxurious. There's a small library with cushy chairs and a roaring fireplace in the winter. Outside, you can enjoy a full beakfast on sunny mornings, or just relax and sunbathe protected from the summer northwest wind in the sheltered backyard and garden. A short trail leads to the beach below. If Ocean House is booked, consider the Tyee Lodge (with five guest rooms) across the street and also ocean-front. ■ *4920 NW Woody Way (just off Hwy 101 N in Agate Beach, 1 block south of Yaquina Head Lighthouse Rd), Newport, OR 97365; (541)265-6158 or (800)56BANDB; $$$; MC, V; checks OK.*

Artists and others seeking elbow room have moved here from crowded Newport. It's still not much more than a patch of strip development along Highway 101, but within that patch are a few keepers. Some interesting chainsaw art is being created at **Seal Rock Woodworks** (along Highway 101, (541)563-2452). Also along the highway, a tiny storefront with a sign proclaiming "Fudge" sells a variety of light and dark fudge and some tasty ice cream; (541)563-2766. Farther south, **Art on the Rocks** (5667 NW Pacific Coast Highway, 2 miles north of the Alsea Bay Bridge, (541)563-3920) has paintings, carvings, crafts, and jewelry. **Ona Beach State Park** (a mile north of town) provides fishing, swimming, and bird-watching possibilities.

RESTAURANTS

Yuzen ★ You may think you're hallucinating. A Japanese restaurant residing in a Bavarian-styled building, located in Seal Rock, a blink of a town with a Wild West motif? No, Yuzen is for real—the home of the coast's finest Japanese cuisine. Even if raw fish isn't your idea of a delectable morsel, you'll enjoy the mildly flavored tuna, salmon, and prawn served in the sushi sampler appetizer (which you should order anyway, as it may take awhile for your entree to arrive). Sukiyaki is splendid, as are the tempura dishes. Dinners include a decent miso soup and a small salad. There's even a wafu steak, a traditional Japanese grilled New York steak with two sauces and veggies. And if you've never tried sake or matcha (green tea) ice cream, this is the place. ■ *Hwy 101 (8 miles south of Newport), Seal Rock; (541)563-4766; $$; beer and wine; MC, V; checks OK; lunch, dinner Tues–Sun.*

▼

Waldport

▲

Waldport is a town in coastal limbo, overshadowed by its larger, better-known neighbors—Newport to the north and Yachats to the south. Not to worry, Waldport has much to recommend it, including the lovely Alsea River estuary, untrampled beaches at either end of town, and a city center unspoiled by tourism. At the south end of the Alsea Bay Bridge (beautifully rebuilt in 1991) is an interpretive center with historic transportation displays. There's good clamming and crabbing in the bay, and equipment (including boats) can be rented at the Dock of the Bay Marina (1245 Mill, (541)563-2003) in the Old Town section, on the water just east of the highway.

The remote, pocket-sized **Drift Creek Wilderness** is tucked into the Coast Range halfway between Seal Rock and Waldport. Visit the Waldport Ranger District office (south of town, off Highway 101, (541)563-3211) for maps and information.

LODGINGS

Cape Cod Cottages ★ Between Waldport and Yachats, the beach becomes narrower and less frequented. Cape Cod Cottages, sitting on a low bank just off Highway 101, occupies 300 feet of this ocean frontage, with easy beach access. Ten cozy (and spic-and-span) one- and two-bedroom units come with fully equipped kitchens, fireplaces (with wood provided), decks, and picture windows overlooking the ocean. The larger units sleep as many as eight. Some even have garages. All in all, this is a nice, out-of-the-way place where children are welcome. ▪ *4150 SW Pacific Coast Hwy (2½ miles south of Waldport, on Hwy 101), Waldport, OR 97394; (541)563-2106; $$; AE, MC, V; checks OK.*

Cliff House Bed and Breakfast ★ At this bright blue B&B perched atop the Alsea River's mouth, you can watch seals and salmon-hungry sea lions just below, as well as migrating whales and memorable sunsets. Four ultra-posh rooms are available; all include antique furnishings, chandeliers, color TVs, water views, and balcony overlooks. The Bridal Suite (the price is no honeymoon) houses a tufted velvet sleigh bed with canopy, an ocean-front mirrored bath with Jacuzzi, and a shower for two. Unfortunately, we've withheld a star this edition due to numerous reports of uneven service (a vital component of any B&B), but our anonymous spies continue to claim they've witnessed nothing less than topnotch attention. Out back, there's an ocean-view deck with an oversize spa, as well as a sauna and steam room, croquet course, and a hammock for two. Massages can be had in the cliffside gazebo (or in your room) for a fee. ▪ *1450 Adahi Rd (1 block west of Hwy 101), Waldport; (541)563-2506; PO Box 436, Waldport, OR 97394; clifhos@pioneer.net; www.virtualcities.com; $$$; MC, V; checks OK.*

Edgewater Cottages ★ Lots of honeymooners land here, and the place is usually booked from the beginning of the tourist season. The nine units (which are regularly upgraded) are varied and rustic-looking, with lots of knotty pine paneling and a beachy feel throughout. The cute, pint-size Wheel House (a steal at $50–$60) is strictly a 2-person affair, while the Beachcomber can accommodate as many as 15 guests. Every cottage has an ocean view, a fireplace (firewood provided), a kitchen, and a sun deck. There's only one phone on the premises, but other necessities, such as corkscrews, popcorn poppers, and food processors, are plentiful. There are minimum-stay requirements, and kids and pets are fine (the latter by prior approval only; $5 extra, too). The owners live on premises, contributing to the homey atmosphere. ▪ *3978 SW Pacific Coast Hwy (2½ miles south of Waldport, on Hwy 101), Waldport, OR 97394; (541)563-2240; $$; no credit cards; checks OK.*

Yachats (pronounced "ya-hots") means "at the foot of the mountain." Tide pools teeming with marine life dot the rocky shoreline; above loom spectacular headlands affording excellent ocean and whale-watching vistas. The Yachats River intersects downtown and empties into the Pacific, providing a playground for seabirds, seals, and sea lions. Between April and October, sea-run smelt (savory, sardinelike fish) are harvested in the coast's sandy coves (visit Smelt Sands State Park, on the town's north end, for a look). The town has a hip, arts-community flavor, with an interesting mix of aging counterculturalists, yups, and tourists. Good local galleries include the Earthworks Gallery (2222 N Highway 101, (541)547-4300) and the Backporch Gallery (Fourth & Highway 101, (541)547-4500). Yachats is also home to the Oregon Coast's oldest **kite festival**; call (541)547-3530 for information.

Yachats is situated at the threshold of the spectacular 2,700-acre **Cape Perpetua Scenic Area**. Hiking trails lead to isolated coves and rocky ledges constantly bombarded by ocean waves. Other paths head deep into bona fide rain forest. Driving along Highway 101 provides an exhilarating journey, packed with panoramas of rugged cliffs abutting the ever-charging Pacific. The Cape Perpetua Visitors Center (2400 Highway 101 S, (541)547-3289) offers films, displays, maps, and a logical starting point.

▼

Yachats

RESTAURANTS

Restaurants

▲

La Serre ★ Fine dining options drop off drastically south of Newport, but La Serre ("the greenhouse") is one of the central coast's better restaurants. The largest plant collection this side of Cape Perpetua's rain forest highlights a dining area with overhead skylights and a beamed ceiling. Herbal aromas redolent of garlic and saffron drift down from the open kitchen, while an appealing (and roaring in winter) fireplace distinguishes an adjacent lounge. Seafood is a good bet, be it catch-of-the-day Pacific whitefish, Umpqua oysters, or zesty cioppino; vegetarian dishes are top-drawer, too. Come Sunday morning, this is breakfast headquarters. ■ *160 W 2nd (2nd and Beach, downtown), Yachats; (541)547-3420; $$; full bar; AE, MC, V; local checks only; breakfast Sun, dinner every day (closed Jan, closed Tues Oct–June).*

New Morning Coffeehouse ★ A cross section of Yachats society—tourists, hip locals in Gore-Tex and faded jeans, and Eugene weekenders—frequents this pleasant retreat. The muffins, Danishes, pies, and coffee cakes are superb. Savory soups and black bean chili are typical luncheon fare. During summer, the kitchen whips up darn good pasta dinners (a mixed veggie fettuccine, for instance) to complement weekend live music. Enjoy it all by the homey wood stove or, on warmer days, on the sunny and out-of-the-wind back deck. ■ *373 Hwy 101 N (at 4th*

St), Yachats; (541)547-3848; $; beer and wine; DIS, MC, V; checks OK; breakfast, lunch every day, dinner Thurs–Sat in summer (closed Mon–Tues in winter).

LODGINGS

Sea Quest Bed & Breakfast ★★ Few B&Bs on the Oregon Coast are better situated than this (well, the Ziggurat next door, perhaps). At Sea Quest you spend the night in a luxurious, estate-like structure located on a sandy, beach-grassed bluff right above the ocean and nearby Tenmile Creek. Four out of the five guest rooms have spas in their baths, plush queen-size beds, private entrances, and ocean views. Miles of Pacific vistas are yours to enjoy from the spacious living room. Scan the horizon with the spyglass, or plunk down with a good book in one of the commodious chairs. ■ *95354 Hwy 101 (6½ miles south of Yachats on west side of Hwy 101, between mile markers 171 and 172), Yachats; (541)547-3782 or (800)341-4878; PO Box 448, Yachats, OR 97498; www.seaq.com; $$$; MC, V; checks OK.*

Ziggurat Bed & Breakfast ★★ This stunning, four-story glass-and-wood structure takes its name from the Sumerian word for "terraced pyramid." It sits on a sandy knoll, up against the roaring Pacific and the gurgling waters of Tenmile Creek. Scintillating views from all 40 windows keep most guests occupied, especially during storms (the glass-enclosed decks are ideal); however, there are also plenty of books and board games in the 2,000-square-foot living room. The east suite boasts a sauna, while the west suite has a round, glass-block shower and a magnificent view. If you're in the market for a quality B&B, this might just be your place. ■ *95330 Hwy 101 (6½ miles south of Yachats on west side of Hwy 101), Yachats; (541)547-3925; PO Box 757, Yachats, OR 97498; $$$; no credit cards; checks OK.*

The Adobe Resort ★ Ensconced in a private, parklike setting, the Adobe fans out around the edge of a basalt-bumpy shore. At high tide, waves crash onto the rocks below while their thunder echoes through the building. The rooms are sizable and come with refrigerators, TVs, VCRs, and coffee-makers. Most have ocean views and a number have fireplaces. The plusher suites (some with spas and fireplaces) all look out on the ocean. All guests have access to a six-person Jacuzzi and sauna. Children are welcome, and pets are allowed in the northwest wing and the four-person apartment units. The on-site restaurant, as ocean-front as you can get (every table enjoys a water vista), rates a notch above the usual mediocre beachtown fare. ■ *1555 Hwy 101 (downtown), Yachats; (541)547-3141 or (800)522-3623; PO Box 219, Yachats, OR 97498; $$; full bar; AE, DC, DIS, MC, V; checks OK; breakfast, lunch Mon–Sat, dinner every day, brunch Sun. &*

Burd's Nest Inn Bed and Breakfast ★ This is one distinctive roost, perched halfway up a hillside and enjoying a big bird's-eye view of the Pacific. The half-century-old home has a cluttered but comfortable look, especially inside, where antiques, unusual toys, and knickknacks compete for wall and table space. The proprietors lend an animated, friendly ambience and specialize in made-to-order breakfasts. ■ *664 Yachats River Rd (east side of Hwy 101, just before the bridge), Yachats, OR 97498; (541) 547-3683; $$; MC, V; no checks.*

Shamrock Lodgettes Disregard the cutesy name; these rustic log-cabin-like units, sequestered on a grassy, 4-acre ocean-front terrace with easy beach access, are cozy and comfortable. All 19 "lodgettes" (some are cabins, but most are rooms) enjoy fireplaces, while some have small kitchens. Rooms 8–15 and apartment 7 are the best deals. Cabin 6, with two bedrooms and baths, sleeps eight. A separate structure houses a sauna and spa open to all guests, and personal massages can be arranged. Pets are welcome in the cabin units. ■ *On Hwy 101 S (just south of the Yachats River bridge), Yachats; (541) 546-3312 or (800) 845-5028; PO Box 346, Yachats, OR 97498; $$; AE, DC, M, V; checks OK.*

FLORENCE

Florence, intersected by the deep, green Siuslaw River, is surrounded by the beauty of the Oregon Dunes National Recreation Area, several large freshwater lakes and, in spring and summer, bright pink and red rhododendron flowers. The geography here—and for 50 miles south—is devoid of the trademark rugged Oregon Coast headlands. Instead, expansive sand dunes, some of them hundreds of feet high, dominate the landscape.

Florence has transformed itself from a sleepy fishing village to a tourist mecca, but the local catch can still be had at Weber's Fish Market on the main strip (802 Highway 101, (541) 997-8886). The revitalized **Old Town**, a continually upgraded few blocks of shops, restaurants, and some of the town's oldest structures, has become visitor-oriented without selling out to schlock.

The **Oregon Dunes National Recreation Area** (see Reedsport for headquarters info) extends for more than 50 miles from Heceta Beach to Coos Bay—32,000 acres of mountainous sand dunes. Orient yourself to this intriguing ecosystem by exploring the South Jetty Road, just south of Florence, or the Oregon Dunes Overlook, another 11 miles south on Highway 101. The dunes, which reach 600 feet high, hide lakes with excellent swimming potential and mysterious tree islands.

Five miles north of Florence is **Darlingtonia Botanical Wayside**, a bog featuring insect-eating plants called cobra lilies. Their unusual burgundy flowers bloom in May. Another 6 miles farther brings you to **Sea Lion Caves**, 91560 Highway 101, (541) 547-3111 (much less kitschy than the advance hype might suggest). You descend 21 stories to a peephole in a natural, surf-swept cavern, where hundreds of sea lions frolic or doze on the rocks.

Also north of town is **Heceta Head Lighthouse**, the Oregon Coast's most powerful beacon and, perhaps, the most photographed lighthouse on the West Coast. Situated just off Highway 101, the lighthouse itself isn't open to the public, although the former lightkeeper's quarters are. This supposedly haunted but truly lovely house can be reserved for weddings or other gatherings, and now also serves as a weekend-only bed and breakfast with three guest rooms; (541) 547-3696.

RESTAURANTS

Blue Hen Cafe ★ Just try to suppress a cackle when you notice the glass, ceramic, and plastic chickens—blue, naturally—everywhere. What's important, though, is that the place is friendly, the prices are reasonable, the food is tasty, and there's lots of it. As you might expect, chicken (always Oregon-fresh fryers) dominates the menu, and it's available baked, grilled, and fried. You'd be hard pressed to finish off an entire "four-cackle" special. The kitchen also serves some fine breakfasts, a few burger choices, pasta, and a surprising number of vegetarian dishes, such as a spinach-broccoli-carrot lasagne and a "chirps Parmesan," roasted potato slices smothered with cheese. Expect to wait awhile in summer, when the place gets packed. ■ *1675 Hwy 101 (in the north part of town), Florence; (541) 997-3907; $; beer and wine; MC, V; local checks only; breakfast, lunch, dinner every day.* ⅃

International C-Food Market ★ Catch it, cook it fresh, and keep it simple is the plan at this big, sprawling seafood operation right on the Siuslaw River pier at the edge of Old Town. The fish-receiving station and the fishing fleet are just outside the restaurant. It's fun to dine on the deck and watch the boats offload (ask for a table at the bar end of the restaurant for the best views). Fresh fish, crab, oysters, and clams are served any way you like 'em. Visit the attached seafood market if you want to cook it yourself. An entranceway sign announces what's being unloaded. ■ *1498 Bay St (at the Siuslaw River), Florence; (541) 997-9646; $$; full bar; MC, V; checks OK; lunch, dinner every day.* ⅃

LODGINGS

Coast House ★★ To call this place picturesque, exclusive, or even spectacular might be understating the case. Coast House is certainly one of a kind, and it's rented to only one group (one or two couples) at a time. The location couldn't be finer—total seclusion on a forested (1⅓-acre) ocean-front cliff just south of Sea Lion Caves. But you'd never find it on your own, so you need to rendezvous with owners Nancy Archer and Ron Hogeland in

Florence beforehand. The four-level, 1,000-square-foot structure features two sleeping lofts with skylights, a full kitchen, roomy living quarters, and a bath with a claw-footed tub overlooking the ocean. Electric baseboard heat keeps Coast House warm, and an antique wood-burning stove (ample fuel provided) renders it romantic. All necessities (robes, music, a bottle of wine), except food, are provided; but there is no phone or TV. Kids and pets are taboo. ■ *10 miles north of Florence (call for details), Florence; (541) 997-7888; PO Box 930, Florence, OR 97439; $$$; no credit cards; checks OK.*

Johnson House Bed & Breakfast ★★ We can't recommend any hotels in Florence, so we're thankful for the wit, curiosity, and lofty aesthetic standards Jayne and Ron Fraese bring to their perennially popular B&B. Reflecting the Fraeses' interests (he's a political science prof, she's an English teacher), the library is strong on local history, natural history, politics, and collections of essays, letters, cartoons, and poetry. There are six guest rooms, one of which is a cute garden cottage. Breakfasts, which include fresh garden fruit and produce (grown out back) and home-baked bread, are among the best on the coast. The Fraeses live next door, so they're available to assist guests. They also own Moonset, an extraordinary, couples-only lodging north of town (2 miles south of Sea Lion Caves). This spendy ($250 a day) retreat includes a CD library, full kitchen (stocked with staples plus a complimentary bottle of Oregon wine), sauna, and a sizable, ocean-view spa. ■ *216 Maple St (1 block north of the river in Old Town), Florence; (541) 997-8000 or (800) 768-9488; PO Box 1892, Florence, OR 97439; fraese@ pesys.com; $$; MC, V; checks OK.* &

Edwin K Bed & Breakfast ★ Built in 1914 by one of Florence's founders, the Edwin K is set in a quiet residential neighborhood beyond the bustle of Old Town. Inside, the place looks formal but feels warm and homey. Ivory wall-to-wall carpeting contrasts nicely with aged and swarthy Douglas fir woodwork. All six spacious guest rooms (named after the seasons) are fitted with private baths and adorned with antiques. Breakfast is served in the exquisitely appointed dining room, another shrine to the woodcrafter's art. Out back, there's a private courtyard with a waterfall. ■ *1155 Bay St (on the west edge of Old Town, across the street from the river), Florence; (541) 997-8360 or (800) 8ED-WINK; PO Box 2686, Florence, OR 97439; $$; MC, V; checks OK.*

REEDSPORT AND WINCHESTER BAY

Reedsport is a port town on the Umpqua River a few miles inland, while Winchester Bay is at the river's mouth. The real draw along this section of the coast is the 53-mile-long **Oregon Dunes**

National Recreation Area. Because you can catch only glimpses of this sandy wilderness from the highway, plan to stop and explore on foot. Headquarters are in Reedsport at the intersection of Highway 101 and Route 38; 855 Highway Avenue, (541)271-3611.

The numerous lakes in the Oregon Dunes make refreshing, warm-water (in season) swimming holes; the larger lakes such as Siltcoos, Tahkenitch, and Tenmile provide freshwater angling and boating. Large portions of the dunes are open to off-road recreational vehicles. Check a map, available at headquarters, to find out who's allowed where.

The former Antarctic research vessel *Hero* is moored on the Reedsport riverfront and is open to the public (summer only). Adjacent is the **Umpqua Discovery Center Museum**, which features a weather station and exhibits on marine life, ocean beaches, and logging; 409 Riverfront Way, (541)271-4816. The **Dean Creek Elk Reserve**, where you can observe wild elk grazing on protected land, is 4 miles east of town on Route 38.

The **Umpqua Lighthouse** (not open to the public) and Coastal Visitor Center are perched atop a headland overlooking Winchester Bay and the river mouth. Follow the signs to Umpqua Lighthouse State Park.

COOS BAY

The south bay's port city and formerly the world's foremost wood-products exporter, Coos Bay has been undercut by a sagging timber industry and the political struggle to control the Northwest's forests. But it's still the Oregon Coast's largest city and the finest natural harbor between San Francisco and Seattle. It's currently making the painfully slow transition from an economy based on natural resources to one that's more service-based (but still a bit rough around the edges).

The Coos Art Museum, 235 Anderson, (541)267-3901, offers many exhibits of big-city quality. **Southwestern Oregon Community College**, 1988 Newmark, (541)888-2525, schedules art shows and musical performances. The **Oregon Coast Music Festival** happens every summer; (541)267-0938. Score coffee drinks and fresh-baked scones at The Scenery, 190 Central, (541)267-5600; and pizza, pastas, and calzones at Pizza Crazy, at 274 S Broadway, (541)269-2029.

RESTAURANTS

Blue Heron Bistro ★★★ *Voilà,* a real bistro with European flair in the heart of Coos Bay—airy atmosphere, outdoor sidewalk tables, and a reasonably priced, innovative menu. Owner Wim De Vriend keeps people coming back at all times of day. For waffles, breakfast parfaits (yogurt, fruit, and muesli), and good strong jolts of joe in the morning. For an array of salads and sandwiches (such as blackened snapper on a toasted onion roll with green chiles) or a German sausage plate (without nitrates, and served with red cabbage, potatoes, and hot mustard) at lunch. For handcrafted pasta (try the pesto fettuccine or the lasagne) or continent-hopping cuisine for dinner, such as New Orleans blackened oysters and Tex-Mex fare. Salmon, no matter how it's prepared (maybe grilled with fresh salsa and served with rice, black beans, and corn relish), is always a winner here. So are the more than 40 varieties of bottled beer and the desserts that include some fine apple pie, carrot cake, and chocolate tortes. ■ *100 W Commercial (Hwy 101 and Commercial), Coos Bay; (541)267-3933; $$; beer and wine; MC, V; local checks only; breakfast, lunch, dinner every day.* &

Kum-Yon's ★ Kum-Yon has transformed a nondescript eatery into a showcase of South Korean cuisine. Some Japanese (sushi, sashimi) and Chinese (eggflower soup, fried rice, chow mein) dishes are offered, but to discover what really makes this place special, you'll have to venture into the unknown. Try spicy hot chap chae (transparent noodles pan-fried with veggies and beef), bulgoki (thinly sliced sirloin marinated in honey and spices) or yakitori (Japanese-style shish kabob). Get there early on weekends. Or check out the Kum-Yon's in Newport (1006 SW Coast Highway; (541)265-5330). ■ *835 S Broadway (at the south end of the main drag), Coos Bay; (541)269-2662; $; beer and wine; AE, MC, V; local checks only; lunch, dinner every day.* &

Bank Brewing Company This inviting downtown establishment is a bank turned microbrewery. A spacious main floor, high ceilings, huge windows, and the balcony seating (formerly the bank's offices, no doubt) lend themselves nicely to a congenial, pub atmosphere. The restored, late-19th-century ornate bar came from North Bend's Anchor Tavern. Sweet Wheat or Gold Coast Golden ale top the craft-beer list. Enticing pub grub includes calamari, shellfish (mussels and clams), stuffed jalapeño (with cheddar) appetizers, and thin-crusted, hand-tossed pizzas. Check the chalkboard for fresh-fish and pasta specials. ■ *201 Central Ave (corner of 2nd), Coos Bay; (541)267-0963; $; beer, wine; MC, V; checks OK; lunch, dinner every day.* &

LODGINGS

Coos Bay Manor Bed & Breakfast ★ Head up the hill away from the commercial glitz of Highway 101 and you'll discover beautifully restored homes among deciduous and coniferous trees and flowering shrubs. The Coos Bay Manor, a grand Colonial-style structure with large rooms and high ceilings, is such a place, located on a quiet residential street overlooking the waterfront. An open-air balcony patio is situated upstairs, where Patricia Williams serves breakfast on mellow summer mornings. The five guest rooms (three with private baths) are all distinctively decorated (the Cattle Baron's Room is decked out with bear and coyote rugs; the Victorian features lots of lace and ruffles). Mannerly children and dogs who tolerate cats are welcome. ■ *955 S 5th St (4 blocks above the waterfront), Coos Bay, OR 97420; (541) 269-1224 or (800) 269-1224; $$; MC, V; checks OK.*

CHARLESTON

Charleston's docks moor the bay's commercial fishing fleet. Fresh fish is inexpensive, the pace is slow, and there's lots to do.

Oregon Institute of Marine Biology is the University of Oregon's respected research station; (541) 888-2581. Visit Chuck's Seafood, 5055 Boat Basin Drive, (541) 888-5525, for fish and **Qualman Oyster Farms**, 4898 Crown Point Road, (541) 888-3145, for oysters. Hikers, canoeists, and kayakers (no motorboaters) like to explore the **South Slough National Estuarine Research Center Reserve**, 4 miles south of Charleston; (541) 888-5558.

Sunset Bay State Park, with year-round camping (including yurts), has a bowl-shaped cove with 50-foot-high cliffs on either side—a good spot to take a swim, as the water in the protected cove is perpetually calm (although cold); (541) 888-4902. Just down the road at **Shore Acres State Park**, a colorful botanical-gardens complex contains a restored caretaker's house (impressively lit up at Christmas) and an impeccably maintained display of native and exotic plants and flowers; (541) 888-3732. At the park, there's also an enclosed shelter from which to view winter storms and watch for whales. Farther south, **Cape Arago State Park** overlooks the Oregon Islands National Wildlife Refuge, home to birds, seals, and sea lions. The **Oregon Coast Trail** winds through all three parks.

RESTAURANTS

Portside ★ It's dark and cavernous inside, so you'll notice the lighted glass tanks containing live crabs and lobsters—a good sign that the kitchen is concerned with fresh ingredients. From your table, you can watch fishing gear being repaired and vessels coming and going in the Charleston Boat Basin. Naturally, fresh seafood, simply prepared, is the house specialty. For something different, try the "cucumber boat," a medley of shrimp, crab, and smoked salmon accompanied by cucumber dressing. Fridays there's a sumptuous Chinese seafood buffet that includes everything but the anchor. ■ *8001 Kingfisher Rd (just over the Charleston bridge, in the midst of the boat basin), Charleston; (541) 888-5544; $$; full bar; AE, DC, MC, V; local checks only; lunch, dinner every day.*

BANDON

The town of Bandon looks—and feels—newly painted, freshly scrubbed, and friendly. Some locals believe Bandon sits on a "ley line," an underground crystalline structure that is reputed to be the focus of powerful cosmic energies. Certainly there's magic here.

Begin in Old Town, where there are a number of galleries, including the **Second Street Gallery** (210 Second, (541)347-4133) and the **Clock Tower Gallery** (198 Second, (541)347-4721). Also in Old Town, buy fish 'n' chips at Bandon Fisheries (250 First SW, (541)347-4282) and nosh at the public pier. For another treat, try the *New York Times*–touted handmade candies at **Cranberry Sweets**, First and Chicago, (541)347-9475 (they're generous with free samples). At **Brewmaster's** (375 Second, (541)347-1195), you can taste a handful of beers from among the 100 recipes in the repertoire. On Bandon's north end, sample the famous cheddar cheeses (especially the squeaky cheese curds) at **Bandon Cheese** (680 Second, (541)347-2456).

The best beach access is from the south jetty or **Face Rock Viewpoint** on Beach Loop Road. This route parallels the ocean in view of weather-sculpted rock formations and is a good alternative to Highway 101 (especially if you're on a bike). Just north of Bandon, **Bullards Beach State Park** occupies an expansive area crisscrossed with hiking and biking trails leading to uncrowded, driftwood-and-kelp-cluttered beaches. In this park, the yurts are clustered near the park's entrance and not very secluded. Built in 1896, the **Coquille River Lighthouse** (open to the public) is located at the end of the park's main road. Good windsurfing beaches abound on the river and ocean side of the park; (541)347-2209.

Bandon's cranberry bogs make it one of the nation's largest producers. Call (541)347-9616 or (541)347-3230 for a tour (May through November). Six miles south of Bandon, the **West Coast Game Park Safari** is a special "petting" park where you can view lions, tigers, and elk, among others; (541)347-3106.

RESTAURANTS

Andrea's ★★ A piano player at breakfast? It can happen at Andrea's, an Old Town landmark with New Age artwork, lots of greenery, and massive, comfy wooden booths. Breakfast here is first-rate (just ask the ivory-tickler). Omelets, yogurt parfaits, and steaming bowls of oatmeal topped with raisins and bananas are right up there with the best pastries in town. Lunch includes substantial sandwiches (order the fried oyster) on homemade, whole-grain breads, a Cajun fish salad, and deep-dish pizza du jour. For dinner, there are a plethora of unusual choices, such as North African crêpes (with an orange-feta sauce), fettuccine with prosciutto, and charbroiled salmon with a yummy cranberry chutney. ■ *160 Baltimore (1 block east of the ocean in Old Town), Bandon; (541)347-3022; $$; beer and wine; MC, V; checks OK; breakfast, lunch Mon–Sat, dinner every day, brunch Sun (dinner Fri–Sat only during winter).*

Harp's ★★ Don't expect unusual background music. The name comes from the presence of affable chef/owner Michael Harpster. Do expect a new, bigger, spectacular sea-front location (just opening at press time). And do look for some wonderful halibut with hot pistachio sauce. Ditto for the grilled snapper, the pasta with prawns and a hot pepper and lemon sauce, and the charbroiled filet mignon marinated in garlic and teriyaki. Salads, a simple enticing mix of homegrown greens, come with a tantalizing garlicky balsamic house dressing. Harpster also does a good job with his sweet onion soup made with beef broth and vermouth. Be sure to partake of the deep-fried mozzarella appetizers and the excellent wine list. ■ *130 Chicago St (½ block east of the harbor, in Old Town), Bandon; (541)347-9057; $$; beer and wine; AE, MC, V; checks OK; dinner every day (Tues–Sat in winter).*

Lord Bennett's Occasionally, an ocean-front eatery with a killer view serves worthwhile food. Actually, Lord Bennett's is across Beach Loop Drive from Bandon's ocean-front cliffs, but the saltwater vistas are stunning. Sautéed and broiled shellfish selections are darn appetizing, also. In a break from pan-frying, oysters are poached, returned to their shells, and finished with mushrooms and mornay sauce, while snapper comes topped with an unusual walnut-garlic concoction. Jamaican jerked chicken (with pineapple salsa) and a vibrantly colored vegetable plate are other possibilities. Baked prawns with prosciutto, deep-fried calamari, and the French onion soup are first-rate appetizers. ■ *1695 Beach Loop Dr (next to the Sunset Motel), Bandon; (541)347-3663; $$; full bar; AE, DIS, MC, V; checks OK; lunch, dinner every day, brunch Sun.* ⅖

LODGINGS

Lighthouse Bed & Breakfast ★★ Spacious and appealing (although the groundskeeping is uninspired), this contemporary home has windows opening toward the Coquille River, its lighthouse, and the ocean, which is a short walk away. Guests can watch fishing boats, windsurfers, seals, and seabirds cavort in the saltwater surroundings. There are now five guest rooms (four enjoy ocean vistas), all roomy and wonderfully appointed. The Gray Whale Room, up on the third floor, is the real stunner, with a king-size bed, wood-burning stove, TV, and a whirlpool tub overlooking the three-sided, watery panoramas. Breakfasts are topnotch, prepared by amiable hostess Shirley Chalupa. ■ *650 Jetty Rd (at 1st St), Bandon; (541)347-9316; PO Box 24, Bandon, OR 97411; $$; MC, V; checks OK.*

Sea Star Hostel and Guest House Begun years ago as a friendly American Youth Hostel, the Sea Star now includes a four-room Guest House, just across a courtyard from the main building, which offers a comparatively lavish alternative to the informal dormlike accommodations. The former bistro is now an un-usual brew store (see Bandon introduction). A natural wood in-terior, skylights, and a harbor-view deck highlight the second-floor suite, which sleeps four. In-room coffee, tea, and cable TV are part of the package. Beer and wine are available. ■ *375 2nd St (take 2nd St off Hwy 101 into Old Town), Bandon, OR 97411; (541)347-9632; $$; MC, V; local checks only.*

PORT ORFORD

The southern Oregon coast's oldest town, Port Orford is a pre-mier whale-watching location (occasionally an individual or pod of whales spends all year in its quiet, kelp-protected coves). It's a town far removed from big-city nuances—sheep ranching, fish-ing, sea-urchin harvesting, and cranberries dominate town life. Yet it's hip in its own way, especially considering the seasonal prolif-eration of surfers and board sailors, who head for Battle Rock and Hubbard's Creek beaches and the windy waters of Floras Lake. Fishing fanatics should visit the Elk and Sixes Rivers for the salmon and steelhead runs. And—bonus of bonuses—Port Or-ford marks the beginning of Oregon's coastal "banana belt," which stretches to the California border and means warmer winter tem-peratures, an earlier spring, and more sunshine than other coastal areas.

One warning: From here south, poison oak grows close to the ocean. Watch out for it at Battle Rock.

Cape Blanco Lighthouse, situated in Cape Blanco State Park (6 miles west of Highway 101, (541)332-6774), is the most westerly lighthouse in the lower 48 states. The lighthouse, closed to the public, is approached via a windy, narrow, and potholed road. On the west side of the light station, a path through the grass leads to the end of the cape—the edge of the continent. Blanco is the windiest station on the coast, so if the view doesn't claim your breath, the breeze will.

Boice-Cope County Park is the site of the large, freshwa-ter Floras Lake, popular with boaters, anglers, and board sailors; take Floras Lake Road off Highway 101, near Langlois. This area has the coast's best trail system (and one that's little used), per-fect for hiking, running, horseback riding, and mountain biking.

Humbug Mountain State Park, 5 miles south of town, fea-tures a steep and switchbacked trail to a top-of-the-world panorama at the summit.

LODGINGS

Floras Lake House Bed & Breakfast ★ If the hot summer sun beckons you to cool swims in a freshwater lake, choose Floras. This modern two-story house offers four spacious rooms, each with a bath and deck access; two enjoy fireplaces. Most elegant are the North and South Rooms, but you can see Floras Lake and the ocean beyond from all four. Hiking and biking trails abound in this isolated area, and Floras Lake is great for windsurfers (and you might just have the beach to yourself). ▪ *92870 Boice Cope Rd (from Hwy 101, turn west on Floras Lake Loop, 9 miles north of Port Orford, and follow signs to Boice-Cope Park), Langlois, OR 97450; (541)348-2573; $$$; MC, V; checks OK.*

Home by the Sea Bed & Breakfast ★ The ocean view is one of southern Oregon's best, and you can see it from both guest rooms in this modest, homey B&B that sits atop a bluff near Battle Rock. There's easy beach access, and guests have the run of a large, pleasantly cluttered dining/living room area, also with ocean view. Quiche, waffles, omelets, and fresh strawberries are the morning mainstays. You can surf the Internet with chatty Alan Mitchell, a friendly whirlwind of information and a Mac enthusiast. ▪ *444 Jackson St (1 block west of Hwy 101), Port Orford; (541)332-2855; PO Box 606-B, Port Orford, OR 97465; alan@homebythesea.com; www.homebythesea.com; $$; MC, V; checks OK.*

Castaway by the Sea This affordable, bluff-top, 14-unit, two-story motel literally sits on history: ancient Indian artifacts, plus the former sites of both Fort Orford, the oldest military installation on the Oregon Coast, and the Castaway Lodge, once frequented by Jack London. The two three-bedroom units have kitchenettes and glassed-in sun decks with harbor and ocean panoramas. All rooms enjoy ocean views. It's an easy stroll down to the beach, harbor, or shops. ▪ *545 W 5th (between Ocean and Harbor Drives), Port Orford; (541)332-4502; PO Box 844, Port Orford, OR 97465; $$; MC, V; local checks only.*

GOLD BEACH

Named for the gold that was found here in the 19th century, Gold Beach is famous as the town at the ocean end of the Rogue River, a favorite with whitewater enthusiasts (*The River Wild*, with Meryl Streep, was filmed here). It's also a supply town for hikers heading up the Rogue into the remote Kalmiopsis Wilderness Area. The Rogue River enjoys fabulous salmon and steelhead runs. Catch some angling tips, or rent clam shovels and fishing gear at the **Rogue Outdoor Store**, 560 N Ellensburg, (541)247-7142.

Jet boat trips are a popular way to explore the backcountry. Guides will discuss the area's natural history and stop to observe wildlife (look for otter, beaver, blue herons, bald eagles, and deer) on these thrilling forays (between 64 and 104 miles) up the Rogue River. The boats dock at lodges along the way for lunch and, sometimes, dinner. One caution: Prepare for sun exposure, as most of these boats are open. Contact **Jerry's Rogue Jets**, Port of Gold Beach, PO Box 1011, Gold Beach, OR 97444, (541)247-7601 or

(800)451-3645, or **Mail Boat Hydro-Jets**, PO Box 1165-G, Gold Beach, OR 97444, (541)247-7033 or (800)458-3511, for info or reservations. Better yet, call **Rogue River Reservations**, (541)247-6504 or (800)525-2161, for information and bookings on just about any Rogue River outing, jet boat trip, or overnight stay in the wilderness (including info about any of the backcountry lodges).

Hiking trails (such as the Shrader Old-Growth Trail, reachable via Jerry's Flat Road, which follows the Rogue's south shore) cut deep into the Kalmiopsis Wilderness or the Siskiyou National Forest east of town. A jet boat can drop you off to explore part or all of the 40-mile-long Rogue River Trail along the stream's north bank. Spring is the best time for a trek, before 90-degree days heat up the rock-face trail. Pick up maps and information at the Forest Service offices, 1225 S Ellensburg, (541)247-3600. Because water traffic on the all-too-popular lower Rogue is controlled, people interested in unsupervised whitewater trips must sign up for a lottery—held during the first six weeks in the new year—with the Forest Service (same address and phone as above).

The little-used Oregon Coast Trail traverses headlands and skirts untraveled beaches between Gold Beach and Brookings. A portion of trail winds up and over Cape Sebastian, 3 miles south of town. Take the steep drive to the top of the cape for breathtaking (and windy) vistas. Nearby Myers Creek Beach is a windsurfing hot spot.

RESTAURANTS

The Captain's Table ★ This funky-looking structure overlooking the highway (with nice ocean views, too) is Gold Beach's old favorite. Nothing is breaded or deep-fried, so a broiled salmon or halibut is a good choice (although doneness is not always consistent). The corn-fed beef from Kansas City is meat you can't often get on the coast. Scallop- and beef-kabobs (with bacon, bell peppers, and onions) are interesting choices. The dining area, furnished with antiques, is moderately small and can get smoky from the popular bar. The staff is courteous, enthusiastic, and speedy. ■ *1295 S Ellensburg Ave (on Hwy 101, south end of town), Gold Beach; (541)247-6308; $$; full bar; MC, V; local checks only; dinner every day.*

Nor'Wester ★ From the windows of the Nor'Wester you may watch fishermen delivering your meal: local sole, snapper, halibut, lingcod, and salmon. Most seafood is correctly cooked (broiled or sautéed), and served garnished with almonds or some other simple topping. Forgo the more complicated, saucy preparations (such as the snapper Florentine). You can also find a decent steak, or chicken with Dijon or orange glaze (and a cranberry-apple relish). The fish 'n' chips are tasty and the clam chowder respectable. ■ *Port of Gold Beach (on the waterfront),*

Gold Beach; (541) 247-2333; $$; full bar; MC, V; checks OK; dinner every day.

LODGINGS

Inn at Nesika Beach ★★★ Is this secluded inn, located in residential Nesika Beach, the Oregon Coast's finest B&B? Many visitors to the three-story neo-Victorian (built in 1992) think so. A jewel of a structure occupying a bluff overlooking the ocean, the inn boasts lovely landscaping, a relaxing wraparound porch, and, in the back, an enclosed ocean-front deck. The expansive interior, with exposed hardwood floors and attractive area rugs, is grandly decorated. All four guest rooms are upstairs, and all four enjoy fabulous ocean views, uncommonly comfortable (and large) feather beds, and private baths with spas. Up on the third floor, a suite-size room with a fireplace and private deck overlooking the Pacific offers the ultimate night's stay. Wine and nibbles are offered each evening in the parlor and living room. Hostess Ann Arsenault serves a full breakfast (in a dining room facing the ocean) that might include crêpes, scones, gingerbread pancakes, myriad egg dishes, and muffins. ■ *33026 Nesika Rd (west off Hwy 101, 5 miles north of Gold Beach), Gold Beach, OR 97444; (541) 247-6434; $$$; no credit cards; checks OK.*

Tu Tu'Tun Lodge ★★★ The lodge complex, named after a local Indian tribe, is one of the loveliest on the coast, though it's 7 miles inland. Tall, mist-cloudy trees line the north shore of the Rogue River, and hosts Dirk and Laurie Van Zante will help you get a line in for salmon or steelhead (or for trout in the spring-stocked pond a mile upriver). The main building is handsomely designed, with lots of windows and such niceties as private porches overlooking the river, racks to hold fishing gear, and stylish, rustic decor throughout. There are 16 units in the two-story main building and two larger kitchen suites in the adjacent lodge, all with river views. In the apple orchard sits the lovely Garden House, which sleeps six and features a large stone fireplace. The nearby two-bedroom and two-bath River House is the spendiest and most luxurious, with cedar-vaulted living room, outdoor spa, satellite TV, and a washer/dryer. All guests can swim in the heated lap pool, use the four-hole pitch-and-putt course, play horseshoes, relax around the mammoth rock fireplace in the main lodge, hike, or fish. A sweet-smelling, madrona-wood fire is lit every evening on the river-view terrace, and you might spot the two resident bald eagles anytime. Breakfast, hors d'oeuvres, and a prix-fixe dinner are served (for an additional $37.50 per person). The four-course evening meal might include your own fish as the entree, or perhaps chicken breasts with a champagne sauce, or prime rib. Outside guests can dine here also (by reservation only). ■ *96550 North Bank*

Rogue (follow the Rogue River from the bridge up the north bank for 7 miles), Gold Beach, OR 97444; (541) 247-6664; $$$; full bar; MC, V; checks OK (restaurant open May–Oct only).

Jot's Resort ★ The manicured grounds of this rambling resort spread along the north bank of the Rogue River, adjacent to the historic Rogue River Bridge and just across the river from the lights of Gold Beach. The 140 rooms, all with water vistas, are spacious and tastefully decorated, and many have refrigerators. If you just want a standard room, ask for one of the newer ones ($85). The two-bedroom condos ($155), with kitchens, accommodate six. There's an indoor pool, spa, and weight room. Rent a bike (or a boat) to explore the riverfront. Rogue River jet boats and guided fishing trips leave right from the resort's docks. And, of course, all the necessary angling gear can be rented. ■ *94360 Wedderburn Loop (at the Rogue River Bridge), Gold Beach; (541) 247-6676 or (800) 367-5687; PO Box J, Gold Beach, OR 97444; $$; AE, DC, MC, V; checks OK.* &

Gold Beach Resort Stay here for in-town beachfront accommodations. This sprawling complex is close enough to the ocean that roaring surf drowns out the highway noise. All the rooms and condos have private decks and ocean views. There's an indoor pool and spa, and a private, beach-access trail leads over the dunes to the ocean. The roomy condos come with fireplaces and kitchens. ■ *1330 S Ellensburg (Hwy 101, near south end of town), Gold Beach, OR 97444; (541) 247-7066 or (800) 541-0947; $$; AE, DC, MC, V; no checks.* &

BROOKINGS

Situated just 6 miles north of the California line, Brookings enjoys the state's mildest winter temperatures and is encircled by breathtaking beauty. To the north lie **Samuel H. Boardman** and **Harris Beach State Parks**. To the east are the verdant Siskiyou Mountains, deeply cut by the Chetco and Winchuck Rivers, while the ancient redwood groves lie to the south. Because of the favorable climate, most of the Easter lilies sold in North America are grown here. Brookings also boasts the Oregon Coast's safest harbor—and therefore it's a busy port. The entire Brookings area has been inundated by retirees: the hills are hummin' with new housing, and the real-estate market is red hot.

Azalea State Park is just east of Highway 101. Fragrant Western azaleas bloom in May, alongside wild strawberries, fruit trees, and violets; you can picnic amid all this splendor on hand-hewn myrtlewood tables. Myrtlewood (which grows only on the southern Oregon coast and in Palestine) can be seen in groves in **Loeb Park**, 8 miles east of town on North Bank Chetco River Road. The **Redwood Nature Trail** in the Siskiyou National Forest winds through one of the few remaining groves of old-growth coastal redwoods in Oregon (Forest Service offices at 555 5th St; (541)469-2196).

Fishing is renowned here. The fleet operates from the south end of town. Stop in at Sporthaven Marina (16372 Lower Harbor Road, (541)469-3301) for supplies and info or at nearby Tidewind Charters (16368 Lower Harbor Road, (541)469-0337) for ocean-going fishing adventures. Soak up the Chetco Harbor ambience, and scarf an order of halibut 'n' chips, at Pelican Bay Seafoods (16403 Lower Harbor Road, (541)469-7971).

RESTAURANTS

Bistro Gardens ★ With but five tables and three booths, this small storefront scrunched into a tired-looking shopping strip is crowded with diners. The decor is tastefully simple, but the menu is expansive—there are seven salmon choices, for instance (try the grilled salmon piccata). Other seafood options include pan-fried Cajun oysters, scampi, and garlic prawns with andouille sausage. Baked chicken with apples and mozzarella, lamb with Dijon and mushrooms, a slew of pasta dishes, even a grilled-polenta ratatouille and a dynamite crab-cake sandwich, all showcase the culinary talents of chef Dan Baldwin, who pulls it all off with aplomb. The beverage selection (no alcohol) is limited. ■ *1130 Chetco Ave (west side of 101, at the north end of town), Brookings; (541)469-9750; $$; no alcohol; MC, V; checks OK; lunch Mon–Fri, dinner Mon–Sat.*

Chives ★ Here's a place that has the town talking: a top-drawer eatery unceremoniously stuck into a Highway 101 strip mall. Disregard the setting; inside, the mood's casual but upscale. Both the lunch and dinner menus offer lots of variety, including preparations previously unknown on the southern coast. For example, veal is as rare in Brookings as a winter freeze, but Chives purveys a classic osso buco—although it's served with garlic mashed potatoes rather than the traditional risotto. A creamy wild-mushroom risotto accompanies the roast duck, and a rock-shrimp risotto appetizer can be had. ■ *1025 Chetco Ave (north end of town, along the main drag), Brookings; (541)469-4121; $$; full bar; MC, V; checks OK; lunch, dinner Wed–Sun, brunch Sun (closed in Jan).* &

Hog Wild Cafe ★ This boutique-y restaurant has gone a bit wild on the pig theme, what with pig dolls, pig cups, and other swine-like paraphernalia. But the food is worth a pig-out. You'll find jambalaya, veggie lasagne, and Cajun meat loaf on the regular menu, plus a good many blackboard items, such as a vegetable frittata or a prime rib sandwich. The Cajun "kitchen-sink" pasta comes with andouille sausage, snapper, shrimp, and scallops in a pizzazzy marinara sauce. Muffins are giganto, and the cheesecakes a treat. You might even give the Hog Slop (chocolate-caramel) or Hog Heaven (chocolate-coconut) mochas a try. ■

16158 Hwy 101 S (west side of Hwy 101, 1 mile south of Brookings-
Harbor bridge), Harbor; (541) 469-8869; $; beer and wine; AE,
MC, V; local checks only; breakfast, lunch every day, dinner Wed,
Fri, Sat (varies in winter). &

LODGINGS

Chetco River Inn ★★ Expect a culture shock: this secluded, al-
ternative-energy retreat sits on 35 forested acres of a peninsula
formed by a sharp bend in the turquoise Chetco River, 17 miles
east of Brookings (pavement ends after 14 miles). Isolation isn't
a problem, because there are no phones, except for inkeeper
Sandra Brugger's cellular phone. The place is not so remote
that you can't read by safety propane lights and watch TV via
satellite (there's even a VCR). The large, open main floor—done
in a lovely, deep-green, marble finish—offers views of the river,
myrtlewood groves, and wildlife. A full breakfast is included,
and Sandra will pack a deluxe sack lunch or serve an exemplary
five-course dinner on request. Fishermen and crack-of-dawn
hikers (the Kalmiopsis Wilderness is close by) are served early-
riser breakfasts. All told, this is getting away from it all without
roughing it. ■ *21202 High Prairie Rd (follow North Bank Rd 16
miles east, left after South Fork Bridge, take second guest driveway on left), Brookings, OR 97415; (541) 670-1645 or (800) 327-
2688 (Pelican Bay Travel); $$; MC, V; checks OK.*

South Coast Inn ★★ Twin gargoyles guard this handsome,
4,000-square-foot, Craftsman-style home designed in 1917 by
renowned San Francisco architect Bernard Maybeck. It's situ-
ated two blocks above downtown, so traffic noise is audible, but
the structure—one of the city's oldest—is surrounded by
soundproofing trees and shrubs, some of them flowering all
year in the mild Brookings climate. A spacious, partially cov-
ered deck, lighted in the evening, extends around most of the
house. Three guest rooms (two with ocean views) are luxuri-
ously appointed with myriad antiques. The downstairs parlor
sports a stone fireplace and a grand piano, while a workout
room includes a weight machine, sauna, and hot tub. An
unattached cottage (with bedroom and kitchen) lacks the
house's charm. Innkeepers Ken Raith and Keith Popper will
even pick you up at the nearby Crescent City (California) air-
port. No children under 12 or pets. ■ *516 Redwood St (turn east
on Oak St, north on Redwood, 2 blocks above Hwy 101), Brookings,
OR 97415; (541) 469-5557 or (800) 525-9273; scoastin@wave.-
net; www.virtualcities.com; $$; AE, DIS, MC, V; checks OK.*

Beachfront Inn If you want an ocean-front motel room in Brookings, this Best Western right at the mouth of the Chetco River
is the closest you can get. Every unit is beachfront and enjoys
a private balcony. Some are a mere 100 feet away from breaking surf. Microwaves and refrigerators, a heated pool, and an

outdoor spa are all part of the deal. The fishing and pleasure-boat fleet moors next door. ■ *16008 Boat Basin Rd (off Lower Harbor Rd, south of the Port of Brookings), Brookings; (541) 469-7779 or (800) 468-4081; PO Box 2729, Harbor, OR 97415; $$; AE, DC, MC, V; checks OK.* ♿

Willamette Valley and Southern Oregon

North to south roughly along the I-5 corridor from Yamhill and Washington Counties in the north to the Rogue River Valley in southern Oregon.

AURORA

Antique hunters find a fertile field in this well-preserved historic village. In 1856, Dr. William Keil brought a group of Pennsylvania Germans to establish a communal settlement. Called the Harmonites, the commune faded away after the death of its founder; today most people come to the town, on the National Register of Historic Places, to comb through the myriad antique stores that occupy the many clapboard and Victorian houses along the highway.

History-minded visitors also enjoy **Champoeg State Park**, site of one of the first settlements in the Willamette Valley and now a fine place to picnic. And rose lovers will want to wander a few miles farther up the river (west on Champoeg Road and across Highway 219) to **Heirloom Old Garden Roses**, (503)538-1576, one of the country's premier commercial growers of old garden roses.

WILLAMETTE VALLEY WINERIES

So many of Oregon's pinot noirs have achieved international renown that many of the better-known bottlings are quite pricey; however, the ardent wine explorer can still find the up-and-coming producers cheerfully selling fabulous wine at reasonable prices out the winery's front door. The greatest concentration of wineries is in Yamhill County, mostly between Newberg and McMinnville. Here, among rolling oak-covered hills, are increasing numbers of vineyards and enough wineries to keep the touring wine lover tipsy for a week.

While summer weekends, as well as the Memorial Day and Thanksgiving weekends, can be quite busy, many wineries are small family operations well off the beaten track, and visitors are still rare enough that they receive hearty welcomes. But many smaller wineries have limited hours, and a few are not open to visitors at all. The best advice is to arm yourself with a map (it's easy to get lost on the backroads) and the winery guide from the **Oregon Wine Advisory Board**, 1200 NW Naito Parkway, Suite 400, Portland, OR 97209, (800)242-2363, or any member winery. In fine weather take along a picnic lunch: many wineries have tables outside, and some sell chilled wine and picnic supplies.

Driving south on Highway 99W, you will first hit **Rex Hill Vineyards**, (503)538-0666, a decidedly upscale winery with a splendid tasting room and outstanding (if pricey) pinot noir. In the hills west of Newberg is **Autumn Wind Vineyard**, (503)538-6931, a small place beginning to turn out fine pinot noir.

Just outside Dundee, **Duck Pond Cellars**, (503)538-3199, makes a pleasant stop and has a number of good value wines. In Dundee, you can't miss the tasting room of **Argyle**, (503)538-8520, which is producing some of the best sparkling wines in the region as well as fine dry riesling. Behind Dundee is **Lange Winery**, (503)538-6476, where you can try an interesting pinot gris. Nearby are two much larger wineries: **Knudsen Erath Winery**, (503)538-3318, one of the oldest and largest in the state (nearby Crabtree Park makes a nice midday stop), with a full lineup of wines in a variety of price and quality categories (one of the best values in pinot noir); and **Sokol Blosser Winery**, (503)864-2282, another large and high-quality producer with a most handsome tasting room. Just south, outside Lafayette (home of a Trappist monastery, Our Lady of Guadeloupe), **Chateau Benoit**, (503)864-3666, sits right on the crest of a ridge, with spacious visitor facilities. They specialize in Müller Thurgau (a great picnic wine).

Driving south of McMinnville on Highway 18 to the ocean you will pass **Yamhill Valley Vineyards**, (503)843-3100, a lovely winery that makes sturdy pinot noir and is set among old oaks, which provide good shade for lunch on a hot day. Just a bit farther along is the **Oregon Wine Tasting Room**, (503)843-3787, which stocks a huge variety of wines for sale and always has an interesting assortment to taste. You'll find wines from places such as topnotch producer **Eyrie Vineyards** that are not open to the public on a regular basis. If you take 99W out of McMinnville, you will drive past the Eola Hills, home to another half-dozen or so wineries, including **Amity Vineyards**, (503)835-2362, a rustic winery that consistently produces excellent pinot noir, gewürztraminer, and dry riesling. Continuing south you will see signs for **Bethel Heights Vineyard**, (503)581-2262, another winery high on a hill (one of the oldest vineyard sites in the area) that makes tasty chenin blanc and fine pinot noir in several price ranges. **Eola Hills Winery**, (503)623-2405, in Rickreall, makes good cabernet sauvignon, a rarity for the Willamette Valley.

Farther south in a small valley near Highway 99W are two neighboring wineries, both very small and off the beaten track. **Airlie Winery**, (503)838-6013, makes excellent Müller Thurgau and has well-priced wines (take some extra time and visit the birds at the winery's pond). **Serendipity Cellars**, (503)838-4284, makes some unusual wines, including Maréchal Foch, a very good (and rare) red. **Tyee Wine Cellars**, (541)753-8754, south of Corvallis, makes excellent pinot gris and gewürztraminer. Right in Monroe is **Broadley Vineyards**, (541)847-5934, a storefront winery that's not much to look at but has some powerful pinots. In the hills to the west is picturesque **Alpine Vineyards**, (541)424-5851, about the only winery in the Willamette Valley to make good cabernet consistently (as well as a fine riesling).

Don't overlook the wineries in the **Tualatin Valley** that lie in the suburbs just west of Portland. Beaverton's **Ponzi Vineyards**, (503)628-1227, is an excellent close-in destination that produces powerful pinot noir, elegant chardonnay, and fine pinot gris and dry riesling (an outstanding lineup). **Cooper Mountain Vineyards**, (503)649-0027, has a beautiful hilltop site and makes tasty pinot gris and promising pinot noir. South of Hillsboro, **Oak Knoll Winery**, (503)648-8198, in an old dairy barn, maintains an Oregon tradition of fruit wines (these are very good) but also produces fine, fruity pinot noir and a variety of other wines at good prices.

Several wineries are open only during the special wine weekends and Memorial Day and Thanksgiving: good bets in this category would be **Chehalem**, (503) 538-4700, in Newberg; **Adelsheim Vineyard**, (503) 538-3652, northwest of Newberg; **Cameron Winery**, (503)538-0336, outside Dundee; **Ken Wright Cellars**, (503) 852-7070, in Carlton; **Panther Creek Cellars**, (503) 472-8080, and **Eyrie Vineyards**, (503) 472-6315, in McMinnville; and **Tempest Vineyards**, (503) 252-1383, in Amity.

NEWBERG

RESTAURANTS

Ixtapa ★ After the long string of fast-food places along 99W, this little restaurant right in town is a refreshing change. You'll be given a hearty welcome as you're ushered into this narrow but colorful and lively place. The service really hustles: you won't get much time to peruse the long menu. Some like their Mexican food a little spicier, but most appreciate the freshness and lightness of the dishes. Grilled chicken is excellent, and the beans, the real test of a Mexican place, are just right. ■ *307 E 1st St (on Hwy 99W northbound, in town), Newberg; (503)538-5956; $; full bar; MC, V; checks OK; lunch, dinner every day.* ♿

LODGINGS

Springbrook Hazelnut Farm ★★ Informal Oregonians will be surprised to step into the colorful elegance of this landmark farmhouse. Owner Ellen McClure is an artist, and it shows. The large, paneled dining room makes you feel as if you're in some Italian palazzo. The B&B guest wing upstairs is spacious, with two shared bathrooms furnished in green wicker. Two downstairs guest rooms offer half-baths, and there's a library and a TV room devoted to guests. The carriage house out back beyond the pond has a perfect little apartment with a well-stocked kitchen (even fixings for breakfast). Guests explore the 60-acre filbert orchard, take a swim in the pool, or play tennis on the private court. ■ *30295 N Hwy 99W (just off Hwy 99W, north of Newberg), Newberg, OR 97132; (503) 538-4606 or (800) 793-8528; $$$; no credit cards; checks OK.*

The Partridge Farm Bed & Breakfast Inn ★ Yes, they do raise partridges and other exotic and not-so-exotic birds, and the eggs you have for breakfast are fresh. In fact, many of the ingredients for breakfast—fruits, vegetables, and herbs—are likely to be right out of the garden. The farmhouse is just off the highway, but the broad lawn and garden in back help you feel way out in the country. The three rooms are furnished in dark antiques and have in-room sinks (the east bedroom is a little larger than the others). A separate parlor downstairs has a TV. The inn is owned by the folks at Rex Hill Vineyards (about a mile away); romantics can arrange a soar in the winery's hot-air balloon. ■ *4300 E Portland Rd (just off Hwy 99W, north of Newberg), Newberg, OR 97132; (503) 538-2050; $$; MC, V; checks OK.*

DUNDEE

RESTAURANTS

Red Hills Provincial Dining ★★★ In many ways, this is an ideal wine-country stop. You'll be received warmly by jovial co-owner Alice Halstead in this country-house-turned-restaurant, while chefs Nancy and Richard Gehrts preside in the kitchen. The simple dinner menu of a half-dozen items changes weekly, and the choices are all intriguing. Penne with olives, capers, and Montrachet cheese is perfectly balanced; beef tenderloin is thick and succulent; pork medallions on white beans are simple but flavorful. You get the idea: the best of European country cooking. And all the details are just right, whether it's bread dusted with fresh rosemary or a crisp salad of greens or lightly cooked vegetables. Desserts are interesting, too, like a rich, chewy fennel cake or raspberry-filled chocolate cake. Add to this an outstanding wine list, with a huge selection from all over the world, and you have a meal you'll want to linger over. ■ *276 Hwy 99W (at the north edge of town), Dundee; (503) 538-8224; $$; beer and wine; MC, V; checks OK; lunch Wed–Fri, dinner Wed–Sun.*

Tina's ★★ Owners Tina Landfried and her husband, David Bergen, work their magic in a small, squat building by the side of the road: a vest-pocket herb-and-salad garden outside, plain white walls inside. As for the food, there's a spirit of innovation

and creativity. The half-dozen entree choices are on the chalk-board: try rabbit risotto or grilled pork tenderloin in port-garlic sauce. Soup might be a flavorful cream of cucumber with dill and cilantro, and the green salad is simple and absolutely fresh. Wines by the glass offer a good selection of local picks, all reasonably priced. There's not much elbow room, but it's a surprisingly good place to relax and unwind after a day on the road.
■ *760 Hwy 99W (center of town, across from the fire station), Dundee; (503)538-8880; $$; beer and wine; AE, MC, V; checks OK; lunch Tues–Fri, dinner every day.* &

LODGINGS

Wine Country Farm ★ In the Red Hills of Dundee (the soil really is red), just past the unmarked entrance to Domaine Drouhin (makers of the Northwest's finest pinot noir and France's outpost in Oregon wine country—no visitors) and surrounded by vineyards, you'll find the Wine Country Farm. From the hilltop watch clouds (or Oregon's trademark rain squalls) drift across the valley below. Three of the five eclectically furnished bedrooms have spectacular views, while a more spacious two-room suite resides over the tasting room. Owner Joan Davenport raises Arabian horses and can take you on a buggy ride. Guests take breakfast (home-baked goodies with Joan's own pinot noir jelly) in warm weather on the deck of this restored 1910 white stucco house. Wine lovers appreciate the attached commercial winery, Wine Country Farm Cellars, which is open for tasting.
■ *6855 Breyman Orchards Rd (from Hwy 99W southbound, turn right onto McDougall just past Sokol Blosser Winery, then right again to Breyman Orchards Rd), Dayton, OR 97114; (503)864-3446 or (800) 261-3446; $$; no credit cards; checks OK.*

YAMHILL

LODGINGS

Flying M Ranch ★★ The terrific setting is what draws people: literally at the end of the road in the Coast Range—there's nothing around but mountains and forest. Ponds for swimming and fishing, tennis courts, and miles of hiking and horse trails (you can actually follow trails all the way to the coast) should keep anyone busy. The motel-style rooms are pretty ordinary. Savvy visitors rent one of the cabins (one of which has 10 beds); they have their own kitchens and are plenty rustic, with no phones or TVs ($75–$200). And for a really large group (up to 20), you might check out the small lodge on Trask Mountain (highest peak in the Coast Range) or set up camp (considerably cheaper, of course) along the little creek. You can even fly in—there's an airstrip. For a fee, local cowboys can take you trail riding on one of the Flying M's horses and maybe even grill you a steak on the way. The lodge has a Western-style lounge (with a bar made from 6-ton logs) and a restaurant that serves the standards but experiments with more exotic fare. ■ *23029 NW Flying M Rd (10 miles west of Yamhill; follow the little red flying Ms), Yamhill, OR 97148; (503) 662-3222; $$; AE, DC, MC, V; checks OK.*

McMINNVILLE

McMinnville is growing up: the feed stores and steel mill are still here, but so are the high-tech companies and espresso hangouts. And the growing wine industry has had a positive effect, especially on the food scene: there's a better concentration of interesting places to eat here than elsewhere in wine country. Along with its central location, that makes this town a good headquarters for wine touring. Serious wine lovers can OD on great wine and food while hobnobbing with wine celebrities (including some of France's hot young winemakers) at the three-day **International Pinot Noir Celebration** in late July or early August on the grounds of gracious old Linfield College; call (503) 472-8964 for information.

RESTAURANTS

Nick's Italian Cafe ★★★ Other local restaurants are giving Nick's a run for its money in exciting cooking, but this is still the one to beat. Nick's has settled into its role as local institution and winemakers' culinary headquarters, and owner Nick Peirano sticks to the Northern Italian cooking he learned at his mother's knee. The fixed-price five-course meal includes a second-course tureen of his grandmother's heavenly, rich, garlicky minestrone, followed by a simply dressed green salad and chewy French bread. Seasonal antipasto might include shellfish in winter or prosciutto and melon in summer. The fourth course is always pasta—homemade, and delicious. Entrees might include a perfectly grilled shark steak or a sirloin steak with capers. Nick's mama will insist you try one of her Italian specialties for dessert. Service can be inconsistent, and the setting, a former luncheonette, is far from fancy. But the food and a fabulous, well-priced wine list (with many local treasures unavailable elsewhere) keep packing them in. ■ *521 E 3rd St (downtown, across from the movie theater), McMinnville; (503) 434-4471; $$; beer and wine; no credit cards; checks OK; dinner Tues–Sun.*

Cafe Azul ★★ Don't think Tex-Mex here: think exotic flavors that just happen to come from Mexico—in this case, southern Mexico. Sisters Claire and Shawna Archibald combine a panoply of peppers, herbs, and cheeses with fresh local produce and handmade tortillas to produce a constantly changing menu of great creativity. Specialty moles are dark and rich, with intriguing flavors that are sweet, tart, hot, and herbaceous all together. Well-cooked pork may show up in a tamale with a rich red sauce or covered with a chile-and-tomatillo sauce—again, you'll keep trying to guess all the flavors. Desserts (if they don't run short) are fabulous, too—like angel food cake of Mexican chocolate, with rich raspberry sauce and whipped cream. Divine. Unfortunately, the narrow storefront location, even with sunny colors, isn't quite up to the food. The wine list is very limited, but beer's a better choice here anyway. Plan ahead and call for reservations—this place has been discovered. ■ *313 3rd St (right downtown), McMinnville; (503)435-1234; $$; beer and wine; MC, V; checks OK; lunch Mon–Sat, dinner Tues–Sat.* &

Third Street Grill ★★ Probably the most elegant setting for dinner in McMinnville. The interior of this Victorian-style house is a bit of a rabbit warren, with numerous intimate spaces, but the tables are comfortable and the nooks and crannies offer a measure of privacy. The menu, as the name suggests, is oriented toward meats, but with interesting combinations of flavors. The richness of duck is balanced with the leanness of lentils and the tart sweetness of apple; the subtle flavors of pork tenderloin with the gentle bite of sun-dried cherries. Portions are generous, and fresh vegetables like red chard accompany dinners. Service is eager but well-informed, and considerable attention has been paid to the wine list, which has an excellent selection of local wines as well as wines by the glass. ■ *729 E 3rd St (just east of downtown), McMinnville; (503)435-1745; $$; beer and wine; MC, V; checks OK; dinner Tues–Sun.*

Golden Valley Brewpub and Restaurant ★ This recycled bottling plant is a happening place in McMinnville. The former warehouse space is fitted out with high beams, lots of potted trees, and a huge wooden bar. Half is pub and half is restaurant, though you can eat in either. The menu is extensive, from pizza to burgers to a few attempts at fussier dishes. Stick with the basics: burgers are huge and come with interesting toppings; the sausage sandwich bites back. There's a good selection of their own brews and wines. A killer root beer is made on the premises, too. ■ *980 E 4th St (at E 3rd and N Johnson), McMinnville; (503)472-2739; $; beer and wine; AE, MC, V; checks OK; lunch, dinner every day.* &

Kame ★ McMinnvilleites aren't used to getting their change counted out in Japanese, but for food this good and this inexpensive, they don't seem to mind one bit. A tiny storefront place, Kame has white walls, plain wooden tables and chairs, a few artfully placed decorations, and simple Japanese food served graciously. Owner Mieko Nordin learned to cook family style from her mother. A basic (and satisfying) meal might include tasty miso soup, a small salad of pickled cabbage, and chicken or pork with vegetables on a bed of steaming rice. Tempura and teriyaki are available for dinner, too. ■ *228 N Evans,*

▼

▲

(at 3rd), McMinnville; (503) 434-4326; $; beer and wine; MC, V; local checks only; lunch Tues–Fri, dinner Tues–Sat.

LODGINGS

Mattey House ★★ Lovers of old homes find this B&B delightful. Denise and Jack Seed, world wanderers originally from England, have tenderly restored an 1890s Victorian farmhouse to its accustomed elegance, with careful attention to detail. The new look retains the house's glories, but with a lighter, less formal, more country feel: lace curtains, flowered wallpaper, comfortable armchairs, lots of flowers. Rooms are (authentically) small, but there are nice touches like a couple of claw-footed bathtubs (only one room has a private bath), a cozy fireplace in the living room, and lots of board games. After a breakfast that might include compote, frittata, or Dutch pancakes, you can wander through the small vineyard and pick your own grapes. You're far enough off the highway that you'll feel you're in the middle of the country. ■ *10221 NE Mattey Lane (just south of Lafayette on Hwy 99W), McMinnville, OR 97128; (503) 434-5058; $$; MC, V; checks OK.*

Steiger Haus Inn ★★ Susan and Dale DuRette have followed in the footsteps of the retired owners quite well. The house, tucked away on a back street, next to a creek, was designed to be a B&B, so all the downstairs rooms have private decks, offering plenty of opportunities to sip coffee outside and enjoy the large, woodsy backyard. Though you're right in town (and close to Linfield College), it's a peaceful oasis. Five rooms (three downstairs, two up) all have private baths, and a conference room is available. The house has a comfortable, Northwest feel, with lots of light. A full breakfast might include fresh poached pears, raisin muffins, and German pancakes, and the DuRettes have their coffee roasted specially for them. Children over 10 are welcome. ■ *360 Wilson St (from Hwy 99W, turn east on Cowls at the hospital), McMinnville, OR 97128; (503) 472-0821; $$; MC, V; checks OK.*

Youngberg Hill Vineyard Bed and Breakfast ★★ We're happy to see this place back in business after a period of uncertainty. New owners Martin and Jane Wright, who hail from South Africa, are serious wine lovers who fell in love with the property as soon as they saw it and are determined to make it a first-class establishment. The setting can't be beat: from the crest of a 700-foot hill you have views that stretch 180 degrees across the Willamette Valley. Even in the dead of winter guests want to take their coffee and sit out on the wraparound porch. A producing vineyard skirts the house, and the Wrights can offer tastings of their own wines as well as those of many other local producers. The five spacious rooms (two with their own fireplaces) in the rambling country-style house all have fabulous views and are very comfortably furnished. The three-course breakfast in the bright dining room includes as many local fresh ingredients as possible: a fruit plate, homemade bread or muffins, perhaps German puffed apple pancakes or eggs and crab in pastry. The quiet of the place is deeply refreshing, and guests can also take advantage of miles of old logging roads for walking through the woods. This is a perfect place for a restful weekend. ■ *10660 Youngberg Hill Rd (from Hwy 99W south from McMinnville, turn right onto Old Sheridan Hwy, then right on Peavine Rd and left on Youngberg Hill Road), McMinnville, OR 97128; (503) 472-2727; martin@youngberghill.com; www.young berghill.com; $$$; MC, V; checks OK.* ⅙

Safari Motor Inn ★ Some chain motels have come to McMinnville, but for location and price, it's hard to beat this long-established place. An unassuming motor lodge just off Highway 99W as you enter town, it doesn't offer anything fancy, but it's a nice alternative for visitors who shy away from the B&B scene. The rooms are quiet and the beds are comfortable. The former motel pool is now pushing up daisies, but if you want to cool off on a hot afternoon, head a quarter mile south on 99W to McMinnville's modern Aquatic Center where, for a couple of bucks, you can frolic in a large pool. A small exercise facility with Jacuzzi is available at the motel. ■ *345 N Hwy 99W (at 19th St), McMinnville, OR 97128; (503) 472-5187; $; AE, DC, MC, V; no checks.* ⅙

BELLEVUE/SHERIDAN

Bellevue, a tiny crossroads, is the site of three fine establishments, all under one roof. The **Oregon Wine Tasting Room**, ·(503) 843-3787, offers tastes of the best bottlings from two dozen Oregon wineries. The **Lawrence Gallery**, (503) 843-3633, is an excellent showcase of fine regional talent in all media. Upstairs is **Augustine's**, one of the region's better restaurants.

RESTAURANTS

Augustine's ★★ Here's an ideal place to take a break and refresh yourself along the road to the beach. The informal, open space has scenic views out both sides: farmland on one side and down into the Lawrence Gallery on the other. You could start your meal with a smoked seafood platter (salmon, mussels, halibut, and cream cheese) or some of the excellent creamy clam chowder. Soup or green salad (veggies and greens come from a local organic farm) is included with the entree. For the main course, zero in on the seasonal seafood (a poached salmon fillet, a tender, fresh sturgeon)—the real focus of owner/chef Jeff Quatraro. The legendary hazelnut cheesecake is rich, light, and not too sweet; citrus tart (orange, lemon, and grapefruit curd) is tangy and refreshing. A good selection of Oregon wines are available by the bottle and the glass. ■ *19706 Hwy 18*

(7 miles west of McMinnville), Bellevue; (503)843-3225; $$; full bar; MC, V; checks OK; lunch Wed–Sat, dinner Wed–Sun, brunch Sun.

LODGINGS

Sheridan Country Inn Sheridan isn't exactly a tourist destination, but you're not far from either the wine country or the ocean, and the Spirit Mountain Casino is just down the highway. This old house on the outskirts of town is now an inn with 12 rooms, 8 in the funky but spacious mansion and 4 in additional duplexes. The rooms are large and comfortable and look out on the surrounding acre of grounds. Some rooms come with microwaves, private baths, and TVs; all have refrigerators. Room 7 is a huge suite with a private Jacuzzi. The inn is a friendly place, and kids are welcome. ■ *1330 W Main (1 mile west of Bridge St on Hwy 18 business loop), Sheridan, OR 97378; (503)843-3151; $$; AE, DC, MC, V; local checks only.* &

MOUNT ANGEL

Visit **Mount Angel Abbey**, a 100-year-old Benedictine seminary, on a foggy morning, when its beautiful setting atop a butte sacred to the Indians makes it seem as if it's floating in the clouds. And don't miss the library, a gem by the internationally celebrated Finnish architect Alvar Aalto. For hours, call (503)845-3030.

SALEM

Recent remodeling and restoration has spruced up both the state capitol and the surrounding blocks, the most attractive part of town. The 1938 capitol has an art-deco-cum-grandiose-classical look and is worth a visit, especially since the fix-up from earthquake damage earlier this decade. Handsome parks flank the building, and just behind is **Willamette University**, the oldest university in the West. The campus is a happy blend of old and new brick buildings, with a small stream, Mill Creek, nicely incorporated into the landscape. It's a pleasant place to stroll, and plant lovers should visit the small but well-tended botanical gardens on the east side of the campus.

Across the road from Willamette University is **Historic Mission Mill Village**, 1313 Mill Street SE, (503)585-7012. The impressive 42-acre cluster of restored buildings from the 1800s includes a woolen mill, a parsonage, a Presbyterian church, and several homes. The mill, which drew its power from Mill Creek, now houses a museum that literally makes the sounds of the factory come alive. The **Jason Lee House**, dating from 1841, is the oldest remaining frame house in the Northwest; regular tours of the premises run from 10am to 4:30pm, Tuesday–Saturday. Picnic along the stream and feed the ducks, if you like. The **Salem Visitor**

Information Center is part of the complex, as are several shops selling handcrafted clothing, gifts, and antiques.

Bush House, 600 Mission Street SE, (503)363-4714, is a Victorian home built in 1877 by pioneer newspaper publisher Asahel Bush. It sits in a large park complete with conservatory, rose gardens, hiking paths, and barn turned art gallery. Tours are available.

Gilbert House Children's Museum, (503)371-3631, on the downtown riverfront between the bridges, has a variety of hands-on learning activities for young children. Children also appreciate Enchanted Forest, (503)371-4242, a nicely wooded storybook park with space for picnicking, just off I-5 south of town.

Salem is off the beaten winery track, but Willamette Valley Vineyards, (503)588-9463, a big investor-owned winery offering a broad range of wines, is just off I-5 south of town and commands a spectacular view of the countryside. Just to the north of the city off Highway 221 is Redhawk Vineyard, (503)362-1596, with a variety of good red wines and humorous labels.

Old-fashioned ferries, operated by cable, still cross the Willamette River in a few places and offer a fun alternative to bridges, if you've got some extra time. Two run in the Salem area: the Wheatland ferry, just north of town in Keizer (follow Highway 219 north from downtown and turn off on Wheatland Road), and the Buena Vista (from I-5 take exit 243 and follow Talbot Road west). They run every day (except during storms or high water) and cost very little.

If you're in the area during the 10 days of the Oregon State Fair (around Labor Day), don't miss it—it's the biggest in the Northwest and there's enough room so you don't feel jammed in; (503)378-3247.

RESTAURANTS

Alessandro's Park Plaza ★★ Easily the most elegant place to eat in Salem, this lovely urban oasis overlooks Mill Creek Park just next to the downtown business district. Owner Alessandro Fasani calls it Roman; most diners would call it upscale Italian, with quiet, professional service and a menu that emphasizes elegant pasta and seafood dishes. Nothing particularly original, but the classics are done with flair: perfectly cooked veal piccata, rich meat-stuffed tortellini in light cream sauce. In addition to the regular menu, a multicourse dinner is offered daily; the staff asks only if there's a particular dish you don't like, and they surprise you with the rest. A delight, indeed. ■ *325 High St SE (at Trade St), Salem; (503)370-9951; $$; full bar; AE, MC, V; local checks only; lunch Mon–Fri, dinner Mon–Sat.* ♿

DaVinci's ★ At this very ambitious, very popular pizza place, individual pizzas come with an interesting assortment of toppings, and there are different homemade whole-wheat pastas each day. An appetizer of thin, light bread covered with garlic and herbs is simple and flavorful. The ravioli might be cheese-and-artichoke, covered with a sauce of scallops and tomatoes and herbs—rich and flavorful, but too many disjointed flavors. Eggplant on top of polenta, covered with a tangy tomato sauce, is less complicated and more successful. Wine by the glass comes dear: you're better off making a selection of one of the well-priced bottles. The brick-and-dark-wood building opens into two stories inside—avoid sitting near the bustling staircase. ■ *180 High St (near Ferry St), Salem; (503)399-1413; $$; full bar; AE, MC, V; checks OK; lunch Mon–Fri, dinner every day.* &

La Margarita ★ This is definitely one of the livelier spots downtown. The unassuming front opens to a colorfully decorated, two-storied interior, with lots of mirrors to make it look bigger than it is and music to keep it hopping. The staff hops, too— this place is busy. The menu has all the usuals, but the specialty is mesquite grilling, especially the tender and lightly cooked beef and chicken. Sauces are subtle, with the emphasis on eating healthy. The mammoth margaritas blow all those good intentions out the door. ■ *545 Ferry St SE (near corner of High and Church Sts), Salem; (503)362-8861; $; full bar; AE, DC, MC, V; checks OK; lunch Mon–Sat, dinner every day.* &

McGrath's Publick Fish House ★ This sharp-looking restaurant might be just a knockoff of more famous Seattle and Portland fish houses, but in restaurant-poor Salem it has a fresh feel. Good prices and special attention to children should keep families happy. Crowds pack this glass-fronted, multi-tiered building. The menu's diverse, but order the seafood off the daily fresh sheet. The blackened oyster appetizer is almost a meal in itself—plump oysters, plenty spicy. Mesquite-broiled salmon and the trout are cooked perfectly, though sauces tend to be uninteresting. No complaints on the chubby marionberry cobbler. The young service staff lacks real expertise but is cheerful and eager. ■ *350 Chemeketa (at Liberty St), Salem; (503)362-0736; $$; full bar; AE, DC, MC, V; checks OK; breakfast, lunch, dinner every day.* &

Morton's Bistro Northwest ★ Clever design puts the diner below roadway level, looking out on an attractive courtyard backed by an ivy-covered wall. The interior is intimate, with dark wood beams and soft lighting. The menu is probably one of the most ambitious in Salem—predominantly Northwest cuisine with hints of international influences, featuring fresh seafood, veal, and a short list of pasta dishes. The service is expert and pleasant, and there's a very good selection of reasonably priced Northwest wines. ■ *1128 Edgewater (across the Marion St bridge from downtown), West Salem; (503)585-1113; $$; full bar; MC, V; checks OK; dinner Tues–Sat.* &

LODGINGS

Marquee House Bed and Breakfast ★ You're a half-dozen blocks from the capitol, but because the house sits away from the street with a broad yard sloping down to Mill Creek, it feels like the country. Owner Rickie Hart, a veteran of Long Beach's Shelburne Inn, has developed a movies theme in this Colonial-style B&B: you might stay in the "Topper" room, with a collection of old hats, or among old Western prints and memorabilia in the "Blazing Saddles" room. Evenings, settle back for movies and popcorn in the living room. Request a room with a view of the creek and a fireplace. Watch for beaver, or for spawning salmon in the fall. Breakfast will probably include local fresh fruits and a plentiful supply of egg or pancake dishes, potatoes, pastries, and fresh breads. ■ *333 Wyatt Ct NE (off Center St, just west of intersection with 17th), Salem, OR 97301; (503)391-0837; $$; MC, V; checks OK.*

INDEPENDENCE

The town looks pretty untouched by modern times, and if you want to remind yourself what an old-fashioned fountain was like, **Taylor's Fountain and Gift**, on the corner of Main and Monmouth, is the perfect place. Marge Taylor, her daughter, and two granddaughters have been serving up burgers, shakes, and malts, as well as breakfasts, pretty much the same way for over 50 years.

RESTAURANTS

Amador's Alley ★ Here's an unexpected find that produces some of the most honest Mexican fare around. Brothers Manuel and Antonio Amador do the cooking, while their families (down to the youngest children) wait on the customers. Nothing elaborate in the way of decor: a whitewashed space, a few Mexican fans, paper flowers. But you know it's going to be good as soon as the first basket of chips arrives (thick, crunchy, homemade) along with a fresh salsa; you can taste the corn and tomatoes. Nothing is fancy or unusual, but everything from tacos to enchiladas is exquisitely fresh, piping hot, and lavishly garnished with sour cream, avocado, fresh tomatoes, and green onions. A second Amador's is in Lincoln City; 828 NE Hwy 101, (503)996-4223. ■ *870 N Main St (at Hoffman Rd), Independence; (503)838-0170; $; full bar; MC, V; checks OK; lunch, dinner Mon–Sat.* ♿

ALBANY

Time and I-5 have both bypassed Albany, which is probably a blessing. Once you get off the freeway (ignore the smell of the nearby pulp mill), you'll discover a fine representative of the small-town Oregon of an earlier era, with broad, quiet streets, neat

▼ Albany ▲

houses, and a slow pace. Once an important transportation hub in the Willamette Valley, the town has an unequaled selection of historic homes and buildings in a wide variety of styles, many of them lovingly restored.

Historic buildings. A self-guided tour displays 13 distinct architectural styles in the 50-block, 368-building Monteith Historic District alone. Then there are the Hackleman District (28 blocks, 210 buildings) and downtown (9½ blocks, 80 buildings). Many of the buildings are open for inspection on annual tours—the last Saturday in July and the Sunday evening before Christmas Eve. A handy guide is available free of charge from the Albany Chamber of Commerce, 435 W First Avenue, (541)926-1517, or the Albany Convention and Visitors Center at 300 SW Second, PO Box 965, Albany, OR 97321, (800)526-2256.

Covered bridges. The covered bridges that were so characteristic of this area are disappearing. From 450 their number has dwindled to less than 50, but that's still more than in any state west of the Mississippi. Most of the remaining bridges are in the Willamette Valley counties of Lane, Linn, and Lincoln, and local preservationists are fighting to save them. Best starting points for easy-to-follow circuits of the bridges are Albany, Eugene, and Cottage Grove; in addition, many handsome bridges dot the woods of the Oregon Coast Range. Six of these bridges lie within an 8-mile radius of Scio, northeast of Albany; for a map, contact the Albany Convention and Visitors Center. For other tours, send an SASE with two first-class stamps to the Covered Bridge Society of Oregon, PO Box 1804, Newport, OR 97365, or call (541)265-2934.

▼

Albany

▲

RESTAURANTS

Novak's Hungarian Paprikas ★★ Don't be put off by the strip-mall setting—you'll get a warm welcome from Joseph and Matilda Novak, Hungarian refugees who run this quaintly decorated place with help from their family (your waitress will help you pronounce the Hungarian dishes). The housemade sausages are mild and delicately spiced, the stuffed cabbage is oozing with flavor, and the sides of tangy spiced cabbage are to kill for (though, surprisingly, the signature chicken paprikas is bland). Huge servings come with lots of vegetables and potatoes, and small prices. Don't forget dessert: the pastry chef is full-time and the dessert menu is longer than the main one. ■ *2835 Santiam Hwy SE (take exit 233 toward town), Albany; (541)967-9488; $; no alcohol; MC, V; checks OK; lunch Sun–Fri, dinner every day.* ₺

CORVALLIS

Corvallis is a pleasant mix of old river town and funky university burg. The Willamette River lines the small downtown area, which is noticeably livelier than in most small towns of the area. You can poke around in interesting shops and stop in for an outrageously big pastry and a cup of coffee at **New Morning Bakery**, 219 SW Second, (503)754-0181, where you can also get a light lunch or dinner. The **Oregon State University** campus is typical of Northwest megaversities, with a gracious core of old buildings, magnificent giant trees, and lots of open space, surrounded by a maze of modern, boxlike classroom and residential buildings of little character. Sports are big here, especially basketball and gymnastics, but the basement of Gill Coliseum also houses the **Horner Museum**, which has a wonderfully eclectic, rather dilapidated collection that relates the history of Oregon's development, from Native Americans to the Oregon Trail to economic growth—a grand place for kids, with lots of nooks and crannies and large artifacts from yesteryear. Unfortunately, it's only open weekends; (541)737-2951. **Corvallis Art Center**, 700 SW Madison, (541)754-1551, located in a renovated 1889 Episcopal church off Central Park, displays local crafts and hosts weekly lunchtime concerts.

Corvallis is ideal for biking and running; most streets include a wide bike lane, and routes follow both the Willamette and Mary's Rivers. Avery Park, 15th Street and US 20, offers a maze of wooded trails as well as prime picnic sites and a rose garden. Tree lovers may also enjoy OSU's 40-acre **Peavy Arboretum**, 8 miles north of town on Highway 99W—it has hiking trails and picnic facilities.

A local winery of interest is **Tyee Wine Cellars**, (541)753-8754, just south of the airport off Highway 99W, a small producer of impeccable quality.

▼

Corvallis

Restaurants

▲

RESTAURANTS

The Gables ★★ While you won't find the culinary creativity of some other offbeat eateries in town, this is still the best place for more formal occasions. Its strip-mall exterior belies a dark and comfortable wood-paneled and crisp-linen interior. The menu is a simple, tried-and-true formula: prime rib, steaks, lamb, and seafood, with an occasional oddity like buffalo. Dinners are huge and come with all the expected trimmings: sourdough bread, relish tray, salad or chicken bisque, veggies, rice or potato. Expect the meat to be perfectly cooked and the service to be quietly efficient. Reserve a table in the wine cellar for special group occasions. ■ *1121 NW 9th St (follow Harrison to 9th), Corvallis; (541)752-3364; $$; full bar; AE, DC, MC, V; checks OK; dinner every day.* &

Bombs Away Cafe ★ This is a tacqueria with an attitude. You'll find all your Tex-Mex favorites, but with a wholesome twist: heaps of herb-flavored brown rice and black beans and hardly any fat in sight. Check this out: a chimichanga stuffed with duck confit and covered with tomatoes and tomatillos. Or how about a goat cheese and black bean quesadilla? Lots of vegetarian choices are available. In the front room you order at the counter, and the ambience is your basic college-town cafeteria, but the help is friendly and service is speedy. In back there's a full-service room that's quieter, with a slightly fancier menu, where you can also order from an impressive variety of tequilas. ■ *2527 NW Monroe (at 25th), Corvallis; (541)757-7221; $; full bar; MC, V; checks OK; lunch Mon–Fri, dinner every day.* &

Nearly Normal's ★ There's nothing normal about Nearly Normal's (they've chosen the flamingo as their official bird). The aging hippies who run the place advertise their food as "gonzo cuisine": vegetarian food, organically grown, but prepared with originality and panache. There's lots of Mexican on the menu, plus a few Middle Eastern items and excellent veggie burgers. Try the falafel, a hearty mix of spicy garbanzo patties packed into pita with fresh veggies and a cool yogurt sauce, or the Acapulco sunburger, with avocado and salsa. The fresh fruit drinks are great. This place can get crowded, and you bus your own dishes. ■ *109 NW 15th St (near the corner of Monroe), Corvallis; (541)753-0791; $; beer and wine; no credit cards; checks OK; breakfast, lunch, dinner Mon–Sat.*

LODGINGS

Hanson Country Inn ★★ The inn is just a few minutes from town, but you'll feel you're in the country as you drive up to this wood-and-brick 1928 farmhouse. Formerly a prosperous poultry-breeding ranch, it's now, thanks to an extensive renovation by former San Franciscan Patricia Covey, a registered historic home. The gleaming living room (with piano and fireplace), sun room, and library are often used for weddings. Step outside into a formal lawn and garden. Upstairs are four guest rooms, luxuriously wallpapered and linened. The best suite has a four-poster bed, a private bath, and a study. After breakfasting on crêpes with blackberries or a fresh frittata, explore the grounds and the original egg house. Bring the kids; a two-bedroom cottage behind the main house has a fully equipped kitchen, private bath, and living area perfect for families. ■ *795 SW Hanson St (5 minutes west of town off West Hills at 35th), Corvallis, OR 97333; (541)752-2919; $$; AE, DC, MC, V; checks OK.*

ELMIRA

LODGINGS

McGillivray's Log Home Bed and Breakfast ★ This spacious log home on 5 wooded acres makes a lovely, pastoral retreat for urbanites and a fine introduction to the beauties of Western Oregon for out-of-staters. The two large guest rooms (one with a king-size bed and two twins—perfect for families) both have private baths. A hearty breakfast is prepared on the wood cookstove with antique griddle, and there are fresh Northwest berries in season. ■ *88680 Evers Rd (14 miles west of Eugene off Hwy 126), Elmira, OR 97437; (541)935-3564; $$; MC, V; checks OK.* &

EUGENE

Although it's the state's second-largest urban area, Eugene is still very much Portland's sleepy sister to the south. There's no skyline here—unless you count the grain elevator (well, okay, there's a 12-story Hilton, too)—and a Eugenean's idea of a traffic jam is when it takes more than five minutes to traverse downtown. There's always parking; people smile at you on the street; and, even in its urban heart, Eugene is more treed than paved.

Still, this overgrown town has a sophisticated indigenous culture, from its own symphony to homegrown ballet, opera, and theater companies. There are more speakers and events (courtesy of the University of Oregon, the state's flagship institution) than one could possibly ever attend. There are good bookstores (don't miss **Smith Family Bookstore**, (541)345-1651 or (541)343-4714), the requisite number of coffeehouses, trendy brewpubs (try **Steelhead** in Station Square, (541)686-2739, or the new local favorite, **The Wild Duck**, on West Sixth, (541)485-3825), two serious chocolatiers (**Euphoria**, (541)345-1990, and **Fenton & Lee**, (541)343-7629), and enough local color—from persevering hippies to backcountry loggers—to make life interesting.

▼

Eugene

▲

Whatever else you do in Eugene, here are the musts: a hike up **Spencer's Butte**, just south of town, for a spectacular view of the town, valley, and its two rivers; a morning at Saturday Market (April–December), the state's oldest outdoor crafts fair; an afternoon shopping and eating your way through the Fifth Street Public Market; an evening at the Hult Center for the Performing Arts. If you're in town in early July, don't miss the area's oldest and wildest countercultural celebration, the **Oregon Country Fair**; (541)484-1314.

Hult Center for the Performing Arts is the city's world-class concert facility, with two architecturally striking halls. The 24-hour concert line is (541)342-5746.

University of Oregon features a lovely art museum with a permanent collection of Orientalia, a natural history museum, several historic landmark buildings, and a wide variety of speakers and events; (541)346-3111. The university has a good bookstore, too; (541)346-4331.

Wistec, a small but nicely conceived hands-on science and technology museum (with accompanying laser light–show planetarium), is the place to take kids on rainy afternoons; 2300 Leo Harris Parkway, (541)687-3619.

Saturday Market, a thriving open-air crafts and food fair, is the ultimate Eugene experience: unique crafts sold by the artisans themselves, continental noshing, eclectic music, and inspired people-watching; open April through December on High Street at Broadway.

Fifth Street Public Market, three levels of shops and upscale crafts booths surrounding a pretty brick courtyard, is a great place to spend a lazy Sunday morning, just you, the *New York Times* (courtesy of **Marketplace Books**), a latte, and a sinful *pain au chocolat* from **Metropol**, the city's best bakery (on the ground floor).

Outdoors. Two rivers that run through town, the Willamette and the McKenzie, provide opportunities for canoeists and rafters, both first-timers and whitewater enthusiasts. Hikers find miles of forest trails just outside the city limits. Runners love the city's several groomed, packed running trails.

Parks. Run along the banks of the Willamette through Alton Baker Park on the 6³⁄10-kilometer groomed Prefontaine Trail. Women will feel safer on the sloughside 1⅗-kilometer circuit that borders Amazon Park, site of spirited outdoor concerts in the summer. Hendricks Park, the city's oldest, features an outstanding 10-acre rhododendron garden (best blooms in May and early June). Skinner's Butte Park, which skirts the Willamette, includes a lovely rose garden, several playgrounds, picnic areas, and a 12-mile bike/running path. Spencer's Butte, just south of town, offers sweeping urban and pastoral views to those who hike up the two relatively easy trails to the top.

▼

Eugene

▲

RESTAURANTS

Adam's Place ★★★ This is Eugene's most elegant restaurant. Adam Bernstein, a third-generation restaurateur who trained at the Culinary Institute of America, has tastefully redecorated this intimate downtown spot on the mall (formerly the Grapevine) by adding mahogany wainscoting, arches, pillars, sconces, and a lovely fireplace to the dining room. The result is a quietly sophisticated place, unpretentious yet classy, with attentive service, lovely presentation, and inventive cuisine (menu changes weekly). Catch the salmon and dill potato pancake with dill crème fraîche and salsa appetizer, or the grilled eggplant, tomato, and warm duck salad. For an entree, consider the wild North Atlantic salmon, perfectly undercooked, and topped with a sweet, tangy chutneylike orange glaze, or the generously portioned polenta lasagne. For dessert, the fall bread pudding is so caramelly and buttery you never want it to end. A nice selection of Oregon and California wines, many by the glass, as well as a full (and pretty) bar, add to the experience. ■ *30 E Broadway (on the downtown mall), Eugene; (541)344-6948; $$; full bar; MC, V; checks OK; lunch, dinner Tues–Fri, dinner only Sat.* ♿

Chanterelle ★★★ Understated, sophisticated, and unfailingly wonderful, chef Ralf Schmidt's intimate restaurant offers the very freshest of every season, cooked with respect and restrained imagination. The small menu with its delicate basil scallops and richly sauced tournedos of beef is supplemented by a wide selection of chef's specials—whatever is fresh and appeals to the chef's sense of adventure. In the spring, there's chinook salmon and local lamb. In the winter, Schmidt's deeply satisfying onion soup warms the inner you. The chef does it all, alone in a kitchen the size of a walk-in closet—and comes out smiling at the end of the evening to greet his loyal patrons. You'll find a respectable wine list and extraordinary desserts. ■ *207 E 5th (across from 5th St Public Market), Eugene; (541) 484-4065; $$; full bar; AE, DC, MC, V; checks OK; dinner Tues–Sat.* ⅄

Zenon Cafe ★★★ A compelling combination of culinary imagination and rock-solid consistency has made Zenon into one of the best restaurants in Eugene. Urbane, noisy, crowded, and invariably interesting, Zenon offers an ever-changing international menu featuring, on any given night, Italian, Greek, Middle Eastern, Cajun, Caribbean, Thai, and Northwest cuisines. Nothing disappoints here, from the hazelnut-encrusted pork tenderloins with raspberry sauce to the Jamaican-spiked ahi with tropical fruit salsa to a lovely eggplant-based vegetarian dish named "The Priest Fainted." A good selection of regional wines by the glass is available. Do leave room for dessert; Zenon's are perhaps the city's best. ■ *898 Pearl St (corner of E Broadway), Eugene; (541) 343-3005; $$; beer and wine; MC, V; checks OK; breakfast, lunch, dinner every day.* ⅄

Cafe Soriah ★★ What a wonderful and well-deserved success for chef/owner Ibrahim Habib, a veteran Eugene restaurateur who established the city's first hole-in-the-wall Middle Eastern eatery years ago. Soriah, a favorite with locals, is a classy but unpretentious Mediterranean and Middle Eastern restaurant where a diner can feel equally at home in Saturday night finery or jeans. The pretty, well-appointed dining room is intimate without being claustrophobic, and in good weather the outside terrace seating is a treat. The lamb sautéed with garlic and mushrooms in cream and turmeric is an excellent choice, as are the simple but succulent rosemary chicken, the moussaka, and the spanakopita. Ib, as everyone calls the popular owner, also makes the best hummus, baba ghanouj, and stuffed grape leaves this side of Beirut. Memorable desserts include a fabulous pecan-crusted, chocolate-ganache, espresso-whipped-cream pie that should be outlawed. ■ *384 W 13th (corner of Lawrence), Eugene; (541) 342-4410; $$; full bar; AE, MC, V; checks OK; lunch Mon–Fri, dinner every day.* ⅄

The LocoMotive Restaurant ★★ Owners Lee and Eitan Zucker come to Eugene via Israel, the Caribbean, and Manhattan, and they are bringing sophistication and subtlety to vegetarian cooking in their friendly restaurant across from the Fifth Street Public Market. The menu is 100 percent vegetarian (vegan on

▼

▲

request), the ingredients are 100 percent organic, and the results are 100 percent delicious. While the menu changes weekly, it always includes a variety of wonderful soups (try the shorba al hummus, a hearty, peppery chickpea and vegetable mix). Musts include the portobello mushrooms in reduced red wine sauce with garlicky mashed potatoes, and the thick and richly flavored Ottoman Stew. The breads are baked fresh daily, as are the lovely desserts. ■ *291 E 5th (across the street from the 5th Street Public Market), Eugene; (541)465-4754; $$; beer and wine; MC, V; checks OK; dinner Tues–Sat.* &

Ambrosia ★ The pizzas are wonderful here: small, crisp pies topped with rich plum tomato sauce and your choice of trendy ingredients (sun-dried tomatoes, artichoke hearts, roasted eggplant) and baked in a huge wood-burning oven. But Ambrosia is much more than a designer pizzeria; take, for example, the angel hair pasta topped with grilled, marinated vegetables, or the zucchini and fennel lasagne. Fresh fish specials might include a grilled halibut in tomato-caper butter or Chilean sea bass finished in dry wine and topped with Dungeness crab and toasted almonds. Gelato cools the evening. ■ *174 E Broadway (corner of Pearl), Eugene; (541)342-4141; $; full bar; MC, V; checks OK; lunch Mon–Sat, dinner every day.* &

Cafe Navarro ★ Like the world beat music that plays on the sound system, Jorge Navarro's restaurant is a rich cross-cultural experience, with dishes ranging from Africa and Spain to Cuba and the Caribbean. Navarro freely combines cuisines, often arriving at extraordinary results such as his Caribbean interpretation of cioppino made here with cilantro, chiles, and roasted tomatoes. There are no bad choices. For lunch, Navarro's version of arroz con pollo, with seared chicken chunks, red peppers, capers, and cilantro, is a good bet. For breakfast, the hands-down favorite is chilaquiles—eggs scrambled with corn tortillas, chipotle salsa, and Monterey Jack cheese. ■ *454 Willamette St (at the foot of Willamette St), Eugene; (541)344-0943; $; beer and wine; MC, V; checks OK; breakfast Sat–Sun, lunch Tues–Fri, dinner Tues–Sat.* &

Mekala's ★ A pretty Thai restaurant with its light-filled dining area overlooking the Fifth Street Public Market courtyard (outside seating, weather permitting), Mekala's features a six-page menu with more than a dozen fiery curries and two dozen vegetarian dishes. Chef/owner Payung Van Slyke is an inventive cook who shows sensitivity to a wide range of palates: magnificent angel wings (deboned chicken wings stuffed with ground pork, glass noodles, and bean sprouts), a flavor-packed homoke soufflé (shrimp, scallops, and fish in a curry-and-coconut sauce with fresh lime leaves, green pepper, and cabbage). End the meal with a dish of velvety homemade coconut ice cream. ■ *296 E 5th St (in the 5th St Public Market Building), Eugene;*

(541)342-4872; $; beer and wine; AE, MC, V; checks OK; lunch, dinner every day. ㄥ

Mona Lizza ★ Part of Eugene's downtown renaissance, this pleasing restaurant with full bar offers many choices. Come for one of the dozen wood-oven designer pizzas, a glass of the local microbrew, and a game of pool (there are a few quiet tables in the back dining room). Come with your kids (the waitstaff is obliging, and atmosphere is casual). Or come for more serious dining, choosing from a diverse nouveau-Italian menu that features fish (try the wood-roasted mahi-mahi topped with leeks, roasted bell peppers, olives, and feta), chicken, meat (the baked rigatoni with homemade sausage is pure comfort food), or vegetarian fare. The typically indulgent desserts greet you when you walk in. Various renditions of the Mona Lisa line the walls, all painted by local artists commissioned by the restaurant. ■ *830 Olive St (on the downtown mall), Eugene; (541)345-1072; $; full bar; AE, DC, MC, V; checks OK; lunch, dinner every day.* ㄥ

Oregon Electric Station ★ The Electric Station narrows the culinary generation gap between the prime-rib-and-baked-potato crowd and the yellowfin-tuna-in-roasted-pepper-butter folks. While there is nothing spectacular about the diverse menu—no great risks taken—there are also few failures. The seafood is never overcooked; the steak is invariably juicy. You eat in converted railroad cars parked behind the lovely brick station that gives the restaurant its name. The historical station building with its 30-foot ceilings and arched windows houses the city's prettiest bar, with live jazz on weekends. ■ *27 E 5th (1 block north of the Hult Center), Eugene; (541)485-4444; $; full bar; MC, V; local checks only; lunch Mon–Fri, dinner every day.* ㄥ

Shiki ★ It's about time Eugene had a noteworthy Japanese restaurant, and Shiki—with its extensive sushi bar, authentic menu, and subtle service—is it. The location (a little box of a building, a former Sizzler, plunked down in the middle of a parking lot) is the only unpromising thing about this smartly run restaurant. Inside, the decor is pleasingly spare, and the menu has something for everyone, from the neophyte who wants to stay with tempura and teriyaki (the wonderful sanshoku bento is your choice) to those with a more adventuresome palate (the *dengaku zanmai*, portions of creamy steamed eggplant, tofu, and potato in sweet miso sauce). The sushi bar features 50 different items, cooked, smoked, and raw. ■ *81 Coburg Rd (Ferry Street Bridge to Coburg Rd), Eugene; (541)343-1936; $; beer and wine; MC, V; checks OK; lunch Tues–Fri, dinner Tues–Sun.*

Excelsior Cafe Eugene's grande dame of nouvelle cuisine is just not what it used to be during the Stephanie Pearl regime. It is still Eugene-style elegant with generally wonderful soups and inspired desserts. But the consistent excellence and intriguing innovation of the past are mostly gone. On occasion, it is possible to eat quite well here—the ambience is lovely, the service professional—but those who knew the "Ex" of yesteryear may be disappointed. ■ *754 E 13th (across from Sacred Heart Hospital), Eugene; (541)342-6963; $$; full bar; AE, DC, MC, V; checks OK; breakfast, lunch, dinner every day.* ⅋

Keystone Cafe This is the place to get back to where you once belonged. If that makes no sense to you, then Keystone is not your kind of eatery. Come here to mix and mingle with the card-carrying counterculturalists and dig into the best breakfast in town. There's an organic bakery in back and funky outside seating in nice weather. ■ *395 W 5th (corner of Lawrence), Eugene; (541)342-2075; $; no alcohol; no credit cards; local checks only; breakfast, lunch every day.* ⅋

LODGINGS

Campbell House ★★★ Built in 1892 and restored as a grand bed-and-breakfast inn, the Campbell House has everything going for it: a location that's quiet (an acre of beautifully landscaped grounds) yet convenient (two blocks from Fifth Street Market); elegant, light-filled rooms with old-world charm (four-poster beds, high ceilings, dormer windows) and modern amenities (TVs, VCRs, phones with data ports, stocked minirefrigerators); and smart, attentive service. Each of the inn's 14 rooms has a private bath, several have gas fireplaces, and one, the Dr. Eva Johnson Room, has a luxurious bathroom alcove with jetted tub for two. The inn is designated nonsmoking, but the Cogswell Room offers a private entrance that opens onto a pretty patio for those who must light up. If you like the personalized service of a B&B but don't like to feel hovered over, if you love country-cottage decor but lament the day Laura Ashley was born, this is your kind of place. Coffee and tea delivered to your room in the morning are followed by a full breakfast featuring waffles, homemade granola, and a special egg dish. ■ *252 Pearl St (2 blocks north of 5th St Public Market, on the east side of Skinner's Butte), Eugene, OR 97401; (541)343-1119 or (800)264-2519; www.campbellhouse.com; $$$; AE, MC, V; checks OK.* ⅋

Excelsior Inn ★★ Sitting atop the Excelsior restaurant (a convenient two blocks from the University of Oregon campus) is this European-style inn. Each of the 14 guest suites is charmingly decorated and features hardwood floors, arched windows, vaulted ceilings, and marble-and-tile private baths. The Bach Room, with its king-size sleigh bed, pretty sitting area, and Jacuzzi tub, is a favorite. All rooms have TVs, VCRs, and computer hookups. Complimentary breakfast is served downstairs at the restaurant, where inn guests order from the regular menu. ■ *754 E 13th (2 blocks west of UO), Eugene, OR 97403;*

(541)342-6963; excelinn@pacinfo.com; $$$; AE, DC, MC, V; checks OK. ᗺ

Valley River Inn ★★ The Inn's neighbor is a regional shopping mall with acres of parking lots, but the Inn looks toward the Willamette River for its ambience. With pretty inner court-yards, lovely plantings, and an inviting pool area, this sprawling complex effectively creates a world of its own. The rooms are oversize and well decorated, with the best ones facing the river. The outdoor dining area hard by the river is wonderful for drinks and hors d'oeuvres. ■ *1000 Valley River Way (exit 194B off I-5 to 105 (west) to exit 1), Eugene, OR 97401; (541)687-0123; $$$; AE, DC, MC, V; checks OK.* ᗺ

The Oval Door ★ This spacious, farm-style home with an inviting wraparound porch is nicely located on a quiet, tree-lined street just a stroll from downtown. The four guest rooms, all with private baths, are pretty and light-filled. The Cecilia, with its gorgeous mahogany bed and roomy sitting area, is particularly nice. Guests may also indulge themselves in the Jacuzzi room with its oversize tub, heated towels, soft music, and enough emollients to appease Cleopatra. A full breakfast is served. ■ *988 Lawrence St (corner of 10th), Eugene, OR 97401; (541)683-3160 or (800) 882-3160; $$; AE, MC, V; checks OK.*

Eugene Hilton For convenience to downtown, the Hilton fills the bill. It's attached to the Eugene Conference Center, across a brick courtyard from the Hult Center for the Performing Arts, a block from the downtown mall, and within easy strolling distance of a half-dozen good restaurants. The rooms are pre-dictable, but there are nice city views from south-facing rooms and quieter butte views from the north. Amenities include a (very small) indoor pool along with a sauna, Jacuzzi, and fitness room. Don't plan to eat at either of the hotel's two lackluster restaurants. ■ *66 E 6th Ave (exit 194B off I-5, then exit 1 to city center), Eugene, OR 97401; (541)342-2000; $$$; AE, DC, MC, V; checks OK.* ᗺ

Phoenix Inn No lodging is more convenient to the UO campus than the Phoenix Inn, one of a small chain of moderately priced minisuite hotels. The rooms are large and airy (though char-acterless), with defined sleeping and sitting areas. Each comes equipped with microwave, refrigerator, wet bar, and coffee-maker, and some have big Jacuzzi tubs. There's also a reason-ably sized indoor pool with adjacent spa and a small fitness center. Complimentary continental breakfast buffet and news-paper start off your day right. Ask for one of the rooms that face the Millrace (a little canal). ■ *850 Franklin Blvd (exit 194B off I-5, then UO exit to Franklin Blvd), Eugene, OR 97403; (541)344-0001 or (800)344-0131; $$; AE, DC, MC, V; checks OK.* ᗺ

SPRINGFIELD

RESTAURANTS

Kuraya's ★ Although its location is off the beaten path, Kuraya's remains a popular spot with local Thai-food lovers. The casual atmosphere, friendly service, and large, inventive menu keep people coming back. So do the seafood basket—shrimp and scallops in a hot, coconutty sauce—and the Bangkok prawns, charcoal broiled and served with a crabmeat-and-peanut dipping sauce. ■ *1410 Mohawk Blvd (at Market), Springfield; (541) 746-2951; $; beer and wine; MC, V; checks OK; lunch Mon–Sat, dinner every day.* &

Spring Garden ★ This resolutely uncharming spot on Springfield's decaying Main Street serves some of the best Chinese food south of Portland. Although you dine with a panoramic view of a Goodwill Industries outlet, you can feast on truly inspired sizzling rice soup, egg rolls that are simultaneously crunchy and eggy, and a variety of fresh, flavorful entrees. Seafood lovers should make a beeline for the stuffed garlic prawns or the pan-fried shrimp, two of the best items on the menu. David Tofu, with chicken or vegetarian, is divine. Try to ignore those around you who order the combination plates. ■ *215 Main St (downtown), Springfield; (541) 747-0338; $; full bar; AE, MC, V; local checks only; lunch, dinner every day.*

LEABURG

LODGINGS

Marjon Bed and Breakfast ★ Thirty minutes east of Eugene, just off the road that threads its way through the Oregon Cascades, sits Margie Haas's immaculate contemporary home on 2 private acres by the banks of the pristine McKenzie, dotted with 2,000 azaleas and 7,000 rhododendrons. The junior room ($95 a night) is a nice-size bedroom with bath (including fishbowl shower) across the hall. The French Provincial suite ($125) has a crystal chandelier, a 7-by-12-foot bed, an adjoining bath with sunken tub, and a view of the Japanese garden. Breakfasts are five-course affairs served with seasonal flair. ■ *44975 Leaburg Dam Rd (3 miles east of Leaburg on McKenzie Hwy, turn at Leaburg Dam Rd (milepost 24), ignore the dead-end signs), Leaburg, OR 97489; (541) 896-3145; $$$; no credit cards; checks OK.*

OAKLAND

RESTAURANTS

Tolly's ★ Tolly's is a bit of an oddity. Downstairs there's an old-fashioned ice cream parlor, candy counter, and antique gift shop. Upstairs the Tollefsons get a bit more serious with a special-occasion place for locals. One elegant room, with high-backed wing chairs and candlelight, is reserved for couples only. Chefs change from time to time, but the execution of dishes like chicken Mediterranean and classic bacon-wrapped filet mignon is respectably consistent. The wine list is the region's longest, at close to 100 labels. ■ *115 NE Locust St (exit 138 off I-5 to middle of town), Oakland; (541) 459-3796; $$; full bar; AE, MC, V; local checks only; lunch, dinner every day.*

STEAMBOAT

LODGINGS

Steamboat Inn ★ On the banks of a fly-only fishing stream is the plain-seeming lodge run for many years by Jim and Sharon Van Loan. Linked by a long veranda paralleling the North Umpqua River are eight small guest cabins, remodeled in 1997; rooms have knotty pine walls, and just enough space (adults only in these). In the woods are five secluded cottages with living rooms and kitchens, suitable for small families. Back down by the river are two riverside suites. No pets, please; enjoy the Van Loans' pets instead. Remarkably good family-style dinners are served in the main building each night a half hour after dark, by reservation only ($35 per person, including premium Oregon wines). That's just enough time to prepare your fishing stories. The inn also serves breakfast and lunch daily, and is now entirely nonsmoking. ■ *42705 N Umpqua Hwy (Hwy 138, 38 miles east of Roseburg), Steamboat, OR 97447-9703; (800) 840-8825; steamboat.n@-worldnet.att.net; $$$; MC, V; checks OK (closed Jan–Feb; weekends only Nov–Dec, Mar–Apr).*

ROSEBURG

The Roseburg area now has eight **wineries,** all open for tours and tastings much of the year: Callahan Ridge, 340 Busenbark Lane, (541) 673-7901; Davidson, 2637 Reston Road, (541) 679-6950; Girardet, 895 Reston Road, (541) 679-7252; Henry, 687 Hubbard Creek Road, Umpqua, (541) 459-5120; HillCrest, 240 Vineyard Lane, (541) 673-3709; La Garza, 491 Winery Lane, (541) 679-9654; Lookingglass, 6561 Lookingglass Road, (541) 679-8198; and Umpqua River (Denino), 451 Hess Lane, (541) 673-1975. Henry and Hill-Crest are open all year. The others have more limited hours in winter. La Garza also has a tasting-room restaurant, the first in the region, serving lunch Wednesday through Sunday, May through September.

Wildlife Safari allows you to drive through rolling country to see a quasi-natural wildlife preserve, with predators discreetly fenced from their prey, and to watch baby animals up close. Open daily; Route 99, 4 miles west of I-5, exit 119, (541) 679-6761, www.maserith.com/safari.

Douglas County Museum of History and Natural History imaginatively displays logging, fur-trapping, and pioneer items in one of the handsomest contemporary structures you'll find. There's a modest admission charge. It's open daily; off I-5 at the fairgrounds, exit 123, (541)440-4507, museum@rosenet.net.

K&R's Drive Inn dishes out huge scoops of Umpqua ice cream. One scoop is really two; two scoops are actually four. It's located 20 miles north of Roseburg, at the Rice Hill exit off I-5.

What started out as the Cow Creek Indians' bingo parlor has grown into the **Seven Feathers Hotel and Gaming Resort** in Canyonville (pop. 1,500), about 25 miles south of Roseburg. Drawn by hundreds of slots, other gaming tables, and a four-story, 156-room hotel that opened in 1996, Seven Feathers patrons often outnumber the Native American proprietors.

RESTAURANTS

Teske's Germania ★ Ernst and Marianne Teske founded Teske's Germania in San Jose, California, some years ago, then sold it and moved to Roseburg to retire. Other ex-Californians in the area prevailed on them to open a new Teske's in Oregon. They did. Good thing. German restaurants appear to be an endangered species in southern Oregon. If you hunger for sauerbraten, red cabbage, and homemade spaetzle, this is the place to go. The fare is hearty and surprisingly inexpensive. ▪ *647 SE Jackson (near Cass, downtown), Roseburg; (541)672-5401; $; full bar; MC, V; local checks only; dinner Mon–Sat.* ♿

LODGINGS

House of Hunter ★ Yes, it's another old house, an Italianate one that dates to circa 1900, but Walt and Jean Hunter restored it in 1990 and have turned it into Roseburg's best B&B, with five bedrooms (two of which are suites). If some of the guest rooms seem a bit small and ordinary, the public Grand Room downstairs is a contrast—bright, roomy, and pleasant, with a mix of antique and contemporary furnishings. Jean Hunter's hearty breakfasts are built around homemade baked goods. No pets are allowed, but children over 10 are welcome. ▪ *813 SE Kane St (near downtown), Roseburg, OR 97470; (541)672-2335 or (800)540-7704; walth@users.wizzards.net; www.server.wizzards. net/hunter/b&b.html; $; MC, V; checks OK.*

WOLF CREEK

LODGINGS

Wolf Creek Tavern An old 1880s stagecoach stop, this inn was purchased by the state and restored in 1979. There are eight guest rooms and one suite. All have private baths. Downstairs there's an attractive parlor and a dining room open to the public. The menu changes from time to time, but the fare, while standard, is usually hearty and inexpensive. Children are okay, pets are not. ■ *100 Railroad Ave (exit 76 off I-5), Wolf Creek, OR 97497; (541) 866-2474; $; no alcohol; DIS, MC, V; local checks only; breakfast, lunch, dinner every day.* ♿

GRANTS PASS

The **Rogue River** is one of Oregon's most beautiful rivers, chiseled into the coastal mountains from here to Gold Beach, protected by the million-acre Siskiyou National Forest, flecked with abandoned gold-mining sites, and inhabited by splendid steelhead and roaming Californians. Two companies offer **jet boat tours**. Hellgate Excursions, (541) 479-7204, departs from the Riverside Inn in Grants Pass. Jet Boat River Excursions, (541) 582-0800, leaves from the city of Rogue River, 8 miles upstream. One guide service that conducts wild and daring whitewater trips is Orange Torpedo Trips, (541) 479-5061. Or you can hike the Rogue, a very hot trip in the summer; see Gold Beach listing in the Oregon Coast chapter.

RESTAURANTS

Hamilton House ★ Chef/owner Doug Hamilton grew up in this house, hidden in the trees east of town. Now it is sandwiched between Fred Meyer and Wal-Mart, where it survives as a handsome dinner house. Count on the salmon being moist and exquisite, and the creamy Jamaican jerk chicken over angel hair pasta quite rich. A daily fresh sheet is often likely to feature lingcod, snapper, and halibut, and there are all the usual steaks. Grants Pass is noted for inexpensive dining, and Hamilton House fits the mold. Two can often get by for $30 (except when Hamilton House offers dinner-theater productions). ■ *344 NE Terry Lane (south Grants Pass exit off I-5, 3 blocks to Terry Lane, left 1 block), Grants Pass; (541) 479-3938; $; full bar; AE, DIS, MC, V; checks OK; dinner every day.* ♿

Legrands ★ The fare is surprisingly good and inexpensive at this French/European restaurant in a converted residence near downtown Grants Pass. The two-course veal piccata dinner soars in at less than $11. Other local favorites include medallions of pork with ginger sauce and sauté of squid with shrimp eggplant. That is, if you haven't filled up on their fresh-baked breads: baguettes, onion bread, or a sun-dried-tomato-and-jalapeño variation. ■ *323 NE E St (3 blocks east of the center of town), Grants Pass; (541) 471-1554; $; full bar; MC, V; checks OK; breakfast Fri–Sun, lunch, dinner every day.* ♿

LODGINGS

Flery Manor ★★ This classy two-story, 5,000-square-foot 1990s rural home on 7 acres of wooded mountainside became a B&B in 1996. Owners John and Marla Vidrinskas did much of the finishing work themselves. The showpiece is the Moonlight Suite, favored by honeymooners and second-honeymooners. Its king-size canopied bed sits in front of a fireplace. French doors open to a private balcony. The bath has a double vanity, double Jacuzzi, and glassed-in shower. It's one of four guest rooms. Some have walk-in closets. Marla serves a three-course breakfast in a formal dining room, featuring baked goods, quiches, frittatas, and beignets. No pets are allowed, but children over 8 are accommodated. ■ *2000 Jumpoff Joe Creek Rd (Hugo exit 66 off I-5, east 1⁷⁄₁₀ miles), Grants Pass, OR 97526; (541)476-3591 or (541)471-2303; flery@chatlink.com; www.grantspass.com/b&b/flery; $$; MC, V; checks OK.*

Morrison's Rogue River Lodge ★ This is the best of the Rogue River lodges favored by fishermen and river-runners. It also happens to be the easiest to reach. While others are accessible only by boat or plane, Morrison's is accessed via a road (paved, no less). The lodge, dating back to the 1940s, has four guest rooms and nine cottages (most people prefer the latter). Start your Rogue River rafting adventures here and you'll be following in the footsteps of George Bush and Jimmy Carter. Overnight rates include a four-course dinner and breakfast. The dining room is open to nonguests; dinners, which always taste best when they're served on the deck, may feature dishes such as cucumber soup, roasted chicken, and a napoleon. ■ *8500 Galice Rd (15 miles west of I-5, Merlin exit), Merlin, OR 97532; (541)476-3825 or (800)826-1963; mlrrt@chatlink.com; $$; DIS, MC, V; checks OK (closed Dec–Apr).*

Paradise Resort ★ The onetime working dude ranch (formerly called Paradise Ranch Inn) continues as a full-service resort, right in the heart of the verdant Rogue River valley. Activities abound: swimming in a heated pool, boating on a 3-acre lake, playing tennis on two lighted courts, golfing on a three-hole course, riding bicycles or hiking along miles of trails, relaxing in a hot tub. With all this planned action, you might expect a sprawling modern resort, but Paradise defies that image: there are only 15 large Early American–style guest rooms. Best are those that overlook one of the three ponds. The emphasis is on peace and quiet: no TVs or phones in rooms (but good message-takers in the office). Overnight guests are served a continental breakfast. The resort's restaurant is open nightly to the general public, with dishes like chicken with brandy-sherry cream sauce, and rack of lamb. Food quality slumped for a time, but has improved. All in all, this continues to be a pleasant getaway. ■ *7000-D Monument Dr (Hugo or Merlin exit off I-5, west to Monument Dr), Grants Pass, OR 97526; (541)479-4333; $$; full bar; MC, V; checks OK; dinner every day, brunch Sun.*

Pine Meadow Inn ★ Maloy and Nancy Murdock built this elegant two-story, 2,600-square-foot country home in 1991 and styled it after a Midwestern farmhouse. The home sits in the middle of a 9-acre estate surrounded by gardens, a fishpond, graveled paths, and park benches. Four upstairs guest rooms feature turn-of-the-century antiques. The Willow Room is the largest, complete with sitting area, love seat, and double vanity bathroom. In the morning the Murdocks are likely to whip up a fresh veggie frittata and strawberry frappé. No pets. ■ *1000 Crow Rd (1 mile north of Merlin-Galice Rd, 5 miles west of I-5 Merlin exit), Merlin, OR 97532; (541) 471-6277 or (800) 554-0806; pmi@pinemeadowinn.com or www.pinemeadowinn.com; $$; DIS, MC, V; checks OK.*

JACKSONVILLE

The town started with a boom when gold was discovered in Rich Gulch in 1851. Then the railroad bypassed it, and the tidy little city struggled to avoid becoming a ghost town. Much of the 19th-century city has been restored; Jacksonville now boasts 85 historic homes and buildings, some of which are open to the public. The strip of authentic Gold Rush–era shops, hotels, and saloons along California Street has become a popular stage set for films, including *The Great Northfield, Minnesota Raid* and the TV-movie version of "Inherit the Wind." Jacksonville is renowned for antique shops.

Britt Festival, an outdoor music and arts series, runs from late June through September on the hillside field where Peter Britt, a famous local photographer and horticulturist, used to have his home. Listeners gather on benches or flop onto blankets on the grass to enjoy open-stage performances of jazz, bluegrass, folk, country, classical music, musical theater, and dance. Quality of performances varies, but the series includes big-name artists from the various categories, and listening to the music under a twinkling night sky makes for a memorable evening. Begun in 1963, the festival now draws some 50,000 viewers through the summer. For tickets and information, contact the Britt Festival office, (541) 773-6077 or (800) 882-7488; brittfest@aol.com; www.mind.net/britt.

Jacksonville Museum, housed in the stately 1883 courthouse, follows the history of the Rogue Valley with plenty of photos and artifacts. Another section displays some works by Peter Britt. The adjacent children's museum lets kids walk through various miniaturized pioneer settings (jail, tepee, schoolhouse). There's a small admission charge for nonresidents; (541) 773-6536.

Valley View Winery, the area's oldest, is at Ruch, 5 miles west of here; (541) 899-8468. The winery maintains another tasting room in town, in Anna Maria's, 130 W California Street, (541) 899-1001.

Jacksonville Inn ★★★ Ask a native to name the area's best, and the answer will often be the Jacksonville Inn. The staff is considerate, and the antique-furnished dining room, housed in the original 1863 building, is elegant and intimate. Executive chef Diane Menzie expertly creates the full realm of continental cuisine—steak, seafood, pasta—plus health-minded low-cholesterol fare and an expanded variety of vegetarian entrees. Dinners can be ordered as leisurely seven-course feasts or à la carte (or save money by ordering from the bistro menu in the lounge). À la carte is substantial enough. The petrale sole is a favorite, as are the veal piccata and the baked polenta with tomatoes, garlic, cheese, and pesto; or try the chicken with portobello mushrooms in a creamy wine sauce. Desserts are lovely European creations. The place is full of locals during weekday lunch. Jerry Evans maintains one of the best-stocked wine cellars in Oregon, with more than 1,500 domestic and imported labels on hand.

Upstairs, eight refurbished rooms are decorated with 19th-century details: antique four-poster beds, patchwork quilts, and original brickwork on the walls. Modern amenities include private bathrooms and air conditioning (a boon in the 100-degree summer swelter). The inn also has three honeymoon cottages nearby, one with king-size canopied bed and two-person Jacuzzi. Guests enjoy a full breakfast. Reserve rooms in advance, especially during the Britt Festival. ■ *175 E California St (the town's main thoroughfare), Jacksonville; (541)899-1900; jvinn@mind. net; www.mind.net/jvinn; $$; full bar; AE, DC, DIS, MC, V; checks OK; breakfast, dinner every day, lunch Tues–Sat, brunch Sun.*

▼
Jacksonville

Restaurants

▲

McCully House Inn ★★ First a popular B&B, the McCully House has also become a respected restaurant serving interesting combinations like pistachio-and-almond-crusted lamb chops with wild mushrooms and wild rice medley. Or how about mahogany duck with vegetable pancakes, shiitakes, and an orange-and-candied-garlic sauce? Some of it's just flowery language, but in general the fare has flavor as well as flair. The restaurant (on the verge of gaining its third star until we discovered its excellent chef, William Prahl, had departed) is a favorite of Hollywood types.

One of the first six homes in the city, McCully House was built in 1861 for Jacksonville's first doctor and later housed the first girls' school. It's elegant inside, with hardwood floors, lace curtains, and lovely antiques. Of the three guest rooms, the best flaunts a fireplace, a claw-footed pedestal tub, and the original black-walnut furnishings that traveled 'round the Horn with J. W. McCully. ■ *240 E California St (follow signs from I-5 to 5th and E California), Jacksonville; (541)899-1942;*

mccully@wave.net; www.wave.net/upg/mccully; $$; full bar; AE, MC, V; checks OK; dinner every day. ዼ

Bella Union ★ This restaurant, in the original century-old Bella Union Saloon (half of which was reconstructed when *The Great Northfield, Minnesota Raid* was filmed in Jacksonville in 1969), has everything from pizza and pasta to elegant dinners to picnic baskets for the summertime Britt Festival. The place usually has a good fresh sheet, with choices such as salmon with chile butter, bass with lime salsa, sole with Romano fettuccine, and ahi tuna. The garden out back is pleasant in warm weather. Proprietor Jerry Hayes, a wine fancier, pours 35 labels by the glass as well as by the bottle. ▪ *170 W California St (center of town), Jacksonville; (541)899-1770; $$; full bar; AE, DIS, MC, V; checks OK; lunch, dinner every day, brunch Sun.* ዼ

LODGINGS

TouVelle House ★★ Frank TouVelle and his new bride built this stately mansion in 1916 after moving to Oregon from Ohio. They lived there for years as Frank became a noted orchardist and politician. Today, it's a Jacksonville landmark, which Carolee and Dennis Casey run as a six-room B&B. The three-story Craftsman features 5,400 square feet of floor space, extensive wood paneling, and square-beamed ceilings. One room's a suite that can accommodate up to four. There's a swimming pool and spa out back. Carolee caters to the corporate trade, and even handles guests' laundry and dry cleaning. In the morning she will not only feast you, but also bring you up to date on town gossip and last night's TV fare. ▪ *455 N Oregon St (4 blocks north of California), Jacksonville, OR 97530; (541)899-8938 or (800)846-8422; touvelle@wave.net; www.wave.net/upg/touvelle; $$; AE, DIS, MC, V; checks OK.*

SHADY COVE/TRAIL

RESTAURANTS

Bel Di's ★★ Ray and Joan Novosad's riverside country dinner house is a lovely place with a dining room that boasts a grand view of the Rogue River. The full dinner is served with elegance, but you're out in the boonies and you don't need to dress up. The overall ambience, the attentive service, and the fine soups and salad dressing are more special than many of the entrees, but try the scampi or the Louisiana stuffed prawns. ▪ *21900 Hwy 62 (north side of Shady Cove's bridge), Shady Cove; (541)878-2010; $$; full bar; MC, V; checks OK; dinner Tues–Sun.* ዼ

Rogue River Lodge ★ The oldest dinner house in Jackson County has been owned by ex-Navy man Ken Meirstin since the 1970s. The walls are decorated with his collection of ship paintings. Dory, his wife, supervises the cooking here and maintains consistent quality with a somewhat predictable menu: steaks, scampi, teriyaki chicken, and prime rib (on weekends). The view of the Rogue isn't as good as at Bel Di's down the road, but the locals like the ambience, food, and piano bar. ■ *24904 Hwy 62 (25 miles north of Medford), Trail; (541)878-2555; $$; full bar; DIS, MC, V; checks OK; dinner every day (closed Tues in winter).*

MEDFORD

Southern Oregon's largest city may not win any contests with nearby towns for prettiness, but it is the center of things in this part of the world. The city is well known across the nation, due to the marketing efforts of Harry and David's, the mail-order giant known for its pears, other fruit, and condiments.

Harry and David's Original Country Store, South Gateway shopping center near Medford's southern I-5 exit (1314 Center Drive), offers "seconds" from gift packs and numerous other items, as well as tours of the complex, which is also the home of **Jackson & Perkins**, the world's largest rose growers. The firm ships from Medford, although most of the flowers are grown in California; (541)776-2277.

The **Craterian Ginger Rogers Theater**, 39 S Central Avenue, is Medford's newest showpiece, a downtown performing arts center with a 742-seat theater that opened in 1997. The former Craterian movie theater dated back to the 1920s. Why Ginger Rogers? The actress owned a ranch on the nearby Rogue River for many years, once danced on the Craterian stage, and in the last couple of years before her death helped raise money for the theater's $5.3 million renovation; (541)779-3000.

CK Tiffin's, a lunchtime cafeteria, has become a mecca for fanciers of vegetarian and low-fat cuisine; 226 E Main Street, (541)779-0480. Locals also like the goodies at **Samovar**, a Russian cafe nearby; 101 E Main Street, (541)779-4967. And for Thai food they flock to **Ali's Thai Kitchen**, a humble spot north of town but one with good, inexpensive fare; 2392 N Pacific Highway, (541)770-3104.

River rafting on a nearby stretch of the Rogue, between Gold Hill and the city of Rogue River, is safe for beginners. You can rent a raft at River Trips in Gold Hill, (541)855-7238, or try one of the shop's Rogue Drifters, a large sack filled with Styrofoam balls.

RESTAURANTS

Genessee Place ★ In a town not noted for great food, Genessee is an oasis. At first, chef-owner Michael Isaacson began with lunch and the lure of quiche, potpies, and cheese bread. Then he moved into dinners, with entrees like homemade cannelloni with ground chicken and cheese in a Pernod-infused tomato sauce, tournedos with red-pepper herb butter, fresh seafood, and veal specialties. The baguette comes with "holy oil," olive oil in which Italian spices have been marinated for three weeks. Isaacson is semiretired now, but other family members carry on, and even opened a second Genessee in Grants Pass in 1996. Lunches are still the most popular with Medford locals. ■ *203 Genessee St (2 blocks east of I-5, between Main and Jackson Sts), Medford; (541) 772-5581; $$; full bar; MC, V; local checks only; lunch, dinner Mon–Sat.*

Hungry Woodsman ★ Bob LaFontaine, owner of a Medford hardware store, tired of the rowdy nightclub next door, bought it in the early 1970s, tore it down, and erected the Hungry Woodsman. The building is a testimonial to the forest products industry. Old saws, photos, and other logging memorabilia adorn the walls. The menu is pretty basic: steak, prime rib, shrimp, crab, lobster. You're probably best off with a steak or an English cut of prime rib; crab tends to be too pricey here. Locals like the Woodsman, as they call it. Few patrons dress up; the waiters wear jeans. ■ *2001 N Pacific Hwy (3 blocks west of the Rogue Valley Mall), Medford; (541) 772-2050; $$; full bar; AE, MC, V; no checks; lunch Mon–Fri, dinner every day.* &

LODGINGS

Under the Greenwood Tree ★★★ Innkeeper Renate Ellam—a Cordon Bleu chef and former interior designer—will have you relaxing in the lap of luxury amid green lawns and 300-year-old trees on her 10-acre farm with an orchard, riding ring, beautiful rose gardens and gazebo, and antique farm buildings. The 1862 home has four guest rooms, each with private bath, Persian rugs, elegant linens, and fresh flowers. Guests who arrive by 4:30pm receive British-style afternoon tea, and Ellam's elaborate three-course breakfasts may include dishes such as vanilla-poached pears with Chantilly cream. Turn-down service includes truffles. The B&B is a popular wedding site. And don't be surprised if you see a familiar face: celebs like Kirstie Alley have stayed here. ■ *3045 Bellinger Lane (exit 27 off I-5, Barnett to Stewart, left on Hull, right on Bellinger), Medford, OR 97501; (541) 776-0000; grwdtree.cdsnet.com; $$$; V; checks OK.*

▼

TALENT

RESTAURANTS

Arbor House ★★ Aging granola types consider this place a find, as it remains surprisingly congenial—one of the most comfortable restaurants in the Rogue Valley, with both indoor and outdoor dining. The menu ranges the world—vegetarian plates, curries, stroganoff, sauerbraten, jambalaya, enchiladas, eggplant Parmigiana, fresh seafoods, and good old American steak. Try the shrimp with curry and a wealth of vegetables. ■ *103 W Wagner St (Hwy 99 to W Valley View Rd, left on Talent Ave, right on Wagner), Talent; (541)535-6817; $$; beer and wine; no credit cards; checks OK; dinner Tues–Sat in summer, Wed–Sat rest of year.* &

New Sammy's Cowboy Bistro ★★ Proprietors Vernon and Charleen Rollins do no advertising, rely entirely on word of mouth, and appear amused when you find them. There's no sign other than a flashing light at night. And the outside looks barely a cut above a shack. Inside, though, is as charming a dinner house as you're likely to find in southern Oregon. There are just six tables; reservations are a must, and you may have to wait a couple of weeks to get in. The French-inspired menu usually lists just a handful of entrees, like duck breast with spinach, chicken with spicy couscous, and salmon with dill sauce and vegetables (perfectly cooked). The wine list is extensive: 40 choices from Oregon, California, and France. ■ *2210 S Pacific Hwy (halfway between Talent and Ashland on Hwy 99/Pacific Hwy), Talent; (541)535-2779; $$; wine only; no credit cards; checks OK; dinner Thurs–Sun (Fri–Sat only in midwinter).*

▼

Talent

Restaurants

▲

ASHLAND

The remarkable success of the **Oregon Shakespeare Festival**, now well over 50 years old, has transformed this sleepy town into one with, per capita, the best tourist amenities in the region. The festival draws a total audience of some 350,000 through the nine-month season, filling its theaters to an extraordinary 97 percent capacity. Visitors pour into this town of 18,000, and fine shops, restaurants, and bed-and-breakfast places spring up in their wake. Amazingly, the town still has its soul: for the most part, it seems a happy little college town, set amid lovely ranch country, that just happens to house one of the largest theater companies in the land. And people still walk downtown at night.

The festival mounts plays in three theaters. In the outdoor Elizabethan Theater, which seats 1,200, appear the famous and authentic nighttime productions of Shakespeare (three different plays each summer). The outdoor theater was remodeled in the early 1990s to improve acoustics. Stretching from February to October, the season for the two indoor theaters includes comedies, contemporary fare, and some experimental works. Visit the Exhibit Center, where you can clown around in costumes from plays past. There are also lectures and concerts at noon, excellent backstage tours each morning, Renaissance music and dance nightly in the courtyard—plus all the nearby daytime attractions of river rafting, picnicking, and historical touring. The best way to get information and tickets (last-minute tickets in the summer are rare) is through a comprehensive agency: Southern Oregon Reservation

Center, (541)488-1011 or (800)547-8052, PO Box 477, Ashland, OR 97520. Festival box office is (541)482-4331, or www.mind.net/osf/.

Ashland is also home to a growing number of smaller theater groups, whose productions are often called **Off Shakespeare** or **Off Bardway**. They are worth checking into. Festival actors often join in these small companies, giving audiences a chance to see Shakespearean actors having a bit of fun and going out on a theatrical limb. Oregon Cabaret Theater presents musicals and comedies through much of the year, with dinners, hors d'oeuvres, and desserts for theater patrons; First and Hargadine Streets, (541)488-2902. Others include Actors' Theater, in nearby Talent, (541)535-5250, and Ashland Community Theater, (541)482-7532, in the Town Hall building at 300 N Pioneer Street.

Touring. The Rogue River Recreation Area has fine swimming for the sizzling summer days, as does the lovely Applegate River. Twenty-two scenic miles up Dead Indian Memorial Road is Howard Prairie Lake Resort, where you can camp, park your trailer, shower, rent a boat, and fish all day; (541)482-1979.

Mount Ashland Ski Area, (541)482-2897, 18 miles south of town, offers 22 runs for all classes of skiers, Thanksgiving to April. It's going strong since a 1992 fund drive raised $1.7 million to buy it from an out-of-town owner who had threatened permanent closure.

Lithia Park. Designed by the creator of San Francisco's Golden Gate Park, Ashland's central park runs for 100 acres behind the outdoor theater. Yes, it was damaged in the 1997 New Year's flood, but has made a comeback, providing a lovely mix of duck ponds, Japanese gardens, grassy lawns, playgrounds, groomed or dirt trails for hikes and jogging, and the pungent mineral water that gave the park its name. There's even an ice-skating rink in winter. In warm weather, it's great for picnicking, especially after stocking up at nearby Greenleaf Deli, 49 N Main, (541)482-2808.

Schneider Museum of Art, at the south end of the Southern Oregon State College campus, is the town's best art gallery, usually with several rotating exhibits. It's open Tuesday through Saturday; (541)552-6245.

The **Pacific Northwest Museum of Natural History** offers 16,000 square feet of dioramas, hands-on science labs, and interactive exhibits, popular with school groups. There's a modest admission charge; 1500 E Main Street, daily (closed Monday and Tuesday in winter), (541)488-1084.

Weisinger Ashland Winery and **Ashland Vineyards** offer opportunities to sample Ashland vintages. The Weisinger winery is snuggled in a Bavarian-style building; the gift shop offers jams, jellies, sauces, and, of course, their wines for sale; Highway 99 just south of Ashland, (541)488-5989; ysingers@oregonwine.org; www.weisingers.com. Ashland Vineyards is near the Highway

66 exit from I-5. Turn north onto E Main Street and follow signs; (541)488-0088 or www.winenet.com.

RESTAURANTS

Chateaulin ★★★ Less than a block from the theaters, you'll find a romantic cafe reminiscent of New York's upper West Side. During the Shakespeare season, the place bustles with before- and after-theater crowds gathered for the fine French cuisine or for drinks at the bar. House specialties are pâtés and veal dishes, but seafood and poultry are also impressive: the delicate butterflied shrimp in a subtle sauce of sherry, cream, tomato, and brandy are delicious, and the chicken breast stuffed with cream cheese and green onions, topped with hazelnuts and champagne sauce, is grand. Chef David Taub and co-owner Michael Donovan change the menu seasonally, and several daily specials feature seasonal entrees prepared with classic French flair. The cafe menu is a favorite of the after-show crowd: baked goat cheese marinated in olive oil on feather-weight squares of toast, an outrageous onion soup, many coffee and other specialty drinks. Service is polished and smooth even during the rush of theater crowds. ■ *50 E Main St (down the walkway from Angus Bowmer Theater), Ashland; (541)482-2264; chateau@jeffnet.org; www.jeffnet.org/chateaulin; $$; full bar; AE, DC, DIS, MC, V; checks OK; dinner every day.*

Firefly ★★ Prepare for a visual feast as well as interesting fare at this small storefront dinner house, which opened in 1994. Chef/owners Tim and Dana Keller worked at trendy restaurants in the San Francisco Bay area before moving to Ashland, and their innovation shows. Presentation is the most artistic in southern Oregon. The Ashland ahi with fennel–sunflower sprout salad, risotto, and carrot jus was served with carved vegetables and splashes of red (fish eggs) around the plate. And the spicy peanut satay was decorated with circular slices of vegetables resembling paints on an artist's palette, while the middle of the plate looked like an assemblage from the gallery down the street. Lamb, salmon, chicken, and duck entrees are usually a part of the menu as well. Portions tend to be more than ample, so ask for a take-home container and leave room for dessert. You may get ice cream in pastry resembling a swan with a greeting from the chef etched in raspberry sauce. ■ *15 N First St (½ block from Main), Ashland; (541)488-3212; $$; beer and wine; MC, V; local checks only; lunch Wed–Fri in summer only, dinner every day in summer, Wed–Sun rest of year.* ₺

Monet ★★ Pierre and Dale Verger have created a French restaurant that has become the talk of Ashland (and even gets a mention or two in Portland). Before opening this gentrified French restaurant in a gracious house, Pierre Verger had restaurants in Montreal, New York state, and the San Francisco Bay area. Favorite dishes include shrimp sautéed in white wine and Pernod, and veal with wild mushrooms and Madeira. Verger goes out of his way to make interesting vegetarian choices, such as sautéed artichoke hearts with sun-dried tomatoes, olives, mushrooms, garlic, shallots, feta, and Parmesan over pasta, as well as a simple French country dish called *la crique Ardechoise*, a kind of gourmet potato pancake with garlic and parsley. The wine list goes on and on. Try for outdoor dining in summer. ■ *36 S 2nd St (½ block from Main St), Ashland; (541)482-1339; $$; full bar; MC, V; checks OK; lunch, dinner every day in summer (lunch Thurs–Sat, dinner Tues–Sat rest of year).*

Primavera ★★ Even if you find the bold red, blue, and orange decor a bit much, wait for the appetizers—they're among the best in southern Oregon. Ricotta ravioli with cream sauce and browned onions is a meal in itself, and the pâté of chicken, pork, and smoked bacon with cranberry chutney and pumpernickel is grand. Entrees usually include chicken, seafood, and a vegetarian choice or two, on a menu that often changes with the seasons. None of the entrees quite approaches the inspiration or execution of the appetizers, but they are still very good and—like the halibut with mustard and fennel and a tomato coulis—capture intense, clean flavors. Desserts, like everything else, are made on the premises. A thoughtfully selected wine list complements the food. The garden is a gorgeous place for a midsummer night's dinner. ■ *241 Hargadine St (below Oregon Cabaret Theatre), Ashland; (541)488-1994; $$; full bar; AE, MC, V; local checks only; dinner Wed–Sun.* &

The Winchester Country Inn ★★ Pay a visit to the Winchester when you feel like being pampered. You sit amid crisp country furnishings on the slightly sunken ground floor of this century-old Queen Anne–style home and look out on tiers of neatly snipped gardens, complete with pathways and a gazebo. The staff attends to your every need. The menu covers an ambitious range of entrees, from Vietnamese marinated broiled *teng dah* beef to lamb or salmon du jour. The chicken breast is likely to be stuffed with pears, currants, and ricotta and topped with a brandy cream sauce. Owners Michael and Laurie Gibb are locally famous for the Dickens Feasts they present each December.

In addition to being one of Ashland's finer restaurants, the Winchester provides 18 pretty antique-furnished guest rooms, some in the main building, others just next door. Guests are treated to full breakfasts. ■ *35 S 2nd St (½ block from Main St), Ashland; (541)488-1115; $$; full bar; MC, V; checks OK; dinner every day, brunch Sun (closed Sun night and Mon in winter).*

Green Springs Inn ★ Here's an escape from the tourist crowds of Ashland—a cozy, rustic spot dishing up Italian specialties in the midst of the splendid hills. The restaurant doubles as a neighborhood convenience store. The 25-minute drive through the red-soil hills, jutting cliffs, and thick evergreens is worth the trip in itself, especially if you want to hike or cross-country ski along the Pacific Crest Trail, which runs a quarter-mile from the restaurant. The delicious and garlicky black bean soup (lapped up with subtly sweet black bread) makes a perfect lunch. But if you need a little more substance, try the mushroom fettuccine. ■ *11470 Hwy 66 (17 miles east of Ashland), Ashland; (541)482-0614; gspring@cdsnet.net; $$; beer and wine; AE, DIS, MC, V; checks OK; breakfast, lunch, dinner every day.* &

Il Giardino ★ Order the risotto when you place your reservation—it's as close to Italy as you'll get without a plane ticket. It's not on the menu and it's time-consuming to make, but Franco Minniti and Jennifer and staff love to cook and are anxious to please. Even some dishes which might sound a bit unusual—ravioli shells stuffed with ground veal and topped with carrot sauce—result in a delightful meal. The place is intimate and can seem crowded. ■ *5 Granite St (1 block from Shakespeare Festival), Ashland; (541)488-0816; $$; beer and wine; MC, V; checks OK; dinner every day.* &

LODGINGS

Country Willows ★★★ Set on 5 acres of farmland seven minutes from downtown Ashland, this rebuilt 1896 country home offers peace and quiet and a lovely view of the hills. Dan Durant and David Newton offer five rooms, three suites, and a separate cottage, with air conditioning and private baths, plus a swimming pool and a hot tub on the large back deck. The best room is, well, in the barn: the Pine Ridge Suite, opened in 1996, has a bedroom–living room combination with lodgepole pine king-size bed, not to mention a bath bigger than most bedrooms. Breakfast is presented on a pretty sun porch. The grounds outside offer running and hiking trails; the owners keep a small flock of ducks, a gaggle of geese, and even a couple of goats on the property. ■ *1313 Clay St (4 blocks south on Clay St from Siskiyou Blvd), Ashland, OR 97520; (541)488-1590 or (800)945-5697; www.willowsinn.com; $$$; MC, V; checks OK.*

Mount Ashland Inn ★★★ Wind your way up Mount Ashland Road and you discover a huge, custom-made two-story log cabin. It was the dream home of Jerry and Elaine Shanafelt, who designed and built the lodge in 1987, using some 275 cedar trees cut from their 160-acre property in the Siskiyous. Innkeepers Chuck and Laurel Biegert continue what the Shanafelts started, and have added an outdoor spa. The magnificent inn is more posh inside than you'd expect from a log house: golden aromatic-cedar logs, high beamed ceilings, large windows, and a huge stone fireplace. Examples of Jerry's handiwork are seen throughout the house: stained-glass windows, a spiral cedar staircase with madrona railing. Guests sleep in handcrafted beds covered with elaborate patchwork quilts, and each of the five units has a private bath. Try for the Sky Lakes Suite, with a two-person whirlpool bathtub, king-size bed, wet bar, private entrance, and a sitting room, plus views of Mount Shasta and Mount McLoughlin. Be prepared for snow November to April. ■ *550 Mt Ashland Rd (follow signs to Mt Ashland Ski Area), Ashland, OR 97520; (541) 482-8707 or (800) 830-8707; $$$; AE, DIS, MC, V; checks OK.*

Romeo Inn ★★★ This imposing Cape Cod home has four plush guest rooms and two suites decorated in contemporary and antique furnishings. The spacious rooms all have king-size beds—covered with hand-stitched Amish quilts—phones, and private baths. The Stratford Suite is a separate structure with its own bedroom, bath, and kitchen; it features a vaulted ceiling with skylight, a marble-tiled fireplace, and a raised whirlpool bathtub for two. The second suite, the Cambridge, has a fireplace, patio, and private entrance. There's a baby grand piano off the living room, and the heated pool and hot tub on the large back deck are open year-round. In the morning, innkeepers Don and Deana Poltis are likely to serve you freshly squeezed orange juice, melon with blueberry sauce, eggs Florentine, sausage, and baked goods. Their breakfasts reportedly satisfy through dinnertime. ■ *295 Idaho St (at Holly), Ashland, OR 97520; (541) 488-0884 or (800) 915-8899; $$$; MC, V; checks OK.*

Cowslip's Belle ★★ Named after a flower mentioned in *A Midsummer Night's Dream* and *The Tempest*, the home has a cheery charm, with its swing chair on the front porch, vintage furniture, and fresh flowers inside. There are two lovely bedrooms in the main house—a 1913 Craftsman bungalow—and two more in a romantic carriage house in the back, with extra privacy, one of them a suite. Jon and Carmen Reinhardt invite guests to snuggle up with one of the inn's resident teddy bears; some guests bring their own. Turn-down service includes a chocolate truffle. Breakfasts feature Jon's baked goods, which he also wholesales to nearby restaurants. Another main attraction here is proximity to the theaters, downtown, and Lithia Park, three to four blocks away. ■ *159 N Main St (3 blocks north of the theaters on Main), Ashland, OR 97520; (541) 488-2901 or (800) 888-6819; stay@cowslip.com/cowslip; www.cowslip.com/cowslip; $$; MC, V; checks OK.*

Peerless Hotel ★★ Originally a hotel built in Ashland's now-historic railroad district in 1900, the building later fell into disrepair. Chrissy Barnett saved the place, merged old hotel rooms into six new B&B units, two of them suites, and filled them with antiques collected from places as disparate as New Orleans and Hawaii. High ceilings and oversize bathrooms are trademarks. Suite 3 features a bath with his-and-her claw-footed tubs and a glassed-in shower. Several have Jacuzzis. In the morning Barnett serves a buffet. You can walk to the Shakespeare theaters from here. ■ *243 4th St (between A and B Sts), Ashland, OR 97520; (541)488-1082 or (800)460-8758; www.mind.net/peerless; $$$; AE, MC, V; checks OK.* ⅊

Chanticleer Inn ★ One of Ashland's original B&Bs, Chanticleer has changed owners in recent years. It isn't quite what it used to be (the owners are now absentees) but is still one of the town's better destinations even without their personal touch. The home has an uncluttered country charm, with an open-hearth fireplace in the spacious sitting room and carefully chosen antiques throughout, plus scripts of all the plays running at the Shakespeare Festival. In the morning, a hearty breakfast is served in the dining room. Chanticleer is four blocks from the theaters, but surprisingly quiet. ■ *120 Gresham St (2 blocks from the library, off Main St), Ashland, OR 97520; (541)482-1919 or (800)898-1950; $$; AE, MC, V; checks OK.*

Morical House Garden Inn ★ Two elegant garden suites with vaulted ceilings, spas, and private entrances, added in 1996, have enhanced this Ashland old-timer. The other five rooms, furnished with antiques, handmade quilts, and family heirlooms, are in the main house, a former farmhouse that dates to the 1880s. Proximity to busy Main Street detracts somewhat from the ambience, but soundproofing and a garden atmosphere help—the latter with ponds, waterfalls, stately trees, and roses. There are nice views of fields and mountains beyond. Breakfasts are hearty. ■ *668 N Main St (1 mile north of downtown and the-aters), Ashland, OR 97520; (541)482-2254 or (800)208-0960; moricalhse@aol.com; $$; AE, DIS, MC, V; checks OK.*

Pinehurst Inn at Jenny Creek ★ Rumor has it that the old road-house was a bordello in earlier days. Today's lodgings mix rustic with elegant. The country inn has six bed-and-breakfast rooms, two of them suites, and a full-service restaurant that's open to nonguests. Each room has a great view of trees and mountains. The inn is 23 miles east of Ashland, and many of those miles require negotiating a winding, narrow highway up the Greensprings grade, which once challenged travelers in covered wagons on the Applegate Trail. It's a 30- to 40-minute drive, but worth it if you want peace and quiet, mountain air, and some pretty good food. ■ *17250 Hwy 66 (on right, between*

*mileposts 23 and 24), Ashland, OR 97520; (541)488-1002; $$;
full bar; DIS, MC, V; checks OK; dinner, brunch Wed–Sun.*

Woods House ★ This 1908 Craftsman, once the home of a
doctor, boasts a beautiful setting out back, with a half acre of ter-
raced English gardens. Out front is the busy boulevard and
traffic, so try for one of the Carriage House units in the rear. All
six guest rooms have private baths. A big plus is that you can
walk the four blocks to the theaters. Lester and Françoise Roddy
are gracious hosts and serve a nifty spinach-cheese egg bake,
in the garden when weather cooperates. ■ *333 N Main St (4
blocks north of theaters), Ashland, OR 97520; (541)488-1598 or
(800)435-8260; wdshousebnb@eworld.com; $$; MC, V; checks OK.*

Windmill's Ashland Hills Inn For those who prefer motels to
B&Bs, this is the best Ashland has to offer, with 159 rooms, several elegant suites, a pool, and tennis courts. There is also a
nonsmoking unit with nearly 60 suites, B&B style because rates
include breakfast. The food is not bad, sometimes very good;
locals like the Sunday brunch. The banquet area, Ashland's
largest, plays host to everything from wine-tastings to formal
balls. ■ *2525 Ashland St (Hwy 66 exit from I-5, 1 block east), Ash-
land, OR 97520; (541)482-8310 or (800)547-4747; $$; AE, DC,
DIS, MC, V; checks OK.* ＆

CAVE JUNCTION

Though the tight spaces can get awfully packed with tourists, the
Oregon Caves National Monument is a group of intriguing for-
mations of marble and limestone. Tours leave periodically each
day year-round. They are a bit strenuous, and the caves remain a
chilly 41 degrees. Part of the caves walkway is now wheelchair-
accessible, following renovation in early 1997. Children under six
are allowed if they meet the height requirement; however, babysit-
ting service is available. Arrive early during summertime, or you
may have a long wait; (541)592-3400.

The Cave Junction area is home to two of Oregon's better
wineries, Foris (654 Kendall Road, (541)592-3752) and Bridgeview
(4210 Holland Loop Road, (541)592-4688). Both have tasting rooms
open daily.

LODGINGS

Oregon Caves Chateau ★ This fine old wooden lodge is set amid
tall trees and a deep canyon. Doors don't always close properly,
but the place is restful. The sound of falling water from nu-
merous nearby mountain streams helps lull you to sleep. Views
are splendid, the public rooms have the requisite massive fire-
places, and the down-home cooking in the dining room can be
quite good. The wine list features several local bottlings. There

are 22 rooms in the lodge—nothing fancy, but clean. ■ *Oregon
Caves National Monument (Rte 46, 20 miles east of Cave Junction, follow signs), Cave Junction, OR 97523; (541) 592-3400;
$$; beer and wine; MC, V; checks OK; dinner every day (dining
room closes earlier than lodge, which is closed Nov–Apr).*

Oregon Cascades

*The Columbia River Gorge—Troutdale to The Dalles—
followed by two easterly Cascade crossings: Sandy to
Mount Hood in the north, McKenzie Bridge to Bend midstate.
Finally, a southward progression through the heart
of the mountains to Klamath Falls.*

COLUMBIA RIVER GORGE

The wild Columbia has been dammed into near lakehood, but its fjordlike majesty is part magnificent waterfalls, part dramatic cliffs and rock formations cut by the country's second-largest river, and part wind tunnel. Watch for the colorful fleet of board sailors who have made this stretch of the river world-renowned. Most of the traffic is on I-84.

The old **Columbia Gorge Scenic Highway** (Route 30), above and paralleling the freeway, is for take-your-time wanderers. This 22-mile detour traverses the waterfall-riddled stretch from Troutdale to Ainsworth Park. Popular viewpoints and attractions are as follows: **Crown Point**, 725 feet above the river, features an art deco–style vista house. Below, at **Rooster Rock State Park**, one of the attractions is a nude bathing beach. **Larch Mountain**, 14 miles upriver from Crown Point, is even more spectacular than the more famous overlooks. **Multnomah Falls** ranks second-highest in the country, at 620 feet (in two big steps). **Multnomah Falls Lodge**, at the foot of the falls, was designed in 1925 by Albert E. Doyle, of Benson Hotel fame, in a rustic stone-and-timber style. Now a National Historic Landmark, the lodge houses a popular naturalists and visitors center; (503)695-2376. It has a large restaurant that is a good stop for breakfast, but dinners are unremarkable (better to go just for dessert). Oneonta Gorge is a narrow, dramatic cleft through which a slippery half-mile trail winds to secluded **Oneonta Falls. Bonneville Dam**, the first federal dam on the Columbia, offers self-guided tours of the dam, the fish ladders (seen through underwater viewing windows), and the navigational locks; (541)374-8820. You can tour the **Bonneville Fish Hatchery** (next to the dam) year-round; however, the best times are in September and November, when the chinook are spawning; (541)374-8393.

The old highway disappears briefly at Hood River; it picks up again between Mosier and The Dalles, where the forests give way to grasslands and the clouds vanish. Wildflowers abound from February to June.

TROUTDALE

RESTAURANTS

Tad's Chicken 'n' Dumplings A down-home country restaurant, 20 miles east of Portland as you head up the Columbia Gorge, this decades-old Oregon institution is popular with kids, bargain-hungry families, tourists—and fanciers of chicken. Steaks, prime rib, salmon, and halibut are also on the menu. Sit at a window table where you can watch the bottle green river, and top off your meal with ice cream or homemade pie. The place is usually packed, particularly for Sunday dinner, which is served early, so call ahead for hours. ■ *943 SE Crown Point (exit 18 off I-84), Troutdale; (503) 666-5337; $; full bar; AE, MC, V; checks OK; dinner every day.* &

LODGINGS

McMenamins Edgefield ★★ Over the last decade, the McMenamin brothers have enlivened Portland-area neighborhoods with 30 Euro-style pubs, a couple of cigar bars, and restoration of the famous Crystal Ballroom. Here they've purchased a former county poor farm and transformed the grounds into a brewery, a winery, and a 5½-acre pinot-gris-and-shiraz vineyard. The old power station is now a lively pub and movie theater (with eight spare bed-and-breakfast rooms upstairs). The administrator's house, an old Craftsman-style bungalow, has an additional six bedrooms. However, the main lodge is where most people stay. This four-story brick manor has 89 guest rooms, wide verandas, a huge ballroom, and the Mission-style Black Rabbit dining room and bar. All rooms are stocked with beer glasses and a canning jar in which you may carry brew back to your room. Guests are loaned terrycloth robes to make the trek to the shared baths on each wing (which isn't as bad as it sounds). Not surprisingly, the Black Rabbit tends to serve dishes that go admirably with a pint of home brew, such as potted Dungeness crab. A resident glassblower and a potter complete the bacchanalian feel of the place. ■ *2126 SW Halsey (Wood Village exit off I-84, south to Halsey, turn left, drive ½ mile to Edgefield sign), Troutdale, OR 97060; (503) 669-8610, (800) 669-8610, or (503) 492-3086 (restaurant); $$; full bar; AE, MC, V; checks OK; breakfast, lunch, dinner every day.* &

CASCADE LOCKS

Before there were dams here, there were rapids. And before the rapids, there was a natural stone bridge over the river—a sacred and mythical place for Native Americans. The dams smoothed out the waters for riverboats, and a fine little museum at the now steel **Bridge of the Gods** explains the legend of the rapids. There are also the **Port of Cascade Locks Visitor Center**, a sailboard launch, and oodles of picnic spots. The sternwheeler *Columbia Gorge* revives the Columbia's riverboat days; there are three trips daily and extra lunch, brunch, dinner, and dance cruises, mid-June through the end of September, with stops at Bonneville Dam and Stevenson Landing; (541)374-8427.

HOOD RIVER

Fruit orchards are everywhere. Hood River is ideally located on the climatic cusp between the wetter west side and the drier east side of the Cascades, alongside the mighty Columbia, so it gets the sun *and* enough moisture (about 31 inches annually) to keep the creeks flowing and the orchards bearing. Thirty miles to the south, 11,245-foot Mount Hood dominates the horizon; however, from the town itself, the views are of Washington's Mount Adams, the Columbia, and its ubiquitous windsurfers. In town, you're as likely to see orchard workers as boardheads, 2-inch steaks as espresso. New restaurants, inns, and shops are constantly opening (and closing) in flux with the high and low seasons.

Visitors come to hike, fish, climb, and ski on Mount Hood and Mount Adams. And the area has some of the best mountain biking in the Northwest. In between is the Columbia River. And on it are the boardheads who can't get enough of the famous winds that blow in at that ideal opposite-to-the-current direction. Over two dozen local businesses cater to the sailboard crowd; several offer lessons and rentals, and all will tell you where the winds are on any given day. The **Hook** and **Columbia Gorge Sailpark/ Marina** are favorites. The latter also features a marina and a cafe.

As locals strongly attest, there was life in Hood River before board sailors descended. Native American artifacts are on exhibit in the **Hood River County Museum**, (541)386-6772, Wednesday through Sunday, April through October, or when flags are flying. The town's Visitors Information Center/Chamber of Commerce is another good source of information about the area, and is open every day of the week (except winter, when it's closed on weekends); (541)386-2000 or (800)366-3530.

Orchards and vineyards are the valley's other economic mainstays. The wonderful small-town **Blossom Festival** (mid-April) celebrates the flower-to-fruit cycle. From Highway 35 you can catch the vista of the orchards fanning out from the north slopes of Mount Hood. For an old-fashioned trip, take the **Mount Hood Scenic Railroad**, (541)386-3556 (Wednesday through Sunday); the Fruit Blossom Special departs the quaint Hood River depot mid-April through December. You can buy the fruit bounty at **The Fruit Tree**, 4030 Westcliff Drive, (541)386-6688, near the Columbia Gorge Hotel, or at **River Bend Country Store**, 2363 Tucker Road, (541)386-8766 or (800)755-7568; the latter specializes in organically grown produce. Or visit the tasting rooms of the **Flerchinger Vineyards**, 4200 Post Canyon Drive, (541)386-2882, or the **Hood River Vineyards,** 4693 Westwood Drive, (541)386-3772, known for its pear and raspberry dessert wines. Beer aficionados head for the **Full Sail Tasting Room and Pub,** 506 Columbia Street, (541)386-2247, for handcrafted Full Sail ales and appetizers. The outdoor deck provides a fitting place for tired board sailors to unwind while keeping the river in sight. Another great addition to the Hood River scene is the **Big Horse Brew Pub,** 115 State Street, (541)386-4411, which pairs its microbrews with simple pub fare and local musical talent.

For a breath-taker, head a half-mile south of town on Highway 35 to **Panorama Point.** Or go east on I-84, exit at Mosier, and climb to the **Rowena Crest Viewpoint** on old Highway 30; the grandstand Columbia River view is complemented by a wildflower show in the Tom McCall Preserve, maintained by The Nature Conservancy. The **Coffee Spot,** Oak Street and First, (541)386-1772, is a good place to get picnic sandwiches, while **Mike's Ice Cream,** 405 Oak Stree, (541)386-6260, makes a great summer stop for fresh huckleberry shakes. **Waucoma Bookstore,** 212 Oak Street, (541)386-5353, has a good selection of titles, especially on Oregon and the Northwest. Get a custom, made-to-your-measurements swimsuit at **Kerrits,** 316 Oak Street, (541)386-1145, a unique locally owned shop and mail-order business that also has active, equestrian, and baby wear.

RESTAURANTS

Big City Chicks ★ What began as a concession stand is now a real restaurant. Owner and chef Nan Bain (who collected recipes as she traveled with the film crew for the *Love Boat* TV series) has proven that her food works. The menu incorporates satays from Thailand, curries from India, and Mexican moles, Jamaican jerked chicken, and Italian pastas. For dessert there are homemade ice creams or Key lime pie (lime juice is shipped fresh from Florida). The pretty restaurant is furnished in 1930s art deco style, with locally made art lamps. On summer evenings, lineups tend to build after 7:30pm. The sister restaurant, Big City Wraps (212 Force Street), serves internationally-flavored wraps for lunch only; (541)387-5511. ■ *1302 13th St (at B St), Hood River; (541)387-3811; $; full bar; MC, V; local checks only; dinner every day.* &

The Mesquitery ★ The mesquite grill takes center stage here. It's housed in a glass-enclosed frame surrounded by booths and small tables. The barbecue is not superhot, but it's A-OK. There are mounds of baby back ribs, a chicken combo, pollo vaquero (grilled chicken to roll in tortillas with pico de gallo), and fresh fish (maybe a moist halibut in a spicy tomatillo sauce). The apple crisp à la mode is dandy; so are the service and the bill. This is a good place to bring the kids. ■ *1219 12th St (at B St), Hood River; (541)386-2002; $; full bar; AE, MC, V; local checks only; lunch Wed–Fri, dinner Mon–Sat (dinner every day May–Nov).* &

Stonehedge Inn ★ Beyond the funky markers and up a rutted gravel drive to this turn-of-the-century summer estate, owner Jean Harmon makes you instantly at home. She'll get the kids looking through her stereopticon viewer, and then she'll tell the history behind each decoration as she leads you to a table in the fire-warmed and dark-wood-paneled main room, the garden-viewing porch room, the homey library, or the intimate bar. Tender steaks might come buried under whole, fresh chanterelle mushrooms, and the seafood arrives fresh and cooked right— for example, halibut rolled in hazelnuts topped with a blueberry beurre rouge. The famous stuffed potato seems to be right out of Betty Crocker's kitchen. Sincere service and general high quality keep this on our list. ■ *3405 Cascade Dr (exit 62 off I-84), Hood River; (541)386-3940; $$; full bar; AE, DIS, MC, V; checks OK; dinner Wed–Sun (call for summer hours).*

Purple Rocks Art Bar and Cafe Despite its name (a self-evident boarder's term), we like this cafe, from the blue-enameled wood stove to the views out paned-glass windows. Art takes the form of sketchbooks filled with patrons' doodles, and crayons and things for the kids, too. Housed in a cute little cottage on Hood River's main street, this local hangout offers delicious multi-grain walnut pancakes and mostly vegetarian fare (sprout and cottage cheese sandwich, lasagne, quiches, and black bean bur-ritos). A full dinner menu (fillet, duck, fish, and so on) is offered during peak summer months. ■ *606 Oak St (west on Oak from downtown), Hood River; (541)386-6061; $; beer and wine; MC, V; checks OK; breakfast, lunch every day.*

LODGINGS

Hood River Hotel ★★ A careful 1989 restoration revived this hostelry's past as a turn-of-the-century country hotel. Thirty-two rooms, including nine one-bedroom kitchen suites, come with four-poster, sleigh, or brass beds, pedestal sinks, and plenty of cheerful floral chintz. Since it's in the center of town, there's some noise from the street, the railroad, and I-84. **Pasquale's Ristorante**, a small, attractive dining room, serves reasonably priced meals strong on Italian specialties and local fruit and fish (the seafood salad is packed with the good stuff). Enjoy your espresso or after-dinner drink in front of the lobby fireplace or at an outside table. Pasquale's is a casual place with live music on Friday evenings. ■ *102 Oak St (at 1st), Hood River, OR 97031; (541)386-1900 or (800)386-1859; $$; full bar; AE, DIS, MC, V; checks OK; breakfast, lunch, dinner every day.* &

Lakecliff Estate ★★ A historic place and everyone's favorite Hood River bed and breakfast, Lakecliff was created in 1908 by architect Albert E. Doyle (who also designed Multnomah Falls Lodge and the Benson Hotel in Portland) as a summer estate for a Portland businessman. The manse features five fireplaces of locally quarried stone, a large and inviting living room, a sun-warmed porch, and an elegant dining room where guests often linger over their oatmeal with sautéed nectarines or Dutch babies with fruit sauce while watching windsurfers below. Some rooms have fireplaces and private bathrooms, others have views. The forest green home is sheltered by woods to create quiet seclusion with an astonishing view of the Columbia River. A new shuffleboard court on the cliff side and a cozy family room with all the amenities for guests were added in 1996. Fine hospitality in outstanding surroundings. ▪ *3820 Westcliff Dr (exit 62 off I-84, ½ mile west of Hood River), Hood River; (541)386-7000; PO Box 1220, Hood River, OR 97031; $$; no credit cards; checks OK (closed Oct–Apr).*

Columbia Gorge Hotel ★ Lumber baron Simon Benson capped his successful completion of the Columbia Gorge Scenic Highway when he built his luxury hotel in 1921 and brought in his famous chef, Henry Thiele. Instantly the hotel became a favorite of honeymooners and tourists. The old dear (restored a number of times) can't compete with the luxury of 1990s hotels, but it does have some pluses: a stunning structure with a private window on Wah-Gwin-Gwin Falls of the Columbia River; and a colorful past, which included visits by Rudolph Valentino. The public rooms are large and elegant. The guest rooms are rather small (especially for the big price), but the price does include turn-down service, a newspaper in the morning, and an insultingly large breakfast. Aim for a gorge-side room; they're quieter and have the best views. The hotel periodically offers Murder Mystery weekends starring Hood River's best actors, and romance packages that add dinner, roses, and chocolate to your stay. ▪ *4000 Westcliff Dr (exit 62 off I-84), Hood River, OR 97031; (541)386-5566 or (800)345-1921; $$$; full bar; AE, DIS, MC, V; checks OK; lunch Mon–Sat, breakfast, dinner every day, brunch Sun.* ♿

Vagabond Lodge The front building is nothing but a nondescript highway-facing unit. The surprise is in back in the riverfront building; ask for a room there. It's so close to the Columbia Gorge Hotel it could almost be another wing. It's got the same view as (some say a better view than) the CGH, but the rooms are twice the size and a fraction of the price. If there are four of you, get a suite with a fireplace and a separate bedroom (it'll cost you less than the smallest room at CGH). ▪ *4070 Westcliff Dr (exit 62 off I-84), Hood River, OR 97031; (541)386-2992; $; AE, MC, V; no checks.*

THE DALLES

The Dalles is *the* historical stop along this stretch, especially now that the long-awaited $21.6 million Columbia Gorge Discovery

Center has opened at Crate's Point. For centuries, this area was the meeting place for Native Americans. In the early 1800s, Hudson's Bay trappers (Edward Crate was one of them) lived here. In the 1840s, it was the official end of the Oregon Trail. Later it served as the only military fort in the Northwest and the county seat of Wasco County, then a 130,000-square-mile vastness that spread from the Cascades to the Rockies.

At the **Columbia Gorge Discovery Center**, (5000 Discovery Drive, (541)296-8660), you can learn about 40 million years of geology and natural history and the last 10,000 years of human occupation of the Columbia Gorge. Best exhibit (among the covered wagons, longhouses, Lewis and Clark camp, cannery, and boardwalks) is a 33-foot working model of the Columbia River that removes Columbia River dams to expose Celilo Falls, an immense basalt chasm of roaring waterfalls east of The Dalles that was completely submerged and silenced when the dam was built in the 1950s.

Also in the area are Native American petroglyphs marking the canyon walls, the 1850 surgeon's house from the old Fort Dalles (now a museum at 15th and Garrison Streets), the east side's "houses of entertainment," and nicely maintained examples of Colonial, gothic revival, Italianate, and American renaissance architecture. Take a tour by car or on foot; maps are available at The Dalles Convention and Visitor Bureau, 404 W Second Street; (541)296-6616 or (800)255-3385.

Uphill from downtown are irrigated cherry orchards; Wasco County is the largest producer in the United States and celebrates its **Cherry Festival** in mid-April.

RESTAURANTS

Baldwin Saloon ★ The Baldwin Saloon, built in 1876, has been a steamboat navigational office, a warehouse, a coffin storage site, an employment office, and a saddle shop; now it's a restaurant and bar. It's nicely done—stripped to the original brick, with fir floors, wooden booths, light streaming in the windows, a mahogany bar, and large turn-of-the-century oil paintings of Northwest nature scenes hanging on the walls. Piano, cello, and violins (on tape) are a nice background—as is the live piano music on weekends. But the food is what impressed us most: fresh oysters on the half shell, smoked salmon mousse served with homemade bread and fresh vegetables, thick sandwiches, filet mignon, and a dozen or more homemade desserts. ■ *205 Court St (at 1st St), The Dalles; (541)296-5666; $; full bar; MC, V; checks OK; lunch, dinner Mon–Sat.* &

Ole's Supper Club ★ Ole's isn't glamorous. In fact, it's in the industrial west end of The Dalles. But locals have liked it this way for 35 years. The consistent quality of the food and the commitment to good wine make Ole's notable—in spite of the fact that it looks like a double-wide mobile home. The house special turns out to be a superb cut of prime rib. Everything is included: delicious homemade soup, a standard salad, and a little loaf of hot homemade bread. The restaurant has established its reputation on beef, but when fresh razor clams are available it treats them well. The bar is one of the few in Oregon that doubles as a wine shop; it's known regionally for its wide selection. ▪ *2620 W 2nd St (exit 84 off I-84, go west 1 mile), The Dalles; (541) 296-6708; $$; full bar; AE, MC, V; checks OK; dinner Tues–Sat.*

LODGINGS

Williams House Inn ★★ A manicured 3-acre arboretum surrounds this classic 1899 Queen Anne house. The inn has been in the Williams family for more than 70 years and is on the National Register of Historic Places. Nicaraguan mahogany decorates the walls, and Oriental rugs cover the floor of the large living room that contains a piano, Don Williams's bass fiddle, and a fireplace. Two of the three rooms have their own balconies; all have their own baths. We especially like the downstairs Elizabeth Suite with its separate bedroom, writing desk, hideabed, and private bath with marble-topped washbasin and a 6-foot-long, claw-footed tub. The Williamses serve a fine breakfast of fresh or frozen local fruits, including cherries from their own orchard, home-roasted granola, muffins, fresh-ground coffees, and eggs. Don Williams happily shares his love and encyclopedic knowledge of the area's rich history. ▪ *608 W 6th St (corner of Trevett), The Dalles, OR 97058; (541) 296-2889; $$; AE, MC, V; checks OK.*

MOUNT HOOD

At 11,245 feet, Hood may not be the highest in the chain of volcanoes in the Cascades, but it is one of the best developed, with **five ski areas** (Mount Hood Meadows, Summit, Mount Hood Ski Bowl (formerly Multorpor), Timberline, and Cooper Spur) on its base. The Timberline Day Lodge Wy'East, at the 6,000-foot level, has plenty of facilities to equip the mountaineer, hiker, or skier. Chairlifts take you to the Palmer Snowfield, up in the glaciers, where you can ski in the middle of summer. The lower parts are ablaze with rhododendrons (peaking in June) and wildflowers (peaking in July); all are easily reachable from trails that spread out from Timberline Lodge. One of the best trails leads 4½ miles west from Timberline Lodge to flower-studded Paradise Park. Like Rainier, the mountain is girt by a long trail (called Timberline Trail), a 40-mile circuit of the entire peak that traverses snowfields as well as ancient forests.

Mid-May to mid-July is the prime time for **climbing Mount Hood**, a peak that looks easier than it is, since the last 1,500 feet involve very steep snow and ice climbing. Timberline Mountain Guides, 88220 E Government Camp Loop, Government Camp, OR

97028, (800)464-7704, have a retail store and climbing equipment rentals; they also conduct climbers to the summit.

RESTAURANTS

The Brew Pub at Mount Hood Brewing Company The theme is universal—trout fishing and beer—in this knotty pine brew-pub, where you can watch the brewmasters at work and ponder what kind of fly the trout over the bar is biting (a bar fly?). Try an oatmeal stout or the popular Iceaxe IPA with a pizza you design from toppings that include fontina, feta, Gorgonzola, smoked cheddar, andouille sausage, smoked salmon, pesto, capers, and walnuts. The burgers are excellent choices too. ■ *87304 E Government Camp Loop (take Government Camp Loop off Hwy 26), Timberline; (503)272-3724; $; beer and wine; AE, DIS, MC, V; checks OK; lunch, dinner every day.* &

LODGINGS

Timberline Lodge ★★ Built in 1937 as a WPA project, Timberline Lodge is a wonderland of American crafts—carved stone, worked metal, massive beams with adze marks plain to see, rugged fireplaces everywhere, and a huge, octagonal lobby that is an inspiring centerpiece for the steep-roofed hotel. Many of the upholsteries, draperies, rugs, and bedspreads in the public and guest rooms have been re-created in their original patterns—in some cases with the help of the original craftspeople. The best rooms are those with fireplaces (but bargain hunters or savvy parents might want to put their kids in the $65 bunk rooms). The resort is known for its year-round skiing, but during the summer, Timberline offers hiking, picnicking, chairlift rides, and guided nature tours (the staff is a great source for suggestions). There's also a sauna and heated outdoor pool. The lobby's best for lounging (as the rooms are quite small); desk nooks upstairs are the postcard-writing spots. As for the Cascade Dining Room, Northwest cuisine is Leif Eric Benson's strong point. The food in the Ram's Head Lounge is not quite as good, but do take time for a drink while looking into the heart of the mountain. Fast food is available in the Wy'East Lodge.

Adventurers might want to sleep over in the restored Silcox Hut, 7,000 feet up the mountain. Built by the same craftsmen who constructed Timberline, Silcox served as the engine room for the Magic Mile chairlift until 1962. Now you can rent bunk rooms (10 minimum in your party) for $75/person per night (includes dinner, breakfast, and transportation from Timberline). Just bring your sleeping bag. Silcox is open to the public 10am–4pm for sandwiches and snacks when the Magic Mile chairlift is running. ■ *Timberline Ski Area (60 miles due east of Portland off Hwy 26), Timberline, OR 97028; (503)272-3311 or (800)547-1406; www.timberlinelodge.com; $$; full bar; AE, MC, V; checks OK; breakfast, lunch, dinner every day.* &

Falcon's Crest Inn All in all, this is a family-friendly three-story inn, owned by Bob (B. J.) and Melody Johnson. Heat radiates from the wood stove in the living room, and seclusion is yours in any of the three lofty hideaways on the top floor (table games, music, videos, views of Ski Bowl). For the most part, the inn is attractively furnished, but you've got to like teddy bears (there are hundreds) and not mind Christmas ornaments (decorations stick around as long as the snow does, sometimes through March). Rooms are done in themes: lions, tigers, and leopards adorn the Safari; the Cat Ballou has red velvet chairs and an ivory lace comforter; the romantic Master Suite has its own private Jacuzzi deck. B. J. cooks a big breakfast and serves satisfying dinners ($30, open to the public) with 24 hours' notice. A variety of wines and beers are available to sip by the fire after a day of mountain play. ■ *87287 Government Camp Loop (take Government Camp Loop off Hwy 26), Government Camp, OR 97028; (503)272-3403 or (800)624-7384; $$$; beer and wine; AE, DIS, MC, V; checks OK; dinner by reservation only.*

WELCHES

This pretty little town was named after Samuel Welch and his son Billy, who built the Old Welches Inn. For excellent coffee, stop by **Mount Hood Coffee Roasters**, 64235 E Brightwood Loop, (503)622-5153, where Serene Elliott-Graber will show you how she roasts coffee beans from around the world.

RESTAURANTS

Chalet Swiss ★★ Open the door and walk into Oregon's version of Switzerland—a world of peasant dresses, cowbells, and hand-carved wooden furniture. Owners Vicki and Greg Guerrero have maintained the Swiss specialties: *Bundnerfleisch* (paper-thin slices of beef salt-cured in alpine air); traditional fondues; *raclette* (broiled cheese served with pickles and onions); greens dressed with lemon, garlic, and herbs. The *Zürcher Geschnetzeltes* (veal in cream sauce with mushrooms) is a particular standout. Reservations are suggested. ■ *24371 E Welches Rd (Hwy 26 and E Welches Rd), Welches; (503)622-3600; $$; full bar; AE, MC, V; checks OK; dinner Wed–Sun.* ᕃ

LODGINGS

The Resort at the Mountain ★★ At the right time of the year, you can ski one day and play golf the next. Its proximity to Mount Hood and its 27-hole golf course make the Resort at the Mountain a good choice for the active traveler. The 160 rooms are large and quiet. The key is to reserve a fireplace room with a gear closet (a necessity here) and a pool- or forest-facing deck (some rooms aim toward the fairway). And, as if skiing, golf, hiking, and fishing weren't enough, there are six tennis courts, an outdoor heated pool and Jacuzzi, a fitness center, mountain-bike rentals, horseshoes, golf lessons, volleyball, badminton, two professional croquet courts, lawn bowling, and basketball. Of course, it's also a very popular conference center. The Tartans Inn serves breakfast and lunch next to the golf course. The Highlands restaurant provides live piano music Friday and Saturday nights in the bar. ■ *68010 E Fairway Ave (½ mile south of Hwy 26 on E Welches Rd, turn on E Fairway), Welches, OR 97067; (503)622-3101 or (800)669-7666; $$$; full bar; AE, MC, V; checks OK; breakfast, lunch, dinner every day, brunch Sun.* &

Old Welches Inn ★ A hundred years after it opened as the first summer inn on Mount Hood, the Old Welches Inn is still perfectly placed: French windows give views of the Resort at the Mountain's 27-hole golf course, the mountains that ring the valley, and grounds filled with wildflowers that stretch down to the Salmon River. The three upstairs rooms are small, but all are attractive and have big views. Relax by the fire, read in the sun room, or enjoy fresh mountain air on two large patios. Larger groups may prefer to rent the no-frills two-bedroom cabin with fireplace, kitchen, and views. ■ *26401 E Welches Rd (1 mile south of Hwy 26), Welches, OR 97067; (503)622-3754; $$; AE, MC, V; checks OK.*

SANDY

Highway 26 divides into one-way avenues through the town of Sandy on the way to Mount Hood. Named for the nearby river, Sandy offers a white-steepled church, antique shops, a weekend country market, ski rentals, and big fruit stands purveying the local fruits, vegetables, wines, juices, and filberts. In short, this is a nice stop en route to the mountains.

The **Oregon Candy Farm**, 5½ miles east of Sandy on Highway 26, (503)668-5066, features Bavarian truffles along with handdipped chocolates and caramel. Kids can watch the candy makers in action.

Oral Hull Park, actually a conference center and lodge on 23 acres of grounds, is designed for the blind, with splashing water and plants to smell or touch; it is a moving experience even for the sighted. You may walk through the garden only by permission if you aren't a guest; (503)668-6195.

RESTAURANTS

The Elusive Trout Pub Wagonwheel chandeliers hanging over the tables and an old wooden canoe suspended upside down from the ceiling complete the look here. But—surprise, surprise—the theme in Sandy's popular pub is fish and fishing. The menu reflects the slang of the former owner, who lived in hip waders until he spawned the idea for the pub. He's gone fishin' (making his own line of furniture), but the new owners have kept the original menu: the Keeper, Bucktail Caddis, Eastern

Brookie, Red Sider, and German Brown are all names for better-than-average sandwiches. Nineteen brews are on draft—try the ale sampler, six 5-ounce glasses of your choice. This is a non-smoking pub. ■ *39333 Proctor Blvd (corner of Hoffman Ave), Sandy; (503) 668-7884; $; beer and wine; MC, V; checks OK; lunch, early dinner Tues–Sun.*

McKENZIE RIVER

The highway through this river valley is the most beautiful of all the Cascade crossings. Following Highway 126 from Eugene, you pass through farm country alongside the green waters of the McKenzie River. Soon there are lovely campgrounds, waterfalls, and amazingly transparent lakes. At Foley Springs, catch Highway 242 for the original pass (opens about July 1 each year). This is volcanic country, with vast 2,000-year-old lava beds.

McKenzie River runs. Long celebrated for trout fishing, the McKenzie has become known for river runs in rafts or the famous McKenzie River boats, rakish dories with upturned bows and sterns. Dave Helfrich River Outfitter in Vida is one outfitter who conducts springtime day trips on the river and also arranges for fly-fishing expeditions in drift boats; 47555 McKenzie Highway, (541) 896-3786; helfrich@efn.org.

VIDA

LODGINGS

Eagle Rock Lodge ★ A former river-guide dwelling is now a quiet bed and breakfast on the McKenzie River. The laid-back but classy, 10-guest-room Eagle Rock Lodge is great for a weekend retreat during the river-rafting and fishing season. If you want to avoid river traffic, hit it before April and you may have the run of the place. The Fireside Room is a spacious river-view suite with stone fireplace, comfortable living room, TV, and even a small library, in case you want to read up on Poe, Shakespeare, exotic plants, or whitetail deer. Bring a bottle of wine and stretch out in front of the fire, if the weather's appropriate. Breakfast, served in hosts Jerry and Susan Motter's attached quarters, is filling. A masseur is available by appointment. From November to April breakfast and dinner are included with the room; the rest of the year, it's breakfast only. ■ *49198 McKenzie Hwy (36 miles east of I-5 on Hwy 126, near Vida), Vida, OR 97488; (541) 822-3962 or (800) 230-4966; erlodge@erlodge.com; $$; AE, DIS, MC, V; local checks only.*

McKENZIE BRIDGE

Tokatee Golf Club, 3 miles west of McKenzie Bridge, is commonly rated one of the five finest in the Northwest: lots of trees, rolling terrain, and distracting views of the scenery; (541)822-3220 or (800)452-6376. It's open February through November.

RESTAURANTS

Log Cabin Inn The fundamentals of home cooking and clean, comfortable lodging are enshrined here in eight remodeled cabins on the water. Dinners are popular and offer a range as broad as wild boar, buffalo, venison, and quail, as well as the more traditional prime rib. Folks come from miles around to top it all off with marionberry cobbler. ▪ *56483 McKenzie Hwy (50 miles east of I-5 on Hwy 126), McKenzie Bridge; (541)822-3432; $$; full bar; MC, V; checks OK; lunch, dinner every day, brunch Sun (winter hours vary).* &

LODGINGS

Holiday Farm ★ First-time visitors to Holiday Farm wouldn't know at a glance that the resort encloses 90 acres and a hidden lake or three. They would find a main house (an old stagecoach stop), pleasant dining in the restaurant, and some amiable riverside cottages with knockout views of the McKenzie. Open year-round, all of the cabins feature decks and bright windows. Older cabins are green and white (with a rebuilt porch here and there); others are cedar-sided and more contemporary. Big and Little Rainbow is a large, modern pair of units that can be combined for a larger group, such as two families. The restaurant with its porch over the river makes a very enjoyable dining stop. ▪ *54455 McKenzie River Dr (3 miles west of McKenzie Bridge), Blue River, OR 97413; (541)822-3715; $$$; full bar; AE, MC, V; checks OK; breakfast, lunch, dinner every day.*

CAMP SHERMAN

LODGINGS

House on the Metolius ★★ This private fly-fishing resort, set on 200 acres of gorgeous scenery with exclusive access to a half-mile of the majestic Metolius River, usually is open all year. It's hard to get into and is open only to registered guests. Lodgings are limited to seven cabins, each with a fully equipped kitchenette, microwave oven, gas barbecue, fireplace, and king-size bed. Units 3 and 4 have ovens. Reservations are necessary. Don't forget your fly rod. ▪ *Forest Service Rd 1420 (2½ miles north of Camp Sherman), Camp Sherman; (541)595-6620; PO Box 100, Camp Sherman, OR 97730; $$$; MC, V; checks OK.*

Metolius River Resort ★★ Not to be confused with the lower-priced, circa-1923 Metolius River Lodges across the bridge (worn and well-loved, like the Velveteen Rabbit, by generations of guests), these 11 lodgettes on the west bank of the Metolius are elegant wood-shake cabins with large decks and river-rock fireplaces. All cabins have river views, master bedrooms and

lofts, furnished kitchens—and French doors leading to large river-facing decks. Because the cabins are privately owned, interiors differ; we especially like numbers 2 and 10, with natural ponderosa pine interiors, and number 1, spiffed up in country floral. Don't want to cook? Raves for nearby Kokanee Cafe, open the end of May through October, (541)595-6420.
■ *5 Suttle Sherman Rd (5 miles north of Hwy 20), Camp Sherman; (541)595-6281 or (800)81-TROUT; HCR Box 1210, Camp Sherman, OR 97730; $$$; MC, V; checks OK.*

SISTERS

Named after the three mountain peaks that dominate the horizon (Faith, Hope, and Charity), this little community is becoming a bit of a mecca for tired urban types looking for a taste of cowboy escapism. On a clear day (and there are about 250 of them a year here), Sisters is exquisitely beautiful. Surrounded by mountains, trout streams, and pine and cedar forests, this little town capitalizes on the influx of winter skiers and summer camping and fishing enthusiasts.

▼

Camp Sherman

Lodgings

▲

There's mixed sentiment about the pseudo-Western storefronts that are thematically organizing the town's commerce, but then again, Sisters does host 56,000 visitors for each of four shows during its annual June rodeo. It also has the world's largest outdoor quilt show, with 800 quilts hanging from balconies and storefronts, each July. In the early 1970s, Sisters developed the Western theme that by now has grown much more sophisticated. The town, built on about 30 feet of pumice dust spewed over centuries from the nearby volcanoes, has added numerous mini-mall shopping clusters with courtyards and sidewalks to eliminate blowing dust. There are several large art galleries, two yummy bakeries (**Sisters Bakery** for sweets, (541)549-0361, or **Northern Lights** for breads, (541)549-9122), a knowledgeable mountain supply store (**Mountain Supply of Oregon**, (541)549-3251) and excellent fly-fishing shop (**The Fly Fisher's Place**, (541)549-3474), and even a store for freshly roasted coffee beans (**Sisters Coffee Company**, (541)549-0527). Although the population of the town itself is about 1,000, more than 7,500 live in the surrounding area on miniranches.

RESTAURANTS

Hotel Sisters Restaurant and Bronco Billy's Saloon ★ The social centerpiece of Western-themed Sisters, this bar and eatery serves up Western-style ranch cooking, with good burgers and some Mexican fare served by a friendly and diligent waitstaff. Seafood is fresh, the filet mignon grilled perfectly, the chicken and ribs succulent. For a couple of bucks more, they'll split your single dinner into servings for two. Owners John Keenan, Bill Reed, and John Tehan have succeeded in turning old friendships into a going business consortium, re-creating the look of a first-class hotel circa 1900. The upstairs hotel rooms are now private dining rooms. A good place for drinks on the deck. ■ *105 Cascade St (at Fir St), Sisters; (541)549-RIBS; $$; full bar; MC, V; checks OK; lunch, dinner every day (lunch Sat–Sun only in winter).* ᣵ

Papandrea's Pizza ★ Oregonians love this place. The original link in a small chain of pizzerias, Papandrea's has built a quality reputation on fresh dough, homemade sauce, real cheese, and fresh vegetables. Because of all this freshness, the place does seem to abide by its disclaimer sign: "We will not sacrifice quality for speed, so expect to wait a little longer." Actually, you wait quite a bit longer for the original thick-crust pies, but there's a you-bake line for take-out. ■ *E Cascade Hwy (east end of town), Sisters; (541)549-6081; $; beer and wine; MC, V; local checks only; lunch, dinner every day.*

LODGINGS

Black Butte Ranch ★★★ With 1,800 acres, this vacation and recreation wonderland remains the darling of Northwest resorts. Rimmed by the Three Sisters mountains and scented by a plain of ponderosa pines, these rental condos and private homes draw families year-round to swim, ski, fish, golf, bike, boat, ride horses (summer only), and play tennis. The best way to make a reservation is to state the size of your party and whether you want a home (most are quite large and contemporary) or simply a good-sized bed and bath (in the latter case, the lodge condominiums suffice, although some are dark and dated, with too much orange Formica and brown furniture). The main lodge is a handsome but not overwhelming building that serves as dining headquarters. Tables at the Restaurant at the Lodge are tiered so that everyone can appreciate the meadow panorama beyond. ■ *Hwy 20 (8 miles west of Sisters), Black Butte Ranch; (541)595-6211; PO Box 8000, Black Butte Ranch, OR 97759; $$$; full bar; AE, DIS, MC, V; checks OK; breakfast, lunch, dinner every day (restaurant closed Mon–Tues Jan–Apr).* ᣵ

Conklin's Guest House ★★ An expensive remodel of an old farmhouse makes this one of the best B&Bs in central Oregon. Each of the large five rooms is wallpapered and well appointed, and each has a big, private bath with its own claw-footed porcelain tub and separate shower. Rooms have neither phones nor TV—just peace. The Forget-Me-Not Suite, on the first floor, has a gas-log fireplace, sunset view, and deck. The Morning Glory Suite, on the second floor, has a stunning view of the pond and gardens, pastures, and mountains. One room under the eaves has been kept a dorm room, with a queen bed and five single beds, all dressed in red plaid flannel sheets—a favorite for all-night talkfests. Large farm breakfasts are served with espresso on the glass-enclosed sun porch, or next to the outdoor heated pool when the weather warms up. Guests are welcome to use laundry facilities, fish for trout from two ponds, and make themselves at home next to the stone fireplace. The pretty grounds are a perfect backdrop for weddings. ■ *69013 Camp Polk Rd (across the road from the Sisters airport), Sisters, OR 97759; (541)549-0123; $$; no credit cards; checks OK.* &

BEND

Bend was a quiet, undiscovered high-desert paradise until a push in the 1960s to develop recreation and tourism tamed Bachelor Butte (later renamed **Mount Bachelor**) into an alpine playground. Then came the golf courses, the airstrip, the bike trails, the river-rafting companies, the hikers, the tennis players, the rockhounds, and the skiers. Bend's popularity and its population (more than 50,000) have been on a steady increase ever since, propelling it into serious-destination status. The main thoroughfare, 10 miles of uninspired strip development, bypasses the historic town center, which thrives just to the west between two one-way streets, Wall and Bond. Part of the charm of the town comes from the blinding blue sky and the pine-scented air. The other part of its appeal is its proximity to the following attractions.

Mount Bachelor Ski Area (22 miles southwest of Bend). Mount Bachelor, the largest ski area in the Pacific Northwest, now has 7 high-speed lifts (for a total of 13) feeding skiers onto 3,100 vertical feet of dry and groomed skiing. The Skier's Palate at the midmountain Pine Marten Lodge serves excellent lunches: smoked salmon pasta, lime chicken fettuccine, or a hot sandwich of Dungeness crab and bay shrimp (as well as microbrews and margaritas). The 9,065-foot elevation at the summit makes for late-season skiing (open until July 4). High-season amenities include ski school, racing, day care, rentals, an entire Nordic program and trails, and better-than-average ski food at three day lodges. Call (800)829-2442 or the ski report at (541)382-7888.

The **High Desert Museum** (59800 S Highway 97, Bend, OR 97702, (541)382-4754) is an outstanding nonprofit center for natural and cultural history, located 4 miles south of Bend, that includes live-animal educational presentations. Inside, visitors can walk through 100 years of history, featuring excellent dioramas from early Native American times through the 1890s. A "Desertarium" exhibits desert animals, including live owls, lizards, and Lahontan cutthroat trout. Twenty acres of natural trails and outdoor exhibits offer replicas of covered wagons, a sheepherder's camp, a settlers' cabin, and an old sawmill; and support three resident river otters, three porcupines, and about a half-dozen raptors (animal presentations daily). A new curatorial center and two new wings (one featuring an extensive collection of Columbia River Plateau Indian artifacts, and the other focusing on birds of prey) are all just part of a $15 million expansion which takes place over the next few years (at the moment they're still trying to raise funds). The museum's Rimrock Cafe serves better-than-average deli lunches (panini sandwiches, bean burritos with corn salsa, sun-dried tomato pasta) 11am to 5pm.

Pilot Butte (just east of town). This red-cinder-cone state park with a mile-long road to the top is a good first stop, offering a knockout panorama of the city and the mountains beyond. Be wary of pedestrians on the road. Have a shake and a burger at the Pilot Butte Drive-In, at the base of the butte.

The **Deschutes River Trail**. Mountain bike or hike for 9 miles along the Deschutes River, from downtown Bend past the Inn of the Seventh Mountain, taking in a series of waterfalls.

Newberry National Volcanic Monument (between Bend and La Pine on both sides of Highway 97). This 56,000-acre monument in the Deschutes National Forest is only a few years old but showcases geologic attractions tens of thousands of years old. Highlights: **Lava Lands Visitor Center** at the base of Lava Butte (12 miles south of Bend) is the interpretive center for miles of lava beds. Be sure to drive or, when cars are barred, take the shuttle up Lava Butte, formed by a volcanic fissure, for a sweeping, dramatic view of the moonlike landscape. Tour **Lava River Cave**, a mile-long lava tube on Highway 97 (13 miles south of Bend). As you descend into the dark and surprisingly eerie depths, you'll need a warm sweater. **Newberry Crater**, 13 miles east of Highway 97 on Forest Road 21, is the heart of the monument. Major attractions include Paulina Peak, the Big Obsidian Flow, Paulina Falls, and East and Paulina Lakes, each with a small resort on its shores. Seasons for different Newberry attractions vary, depending on snow, but generally they are open May through October. Call (541)593-2421 or (541)388-5664 for details.

Pine Mountain Observatory, 30 miles southeast of Bend on Highway 20, (541)382-8331, is the University of Oregon's astronomy research facility. One of its three telescopes is the largest in the Northwest.

Deschutes Historical Center (corner of NW Idaho and Wall) features regional history and interesting pioneer paraphernalia, but keeps limited hours (open Tuesday–Saturday); (541)389-1813.

Cascade Lakes Highway/Century Drive. This 100-mile scenic tour needs several hours and a picnic lunch for full appreciation; there are stunning mountain views and a number of lakes along the way. Begin in Bend along the Deschutes River, using the Bend Chamber of Commerce's booklet "Cascade Lakes Discovery Tour."

Smith Rock State Park. Twenty-two miles north of Bend in Terrebonne, some of the finest rock climbers gather to test their skills on the red-rock cliffs. Year-round camping is available; (541)548-7501.

The **Crooked River Dinner Train** ambles up the 38-mile Crooked River Valley between Redmond and Prineville with 3-hour scenic excursions and white-tablecloth dinner service. Check the season; special events and theme rides are offered, from murder-mystery tours to champagne brunches to Western hoedowns. Reservations are required; (541)548-8630 or dintrain@empnet.com.

RESTAURANTS

Broken Top Club ★★ The 25,000-square-foot clubhouse of the Broken Top golf course captures an exceptional view of the Cascades with the golf course and lake gracing the foreground. The talents of some of the area's most successful artists are on display everywhere. Make your reservation for a half hour before sunset, and if Mother Nature is accommodating, you'll be treated to a spectacular sunset over the jagged Broken Top and Three Sisters. The food is equally sensational and consistent, in spite of staff turnover. You might start with the shrimp quesadilla with guacamole and tomato, and move to a mixed seafood and spinach lasagne with fresh pesto cream and roasted pine nuts, or grilled salmon with wild rice and sweet pepper relish on a tarragon-pecan sauce. This is elegance in central Oregon. ■ *61999 Broken Top Dr (just off Mt Washington Dr from Century Dr), Bend; (541)383-8210; $$; full bar; MC, V; local checks only; lunch Tues–Sat, dinner Tues–Sat.* &

Cafe Rosemary ★★ This tiny restaurant, with its polished concrete floor, plastic chairs, white tablecloths, twinkle lights overhead, and fine art on the walls, serves up simply wonderful food. Appreciative diners have been known to stand and applaud both the meal and chef Bob Brown, who came out of Southern California catering retirement to serve up simple lunches (savory thick-crusted pizzette and salads of field greens, as well as several on-the-board specials, such as a roast vegetable ravioli). Wind up with full-bodied coffee served in big white porcelain cups. Dinners are pure magic—especially when served prix fixe for, say, Valentine's Day—and might feature caviar on heart-shaped blini; prawns on rosemary skewers; consommé with truffles; smoked duck breast with jalapeño polenta; salads with fresh pears, Gorgonzola and sweet, roasted nuts; peppered chateaubriand of beef; and all finished with chocolate marquise. Street dining is available during the summer (but not recommended the way the dust blows around in this town). And, just in case you'd rather dine elsewhere, all food can be prepared to go. ■ *222 NW Irving (call for directions), Bend; (541)317-0276; $$; wine only; MC, V; checks OK; lunch Mon–Sat, dinner Wed–Sat.* &

Pine Tavern Restaurant ★★ Buttonhole three out of four Bend citizens on the street and tell them you're ready for a fancy night out, with good food, service, atmosphere, and a decent value for your dollar. The recommendation time and again will be the Pine Tavern. This establishment—and 50 years of history make it truly established—has its reputation for quality. Request a table by the window (overlooking the placid Mirror Pond) in the main dining room and marvel at the tree growing through the floor. The prime rib petite cut is ample even for a hungry diner, but prime rib is the forte of the restaurant and few can resist the larger cut. There's great apple butter for the soft rolls. ■ *967 NW Brooks (foot of Oregon Ave downtown at Mirror Pond), Bend; (541)382-5581; $$; full bar; AE, DIS, MC, V; checks OK; lunch Mon–Sat, dinner every day.*

Rosette ★★ Rosette gets the prize for the most unique use of dried reeds, common along the Deschutes River, as decor. With private booths, all painted white, along one cream-colored wall and white-cloth-covered tables filling in, the room looks so light and airy that it's surprising to see such hearty dishes as burgundy braised beef stew (served over mashed potatoes) and seared duck breast made with sun-dried cherries on a mostly meat dinner menu. Wash your dinner down with a stout beer, such as Deschutes's Obsidian Stout. Lunches take a lighter, more Asian turn with such dishes as a warm duck salad made with shiitake mushrooms dressed with garlic-soy vinaigrette, or stir-fries and salads sprinkled with sesame seeds. ■ *150 NW Oregon Ave (between Bond and Wall), Bend; (541)383-2780; $$; beer and wine; MC, V; checks OK; lunch Tues–Fri, dinner Mon–Sat.* &

Scanlon's ★★ Scanlon's adjoins the Athletic Club of Bend, but aside from an aerobic instructor's distant bark and the slightest whiff of chlorine from the pool, you'd never know it. Once you're ensconced in a cozy white-tablecloth booth, your mind will be on the food—meals start right away with sweet homemade breads (Tuscan and focaccia) with virgin olive oil and balsamic vinegar for dipping. Dinners may be dressed up or dressed down: a simple rock shrimp pizza with roasted red peppers, eggplant piccata with lemon, or braised salmon or oven-roasted rack of lamb. Meats are grilled on cherry wood. The wine list is thoughtful. ■ *61615 Mt Bachelor Dr (just off Century Dr on the way to Mt Bachelor), Bend; (541)382-8769; $$; full bar; AE, MC, V; checks OK; lunch Mon–Fri, dinner Tues–Sun.* &

Honkers ★ You're bound to see Canada geese flying low over the Deschutes River just outside the 40-table dining area, so reserve a window seat. Honkers, which housed the first Brooks-Scanlon sawmill, pays homage to the town's bygone lumber mill era with crosscut saws on ponderosa pine walls, exposed rafters, and a stone fireplace near the lounge. Most diners are satisfied with the charbroiled salmon, pork chops with apple and raisin chutney, or the green-peppercorn steak. Add Honkers' cheesy, twice-baked potatoes or their butter rum cake, and you've got yourself a meal worth trumpeting about. ▪ *805 SW Industrial Way (east bank of the Deschutes, just off Colorado Ave), Bend; (541)389-4665; $$; full bar; MC, V; local checks only; lunch Mon–Fri, dinner every day.* ㅤ&

Alpenglow Cafe The Alpenglow they're referring to is probably the warm feeling in your belly after you eat their mountain of breakfast (served all day). Orange juice is fresh squeezed and full of pulp, bacon and ham are locally smoked (salmon is brined and smoked in-house), and breads (even the lunchtime hamburger buns) are homemade. Chunky potato pancakes, made with cheddar and bacon, are served with homemade applesauce or sour cream. The salmon eggs Benedict is huge—two eggs on two English muffin halves, topped with smoked king salmon, fresh basil, tomatoes, and a rich, lemony hollandaise. Even the huevos rancheros have the Alpenglow touch—a generous dollop of cilantro pesto and fresh salsa on top. All entrees come with a pile of home fries and coffee cake or fresh fruit (there's no can opener on the premises). ▪ *1040 NW Bond St (next to the Deschutes Brewery), Bend; (541)383-7676; $; beer only; AE, DIS, MC, V; local checks only; breakfast, lunch every day.* &

Deschutes Brewery & Public House It was only a matter of time before this was no longer the only brewpub in town. But it's still the best. The place was designed by Portland city folk, with urbanites in mind: exposed rafters and dark wood wainscoting. The beer is dark too: a robust Obsidian Stout or a rich Black Butte Porter, and on the lighter side, a hoppy Cascade Golden Ale and the ever-popular Bachelor Bitter. For nondrinkers, a peppery ginger ale is available. The kitchen has created light bar food for midday (French onion soup, veggie burgers, black bean chili, and homemade sausages with sauerkraut) and a full dinner menu. But really, most folks come for the brew. ▪ *1044 NW Bond St (near corner of Greenwood), Bend; (541)382-9242; $; beer and wine; MC, V; local checks only; lunch, dinner every day.* &

LODGINGS

Sunriver Lodge ★★★ More than a resort, Sunriver is an organized community with its own post office, chamber of commerce, realty offices, outdoor mall, grocery store, and more than 1,500 residents. The unincorporated town now sprawls over 3,300 acres, and its own paved runway for private air commuting does a brisk business. Its specialty is big-time escapist vacationing, and this resort has all the facilities to keep families, couples, or groups of friends busy all week long, year-round. Summer months offer golf (three 18-hole courses), tennis (28 courts), rafting, canoeing, fishing, swimming (three pools, two complexes of hot tubs), biking (30 miles of paved trails), and horseback riding. In winter the resort is home base for skiing (both Nordic and alpine), ice-skating, snowmobiling, and indoor racquetball. The marina offers canoe and whitewater raft floats and guided fly-fishing. For the best bargain, deal through the lodge reservation service, request one of the large and contemporary homes (these often have luxuries like hot tubs, barbecues, and decks), and split expenses with another family. If you want access to the pool and hot tub facility, be sure to request a house that has a pass. Even the bedroom units in the lodge village have a small deck and a fireplace and come with privileges such as discounted recreation, depending on the season.

Lodge dining includes the Meadows, a much-acclaimed showplace for lunch, dinner, and Sunday brunch. Elsewhere in the town of Sunriver, choose anything from Chinese to pizza. We like to catch the inexpensive breakfast down at the Trout House at the Sunriver Marina, too. ■ *Off Hwy 97, 15 miles south of Bend, Sunriver; (541)593-1000 or (800)547-3922; PO Box 3609, Sunriver, OR 97707; $$$; full bar; AE, DIS, MC, V; checks OK; breakfast, lunch, dinner every day (seasonal hours vary).* &

Inn of the Seventh Mountain ★★ The Inn offers the closest accommodations to Mount Bachelor and is especially popular with families, no doubt due to the vast menu of activities built into the multicondominium facility and the reasonable price tag ($59–$299). It has the biggest ice rink around (even though it's not full-size), which converts to a rollerskating rink in April; a coed sauna large enough for a dozen friends; three bubbling hot tubs; and two heated swimming pools. In the summer the pools are the center of activity—there's a whole layout complete with water slide and wading pool. The Inn does a terrific job of social planning and offers fabulous off-season rates. An activities roster for the week gives the rundown on tennis, horseback riding, biking, skating, rafting, snowmobiling, skiing, aerobics, frisbee, golf—you name it. There is plenty of good eating at the resort. The Poppy Seed Cafe puts on a plentiful and tasty breakfast. Josiah's offers fine dining and fun in the spacious lounge downstairs. ■ *18575 SW Century Dr (7 miles west of downtown), Bend; (541)382-8711 or (800)452-6810; PO Box 1207, Bend, OR 97702; $$$; full bar; AE, DIS, MC, V; checks OK; breakfast, lunch, dinner every day.* &

Mount Bachelor Village ★★ What this development has over some of its more famous neighbor resorts is spacious rooms. Every unit has a completely furnished kitchen, a wood-burning fireplace, and a private deck. We prefer the newer units, where the color scheme is modern and light and where the soundproofing helps mute the thud of ski boots. Some units look out to the busy mountain road, but the River Ridge addition looks out over the Deschutes River. There are 125 units to choose from. Amenities: two outdoor Jacuzzis, seasonal outdoor heated

▼

Bend

Lodgings

▲

pool, six tennis courts, and a 2⅕-mile nature trail. Scanlon's restaurant (see review) is a good choice for lunch and dinner. ■ *19717 Mt Bachelor Dr (toward Mt Bachelor on Century Dr), Bend, OR 97702; (541)389-5900 or (800)452-9846; $$$; AE, MC, V; checks OK.* &

Pine Ridge Inn ★★ Perched on the edge of the river canyon on Century Drive, this 20-suite inn is smaller than neighboring resorts but big on privacy, luxury, and south-facing bird's-eye views of the Deschutes River. All suites have step-down living rooms with antique and reproduction furniture and gas-log fireplaces, private porches, and roomy, well-stocked baths. The second-floor Hyde Suite is hands-down the best in the house, with luxurious king bedroom, living/dining room, Jacuzzi tub, adjoining powder room, and several decks. Complimentary full breakfasts are served in a small gathering room or delivered to your door. Afternoons, nibble crostini with salmon or smoky cheddar spreads with a glass of wine or a locally brewed beer. And, even amid all this luxury, well-behaved children are welcome; they can choose from a well-stocked library of videos, munch popcorn in their room, and get a special turn-down treat of hot chocolate and cookies before bed (grown-ups get tea, cookies, and fruit). This is a good place for corporate retreats too, as each room has a big desk and data ports. Budget tip: The six rooms that face the parking lot are considerably less expensive. ■ *1200 SW Century Dr (just before Mt Bachelor Village), Bend, OR 97702; (541)389-6137 or (800)600-4095; pineridge@ empnet.com; $$$; AE, DC, DIS, MC, V; checks OK.* &

Rock Springs Guest Ranch ★★ From late June through late August and at Thanksgiving, the emphasis here is very much on family vacations. (The rest of the year, the ranch functions as a topnotch conference center.) Counselors take care of the kids in special programs all day while adults hit the trail, laze in the pool, play tennis, or meet for hors d'oeuvres every evening on the deck. Digs are comfy knotty pine two- and three-room cottages with fireplaces. Only 50 guests stay at the ranch at one time, so it's easy to get to know everyone, particularly since all eat family style in the lodge. The setting, amid ponderosa pines and junipers alongside a small lake, is secluded and lovely. The main activity here is riding, with nine wranglers and a stable of 65 horses. Summer season is booked by the week only ($1,430 per person—kids for less, children under 2 free), which includes virtually everything with your room. Tennis courts are lit; there's a free-form whirlpool with a 15-foot waterfall over volcanic boulders, a sand volleyball court under the tall pines, and fishing in the ranch pond. ■ *64201 Tyler Rd (on Hwy 20, 7 miles from Bend and 20 miles from Sisters), Bend, OR 97701; (541)382-1957; $$; AE, MC, V; checks OK.* &

Entrada Lodge ★ Whether you're a weary traveler or an avid skier just looking for a firm mattress, a dependable shower, a clean room, and decent TV reception, you'll get that and more here. The "more" is a summer pool, a year-round outdoor hot tub, close proximity to the mountain, a spa room, hot chocolate and snacks from 4pm to 6pm by the office fireplace, and free continental breakfast. Friendly owner Brett Evert works hard to personalize this 79-room ranch-style Best Western motel. Pets are allowed, with some restrictions, for $5 a night. The price is thrifty, and the proximity to the mountain is a plus. ■ *19221 Century Dr (3 miles from Bend), Bend, OR 97702; (541)382-4080 or (800)528-1234; $$; AE, DIS, MC, V; no checks.*

Lara House Bed and Breakfast ★ One of Bend's largest and oldest (1910) homes, Lara House is a bright and homey bed and breakfast all newly remodeled and refurnished, with new private bathrooms in all rooms. The main room is perfect for small-group socializing, with a large stone fireplace and a sunny adjacent solarium that looks out over the yard onto the river parkway. A big breakfast is served at small tables on the sun porch as well as at the community oak table. Best of the themed six rooms is the bridal suite on the third floor, with sitting room, huge king bed, and spacious bathroom. The two-bedroom apartment with kitchenette and wood-burning stove on the ground floor is rented nightly or for long-term stays. The spa tub on the south-facing deck, bicycles, and outdoor games are available for guests. ■ *640 NW Congress (at Louisiana), Bend, OR 97701; (541)388-4064; $$; DIS, MC, V; checks OK.*

The Riverhouse ★ The Riverhouse has become an institution in Bend for comfortable stays at more reasonable rates than the recreation resorts. It's really a glorified motel, with a river that runs right by. Amenities are abundant: indoor and outdoor swimming pools, saunas, three whirlpools, exercise room, indoor Jacuzzi, 18-hole golf course with driving range, and tennis courts. The Deschutes creates welcome white noise to mask Highway 97's wall-to-wall traffic. Request a room with a view of the river and away from the yahoos in the hot tub. You can choose from Mai's Chinese Cuisine, the Poolside Cafe, and Crossings at The Riverhouse, the last of which is respected for its continental cuisine. The après-ski lounge rocks with contemporary and Western bands, so avoid nearby rooms unless you plan to dance all night. ■ *3075 N Hwy 97 (across from Bend River Mall), Bend, OR 97701; (541)389-3111 or (800)547-3928; $$; full bar; AE, DIS, MC, V; checks OK; breakfast, lunch, dinner every day.* &

ELK LAKE

LODGINGS

Elk Lake Resort Elk Lake is a small mountain lake about 30 miles west of Bend on the edge of the Three Sisters Wilderness Area. This remote fishing lodge—reached by snow-cat or 10 miles of cross-country skiing in the winter (or by car in the summer months)—consists of a dozen self-contained cabins, most with fireplace, kitchen, bathroom, and sleeping quarters for two to eight people. It's nothing grand, but the place is much favored by Bend dwellers and the scenery is wonderful. There are a small store and a coffee shop/dining room with standard American grub. Phone direct, a year in advance, to make reservations for both cabins and the dining room. Bring your bug juice in summer—mosquitoes can be ravenous. ■ *Century Dr (look for signs to Elk Lake), Bend; (541)317-2994; PO Box 789, Bend, OR 97709; $$; MC, V; no checks.*

MOUNT BAILEY

Mount Bailey Alpine Ski Tours offers a true backcountry skiing experience, with snow-cats instead of helicopters to take you to the top of this 8,363-foot ancient volcano, and experienced guides who stress safety. Diamond Lake Resort, (541)793-3333, is headquarters for the guide service. Also in winter: snowmobiling, cross-country skiing, inner-tube and snowboard hills, and ice-skating when the lake permits. When the snow melts, the operation turns to mountain-bike tours, boating, swimming, and hiking.

WESTFIR

This former logging town flanks the North Fork of the Middle Fork of the Willamette River, excellent for fishing for rainbow trout. The **Aufderheide National Scenic Byway** winds east out of Westfir into the heart of the Cascades, meandering along the river, and is popular with bicyclists, although heavy snowfall closes the route from November until early April.

LODGINGS

Westfir Lodge ★★ Westfir Lodge has long anchored the tiny community of Westfir. For many years it housed the former lumber company offices. Then Gerry Chamberlain and Ken Symons converted the two-story building into a very pleasant seven-room inn, and they continue to close for remodeling for four weeks every year. The bedrooms ring the first floor; in the center are a living area, kitchen, and formal dining room where guests are served a full English breakfast (English bangers and fried potatoes, eggs, broiled tomato topped with cheese, and scones). Cottage gardens outside and a plethora of antiques throughout the lodge lend an English country ambience. The longest covered bridge in Oregon—the 180-foot Office Bridge (1944)—is just across the road. ■ *47365 1st St (3 miles east of Hwy 58 near Oakridge), Westfir, OR 97492; (541) 782-3103; $$; no credit cards; checks OK (closed mid-Feb to mid-Mar).* &

ODELL LAKE

LODGINGS

Odell Lake Lodge and Resort This resort on the shore of Odell Lake is ideal for the fisher, the hiker, and the skier in all of us. The lake's a bit alpine for much swimming; instead, cast for the Mackinaw trout, rainbow, or kokanee. (Most sports equipment—fishing rods to snowshoes—is for rent here.) The small library is the perfect place to sink into an overstuffed chair and read in front of the fireplace. Fresh rainbow trout (of course) is our first choice at the restaurant, which is open year-round for three squares a day. As for accommodations, request a lakeside room, one of seven in the hotel (room 3, specifically; it's a corner suite warmed with knotty pine paneling and views of lake and stream). If you'd rather stay in a cabin, the few additional dollars required to get a lakeside one are well spent. The new, well-lit cabin 10 is the best (and the only wheelchair-accessible one). Or try cabins 6 or 7. Cabin 12 sleeps a friendly crowd of 16. The second-tier cabins are significantly smaller (no views, either). Pets okay in cabins only; minimum stays during peak season. ■ *From Oakridge, head east on Hwy 58 for 30 miles, take E Odell Lake exit; (541) 433-2540; PO Box 72, Crescent Lake, OR 97425; $$; no alcohol; DIS, MC, V; checks OK; breakfast, lunch, dinner every day (Wed–Sun only in winter).* &

LA PINE

LODGINGS

Diamond Stone Guest Lodge & Gallery ★ Diamond Stone is a diamond in the rough. Innkeepers Doug and Gloria Watt, who run a mortgage business, have created a four-room inn near the meandering Little Deschutes River (slow water, great for canoeing) between Sunriver and La Pine. Western art livens up the place (and is for sale). Our favorite is the two-room suite with a view of Mount Bachelor and the Quail Run Golf Course. Cable TV, VCR, and access to a large video library are included. The living room features a fireplace, vaulted ceiling, and CD player—your choice of tunes. Amenities include outdoor hot tub, sauna, and sun decks. Breakfast keeps even the most active traveler going all day. Help yourself to drinks in the fridge. ■ *16696 Sprague Loop (8 miles south of Sunriver and 3 miles west of Hwy 97), La Pine, OR 97739; (541) 536-6263 or (800) 600-6263; $$; AE, DIS, MC, V; local checks only.*

SUMMER LAKE

Take Highway 31 just a few miles south of La Pine and head east to the high desert. You'll pass Fort Rock, where Klamath Indians found refuge when Mount Mazama exploded 6,800 years ago. Woven sandals found in one of Fort Rock's caves carbon-dated to 9,000 years ago; archaeological studies have found Klamath-style artifacts that date back 13,000 years in the old lake bed. Summers, the mom-and-pop grocery store and the small pioneer museum nearby are usually open.

LODGINGS

Summer Lake Bed & Breakfast Inn ★★ If you are looking for luxury in a remote setting, this is the place—110 miles southeast of Bend on the edge of one of Oregon's largest bird refuges. From the inn's hot tub on the wide deck you can see 40 unmarred miles in all directions and, in the black night, more stars than you can count. Stay in one of three upstairs bedrooms in the rustic main house, or in one of three cabin-style condos with kitchens, Jacuzzi tubs, private decks, music, and VCRs. They're all equally attractive. Owners Darrell Seven and Jean Sage serve a big breakfast, and will cook dinner for you with advance notice (good thing, since there isn't a grocery store or restaurant for miles). The area has considerable natural charms, which you'll have mostly to yourself—hiking in the Gearhart Wilderness Area, horseback riding (BYOH), paragliding and hang gliding from sanctioned jump-off areas, fly-fishing for Donaldson trout in nearby rivers and reservoirs, snowmobiling, and cross-country skiing. Or ask Seven, who has lived here since the 1960s, about favorite spots or his own guided three-day camping trips into the high desert. ■ *D-7 Ranch, 31501 Hwy 31 (between mileposts 81 and 82), Summer Lake, OR 97640; (541)943-3983 or (800)261-2778; $$; AE, MC, V; checks OK.*

LAKEVIEW

At an elevation of nearly 4,300 feet, Lakeview calls itself "Oregon's Tallest Town." It's better known for its geyser, Old Perpetual—which doesn't exactly rival Yellowstone's Old Faithful but is Oregon's only geyser. It's located in a pond at **Hunter's Hot Springs**, a 47-acre property dotted by hot-springs pools, on the west side of Highway 395 about 2 miles north of town. The geyser goes off once every 30 seconds or so, shooting 75 feet into the air for 3 to 5 seconds. It's been erupting regularly for some 60 years, apparently unleashed by someone trying to drill a well. Hunter's Hot Springs resort, built in the 1920s, now includes an Italian restaurant and a 33-unit motel; (541)947-2127.

Abert Lake, 20 miles north of Lakeview, is a stark, shallow body of water over which looms **Abert Rim**, a massive fault scarp.

One of the highest exposed geologic faults in North America, the rim towers 2,000 feet above the lake.

CRATER LAKE

Some 6,500 years ago, 15,000-foot Mount Mazama became the Mount St. Helens of its day, blew up, and left behind a deep crater that is now filled with a lake. Plunging to a depth of 1,932 feet, it's the deepest lake in the United States. **Crater Lake National Park** is extraordinary: the impossibly blue lake, eerie volcanic formations, a vast geological wonderland. The **Visitors Center**, at the park headquarters, (541)594-2211, offers a theater, an information desk, and a good interpretive exhibit. Visitors can camp at Mazama Campground or other designated areas around the park. You can take the two-hour boat ride from Cleetwood Cove out to Wizard Island and around the lake. There are dozens of trails and climbs to magnificent lookouts. In winter, when the crowds finally thin out, only the south and west entrance roads are kept open. Cross-country skiing and snowshoe walks are popular winter activities.

LODGINGS

Crater Lake Lodge ★★ Originally built in 1909, the historic wood-and-stone building, perched at 7,000 feet on the rim of the caldera, was weakened considerably by decades of heavy snowfall. The four-story summer lodge was restored in the mid-'90s with a $15 million taxpayer-funded makeover, and features 71 rooms. Even though only 26 rooms face the lake, all have great views. Best are the eight with claw-footed bathtubs in window alcoves. You won't find TVs or in-room phones here. The dining-room motif is 1930s lodge decor, conveying the mood of the original, but the food is contemporary. Nonguests should make reservations many months in advance. The small (71-seat) dining room serves guests who reserve on check-in; if the dining room is full, you can choose between two less-than-grand restaurants at Rim Village, 500 feet from the lodge. ■ *Crater Lake National Park via Hwy 138 or Hwy 62; (541)594-2511 or (541) 830-8700; PO Box 128, Crater Lake, OR 97604; $$$; beer and wine; MC, V; checks OK; breakfast, lunch, dinner every day (closed mid-Oct to mid-May).*

KLAMATH FALLS

This city of 17,000 people, the largest for 70 miles around, is so isolated that it once led a movement to secede from Oregon and become the state of Jefferson. Now its residents happily welcome tourists, bird-watchers, and sportspersons from both Oregon and California (just 25 miles south). It's a pretty drive through the high desert from Bend, or over the mountain passes from Medford or Ashland. Seemingly dormant for years, the geothermally heated town has bubbled to life in the past few years with a flurry of construction, including chain hotels and the $250 million **Running Y Ranch Resort**, with its planned 250-room hotel, Arnold Palmer golf course, and condo development on 9,000 acres 10 miles out of town; (888)797-2624. The Klamath Indian Tribe also shook things up shortly after the last earthquake when they announced plans to build their **Kla-Mo-Ya Casino** on Highway 97 at Chiloquin, which is now open just a few miles north of the Klamath Falls International Airport.

The **Favell Museum of Western Art** is a true Western museum, with arrowheads, Indian artifacts, and the works of more than 200 Western artists; 125 W Main Street, (541)882-9996. The **Klamath County Museum** exhibits the volcanic geology of the region, Indian artifacts from all over Oregon, and relics from the Modoc wars; 1451 Main Street, (541)883-4208. The **Baldwin Hotel Museum**, in a spooky 1906 hotel, retains many fixtures of the era; open June through September; 31 Main Street, (541)883-4207. **Ross Ragland Theater**, a onetime art deco movie theater, now presents stage plays, concerts, and the like an impressive 130 nights a year; (541)884-0651. Take Highway 139 south a few miles south to the **Lava Beds National Monument Visitor Center** in Tulelake, California, and walk through the moonscape where Captain Jack and 60 Modoc Indian men defended themselves and their families during a four-month siege in 1872 by the U.S. Cavalry; (916)667-2282.

Upper Klamath Lake, 143 square miles, lies on the remains of a larger ancient lake system and is the largest lake in Oregon; it's fine for fishing and serves as the nesting grounds for many birds, including white pelicans. The Williamson River, which flows into the lake, yields plenty of trout.

RESTAURANTS

Chez Nous ★ The name may be French, but Achim and Arlette Bassler serve more of a continental menu in this graceful older home on the south side of town. It's a favorite with locals, who go there for dishes like tournedos gourmet Chez Nous, with artichoke bottoms, scampi, and béarnaise atop the fillets. You get béarnaise with the salmon and halibut, too. The veal Marsala comes on a bed of spinach. And they do chateaubriand or giant lobster for two. Otherwise, it's pretty standard, but nicely done. ■ *3927 S 6th St (follow 6th St south, a few blocks past Altamont), Klamath Falls; (541)883-8719; $$; full bar; AE, DIS, MC, V; local checks only; dinner Tues–Sat.* ㅊ

Fiorella's ★ Residents of Klamath Falls appreciate the Northern Italian fare at Fiorella and Renato Durighello's restaurant. On a recent visit we had fine scalloppine Marsala and the house special, pastitsio, both of which came with soup, salad (in summer, it's fresh from their own garden), and garlic bread. The pasta is homemade and delicious. Reservations welcome. ■ *6139 Simmers Ave (S 6th St to Simmers), Klamath Falls; (541) 882-1878; $$; full bar; AE, MC, V; local checks only; dinner Tues–Sat.*

LODGINGS

Thompson's Bed and Breakfast by the Lake ★ Mary and Bill Pohll offer four bedrooms on a separate level with private entrance. All have private baths. Sunsets over the Cascade Range provide a backdrop to the spectacular view of Upper Klamath Lake. Bring your binoculars for bird-watching; bald eagles roost in the backyard. Deer are frequent visitors here too. Mary can cook virtually anything for breakfast, but apple pancakes and French toast are her specialties. Bill sometimes cooks five-course dinners for guests with plenty of advance notice. This was the first B&B in town, launched when Mary's last name was Thompson. Others have come and gone, but this is still the best. ■ *1420 Wild Plum Court (call for directions), Klamath Falls, OR 97601; (541) 882-7938; tompohll@aol.com; $$; no credit cards; checks OK.*

BLY

LODGINGS

Aspen Ridge Resort ★ This complex of log homes appears like a mirage in the high meadows of south-central Oregon, reminding one somewhat of an early-day miniature Sunriver. The resort sits on 160 acres that were once part of 14,000-acre Fishhole Creek Ranch. Five log cabins sleep six each; the two suites and two bedrooms (all with private baths) in the main lodge go for less. Most people come here to be outside, go mountain biking, or ride horseback—but there is a tennis court for those who prefer to stick around the ranch. If you don't like beef, you won't fit in here. The resort is adjacent to a working cattle and buffalo ranch, which provides a view and influences the restaurant's menu. Best meal bargain is the steak dinner, barbecued on the back porch. ■ *Fishhole Creek Rd (18 miles SE of Bly), Bly; (541) 884-8685; PO Box 2, Bly, OR 97622; $$; full bar; no credit cards; checks OK; breakfast, lunch, dinner every day (closed Mar).*

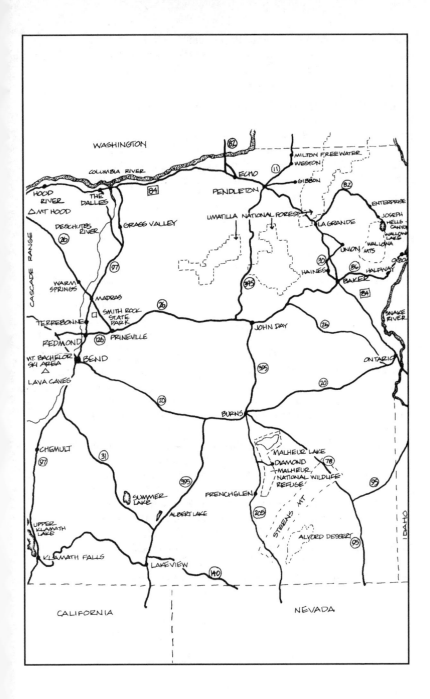

Eastern Oregon

Two major routes: eastward midstate from Warm Springs to John Day, and southeastward along I-84 from Pendleton to the Idaho border (with a diversion into the Wallowas), turning in-state again to Burns and Frenchglen.

WARM SPRINGS

For most highway cowboys, Warm Springs was just a small bend in the road at the bottom of a pine-studded rimrock canyon on Highway 26, until the spectacular **Museum at Warm Springs**, (541)553-3331, opened in 1993. And what a museum it is. The architecture alone has won numerous awards. Built by the three Native American tribes (Wasco, Paiute, and Warm Springs) who live on the 600,000-acre reservation, the museum houses a permanent collection (the largest tribally owned collection in the United States) that includes prized heirlooms protected by families for generations, on view to the public for the first time. The Smithsonian Institution has named it the best of its kind in North America. Look here for stunning beadwork that would have been exchanged in a Wasco wedding, baskets, stories of early reservation days, music, and dance. The museum's art gallery has frequently changing shows of Indian art and artists, a small gift shop, and demonstrations during the summer.

LODGINGS

Kah-Nee-Ta Resort and Village ★★ Over the years, this resort owned by the Confederated Tribes of Warm Springs keeps getting better—incorporating more Indian art into the decor and, in 1996, adding a cultural desk where guests could ask questions about Indian history, religion, and lifestyle. In 1997, after a year of prairie fires and floods, the resort was completely revamped, including rebuilding the old recreation complex next to the river that now includes a European-style day spa and a giant water slide for kids, as well as miniature golf and an 18-hole championship golf course, stables, and river kayaking. New tepees that hold up to 12 overnight guests are decorated with traditional Wasco, Paiute, and Warm Springs designs handpainted by tribal members. The huge swimming pool and spas are fed by sweet-smelling water from the nearby hot springs. New motel units with suites, kitchens, and bedrooms, which can be combined for large groups, overlook the pool; a 65-unit RV park is neatly tucked into a corner of the property. There's a restaurant/deli/general store poolside too.

In the main hotel, high on the hill overlooking the canyon, are 139 newly appointed rooms: all have views of canyon and sky. The Juniper Room's full-service menu satisfies both metropolitan and ranch tastes, with Indian flute music piped in overhead. Fry-bread and huckleberry preserves are served with dinner. Popular outdoor salmon bakes, every Saturday through the summer, feature fillets skewered on alder sticks and baked over a crackling alderwood fire while guests watch Indian powwow-style dancing. And in case you've got the urge to gamble, a two-story casino has been added (quite unobtrusively) to the back of the building. ■ *11 miles north of Warm Springs on Hwy 3, follow the signs from the Simnasho exit on Hwy 26 or turn onto Hwy 3 from the town of Warm Springs; (541)553-1112, (800)554-4786, or (800)831-0100; PO Box K, Warm Springs, OR 97761; $$; full bar; AE, DC, DIS, MC, V; checks OK; breakfast, lunch, dinner every day.* craftedⒼ

REDMOND

LODGINGS

Inn at Eagle's Crest ★★ Sisters has Black Butte, Bend has Sunriver, and Redmond has Eagle's Crest. The private homes at this full resort rim the 18-hole golf course, and visitors choose one of the 75 rooms in the hotel (the best ones have decks facing the golf course) or a condominium. The condos are the better deal, especially if you come with four to eight people. They've got kitchens and access to the recreation center (an additional $5 per day fee to those who stay in the main building) with its indoor tennis, squash, and racquetball courts, workout room, masseuse, tanning salon, heated outdoor pool, and tennis courts; miles of biking and jogging trails; an equestrian center; and playfields. The food at the resort's formal Canyon Club is predictable for such a clubby atmosphere, with rancher-size portions except for breakfast, which is a lighter meal. Service can be slow. The three-tiered deck outside provides a good view. ■ *821 S 6th St (5 miles west of Redmond on Hwy 126, turn south on Cline Falls Rd), Redmond; (541)923-2453 or (800)MUCH-SUN; PO Box 867, Redmond, OR 97756; $$; full bar; AE, MC, V; checks OK; breakfast, lunch, dinner every day (dinner every day in winter).*

JOHN DAY

You are in the midst of dry cattle country in an area loaded with history: John Day is just off the old Oregon Trail, and the whole region was full of gold (during the height of the Gold Rush in 1862, $26 million in gold was mined in the neighboring town of Canyon City).

Kam Wah Chung Museum, next to the city park, was the stone-walled home of two Chinese herbal doctors at the turn of the century. A tour makes for an interesting glimpse of the Chinese settlement in the West: opium-stained walls, Chinese shrines, and herbal medicines are on display, as well as a small general store. Open May to October.

John Day Fossil Beds National Monument lies 40 to 120 miles west, in three distinct groupings: the banded Painted Hills, extremely ancient fossils, and fascinating geological layers; 420 W Main Street, (541) 575-0721, for maps and brochures.

LODGINGS

The Ponderosa Guest Ranch ★★★ If cowboys are your weakness and cattle country beckons, you can't do better than the Ponderosa, 120,000 acres of rolling rangeland in the splendid Silvies Valley. Here's a dude ranch that's a bona fide working ranch, with up to 4,000 head of cattle. No pokey trail rides here; if you're game, you'll join ranch cowboys in the day-to-day management of the herds. (Of course, you're welcome to disappear by yourself to fly-fish in any of the six streams or just soak in the hot tub near the pond.) April is calving season, when you might help "cut" cows and their offspring into new herds and make sure disoriented calves "mother up." In May you can help round up the calves for branding, and in June move herds to high mountain pastures. Ranch manager Garth Johnson is a master at matching one of the ranch's 70 horses to your abilities, and the cowboys offer plenty of encouragement.

▼

John Day

Lodgings

▲

The ranch is a serious and long-standing business, yet the guest lodge is not an afterthought. There are eight log guest cabins with three double units each (request Jump Creek, with its unobstructed view) and a massive main lodge with a spacious dining room, a bar, and plenty of relaxing areas. Tanya Johnson oversees the lodge and its staff, making sure you are well fed and that your special interests—be they bird-watching on ranch wetlands or a hankering for blueberry buckle for dessert—are accommodated. Hearty ranch fare (included in the price) is served family style, and there's plenty of it, starting with eggs and biscuits with sausage gravy and ending with a full steak dinner. In winter, there are 35 miles of groomed cross-country trails to explore. The Johnsons provide a masterful blend of professionalism and casual friendliness that makes this an outstanding experience. And, in case you were wondering, of course they have a calf you can name Norman. Minimum two-night stay in winter (November–April), minimum three-day stay in summer (May–October). ■ *On Hwy 395 halfway between Burns and John Day; (541) 542-2403 or (800) 331-1012; PO Box 190, Seneca, OR 97873; cu@ponderosa.com; $$; full bar; AE, MC; checks OK; breakfast, lunch, dinner every day.*

DAYVILLE

LODGINGS

Fish House Inn Mike and Denise Smith escaped San Diego with two young children in favor of considerably smaller Dayville (population 214). They settled into a century-old house built by Dayville's first liquor-store owner. Denise has turned the tiny original liquor store into a gift shop; Mike remodeled a small cottage in the back into two private guest rooms. There are three more rooms in the main house as well, all decorated with stuff gleaned from farm sales (old rakes, ice tongs, and horseshoes), things piscine (old rods, reels, and creels among them), and baskets Denise wove from river willows. In warm weather a bountiful breakfast (with the best coffee in 4,528 mostly empty square miles) is served in the garden. ■ *110 Franklin Ave (on Hwy 26 west of John Day), Dayville; (541) 987-2124; PO Box 143, Dayville, OR 97825; $; MC, V; checks OK.*

PENDLETON

In these parts, the name of this town is synonymous with the Wild West. Each September the **Pendleton Round-up** rolls around—a big event ever since 1910 that features a dandy rodeo; call (800) 457-6336 for tickets and information. **Hamley's and Company** has been selling Western clothing, boots, hats, tack items, and custom-made saddles since 1883. It's a kind of shrine, the L. L. Bean of the West; 30 SE Court Street, (541) 276-2321.

Pendleton Woolen Mills gives tours Monday through Friday and sells woolen yardage and imperfect versions of its famous blankets at reduced prices; 1307 SE Court Place, (541) 276-6911; penwoolmil@aol.com; www.pendleton-usa.com. **Pendleton Underground Tours** provides a 90-minute walk through Pendleton's history—most of it underground—to view the remains of businesses that date back to the turn of the century: bordellos, opium dens, and Chinese jails. Reservations are necessary and should be made at least 24 hours in advance. Price is $10 per adult; 37 SW Emigrant Avenue, (541) 276-0730.

After a long struggle for funding, the Umatilla tribe will open in late 1998 the $13 million **Tamustalik** (pronounced ta-MUST-ah-luck) **Cultural Institute** on 640 acres behind the **Wildhorse Gaming Resort** (which has a golf course and an overpriced barebones hotel). For the first time ever, the Institute will tell the story of the Oregon Trail—one of the greatest mass migrations in human history, which had an indelible impact on the Indians of the West—from the Indian point of view; PO Box 638, Pendleton, OR 97801.

Raphael's Restaurant and Lounge ★★ In the historic Roy Raley House, across from the landmark Clock Tower, the Hoffmans continue the charming and somewhat eccentric approach to food that they mastered at the Skyroom. Visit the authentic Native American fine art gallery (Raphael Hoffman is a member of the Nez Percé tribe) while waiting for your table. Raphael's husband, Robert, the chef, is not Indian, but some of the dishes show a Native American touch. Emphasis is more on flavor than on presentation. Indian salmon wrapped in spinach and smothered with wild huckleberries appears too dark until the pink of the salmon breaks through with the first fork cut; the flavor is incredible. An applewood-smoked prime rib is the most popular beef entree; many of the patrons are crazy about it. Wild game such as alligator, rattlesnake, and elk is featured during the hunters' months of September, October, and November. The wine list features a good selection of moderately priced Northwest wine. Varietal wines are sold by the 8-ounce glass. ■ *233 SE 4th (Court and Dorion), Pendleton; (541)276-8500; $$; full bar; MC, V; checks OK; lunch Tues–Fri, dinner Tues–Sat.* ☐

LODGINGS

Parker House ★★ In 1917, this magnificent 6,000-square-foot home was more than just a place to live for the prominent L. L. Rogers family; it was a testament to the success of their ranch and their standing in Pendleton society, what with imported Chinese silk wallpaper, a formal ballroom draped in elegance, and a grand porch overlooking an English garden. It all seems out of place in the wheat fields of Eastern Oregon, but somehow the clash is welcome. Of the five rooms, Gwendolyn is the grandest, with its fireplace and French doors; however, all the rooms are brightened with freshly cut flowers and enhanced with thick robes (you never want to get dressed). This is definitely one of the classier stays this side of the Cascades. ■ *311 N Main St (north on Hwy 11, follow City Center signs to downtown, head north on Main, cross Umatilla River to N Main), Pendleton, OR 97801; (541)276-8581 or (800)700-8581; $$; MC, V; checks OK.*

Swift Station Inn Bed and Breakfast ★ Ken and Lorry Schippers both work full-time for the state of Oregon, but their labor of love on weekends and evenings has turned one of Pendleton's white elephants into its finest lodgings. The ground-floor Victorian Room (our favorite) has a private bath. A large hot tub in the backyard melts away the fatigue of driving (and you do a lot of it in these parts). Breakfasts are large, and the Schipperses are so anxious to please that you'll probably leave feeling guilty for not finishing what's on your plate. Well-behaved, courteous children are welcome. Rates are higher during September because of the Round-up. ■ *602 SE Byers (exit 210* *off I-84, north on State Hwy into town, north on 9th St 3 blocks to Byers), Pendleton, OR 97801; (541)276-3739; $$; MC, V; checks OK.*

Indian Hills Motor Inn A little to the south of Pendleton is the Red Lion's Indian Hills Motor Inn, the most lavish motel in town. Amenities include heated pool, lounge, dining room, and coffee shop. There are outsized, gaudy Western bas-reliefs in the reception areas. The view from your balcony over the low mountains and tilled fields of Eastern Oregon can be inspiring—more so than the food. Sunday morning brunch is the best meal of the week. Well-behaved pets are okay. ■ *304 SE Nye Ave (exit 210 off I-84), Pendleton; (541)276-6111; PO Box 1556, Pendleton, OR 97801; $$; AE, DC, MC, V; checks OK.* &

The Working Girl's Hotel Here's the first nonprofit hotel we've ever seen. Its mission? To bring tourism to Pendleton—and at these prices, you'll come back, Round-up or no. The hotel gets its name from its former incarnation as a bordello. The girls are gone, but the five spacious rooms (one long flight up) in this pretty brick building are just as welcoming. Each has 18-foot ceilings and antique furnishings (even the television is cleverly hidden in a vintage radio cabinet). The plumbing's still the original stuff, so you'll need to cross a hall to the bath—but that's a small price to pay for such a fun night's stay. Continental breakfast is served, and if you stay longer, the kitchen is available for your preparations. Young children are discouraged. ■ *17 SW Emigrant Ave (between Main and SW 1st), Pendleton, OR 97801; (541)276-0730 or (800)226-6398; $; MC, V; checks OK.*

ECHO

RESTAURANTS

The Echo Hotel Restaurant and Lounge ★ The Echo's cedar-shake interior is filled with a bar, a split-level dining area, and three blackjack tables. This former rabbit cannery and historic hotel serves up generous portions of 16-ounce prime rib and ranch-wagon specials. Primarily a whiskey-and-ribs place, the Echo is getting more and more attention for its seafood and Northwest wines from Pendletonians, who flock here on weekends. ■ *110 Main St (20 miles west of Pendleton on I-84), Echo; (541)376-8354; $; full bar; DC, MC, V; local checks only; breakfast Sat–Sun, lunch, dinner Tues–Sun.* &

WESTON

RESTAURANTS

Tollgate Mountain Chalet Walla Walla folks often drive 50 miles south through the lovely, waving wheat fields to this rustic eating place in the Blue Mountain forest. Locals order the chili, the prime-rib sandwich on homemade bread, a hamburger, a Reuben sandwich, or a reasonable steak; the pies are homemade and different every day. It makes a particularly good spot for breakfast before a day of hiking or mushroom hunting. ■ *Rt 1 (16 miles east of Weston on Tollgate Mtn Hwy), Weston; (541)566-2123; $; full bar; MC, V; local checks only; lunch, dinner Tues–Thurs; breakfast, lunch, dinner Fri–Sun.* &

MILTON-FREEWATER

RESTAURANTS

The Oasis This isn't a copy of a 1920s Western roadhouse, it's the real thing—and it hasn't ever changed: linoleum floors and lots of chrome. Eat in the bar and eavesdrop on the cowboys swapping stories. Although not every dish on the menu is a culinary triumph, the steaks are uniformly reliable and gigantic. Prime rib is good. On Sundays, chicken and dumplings is served family style, all you can eat, for well under $10 per person—and a fine meal it is. A breakfast platter of biscuits and gravy goes for just over $2. Students from Walla Walla are fascinated with this place. ■ *Old Milton-Freewater Hwy and State Line Rd, Milton-Freewater; (541)938-4776; $; full bar; MC, V; local checks only; breakfast, lunch, dinner Tues–Sun.* &

LA GRANDE

RESTAURANTS

Ten Depot Street ★ Sandy Sorrels (who also owns the popular Mamacita's a block away) has been running La Grande's fussiest restaurant (which, in fact, is not that fussy) for the past decade. Ten Depot has had its up and downs, but it's still the locals' pick for an evening out. The dining room, in an old brick building with antique furnishings, is nice, but most folks still prefer to order dinner in the lounge, with its beautiful carved-wood back bar. Bargain hunters look for the blue plate special—under $5—all week long. Dinners can be as simple as a two-fisted (half-pound) burger to chicken and pesto pasta, to beef tenderloin heaped with sautéed mushrooms. Lunches feature superior salads and meaty sandwiches. Widmer beers are on tap. ■ *10 Depot St (2 blocks west of Adams), La Grande; (541)963-8766; $$; full bar; AE, MC, V; checks OK; lunch, dinner Mon–Sat.* &

The Lifeline Cafe La Grande quickly embraced Marty Hart's restaurant in the former office supply store on Depot Street, which is becoming La Grande's restaurant row. Lunchtime crowds are proof that her open-faced focaccia sandwiches are a big hit in cowboy country. The menu's small, but it has a slight Mediterranean twist (often low-fat). The fresh fruit smoothies and savory breads (from Knead's Bakery next door) are the perfect pick-me-up in the hot afternoon sun. On Fridays and Saturdays you can get the same lunch nibbles until 11pm. This is an Eastern Oregon find for vegetarians too. ■ *111 Depot St (near Adams), La Grande; (541) 962-9568; $; no alcohol; no credit cards; checks OK; lunch every day, dinner Fri–Sat.*

Mamacita's House specials such as the Full Meal Steal (typically two chicken soft tacos with beans and rice) for less than $3 at lunch are usually the best things coming out of the kitchen. Food is not overly spiced and not as fat-laden as Mexican food often is. Local college students provide most of the helpful service. In winter, try to catch Mamacita's on International Night (once a month) for a multicourse meal featuring the foods of another nation. Wine margaritas and an adobe-colored wall adorned with bright splotches of Mexicana complete the experience. ■ *110 Depot St (near Adams), La Grande; (541) 963-6223; $; full bar; no credit cards; checks OK; lunch Tues–Fri, dinner Tues–Sun.* ♿

LODGINGS

Stang Manor Inn ★★ This restored timber baron's house on the hill behind town returns an elegance to this once-booming town. A sweeping staircase leads up to the four bedrooms. The master suite is, of course, the best—and biggest—accommodation, but even if you opt for the former maid's quarters, you won't have to lift a finger. The owners, Marjorie and Pat McClure, have given personal attention to an already nurturing environment. Cookies—madeleines, perhaps—with tea await you at afternoon check-in. Breakfasts are always served on china and crystal. ■ *1612 Walnut St (corner of Spring), La Grande, OR 97850; (503) 963-2400; stang@eoni.com; www.eoni.com/stang; $$; DC, MC, V; checks OK.*

JOSEPH

This is the fabled land of the Wallowas, ancestral home of Chief Joseph, from which he fled with a band of Nez Percé warriors to his last stand near the Canadian border. Although Chief Joseph's remains are interred far from his beloved "land of the winding water," he saw to it that his father, Old Chief Joseph, would be buried here, on the north shore of Wallowa Lake. The town itself is becoming something of an art colony. David Manuel, State of Oregon official sculptor for the Oregon Trail Celebration, opened the **Manuel Museum and Studio** on Main Street, (541) 432-7235. **Valley Bronze of Oregon** has built a foundry and a showroom in Joseph. Tours are offered on weekdays; phone (541) 432-7551 for information.

Wallowa Lake State Park, on the edge of the Wallowa-Whitman National Forest and Eagle Cap Wilderness, is perhaps the only state park in the country where locals still lament the fact that there are "never enough people." An Alpenfest with music, dancing, and Bavarian feasts happens every September, but the peak season is still midsummer, when the pristine lake and its shores are abuzz with go-carts, sailboats, and windsurfers. In winter the attraction is miles and miles of unpeopled cross-country trails throughout the lovely Wallowa highlands.

Wallowa Lake Tramway at the edge of the park takes you by a steep ascent in a four-passenger gondola to the top of 8,200-foot Mount Howard, with spectacular overlooks and 2 miles of hiking trails (summer only); (541)432-5331.

Hells Canyon, 35 miles east of Joseph, is the continent's deepest gorge, an awesome trench cut by the Snake River through sheer lava walls. The best view is from Hat Point near Imnaha, though McGraw Lookout is more accessible if you don't have four-wheel drive. Ask at the ranger station in Joseph. Maps of the region's roads and trails, and information on conditions, are available at the Wallowa Valley Ranger District in Joseph; (541)426-4978.

Hurricane Creek Llamas. Explore the lake-laden Eagle Cap Wilderness with a naturalist, while smiling llamas lug your gear. Hikes vary in length; hearty country meals are included (May to September). Call in advance, (541)432-4455.

Wallowa Alpine Huts. Experienced backcountry ski guides offer 3- to 5-day powder-bound tours for skiers seeking the best of the Wallowa winterland. You stay in spartan tents and dine in a yurt; (208)882-1955.

RESTAURANTS

Vali's Alpine Deli and Restaurant ★ Don't let its "deli" status mislead; a dinner at Vali's usually requires reservations. The food here is Hungarian-German (and so is the decor) interspersed with a few authentic renditions from other cuisines. Paprika chicken and dumplings is not to be missed when offered. Wiener schnitzel is also exceptional. At breakfast time, Maggie Vali's homemade doughnuts are local legend, but don't show up hungry—the morning meal ends there. In the summer, sausage and cheese are available to take out for picnics. An enclosed deck adds a nice touch to the dining experience. ∎ *59811 Wallowa Lake Hwy/Hwy 82 (5 miles south of Joseph, near Wallowa Lake State Park), Joseph; (503)432-5691; $; full bar; no credit cards; checks OK; breakfast, dinner Tues–Sun (closed Labor Day to Memorial Day).*

LODGINGS

Chandlers—Bed, Bread, and Trail Inn ★ Cedar shingles, multi-angled roof lines, and cushiony wall-to-wall carpets make this bed and breakfast resemble an alpine ski lodge—in the middle of Joseph. A log staircase climbs from the comfortable living room to a loft where five simple bedrooms share a sitting room and workable kitchenette. Three of the five bedrooms have private baths. The mountains almost climb into room number 1. The substantial breakfast and the knowledgeable hosts make this a wonderful stopover for area explorers. ■ *700 S Main St (east end of Main St), Joseph, OR 97846; (541)432-9765 or (800)452-3781; $; MC, V; checks OK.*

Wallowa Lake Lodge ★ The rooms in this historic lodge are very small (especially the $50 ones). You'll do best if you reserve one of the originally restored rooms with a lake view. If you plan to stay longer, the rustic (but refurbished) pine cabins on the lake, with a living room, fireplace, and kitchen, allow for a bit more flexibility. Even if the rooms were spacious, we'd spend most of the evening in front of the magnificent stone fireplace in the knotty pine lobby, and the days on the lake or in the mountains. The deck is a splendid addition. Cabins are available year-round; the lodge and restaurant are closed (except for private parties) in winter. ■ *60060 Wallowa Lake Hwy (near Wallowa Lake State Park), Joseph, OR 97846; (541)432-9821; $$; DC, MC, V; checks OK.*

HAINES

RESTAURANTS

Haines Steak House ★ There's no mistaking that you're in cattle country, pilgrim. Most of the vehicles surrounding this ever-busy spot are of four-wheel-drive breed and many of the men wear their cowboy hats while eating. Cowbells add to the ranch-like bedlam about every five minutes to announce a birthday or an anniversary. We particularly like the log cabin–type booths. Stay with the beef; it's well selected, well cut, and well cooked. ■ *910 Front St (on old Hwy 30, a short detour from I-84, exit 285 eastbound or exit 306 westbound), Haines; (541)856-3639; $$; full bar; AE, DC, MC, V; checks OK; lunch Sun, dinner Wed–Mon.* ⚅

BAKER CITY

Baker's restful city park, old-time main street, and mature shade trees may give it a Midwest flavor, but the backdrop is decidedly Northwest. Located in the valley between the Wallowas and the Elkhorns, Baker makes a good base camp for forays into the nearby mountain Gold Rush towns. The **Oregon Trail Interpretive Center**, 4 miles east of I-84 on Highway 86, is worth the detour. The multimedia walk-through brings the Oregon Trail experience to life. Open every day except Christmas and New Year's Day, admission is now $5 per adult (but one day a month it is free); (541)523-1843.

 Ghost towns. The Elkhorn Mountains, west of Baker, contain most of the old mining towns, which you can tour on a 100-

mile loop from Baker (some on unpaved roads). The deserted towns of Granite, Bourne, Bonanza, and Whitney are well worth visiting. There's a restored narrow-gauge steam train in the now revitalized ghost town of Sumpter that operates between Memorial Day and Labor Day.

Anthony Lakes Ski Area, 20 miles west of North Powder, has good powder snow, a chairlift, and cross-country trails; (541)856-3277.

RESTAURANTS

The Phone Company Restaurant Ask any local what's the finest restaurant in town, and the answer is quickly The Phone Company. Keri Whitnah opened her restaurant in the classic 1910 building which once, indeed, housed the phone company (check out some of the old black-and-white photos on the wall). Whitnah's place is the favorite call of the locals less because of its location and more because it's one of the few places in town (if not the only one) that makes everything from scratch—nothing canned or bottled. The menu is small but has a few nice surprises such as warm brie with Northwest apples and tender grilled lamb chops (alongside Eastern Oregon favorites like a caesar and filet mignon). ■ *1926 1st St (at Washington), Baker City; (541)523-7997; $$; full bar; MC, V; checks OK; lunch Tues–Fri, dinner Tues–Sat.* &

LODGINGS

▼

▲

Geiser Grand Hotel [*unrated*] What for a long time has been a sore spot on Baker City's Main Street is now the town's centerpiece. The restored 1889 Geiser Grand Hotel is a massive three-story building that once offered a haven of gentility in a town full of rough-edged gold prospectors and lumberjacks. Restorers Barbara and Dwight Sidway made it their mission to nurse this historic but sagging building to a new—equally showy—beginning. A couple of years and $6 million later, the saloon is reopened and, at press time, the original 70 rooms were about to be unveiled as 30 new ones (bigger, and with private baths). Antiques, period wallpapers, and even a couple of 7-foot Chinese vases all contribute to evoking the 19th-century grace. And if the Sidways pay as close attention to the management of the hotel as they did to the reviving of it, their efforts will be generously rewarded. ■ *1996 Main St (downtown), Baker City, OR 97814; (541)523-1889; $$; full bar; AE, DIS, MC, V; checks OK; breakfast, lunch, dinner every day.* &

HALFWAY

Once just a midway stop between two bustling mining towns, Halfway is now the quiet centerpiece of Pine Valley—stashed between the fruitful southern slopes of the Wallowa Mountains and the steep cliffs of Hells Canyon.

Hells Canyon, the continent's deepest gorge, begins at Oxbow Dam, 16 miles east of Halfway. For spectacular views of the Snake River, drive from Oxbow to Joseph (take Highway 86 to Forest Road 39; summers only). Maps of the region's roads and trails are available from the Forest Service, just outside Halfway; (541)742-7511. The folks at **Wallowa Llamas** lead 3- to 7-day trips along the edge of Hells Canyon or into the pristine Eagle Cap Wilderness high in the Wallowas, while their surefooted beasts lug your gear and plenty of food; for a brochure or information, call (541)742-2961. For those who would rather experience the raging river up close, **Hells Canyon Adventures** in Oxbow arranges jet boat tours or combination excursions leaving from Hells Canyon Dam; call (541)785-3352.

LODGINGS

Birchleaf Bed and Breakfast Horse pastures, peach trees, and solitude are the attractions. This pretty home sits on a south-facing slope above Halfway—a little town on the edge of a big outdoors. The rooms are as simple as the town itself: nothing fancy. If it's summer, the owners are there to greet you. When the weather cools and business slows, they retreat to Baker City and leave the place in the capable hands of friendly local managers. Either way, you'll become part of the family. ■ *Rte 1, Box 91 (4½ miles north of Halfway), Halfway, OR 97834; (541)742-2990; $; no credit cards; checks OK (call ahead for winter schedule).*

ONTARIO

RESTAURANTS

Casa Jaramillo This Mexican cantina gives cool respite from the hot Eastern Oregon desert. Expanded and remodeled, it has a tropical atmosphere perfect for families. Since 1967, John Jaramillo and his family have been turning out authentic Mexican fare. Try the enchiladas rancheros, with fresh crunchy onions and a chile verde sauce that delivers. The guacamole is great. ■ *157 SE 2nd St (2 blocks south of Idaho Ave), Ontario; (541)889-9258; $; full bar; AE, MC, V; checks OK; lunch, dinner Tues–Sun.*

BURNS

The town of Burns, once the center of impressive cattle kingdoms ruled by legendary figures Pete French and William Hanley, is a welcome oasis in this desolate high-desert country. The look of the land, formed by 10 million years of volcanic activity, was branded on the American consciousness in a few decades by the thousands of Western movies filmed in the area.

Malheur National Wildlife Refuge, 37 miles south of Burns on Route 205, is one of the country's major bird refuges—184,000 acres of verdant marshland and lakes. It is an important stop for migrating waterfowl in spring and fall, and the summer breeding grounds for magnificent sandhill cranes (with wingspans approaching 100 inches), trumpeter swans, and many other birds; (541)493-2612; forrest_cameron@mail.fws.gov.

RESTAURANTS

Pine Room Cafe ★ Here's a cafe that has kept the same faithful clientele over the past 30 years, even with an ownership change. Careful preparations and interesting recipes are the reason: the chicken livers in brandy and wine sauce are different and popular, and the Oltmans still refuse to give out the secret ingredients of their German potato-dumpling soup, a local favorite. They also make their own bread and cut their own steaks in the kitchen. ■ *543 W Monroe St (at Egan), Burns; (541)573-6631; $$; full bar; MC, V; local checks only; dinner Tues–Sat.* &

LODGINGS

Best Western Ponderosa With 52 rooms, this is the preferred place to stay in Burns. It's blessed with a swimming pool to cool you off after a hot day's drive. What more? Pets are okay. ■ *577 W Monroe (on Hwy 20), Burns, OR 97720; (541)573-2047 or (800)528-1234; $; AE, DC, MC, V; no checks.* &

DIAMOND

LODGINGS

Diamond Hotel You might mistake Diamond for a ghost town; however, its six residents keep the looming ghosts at bay. Judy and Jerry Santillie, formerly of the Frenchglen Hotel, cater to those exploring Malheur territory. The Diamond now quintuples as hotel, general store (with gas), deli, post office, and late in the afternoon local watering hole. The five small bedrooms upstairs share two baths and a sitting area. The Santillies are full of high-desert stories. Judy used to be a ranch cook (there's always meat, potatoes, vegetables, salad, bread). A platter of tenderloin comes with slabs for every taste from well-done to "so rare that a good vet could get it back up on its feet." Desserts (perhaps a marionberry cobbler with ice cream or Judy's Guadalupe River Bottom Cake) are double—no, triple—the size you need them to be and that's okay with us. ■ *12 miles east of Hwy 205, Diamond; (541)493-1898; Box 10, Diamond, OR 97722; $; beer and wine; MC, V; checks OK; breakfast, dinner every day (hotel guests only).*

FRENCHGLEN

This beautiful little town (population 15) is a favorite stopover for those visiting the **Malheur National Wildlife Refuge** (see Burns introduction) or **Steens Mountain**, Frenchglen's biggest tourist attraction, which rises gently from the west to an elevation of 9,670 feet and then drops sharply to the Alvord Desert in the east. A dirt road goes all the way to the ridge top (summers only), and another skirts this massive escarpment—an adventurous day trip by the vast borax wastelands of the former Alvord Lake, numerous hot springs, and fishing lakes near the northeastern end of the route. Neither route is recommended if there's been much precipitation. Geologically, Steens forms the world's largest block fault, created by volcanic lava flows and glacial action. Contact the BLM office in Hines for information about Steens; (541)573-4400.

LODGINGS

Frenchglen Hotel ★ A small, white frame building that dates back to 1916 has eight small, plain bedrooms upstairs with shared baths, renting for about $48 a night; room 2 is the largest and nicest, and the only one with a view of Steens. Nothing's very square or level here, and that's part of the charm. Downstairs are a large screened-in veranda and the dining room. The current manager, John Ross, cooks up good, simple meals for guests and drop-by visitors. Ranch-style dinner is one seating only (6:30pm sharp) and reservations are a must. But if you miss dinner, John won't let you go hungry (this *is* ranch country). The hotel closes in winter, but will open for group bookings. ■ *60 miles south of Burns, Frenchglen; (541)493-2825; General Delivery, Frenchglen, OR 97736; $; beer and wine; MC, V; checks OK; breakfast, lunch, dinner every day (closed mid-Nov through mid-Mar).*

▼

Frenchglen

▲

WASHINGTON

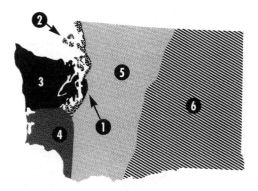

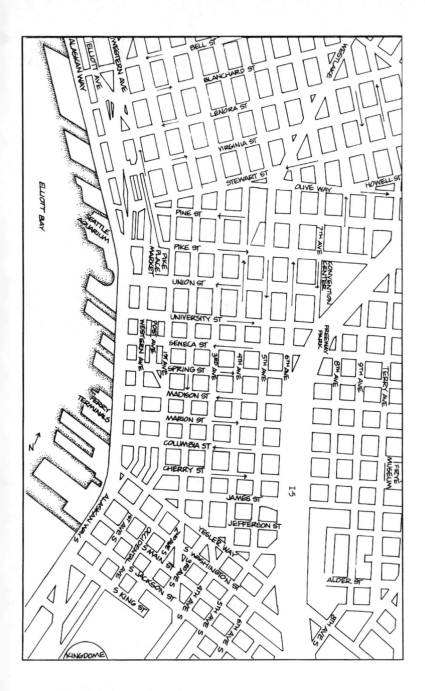

Seattle and Environs

Including Edmonds and Bothell to the north;
Woodinville, Redmond, Kirkland, Bellevue, Mercer Island, and
Issaquah to the east; Bainbridge Island to the west;
and Tukwila, Burien, and Kent to the south.

SEATTLE

Seattle is a charming metropolis grown up in the middle of an evergreen forest. It's a city famous for its enduring relationships with Boeing and Bill Gates, for the Space Needle and Pike Place Market, and for coffee, always coffee, available in steaming cups from mobile espresso carts that sprout on street corners like mushrooms after a good rain.

This is a town where cops ride bikes, farmers and fishmongers hawk their wares at open-air markets, gardeners putter be it January or July, and early-morning kayakers paddle in the wake of log booms and container ships that ply the city's busy waterways. Situated between sparkling Puget Sound and Lake Washington, and dotted with lakes, Seattle is nearly surrounded by water, with mountains just about everywhere you look. On clear days, Mount Rainier's distant snowcapped presence has even been known to halt commuter traffic—which has grown worse as the population grows and the city's bedroom communities spread farther afield.

But rapid growth and international sophistication have brought to this city outstanding restaurants, thriving cultural organizations, impressive athletic teams, and fabulous citywide festivals. What follows are a few highlights of Seattle's entertainment; for a detailed city guide, we refer you to our companion book, *Seattle Best Places*.

THE ARTS

Music. The Seattle Symphony has been a barometer of the city's growing stature in the music world, reaching a new level of consistency and artistic mastery under maestro Gerard Schwarz (and sure to crescendo with the opening of a state-of-the-art concert hall of its own, in 1998); (206) 443-4747. Sellout audiences have come to expect fresh and innovative productions from Seattle Opera, which has become a top-flight company under the leadership of Speight Jenkins, general director since 1983; (206) 389-7676. Chamber music has become a local passion, with the International Music Festival of Seattle in June (showcasing many top Russian and

European musicians, and including orchestral and vocal performances; (206)622-1392) and the Seattle Chamber Music Festival in July (at bucolic Lakeside School; (206)328-5606). Concert series presented by the Early Music Guild, the Northwest Chamber Orchestra, and the International Chamber Music and President's Piano Series at the University of Washington's Meany Hall for the Performing Arts, (206)543-4880, plus a burgeoning number of performances by fine local groups, round out the winter and spring seasons. Choral music is experiencing an upsurge, as evidenced by fine performances of the Tudor Choir, Seattle Men's Chorus, Seattle Choral Company, and many others.

Theater. Touring Broadway blockbusters take the stage at the glamorously refurbished Paramount Theater, while at the splendid 5th Avenue Theatre, the house mainstay is new productions of classic musicals (and an occasional Broadway-bound experiment). The nationally acclaimed Seattle Repertory Theatre ("The Rep") mixes recent off-Broadway and regional theater successes with the occasional updated classic and Broadway-bound "commercial" fare. A Contemporary Theatre (ACT), now at home in the remodeled Eagles Auditorium, sticks mainly to contemporary plays, particularly new works by young American and English playwrights.

An explosion of experimentation has occurred among the dozens of smaller theater companies around town, resulting in funky, campy, classical, and avant-garde theater worth checking out. Half-price tickets are available to both fringe and larger theaters through Ticket/Ticket, by walking up to either location (Capitol Hill and downtown) on the day of the show; call (206)324-2744 for directions.

Dance. Under the guidance of artistic directors Kent Stowell and Francia Russell, Pacific Northwest Ballet has evolved into one of the top regional companies in America. Its regular season mixes masterworks with new pieces, and the Christmas highlight is a breathtaking realization of *The Nutcracker* with sets by Maurice Sendak; (206)292-2787. Dance and other contemporary performance (dramatic, comic, musical, multimedia) can be seen at On the Boards (various venues; scheduled to move to Queen Anne in fall 1998; (206)325-7901); and the World Dance Series presents an ever-thrilling roster of touring companies at Meany Hall; (206)543-4880.

Visual Arts. The Robert Venturi–designed Seattle Art Museum, with Jonathan Borofsky's towering sculpture, *Hammering Man*, at the main entrance, has by now become an established part of the downtown skyline. The building on University Street between First and Second Avenues houses the museum's permanent collections, while the Seattle Asian Art Museum, in the former SAM location in Volunteer Park, offers one of the most extraordinary collections of Asian art in the country; contact both museums at (206)654-3100. The Henry Art Gallery at the

University of Washington mounts thoughtful and challenging shows; (206)543-2280. The city's main commercial art galleries are found predominantly (though not exclusively) in the Pioneer Square area and along First Avenue; most gallery openings are the first Thursday of every month.

OTHER THINGS TO DO

Nightlife. There are clubs all over town, but Seattle's much-ballyhooed music scene is neighborhood-centered. Pioneer Square offers various acts, from jazz to Cajun to rock 'n' roll; Ballard brings in the blues, as well as traditional and new folk music; the alternative music scene makes its mark in the Denny Regrade and Belltown neighborhoods; and DJ-controlled club music has bodies pulsating on Capitol Hill. Dimitriou's Jazz Alley, one of the West Coast's finest jazz clubs, provides an intimate venue and draws an international roster of well-known performers. There are good coffeehouses everywhere, but particularly in the University District and on Capitol Hill (which is also the unofficial playground for Seattle's sizable gay and lesbian community). Fremont, with its many brewpubs, taverns, coffeehouses, and inexpensive restaurants, offers much in the way of nighttime haunts and hangouts.

Exhibits. The Woodland Park Zoo is a world leader in naturalistic displays, as evidenced by its open African savanna and the exotic Asian elephant forest; (206)684-4800. The Museum of Flight, south of the city, is notable for its sophisticated design and impressive collection; (206)764-5720. Pacific Science Center, part of Seattle Center, features engrossing hands-on science exhibits for school-age children, with traveling shows and a planetarium aimed at all age groups; (206)443-2880. Amid the tourist bustle along the downtown waterfront is the Seattle Aquarium, with illuminated displays and convincing re-creations of coastal and intertidal ecosystems, along with a full complement of sharks, octopi, salmon, playful sea otters, and other Puget Sound inhabitants; (206)386-4320.

Parks. Seattle's horticultural climate is among the finest in the world—damp and mild all year—so the parks are spectacular and numerous. Washington Park Arboretum, with 5,500 species of plants and gentle pathways amid azaleas and rhododendrons, is the loveliest, (206)543-8800; Discovery Park, with grassy meadows and steep sea cliffs, is the wildest, (206)386-4236; Green Lake, with its surrounding running/walking/in-line skating track, is by far the most active. Freeway Park, built over I-5 downtown, is the most urban.

Sports. Seattle's professional teams have been known to get less attention than the venues in which they play (thanks to past controversy over the Kingdome and the Mariners' new ballpark). But local fans continue to do the wave for their home teams, particularly the Mariners, (206)628-3555, whose who'd-a-thunk-it successes in recent years brought new life to local baseball. The Seattle SuperSonics continue to tear up the courts from early November to late April, often playing to sellout crowds, (206)281-5850, while the Seahawks don't get as much support these days as the UW Huskies (who play in one of the land's most beautiful football stadiums).

Shopping. The downtown area has designer-name stores, plus some excellent full-line department stores (including the flagship hometown favorite, Nordstrom, and the Bon Marché). Westlake Center, a slick mall smack in the middle of the downtown congestion, is an appealing place to shop, but of the specialty shopping areas, we favor Pike Place Market and Upper Queen Anne (for foodstuffs), Capitol Hill and Fremont (arty, funky, and oh-so-Seattle), and Pioneer Square (for fine arts and crafts and some of the city's best bookshops).

Transportation. The Metro bus is free before 7pm in downtown's commercial core; otherwise, the fare is 85 cents within the city ($1.10 during peak hours) and $1.10 if you cross the city line ($1.60 peak); (206)553-3000. Another common commute (and a cheap thrill for visitors) is a trip on one of the scenic **Washington State Ferries**, which cross Puget Sound frequently to various destinations; (206)464-6400 or (800)843-3779. The **Monorail**, which connects Seattle Center to the downtown retail district, offers a 90-second, 1⅕-mile ride, leaving at 15-minute intervals from 9am to 11pm.

RESTAURANTS

Campagne ★★★★ White linen, hardwood floors, tiny vases of flowers, and wall space dedicated to wine bottles help set the charming yet sophisticated mood at Campagne. Located in a quiet courtyard in Pike Place Market, this gem of a restaurant is inspired by the southern reaches of France, yet takes full advantage of the Northwest's cornucopia of fine foodstuffs. Owner Peter Lewis, the city's most gracious host, oversees a staff composed of Seattle's finest servers. The always-stunning fare reflects the day's catch, the season's offerings, and the influence of French-schooled chef-exec Jim Drohman, long a fixture in Campagne's kitchen, who took over in 1997 where his predecessor, Tamara Murphy, left off. There are many successes here—an inspired wine list not the least among them. Lavender-fried quail and meltingly rich duck confit star in salads. French soul food—sweetbreads, foie gras—is lavished with careful attention, while fish and fowl get delicate, masterful treatment. A cafe and late-night menu is available in the exceptionally romantic bar. Dining at a courtyard table and then slowly sipping a Framboise Sauvage is the next best thing to a trip to France. (See also review for Cafe Campagne.) ■ *86 Pine St (between Stewart and Pine on Post Alley), Seattle; (206)728-2800; $$$; full bar; AE, DC, MC, V; no checks; dinner every day.* ᕗ

Lampreia ★★★★ Scott Carsberg's sleek restaurant exudes sophistication. Although plate-as-palette—with splashes of color and unexpected combinations of flavor dazzling the eye and the tongue—has become practically synonymous with the Seattle food scene, Carsberg offers a gentle reprieve: a minimalist approach for maximum effect. Simplicity is key—from what's on the walls (a warm-toned paint and little else) to what's on the table (heavy silver, a fine linen napkin, a candle) to what's on the plate (food so visually understated that the depth of flavor comes as a shock). Zealous use of seasonal, regional, and organic ingredients is akin to religion here. The intermezzo course acts as a light meal in itself: perhaps a slice of foie gras atop a bed of spicy-sweet red cabbage, or fresh razor clams, simply and perfectly sautéed. Entrees might include a tender veal chop tinged with lemon zest, or the sweetest of spot prawns, resting on a cloud of potatoes and graced with a shaving of truffles. A fine selection of artisan cheeses makes a nice alternative to dessert, and the wine list is carefully wrought and reasonably priced. Some find the service a bit too-too; we find it as polished as the silver. ■ *2400 1st Ave (corner of Battery), Seattle; (206) 443-3301; $$$; full bar; AE, MC, V; no checks; dinner Tues–Sat.*

Rover's ★★★★ French chef Thierry Rautureau is a handsome elf with a warm wit, a world of personality, and a four-star hand in the kitchen. His restaurant, a small house tucked into a garden courtyard near Madison Park, has been expanded. Best of all, the dining room is now elegantly redecorated. Dinners here are marvelously sauced, classically French-inspired treatments of not-strictly-Northwest fare. Rautureau's forte is seafood, and he's adept at finding the best-quality ingredients—even if it means importing turbot directly from France. Portions are served with a generous hand, and when you see what he can do with monkfish liver, you'll never say "never" again. A whole Maine lobster, out of the shell, steamed and served with a truffle purée, will make you savor every mouthful. Tender pink slices of venison with a peppercorn sauce taste surprisingly delicate. Expect utterly professional service, and expect sticker shock when perusing the sublime wine list. For an unforgettable experience, take advantage of the chef's elaborate tasting menus. Dining in the courtyard is enchanting. ■ *2808 E Madison St (1½ blocks from the Arboretum, at 28th), Seattle; (206) 325-7442; $$$; beer and wine; AE, DC, MC, V; checks OK; dinner Tues–Sat.*

Adriatica ★★★ Climbing the challenging flights of stairs leading to the Adriatica may be the culinary equivalent of reaching the summit of Mount Rainier: always worth the effort. It's been nearly 20 years since Jim Malevitsis opened this handsome, romantic, tri-level dinner house, long admired for its

Mediterranean-inspired fare, carefully crafted wine list, and striking eastward view of Lake Union. The menu hasn't changed dramatically over the years, but the once-stunning view is now obstructed by an office complex. Finally, patrons have stopped fighting for a window table and have turned instead to the main event: dinner. In the comfortably cloistered warren of small dining rooms you may sup on herb-kissed grilled meats, fresh seafood, and seductive pastas (fettuccine with smoked duck is a standout). Start with calamari fritti—renowned for the garlic quotient of its skordalia—and finish with a chocolate espresso soufflé. Then head upstairs to enjoy an after-dinner drink in the elegant little bar. ■ *1107 Dexter Ave N (corner of Aloha), Seattle; (206) 285-5000; $$$; full bar; AE, DC, MC, V; checks OK; dinner every day.*

Al Boccalino ★★★ Rustic Al Boccalino is equally good for a business get-together, a special celebration, or a meaningful dinner for two. Intoxicating drifts of herbs and garlic greet you as you enter the old brick building just off Pioneer Square. A skewed shape to the two rooms—accented with dark wood and stained glass—creates an atmosphere of intimacy and intrigue. The menu features the best of southern Italian cuisine with an expanded focus on Italy's other regions. Split for two, any pasta choice would make a great first course. In these times of restraint, the bistecca alla Fiorentina—a perfectly delicious, perfectly broiled, and perfectly *enormous* aged porterhouse—is not for the faint of heart. The chefs know a thing or three about timing, resulting in creamy risotto, moist vitello, and gamberoni that are never sautéed longer than necessary. The wine list is solidly Italian, as is the noise level when things get busy. Special kudos for gracious service and great, low-key, moderately priced lunches. ■ *1 Yesler Way (at Alaskan Way), Seattle; (206) 622-7688; $$$; beer and wine; AE, DC, MC, V; checks OK; lunch Mon–Fri, dinner every day.* &

Andaluca (Mayflower Park Hotel) ★★★ Soulful, sexy, small but splashy, Andaluca is a feast for the senses—a colorful paean to the coastal Mediterranean. Romance is in the air, even when the room is filled with business folk, as it often is at lunch. Glowing rosewood booths, fresh flowers, and textured walls in deep jewel tones that match the fancy glass bread plates create an intimate setting for the lusty dishes put before you. Chef Don Curtiss combines the ingredients of the Northwest with a bit of Spain, a touch of Italy, a soupçon of France, a hint of Greece, and traces of the Levant to create food that is as dramatic on the palate as it is on the plate: broiled ouzo prawns, zarzuela (a shellfish stew), seared lamb loin in vine leaves, Cabrales-crusted beef (Spanish blue cheese and bread crumbs). Linger at the bar over a few "small plates and sharables" enjoyed with a specialty cocktail—perhaps an herb-and-vodka-infused gazpacho Bloody

Mary. Or stop in for dessert. ■ *407 Olive Way (near corner of 4th), Seattle; (206) 382-6999; $$$; full bar; AE, DC, DIS, MC, V; checks OK; breakfast every day, lunch Mon–Sat, dinner every day.* &

Anthony's Pier 66 ■ Bell Street Diner ★★★ Ever since this upscale/midscale, upstairs/downstairs, sprawling restaurant complex opened downtown, seafood with a view hasn't been the same. Upstairs at Anthony's Pier 66 you might drink a bracing ginger-infused martini at the bar while you hold out for a snug booth in the graceful arc of the handsome koa wood–accented dining room. Thrill to such appetizers as the "Poke Trio"—a Hawaiian-style starter that elevates ahi to new heights—or the "Potlatch"—a local shellfish-fest known to cause a swoon—and then make your way through a menu heavy with seafood (don't miss the crab cakes). Presentation points are well earned here, and service deserves a nod, as it does downstairs at the decidedly more casual **Bell Street Diner**. Fans of its sister restaurant, Chinooks (see review), will appreciate the menu and the industrial-style decor that has been cloned here to great effect. Sit at the open kitchen (where stools flank a gleaming stainless-steel counter), in the bar (with seating both indoors and out), or in the bustling dining room, and order the justly popular mahi-mahi tacos or the excellent tempura-fried seafood. For quick-stop cheap eats, there's Anthony's Fish Bar, an adjoining walk-up window on the promenade. ■ *2201 Alaskan Way (at Pier 66), Seattle; (206) 448-6688; $$$ (Anthony's Pier 66), $$ (Bell Street Diner); full bar; AE, DC, DIS, MC, V; local checks only; dinner every day (Anthony's Pier 66); lunch, dinner every day (Bell Street Diner).* &

Cafe Campagne ★★★ Peter Lewis's very French bistro, Cafe Campagne, nestled just below its stylish upscale sibling, Campagne, often proves too small to accommodate those who throng to this Pike Place Market favorite day and night. Whether you sit at a cherry-wood table or at the elegant counter, be sure to utter the most important words spoken here: garlic mashed potatoes. A very French omelet can be had any time of day. At lunch or dinner, the delicate pan-fried oysters, herby rotisserie chicken, or classic steak frites will put you over the edge. Breakfast on brioche French toast or an elegant pastry served with Plugra butter and lavender honey, and you'll be transported to Provence in the time it takes to say *"Plus de cafe, s'il vous plaît."* ■ *1600 Post Alley (at Pine St), Seattle; (206) 728-2233; $$; full bar; AE, DC, MC, V; no checks; breakfast, lunch, dinner Mon–Sat, brunch Sun.* &

Cafe Lago ★★★ Chef/owners Jordi Viladas and Carla Leonardi fuel the fires at this rustic Montlake cafe reminiscent of trattorias that dot the hills of Tuscany. A flaming brick oven, butcher-paper-topped tables nestled together, and prettily stenciled walls entice some of the most discerning pasta-lovers in the city. The menu includes a strong selection of antipasti and thin-crusted pizzas; a short list of pastas; and meat, fish, or fowl, grill-kissed and artfully sided. Start with the astounding antipasto sampler, which might include a multitude of cheeses, roasted red peppers, a head of roasted garlic, a selection of cured meats, and crostini swabbed with olive paste. Fruit-wood imparts a smoky flavor to the fabulous thin-crusted pizzas, while the handmade pastas give new meaning to the word ethereal. (Oh! the lasagne, the gnocchi, the butter-drenched cappellacci con zucca!) The wine list runs the gamut in prices, with a few Northwest offerings and some rather fine Italian bottlings. High ceilings make for a noisy room, but, hey, that's Italian. ■ *2305 24th E (5 blocks south of the Montlake Bridge), Seattle; (206)329-8005; $$; beer and wine; MC, V; checks OK; dinner Tues–Sun.* ⅄

Canlis ★★★ Everyone has an opinion about Canlis. Some say it's Seattle's finest celebratory restaurant, others say it's an anachronism. We say you gotta love a place this dedicated to making the customer feel like visiting royalty. Owners Chris and Alice Canlis, intent on enticing the "next generation" of Canlis-goers, recently sunk $1.5 million into a structural remodel of the nearly 50-year-old restaurant, updated the menu to take better advantage of the Northwest's bounty, traded in their waitresses' cumbersome traditional kimonos for swaying pantsuits, and continue to offer luxe dining in luxe surroundings at luxe prices. Nonetheless, there remains a timeless quality about the place—from the twinkling lights around Lake Union below, to the well-heeled, well-aged patrons sipping martinis, to the sound of "Happy Birthday" being played for the umpteenth time at the splendid piano bar. Yes, you can still order Canlis Steak Pierre, Peter Canlis Shrimp Capri, and the famous Canlis Salad (an overdressed knockoff of a caesar), but the menu also boasts an exceptional sashimi appetizer; crisp, moist, Dungeness crab cakes; and a mixed grill sure to please any carnivore. The wine list makes the phone book look like Cliff Notes, and though you can spend $1,000 on a single bottle, there are options in the $30 range worth savoring. ■ *2576 Aurora Ave N (at Halliday just south of the Aurora Bridge), Seattle; (206)283-3313; $$$; full bar; AE, DC, DIS, MC, V; checks OK; dinner Mon–Sat.* ⅄

Chez Shea ■ Shea's Lounge ★★★ You might walk through the Market a hundred times and not know that Sandy Shea's tiny, romantic hideaway is perched just above, looking out over the Sound. Dinner at Chez Shea is a prix-fixe affair, with four courses prepared by adventurous young chef Peter Morrison, reflecting the bounty of the season and ingredients fresh from the market stalls below. A winter meal might begin with a ricotta-and-Parmesan-rich soufflé set atop a roasted tomato sauce, followed by hubbard squash soup, tangy with diced cabbage and thickened with pearly rice. The main course could be a veal shank, braised in red wine with olives, capers, and rosemary. Or moist Alaskan halibut encrusted with peanuts, bedded over cellophane noodles and perfumed with citrus and ginger. Service is always sure and gracious.

Shea's Lounge is an unpretentious, sexy little bistro and bar wedded to Chez Shea by way of a common door (and a common kitchen). The modest menu offers "lounge pizzas" and other light fare strongly influenced by the flavors of the Mediterranean. It's the perfect place to meet a friend for a little something before or after. ■ *Corner Market Building, Suite 34 (across from the clock in Pike Place Market, 2nd floor), Seattle; (206) 467-9990; $$$ (Chez Shea), $$ (Shea's Lounge); full bar; AE, MC, V; checks OK; dinner Tues–Sun.*

Dahlia Lounge ★★★ Seattle learned much about Northwest foods from kitchen maverick Tom Douglas, and grew accustomed to his clever juxtaposition of cultures within a meal—indeed, within a plate—first at Cafe Sport, where he reigned as head chef, and later here at the Dahlia. Never resting on his laurels, Douglas next opened the fabulous Etta's Seafood, followed by his latest contribution to the local dining-and-drinking scene, Palace Kitchen (see reviews). He now shuttles among the trio of very different restaurants, yet even in his absence, the Dahlia's food is executed with an artist's eye and an epicure's palate. The restaurant's scenic appeal lies in a stylish two-level dining landscape of vermilion, gold, and brocade—and the intriguing presentations on your plate. Plump, grilled, five-spice quail is drizzled with pomegranate jus and sided with a Vietnamese spring roll. Braised lamb shank is complemented by toasted couscous and spicy harissa sauce. And you'll not find a better version of the salty-sweet Japanese specialty, kasu cod, than that served here. As for desserts: they're the best in town—and we'd happily grant a fourth star to the perfect coconut cream pie. ■ *1904 4th Ave (between Stewart and Virginia), Seattle; (206) 682-4142; www.tomdouglas.com; $$$; full bar; AE, DC, DIS, MC, V; checks OK; lunch Mon–Fri, dinner every day.* &

El Gaucho ★★★ Paul Mackay, who managed Seattle's original El Gaucho (known for its mink-lined booths, flaming shish kabobs, cafe Diablo, and other tableside hanky-panky), has resurrected the gone-but-not-forgotten steak house in a new venue: Belltown. The '90s version—a big, dark, dramatic, windowless space—brings a kitschy chicness to the memory of the hallowed haunt where Sinatra would have felt at home. The bar crowd sip martinis as jazz standards emanate from a baby grand; those inclined head into the cigar lounge to puff a stogie. Patrons seated at comfy banquettes in the theater-in-the-round-style dining room share chateaubriand-for-two or custom-aged steaks and big, honking baked potatoes with all the trimmings. They watch in awe as swords of lamb tenderloin are vodka-flamed before their eyes. Seafood lovers don't get short shrift here, either: they can dredge garlic bread in buttery Killer Shrimp or spoon saffron-scented broth from an artful bouill-abaisse. Bananas Foster proves both decadent and sublime. ■ *2505 1st Ave (near Wall), Seattle; (206) 728-1337; $$$; full bar; AE, DC, MC, V; checks OK; dinner every day.* &

Etta's Seafood ★★★ Tom Douglas's '90s-style seafood house—with one small, conversation-friendly dining room and another larger and much noisier noshery complete with a bar and counter seating—occupies the husk of the late Cafe Sport (where Douglas first made his mark before achieving culinary fame). Only Tom Douglas would have the chutzpah to list starter courses like fire-grilled tamales with Jack cheese and an-cho chiles ($3 each) alongside beluga caviar ($45 an ounce). His lengthy menu dares you to choose between such wonders as a simple wedge of iceberg lettuce topped with an extraordinary blue cheese dressing or steamed, chilled octopus with green-papaya slaw and fried ginger. Choosing from among the many "sides" to go along with his signature pit-roasted king salmon or whole fried tilapia is even more daunting. (Hint: Don't miss the red bliss mashed potatoes.) Start with an ass-kicking Bloody Mary, and save room for dessert. ■ *2020 Western Ave (north end of Pike Place Market), Seattle; (206) 443-6000; www.tomdoug las.com; $$$; full bar; AE, DC, JCB, MC, V; checks OK; lunch, dinner every day, brunch Sat–Sun.* &

Flying Fish ★★★ Fans have been storming the doors since this colorful, imaginative fish house opened, and why not? Chef/owner Christine Keff assembles a daily fresh sheet that pays lavish homage to seafood—and to Asian seasonings. Expect sparkling renditions of the usual Northwest players: Dun-geness crab (in a fiery Sichuan pepper sauce), grilled king salmon (in a tomato-ginger broth), and halibut (cheeks, treated to a Thai curry). But you'll also find exotic imports: fillet of arc-tic char in a rich chanterelle sauce; moist escolar with chipotle vinaigrette; or firm opah swathed with red pepper oil. Most fun is ordering by the pound. Platters meant for sharing often in-clude "sister-in-law" mussels, spicy Texas barbecue shrimp, or Keff's pièce de résistance—whole, fried, lemongrass-marinated snapper served with fresh herbs and Vietnamese rice pancakes. This airy, clattering place proves too loud for some, but the hip-sters that crowd the bar and case the joint from tables perched high above the dining room don't seem to mind. ■ *2234 1st Ave (at Bell), Seattle; (206) 728-8595; $$; full bar; AE, DC, MC, V; checks OK; dinner every day.* &

Fullers (Seattle Sheraton) ★★★ A hushed elegance complements the stunning display of contemporary Northwest glass
and artwork. You sink into a high-backed, almost-private banquette, or into the cushioned comfort of a table next to the
calming waterfall of a George Tsutakawa–designed fountain.
"Hmmmm," you say. "Nice, in a stuffy, museum-ish way." Prepare for an attitude adjustment. Your taste buds will be spun in
all directions by chef Monique Barbeau. Bite-size sashimi-grade
tuna, flavored with shiso leaf and tossed with wasabe vinaigrette, shows up in an edible potato-parsnip basket; a composed
salad of watermelon and feta cheese sports tart red sumac and
sage pesto; and a brace of lightly stuffed Moroccan-spiced quail
comes perfumed with preserved lemons. Some diners would
be better off with a trio of Ellensburg lamb chops in a port
demiglace with a luscious potato–goat cheese tart—staid by
comparison. You'll appreciate the fabulous molten-chocolate
dessert, the fussy press-pot coffee service, and the chance to
prove to yourself that hotel-restaurant fine dining is not a con-
tradiction in terms. ■ *1400 6th Ave (between Pike and Union),
Seattle; (206)447-5544; $$$; full bar; AE, MC, V; checks OK;
lunch Mon–Fri, dinner Mon–Sat.* &

Georgian Room (Four Seasons Olympic Hotel) ★★★ A grand
space for those grand occasions, the Georgian Room, with its
high ceilings, ornate chandeliers, and all the accoutrements of
fine dining, will take you back in time to a place that—believe
it or not—still exists. A tuxedoed maître d' pours your martini
from an elegant shaker, a staff of professional waiters dressed
in full *Love Boat* regalia tend to your every need, and a pianist
tinkles the ivories in the center of the room. Come prepared to
pay a lot for the experience. Chef Kerry Sear composes a warm
salad of winter cabbage speckled with duck cracklings and
wearing a perfect slice of foie gras. White truffle risotto with
black truffle sauce is heaven with each bite. Entrees appear as
objets d'art: a rack of lamb might crown a plate garnished with
garlic-stuffed olives and Swiss chard, and four joints of tender
pheasant come sauced with caramelized onions. Private parties
can reserve the Petite Georgian. Afterward, step into the Geor-
gian Terrace for a very civilized Cognac and cigar. ■ *411 Uni-
versity St (in the Four Seasons Hotel, at 4th and University),
Seattle; (206)621-7889; $$$; full bar; AE, DC, MC, V; no checks;
breakfast every day, dinner Mon–Sat.* &

The Hunt Club (Sorrento Hotel) ★★★ The Hunt Club remains
yet another fine example of Seattle's excellent hotel dining
tradition. The clubby bar and carefully partitioned dining
room—considered a bit dark and cloistered by some—are
warmed with burnished mahogany paneling and deep red
brickwork. Chef Brian Scheeser is now overseeing this stel-
lar kitchen—and a menu whose rich reductions and careful

▼

Seattle

Restaurants

▲

flavorings continues to impress. We've been wowed with the naturally sweet and artfully spiced butternut squash ravioli; a deep, lavender-stoked loin of lamb; the roasted smokiness of a fillet of king salmon; and the solicitous yet affable service. After dinner, savvy patrons retire to the Sorrento's elegant fireplace lounge for after-dinner refreshment enjoyed with a piano accompaniment. ■ *900 Madison St (at Terry), Seattle; (206)343-6156; $$$; full bar; AE, DC, DIS, MC, V; checks OK; breakfast, lunch, tea, dinner every day, brunch Sat–Sun.* &

Il Bistro ★★★ Through the years, Il Bistro has been a cherished refuge down a narrow cobblestone street in the crook of the arm of Pike Place Market. The low-ceilinged intimate rooms, rounded arches, and whitewashed walls make this sexy Euro-bistro—now moving into its third decade—a great place to enjoy food, wine, and the company of friends. The lower-level bar is a favorite spot to linger over an aperitif or share a late-night supper. There are always interesting specials (such as tiny morel mushrooms playing inspired complement to a tangle of tagliatelle), but this is a place where many patrons know what to order before they leave home. Il Bistro consistently serves one of the best racks of lamb in Seattle—and just the right wines to go along with it (there's a lengthy list of Chiantis). ■ *93-A Pike St (just below Read All About It in Pike Place Market), Seattle; (206)682-3049; $$$; full bar; AE, DC, MC, V; no checks; dinner every day.*

Il Terrazzo Carmine ★★★ Dining at Carmine Smeraldo's venerable Italian restaurant is an event, whether you come for lunch or for dinner. Graze through the antipasti and watch for Seattle's rich and famous, who are likely to be dining beside you in this comfortably airy restaurant or on the outside terrace. Deciding among the many pastas is a feat (consider ordering a half portion as a first course). As for the main courses, sweetbreads with prosciutto and peas arrive lightly smothered in a wonderful wine sauce. Fork-tender scaloppine of veal is dressed with a buttery lemon sauce and capers. Wine-braised osso buco happily appears with grilled polenta (the better to soak up the last of that glorious "gravy"). Those looking for a light meal might sit in the bar, share a couple of antipasti, choose a bottle of wine from the extensive list, and call it dinner. ■ *411 1st Ave S (near King), Seattle; (206)467-7797; $$$; full bar; AE, DC, DIS, MC, V; no checks; lunch Mon–Fri, dinner Mon–Sat.* &

Kaspar's ★★★ Convenient to Seattle Center (hallelujah for valet parking!), this handsomely appointed dinner house is a great opening act for the pre-theater/opera/ballet crowd—and an elegant place to settle in for the evening whatever the occasion. Swiss-born and -trained chef Kaspar Donier imaginatively couples classic international cooking styles with seasonal Northwest ingredients. The best of the results can be astonishing, and hard-core fans might reserve a seat at the "chef's table" in the kitchen to watch him at work. Expect such dishes as Muscovy duck breast with a gingery fruit salsa, or perfectly sautéed sea scallops with a spicy bacon sauce over fresh spinach. Desserts consistently reveal the deft hand of a classical pro. Kaspar's wife, Nancy, keeps a watchful eye up front, while his brother, Markus, acts as sommelier. In the small but comfortable wine bar, dozens of wines by the glass are complemented by a short bar menu and a drop-dead gorgeous array of inexpensive "tastes." ■ *19 W Harrison (at 1st Ave W), Seattle; (206)298-0123; $$$; full bar; AE, MC, V; no checks; dinner Mon–Sat.* ⅋

Le Gourmand ★★★ Seattle's foodies always seem to be buzzing about some more fashionable place. But this unprepossessing Ballard storefront is where Bruce Naftaly, one of the founding fathers of Northwest regional cooking, quietly and carefully employs classic French techniques while relying on the freshest local ingredients. A pair of capable servers attend a diminutive dining room—its trompe l'oeil wall replete with trees and flowers, its ceiling painted like a clear spring day—and deftly answer questions about the small seasonal menu and the French/Northwest wine list. Dinner here is a three-course prix-fixe affair including appetizer, entree, and salad (cost is based on the main course, and it is a steal). You might begin with creamy blintzes enfolding Sally Jackson's sheep's cheese, or order mussels infused with the herbal flavors of sweet cicely and lovage. Among the entrees, perhaps a delicately poached salmon fillet, roast duck with an intense black currant sauce, or a noble rack of lamb. You'll finish with a salad of wild greens feathered with calendulas, nasturtiums, and rose petals from the backyard garden. ■ *425 NW Market St (corner of 6th), Seattle; (206)784-3463; $$$; beer and wine; AE, MC, V; checks OK; dinner Wed–Sat.*

The Painted Table (Alexis Hotel) ★★★ The gorgeous hand-painted plates are just for looks, but once the artwork's removed from the table you won't be let down by its replacement. Here in this deeply colorful, two-tiered dining room, Asian influences abound, and desserts are as lovely in every way as that which comes before them. Don't miss chef-exec Tim Kelley's by-now-famous goat cheese and vegetable "salad"—a layered tower of grilled eggplant, creamy chèvre, oven-dried tomatoes, and onion confit. On a seasonally changing menu, mango glaze moistens a baby quail while Chinese five-spice adds depth of flavor. Chile-garlic broth clings to fine strands of pasta but never overwhelms choice morsels of rock shrimp. Side dishes refuse to play second fiddle to such melodic renderings as mustard-glazed Oregon rabbit, pan-roasted monkfish, or crisp breast of Muscovy duck. At lunch, there's a knockout hoisin chicken club among other tonier offerings, but well-meaning service is far less polished than at dinner. ■ *92 Madison St (at 1st), Seattle; (206) 624-3646; $$$; full bar; AE, DC, MC, V; no checks; breakfast every day, lunch Mon–Fri, dinner every day.*

Palace Kitchen ★★★ The latest Tom Douglas invention marries a palatial open kitchen and a serious bar scene in a dramatic setting that's as casual as it is sophisticated. Whether you're seated at the enormous tile-topped bar (where martinis come in individual mini-shakers), in a wooden booth, a storefront banquette, or the private room (all with a view of the action—of which there is plenty), you can eat and drink yourself into ecstatic oblivion. Make a meal of finger foods without spending a fortune: fat, spicy, grilled chicken wings; crisp-fried, semolina-coated anchovies; housemade sopressata sausage; a killer cheese plate. Up the ante and order the night's applewood-grilled special—spit-roasted meat, poultry, or whole grilled fish. Seafood gets special treatment here, as does dessert (you'll recognize your favorites from the Dahlia and Etta's; this is the dessert kitchen for all of Douglas's restaurants). The fun, informative wine list is the most entertaining in town. ■ *2030 5th Ave (corner of Lenora), Seattle; (206) 448-2001; www.tom-douglas.com; $$; full bar; AE, DC, MC, V; checks OK; dinner every day.* &

Pirosmani ★★★ Set in a turn-of-the-century home, with a warren of small, candlelit rooms, Pirosmani both intrigues and delights. Chef Laura Dewell's menu offers a spirited interpretation of the foods of the former Soviet Republic of Georgia, whose latitudinal kinship with the Mediterranean provides the impetus for a menu that also borrows from that culinary treasure trove. Well-schooled servers will introduce you to a trio of Georgian condiments. You might spoon the plummy, sweet-spicy *tkremali* onto *khachapuri* (rounds of flat bread oozing feta and mozzarella), or sass up knobs of *khinkali* (meat-stuffed dumplings) with the potent chile-and-garlic-spiked ajika. *Svaneti*, a beguiling mix of dry seasonings, can be sprinkled on just about everything. A Georgian classic, braised duck Satsivi, is smothered in a thick walnut sauce with the nuances of coriander, cinnamon, cayenne, paprika, and fenugreek. At press time, Dewell has announced plans to close the restaurant, but to reopen later in a new location and with a broader menu. A unique and special place, watch for this change. ■ *2220 Queen Anne Ave N (between Boston and McGraw), Seattle; (206) 285-3360; $$$; beer and wine; AE, MC, V; checks OK; dinner Tues–Sat.*

Place Pigalle ★★★ Long on charm, short on space, this classic Seattle bistro with a peekaboo Puget Sound view is everything a stylish Northwest restaurant should be, and more. Small wonder, then, that locals find owner Bill Frank's hideaway in Pike Place Market the perfect spot to sip an eau-de-vie, lunch with a friend, or engage in a romantic dinner à deux. A range of intriguing dishes combines the freshness of Northwest ingredients with recipes that speak here of France and Italy, there of Mexico and Japan, all filtered through the imagination of very capable chefs. You may sample something as simple as onion soup gratinée (with its beefy broth, silky onions, and chewy Gruyère) or as sophisticated as a saddle of rabbit, rolled with roasted eggplant, red pepper, spinach, and feta, and treated to a side of sweet root vegetables. On sunny days, a small crowded skyway offers outdoor seating used by those anxious to catch every daylight ray. When it's gray, there's no better place to perch than at the jewel of a bar. ■ *81 Pike St (under the clock and down the walkway behind the pig at Pike Place Market), Seattle; (206) 624-1756; $$$; full bar; AE, MC, V; no checks; lunch, dinner Mon–Sat.*

Ponti Seafood Grill ★★★ Ponti, tucked almost under the Fremont Bridge, might inspire dreams of the Mediterranean, with its canalside perch, stucco walls, red-tiled roof, and elegantly understated dining rooms. But its true inspiration is defined by its food, not its mood. Call it pan-Asian, call it fusion cuisine, but give credit where it is due: to chef Alvin Binuya, who continues to oversee the menu here as he sets his sights on a new sibling venue, Axis, which opened in Belltown at press time. The menu borrows from an array of ethnic flavors (with more than a passing nod to Asia): expect cross-cultural magic with such signature dishes as black pepper tuna carpaccio (drizzled with soy vinaigrette) and Thai curry penne (with broiled scallops, Dungeness crabmeat, spicy ginger-tomato chutney, and basil chiffonade). Dine outdoors in warm weather, or take advantage of the view during a lovely, leisurely Sunday brunch. ■ *3014 3rd Ave N (behind Bleitz Funeral Home on the south side of the Fremont Bridge), Seattle; (206) 284-3000; $$$; full bar; AE, DC, MC, V; local checks only; lunch Mon–Fri, dinner every day, brunch Sun. &*

Queen City Grill ★★★ Long before the words "Belltown" and "hip" were inevitably spoken in the same sentence, Queen City made its mark as a hip Belltown cafe with a romantic, Euro-bistro atmosphere, where the grilled fare was every bit as good as the drinks that went with it. Though lately we've found lapses in the execution of a number of entrees, the allure is the same. You slide into a high-backed wooden booth and schmooze with friends. Fashionably chic people perch at the bar with cigarettes and cocktails. The wine list offers a broad selection, including an extensive variety of vintages from the Northwest's best winemakers. And servers are professionals well suited to the task. Let them steer you to a melting tuna carpaccio appetizer, an enticing gumbo, or a caesar salad: whole-leaf hearts of romaine, simply dressed in olive oil, lemon, and Worcestershire. Consider the day's seafood or chop special; or choose grilled fresh ahi, an aged New York steak, or a great burger. ■ *2201 1st Ave (corner of Blanchard), Seattle; (206)443-0975; $$$; full bar; AE, DC, MC, V; checks OK; lunch Mon–Fri, dinner every day.* &

Saleh al Lago ★★★ Saleh Joudeh is a native of the Middle East who left his heart in central Italy 20-some years ago. Self-taught and earnest about his restaurant, Joudeh has put out some of the most consistently good central Italian food in Seattle here at Green Lake since 1982. The two-tiered, pink-hued destination dining place is more popular with Seattle's moneyed muck-a-mucks than with the city's youthful trend-seekers (who may find the room too bright, the menu too traditional). But what Saleh al Lago might lack in excitement, it makes up for in execution. You're not likely to find a better plate of calamari than this lightly floured version sautéed with lemon, garlic, and parsley. Risotto is done to chewy perfection here, perhaps with a rich red sauce and bits of filet mignon or with chicken, arugula, and Gorgonzola. Try the sautéed Provimi veal with its delicate quattro formaggi sauce, or the excellent house-made ravioli. Bored with tiramisu? Think again before you pass up Saleh's. ■ *6804 E Green Lake Way N (on the east side of Green Lake), Seattle; (206)524-4044; $$$; full bar; AE, DC, MC, V; checks OK; lunch, dinner Tues–Sat.* &

Shiro's ★★★ To the delight of legions of fans, Seattle's best-known sushi chef, Shiro Kashiba, opened Shiro's. Graced with a blond hardwood sushi bar, linen-draped tables, and the presence of the master, this immaculate, simply decorated Belltown storefront was an immediate hit. Though the small menu offers full-course dinner entrees as well (tempura, sukiyaki, and teriyaki with accompanying rice, salad, and miso soup), it's the sushi that commands full sensual attention: this is the most lustrously gleaming fish you'll see in this town, and you'd do best to heed the call. Ask about seasonal specialties. At lunch, the bento box offers an opportunity for serious sampling and sushi is decidedly more affordable. ■ *2401 2nd Ave (corner of Battery), Seattle; (206)443-9844; $$$; full bar; AE, MC, V; no checks; lunch Mon–Fri, dinner Mon–Sat.* &

Szmania's ★★★ Magnolia Village may be a bit out of the way and hard to find, but Szmania's makes it worth the trouble. This modern restaurant, run by Ludger and Julie Szmania (pronounced *Smahn-ya*), is now one of the city's most sought out destination-dining spots. The open kitchen provides a stage set where German-born Ludger uses Northwest ingredients to create such wide-ranging dishes as Jäegerschnitzel with spaetzle and herb-crusted mahi-mahi with pinot noir sauce. Servings are generous, and many entrees are offered in half portions. Expect strong flavors that work well together—such as grilled duck with raspberry barbecue sauce—and take note of the loveliest array of vegetables ever to garnish a plate. For dessert: the signature crème brûlée trio. A remodel, including the addition of a fireside lounge, was underway at press time. ■ *3321 W McGraw St (at 34th Ave W), Seattle; (206)284-7305; $$; full bar; AE, DC, MC, V; local checks only; lunch Tues–Fri, dinner Tues–Sun.* &

Theoz ★★★ Theoz, in the historic Decatur Building, opened in a space notable for its graceful architectural elegance: high ceilings, a sweeping staircase, and sea-green walls. In the burnished wood bar, the before-and-after crowd might sip cocktails and partake of smoky duck tamales wrapped in banana leaf, mussels steamed with lime leaf and spicy sambal, or beautifully crafted desserts. Chef Emily Moore—whose bold stylings previously earned her acclaim at the Painted Table—creates "new American cuisine with a Ring of Fire twist" (don't ask, just eat). This marriage of spices and flavorings—whose accents evoke the culinary cultures of Indonesia, coastal China, the South Pacific, South America, and Mexico—translates as theatrically presented dishes such as a fire-roasted range veal chop with potato–black bean cakes, merlot sauce, and strips of chile poblanos, or an elaborate black Thai rice soufflé (sure to pique the palate of the sophisticated vegetarian). ■ *1523 6th Ave (between Pike and Pine), Seattle; (206)749-9660; $$$; full bar; MC, V; local checks only; lunch Mon–Fri, dinner every day.* &

Tulio (Hotel Vintage Park) ★★★ Tulio's neighborhood Italian charm belies its elegant, downtown hotel location. Tables are packed in tightly, and the sweet scent of roasted garlic hangs in the air. A busy little bar attracts the after-work/pre-theater/smoke-and-drink crowd, and an upstairs dining room, reached by a spiral staircase, provides additional seating (as well as a venue for private parties). Fronting the exhibition kitchen is a handful of counter seats where you might watch chef Walter Pisano conduct his well-tuned orchestra. The action reaches fever pitch back here, where whole prosciutti hang from above (prosciutto punctuates the menu—wrapped around roasted asparagus, adding a touch of salt to mushroom-scented pansotti, or stuffed into a gorgeous veal chop). Service is swift, knowledgeable, and attentive. The menu offers such *primi* courses as smoked salmon ravioli in a lemon-spiked cream sauce, and excellent risotti whose ingredients change to reflect the season. Roasted or grilled cuts of meat, poultry, and fish round out the dinner menu, while thin-crusted pizzas and cheesy calzones add a casual note to the lunch menu. At breakfast, expect to rub elbows with hotel guests over expensive omelets. ■ *1100 5th Ave (at Spring), Seattle; (206)624-5500; $$; full bar; AE, DC, DIS, MC, V; no checks; breakfast, lunch, dinner every day.* &

Virazon ★★★ Virazon presents classical French cookery, tweaked with the homegrown flavors of the Northwest by the passionate, well-schooled hand of chef Astolfo Rueda. On this busy south-of-Pike-Place-Market corner near Seattle Art Museum, business folk and ladies-who-lunch can choose to dine at one of a handful of outdoor tables. Shoppers find respite from gray weather in the pretty, golden-hued bistro setting overseen by co-owner Judy Schocken. Romance-seekers will be at home here on a candle-lit evening, indulging in a five-course ménu de dégustation and sipping something from a wine list offering many half-bottles and interesting by-the-glass options. The oft-changing menu relies on Northwest purveyors for such local ingredients as handcrafted cheeses, baby root vegetables, and fresh Willapa Bay sturgeon—though such imported luxuries as Périgord black truffles may complement the artfully sauced, locally inspired fare. ■ *1329 1st Ave (at Union), Seattle; (206)233-0123; $$$; beer and wine; AE, DC, MC, V; checks OK; lunch Mon–Sat, dinner Tues–Sat.* &

Wild Ginger ★★★ The Wild Ginger is wildly popular. Basking in the glow of much national attention are owners Rick and Ann Yoder, whose culinary vision has left a lasting impression on the Seattle restaurant scene (and inspired more than a few imitators). Just as the restaurants and markets of Bangkok, Singapore, Saigon, and Djakarta offer a wide range of multi-ethnic foods, so does the Wild Ginger, which brings together some of the best dishes from these Southeast Asian cities. At the mahogany satay bar, order from a wide array of sizzling skewered selections, but don't miss the coconut milk–basted Bangkok boar. Wherever you sit, try the succulent Singapore-style stir-fried crab, fresh from live tanks and redolent with ginger and garlic; exceptional, crisp-skinned "fragrant duck" spiced with star anise and cinnamon; and laksa, a spicy Malaysian seafood soup whose soft, crunchy, slippery textures and hot and salty flavors encompass everything good about Southeast Asian cookery. Great live jazz makes the Ginger the city's most happening scene on Monday nights. ■ *1400 Western Ave (just below and south of Pike Place Market, at Western and Union), Seattle; (206)623-4450; $$; full bar; AE, DC, MC, V; no checks; lunch Mon–Sat, dinner every day.* &

Brie & Bordeaux ★★ Green Lake's neighborhood wine-and-cheese shop has stepped across the street, added a kitchen and cheery bistro, and proven definitively that bigger (in this case, at least) is better. Drop by the retail shop for a to-go run on the essentials—a bottle of wine, a choice wedge of cheese—or step into the colorful cafe to sample such cheese-centric offerings as a French Brie omelet, a smoked turkey and Cotswold sandwich, or a pâté-and-cheese-filled ploughman's plate. The mood turns delightfully serious at dinner, as does the kitchen. The small menu entices with seasonal fare: Oregon rabbit, pan-seared sea bass, or a rack of lamb glazed with a reduction of cabernet and shallots. Nothing on the lengthy wine list suits you? Owner Alison Leber will gladly step into the shop and pull something off the shelf—or steer you toward something unfamiliar that you're sure to love. And, yes, you can have a cheese course in lieu of dessert. ■ *2227 N 56th St (corner of Kirkwood), Seattle; (206)633-3538; $$; beer and wine; AE, DC, MC, V; local checks only; breakfast, lunch Tues–Fri, dinner Tues–Sat, brunch Sat–Sun.* &

Cactus ★★ The sun-drenched cuisines of Mexico and the Southwest are a great antidote to yet another gray Seattle day. Whatever the weather, this colorful, comfortable cafe, with its outdoor tables and faux-Southwest decor, packs 'em in. Folks sit at the tapas bar and share *gambas al ajillo* (spicy garlic shrimp bathed in sherry, lemon, and herbs) or *berengena asada* (roasted eggplant with cilantro pesto), among many other flavorful tidbits that make a satisfying light meal. The familiar Mexican reliables—fajitas, enchiladas, chimichangas—are well done, but other choices (say, ancho-and-cinnamon-roasted chicken) can offer more interesting options. Navajo fry-bread or tortillas accompany the main dishes. There's a no-reservations policy, but loaned beepers let you stroll the neighborhood while you wait. ■ *4220 E Madison St (between 42nd and 43rd), Seattle; (206)324-4140; $$; full bar; DC, DIS, MC, V; checks OK; lunch Mon–Sat, dinner every day.* &

Cafe Flora ★★ When it opened, Cafe Flora's meatless, smokeless, boozeless ethic was rooted in a larger vision: multiculturalism, responsible global stewardship, and a fervid righteousness about healthy eating. Political and social agendas aside, this very attractive restaurant became a mecca for vegetarians and carnivores alike. Since then, concessions have been made for those who choose to sip something more potent than rosemary-laced lemonade, so these days you can enjoy a glass of merlot with your Portobello Wellington (a mushroom-pecan pâté and grilled portobellos, wrapped in pastry) or drink a beer with your Oaxaca Tacos (corn tortillas stuffed with spicy mashed potatoes and cheeses, set off by a flavorful black bean stew and sautéed greens). Soups are silky and luscious; salads sport interesting, often organic ingredients; and those who don't do dairy will always find something cleverly prepared to suit their dietary needs. Never hesitate when the dessert tray makes the rounds. ■ *2901 E Madison (at 28th), Seattle; (206)325-9100; $$; beer and wine; MC, V; checks OK; lunch Tues–Fri, dinner Tues–Sun, brunch Sat–Sun.* &

Chinook's at Salmon Bay ★★ It's big, busy, and formulaic, but the Anthony's HomePort folks are certainly using the right bait here in the heart of Fishermen's Terminal. The industrial design, with very high ceilings, steel countertops, and visible beams and ventilation ducts, fits well with the bustle around the working marina. The seemingly never-ending menu ranges from broiled, steamed, fried, sandwiched, and pasta-tossed seafood to Japanese stir-fries and teriyaki chicken burgers. We suggest you nab a few things off the regular menu (tempura onion rings and a half-dozen raw oysters) and pay close attention to the daily special sheet (say, wild chinook salmon, alder-planked and swabbed with a sweet bell pepper butter sauce). For dessert, try a big piece of blackberry cobbler—if you haven't already overdosed on the warm focaccia brought to you in basketsful by friendly servers. If it's a quick fish 'n' chips fix you're after, head next door to **Little Chinook's.** ■ *1900 W Nickerson St (at Fisherman's Terminal), Seattle; (206)283-4665; $$ (Chinook's at Salmon Bay), $ (Little Chinook's); full bar (Chinook's at Salmon Bay), no alcohol (Little Chinook's); AE, DC, DIS, MC, V; checks OK; breakfast Sat–Sun (Chinook's at Salmon Bay only), lunch, dinner every day.* &

Chutneys ★★ If you're not yet familiar with the flavors of the Asian subcontinent, this surprisingly elegant Lower Queen Anne dining room is an excellent place to begin. Servers are happy to explain dishes and make recommendations. Before you can scan the menu, a basket of pappadams appears with two of the restaurant's namesake chutneys. Among the worthy starters are Onion Bhaji—a variation on onion rings—and remarkably light vegetable pakoras. Entrees can be ordered at varying degrees of heat, to be chased with a cocktail, an Indian beer, or a mug of milky, cardamom-infused tea. Though Indian food can be fiery, even the curry vindaloo—synonymous in some restaurants with tongue-searing heat—is spicy without going overboard. Main-dish selections include chicken tikka masala (which combines the appeal of the tandoor with a creamy tomato-yogurt sauce) and a mixed tandoori grill (with succulent lamb chops, chicken, and fish among the generous offerings). Portions of basmati rice are served in individual copper pots, and there are many appealing vegetarian options. Don't overlook the breads, or the lunch buffet—it's a considerable bargain. Chutneys also has outposts on Capitol Hill (605 15th Ave E, (206)726-1000) and in Wallingford Center (1815 N 45th St, (206)634-1000). ■ *519 1st Ave N (between Mercer and Republican), Seattle; (206)284-6799; $$; full bar; AE, DC, DIS, MC, V; checks OK; lunch, dinner every day.* &

Coastal Kitchen ★★ Neighborhood restaurant kingpins Peter Levy and Jeremy Hardy have launched their third joint, on the eastern reaches of Capitol Hill. We think it's their best effort to date. This is the food of the coast—any coast—tweaked with a Jersey diner/Mom-for-the-'90s sensibility. The regular menu sports some serious winners, like a tender half of roast chicken and a grilled pork chop dinner plate with juicy, spicy chops nudging up against mashed potatoes and gravy so good you'll be begging for seconds. There's fresh fish, simply grilled, and the All Day Long Breakfast, with maple-smoked bacon, hashbrowns, toast, and eggs. The kitchen cooks up quarterly-changing getaways to far-flung coastal locales, and this is where the cooks get rowdy and imaginative. We've scarfed Gulf Coast fried green tomatoes with aioli and crowder peas; epazote-and-lime-laced Michoacan seafood stew; and Thai-style spring rolls. Exotic cocktails like the Blue Moon Martini (it's very, very blue) make imbibing more fun than usual. Be forewarned: The menu is written in such fractured, Huck Finnified vernacular (y'all know they're duckin' and dippin' and tryin' to be interestin') that it may get on your nerves as much as the clattery din. ■ *429 15th Ave E (between Harrison and Republican), Seattle; (206)322-1145; $$; full bar; MC, V; checks OK; breakfast, lunch, dinner every day.* ♿

Dulces Latin Bistro ★★ Owner/chef Julie Guerrero cooks most nights in a cut-away kitchen in one corner of this handsome Madrona bistro, while her partner, Carlos Kainz, acts as host. Their low-ceilinged, rust-toned dining room, with its soft, jazzy Latin guitar pulsing in the background, offers the perfect place to relax on a rain-soaked night. Candle-lit and comfortable, the atmosphere warms patrons in any weather. Though the owners' Latin heritage—and dishes such as chiles rellenos, prawns a la diabla, and saffron-scented paella—lend the menu its Latin beat, Guerrero paints with a far broader palette. You might sample New England clam chowder one night, black bean soup the next. Homemade ravioli may arrive stuffed with chorizo and sauced with tomatillos—or enfolding salmon, capers, and herbs. A rack of Ellensburg lamb, finished with pomegranate demiglace, is first-class. Be sure to sample something from the dessert tray, and take note: there's a small bar and cigar lounge too. ■ *1430 34th Ave (corner of E Pike), Seattle; (206)322-5453; $$; full bar; AE, DIS, MC, V; checks OK; dinner Tues–Sun.* ♿

El Camino ★★ Alice Hughes and James Weimann (who also own the funky Triangle Tavern just a shout away) have given the city what it's long been waiting for: an upscale Mexican joint that nods to Mexico's regional cuisine while snubbing the Tex-Mex schlock that we've been forced to grow used to. Their mood's-right Fremont cantina is divided into bar (serious social scene, superb fresh-juice margaritas) and dining room (festive vinyl tablecloths, great casual service). Beyond the bar, an outdoor patio doesn't quite look out on the nearby Ship Canal. But why pay attention to what's going on *outside*, when there is so much happening within? Standouts include a killer chile relleno, tacos carne asada (with house-made masa tortillas), quesadillas de camarones (stuffed with cheese, rock shrimp, and cilantro paste), and a mile-high chocolate torte. For breakfast, don't miss the El Camino Hash, the huevos rancheros, or the house-made chorizo. ■ *607 N 35th St (near Fremont Ave), Seattle; (206) 632-7303; $$; full bar; AE, MC, V; dinner every day, brunch Sat–Sun.* &

The 5 Spot ★★ Most mornings there's a line under the big neon coffee cup outside this Queen Anne landmark. It's a Big Fun kind of place at the top of the Counterbalance and, in fact, it counterbalances an architecturally pretty cafe with a kitschy menu and solid service. Expect such standard regional American fare as Southwestern tostadas, Southern-style country ham with sautéed greens, Northwest halibut 'n' chips, and New England roast chicken supper. A Food Festival Series mixes in a regionally oriented menu (say Florida or Texas) on a rotational basis. A great pair of dinner pork chops come with rib-sticking mashed potatoes and gravy, though we know folks who can make a meal out of an order of french fries and a Pabst Blue Ribbon in the bar. The updated red flannel hash served at breakfast may be the best you'll ever eat. ■ *1502 Queen Anne Ave N (at the top of the Counterbalance), Seattle; (206) 285-SPOT; $$; full bar; MC, V; checks OK; breakfast, lunch, dinner every day.* &

I Love Sushi ★★ Silly name? Don't be so sure. Chef Tadashi Sato offers two premier Japanese restaurants, one on each side of Lake Washington. Both feature bustling, bright, high-energy sushi bars with exquisitely fresh fish—and a friendly, helpful young staff to keep things running smoothly. Sato and his fishmasters attract many Japanese customers who know a good thing when they eat one. The sushi combinations are a veritable bargain (particularly at lunch); traditional specialties such as sea urchin, abalone, and fermented bean paste may raise the stakes somewhat. Flame-broiled fish cheeks, myriad udon and yakisoba options, the ubiquitous tempura, and chawanmushi—a steamed custard that is the ultimate in Japanese comfort food—are always good. The Lake Union branch is nonsmoking at lunch (you take your chances at dinner). The Bellevue version has been remodeled to allow for more dining space. ■ *1001 Fairview Ave N (on the Yale St Landing off Fairview), Seattle; (206) 625-9604; $$; full bar; AE, MC, V; no checks; lunch Mon–Fri, dinner every day.* & ■ *11818 NE 8th St (at 118th Ave NE), Bellevue; (206) 454-5706; $$; full bar; AE, MC, V; no checks; lunch Mon–Sat, dinner every day.* &

Kabul ★★ In ancient Afghanistan, the king's cooks marinated and grilled the finest meats, infusing dishes with mint, cilantro, and dill, and applying the cooling touch of yogurt and the zing of scallions. Recipes were guarded jealously and passed down through the generations. Today, Sultan Malikyar—who emigrated from Kabul, Afghanistan, in the late '70s—prepares his family's recipes here in Wallingford. His father's kabob recipe and his mother's chaka (garlic yogurt sauce) are menu staples. This is fragrant, elegant food: crisp *bolani* (scallion-potato turnovers); *jan-i amma* (an Afghan version of tzatziki); and *ashak* (delicate scallion dumplings topped with either a beef sauce or a vegetarian tomato sauce). Service is unfailingly friendly, and the room—with its simple decor, glass-topped tables, and colorful accents—is almost as soothing as the cardamom-and-rosewater-flavored custard served as dessert. There's live sitar music on Tuesday and Thursday. ▪ *2301 N 45th St (corner of Corliss), Seattle; (206)545-9000; $; beer and wine; AE, DC, DIS, MC, V; local checks only; dinner Mon–Sat.*

Macrina Bakery and Cafe ★★ Leslie Mackie has gained national acclaim as a bread baker, first as originator of the rustic bread program at Grand Central Bakery and later with her own ovens at Macrina. Today, she and her small army of bakers can hardly keep up with the demand for her gutsy, exceptional breads, which you'll find on the tables at the city's finest restaurants. Mornings, Belltown regulars show up for buttery pastries, bowls of fresh fruit and house-made granola, and creamy lattes, enjoyed in the sunny Euro-chic cafe setting. Others make haste with a loaf of potato bread, warm from the oven. Lunch brings simple, artful soups, salads, and panini, and a classy meze trio of daily-changing Mediterranean-inspired noshes. ▪ *2408 1st Ave (near Battery), Seattle; (206)448-4032; $; beer and wine; MC, V; checks OK; breakfast, lunch Mon–Fri, brunch Sat–Sun.* ⅃

Madison Park Cafe ★★ Indulging in a morning repast at this charming house-turned-cafe has been a local ritual for nearly 20 years. Seated at one of too few tables inside—or out in the brick courtyard in warm weather—you might wrap your hands around a latte, smear butter on a warm scone, and await baked eggs bubbling with ham and cheese, or a grand, soufflé-like strata. Neighbors gossip while children toy with their coloring books, eat homemade granola, and wipe sticky hands on checkered tablecloths. At lunch, real estate agents do soup and salad with clients, shopkeepers share inventive sandwiches, and you can still get a proper quiche and a glass of wine to go with it. On Friday and Saturday evenings, this longtime breakfast-and-lunchery turns into a country-French bistro, when oysters sing with Pernod cream sauce, rack of lamb shares the plate with celeriac-flavored mashed potatoes, and such French classics as steak au poivre and cassoulet give credence to the restaurant's Gallic aspirations. Moderate prices at dinner carry over to the small, mostly French wine list. ▪ *1807 42nd Ave E (across from the tennis courts), Seattle; (206)324-2626; $$; beer and wine; MC, V; checks OK; breakfast Tues–Sun, lunch Tues–Sat, dinner Fri–Sat.*

Marco's Supperclub ★★ When Marco Rulff and Donna Moodie opened this groovicidal Belltown bistro, they crossed their fingers in hope that years of tableside experience, an adventurous and capable chef, and a strong staff of personable, sophisticated servers would bring business their way. And it was clear from day one that the husband-and-wife team had more than luck going for them. In the years since, their sexy, noisy, and *busy* restaurant has welcomed hordes of savvy diners who come for the warm, funky atmosphere and the trip-around-the-world menu. To start, try the innovative fried sage appetizer or the Thai-style mussels. Among the terrific standards is a subtly spiced Jamaican jerk chicken served up with sautéed greens and mashed sweet potatoes. Pork and beef get treated right whatever the preparation. A bar running the length of the room is a great perch for those dining alone. In summer, a colorful deck out back practically doubles the seating capacity. ■ *2510 1st Ave (between Vine and Wall), Seattle; (206) 441-7801; $$; full bar; AE, MC, V; checks OK; lunch Mon–Fri, dinner every day.*

Metropolitan Grill ★★ This handsome, money-colored haunt in the heart of the financial district does a booming business among stockbrokers, Japanese tourists, and others willing to shell out plenty for a big, thick steak. The bovine is divine here at Suit Central, so you'd do well to stick with the beef. Pastas and appetizers are less well executed, but a list of large, appealing salads, sandwiches, and a daily fish special present good alternatives for the lunch crowd. Professional, white-coated waiters are of the no-nonsense school, which suits the table-hopping power brokers just fine. Financiers count on the Met's 32-person private room as a dependable dinner venue, and the bar is a splendid watering hole for imbibers from the old-school, loosen-your-tie-and-pour-me-a-Scotch era—with classic barmen always in top form. ■ *820 2nd Ave (at Marion), Seattle; (206) 624-3287; $$$; full bar; AE, DC, DIS, MC, V; checks OK; lunch Mon–Fri, dinner every day.* &

Nikko (Westin Hotel) ★★ In a city filled with small mom-and-pop Japanese restaurants, this corporate behemoth stands out with what is surely the largest, and arguably the most attractive, Japanese dining room in Seattle—though we've been less than enamored of its service lately. Sleek, colorful, and designed with a contemporary bent, it also offers one of the city's lengthiest sushi bars: a great place to enjoy raw-fish delicacies including nearly two dozen nori-wrapped rolls (the astounding Nikko Roll sports seven different varieties of fish). You can expect to rub elbows with hotel guests, who find no need to look elsewhere for steaming shabu-shabu, crisp soft-shell crab, or black cod kasazuke broiled to flaky perfection. Enjoy a plate of grilled thises and thats from the robata bar, or steal away for a private meal in a tatami room. Locals know to head straight for

▼
Seattle

Restaurants

▲

the bar after work for a tall Japanese beer and free nibbles (Mon–Fri). ■ *1900 5th Ave (in the Westin Hotel, at Westlake), Seattle; (206)322-4641; $$$; full bar; AE, DC, MC, V; local checks only; lunch Mon–Fri, dinner Mon–Sat.* ⅁

ObaChine ★★ Wunderchef Wolfgang Puck is as famous for his multitude of chic restaurants as for his chic frozen pizzas. Now he's part of the local lingo, having brought ObaChine number two (the first lives in Beverly Hills; more are in the offing) into the megawatt Meridian complex. There's a small, less-conspicuous bar downstairs, but the action's above in the oversized dining room dominated by an exhibition kitchen and satay bar, Asian art and artifacts, and entirely too much purple. We give the nod to Puck's interesting, well-executed, taste-of-Asia fare: crisp lamb samosas and shiitake-filled pot-stickers; moist, tea-leaf-baked ten-spice salmon; tandoori murgh chicken that puts local Indian joints to shame; exotic, colorful side dishes and desserts that never get short shrift; and an appealing, Northwest-heavy wine list. Tables along the far wall may prove too close for comfort for the business-lunchers who flock here by day. ■ *1518 6th Ave (between Pike and Pine), Seattle; (206)749-9653; $$; full bar; AE, DC, MC, V; no checks; lunch Mon–Sat, dinner every day.* ⅁

Palisade ★★ Inside, with a waterfall and a seawater tidal pool, tropical-looking plants and trees, chandeliers festooned with glass balls, and a player piano perched on a ledge *over* the bar, Palisade might be mistaken for the Hyatt Regency in Maui. Outside, beyond the Elliott Bay Marina to the grandstand view of the city and the Sound, it's definitely Seattle. Step over the cobblestone bridge into the expansive dining area, where there's not a bad seat in the house. The menu, too, is vast and highlights contemporary grilling, searing, and rotisserie cooking styles for a variety of fish, meat, and poultry. Order the pupu platter for a sampling of appetizers; try the shellfish chowder and you'll be well rewarded. Imaginative entree preparations favor Polynesian inspirations like macadamia nut chicken with banana-papaya chutney. Consider a simple fish dish—perhaps an apple-wood-grilled steelhead or rotisserie-smoked lingcod. One standout combination is the spit-roasted prime rib paired with grilled hazelnut prawns. Palisade's "Cityview" brunch is the hottest ticket in town.

Downstairs is the inexpensive waterside grill, **Maggie Bluffs**, (206)283-8322, whose casual atmosphere—with a menu to match (big burgers, pastas, salads, and a host of finger foods)—offers respite from the South Pacific schmaltz. ■ *2601 W Marina Pl (at the Elliott Bay Marina), Seattle; (206)285-1000; $$$; full bar; AE, DC, DIS, MC, V; no checks; lunch Mon–Sat, dinner every day, brunch Sun.* ⅁

Phoenecia at Alki ★★ At this, Phoenicia's third incarnation, it's easy to feel at home among the regulars when you're seated in a room that's part souk, part bistro, with ornate silk flower arrangements and magic carpets hung on sunshine-colored walls that seem to glow with Mediterranean sunshine (even when the sun's not setting over Alki Beach). Owner Hussein Khazaal moves from table to table, suggesting wines, directing servers, and taking orders for dishes that he swears will be "the best you've ever had!" (Watch out—your bill can mount swiftly.) The standard hummus, tabouli, and baba ghanouj are here, but then it's off on pan-Mediterranean explorations: saffron and pine-nut risotto with shellfish; Moroccan eggplant with penne and tomatoes; excellent, inventive thin-crust pizza. To round it all off you may choose, appropriately, between espresso and Turkish coffee, tiramisu and baklava. ■ *2716 Alki Ave S (between 59th and 60th), Seattle; (206) 935-6550; $$; beer and wine; MC, V; checks OK; lunch Tues–Fri, dinner Tues–Sat.* ⑤

The Pink Door ★★ The low-profile entrance (just a pink door off Post Alley) to this Italian trattoria hidden away in Pike Place Market belies the busy scene within. In the winter, the dining room grows noisy, but come warmer weather, everyone vies desperately for a spot on the trellis-covered rooftop terrace, with its breathtakingly romantic view of the Sound. Owner Jackie Roberts offers hefty plates of pasta and a short list of fish/meat/poultry dishes. Or you can construct a fine meal from the limited bar menu (the antipasto is a Tuscan feast, and the aglio al forno—roasted garlic with a scoop of ricotta-Gorgonzola cheese spread accompanied by excellent bread—is a most slatherable nosh). The Pink Door overflows with Italian kitsch, which is not lost on the arty, under-30 set that calls the place home. There's often live music at night. ■ *1919 Post Alley (between Stewart and Virginia), Seattle; (206) 443-3241; $$; full bar; AE, MC, V; no checks; lunch, dinner Tues–Sat.*

Ray's Boathouse ★★ With its gorgeous view of Shilshole Bay and the Olympics beyond, Ray's has long been *the* place for waterfront dining—one favored by locals and tourists alike. These days, with hip seafooderies abounding and new restaurants taking up residence on shores in and around Seattle, Ray's is facing some real competition (and not always living up to its once-sterling reputation). The departure of several longtime staffers may be the wake-up call needed to set things straight. Meantime, you can't beat the view, the superb wine list (with a page devoted to splits), or the freshest oysters, salmon, and halibut in season, and don't miss the opportunity to order grilled Chatham Straits black cod in sake kasu—a menu staple. Lunch is served upstairs at the more casual **Ray's Cafe**, especially popular at happy hour and in warm weather, when the deck (and the bar) draws a crowd. ■ *6049 Seaview Ave NW (at 60th NW),*

*Seattle; (206) 789-3770; $$$; full bar, AE, DC, MC, V; local
checks only; lunch (Ray's Cafe only), dinner every day.* ✆

Salvatore ★★ Salvatore Anania's neighborhood dinner spot
continues to impress by getting all the essentials right—the
old-fashioned, Southern Italian way. This is one of those warm,
inviting trattoria-style joints whose garlicky aroma and "That's
Amore" atmosphere draw a loyal audience looking for Italian
comfort food. They've come to the right place. Service is
friendly and more than helpful (you might *need* help choosing
from among the many Italian wines offered). We suggest you
start with one of the thin-crusted pizzas and then take your
waiter's cue when it comes to specials—or order the spicy, al-
ways-satisfying penne puttanesca. On busy nights, Salvatore's
no-reservations policy often leaves wannabe diners crowded
and waiting in a tight space. ■ *6100 Roosevelt (1 block north of
Ravenna Blvd), Seattle; (206)527-9301; $$; beer and wine; DIS,
MC, V; checks OK; dinner Mon–Sat.* ✆

Sanmi Sushi ★★ Misao Sanmi was a Buddha-like presence behind a few well-known sushi bars before he opened his own
Sanmi Sushi in the shade of towering Palisade. Sit in the serene,
sunny dining room and view the pleasure craft docked in the
marina, or head directly to the sushi bar where Sanmi presides
over a fine view of some great-looking fish. The menu features
a lengthy list of appetizers, including glistening, salty-sweet,
black cod kasazuke (also available as an entree), and marvelous
albacore tuna, seared, sliced, and resting atop vinegar-dressed
onions. A number of soups, combination dinners (with raw fish
or cooked meat and seafood components), oodles of Japanese
noodles, and grilled meats and fish round out the menu. Bring
your appetite to lunch and order the makanouchi bento to sample a superb array of Sanmi's finest treats. ■ *2601 W Marina
Place, Suite S (at Elliott Bay Marina), Seattle; (206)283-9978; $$;
beer and wine; AE, MC, V; no checks; lunch, dinner every day.* ✆

Shanghai Garden ★★ Owner/chef Hua Te Su attracts diners
from every Chinese province (and every Seattle neighborhood)
with exceptional regional Chinese dishes at this very pink In-
ternational District restaurant. His vast, adventurous menu is
filled with exotica such as black-moss-and-bamboo-fungus soup,
sautéed hog maw, and fish-head casserole. Come prepared to
be wowed by anything made with pea vines or with the chef's
special hand-shaved noodles. The vivid tendrils of the sugar pea
plant resemble sautéed spinach, and they cook up tender and
clean-tasting, never more so than when paired with plump
shrimp. The noodles, shaved off a block of dough, are the main
ingredient in a dozen different dishes. Try them in what may
be the best chow mein you'll ever eat.

Shanghai has been perfectly cloned in Issaquah, giving East-siders cause to rejoice. The menu and decor mimic the I-District version, but here there's an adjoining cocktail lounge (vestiges of its former incarnation), and you might order a mai-tai with your mu-shu. ■ *524 6th Ave S (corner of S Weller St), Seattle; (206) 625-1689; $; beer and wine; MC, V; no checks; lunch, dinner every day.* ⅔ ■ *80 Front St (downtown), Issaquah; (425) 313-3188; $; full bar; MC, V; no checks; lunch, dinner every day.* ⅔

Snappy Dragon ★★ Owner Judy Fu is a one-woman Chinese noodle factory and wokmeister extraordinaire whose quiet, competent elegance permeates the kitchen at this quaint North End house-turned-restaurant. This is arguably the best Chinese food north of the International District, distinguished not only for the quality of the many fresh, inexpensive dishes, swift take-out and delivery service, and Fu's exceptional handmade noo-dles, but for the city's only *jiao-zi* bar. Fu cooked professionally for others for 25 years before opening the Snappy Dragon. Here, with the help of her son and daughter-in-law (who man-age the phone and the floor), she turns out a sampling of au-thentic clay hot pots and well-executed versions of the standard wokked-up chicken, pork, beef, and vegetable dishes as well as some of the city's finest mu-shu. Appetizers include *jiao-zi* (boiled meat- and veggie-filled dumplings with a fragrant dip-ping sauce) and a delicate green onion pancake (think: Chinese focaccia). Big bowls of comforting soups star Fu's thick, tender noodles. ■ *8917 Roosevelt Way NE (at 89th), Seattle; (206) 528-5575; $; full bar; AE, DC, MC, V; checks OK; lunch Mon–Sat, dinner every day.* ⅔

Sostanza ★★ The second coming of Sostanza is a lot like the first coming. And that's a good thing, since this romantic trat-toria, now owned by chef Lorenzo Cianciusi, was—and re-mains—an extension of its loyal patrons' home dining rooms. Sostanza's inviting main salon is warmed by papaya-colored walls, exposed brick, and a cozy fireplace. A second, smaller dining room and bar are new additions, as is a deck affording a lovely view of Lake Washington. The rustic Italian fare is or-chestrated by Cianciusi, and executed in a kitchen whose staff greet customers with friendly hellos. Expect fine renditions of such traditional first courses as *carpaccio di manzo* or *zuppetta Toscana* (a superb cannellini bean soup). Pasta and risotto are among Cianciusi's many successes, while gentle grilling does well by poultry and seafood. Meat and game wear reduction sauces that are often accented with barolo and Chianti, garlic and rosemary. A descriptive wine list is heavy with Italian op-tions. ■ *1927 43rd Ave E (just off Madison), Seattle; (206) 324-9701; $$; full bar; AE, DC, MC, V; checks OK; dinner Mon–Sat.* ⅔

Swingside Cafe ★★ Owner/chef Brad Inserra (he's the guy working his buns off in the absurdly small kitchen) produces a world of big flavors and an always-inventive menu. There are hearty stews and sautés and pasta dishes spiced with unpredictable North African, Creole, and nouvelle-American accents. The brown Moroccan sauce caresses the mouth; tangy seafood dishes sing of the sea; the gumbo is extraordinary, and spicy enough to cure what ails you. Everything's rich, delicious, and amply portioned; don't over-order, or you may have to be carried home. As for atmosphere, you've probably forgotten eating out could be as simple, casual, and friendly as this. Dinner in the "fish room"—a tiny, aquarium-like atrium attached to the back of the house—is an experience all its own. ■ *4212 Fremont N (across from the Buckaroo Tavern, at 42nd), Seattle; (206)633-4057; $$; beer and wine; MC, V; local checks only; dinner Tues–Sat.* &

Union Bay Cafe ★★ Long a sweetly funky neighborhood cafe, the Union Bay has moved into a new complex a few doors down from its longtime Laurelhurst location. The upscale contemporary design relieves the cafe of any of its arty funk, adding a far larger kitchen where talented chef/owner Mark Manley presides. Etched glass "walls" divide the entranceway from twin dining rooms that provide a gallery setting for the work of Manley's artist-wife. As ever, folks are as likely to be celebrating a birthday or anniversary as stopping in for a relaxing dinner after a day's work. A starter of mussels scented with lemongrass, ginger, and tamarind proves that although the small, seasonal menu leans toward Italian (try the calamari saltati or the rabbit alla Calabrese), Manley can do Asian too. Fruit finds its way into many dishes: Muscovy duck breast with dried cherries, pork tenderloin with rhubarb, venison with huckleberries. Expect several pasta and vegetarian options, fine desserts, and an appealing wine list. ■ *3513 NE 45th St (2 blocks east of University Village), Seattle; (206)527-8364; $$; beer and wine; AE, DC, MC, V; checks OK; dinner Tues–Sun.* &

El Puerco Llorón ★ This place transports you back to that cafe in Tijuana, the one with the screaming hot pink and aquamarine walls and the bent, scarred "Cerveza Superior" tables. Remember the wailing jukebox and the cut-tin lamps and the woman quietly making corn tortillas by the door? They're all here. Belly up to the cafeteria line, place your order, and fight for a table: in warm weather, those outdoor ones are as hard to get as parking spots. Try the taquitos plate, three excellent corn masa tortillas rolled around a filling and served with rice, beans, and a scallion. The chiles rellenos, so often bungled by American chefs, are fresh and bright with flavor. At the end of the counter, pick up fresh lemonade or a Mexican beer. ■ *1501 Western Ave (on the Pike Place Market Hillclimb), Seattle;*

(206)624-0541; $; beer and wine; AE, MC, V; no checks; lunch, early dinner every day.

Pagliacci Pizza ★ All three Pagliacci pizzerias (Capitol Hill, Queen Anne, and University District) offer the same simple yet eternal lure: excellent thin-and-tangy cheese pizzas. The true test of the exceptional crust is the original cheese pizza, which is unadorned except for a light, fresh tomato sauce and good mozzarella. Hot from the oven, it's hard to beat. Skip the salads (blah, one and all) and go straight for the pies; this place is about pizza, and that's it. You can take out or eat in. Comfortable, echoing, and sometimes hectic, they're all fine places for a quick solo meal. A phone call to Pagliacci's primo central delivery service, (206)726-1717, will get you delivery from any of a fast-growing number of neighborhood pizza kitchens. ■ *426 Broadway Ave E (across from the Broadway Market), Seattle (and branches); (206)324-0730; beer and wine; AE, MC, V; checks OK; lunch, dinner every day.* &

Red Mill Burgers ★ When Babe and John Shepherd were school kids, they often hung out at the Red Mill—an old diner-style restaurant. Thirty years after the Red Mill served its last meal, the brother-and-sister team opened their tiny, namesake burger joint in a corner of an old brick building. Within weeks they were attracting crowds of worshippers who came for one of their 18 varieties of the all-American favorite. Within months they expanded into an adjoining space to accommodate the hordes. Today they own the building. This is not a fast-food joint, and the wait is worth it, as you'll see when you sink your teeth into a burger topped with thick slices of pepper bacon, anointed with a smoky house-made mayo, and sandwiched in a big, warm bun with the freshest of lettuce and tomatoes. Those who don't do red meat will find a terrific array of veggie and chicken burgers. Don't miss the killer onion rings, and knock 'em back with a milk shake. ■ *312 N 67th St (where Phinney meets Greenwood), Seattle; (206)783-6362; $; no alcohol; no credit cards; checks OK; lunch, dinner Tues–Sun.* &

Sea Garden ■ Sea Garden of Bellevue ★ The name says it all: the best efforts are put into anything that comes from the sea—particularly if it spent its last minutes in the live tank up front. The place is nothing fancy, but we've always been enamored of Sea Garden's ability to keep such consistently excellent seafood so reasonably priced. Expect subtle Cantonese fare (the tamely spiced stuff we all enjoyed before we developed our culinary crush on fiery Sichuan or Hunan food). Choose lobster or crab and they'll bring it snapping mad in a bucket to your table for inspection. Minutes later it arrives, perfectly turned out, chopped into tender pieces and served with a consistently finger-lickin'-good black bean sauce, or a refreshing ginger and green onion sauce. Big, succulent sea scallops populate a plate with honey-glazed walnuts. Naturally sweet spot prawns on wooden skewers burst with flavor. The extensive menu offers plenty of vegetarian options, plus exotics like jellyfish, sea cucumber, or fish maw. Larger parties fill the somewhat dreary upstairs room. Open late every day.

When the Sea Garden decided to open a second branch in Bellevue, the owners, an extended family, built from the ground up. It's not a grand place, but it is smart and bright. Service (at both restaurants) ranges from adequate to exasperating. ■ *509 7th Ave S (at Jackson), Seattle; (206)623-2100; $; full bar; AE, MC, V; no checks; lunch, dinner every day.* ■ *200 106th Ave NE (corner of NE 2nd), Bellevue; (425)450-8833; $; full bar; AE, DC, MC, V; no checks; lunch, dinner every day.* &

Siam on Broadway ■ Siam on Lake Union ★ Among Seattle's multitude of Thai restaurants, tiny Siam wins the popularity contest, hands down. Working the woks and burners in a tiny open kitchen fronted by counter seating, a quartet of women move with utmost grace, portioning meats and vegetables, dipping into salty potions. They produce, among other flavorful dishes, what might be the city's best *tom kah gai*—the chicken soup spicy with chiles, sour with lemongrass, and soothed with coconut milk. The menu doesn't stray far from the Bangkok standards, but the dishes created by the deft hands in the kitchen are distinctive. Sit at the counter and enjoy the show, or wait for one of only 15 tables in the back. You won't have to wait at **Siam on Lake Union**, a newer, larger outpost with outdoor seating. Nor will you have to search for a parking space (they've got a private lot). Though good, the food here doesn't quite live up to its Broadway sibling's. ■ *616 Broadway (on Capitol Hill), Seattle; (206)324-0892; $; beer and wine; AE, MC, V; checks OK; lunch Mon–Fri, dinner every day.* ■ *1880 Fairview Ave E (on the east side of Lake Union), Seattle; (206)323-8101; $; full bar; AE, MC, V; checks OK; lunch Mon–Fri, dinner every day.* &

Thai Restaurant ★ You can't help but play the Thai version of "Who's on First?" at this aptly and simply named Thai favorite: "Which Thai restaurant?" "Thai Restaurant." "Yeah, but which one?" "The Thai restaurant near Seattle Center." "Which Thai restaurant is that?" "Thai Restaurant!" Here's a hint: locals call it "the Thai restaurant at First and John." With its alluring aromas of basil, garlic, and lemongrass, decor rich with orchid colors and textile hangings, soothing Thai music, and gracious, exceedingly polite service, this longtime favorite is a tranquil oasis. The kitchen offers a few innovations to the standard Thai menu, including an appetizer of spinach leaves (meant to be rolled around various condiments and dipped in a sauce), and a fine Thai curry featuring chicken and cashews. Expect tender beef in a salad fragrant with mint and onions, and beware anything above three stars on the heat-factor scale. Vegetables

▼

Seattle

Restaurants

▲

are treated as carefully as the customers. Homemade coconut ice cream will put out any tonsil fires. ▪ *101 John St (corner of 1st), Seattle; (206) 285-9000; full bar; AE, MC, V; checks OK; lunch Mon–Fri, dinner every day.*

Zeek's Pizza ★ Zeek's—known for its absurd pizza toppings and too-nice-to-be-for-real staff of pizza-throwers, salad-makers, and money-takers—offers two locations. The original, near Seattle Pacific University, has a decidedly hip, industrial look; the second is on Phinney Ridge. At either of these busy spots, run by young pizza impresarios Doug McClure and Tom Vial, you should not hesitate to order the Thai-One-On, a pizza doused with the makings of phad Thai: chunks of chicken, slivers of carrot, crunchy mung bean sprouts, and fresh cilantro atop a spicy hot peanut sauce that'd do a satay proud. Purists might lean toward the Frog Belly Green, with pesto, fresh tomatoes, and whole-milk mozzarella layered over a very white, slightly doughy crust with an olive oil glaze. Then there's the weird-but-wonderful Texas Leaguer (barbecued chicken, red onion, and cilantro), and El Nuevo Hombre (salsa, refried beans, and fat slices of jalapeño). Eat in, take out, and delivery, too. ▪ *41 Dravus St (near corner of Nickerson), Seattle; (206) 285-6046; $; beer and wine; MC, V; checks OK; lunch, dinner every day.* ▪ *6000 Phinney Ave N (at 60th), Seattle; (206) 789-1778; $; beer and wine; MC, V; checks OK; lunch Mon–Fri, dinner every day.* ᕫ

LODGINGS

Four Seasons Olympic Hotel ★★★★ Elegance is yours at Seattle's landmark hotel, where grand borders on opulent, and personal around-the-clock service means smiling maids, quick-as-a-wink bellhops, and a team of caring concierges who ensure your every comfort. Luxury pervades the 450 handsome guest rooms and suites tastefully furnished with period reproductions (executive suites feature down-covered king-size beds, separated from an elegant sitting room by French doors). It also pervades the venerable Georgian Room (see review), where the talents of chef Kerry Sear, the decorum of liveried waiters, and the strains of a grand piano create a fine-dining experience you won't soon forget. Enjoy afternoon tea in the Garden Court, or relax in the solarium spa and pool (where a licensed masseuse is on call). The hotel even goes out of its way for kids, right down to a teddy bear in the crib and a step stool in the bathroom. There are several elegant meeting rooms and fine shops in the retail spaces off the lobby. Prices are steep, especially considering that there are few views, but this is Seattle's one world-class contender. ▪ *411 University St (at 5th), Seattle, WA 98101; (206) 621-1700 or (800) 821-8106; $$$; AE, DC, JCB, MC, V; checks OK.* ᕫ

Alexis Hotel ★★★ When the Sultan of Brunei showed up in Seattle on business, this is where he stayed. And if it's good enough for the one of the richest men in the world, you'll probably like it too. The Alexis is a gem carved out of a lovely turn-of-the-century building in a stylish section of downtown near the waterfront. You'll be pampered here, with Jacuzzis and real-wood fireplaces in some of the suites, and nicely insulated walls between rooms to ensure privacy. Request a room that faces the inner courtyard; rooms facing First Avenue can be noisy, especially if you want to open your window. A recent renovation turned the adjacent Arlington Suites into additional guest rooms, bringing the total number of rooms to 109, but the Alexis retains its intimate, boutique-hotel feel. We especially love the bright mix of patterns and colors in the newer rooms. For a splurge, book one of the new spa suites: the bathroom—complete with a deep Jacuzzi—is as big as some hotel rooms. In addition to a much-welcomed "no tipping" policy, amenities include complimentary continental breakfasts, a morning newspaper of your choice, shoeshines, and a guest membership in the nearby Seattle Club ($15 per day). There's a steam room that can be reserved just for you, and a new Aveda Spa, where you can have such treatments as massages and facials (request an in-room massage, if you prefer). The Painted Table serves innovative Northwest cuisine (see review); the Bookstore Bar is a cozy, if smoky, nook in which to enjoy a libation and a light meal. ■ *1007 1st Ave (at Madison), Seattle, WA 98104; (206) 624-4844 or (800) 426-7033; $$$; AE, DC, MC, V; checks OK.* ⅄

Gaslight Inn and Howell Street Suites ★★★ Stately and exquisitely kept, the Gaslight is one of the loveliest, most reasonably priced, and friendliest bed and breakfasts in town. Innkeepers Trevor Logan, Steve Bennett, and John Fox have polished this turn-of-the-century mansion into a 10-guest-room jewel. Each room is decorated in a distinct style—some contemporary, some antique, some art deco, some Mission; five have private baths (the rest share two baths), and you might opt for a room with a view, a fireplace, or a deck, depending on availability. A deck now spans the rear of the main house, allowing views of downtown, Puget Sound, and the Olympics. Relax outdoors in the heated pool, or hunker down in the handsomely appointed common rooms (perhaps in the well-stocked library or by the fireplace in the living room). Next door, the Howell Street Suites—six full and one studio—come outfitted with wet bar, contemporary furnishings and antiques, coffeemaker, wineglasses, fruit, and flowers. A new guest suite, replete with Northwest art glass, features a fireplace and city/mountain view; another new addition has a private garden. The suites also offer phones, fax availability, off-street parking, maid service, and laundry facilities. No pets, kids, or smoking. ■ *1727 15th*

*Ave (at Howell), Seattle, WA 98122; (206) 325-3654; $$; AE,
MC, V; checks OK.*

Hotel Vintage Park ★★★ The Vintage Park, part of the San
Francisco–based Kimpton Group, is a personable, well-run,
classy downtown hotel, with genuinely attentive service. There
are two kinds of rooms: those facing inward and those facing
outward (the exterior rooms tend to have a little more space,
but forget about a view). Unfortunately, the hotel is located
alongside a busy I-5 entrance ramp, and soundproofing seems
to help only on the upper floors. The hotel's grand suite, occu-
pying the entire top floor, gives a new fun twist to elegance.
Everywhere else, they've carried their "vintage" theme to the
limit, with rooms named after wineries, burgundy upholstery,
and green-and-maroon bedspreads. All rooms have robes, hair
dryers, irons and ironing boards, and phones in the bathrooms.
There's lightning-fast 24-hour room service from their excellent
Italian restaurant, Tulio (see review). The hotel provides coffee
in the morning and complimentary fireside wine-tasting in the
evening—classic Kimpton. ■ *1100 5th Ave (corner of Spring),
Seattle, WA 98101; (206) 624-8000 or (800) 624-4433; sales@
hotelvintagepark.com; www.hotelvintagepark.com; $$$; AE, DC,
DIS, JCB, MC, V; checks OK.* &

Inn at the Market ★★★ The setting—perched just above the
fish, flower, and fruit stalls of Pike Place Market, with a view
of Elliott Bay and adjacent to Seattle's oh-so-special French-
inspired restaurant, Campagne (see review)—is unsurpassed.
This small hotel (65 rooms) features personalized service that
approximates that of a country inn. Despite the downtown location, you won't feel oppressed by conventioneers (conference
facilities consist of one meeting room and one outdoor deck).
The architecture features oversize rooms, bay windows that let
occupants of even some side rooms enjoy big views, and a comfortable, pretty lobby. There is no complimentary breakfast
(just coffee), but a room-service breakfast can be ordered from
Bacco in the courtyard; dinner comes from Campagne. ■ *86 Pine
Street (between 1st and Market), Seattle, WA 98101; (206) 443-
3600 or (800) 446-4484; usa.nia.com/innmarket; $$$; AE, DC,
MC, V; checks OK.* &

Sorrento Hotel ★★★ Occupying a corner just east of downtown
in Seattle's First Hill neighborhood, the Sorrento is an Italianate
masterpiece that first opened in 1909, was remodeled to the
tune of $4.5 million in 1981, and is now preparing for a floor-
by-floor makeover for the millennium, adding top-notch service
touches like fax machines, in-room voice mail, and a small on-
site exercise facility. The 76 rooms are decorated in muted good
taste with a slight Asian accent. We recommend the 08 series
of suites, in the corners. Suites on the top floor make elegant
quarters for special meetings or parties—the showstopper

being the 3,000-square-foot, $1,200-a-night penthouse, with a grand piano, a patio, a Jacuzzi, a view of the bay, and several luxurious rooms. A comfortable, intimate fireside lobby lounge is a civilized place for afternoon tea or sipping Cognac while listening to jazz piano or classical guitar. Chef Eric Lenard showcases Northwest lamb, among other local culinary treasures, at the manly Hunt Club (see review). Some guests may find the location—uphill five blocks from the heart of downtown—inconvenient, but we find it quiet and removed. ■ *900 Madison St (at 9th), Seattle, WA 98104; (206) 622-6400 or (800) 426-1265; $$$; AE, DC, MC, V; checks OK.* ♿

The Bacon Mansion ★★ Built by Cecil Bacon in 1909, this Edwardian-style Tudor mansion is now a fine bed and breakfast. Most of the original wood was destroyed in a fire more than a dozen years ago, but the mansion has been skillfully restored. Eight rooms in the main guest house (five with private baths) are appointed with antiques and brass fixtures. The top of the line is the Capitol Room, a huge suite on the second floor with a sun room, fireplace, French doors, and a view of the Space Needle. The basement Garden Room (which stays pleasantly cool in summer) has 8-foot ceilings and a kitchenette. The unique Carriage House, a separate, two-story building with hunter green decor, is appropriate for a small family or two couples. An expanded continental breakfast might be served on the spacious patio between the main house and carriage house. Proprietor Daryl King is an enthusiastic, friendly host. ■ *959 Broadway E (corner of E Prospect St), Seattle, WA 98102; (206) 329-1864 or (800) 240-1864; $$; AE, MC, V; checks OK.*

Chambered Nautilus ★★ In a woodsy hillside setting in the University District, this 1915 Georgian colonial is comfortingly funky, offering six airy guest rooms furnished with antiques. All have private baths (though two rooms require you to step into the hall for access); some open onto porches with tree-webbed views of the Cascades. All rooms have robes, desks, flowers, and reading material. The location—just across the street from shared student housing units, and a few blocks from Fraternity Row—can get noisy during rush. Other times, though, it's surprisingly quiet. New innkeepers Steve Poole and Joyce Schultze serve a full breakfast and complimentary afternoon tea. There's a small library area, a large dining room, and an enclosed sun porch that invites lingering. Smoking is allowed on the porches and outside. Make prior arrangements for kids under 12. ■ *5005 22nd Ave NE (east on NE 50th St to 21st Ave), Seattle, WA 98105; (206) 522-2536; $$; AE, DC, MC, V; checks OK.*

The Edgewater Inn ★★ Alas, you can't fish from the famous west-facing windows of this waterfront institution anymore. You can, however, still breathe salty air and hear the ferry horns toot. The lobby and rooms have a rustic tone, with bleached oak and overstuffed chairs, plaid bedspreads, and lots of duck motifs and antler art. It's like a lodge on a busy (and sometimes noisy) Northwest waterfront, but with a reputable restaurant (Ernie's Bar and Grill, whose cruise ship–style Sunday brunch is a veritable extravaganza), a decent bar with a piano, and an uninterrupted view of Elliott Bay, Puget Sound, and the Olympic Mountains. Waterside rooms have the best views but can get hot on summer afternoons. At the moment, the Edgewater remains the only hotel on the waterfront, allowing it to command prices approaching outrageous. It's a short walk to the newly developed Bell Street Pier (Pier 66), with a trio of seafood restaurants (see Anthony's Pier 66 review) and an overpass for easier access to nearby Pike Place Market. ■ *Pier 67, 2411 Alaskan Way (Pier 67 at Wall St and Alaskan Way), Seattle, WA 98121; (206)728-7000 or (800)624-0670; $$$; AE, DC, MC, V; checks OK.* ♿

Lake Union B&B ★★ Take off your shoes and sink into the white cloud of carpet and inviting couches in this modern, three-story house near Gas Works Park, where you can enjoy a glass of wine by the fireplace. There are three rooms, each with TV/VCR, telephone, queen-size feather bed, and carefully ironed sheets. Upstairs, two stunning rooms offer Lake Union views. The larger suite also boasts a solarium, fireplace, Jacuzzi, and private bath (the sauna in the bathroom downstairs has piped-in music). Owner Janice Matthews, a former restaurateur, gladly prepares private dinners on request. In affiliation with her B&B, Matthews also offers overnight accommodations and romantic cruises on an elegant yacht, complete with private stateroom. ■ *2217 N 36th St (3 blocks north of Gas Works Park), Seattle, WA 98103; (206)547-9965; $$; MC, V; checks OK.*

Madison Renaissance Hotel ★★ This large hotel at the southeast edge of downtown successfully conveys a sense of warmth and intimacy inside. The lobby is tasteful and uncluttered, upstairs hallways are softly lit, and the rooms are elegantly furnished, with lots of marble and wood; most offer great city views. Avoid rooms on the freeway side; although the windows are soundproofed, the hum of traffic seeps in. Guests enjoy complimentary coffee and morning newspaper, a rooftop pool, and free in-town transportation. The pricey "Club Floors" (25 and 26) offer exclusive checkin privileges, concierge services, hors d'oeuvres and continental breakfast at Club Lounge, a library, and the best views. Prego, on the 28th floor, offers a fine selection of seafood to complement the view. ■ *515 Madison St (at 6th), Seattle, WA 98104; (206)583-0300; $$$; AE, DC, MC, V; checks OK.* ♿

Mayflower Park Hotel ★★ Renovations have paid off at this handsome 1927 hotel right in the heart of the downtown shopping district. A coolly elegant lobby opens onto Oliver's (a bar and lounge, famous for its outstanding martinis) on one side and Andaluca (a sexy, new, jewel-colored Mediterranean restaurant with a great little bar; see review) on the other. Rooms are small, still bearing charming reminders of the hotel's past: lovely Oriental brass and antique appointments; large, deep tubs; thick walls that trap noise. Taupe-toned and tastefully decorated, suites offer comfortable sitting areas and private sleeping quarters with king-size bed. Modern intrusions are for both better and worse: double-glazed windows in all rooms keep out traffic noise, but there are undistinguished furnishings in many of the rooms. The deluxe rooms are slightly bigger and have corner views; aim for one on a higher floor or you may find yourself facing a brick wall. ■ *405 Olive Way (at 4th), Seattle, WA 98101; (206) 623-8700 or (800) 426-5100; $$$; AE, DC, MC, V; checks OK.* &

The Paramount Hotel ★★ A new addition to downtown's lodging scene (and yet another feather in the cap of the WestCoast hotel chain), the Paramount, which opened in 1996, is kitty-corner from the theater that shares its name and convenient to the Convention Center and midtown shopping. Step inside, and the cozy faux-library look of the lobby (think: arty hunting lodge with grand fireplace) is in keeping with the hotel's intended "European chateau" ambience. The Paramount's modest size— there are 146 guest rooms, two small meeting rooms, and a tiny fitness center—will appeal to those who eschew megahotels. Standard guest rooms are prettily appointed, though rather small, as are the bathrooms. Consider splurging for an "executive" room, whose corner location means a bit more space and whose bathroom boasts a whirlpool tub. The adjoining restaurant, Blowfish—home to a robata bar and a wall of pachinko machines—joined Seattle's growing pan-Asian restaurant roster in the summer of '97. ■ *724 Pine St (corner of 7th), Seattle, WA 98101; (206) 292-9500 or (800) 426-0670; $$$; AE, DC, DIS, JCB, MC, V; checks OK.* &

Pioneer Square Hotel ★★ Regentrification is the name of the game along this lovely block in Pioneer Square, and this (shhh: you'd never know) Best Western property offers just that. Renovations have transformed a formerly seedy hotel into a handsome, comfortably appointed, moderately priced lodging—a boon for budget-minded travelers intent on staying in the heart of Seattle's old town among galleries, bookstores, boutiques, restaurants, and nightclubs. In each guest room you'll find rich, elegant cherry-wood furniture and two armoires (one to use as a closet—since the former closets have been transformed into spacious bathrooms—and one for the TV). There's a small sitting alcove in these surprisingly quiet rooms (the hotel is in close proximity to the busy Alaskan Way Viaduct). Quibbles? The front desk staff could use some polish, and the complimentary

▼

▲

continental breakfast may be pretty picked over if you sleep past 7:30am. The neighborhood may not suit timid travelers, but for those willing to embrace the urban melting pot, this is a great new choice. *77 Yesler Way (between 1st St and Alaskan Way), Seattle, WA 98104; (206)340-1234 or (800)800-5514; info@pioneersquare.com; www.pioneersquare.com; $$; AE, DC, DIS, MC, V; no checks.* &

Roberta's ★★ Roberta is the gracious, somewhat loquacious lady of this Capitol Hill house near Volunteer Park and a few blocks from the funky Broadway district. Inside, it's lovely: refinished floors throughout, a comfortable couch and an old upright piano, books everywhere, and a large oval dining table and country-style chairs. Of the five rooms, the Hideaway Suite (the entire third floor), with views of the Cascades from the window seats, a skylight, a sitting area with a futon couch and a small desk, and a full bath with a tub, is our favorite. Others prefer the Peach Room, with its antique desk, bay window, love seat, and queen-size oak bed. Early risers will enjoy the Madrona Room, with its morning sun and private bath. All five rooms have queen-size beds; four have private baths. In the morning, Roberta brings you a wake-up cup of coffee, then later puts out a smashing full breakfast (no meat). No children. No smoking except on the porch. ■ *1147 16th Ave E (north of Prospect), Seattle, WA 98112; (206)329-3326; www.robertasbb. com; $$; MC, V; checks OK.*

Sheraton Seattle Hotel and Towers ★★ Seattle's Sheraton is an 840-room tower rising as a sleek triangle, the Convention Center in its shadow. It, too, aims at the convention business, so the guest rooms are smallish and standard, and much emphasis is placed on the meeting rooms and the restaurants. The summer of 1996 saw the completion of a nearly $7 million renovation featuring a newly designed lobby lounge and oyster bar, as well as the reenvisioning of the casual Pike Street Cafe (famous for its 27-foot-long dessert spread), and the transformation of a disco bar into Schooners Sports Pub (big-screen TVs, Northwest microbrews, pub fare). The outstanding fine-dining restaurant, Fullers, remains an oasis of serenity adorned with fine Northwest art (see review). Service here is quite efficient. Convention facilities are complete, and the kitchen staff can handle the most complex assignments. Discriminating business travelers can head for the upper four "VIP" floors (31–34), where a hotel-within-a-hotel offers its own lobby, concierge, club lounge (with its own bar and complimentary continental breakfast, afternoon tea, and evening hors d'oeuvres), and considerably more amenities in the rooms (although they're the same size as the economy ones). The hotel's top-floor health club has a heated pool and a knockout city panorama. *1400 6th Ave (at*

*Pike), Seattle, WA 98101; (206) 621-9000 or (800) 204-6100;
$$$; AE, DC, MC, V; checks OK.* &

University Inn ★★ A remodel in 1993 added a south wing, more
than doubling the number of guest rooms at this bright, clean,
well-managed University District establishment. Rooms in the
newer wing are more spacious and have king-size beds. North-
wing rooms, even after a remodel of their own, are standard,
with shower stalls in the bathrooms (no tub). Some have small
balconies overlooking the heated outdoor pool and hot tub.
Other amenities include complimentary continental breakfast,
morning paper, a small fitness room, and free off-street parking.
Whether or not you have business at neighboring University of
Washington, the exceptionally beautiful, parklike campus (don't
miss the renovated Henry Gallery, the Suzzallo Library, or the
Mount Rainier vista) is worth a visit. ■ *4140 Roosevelt Way NE
(corner of NE 42nd St), Seattle, WA 98105; (206) 632-5055 or
(800) 733-3855; univinn@aol.com; www.travelweb.com; $$; AE,
DC, DIS, MC, V; checks OK.* &

WestCoast Plaza Park Suites ★★ For better or for worse, Plaza
Park is but a step away from the Washington State Convention
Center. In addition to the 25 standard rooms, all other accommodations are, in one way or another, suites, with a living room,
dining area, kitchenette, and a bedroom (sporting a second
TV). Some have fireplaces and some even have Jacuzzis. While
all are large, the somewhat bland decor could use a splash of
something. Expect all the amenities of a full-service hotel: conference rooms, exercise rooms (sauna and Jacuzzi, too), laundry and valet service. By early 1998, an Outback Steakhouse
will adjoin the hotel, which for now has no restaurant (though
an extensive continental breakfast is included in the rates). The
Plaza Park is great for corporate clients on long-term stays or
families on vacation wanting a little room to spread out (and an
outdoor pool for the kids). ■ *1011 Pike St (at Boren), Seattle, WA
98101; (206) 682-8282 or (800) 426-0670; $$$; AE, DC, DIS,
MC, V; checks OK.* &

Westin Hotel ★★ Westin's international headquarters is in Seat-
tle, so this flagship hotel has quite a few extras. The twin cylin-
drical towers, called "corncobs" by the natives, nonetheless
afford spacious rooms with superb views, particularly above the
20th floor. The size of the hotel (with 877 rooms and 48 suites)
contributes to some lapses in service, however; we can attest
to long lines for checkin and occasional difficulties getting at-
tention from the harried concierge staff. Convention facilities,
spread over several floors of meeting rooms, are quite com-
plete. There is a large pool, along with an exercise room. On the
top floors are some ritzy, glitzy suites. The location, near West-
lake Center and the Monorail station, is excellent. Two notable
restaurants—Nikko (with a great sushi bar; see review) and

Roy's Seattle (the 12th of chef Roy Yamaguchi's international "Euro-Asian" empire)—are on the premises. ■ *1900 5th Ave (between Stewart and Virginia), Seattle, WA 98101; (206) 728-1000 or (800) 228-3000; $$$; AE, DC, MC, V; checks OK.* &

The Claremont Hotel ★ Travelers from all over keep the Claremont heavily booked year-round. The location can't be beat: three blocks from the Market, a block and a half from Westlake Center and the Monorail. A recent makeover has added an elegant touch to many of the rooms. Kitchen suites are available, and whole families can comfortably fit in the apartment suites, which feature a full kitchen, a separate bedroom, and a living area where twin beds may be added on request. For a moderately priced splurge, spring for one of the corner king bedroom suites on an upper floor with a view of downtown and the Market. The very popular Italian restaurant Assaggio adjoins the hotel. ■ *2000 4th Ave (at Virginia), Seattle, WA 98121; (206) 448-8600 or (800) 448-8601; $$; AE, DC, DIS, JCB, MC, V; checks OK.*

MV Challenger ★ A luxury liner it's not, but if you've got a thing for tugboats, the boat-and-breakfast MV *Challenger*, Captain Jerry Brown's handsomely restored, 96-foot workhorse, is for you. Everything—from the spotless galley to the eight cabins—is shipshape. Lounge topside on a deck chair, or inside around the fireplace, or step out and explore the docks, restaurants, and shops just a stroll away. For utmost quiet and comfort, reserve one of the cabins on the tug's upper deck, or consider renting space aboard one of two yachts moored alongside the tug (rates include an exceptional breakfast aboard the *Challenger*). ■ *1001 Fairview Ave N (at Yale St Landing), Seattle, WA 98109; (206) 340-1201; $$; AE, MC, V; checks OK.*

Pacific Plaza Hotel ★ The midsize Pacific Plaza offers a welcome respite from astronomical downtown hotel prices. For those who care more about location and budget than amenities, this is the perfect place. Rooms start at well under $100, even in summer, and include a generous continental breakfast. The ambience brings to mind a good budget hotel in a European city: long hallways; simple, comfortable rooms; and small, clean bathrooms. Light sleepers may wish to stay elsewhere, as the hotel is not air-conditioned and opening the windows invites traffic noise. ■ *400 Spring St (corner of 4th), Seattle, WA 98104; (206) 623-3900 or (800) 426-1165; $$; AE, DC, DIS, MC, V; checks OK.*

Pensione Nicols ★ Its location is both the best and the worst feature of Pensione Nicols. Its perch, just above the Pike Place Market, outweighs the fact that its entrance is right next to an X-rated movie theater on an otherwise boutique-and-restaurant-filled block of First Avenue. Some of the rooms facing this busy street can be quite noisy, and though the other rooms don't have windows, they do have skylights and are much quieter. Ten guest rooms share four bathrooms. The large common room at the west end of the third floor has a gorgeous view of the Market's rooftops and Elliott Bay beyond; it is here that the bountiful continental breakfast—including fresh treats from the Market—is served. Unusual antiques abound (the Nicolses also own N. B. Nicols, a charming antique store in Post Alley, below). Also available: two wonderful suites, each with private bath, full kitchen, bedroom alcove, and a living room with that great view. ■ *1923 1st Ave (between Stewart and Virginia), Seattle, WA 98101; (206) 441-7125 or (800) 440-7125; $$; AE, DC, DIS, MC, V; checks OK.*

Residence Inn by Marriott—Lake Union ★ It's not exactly on the lake, but rather across busy Fairview Avenue. Still, the 234 rooms, half of which boast lake views (request one on the highest floor possible), are spacious and tastefully decorated. All rooms have fully outfitted kitchenettes, and a continental breakfast and evening dessert are presented in the lobby—a light, plant-filled courtyard with an atrium and waterfall. There isn't a hotel restaurant, but guests may charge meals to their room at any number of lakeside eateries across the street. Amenities include meeting rooms, lap pool, exercise room, sauna and steam room, and spa. ■ *800 Fairview Ave N (at Boren, at the south end of Lake Union, across from the marina), Seattle, WA 98109; (206) 624-6000 or (800) 331-3131; $$$; AE, DC, MC, V; checks OK.* ৬

The Williams House ★ At various times in its lengthy history, this south-slope Queen Anne turn-of-the-century residence has been a gentlemen's boardinghouse and an emergency medical clinic for the 1962 Seattle World's Fair. Today, owners Doug and Sue Williams offer five guest rooms, four with views (three have private baths; the other two have a bath each, down the hall). The enclosed south sun porch is a nice gathering spot, and you can relax with a book out in the colorful, well-kept garden. Brass beds, original fixtures, fireplaces, ornate Italian tiles, and oak floors mirror the home's Edwardian past. A full breakfast is served in the first-floor dining room. ■ *1505 4th Ave N (at Galer), Seattle, WA 98109; (206) 285-0810 or (800) 880-0810; innkeepr@wolfenet.com; useattle.uspan.com/williamshouse; $$; AE, DC, DIS, MC, V; checks OK.*

Hotel Monaco [*unrated*] What the Greek Isles have to do with Seattle is beyond us, but we like what the Monaco, with its bright, Mediterranean look, has done to Seattle. The domed lobby with a nautical mural of dolphins playing in the Aegean circa 2000 BC, white marble floors, and images of steamer trunks evoke another travel era altogether. Press time marks the introduction of the 21st Kimpton Group hotel (and the third in Seattle), and this 189-room hotel is bound to give Seattle's top establishments a run for their money. As at many local hotels, the views take a backseat (this used to be a nondescript telephone switching center): service and design are to be the focal points here for individual travelers and businessmen alike (there are 6,000 square feet of meeting space). Those who insist on a view should request south-facing rooms on floors 6 through 11, and those who insist on bringing a pet, may. And if you don't have a pet, you might consider asking about their loaner goldfish. Adjacent to the hotel will be the 175-seat Sazerac restaurant, featuring Southern-inspired cuisine. ■ *1101 4th Ave (at Spring St), Seattle, WA 98101; (206) 621-1770 or (800) 945-2240; www.monaco-seattle.com; $$$; full bar; AE, DC, DIS, MC, V; checks OK; breakfast, lunch, dinner every day.*

Houseboat Hideaway [*unrated*] A stay on one of these floating hideaways could be the quintessential Seattle experience. You're moored on sparkling south Lake Union, with unencumbered lake vistas and all the comforts of home. Houseboat Hideaway is a family-owned and -operated rental company providing overnight houseboat accommodations (among them a tug, small houseboats, a 28-foot European-style canal barge, and even some true floating homes à la *Sleepless in Seattle*). All have kitchen or kitchenette; some have hot tubs, barbecues, and hammocks ripe for lounging. Prices range from $125 to $350 per night, with room for 2 to 10 "passengers" depending on the accommodation. Daily maid service is available for an additional fee, but this is, first and foremost, a make-yourself-at-home-in-Seattle private marine hideaway. ■ *Multiple locations; mail: 2226 Eastlake Ave E, Seattle, WA 98102; (206) 323-5323; $$$; AE, MC, V; checks OK.*

Inn at Harbor Steps [*unrated*] Just open at press time, this Four Sisters property is the second in the Northwest (Saratoga Inn was the first), offering Four Sisters' hallmark country-inn ambience in a decidedly urban setting. Tucked into the swanky new high-rise commercial-and-condo complex at Harbor Steps, the inn is both intimate and elegant, catering to the discerning business or holiday traveler with 20 rooms (most overlooking a garden courtyard). Each has a fireplace, king or queen bed, wet bar, fridge, and sitting area; deluxe rooms include spa tubs. Furnishings are contemporary and tasteful. Among the many amenities are 24-hour concierge/innkeeper services, afternoon tea, complimentary hors d'oeuvres and wine, and a breakfast buffet. Guests have access to an indoor pool, sauna, Jacuzzi, exercise room, and meeting room. ■ *1221 1st Ave (between University and Seneca), Seattle, WA 98101; (206) 748-0973 or (888) 728-8910; $$$; AE, DC, MC, V; checks OK.* &

The area thought of as Edmonds is just a small village in a much larger city. "Downtown Edmonds" is a throwback to another era, with a small movie theater, friendly shopkeepers, wide sidewalks, and waterfront views that encourage evening strolls. The ferry here departs to Kingston; for information, call (425)464-6400. Edmonds bills itself as the City of Celebrations. Most popular are the **Edmonds Art Festival** (in June) and **A Taste of Edmonds** (third weekend in August).

Brackett's Landing, just north of the ferry terminal, has a jetty and an underwater marine-life park that draws scuba enthusiasts. **Edmonds Historic Walk** was prepared by the Centennial Committee and offers a look at old Edmonds; stop by the Chamber of Commerce, 120 N Fifth Avenue, (425)776-6711, for a free map of the walk.

RESTAURANTS

Ciao Italia ★★ Owner Patrick Girardi, a friendly, earnest young restaurateur, can be found working the room at this Edmonds favorite. Ciao Italia's strip-mall location aside, the pleasant atmosphere—at once candle-lit and casual—works to fine effect. The menu is full of Italian meat-and-pasta standards done in better-than-standard fashion. Order the simple, elegant pizza Margherita, or an artichoke-and-olive-speckled pizza capricciosa, perhaps split as a first course. The thin crusts are perfectly yeasty and chewy. Consider choosing pastas from the specials list, which here always seems to yield the chef's best efforts. Pasta, chicken, and veal entrees come with complimentary (and sometimes too garlicky) salads; other meat dishes include worthy sides (creamy polenta if you're lucky). ■ *546 5th Ave S (in the shopping center, south of 5th and Walnut), Edmonds; (425)771-7950; $; beer and wine; MC, V; local checks only; dinner Mon–Sat.* &

▼

Edmonds

Restaurants

▲

Provinces Asian Restaurant & Bar ★★ Today, the idea of a pan-Asian restaurant is accepted even in the quiet hamlet of Edmonds—where a serene and decidedly older crowd enjoys a range of Asian cuisine in an attractive, oversize dining room set in a quaint shopping mall. We like the swift, efficient service, the Vietnamese salad rolls, and the Bangkok hot and sour soup—served in a clay pot brimming with shellfish and straw mushrooms, fragrant with lemongrass, and large enough to feed four. The Cantonese-style seafood lobster sauce is dense with shellfish and vegetables and flavored with Chinese black beans. Mongolian ginger beef is a touch sweet but pleasantly potent with ginger and garlic. An abbreviated lunch menu—including humongous bowls of udon with various meats, vegetables, and seafood—is a bargain and a half considering the quality of the ingredients. In the adjoining cocktail lounge, folks meet to bend an elbow, smoke a cigarette, and make merry. ■ *201 5th Ave S (upper level in Old Mill Town Mall at 5th and Maple), Edmonds; (425) 744-0288; $$; full bar; AE, DC, MC, V; local checks only; lunch Mon–Sat, dinner every day. ₷*

Brusseau's ★ Though original owner Jerilyn Brusseau is long gone, her eponymous cafeteria-style bakery and cafe remains an Edmonds favorite. Ferry-bound folks vie for a spot outdoors at umbrellaed picnic tables, while local families and elderly patrons relax inside at glass-topped tables over coffee and sweets. The day's menu always includes a couple of soups—perhaps cilantro-and-cumin-spiked black bean, meant to be sopped up with a house-baked sourdough roll. Create a sandwich from a short list of options (yes, you may have a half), or choose among a sampling of salads lining a glass display case. Save room for a slice of seasonal fruit pie, and don't leave without buying a loaf of fresh bread to savor at home. ■ *117 5th Ave (at Dayton), Edmonds; (425) 774-4166; $$; no alcohol; MC, V; checks OK; breakfast, lunch every day.*

LODGINGS

Edmonds Harbor Inn ★ Strategically located near the Edmonds ferry and train terminals, the inn is an attractive choice for a night in this charming, waterside Seattle suburb. It features 61 large rooms (with views, unfortunately, of the surrounding business park rather than the picturesque Sound), oak furnishings, continental breakfast, and access to an athletic club just next door. If you're traveling with youngsters in tow, the rooms with modern kitchenettes, coupled with the inn's extremely reasonable rates, will be particularly appealing. Get directions—the place is near the harborfront, but is a little difficult to find in the gray sea of new office and shopping developments. ■ *130 W Dayton St (at Edmonds Way), Edmonds, WA 98020; (425) 771-5021 or (800) 441-8033; $$; AE, DC, MC, V; checks OK. ₷*

GREATER SEATTLE: BOTHELL

The town stands at the north end of Lake Washington, on the way into more open country. **Sammamish River Park** is a pleasant spot, and from here you can take a 9½-mile hike, bike ride, or in-line skating tour along the Sammamish River (often called the Sammamish Slough), which extends from Bothell to Marymount Park in Redmond, stopping part of the way at Chateau Ste. Michelle winery (see Woodinville introduction).

RESTAURANTS

Relais ★★★ For the culinarily conscious, Bothell has always meant one thing: Gerard's Relais de Lyon. In 1996, after 20 years as the man behind the restaurant's name (and its stoves),

Gerard Parrat—whose outpost and bastion of French cuisine offered the last great hope for lovers of formal French dining— tossed his toque to a new chef/owner, Eric Eisenberg. French-trained and New York–driven, Eisenberg and his best friend, co-owner Joseph Miglino (late of Columbia Winery), strive to continue the traditions that made Gerard's a worthy destination. This handsome converted home offers a warren of small dining rooms, though the best seat in the house can be had only when the weather's fine—in the always-romantic courtyard. Fireplaces warm the somewhat austere interior decor. As for the new menu, all the classic French ingredients are accounted for, as is a multicourse ménu de dégustation. Escargots are chopped with hazelnuts and stuffed into pasta; lobster enriches a bisque or comes steamed in an herb broth; roasted squab is paired with foie gras; and tournedos of beef wear sauce béarnaise, *bien sûr*. Allow Miglino to match your meal with a trio of fine wines by the glass. There's Sunday brunch now, too. ■ *17121 Bothell Way NE (near 96th Ave NE), Bothell; (425) 485-7600; $$$; full bar; AE, MC, V; checks OK; dinner Tues–Sun, brunch Sun.* &

Environs

GREATER SEATTLE: WOODINVILLE

The suburbs have caught up with this formerly rural outback, paving the dirt roads and lining them with strip malls. Some of the country ambience remains, however, especially to the east, where Woodinville fades into the dairy farms of the Snoqualmie Valley. Woodinville's claim to fame is **Chateau Ste. Michelle**, the state's largest winery (though many other wineries and microbreweries now dot the landscape). The grapes come from Eastern Washington, but experimental vineyards are on-site, and tours of the operation, complete with tastings, run daily every half hour between 10am and 5pm; 14111 NE 145th, (425) 488-3300. Just across the street from Ste. Michelle is **Columbia Winery**, the state's oldest premium-wine company. Columbia offers tours on weekends between 10am and 4pm, and the tasting room is open daily from 10am to 7pm; 14030 NE 145th, (425) 488-2776.

Gardeners from around the region flock to **Molbak's**, the massive nursery and greenhouse at 13625 NE 175th; (206) 483-5000.

Woodinville

Restaurants

▲

RESTAURANTS

The Golden Goat Cafe Med ★★ The Golden Goat would be a great neighborhood cafe, if there were a neighborhood anywhere in sight. Owner/chef Jeff Boswell is a most genial host, running on inspiration and whimsy. He'll sometimes crank up a jazz tune while piecing together bountiful antipasto plates with smoked salmon crostini and frittatas of artichoke, arugula, and chiles. The chef's two favorite liquids appear to be balsamic vinegar, which he uses generously, and wine, Italian and Washington, on which he imposes a very modest markup. Fill up on your choice of such dishes as roasted chicken, wonderful braised lamb shanks, and a half-dozen fresh pasta options, because often he just doesn't feel like making desserts. ■ *14471 Woodinville-Redmond Rd (at 145th), Woodinville; (425) 483-6791; $$; beer and wine; AE, DC, DIS, MC, V; checks OK; dinner Tues–Sat.* ⧖

Armadillo Barbecue ★ Leave refinement behind when you enter this West Texas barbecue joint plopped down in the wilds of Woodinville. Brothers Bob and Bruce Gill serve up their own brand of perverse humor along with tender, lean pork and extra-moist chicken, thoroughly and powerfully smoked, with a rich hot-sauce tang, and sides of molasses-heavy beans and cakey corn bread. It all adds up to a fine Texas feast. Sit at the counter and you can jaw with the cooks—all schooled in rapid repartee—sip one of 40 beers, and order a "Snake Plate," which gives you "three bucks worth o' stuff," for $4. Salads won't convert anyone to vegetarianism. The massive oven/smoker, right behind the counter, cannot seem to contain all the smoke it produces, so customers usually go home lightly smoked outside as well as in. ■ *13109 NE 175th St (take Woodinville exit from Hwy 522E), Woodinville; (425) 481-1417; $; beer and wine; AE, MC, V; checks OK; lunch, dinner every day.* ⧖

▼

▲

GREATER SEATTLE: MALTBY

RESTAURANTS

Maltby Cafe ★★ Upstairs, the 1937 WPA-project Maltby School gymnasium remains as it was. Downstairs, in what used to be the school cafeteria, the Maltby Cafe dishes up outstanding country breakfasts and equally satisfying lunches. Finding the place the first time might be tough, but you'll never forget the way. A Saturday-morning repast can fill you for the weekend. Unhurried, bountiful breakfasts feature delicious omelets—the Maltby is a huge affair, stuffed with more than a cup of assorted veggies, ham cubes, even pieces of roast beef—good new potatoes, old-fashioned oatmeal, and thick slices of French toast. If you have to wait for a table (which is usually the case on weekends), order one of the legendary cinnamon rolls and savor it on the steps outside. At lunch, there're great sandwiches and soups (try a Reuben, made with their own corned beef). ■ *8809 Maltby Rd (Hwy 522 and Hwy 9), Maltby; (425) 483-3123; $; beer and wine; MC, V; checks OK; breakfast, lunch every day.* ⧖

GREATER SEATTLE: REDMOND

Once a bucolic suburban destination, now known worldwide as the headquarters for mighty **Microsoft**, this city at the north end of Lake Sammamish is also the hub of a lot of local (and national) cycling activity. The **Marymoor Velodrome in Marymoor Park,** a 400-meter concrete track built for the 1976 Olympic trials, draws world-class bicyclists for twice-weekly races from mid-May through September. The park itself, on the north shore of Lake Sammamish, is a huge expanse of ball fields and semiwild grassland that makes for great bird-watching. On weekends, hundreds of dog owners bring their pets to the vast and legally leashless dog run in the fields along the Sammamish River. Less-ambitious bicyclers enjoy the **Sammamish River Trail,** which runs north along the river.

RESTAURANTS

Il Bacio ★★ In the kitchen is chef Rino Baglio—a native of Como, Italy, whose list of credentials runs longer than uncut linguine (he helped prepare the wedding feast for Chuck and Di, and cooked for Princess Caroline of Monaco). Handling the dining room—decorated to resemble the Italian countryside, with faux grape arbor, faux slate roof, and faux rolling hills—is his wife, Patsy, smiling cheery hellos, handling the ringing telephone, and directing traffic. Sometimes it seems as if half of Redmond is here, spooning up *pasta e fagioli*, soaking rustic bread in garlicky *vongole in brodetto*, forking into breaded veal cutlet topped with prosciutto and fontina, or twirling strands of soul-satisfying spaghetti Bolognese—rustic fare whose rich tomato sauce offers ground beef, veal, and pork bolstered by herbs, garlic, and a fine dice of carrot. Baglio's adjacent pasticceria is long gone (an additional dining room has taken its place), but you probably won't have room for dessert anyway. ■ *16564 Cleveland St (downtown, on the main eastbound drag), Redmond; (425)869-8815; $$; beer and wine; MC, V; local checks only; lunch Mon–Fri, dinner Mon–Sat.* &

▼
Redmond

Restaurants

▲

Si Señor ★ The influences of the cuisines of Peru and the area of northeastern Mexico centering on the city of Monterrey help account for much of the originality on this menu. And though you can order the usual south-of-the-border standbys, why miss out on exotica? *Lomo de almendra* is marinated pork loin in a deliciously dark, almond-flavored sauce; *seco,* a Peruvian lamb dish, comes sauced with a blend of cilantro and onions. *Anticuchos,* a dinner-size appetizer, will astound those frustrated by skimpy little sticks of beef satay; here you get a platter with baked potatoes flanking skewers laden with flat slabs of tender, marinated, charred beef heart (don't balk: if you didn't know it, you'd never guess). The staff is lively and lighthearted, occasionally barreling into the dining room with a platter and hollering "Cheeseburger!" Live music accompanies dinner on weekends. ■ *2115 Bellevue-Redmond Rd (behind Sears), Redmond; (425)865-8938; $; full bar; AE, DC, MC, V; checks OK; lunch, dinner every day.* &

This city's comfortable downtown on Lake Washington's Moss Bay is a popular strolling ground, especially in summer. Art galleries, restaurants, and boutiques line the two-story main street. Several restaurants look out over boats docked at the marina. Grab a latte and walk a block to the waterfront park, where ducks beg scraps and dodge children on the sandy beach.

On Yarrow Bay at the south end of town lies **Carillon Point**, a glitzy hotel-and-shopping complex lining a round, red-brick courtyard with views of the lake and the Olympic Mountains in the distance.

To the north, just outside of Kirkland, at **Saint Edward State Park**, spectacular rolling trails amble through old stands of Douglas fir and Western red cedar, eventually winding up on the lakefront.

RESTAURANTS

Cafe Juanita ★★★ Owner/host Peter Dow is devoting more time to his winery these days. His Cavatappi label is in such demand that the wines, made on the premises, are not always listed on the Juanita's excellent, Italian-heavy wine list. Dow's kitchen is in the capable hands of chef/manager John Neumark, his dining room run with professional grace by well-versed servers. This dimly lit converted creekside house hasn't changed much since 1979: it's still a most unpretentious space, with a few etchings and many wine bottles by way of decor. One can't help but think that candlelight and music would help warm the room tremendously, but the loyal Eastside contingent here for the country-Italian fare doesn't seem to mind the lack of chic or romantic ambience. There's no printed menu, just oversize blackboards (touting, as ever, pollo pistacchi, agnello verdure, anitra affumicata, and pasta puttanesca). Servers offer detailed explanations, and from there it's a pleasurable glide through dinner. The house-made olive and rosemary bread will help you swab every drop of luscious sauce that perfects a tender rabbit, a smoky duck breast, or a lusty homemade pasta. Finish with biscotti and Vin Santo. ■ *9702 NE 120th Pl (116th off I-405, west to 97th), Kirkland; (425)823-1505; $$; full bar; MC, V; checks OK; dinner every day.*

Third Floor Fish Cafe ★★★ Now that chef Scott Staples is working culinary magic at the formerly hit-or-miss Third Floor, no one can complain any longer that there's no place to eat dependably fabulous food on the Eastside. Burnished wood creates a handsome, masculine look throughout this terraced arc of a dining room. Expense-accounters (and types who are just off the SS *We've-Got-Money*) finally have a worthy perch for fine dining, and nearly every table affords a Moss Bay view. Seafood scores big, with caramelized scallops dancing around creamy

▼ Kirkland ▲

risotto in a pool of vanilla-and-citrus-scented brown butter, or pan-seared sturgeon strewn with shiitakes and set atop a creamy-centered rice cake. Infused oils and a vast store of imaginative vinaigrettes make for artful, eminently edible dishes. Cabernet-braised lamb shank, peppercorn-crusted beef tenderloin, and such specials as salt-crusted venison offer carnivores something to talk about. As does the splendid view, shared with patrons hoisting one in the bar. ■ *205 Lake St S (downtown), Kirkland; (425)822-3553; $$$; full bar; AE, MC, V; checks OK; dinner every day.* &

Bistro Provençal ★★ You won't find a more reliable restaurant on the Eastside. The cozy, country-inn atmo remains, as does the creaky old dessert tray, which could have served napoleons to Napoleon. You're likely to be waited on by one whose native tongue is French and whose service may prove erratic, but the food has been, is, and probably always will be well worth a minor inconvenience. The menu emphasis is bistro, though you can also choose from more upscale items on the à la carte menu. Or try the deluxe, five-course, prix-fixe "ménu de gastronomie." We like the inexpensive four-course bistro menu, which begins with a full and flavorful onion soup, followed by a good crisp salad with a sprinkling of goat cheese. Among the main-course selections is the *daube avignonnaise,* a simple, comforting Provençal-style beef stew that chef Philippe Gayte has been preparing since the day his restaurant opened decades ago. ■ *212 Central Way (downtown), Kirkland; (425)827-3300; $$; full bar; AE, DC, MC, V; local checks only; dinner every day.* &

City Thai Cuisine ★★ Who could expect to find harmony in a strip mall? Perhaps the hungry soul who braves the harried crowds at Kirkland's Parkplace Center, headed for City Thai. The atmosphere here is elegant and refined, from the white linen napkins to the antique wooden tables and chairs, but the true mood is reflected in the food. By focusing on the subtle symmetry of seasonings, owner Joe Suwanvichit has created elegant meals with just the right balance of spicy and sweet flavors. Those seeking enlightenment might begin with the *tom mun*—fish cakes dipped in a dainty sauce of sliced cucumbers, chopped peanuts, and red onions—or the *tom yum* soup, in which flavors blend rather than compete for dominance. Portions are plentiful and pretty. City Thai in Bellevue is under separate ownership. ■ *134 Parkplace Center (near KeyBank, across from QFC), Kirkland; (425)827-2875; $; beer and wine; AE, DIS, MC, V; checks OK; lunch, dinner Tues–Sun.* &

Ristorante Paradiso ★★ Owner/chef Fabrizio Loi's labor of love, just off Kirkland's main drag, is a surprisingly sophisticated culinary treat in unpretentious digs. Much of the menu remains constant from its 1991 debut. Openers include a beautifully arranged plate of grilled vegetables for two, or a generous bowl of fresh, perfectly cooked mussels and clams in a wine-based broth. There's a range of meat dishes, including a delicate saltimbocca, and a long list of pastas. We like the *scaloppine alla pizzaiola* (veal with a veil of oregano-scented tomato sauce and capers) and the *pollo alla mia maniera* (Marsala-sauced chicken stuffed with spinach, mozzarella, and prosciutto). There's a great selection of wines, featuring many Italian labels, priced from the midteens and up. ■ *120A Park Lane (off Lake Washington Blvd, across from Moss Bay), Kirkland; (425)889-8601; $$; beer and wine; AE, DC, DIS, MC, V; checks OK; lunch Mon–Fri, dinner every day.* &

Shamiana ★★ Brother-and-sister team Eric Larson and Tracy Larson DeVaan grew up as foreign-service kids in East Pakistan (now Bangladesh), and after their return to the United States found themselves hankering for the food they remembered. At Shamiana, you'll find Eric in the kitchen while Tracy runs the front of the house. Eastern cooking meets Western chefs here in the happiest of ways: stunning creations include a velvet butter chicken wallowing in cumin-scented butter, tomato, and cream sauce. A Pakistani barbecue turns out flame-broiled meats, and there are mouth-watering versions of traditional Indian curries. Vegetarians can select from crisp samosas stuffed with crunchy potatoes or *aloo dum Kashmiri*, potatoes simmered in spicy yogurt sauce. The menu notes which dishes are made without dairy products and gives a heat guide to ordering curries. Lunch is bargain city, with a buffet that changes daily. ■ *10724 NE 68th St (in Houghton Village, at 108th Ave NE), Kirkland; (425)827-4902; $$; beer and wine; AE, DC, MC, V; checks OK; lunch Mon–Fri, dinner every day.* &

▼

Kirkland

Restaurants

▲

Yarrow Bay Grill and Beach Cafe ★★ There are two restaurants here, one on top of the other, each with a gorgeous Lake Washington view. Originally intended to be an Eastside version of Ray's Boathouse in Shilshole (three of the four Ray's owners started Yarrow Bay), these siblings have evolved over the years into fine, unique dining spots whose menu offers "world fare" (read: all over the map). With chef Vicki McCaffree in charge, the upstairs grill is better than ever. A piece of fresh Atlantic salmon could not be more perfectly done, steamed in sake and ginger and topped with a sesame-kissed shiitake-ginger-butter sauce. Half the entree menu comes from the sea, with such Pacific Rim touches as panko-fried calamari, Korean beef satay, or a Thai-style crab cake. All this is complemented by a deep wine list and plenty of wines by the glass.

Downstairs, the casual **Beach Cafe** is lively. Knock a few bucks off the upstairs prices and sample a jazzed-up United Nations menu, with Greek horiatiki salad, Cajun-fried rock shrimp, Jamaican jerk chicken, "mom's" meat loaf, or selections from the country of the month. ▪ *1270 Carillon Point (in the Carillon Point Plaza), Kirkland; (425)889-9052; $$$ (Yarrow Bay Grill), $$ (Beach Cafe); full bar; AE, DC, MC, V; checks OK; lunch, dinner every day, brunch Sun.* ઠ

DaVinci's Flying Pizza and Pasta ★ It could be 1969, judging from the trippy Day-Glo and black-light decor, tempered with a touch of modernity—big-screen TVs in the bar, which jumps with young singles looking for pizza, pasta, and perhaps other things as well. DaVinci's fronts two streets, wrapping around the corner of a building, with retractable walls that open in fine weather. The back room is the lake-view restaurant proper, only a little more sedate than the bar. Avoid the loathesome barbecue smoked-chicken pizzas. Much better are the more classic pies—the Leonardo's pizza with aged salami, Greek olives, chèvre, peppers, and tomatoes saucelessly combined with olive oil on a bready crust is a clean marriage of flavors. Better still are the pastas, including excellent lasagne and cannelloni. Sandwiches are unusually satisfying, desserts heavenly. ▪ *89 Kirkland Ave (at Lake St), Kirkland; (425)889-9000; $; full bar; AE, DC, DIS, MC, V; checks OK; lunch, dinner every day.*

LODGINGS

Woodmark Hotel ★★★ On the eastern shore of Lake Washington, this hotel claims the title of the only lodging actually on the lake. From the outside, it resembles a modern office building, but on the inside one encounters the soft touches of a fine hotel: 100 plush rooms (the best have lake views and sounds of geese honking and ducks quacking) with fully stocked minibars and refrigerators, terrycloth robes, oversize towels, and service (from laundry to valet) to match. You'll get a complimentary newspaper with the full breakfast and a chance to "raid the pantry" for late-night snacks and beverages. Downstairs on the lake level there's a comfortable living room with a grand piano and a well-tended fire. The hotel has its own restaurant, Waters, featuring Northwest cuisine and an appealing terrace with a sumptuous view. Check out the nearby specialty shops (including a plush day spa), or rent a boat from the marina. Business travelers may take advantage of extra amenities such as a pager for off-site calls, a cellular phone, and complimentary use of a laptop computer and printer. Parking access is a bit of a maze. ▪ *1200 Carillon Point (Kirkland exit off SR 520, north on Lake Washington Blvd NE to Carillon Point), Kirkland, WA 98033; (425)822-3700 or (800)822-3700; $$$; AE, DC, MC, V; checks OK.* ઠ

Shumway Mansion ★★ When Richard and Salli Harris heard that developers wanted to demolish this historic 1909 building to make room for condos, they hauled the four-story house to a safe location near Kirkland's Juanita Bay. Now it's a gracious bed and breakfast, with an equal emphasis on seminars and receptions. The eight guest rooms are furnished with antiques, and public rooms overlook the bay (just a short walk away) and the lower parking lots. The ballroom downstairs, opening onto a flowering patio in summer, is often used for weddings or special meetings. A full breakfast is served in the dining room on linen-clad tables. Guests can use the Columbia Athletic Club a block away for no charge. Children over 12 are welcome. No pets or smoking. ■ *11410 99th Pl NE (near NE 116th), Kirkland, WA 98033; (425)823-2303; $$; AE, MC, V; checks OK.* &

GREATER SEATTLE: BELLEVUE

Bellevue continues to boom at a seemingly endless pace. This erstwhile hamlet, which can now rightfully be called Seattle's sister city, boasts its own downtown skyline, a growing population, and more shop-till-you-drop options than you'd care to shake a credit card at. Bellevue is the heart of the "Eastside"—the former suburbs of Seattle, east of Lake Washington, that now stand on their own. As many commuters now leave Seattle in the morning for work on the Eastside as make the traditional suburbs-to-Seattle trek—causing, incidentally, some serious bridge-crossing standstills whatever the direction.

At the core of downtown Bellevue is **Bellevue Place**, a hotel, restaurant, and shopping complex.

Nearby, the ever-growing mega-mall **Bellevue Square** hosts Nordstrom and hundreds of other stores, but it's also one of the first malls in the country to house a museum: the **Bellevue Art Museum**, specializing in Northwest crafts (plans are in the offing for a move into a new stand-alone venue); (425)454-6021.

Much of what makes Bellevue such a livable city are the quiet neighborhoods that ring downtown. The neighborhood surrounding **Bridle Trails State Park** on the Kirkland border looks like a condensed version of Virginia equestrian country, with backyards of horses and stables. The park features miles of riding and hiking trails through vast stands of Douglas fir. Day hikers can head east toward Issaquah to explore **Cougar Mountain**, the forested, westernmost hill of an ancient mountain range that stretches from Lake Washington to the younger Cascades.

RESTAURANTS

Azaleas Fountain Court ★★★ There is no more romantic dining spot in Bellevue than Azaleas. On weekends, live jazz accompanies dinner; in summer, the courtyard—complete with small fountain—beckons. Any time, the dining room's country/continental ambience provides a warm backdrop for chef Dan Sullivan's seasonal menus (offering, perhaps, lamb sirloin bedded on white beans and flavored with garlic and mint, beef tenderloin encrusted with roasted garlic, or ahi tuna treated to a colorful toss of sweet red pepper and leeks). A bistro menu, served limited hours, is meant to draw those in search of a more casual, inexpensive repast via the pasta/risotto, pizza/focaccia, steamed clams/spinach salad route. Count on sophisticated service, a worthy wine list, and delicious homemade sorbets and ice creams. ■ *22 103rd NE (off Main St), Bellevue; (425) 451-0426; $$$; full bar; AE, MC, V; checks OK; lunch Tues–Fri, dinner Mon–Sat.* &

Andre's Eurasian Bistro ★★ Chef/owner Andre Nguyen has a serious Eastside following. This is the second incarnation of the original Andre's Gourmet Cuisine, which was ravaged by fire early in 1996 but reopened, a few doors down, later that year. Clean lines, warm colors, and tasteful Southeast Asian artwork make this strip-mall space surprisingly appealing. Counter seats front an open kitchen. To one side, a fireplace warms the room, while a smaller, quieter salon provides additional seating. Soup may be Japanese miso, Vietnamese pho, or a richly aromatic cream-of-five-onion that whispers of France. Shrimp-filled, rice paper–wrapped salad rolls share space on the menu with a caesar and a rather ordinary "Indochine" chopped salad. Chinese dishes sometimes prove ho-hum. Consider the daily specials—perhaps wok-fried catfish or a merlot-braised lamb shank. Eurasian pork (spiked with curry, ginger, and Marsala) earns much applause, as does Andre's wife Noel's caramel flan. ■ *14124 NE 20th St (near 140th), Bellevue; (425) 747-6551; $$; beer and wine; AE, DC, MC, V; no checks; lunch Mon–Sat, dinner every day.* &

▼

Bellevue

Restaurants

▲

Daniel's Broiler (Bellevue) ★★ Noisy steak-house chains might hold more appeal for family-oriented Eastsiders (and their pocketbooks), but we say, forget the rest and go for the best. Daniel's corn-fed USDA prime steaks, offered in appropriately masculine surroundings, with a panoramic view from the 21st floor of the Seafirst Building, put other grillmeisters to shame. Perhaps your server will suggest cutting into your filet mignon or well-marbled rib-eye (a bargain at lunch) to see if it's seared to your liking (laughing, knowing it will be). The day's fresh catch is among the worthy options for those who don't do red meat. Expect straightforward steak-house fare with all the trimmings: potatoes mashed, baked, or shoestringed beyond compare. To start, there are prawn cocktails, oysters on the half shell, or a velvety cup of clam chowder. The wine list is praiseworthy. So is Daniel's Seattle twin restaurant, perched across Lake Washington at Leschi Marina. ■ *10500 NE 8th St (in the Seafirst Building), Bellevue; (425) 462-4662; $$$; full bar; AE, DC, DIS, MC, V; checks OK; lunch Mon–Fri, dinner every day.* ■ *200 Lake Washington Blvd (at Alden St), Seattle; (206) 329-4192; $$$; full bar; AE, DC, DIS, MC, V; checks OK; lunch Mon–Fri, dinner every day.* &

Firenze ★★ Owner Salvatore Lembo squeezes considerable Mediterranean atmosphere out of this small mall restaurant, just a ravioli toss from Crossroads Cinema: terra-cotta floor, sun-yellow stucco walls, one antique sideboard, one old chandelier, and many, many wine bottles. Sinatra knocks out a tune to the crash of dishes dumped in a serving station just outside the kitchen. Expect traditional Italian offerings among the pasta, veal, and chicken dishes, but don't expect much from the pizza. Spaghetti carbonara is dreamily creamy, generously spiced, and loaded with pancetta. A tender chicken breast or veal fillet rests in a lake of Gorgonzola sauce. Skip the veal Marsala and move on to a veal piccante, sauced with sun-dried tomatoes, capers, and lemon—simple, elegant, sublime. Nightly specials can include osso buco, risotto, and the occasional salmon. Servers know their stuff and don't try to force a dessert on you, though you wouldn't mind being forced to eat the dainty little tiramisu. ■ *15600 NE 8th (at Crossroads Mall), Bellevue; (425)957-1077; $$; full bar; AE, MC, V; local checks only; lunch Mon–Fri, dinner every day.* &

Golkonda ★★ There's no fuchsia-tinted tikka chicken here, or even a tandoori oven. Naan? None. Golkonda, a restful restaurant with white linen and comfortable booths, serves up spirited Indian food from the southern part of the country. These include the filling, crêpelike dosas that owners Usha and Lakshma Reddy have been selling for years at their nearby Crossroads food court place, A Bite of India. Everyone starts with complimentary rasam, a spicy tomato and tamarind soup. The biryanis—veggie, chicken, or lamb—are excellent, basmati rice–based casseroles. *Dum-ka-murcha,* a garlicked, gingered game hen marinated overnight in a yogurt sauce, is an incredibly messy, delicious feast. Good desserts here, especially the *pala mayasam,* a sort of tapioca pudding with grated carrots, vermicelli, and bursts of cardamom. ■ *15600 NE 8th (at Crossroads Shopping Center), Bellevue; (425)649-0355; $$; beer and wine; AE, DC, DIS, MC, V; checks OK; lunch, dinner Mon–Sat.* &

Raga Cuisine of India ★★ Most East Indian restaurants in America put more effort into ethnic decor than authentic cooking. Raga puts the emphasis where it belongs: in the charming copper pans and warmers on your table, and on the luscious food in them. Try the symphonic smoked eggplant in a chunky purée; tandoori oven–baked rack of lamb or chicken breast, all the juices sealed and simmering within; succulent prawns complemented by a flaming-hot spinach-tomato sauce; mussels sautéed in fragrant curry sauce; or piping hot breads streaked with fresh garlic and basil. Owner Kamal Mroke sets a standard for every other Indian kitchen in the area; even the inexpensive steam-table lunch so popular with the Eastside software crowd

▼

Bellevue

Restaurants

▲

is several cuts above those of its many competitors. Dinner is more than worth the trip across Lake Washington. ▪ *555 108th Ave NE (at 5th Ave NE), Bellevue; (425) 450-0336; $$; full bar; AE, DC, MC, V; checks OK; lunch, dinner every day.* ♿

Tosoni's ★★ To its many loyal regulars, some of whom have been dining here since its 1983 inception, it's known as "Walter's place." They know that the humble, strip-mall exterior belies the Old World delights awaiting inside, where the man wearing the toque (literally) is Austrian chef Walter Walcher, who works in the open kitchen presiding over a small booth-lined room filled with antique cabinets and armoires. Lending a hand prepping salads and Walter's delightful desserts—and warmly welcoming their steadfast devotees—is his wife, Wendy. Of the dozen or so entrees and nearly as many appetizers, many do the Continental (escargots, steak tartare, flambéed Muscovy duck), but you can expect a taste of Italy (ravioli, pasta puttanesca) and Japan (shiitake mushrooms, grilled ahi tuna) too. Vegetarians appreciate artful dishes such as the porcini risotto and the goat cheese–stuffed morels. Meat eaters have kept the garlic lamb—tender strips sautéed in olive oil, heavily garlicked, and smartly peppered—on the menu for more than a dozen years. ▪ *14320 NE 20th St (off 148th Ave NE), Bellevue; (425) 644-1668; $$; beer and wine; MC, V; local checks only; dinner Tues–Sat.* ♿

California Pizza Kitchen ★ This is the first Northwest incursion of the chain that arguably introduced the country to the nouveau, anything-goes pizza. Though Thai and barbecue-chicken pizza are now almost ubiquitous, not so the Peking duck pizza, the burrito pizza, the tandoori pizza, nor the (ugh) potato pizza. They're baked in a super-hot, wood-fired oven; the crust comes out crisp, the quality high. Only the quantity is an issue (don't expect to take home leftovers). You could call the place California Pasta Kitchen, too, given the multitude of varieties offered. Among the best, the chipotle chicken fettuccine mixes chunks of poblanos and colorful bell peppers in a spicy chipotle cream sauce. ▪ *595 106th Ave NE (near NE 8th), Bellevue; (425) 454-2545; $; full bar; AE, DC, DIS, MC, V; checks OK; lunch, dinner every day.* ♿

Dixie's BBQ ★ Finding Dixie's BBQ requires a little faith. Despite the streetside sign, this tan steel building looks for all the world like an automotive repair garage. Guess what? It is. Hours before cracking open a crankcase at Porter's Automotive Service, Gene Porter fires up his smoker, descriptively named Dino, in a converted 1,500-gallon tank. It was faith that launched this enterprise: Gene and his wife, Dixie, started barbecuing for their family's church. Eventually, they partitioned off 600 square feet of the garage and opened for business. The brief menu lists five dinner options—pork ribs, beef ribs, chicken wings, turkey wings, and a combo plate—along with a brisket sandwich, a few sides, and dessert. On a lucky day, you'll find Dixie has baked a lemon cake or a sweet potato pie. It's primarily take-out, but with a few tables in the garage/waiting room and outside in the driveway, it's the only place we know where you can get brisket and a brake job at the same time. ■ *11522 Northup Way (near 116th NE), Bellevue; (425) 828-2460; $; no alcohol; no credit cards; checks OK; lunch, dinner Mon–Sat.* と

Gilbert's Main Street Bagel Deli ★ Gilbert's looks smart and urbane enough for Belltown, but instead it's in Old Bellevue, offering shoppers and neighborhood condo-dwellers a lot more than big, crisp-skinned bagels. They sell sandwiches (great Italian beef) and salads (feta-and-kalamata-loaded Greek), plus pizzas (big slices, limited options) and a range of baked goods (terrific low-fat chocoholic's delight). Gilbert's suffers a bit from its all-things-to-all-people approach, especially in the evening, when a sandwich is still a better choice than most of the dinnertime fresh sheet—which might offer a rubbery low-fat tequila-lime chicken, or a decent smoked salmon ravioli. The cavernous place is a bit drafty in cold weather, but it's still a cool spot for a bite and a chat. ■ *1004 Main St (at 101st SE), Bellevue; (425) 455-5650; $; beer and wine; AE, MC, V; checks OK; breakfast, lunch every day, dinner Fri–Sat.* と

Noble Court ★ During the week, when it's not so crowded, request one of the tables lining the windows looking out on the small creek—and you're less likely to notice the worn interior and slightly uncomfortable seating. The menu ranges from standard kung pao and fried rice to the more exotic shark's-fin soup, stewed abalone, and bird's-nest-with-crabmeat soup. Live tanks at the entrance display fish and crustaceans ready for a little black bean sauce. The restaurant is a favorite with the Eastside's many Chinese residents, who show up on weekends for what most consider to be the best dim sum on either side of the Lake Washington bridges. Expect to wait for up to an hour. Noble Court serves dim sum during the week as well, though the range of selections is somewhat limited and the ambience can't match those weekend feeding frenzies. ■ *1644 140th NE (off Bellevue-Redmond Rd), Bellevue; (425) 641-6011; $$; full bar; AE, MC, V; no checks; lunch, dinner every day.* と

LODGINGS

Bellevue Club Hotel ★★ The new hotel addition at the former Bellevue Athletic Club (now the Bellevue Club) promises to give the Hyatt Regency a run for its money, especially among well-heeled business travelers. Each of the 67 rooms is beautifully decorated, featuring striking modern furnishings and pieces by Northwest artists. The oversize limestone and marble bathrooms are absolutely fabulous, complete with spalike tubs and separate shower stalls. The lovely garden rooms open onto private patios; other rooms overlook the five tennis courts. All of the extensive athletic facilities are available to hotel guests, including an Olympic-size swimming pool, indoor tennis, racquetball, and squash courts, and aerobics classes. ■ *11200 SE 6th St (near 114th), Bellevue, WA 98004; (425)454-4424 or (800)597-1110; $$$; AE, MC, V; checks OK.* ♿

The Bellevue Hilton ★★ With every amenity in the book, the Bellevue Hilton is the best bet on the Eastside's Hotel Row. Rooms are tastefully done in warm colors. Amenities include use of a nearby health-and-racquet club, free transportation around Bellevue (within a 5-mile radius), room service until 10pm weekdays and 10:30pm weekends, a Jacuzzi, a sauna, a pool, several free cable channels in every room, and two restaurants. Working stiffs will appreciate the modem hookups and desks in every room; computer, fax machine, and copy machine are also available. Parlor suites have a sitting room, a wet bar and refrigerator, and a dining table. ■ *100 112th Ave NE (at Main), Bellevue, WA 98004; (425)455-3330 or (800)BEL-HILT; $$$; AE, DC, MC, V; checks OK.* ♿

Hyatt Regency at Bellevue Place ★★ The Hyatt Regency is just one part of Kemper Freeman's splashy, sprawling retail-office-restaurant-hotel-health-club complex called Bellevue Place. The 382-room hotel (at 24 stories, the highest in Bellevue) offers many of the extras: pricier "Regency Club" rooms on the top two floors, two big ballrooms, several satellite conference rooms, use of the neighboring Seattle Club (for a $10 fee), and a fine restaurant, Eques. The best rooms are on the south side above the seventh floor. ■ *900 Bellevue Way (at NE 8th St), Bellevue, WA 98004; (425)462-1234 or (800)233-1234; $$$; AE, DC, MC, V; checks OK.* ♿

Residence Inn by Marriott—Bellevue ★★ A quiet cluster of suites just off Highway 520 in east Bellevue, the Eastside version of the Residence Inn feels more like an apartment complex than a hotel. Well suited to business travelers, the place is also great for families. All suites have fireplaces, full kitchens, and separate living rooms and bedrooms; a complimentary continental breakfast is provided in the main building. The complex has an outdoor pool, three spas, and a sports court; in addition, passes to three nearby health clubs are provided. They'll even do your grocery shopping for you. Travelers with smaller budgets might try the moderately priced basic hotel rooms next door at the Courtyard by Marriott; (425)869-5300. ■ *14455 NE 29th Pl (near 148th Ave NE), Bellevue, WA 98007; (425)882-1222 or (800)331-3131; $$$; AE, DC, DIS, JCB, MC, V; checks OK.* ♿

WestCoast Bellevue Hotel ★ Part of the ever-expanding West-Coast chain (which seems to be buying up hotel properties faster than you can say "bargain rates"), this midscale hotel just a jump off I-405 offers, in addition to 176 very reasonably priced guest rooms, 16 two-level townhouse suites featuring loft bedrooms with king-size beds. Rooms flaunt new carpeting and draperies, and the lobby furnishings have been recently updated. Rooms facing the courtyard are more appealing, of course, than those with parking-lot vistas. There's a small exercise facility and an outdoor pool (heated in summer, closed in winter). Eats and drinks are available here at the Eastside Bar & Grill. ■ *625 116th Ave NE (near NE 8th), Bellevue, WA 98004; (425)455-9444 or (800)426-0670; $$; AE, DC, DIS, MC, V; checks OK.* ♿

GREATER SEATTLE: MERCER ISLAND

RESTAURANTS

Pon Proem ★ Sheer, unadulterated capsicum is not the story at Mercer Island's nifty little Thai joint, though the seasoning is there in a no-nonsense star scale (*"chok dee"* next to five stars means "good luck"). While the red curry chicken lacks a certain oomph, everything else sampled here displays balance and a deft touch at the wok. Three kinds of soy sauce, plus chile paste, give the chicken dish called *gai pahd met ma muang* better balance than a gymnastics team. Vegetarian phad Thai is freshened by red cabbage, carrots, and sprouts. Deep-fried dishes are consistently pleasing, especially the gai Pon Proem—mildly spicy chunks of chicken for finger-dipping (call it McNuggets for grown-ups). Modest digs in a strip-mall setting are warmed by the owner's hand-sewn seat-cushion covers and window treatments. ■ *3039 78th Ave SE (on the south edge of downtown, next to PayLess), Mercer Island; (206)236-8424; $; beer and wine; AE, DIS, MC, V; local checks only; lunch Mon–Fri, dinner every day.* ♿

GREATER SEATTLE: ISSAQUAH

Fast-food franchises now line I-90, but the center of this old coal-mining town still resembles small-town America, complete with a butcher shop, a well-respected community theater, and a working dairy. On good days, Mount Rainier appears between the hills that form the town's southern and eastern borders. Whatever the weather, locals flock to the swell, new, 33,000-square-foot community center to run the indoor track, take aerobics classes, or root for the hometown team playing at one of three basketball courts in a gym that holds up to 1,000 screaming suburban fans.

The **Issaquah Farmers Market**, adjacent to the community center (at the intersection of First and Bush), is held Saturdays, mid-April to mid-October, from 9am to 3pm.

Gilman Village on Gilman Boulevard is a shopping complex with a twist: the developers refurbished old farmhouses, a barn, and a feed store, then filled them with craft and clothing shops, restaurants, and a woodworking gallery; (425)392-6802. **Boehm's Chocolates** on the edge of town still dips its chocolates by hand and offers tours for groups (reservations are needed); (425)392-6652.

Lake Sammamish State Park, between town and Lake Sammamish, offers swimming and boat access; (425)455-7010. **Tiger Mountain**, the sprawling 13,000-acre state forest that looms to the east, is a favorite weekend destination for hikers and mountain bikers. Trails wind through alder and evergreen forests and past old coal-mine shafts.

RESTAURANTS

Mandarin Garden ★ Mandarin Garden now offers a handsome cocktail lounge where you can snack on Chinese appetizers and knock one back. The restaurant itself isn't much to look at, but the menu makes up for the characterless interior. Chef Andy Wang, a native of Shanghai, handles equally well the delicate flavors of Mandarin and the heat and spice of Sichuan and Hunan. But be assured that if you order a starred dish, you're going to get hot and spicy. Hunan chicken packs a wallop as well as a mess of delectable chicken. Praiseworthy dishes include mixed seafood Sichuan, melt-in-your-mouth kung pao chicken, and variations on bean curd. Large private rooms are available for banquets. Order Peking duck a day in advance. ■ *40 E Sunset Way (exit 17 off I-90), Issaquah; (425)392-9476; $; full bar; MC, V; local checks only; lunch Mon–Sat, dinner every day.*

Nicolino ★ On warm days, the sunny brick courtyard is the place to be. On cold or rainy days, head for the cheerful little dining room, pleasantly cluttered with wine bottles and family pictures, maps and mandolins, for a steaming plate of soul-warming pasta. Though they've been known to heavy-hand the prawns and chicken, Nicolino's pasta (and its low prices) continue to fuel its reputation and attract crowds. You won't find showy dishes, yet a simple pasta can be stunningly executed, while the fork-tender veal shank in the osso buco Milanese comes atop fettuccine so buttery the taste comes right through the tomato sauce and orange zest. Hearty slices of peasant bread are meant to be dredged in herb-, garlic-, and chile-spiked olive oil and accompanied by a soothing glass of Chianti. ■ *317 NW Gilman Blvd (in Gilman Village), Issaquah; (425)391-8077; $$; beer and wine; DC, MC, V; checks OK; lunch, dinner every day.* &

Once a major logging center, Bainbridge Island is now a semi-rural haven for city professionals (who don't mind the half-hour commute via ferry from downtown Seattle), writers, artists, and people seeking simpler lives. It makes a pleasant tour by car or bike, during which you can see small pastoral farms, enviable waterfront homes, and spectacular cityscapes (especially from **Fay Bainbridge State Park** on the northeast corner of the island; (206) 842-3931). The wooded and waterfront trails in **Fort Ward State Park**, on the south end of the island, make for a nice afternoon stroll (good picnic spots, too); (206) 842-4041. Or just walk off the ferry to **Waterfront Park**— a good place for a picnic and, if so inclined, a paddle (you can rent canoes and kayaks from Bainbridge Island Boat Rentals; (206) 842-9229).

Bloedel Reserve encompasses 150 acres of lush, tranquil gardens, woods, meadows, and ponds. Plants from all over the world make the grounds interesting any time of the year. Open Wednesday through Sunday; reservations are required and limited; (206) 842-7631.

The small, family-owned **Bainbridge Island Winery**, on State Highway 305, (206) 842-WINE, makes a number of good wines, including a superb strawberry. **Pegasus Coffee**, at the foot of Madison Avenue S, (206) 842-3113, or **Bainbridge Bakers**, in Winslow Green, (206) 842-1822, both make good stops for coffee and pastries. The **Harbour Public House**, overlooking Eagle Harbor, is the locals' pick for a casual evening of beer, fish 'n' chips, and music; (206) 842-0969.

RESTAURANTS

Cafe Nola ★★ Imagine yourself holding a bowl of cafe au lait with both hands, indulging in a strawberry-rhubarb crisp, and having a heart-to-heart with a friend. Cafe Nola is the perfect setting. Uniting their culinary talents, sisters Melinda Lucas and Mary Bugarin have transformed a former Puget Power office into a stylish refuge decorated in soft wheat-colored tones. "Organic and very local" describes the ingredients that make up their small, beautifully presented menu. Breakfasts (locally gathered eggs, a simple bowl of stunning fresh fruit, an array of house-baked breads and sweets) and lunches (panini and outstanding salads composed with, say, marinated portobellos and butternut squash) come carefully prepared. At dinner, served a couple of nights each week, you might encounter spicy agnolotti with tomato sauce or a sublime rack of lamb with parsnip-potato gratin. Dine outside when it's warm, and don't miss dessert. Distracted service complements the artistic, somewhat European setting. ■ *101 Winslow Way E (at Madison), Bainbridge Island; (206) 842-3822; $$; beer and wine; MC,*

V (at dinner only); checks OK; breakfast, lunch Tues–Sun, dinner Fri–Sat. &

Pleasant Beach Grill ★★ Under the direction of chef Hussein Ramadan, meals here are executed with a pleasant consistency much appreciated by Bainbridge Island locals. His menu may include a sauté of prawns, scallops, and whitefish (in a Thai-style sauce of curry, lemongrass, and coconut milk) and an excellent 10-ounce slab of New York pepper steak, plus specials inspired by fresh seasonal ingredients. Stick with the simpler grills and seafoods and enjoy the ample portions and skilled service. At press time, the island's only white-linen restaurant is quietly tucked away in a large tudor house on the island's southwest corner. Lease problems, however, are forcing the Grill to look for a new location; islanders are keeping their fingers crossed for another warm and cozy spot. ■ *4738 Lynwood Center Rd (follow signs toward Fort Ward State Park boat ramp), Bainbridge Island; (206)842-4347; $$; full bar; AE, MC, V; no checks; dinner every day.*

Ruby's on Bainbridge ★★ Maura and Aaron Crisp have turned this location next door to the island's only movie theater into a mini–destination restaurant. It's a steamy, garlicky little place a hobbit might love—just casual enough for the locals, just sumptuous enough for weekend guests and day trippers. The menu changes often, but you'll encounter such entrees as fettuccine tossed with wild mushrooms, swordfish dressed in soy and ginger, and pork tenderloin with a raspberry reduction. Salads are exceptional. ■ *4569 Lynwood Center Rd (in Lynwood Center; follow signs toward Fort Ward State Park boat ramp), Bainbridge Island; (206)780-9303; $$; beer and wine; MC, V; checks OK; lunch, dinner Tues–Sun, brunch Sat–Sun.*

▼

Bainbridge Island

Restaurants

▲

Sawatdy Thai Cuisine ★★ Bainbridge Islanders don't need to ferry over to the big city for a taste of Thailand: they're mightily convinced that some of the best Thai food in the Seattle area can be found here at home. Island life is a trade-off, with residents often settling for mediocre dining experiences in exchange for convenience. The place runs like clockwork, and you can rest assured that every fragrant dish, from the eggplant lover's platter to the coriander beef with sticky rice, is well executed and every customer well cared for. Hold your decision until you've had a chance to talk to your server, who can give you the inside scoop on what dish "mom" is cooking best that night. Reservations are a good idea. ■ *8770 Fletcher Bay Rd (take Hwy 305, turn west on High School Rd, then north on Fletcher Bay Rd to Island Center), Bainbridge Island; (206)780-2429; $; beer and wine; MC, V; checks OK; lunch Mon–Fri, dinner every day.*

Streamliner Diner On weekdays at this Bainbridge Island club-house, locals have been known to swill coffee for hours on end (although the new owners seem to be trying to change that). On weekends, locals make way for Seattleites in search of a piece of island life. The room is pretty and light, with a few hip-pified diner-ish touches like the long, curving, wooden counter and the 1940s tablecloths. And even when the service goes awry, the breakfasts are good, featuring a funky mixture that fits right in with the decor: hearty omelets, lots of fresh-baked goods, perfect waffles, a veggie tofu scramble, a fabulous fried-egg sandwich. The potatoes are old-fashioned and delicious. ■ *397 Winslow Way (at Bjune), Bainbridge Island; (206)842-8595; $; no alcohol; no credit cards; checks OK; breakfast every day, lunch Mon–Sat.*

LODGINGS

The Bombay House ★★ Set in a lavish flower garden with a rough-cedar gazebo overlooking scenic Rich Passage, this sprawling turn-of-the-century house is just a sweet stroll from Fort Ward State Park. With a hearty dose of island-hideaway at-mosphere, the Bombay House has five bedrooms done up in country antiques. Three have private baths, and the vast sec-ond-floor Captain's Suite has a wood-burning parlor stove and a claw-footed tub. The living room has a large fireplace. The Kanchuks are friendly hosts. In the morning, you'll have the good fortune to follow your nose to one of Bunny's morning feasts with fresh-baked goodies. Children over 6 years are wel-come. ■ *8490 Beck Rd NE (4 miles south of the ferry, just off W Blakely Ave), Bainbridge Island, WA 98110; (206)842-3926 or (800)598-3926; $$; AE, MC, V; checks OK.*

▼ Bainbridge Island

Restaurants

▲

GREATER SEATTLE: SEA-TAC

LODGINGS

Seattle Airport Hilton Hotel ★★ In this streamlined, four-winged building, camouflaged by trees and plantings, the Seattle Airport Hilton manages to create a resort atmosphere along an airport-hotel strip. The 178 plush, larger-than-standard rooms (at posh prices) are set around a landscaped courtyard with pool and in-door/outdoor Jacuzzi; they feature desks and computer hook-ups, irons, ironing boards, and coffee-makers. An exercise room and numerous meeting and party rooms are available. So is a 24-hour business center, complete with fax, copy machine, com-puter, and laser printer. The Great American Grill serves break-fast, lunch, and dinner. ■ *17620 Pacific Hwy S (188th St exit off I-5, north 1 mile), Seattle, WA 98188; (206)244-4800 or (800)HILTONS; $$$; AE, DC, MC, V; checks OK.* &

Seattle Marriott at Sea-Tac ★★ Business travelers (and folks who prefer to spend a night near the airport rather than fight traffic to catch an early-morning flight) will appreciate the swift, courteous service at this 459-room megahotel about a block from the airport strip. The lobby, with its warm Northwest motif, opens up into an enormous, covered atrium complete with indoor pool and two Jacuzzis. There's also a sauna and a well-equipped exercise room. As for the accommodations, why bother with a standard room? For slightly higher rates, more spacious, handsomely appointed suites are available on the concierge floor. These include such amenities as higher-quality linens, robes, turn-down service, hair dryers, iron and board, and access to a lounge that serves continental breakfasts and nightly nibbles. A casual dining room offers all the usual hotel fare—from sandwiches to steaks. ■ *3201 S 176th St (just east of Pacific Hwy S, at 32nd Ave S), Seattle, WA 98188; (206) 241-2000 or (800) 228-9290; $$$; AE, DC, MC, V; checks OK.* &

GREATER SEATTLE: BURIEN

RESTAURANTS

Filiberto's ★★ Filiberto's has been around for more than 20 years, and it remains among the most authentic and—on a good day—among the best of the many local Italian restaurants. The look is cheery and trattoria-perfect (even the dishwashing area in back is finished in imported tile). Service can be erratic, but the food is the primary focus here, with good attention to the basics. The long menu emphasizes Roman preparations of pasta (including delicious gnocchi), veal, poultry, and rabbit, right down to the *real* stracciatelle alla Romana. A large, well-priced selection of Italian wines is stacked in a help-yourself wall display; a real pizza oven turns out noteworthy pizza and calzone; and a bocce court resides out back, complete with lighting for evening play. ■ *14401 Des Moines Memorial Dr S (off Hwy 518), Burien; (206) 248-1944; $$; full bar; AE, MC, V; checks OK; lunch, dinner Tues–Sat.* &

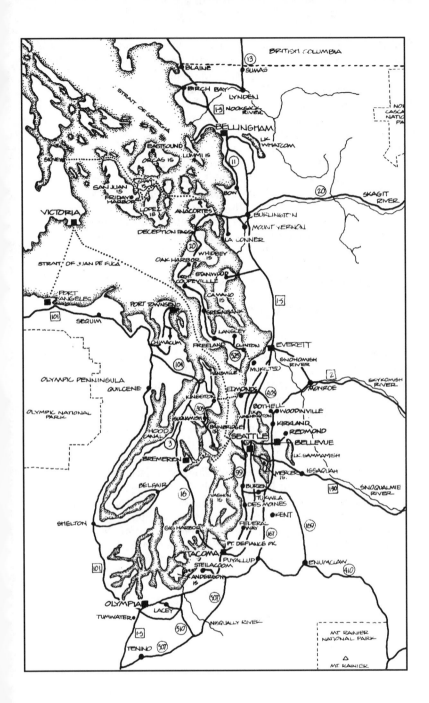

Puget Sound

*North to south along the I-5 corridor,
including side trips to the islands.*

BLAINE

LODGINGS

Inn at Semi-ah-moo ★★★ Semi-ah-moo Spit is a stunning site for a resort, with beachward views of the sea and the San Juans from many of the buildings. It sports lots of amenities: a 300-slip marina convenient to the inn; a house cruise vessel on which you can book excursions through the San Juans or scenic fishing trips; a thoroughly outfitted athletic club (a heated indoor/outdoor swimming pool, racquetball, squash, tennis, aerobics, weight lifting, tanning, massage, sauna, and Jacuzzi); an endless stretch of beach. Three restaurants (Stars, the expensive Northwest gourmet dining room, plus two more casual spots) provide the necessary range of culinary alternatives that you'd be hard-pressed to find in Blaine. The golf course, designed by Arnold Palmer, has long, unencumbered fairways surrounded by dense woods, excellent use of water, and lovely sculptural sand traps. The adjacent convention center, where revamped cannery buildings make topnotch meeting arenas, is really Semi-ah-moo's greatest strength. The rooms are prettily laid out and spacious. Be sure to ask for a bayside room if you want a view (and a fireplace for added ambience); otherwise, you'll be looking out at the parking lot. ■ *9565 Semi-ahmoo Pkwy (take exit 270 off I-5, travel west, watch for signs), Blaine; (360)371-2000 or (800)770-7992; PO Box 790, Blaine, WA 98230-0790; $$$; full bar; AE, DC, DIS, MC, V; checks OK; breakfast, lunch, dinner every day.* &

BIRCH BAY

It's just the place for 1950s teenage nostalgia. The crescent-shaped beach draws throngs of kids—cruising the strip, go-carting, hanging out in the arcade (open Memorial Day through Labor Day). Frankie and Annette would be right at home. There's a state park for camping and lots of sandy beach to wiggle between your toes. Off season can be very quiet.

LODGINGS

Birch Bay Vacation Rentals ★★ This is the best of the condo developments, right in the middle of town, across the main street from the beach. Units are set at angles among the beautifully maintained grounds, affording some of them better water views than others. Suites (one-, two-, and three-bedroom units) are modern and deluxe, with fireplaces, kitchens, and washers and dryers. There are outdoor tennis courts, an indoor heated pool, a Jacuzzi, and racquetball courts to keep everyone busy. ■ *7824 Birch Bay Dr (take exit 270 off I-5, head west for 5 miles, follow signs), Birch Bay, WA 98230; (360)371-7633; $$; AE, MC, V; checks OK.*

LYNDEN

This neat and tidy community, with immaculate yards and colorful gardens lining the shady avenue into downtown, has adopted a Dutch theme in tribute to its early inhabitants. Be sure to visit the charming **Pioneer Museum**, full of local memorabilia and antique buggies and motorcars; (360)354-3675.

RESTAURANTS

Hollandia Riding on the tail of bigger Dutchified establishments is a slightly more tasteful bistro with authentic fare imported from The Netherlands. Chef Dini Mollink works competently on what is, to the American palate, rather heavy cuisine. A safe choice is the Toeristen menu: *Groentesoep* (firm, tasty meatballs in a luscious vegetable broth), *Schnitzel Hollandia* (lightly breaded chicken breast), and dessert (little almond tarts). A less filling selection would be the *Koninginnesoep* met crackers (the Queen's cream soup, a rich chicken soup served with fresh raisin bread and thin slices of Gouda cheese). A small spice cookie accompanies your after-dinner coffee. ■ *655 Front St (in the Dutch Village at Guide Meridian and Front St), Lynden; (360)354-4133; $; beer and wine; MC, V; local checks only; lunch Mon–Sat, dinner Thurs–Sat.*

LODGINGS

Dutch Village Inn One might question an inn located in a windmill in a Dutch-theme village. This particular inn, however, provides six tastefully furnished and luxuriously appointed rooms to please all but the most jaded of travelers. Not surprisingly, the rooms are named for the Dutch provinces; the Friesland Kamer room, named after the northernmost province, occupies the top of the windmill. Views are lovely, but interrupted rhythmically as the giant blades of the windmill pass by (turning, fully lit, until 9pm). There are special touches in all the rooms: two have extra beds fitted into curtained alcoves in true Dutch fashion, and two have two-person tubs. Breakfast is on the house. ■ *655 Front St (at Guide Meridian), Lynden, WA 98264; (360)354-4440; $$; AE, MC, V; checks OK.*

RESTAURANTS

Black Forest Steakhouse Jack Niemann has brought his mesquite-grill technique down from his popular White Rock, BC, eatery to the hamlet of Everson, 30 minutes northeast of Bellingham. Decor is a quirky combination of rough-wood rustic and ivy-twined beer garden—setting just the right mood for the food, which includes the trademark steaks, grilled meats, and outstanding sauerbraten and schnitzels. They don't take reservations and diners tend to linger, so don't be in a rush. ■ *203 W Main St (on main drag), Everson; (360)966-2855; $; full bar; AE, MC, V; checks OK; dinner every day.*

BELLINGHAM

The mishmash grid of Bellingham's streets is a reminder of its former days as four smaller towns. In recent years, however, the cityscape, situated where the Nooksack River flows into the Bellingham Bay, has been rediscovered: the town is full of fine old houses, award-winning architecture at Western Washington University, stately streets, and lovely parks. An economic boom is bringing change and expansion to Whatcom County, most notably at the handsome port facility that houses the southern terminus of the **Alaska Marine Highway System**; (360)676-8445 or (800)642-0066. Bellingham is where many travelers begin the long journey up the coast and through Alaska's famed Inside Passage. Sticking closer to home, the **Island Shuttle Express** provides passenger-only ferry service from Bellingham to the San Juan Islands, May through September; whale watching and overnight cruises are also offered; (360)671-1137.

▼

Bellingham

▲

Western Washington University, on Sehome Hill south of downtown, is a fine expression of the spirit of Northwest architecture: warm materials, formal echoes of European styles, respect for context and the natural backdrop. Also stop at the visitor parking kiosk on the south side of campus for a map of the university's outdoor sculpture collection; (360)650-3000.

The **Old Town** around W Holly and Commercial Streets hosts antique and junk shops and some decent eateries. **Bellingham Farmers Market** features produce (including the county's famed berry harvests), fresh seafood, herbs, flowers, and crafts on Saturdays from April through October, downtown at Railroad Avenue and Chestnut Street; (360)647-2060. The **Fairhaven** neighborhood, the product of a short-lived railroad boom from 1889 to 1893, is good for exploring. **The Marketplace**, the grand dame and central figure among the attractive old buildings, was restored in 1988 and houses a number of interesting shops and dining options. The district is rich with diversions: crafts galleries, coffeehouses, bookstores, a charming garden/nursery emporium, and a lively evening scene unique to Bellingham. Village Books, (360)671-2626, carries an eclectic mix of new and used bestselling, childrens, and regional titles, and has a knowledgeable staff and an attached cafe. Tony's Coffees is the local beanmeister, 1101 Harris, (360)738-4710; the Village Cafe and Bakery has a tantalizing array of lovely pastries, as well as salads and sandwiches, 1307 Harris, (360)671-7258. Stop in at the attractive Archer Ale House for a wide selection of brews, including hard-to-find Belgian beers, and some tasty Cornish pasties, 1212 10th, (360)647-7002.

Breweries and Vineyards. Bellingham now has two attractive brewpubs, the Boundary Bay Brewery downtown (1107 Railroad, opposite the Farmers Market, (360)647-5593) and the Orchard Street Brewery, north of downtown off Meridian in an office park (709 W Orchard, (360)647-1614). Orchard Street is as popular among locals for its food as for its beer; Boundary Bay also serves up some tasty pub grub (try the delicious lamb burger). Mount Baker Vineyards is an attractive, cedar-sided, skylit facility that specializes in some of the lesser-known varietals, such as Müller Thurgau and Madeleine Angevine. Their plum wine, made from local fruit, is delightful; their 1994 cabernet sauvignon was recently awarded a gold medal by the Tri-Cities Oenological Society; 11 miles east of Bellingham on Mount Baker Highway, (360)592-2300.

The Arts. The Whatcom Museum of History and Art, 121 Prospect Street, (360)676-6981, a massive Romanesque building dating from 1892, was used as a city hall until 1940. It has permanent exhibits on historic Bellingham as well as an adventurous art exhibition schedule. Check out the presentations on local wildlife and Native American culture in the education center down the block, and the Children's Museum Northwest, an associated facility, a few doors farther north. One block from the museum is Henderson Books, one of the finest used bookstores in the state; 112 and 116 Grand Avenue, (360)734-6855. The **Bellingham Music Festival** has quickly become an institution, featuring more than two weeks of orchestral, chamber, and jazz performances, beginning the third week of August; (360)676-5997. The Mount Baker Theater, built in 1927 and renovated in 1995, is home to the Whatcom Symphony Orchestra and the site of a wide array of concerts, plays, and films; 104 N Commercial, (360)734-6080.

Parks and Gardens. Sehome Hill Arboretum, adjacent to the WWU campus, sports over 3 miles of trails, with prime views of the city, Bellingham Bay, and the San Juans. Whatcom Falls Park, to the east of the city off Lakeway Drive at 1401 Electric Avenue, has more than 5 miles of trails overlooking several scenic falls. Big Rock Garden Park is a wonderful woodland site with a vast array of azaleas, rhododendrons, and Japanese maples (open daily from April to October, 2900 Sylvan, near Lake Whatcom).

Lake Whatcom Railway, located not on Lake Whatcom but on Highway 9 at Wickersham, makes scenic runs on Saturdays in July and August using an old Northern Pacific engine; (360)595-2218.

The **Ski-to-Sea Race** attracts teams from all over the world to participate in this annual seven-event relay race over Memorial Day weekend; (360)734-1300.

RESTAURANTS

il fiasco ★★ il fiasco (Italian for "the flask") continues to attract kudos from locals and visitors alike for its excellent Northern Italian cuisine, from the squid with artichoke aioli through the penne with chicken and Gorgonzola to the almond flan. Side dishes are particularly satisfactory: crusty, chewy bread with a dip of herb-infused olive oil, perfectly dressed salads, intensely flavorful three-mushroom soup. Occasionally, kitchen experiments go astray, as with a duck ravioli with a too-sweet sauce, but such lapses are rare. ▪ *1309 Commercial St (off Holly), Bellingham; (360)676-9136; $$; full bar; AE, DC, MC, V; local checks only; lunch Mon–Fri, dinner every day.* &

Pacific Cafe ★★ Tucked into the historic Mount Baker Theater building, the Pacific Cafe has been a leader on Bellingham's gastronomic front since 1985. The ambience is civilized and modern: good abstract watercolors on the walls, quiet jazz on the speakers. The menu reflects a bit of co-owner Robert Fong's Asian influence (he comes to Washington via Hawaii, supplemented with years of travel in Europe, India, China, and Malaysia). The satay sauces are complex, light, and fragrant, and the seafood is noteworthy. Both oysters and squid respond beautifully when matched with shiitakes and Thai chiles. Fong is a serious wine collector, and the quality of the vintages presented reflects a fine-tuned palate. Note especially the selection of dessert ports. ▪ *100 N Commercial (near Champion), Bellingham; (360)647-0800; $$; beer and wine; MC, V; local checks only; lunch Mon–Fri, dinner Mon–Sat.*

▼

▲

Pepper Sisters ★★ Cheerful, knowledgeable service, a great location in one of Bellingham's vintage brick commercial buildings, and a wide-awake kitchen have turned Pepper Sisters into an institution, well known for its Southwestern fare. Daily seafood specials are a showcase for the chefs' ability to combine local provender with what the owners call High Desert cuisine: say, oysters in pumpkinseed sauce. The kitchen shows the same verve with plainer fare: roasted potato and garlic enchilada with green chile sauce, or an unctuous, spicy eggplant tostada. Coffee flan is a standout dessert, and the coffee itself, the local Tony's brand, is brewed with a dusting of cinnamon on the filter. ▪ *1055 N State St (south of Holly), Bellingham; (360)671-3414; $; beer and wine; MC, V; checks OK; dinner Tues–Sun.*

Cafe Toulouse ★ Toulouse continues with its original claim to fame: huge, well-orchestrated breakfasts and lunches for the local office crowd. This quietly remodeled corner of the old Bon Marché is the best place in town for Sunday brunch. The breakfast and lunch menus offer favorites familiar to Toulouse regulars: Greek and Provençal frittatas, huevos rancheros, hefty sandwiches, soups, and pastas. If there's a weak spot, it's the soups. ■ *114 W Magnolia St (downtown near Cornwall, next to the Federal Building), Bellingham; (360) 733-8996; $; no alcohol; MC, V; checks OK; breakfast, lunch every day.*

Thai House ★ Peggy Rieschl has fashioned a most comfortable spot, located (as many of the great Thai restaurants seem to be) in a strip mall. It's a nice environment in which to savor one's fish cakes or linger over the flavorful hot-and-sour soup chock-full of tender seafood and scented with fresh lemongrass. Tried-and-true favorites include a whole flatfish, deep-fried and smothered in a spicy red sauce, or any one of the curries. But the real finds are likely to be the daily specials posted on the blackboards. Catering, too. ■ *3930 Meridian Village (across from Bellis Fair Mall), Bellingham; (360) 734-5111; $; beer and wine; MC, V; checks OK; lunch Mon–Fri, dinner every day.*

Colophon Cafe Located in the best bookstore in town, Colophon offers table service and an outdoor wine garden on its lower level, booths and sidewalk tables above. The African peanut soup (in vegetarian and nonvegetarian versions) is justly famous: chunky with fresh tomatoes, grainy with peanuts, and pungent with fresh ginger root. Real cream pies—rich, light, and wonderful—are another specialty: Key lime, chocolate brandy, and peanut butter. The Colophon encourages patrons to tarry over their espresso. ■ *1208 11th St (in Village Books, near Harris St in Fairhaven), Bellingham; (360) 647-0092; $; beer and wine; DIS, MC, V; checks OK; breakfast, lunch, dinner every day.* ♿

Taste of India Tandoori meats and breads and other Punjabi creations are a specialty. The shrimp tandoori is terrific, with sweet, tender-firm shrimp, a perfect masala, and a mint chutney. The vegetarian combination is another triumph of flavor-blending. These are meals for lingering, which allows time to polish off a 22-ounce Taj Mahal beer. The lunch buffet, a bargain, is justly popular with the locals. ■ *3930 Meridian St, #J (across from Bellis Fair Mall, 2 doors south of Thai Kitchen), Bellingham; (360) 647-1589; $; beer and wine; DIS, MC, V; local checks only; lunch, dinner every day.*

LODGINGS

Schnauzer Crossing ★★★ Sophisticated and unique, this B&B overlooking Lake Whatcom attracts a surprising range of visitors, from newlyweds to businesspeople to discerning foreign travelers, and graciously accommodates them all. Many of Donna and Monty McAllister's guests return again and again to this lovely contemporary home and its gardens and grounds. Three accommodations are available: while the spacious and elegant Garden Suite, with fireplace, Jacuzzi, TV/VCR, and a garden view, and the separate cottage overlooking the lake are the most luxurious options, guests staying in the simpler Queen Room enjoy the wonderful surroundings without the pricey amenities. The McAllisters are sensitive to guests' needs for privacy and have a finely tuned sense of hospitality that's obvious in the small details: extra-thick towels, bathrobes and slippers, and gorgeous flowers year-round. A superior breakfast might include homemade quiche, fresh fruit parfait, and fresh-baked lime scones. There's a hot tub in a Japanese garden setting. Reserve several months in advance for summer and weekend stays. ■ *4421 Lakeway Dr (take exit 253 off I-5, go 2⅘ miles on Lakeway Dr and turn left), Bellingham, WA 98226; (360) 734-2808 or (800) 562-2808; schnauzerx@aol.com; fairfax2.laser.et/~hatchm/schnauzerx.html; $$$; MC, V; checks OK.*

Best Western Heritage Inn ★★ Three tasteful, Wedgwood blue, shuttered and dormered structures nestling amid a small grove of trees and a stream seem incongruous adjacent to I-5 and a conglomeration of malls; however, this Best Western is one of the most professionally run hotels in the area. Rooms are elegantly furnished with exquisite cherry-wood four-poster beds, high- and lowboys, wing chairs in rich fabrics, and stylish desks with a comfortable chair. Other thoughtful touches include in-room coffee and tea, hair dryers, guest laundry facility, an attractive outdoor pool (in season), and an indoor hot tub. Request a room away from the freeway. Free continental breakfast is offered. ■ *151 E McLeod Rd (take exit 256 off I-5), Bellingham, WA 98226; (360) 647-1912 or (800) 528-1234; $$; AE, DC, MC, V; checks OK.* ♿

Big Trees Bed & Breakfast ★ Occupying a lovely 1907 Craftsman home in a quiet residential neighborhood just above Lake Whatcom, Big Trees is surrounded by just that: big trees (cedars and firs). The wide covered porch and the stone fireplace are two inviting places to relax. Upstairs, there are three bedrooms; two share a bath. Feather beds and down pillows help ensure a good night's rest. In the morning, enthusiastic innkeeper Jan Simmons serves up a hearty full breakfast, and a plateful of ideas of things to do around Bellingham. ■ *4840 Fremont St (take exit 253 off I-5 and head east on Lakeway Dr), Bellingham, WA 98226; (360) 647-2850 or (800) 647-2850; $$; MC, V; checks OK.*

North Garden Inn ★ This Victorian house (on the National Register of Historic Places) is especially popular with visitors to the nearby WWU campus. The Inn has 10 guest rooms, most with private bath. Some have lovely views over Bellingham Bay and the islands. All the rooms are attractive and clean and have a bit more character than usual—due partly to the antique house, partly to the influence of the energetic, talented, and well-traveled hosts. Barbara and Frank DeFreytas are both musical: there's a grand piano in one of the parlors, and musical or dramatic evenings take place here just as they probably did at the turn of the century. Guests who want to practice the piano privately should request the room that has its own piano. ■ *1014 N Garden St (at Maple), Bellingham, WA 98225; (360) 671-7828 or (800) 922-6414; $$; MC, V; checks OK.*

Stratford Manor ★ Set somewhat incongruously amid the farmland to the northeast of Bellingham, this rambling English Tudor–style home sits on a knoll overlooking the surrounding countryside. The three guest rooms occupy their own wing of the house; they all have Jacuzzis and gas fireplaces. Our favorite is the downstairs Garden Room, which has a spacious sitting area and a double Jacuzzi tub overlooking the garden. The common area in the guest wing has a TV and VCR with a selection of movies. There's an indoor hot tub, and a full breakfast is served in the dining room, after wake-up coffee is delivered to your door. ■ *1416 Van Wyck Rd (take Sunset Dr exit off I-5 and go northeast to Van Wyck), Bellingham, WA 98226; (360) 715-8441; $$$; MC, V; checks OK.*

LUMMI ISLAND

Located just off Gooseberry Point northwest of Bellingham, Lummi is one of the most overlooked islands of the ferry-accessible San Juans. It echoes the days when the San Juan Islands were still a hidden treasure, visited only by folks who preferred bucolic surroundings and deserted beaches to a plethora of restaurants and gift shops. Private ownership has locked up most of this pastoral isle, so you won't find state parks or resorts. To stretch your limbs, bring bikes and enjoy the quiet country roads. Plan ahead; dining options tend to be seasonal.

Lummi is serviced not by Washington State Ferries but by the tiny **Whatcom County ferry**, which leaves Gooseberry Point at 10 minutes past the hour from 7am until midnight (more frequently on weekdays). It's easy to find (just follow the signs to Lummi Island from I-5, north of Bellingham), cheap ($4 round trip for a car and two passengers), and quick (a 6-minute crossing; call ahead for schedule, (360) 676-6730. The ferry returns from Lummi on the hour.

LODGINGS

The Willows Inn ★★★ Run as a resort since the late 1920s, the old Taft family house perches on a knoll 100 feet above the accessible beach, offering sweeping views of the San Juan and Gulf Islands. There are four rooms in the main building (available weekends only, mid-February to mid-October), a small cottage for two with a kitchen (decor is a bit precious, but the view and privacy are terrific), and a two-bedroom guest house that looks out over the rose garden to the ocean (with a little of the kitchen roof in between). For couples traveling together, the last is our favorite; it also boasts a gas fireplace and a Jacuzzi. On weekends, arrive in time for complimentary afternoon tea at 3:30. Breakfast is also served weekends only, beginning with a knock on your door at 8am, as innkeepers Gary and Victoria Flynn deliver a beautiful tray with coffee and a loaf of hot Irish soda bread. A plentiful breakfast is served promptly at 9am. Weekdays, breakfast fixings are left in the kitchens of the cottage and the guest house. Saturday-night dinners are now open primarily to guests staying at the inn (a few nonguests may be accommodated; call ahead). Everything about the evening-long meal is sumptuous, and each dish incorporates the freshest ingredients, with many herbs and edible floral accents from the Flynns' garden. ■ *2579 W Shore Dr (from ferry, north on Nugent for 3½ miles), Lummi Island, WA 98262; (360) 758-2620; willows@pacificrim.net; www.pacificrim.net/-willows; $$$; beer and wine; MC, V; checks OK; dinner Sat (summer only).*

CHUCKANUT DRIVE

This famous stretch of road between Bellingham and Bow used to be part of the Pacific Highway; now it is one of the prettiest drives in the state, curving along the Chuckanut Mountains and looking out over Samish Bay and its many islands. Unfortunately, if you're in the driver's seat you'll have to keep your eyes on the road and wait for turnoffs for the view; the road is narrow and winding. Take the Chuckanut Drive exit off I-5 north, or follow 12th Street south in Bellingham.

Teddy Bear Cove is a lovely beach on a secluded shore along Chuckanut Drive just south of the Bellingham city limits. Watch for a parking lot on the left side of the road as you drive south from Bellingham.

The Interurban Trail, once the electric rail route from Bellingham to Mount Vernon, is now a 5-mile running, walking, riding, and mountain-biking trail connecting three parks on Chuckanut Drive: Fairhaven Park (in town) to Arroyo Park to Larrabee State Park.

Larrabee State Park, 7 miles south of Bellingham, was Washington's first state park. Beautiful sandstone sculpture along the beaches and cliffs provides a backdrop for exploration of the abundant sea life. There are good picnic areas and camping; (360) 676-2093.

As you wend your way north from Bellingham through these bucolic communities of the Skagit Valley, it's hard to believe that I-5 is only minutes away. Removed from traffic and shopping malls, you'll discover orchards, oyster beds, slow-moving tractors, and fields of mustard. In Bayview, visit the **Breazeale-Padilla Bay National Estuarine Research Reserve and Interpretive Center**. Learn about the Padilla Bay estuary through displays, saltwater tanks, and a library. Open Wednesday through Sunday, 10am–5pm; 1043 Bayview-Edison Road, (360)428-1558. A 2-mile shoreline trail begins just a short drive south of the Center. Nearby **Bayview State Park** is open year-round with overnight camping and beachfront picnic sites, perfect for winter bird-watching; (360)757-0227.

Permanent and part-time residents inhabit **Samish Island**, as do numerous oyster beds. **Blau Oyster Company** has been selling Samish Bay oysters, clams, and other seafood since 1935. Open Monday through Saturday; 7 miles west of Edison via Bayview-Edison Road and Samish Island Road, follow signs to the shucking sheds; 919 Blue Heron Road, Samish Island, (360)766-6171. If you're hungry or thirsty as you make your way through Edison, stop at the (smoky) Longhorn Saloon for tasty burgers, local oysters, and a huge selection of beers, both on tap and in the bottle; (360)766-6330.

▼

Bayview,
Samish
Island,
Edison, Bow

▲

RESTAURANTS

The Oyster Bar ★★★ This Samish Bay restaurant with a spectacular view is an institution on Chuckanut Drive. The award-winning wine list can be a bit intimidating, but a veteran server steers you in the right direction. The small menu focuses on local bounty: start with a half-dozen raw oysters fresh out of Samish Bay. The mixed green salad is nicely accented by a goat cheese garnish. The main course might be a perfectly cooked filet mignon with Dijon mustard, or a generous fillet of king salmon. A light cheese soufflé accompanies each meal. A creamy and delicious espresso cheesecake will keep you awake for the drive back down Chuckanut. No young children, please. ■ *240 Chuckanut Dr (north of Bow), Bow; (360)766-6185; $$$; beer and wine; AE, MC, V; local checks only; dinner every day.*

Oyster Creek Inn ★ The windows of this creekside restaurant open onto views of lush, green trees and rippling water. Adjacent to the Samish Bay Shellfish Farm, the Inn has a long history of dedication to seafood. The menu is a bit overwhelming, so keep it simple and start with a glass of house wine made by manager Doug Charles and, unless you're famished, stay with the small side of the menu (large meals include a spinach timbale and stuffed potato). A pea-cucumber salad in a dill dressing starts the meal a bit slowly, but the mussels in garlic herb sauce served with cold vegetables in a creamy tarragon sauce is a potent entree. You must try the wild blackberry pie. ■ *190 Chuckanut Dr (about a half hour's drive south of Bellingham), Bow; (360) 766-6179; $$; beer and wine; AE, MC, V; local checks only; lunch, dinner every day.* ᕷ

The Rhododendron Cafe ★ The Rhododendron Cafe is the perfect starting or ending point for a scenic trek on Chuckanut Drive. It may not have the view other Chuckanut eateries boast, but it serves up some awfully good food. Once the site of the Red Crown Service Station in the early 1900s, the Rhody serves homemade soup (the chowder is excellent), a tasty portobello mushroom burger, or lightly breaded and pan-fried Samish Bay oysters for lunch. The dinner menu is eclectic, ranging from four-cheese cannelloni to grilled pork loin to Italian oyster stew. Whatever you do, don't skip the desserts. The Rhody Express serves up to-go dishes, while the Rhody Too is an art gallery and gift shop. ■ *553 Chuckanut Dr (at the Bow-Edison junction), Bow; (360) 766-6667; $$; beer and wine; AE, MC, V; checks OK; breakfast Sat–Sun, lunch Fri–Sun, dinner every day (closed late Nov–Dec).* ᕷ

LODGINGS

Samish Point by the Bay ★★ Theresa and Herb Goldston have fashioned a tranquil getaway on their estatelike property at the west end of Samish Island. Solitude and privacy are assured to those staying at the Guest House, a new three-bedroom house with a gas fireplace in the cozy living room and a hot tub on the back deck. If you reserve the entire house (a pricey option except when shared with another couple or two, but one we recommend), you also have use of the fully equipped, gleaming modern kitchen. A continental breakfast is provided. There's an additional guest room in the main house. The grounds have miles of wooded trails, and there's access to a beach with a picnic table and a great view of the mountains lining Chuckanut Drive. ■ *447 Samish Point Rd (at the end of Samish Point Rd on Samish Island, west of Bow), Bow, WA 98232; (360) 766-6610 or (800) 916-6161; $$$; AE, MC, V; checks OK.*

Benson Farmstead Bed & Breakfast As you walk through the back door, you may wonder where John Boy is. But this is for real, not fiction. Once part of a working dairy farm, the large 17-room house is packed with antiques and Scandinavian memorabilia. The four upstairs guest rooms are outfitted with iron beds and custom quilts. Best are the English Garden Room and the Forget-Me-Not Room. In the evening, relax in the hot tub or in the parlor, sharing Sharon Benson's desserts and coffee. Jerry Benson cooks a country breakfast. And don't be surprised to hear music in the air; the Bensons are talented pianists and violinists (as are their four sons). Kids like this place, especially the playroom and the three cats. ▪ *1009 Avon-Allen Rd (exit 231 off I-5 north of Burlington), Bow, WA 98232; (360) 757-0578; $$; MC, V; checks OK (open weekends only Oct–Mar, except by special arrangement).*

ANACORTES

Anacortes, the gateway to the San Juans, is itself on an island: Fidalgo Island. Though most travelers rush through here on their way to the ferry, this town adorned with colorful, life-size cutouts of early pioneers is quietly becoming a place where it's worth it to slow down. For picnic or ferry food, try **Geppetto's** (3320 Commercial Avenue, (360) 293-5033) for Italian take-out. Those with a little more time head to **Gere-A-Deli** (502 Commercial Avenue, (360) 293-7383), a friendly hangout with good homemade food in an airy former Bank of Commerce building, or the **Anacortes Brewhouse** (320 Commercial Avenue, (360) 293-2444), with its own brews and wood-oven pizzas. And don't forget the **Calico Cupboard**, offshoot of the well-known cafe and bakery in La Conner (901 Commercial Street, (360) 293-7315).

If you need reading material for the ferry line, stop by **Watermark Book Company** (612 Commercial, (360) 293-4277), loaded with interesting reads. Seafaring folks should poke around **Marine Supply and Hardware** (202 Commercial Avenue, (360) 293-3014); established in 1913, it's packed to the rafters with basic and hard-to-find specialty marine items. And for the history of Fidalgo Island, visit the **Anacortes Museum** (1305 Eighth Street, (360) 293-1915).

For those who plan to go kayaking in the islands, first stop by **Eddyline Watersports Center** (1019 Q Avenue, (360) 299-2300); it is located at the Cap Sante Marina just before Anacortes (take a right on R Avenue off SR 20). Test-paddle a kayak in the harbor, then rent one for the weekend in the San Juans; reservations are necessary.

Washington Park is less than a mile west of the ferry terminal. Here you'll find scenic picnic areas and a paved 2½-mile trail looping through an old-growth forest with great views of the San Juans. Back at the ferry terminal, try the seafood pizza at the Compass Rose, (360) 293-6600 (but watch the clock, the pizzas can take a while).

RESTAURANTS

La Petite ★★ The Hulscher family, longtime owners of this restaurant at the Islands Inn motel, continues to deliver French-inspired food with a touch of Dutch. With only six entrees to choose from, quality is high. Try the lamb marinated in sambal or the popular pork tenderloin served with a mustard sauce. If chateaubriand is on the menu, order it; it's delicious. Soup, salad, and oven-fresh bread come with each meal. La Petite has an interesting dessert list, with plenty of options for chocolate lovers. A fixed-price Dutch breakfast is intended primarily for (but not exclusive to) motel guests. ■ *3401 Commercial Ave (at 34th), Anacortes; (360) 293-4644; $$; full bar; AE, DC, DIS, MC, V; local checks only; breakfast every day, dinner Tues–Sun.* 🕭

The Salmon Run (Majestic Hotel) ★★ It's the most elegant dining room in Anacortes, where diners are welcomed to a cathedral-ceilinged room filled with white tablecloths and tall-paned windows overlooking a garden and patio. The bistro has succeeded in combining the harvest of the Pacific Northwest with classic French cuisine and a Pacific Rim flair. At dinner, begin with grilled scallops served with a Thai peanut sauce. Mahi-mahi with an almond crust was fresh, moist and flavorful. There's also a Sunday champagne brunch, and live jazz Friday and Saturday nights in the pub. ■ *419 Commercial Ave (between 4th and 5th), Anacortes; (360) 299-2923; $$; full bar; AE, DIS, MC, V; local checks only; lunch, dinner every day (closed Tues in winter).* 🕭

LODGINGS

Channel House ★★ Just a mile and a half from the ferry dock, Dennis and Pat McIntyre's Channel House is a 1902 Victorian home designed by an Italian count. Each of the four antique-filled rooms has at least a peekaboo view of Guemes Channel and the San Juan Islands (best views are from the Canopy Room and the Island View Room). A cottage contains our two favorite rooms, however, each complete with a wood-burning fireplace and private whirlpool bath; the Victorian Rose has its own deck. There is a large hot tub out back, and the McIntyres serve cozy candlelit breakfasts (stuffed French toast is a specialty). Freshly baked oatmeal cookies and Irish Cream coffee await guests returning from dinner. The McIntyres gladly accommodate guests who need breakfast early in order to catch a ferry to the San Juans, but the Channel House is worthy of a longer stay. ■ *2902 Oakes Ave (at Dakota), Anacortes, WA 98221; (360) 293-9382 or (800) 238-4353; beds@sos.com; $$; AE, MC, V; checks OK.*

The Majestic Hotel ★★ Truly majestic, this 1889 hotel has been through a number of incarnations, but this is surely the grandest. It belongs on a bluff overlooking the Pacific, but provides a fine night's stay even in the middle of Anacortes. Every one of the 23 rooms is unique, all with English antiques; some have oversize tubs with skylights above, some have decks, others have VCRs, and a few have everything. The best rooms are the showy corner suites. On the second floor (the only smoking level) is a small library with a chess table. And up top, there's a cupola with a 360-degree view of Anacortes, Mount Baker, the Olympics, and the San Juans. There's no better perch in sight for a glass of wine at sunset. ■ *419 Commercial Ave (between 4th and 5th), Anacortes, WA 98221; (360)293-3355 or (800)588-4780; $$$; AE, DIS, MC, V; checks OK.* &

SAN JUAN ISLANDS

There are 743 at low tide and 428 at high tide; 172 have names; 60 are populated; and only 4 have major ferry service. The San Juan Islands are varied, remote, and breathtakingly beautiful. They are also located in the rain shadow of the Olympic Mountains, and most receive half the rainfall that Seattle receives. Of the four main islands, three—Lopez, Orcas, and San Juan—have lodgings, eateries, and some beautiful parks and are discussed below. The fourth, Shaw, has little on it other than the world's only ferry landing run by nuns, who also run a certified dairy—three cows—and a state campground with 12 sites.

Getting There. The most obvious and cost-effective way of getting to the San Juans is via the **Washington State Ferries**, which run year-round from Anacortes, 1½ hours north of Seattle; for schedule and fare information, call (206)464-6400. Keep in mind, however, the sparsely populated islands are rather overrun in the summer months, and getting a ferry out of Anacortes can be a long, dull 3-hours-and-up wait. Bring a good book—or park the car and board with a bike. Money-saving tip: cars only pay westbound. If you plan to visit more than one island, arrange to go to the farthest first (San Juan) and work your way east.

During the summer, there are other options for those who don't need to bring a car. The **Victoria Clipper** makes a once-a-day trip from downtown Seattle to Friday Harbor (with seasonal stops at Rosario Resort on Orcas Island). The ferry departs Pier 69 at 7:30am; (206)448-5000.

Another option, summer only, is via Bellingham; the **San Juan Island Shuttle Express** provides passenger-only ferry service to the San Juan Islands, May through September. Call for reservations: (360)671-1137 or (888)373-8522.

You can also fly to the islands. **Kenmore Air** schedules five flights a day during peak season. Round-trip flights start at about $112 per person and leave from Lake Union in Seattle; for more information, call (206)486-1257 or (800)543-9595.

For an active, exciting education about the San Juan Islands ecosystem, immerse yourself in a week of marine science activities at the **Island Institute's** Family Marine Adventure Camp, now based on Orcas Island (PO Box 358, Eastsound, WA 98245; (360)376-6720 or (800)956-ORCA).

SAN JUAN ISLANDS: LOPEZ

Lopez Island, flat and shaped like a jigsaw-puzzle piece, is a sleepy, rural place, famous for its friendly locals (drivers always wave) and its cozy coves and full pastures. It has the easiest bicycling in the islands: a relatively level 35-mile circuit suitable for the whole family to ride in a day. If you don't care to bring your own bikes, **Cycle San Juans**, (360)468-3251, will deliver rented 21-speed bikes to wherever you're staying. The company also offers full- and half-day bicycle tours.

There are numerous public parks. Two day parks (**Otis Perkins** and **Agate County**) are great for exploring, with good beach access. You can camp at **Odlin County Park**, (360)468-2496, (80 acres) or **Spencer Spit State Park**, (800)452-5687, (130 acres), both on the island's north side. Odlin has many nooks and crannies, and grassy sites set among Douglas firs, shrubs, and clover. Spencer Spit has around 30 conventional campsites, and more primitive sites on the hillside. Both parks have water, toilets, and fire pits. Seals and bald eagles can often be seen from the rocky promontory off **Shark Reef Park**, on the island's western shore.

Lopez Village is basic but has a few spots worth knowing about, such as **Holly B's Bakery** (in the Lopez Plaza, (360)468-2133), with celebrated fresh bread and pastries and coffee to wash them down (open April through December), and **Gail's** (Village Center, (360)468-2150), for soups and sandwiches.

RESTAURANTS

The Bay Cafe ★★★ For years the twinkling Bay Cafe has been reason alone to come to this serene isle, and we hope that remains true under new owners. The chefs remain the same, however, and pledge to maintain their winning way with ethnic preparations from around the world. The menu might include pork and blue corn posole, grilled tofu with chickpea-potato cakes (vegetarians never suffer here), or a marvelous beef fillet draped in sweet caramelized onions and a roasted garlic Roquefort sauce. Usually there are seafood tapas, which in a recent incarnation included basil-and-goat-cheese-stuffed prawns with saffron rice and a delectable ricotta corn cake with smoked salmon and blackberry sauce. Prices are reasonable, especially considering the inclusion of both soup (perhaps a delicate chanterelle-spinach) and a fresh tossed salad. Service is warm and proficient, atmosphere funky and relaxed. ▪ *Junction of Lopez Rd S and Lopez Rd N, Lopez Village; (360)468-3700; $$; beer and wine; DIS, MC, V; checks OK; dinner every day (weekends only in winter).*

LODGINGS

Inn at Swifts Bay ★★★ The most appealing accommodation on Lopez is this handsome Tudor inn, formerly a summer home, set among the cedars above Swifts Bay. Though new innkeepers were just finding their feet as we visited, they appear committed to maintaining the fine blend of pampering guests and letting them be that has established the inn's reputation for a decade. Public rooms are cozy and charming. Choose from two large, comfortable bedrooms (with shared bath) or three suites (with gas log fireplaces). Our favorite, the Red Cabbage Suite, is a very private space with a separate sitting area, an afternoon-sun deck, and a VCR. There's also a secluded outdoor hot tub that can be scheduled for private sittings (towels, robes, and slippers provided); a first-class selection of movies on tape; and a tiny exercise studio with a two-person sauna. You will need it after breakfast, an elegant presentation of fruit, home-baked pastries, and an elaborate entree that might range from salmon potato cakes to a Brie and apple omelet. The windswept bay is a five-minute walk away. ■ *3402 Rt 2 (head 1 mile south of ferry to Port Stanley Rd, left 1 mile), Lopez Island, WA 98261; (360) 468-3636; innatswiftsbay.com; www.swiftsbay.com; $$$; AE, DIS, MC, V; checks OK.*

Edenwild Inn ★★ The majestic Victorian centerpiece of Lopez Village, this B&B features eight individually decorated rooms, some with fireplaces, all with private baths and beautifully stained hardwood floors. Though it's not on the water, the front rooms on the upper floor have fine views: Room 6 features vistas of the bay and has a fireplace and sitting area. Breakfast is served at individual tables in the dining room. The only B&B on the island to accept children, it is also walking distance from the restaurants in town. ■ *Eads Lane and Lopez Village Rd, Lopez Village; (360) 468-3238; PO Box 271, Lopez Island, WA 98261; edenwildinn@msn.com; $$$; MC, V; checks OK.* &

Blue Fjord Cabins ★ Lopez is the most secluded and tranquil of the three ferry-accessible islands, and the Blue Fjord Cabins are the most secluded and tranquil getaway on Lopez. The two log cabins are tucked away up an unmarked dirt road, each concealed from the other by thick woods. They're of modern chalet design, clean and airy, with full kitchens. There's a three-night minimum stay in July and August. Doing nothing never had such a congenial setting. ■ *Elliott Rd at Jasper Cove; (360) 468-2749; Rt 1, Box 1450, Lopez Island, WA 98261; $$; no credit cards; checks OK.*

Lopez Farm Cottages ★ Amid sheep and cedars on 30 acres of prime Lopez pastureland, John and Ann Warsen built four cozy (read: tiny) cottages and fitted them with stylish pine interiors and plenty of windows. Each has a fireplace, a queen-size bed, front and back porches, and a minikitchen (fridge, microwave, sink, and dishes), making them suitable for extended getaways. But they're not bad for weekend romance either, with double-headed showers in every bathroom and a basket of continental breakfast delivered each evening for the next morning. The Warsens are gracious hosts. Unless you're from Iowa, the field setting may lack a feeling of landscape, but the acreage is a work in progress: look soon for a wildlife pond, campsites, and four more cottages. ■ *Fisherman Bay Rd (2⁷⁄₁₀ miles from the* *ferry), Lopez Island, WA 98261; (360) 468-3555 or (800) 440-3556; $$; MC, V; checks OK.*

MacKaye Harbor Inn ★ Location, location, location. Bicyclists call it paradise after their sweaty trek from the ferry to this little harbor. The tall powder-blue house sits above a sandy, shell-strewn beach, perfect for sunset strolls or pushing off in one of their rented kayaks to explore the scenic waterways. The Harbor Suite is our top choice, with its fireplace, private bath, and enclosed sitting area facing the beach. Rent kayaks or mountain bikes, ask the very friendly innkeepers, Mike and Robin Bergstrom, to share their secrets about the island, and you're off to explore. Return in the afternoon for freshly baked cookies. If you do come by bike, be warned: the closest restaurant is 6 miles back in town. Breakfast gets you started before a long morning of paddling out to the otters. ■ *12 miles south of the ferry landing on MacKaye Harbor Rd; (360) 468-2253; Rt 1, Box 1940, Lopez Island, WA 98261; $$$; MC, V; checks OK.*

SAN JUAN ISLANDS: ORCAS

Named not for the whales (the large cetaceans tend to congregate on the west side of San Juan Island and are rarely spotted here) but for a Spanish explorer, Orcas has a reputation as the most beautiful of the four main San Juan islands. It's also the biggest (geographically) and the hilliest, boasting 2,400-foot **Mount Constitution** as the centerpiece of Moran State Park. Drive, hike, or, if you're feeling up to it, bike to the top, but get there somehow; from the old stone tower you can see Vancouver, Mount Rainier, and everything between. The 4,800-acre **Moran State Park**, about 13 miles northeast of the ferry landing, also has one lake for freshwater swimming, two more for boating, five for fishing, and nice campsites, but you must call a central reservation service at least two weeks ahead for reservations: (800) 452-5687.

The man responsible for the park was shipbuilding tycoon Robert Moran. His old mansion is now the centerpiece of **Rosario Resort**, just west of the park. Unfortunately, the resort doesn't live up to its extravagant billing and prices. But the mansion, decked out in period memorabilia and mahogany trim and featuring an enormous pipe organ (still in use; check for concert dates), is certainly worth a sightseeing stop; (360) 376-2222.

Although you probably won't see whales around Orcas, there's a plethora of other wildlife, including bald eagles and seals. One good way to get up close: **kayak trips**. Try Shearwater Sea Kayak Tours, (360) 376-4699, which push off from many locales, including beautiful Doe Bay. Doe Bay Resort, a funky former artists' colony, offers threadbare accommodations and campsites for those visiting the (clothing optional) hot mineral springs; 26 miles northeast of ferry landing, (360) 376-2291.

Or you can **rent bicycles** by the hour, day, or week from Dolphin Bay Bicycles, (360)376-4157, at the Orcas ferry landing, or Wild Life Cycles, (360)376-4708, in Eastsound.

Every small, hip town has to lay claim to a small, hip bakery, and Eastsound has **Roses Bakery Cafe**, (360)376-4220. Roses features simple breakfasts and lunches; locals prefer the outdoor patio for fresh blueberry scones, muffins, savory soups, and lattes served in enormous bowls.

Orcas Island is the perfect place to relax with a good book in hand, and **Darvill's Book Store**, (360)376-2135, in Eastsound, houses an impressive stock of reading material for any and all interests. Pacific Northwest authors are well represented here.

RESTAURANTS

Christina's ★★★ Built above a 1930s gas station in Eastsound, Christina's offers the bewitching blend of provincial locale and urban sophistication that marks the finest rural destinations. The view of the bay and craggy islet from dining room and deck is sublime; more often than not, Christina Orchid's classic continental food is, too. Singing scallops, gathered off Guemes Island, might be gently steamed in their elegant shells with fragrant hints of thyme and garlic; king salmon might arrive adorned with tender coils of fiddlehead fern. A recent fillet of beef in Gorgonzola cream was a masterpiece of flavor and texture, the kind of dish that has made Christina's reputation as the finest dining room in the islands. Occasional missteps— salmon so minimally adorned as to be monotonous, long lapses in the server's attention—wouldn't bother so much if you weren't dropping an easy $100 (for two) to eat here. Servings tend toward the generous, with a nice selection of appetizers sized right to split or enjoy as your own light meal. ■ *North Beach Rd and Main St, Eastsound; (360)376-4904; greendolphin@msn. com; $$$; full bar; AE, DC, MC, V; checks OK; dinner every day (Thurs–Mon in winter).*

Ship Bay Oyster House ★★ Ship Bay has developed a reputation as a great spot for fresh fish and local oysters. Lovers of the briny mollusks will be in oyster heaven: baked, stewed, panfried, or au naturel (try an oyster shooter, served up in a shot glass with Clamato and sake), there's a 'ster for every palate. The Pacific Coast locale (a comfortable old farmhouse with a view of Ship Bay) belies the Atlantic Coast ambience. The clam chowder—a New Englandy version, included with every entree—might be the best in the West, and the kitchen obviously never learned about portion control (just order a small slab of spicy-hot barbecue baby back ribs with its exceptional accompaniment of black beans and salsa, and you'll get our drift). ■ *Just east of Eastsound on Horseshoe Hwy; (360)376-5886; $$; full bar; AE, MC, V; checks OK; dinner every day (Tues–Sun off-season; closed Dec–Feb).* &

Bilbo's Festivo ★ Orcas Islanders speak of this cozy little place with reverence. Its decor and setting—mud walls, Mexican tiles, arched windows, big fireplace, handmade wooden benches, spinning fans, in a small house with a flowered courtyard—are charming, and the Navajo and Chimayo weavings on the walls are indeed from New Mexico. The fare includes a combination of Mexican and New Mexican influences, with improvisation on enchiladas, burritos, chiles rellenos, and mesquite-grilled specials. In summer, lunch is served taqueria-style, grilled to order outdoors, then heaped with the condiments of your choice. ■ *North Beach Rd and A St, Eastsound; (360) 376-4728; $; full bar; MC, V; local checks only; lunch, dinner every day (dinner only off-season).*

Cafe Olga ★ You're likely to experience a wait at Cafe Olga, a popular midday stop for locals and visitors alike. Luckily, this country kitchen is part of the Orcas Island Artworks, a sprawling cooperative crafts gallery in a picturesque renovated strawberry-packing barn, so you can browse while you work up an appetite. The wholesome international home-style entrees range from a rich Sicilian artichoke pie to a chicken enchilada with black bean sauce to a Greek salad. For dessert, try a massive piece of terrific blackberry pie. ■ *East of Moran State Park at Olga Junction, Olga; (360) 376-5098; $; beer and wine; MC, V; local checks only; lunch every day (closed Jan–Feb).* ♿

Deer Harbor Lodge and Inn ★ This expansive, rustic dining room with a large view deck is a cozy, soothing place, despite its size. Pam and Craig Carpenter rescued the inn from its long career as a purveyor of battered chicken and made it home to some good seafood, with generous portions. Eight or so entrees are outlined on the blackboard at the door and vary according to what's in season. Soups and salads arrive in large serving bowls, and the accompanying bread is homemade. Both the wine list and the beer list are thoughtfully conceived. Unfortunately, our endorsement does not extend to the adjoining inn, which on our latest visit showed signs of inattention. ■ *From ferry landing, follow signs to Deer Harbor; (360) 376-4110; www.onlinefx.com/orcas/DHInn; $$; beer and wine; AE, MC, V; checks OK; dinner every day (closed Jan, and variable off-season).* ♿

LODGINGS

Chestnut Hill Inn Bed & Breakfast ★★★ Every romantic stereotype of B&B elegance is fulfilled in this renovated farmhouse, perched atop a pastoral rise not far from the ferry. Marilyn Loewke (Islanders call her "Ms. Romance") and her husband, Dan, have fitted the five guest rooms with luxurious appointments large and small: feather beds, fireplaces, Egyptian-cotton linens, robes, slippers, liqueurs, loofahs. The fanciest, the Chestnut Suite, boasts a TV/VCR, stocked fridge, and two-person

Jacuzzi bath with dimmer switch. Suffice it to say, folks either love the romance overkill or loathe it. But even hardened chinz-haters appreciate the attention and good taste that have gone into every facet of this inn. Each of the rooms (an additional private cottage is under construction) has been individually conceived and appointed. We favor the Chapel Room, with its double shower and view of the charming steepled chapel in the pear orchard. There's also a pond (complete with rowboat), a stable (complete with horses), and a gazebo (complete with a full schedule of weddings). Marilyn is a gifted cook: in addition to lavish breakfasts and picnic hampers, she prepares dinners as good as anything else on the island for guests in the off season. ■ *Not quite 2 miles east of ferry landing off Laporte Road, Orcas; (360)376-5157; PO Box 213, Orcas, WA, 98280; chestnut@ pacificrim.net; www.pacificws.com/orcas/chestnut.html; $$$; AE, DIS, MC, V; checks OK.*

Spring Bay Inn ★★★ It's a long dirt road getting here, but rarely is a drive so amply rewarded. Situated where 57 wooded acres meet the sea is the handsome Spring Bay Inn, as stylishly appointed indoors as it is scenic outside. The interior reflects the naturalist sensibilities of innkeepers Sandy Playa and Carl Burger, an engaging and youthful pair of retired state park rangers whose crunchy-granola lifestyle sets them apart from other upscale B&B owners. The angular great room, with its fieldstone fireplace and vaulted ceiling, showcases a stunning view of Spring Bay. Upstairs are four thoughtfully decorated guest rooms, each with its own bath and Rumford fireplace; two have private balconies. Downstairs is the Ranger's Suite, with 27 windows and its own hot tub. Come morning, coffee, muffins, and fresh fruit are delivered to each door—a little sustenance for the two-hour guided kayak tour around Obstruction Island. (Beginners are welcome, kayaks and equipment provided, harbor seal and eagle sightings free of charge.) Return to the lodge for a big healthy brunch. The property is adjacent to Obstruction Pass State Park, and is laced with hiking trails and teeming with wildlife. (Did we mention this is the place to come for a straight shot of fabled Northwest outdoorsiness?) After dark, ease tired muscles with a private soak under the stars in the bayside hot tub. ■ *Follow Obstruction Pass Rd to Obstruction Pass Park trailhead, take right fork onto dirt road to Spring Bay gate, Olga; (360)376-5531; PO Box 97, Olga, WA 98279; $$$; AE, DIS, MC, V; checks OK.*

Cascade Harbor Inn ★★ Now *this* is the way to stay at Rosario, particularly if you have kids in tow. Forty-eight modern units—some studios with Murphy beds, some two-queen rooms, some in-between—all have decks and water views, and many configure into multiunit suites with fully equipped kitchens. Once managed by Rosario, this inn now shares only its vistas of pristine Cascade Bay and its beach access. Continental breakfast is included. ■ *Just east of Rosario along shore of Cascade Bay, Eastsound; (360)376-6350 or (800)201-2120; HC 1, Box 195, Eastsound, WA 98245; www.pacificws.com/orcas/cascade.html; $$$; MC, V; local checks only.*

Turtleback Farm Inn ★★ Located inland amid tall trees, rolling pastures, and private ponds, Turtleback offers seven spotless rooms dressed in simple sophistication and stunning antiques. It also offers efficiency: Turtleback's veteran innkeepers Bill and Susan Fletcher have thought of everything, from cocoa, coffee, and fresh fruit for nibbling to flashlights for evening forays. Their curt personal style may leave them wanting in bed-(and breakfast)side manner, but it didn't cramp us too much on a recent visit. What did cramp us was our room, the aptly named Nook. It really is worth the extra $50 or more to go up a notch or two: choose either one of the larger upstairs rooms or one of two downstairs rooms with private decks overlooking the meadow and the lambs a-prancing. Susan cooks magnificent breakfasts, and serves them on the deck in sunny weather. Members of the Turtleback Fan Club, take note: as we went to press, construction was underway on an adjacent four-suite building. ■ *10 minutes from the ferry on Crow Valley Rd, Eastsound; (360)376-4914; Rt 1, Box 650, Eastsound, WA 98245; www.specialplaces.com; $$$; DIS, MC, V; checks OK.*

Beach Haven Resort ★ Regardless of the time of year, this funky family retreat with its long pebble beach, canoes and rowboats, and lack of maid service reminds us of summer camp. No TV. No telephones. No fussy amenities. Expect a seven-day minimum stay in summer, and consider coming in the off season, when rates prove especially affordable (and you'll likely encounter fewer "campers"). Accommodations range through various grades of rustic—the wood stove–heated cabins, shielded by old-growth forest, are of the genuine log variety—to modern apartments, a "Spectacular Beachcomber" four-bedroom house, and a brand-new "Honeymoon Cabin" all decked out with a Jacuzzi and a heated bathroom floor. A designated family section sports a wonderful playground. ■ *8½ miles NW of the ferry at President Channel off Enchanted Forest Rd, Eastsound; (360)376-2288; Rt 1, Box 12, Eastsound, WA 98245; beachvn@ aol.com; $$; MC, V; checks OK.* &

North Beach Inn ★ If you like funky, private settings with history and personality, North Beach Inn is the spot. Originally an apple orchard, then converted into a resort in the early '30s, North Beach Inn has remained relatively unchanged ever since. Eleven worn cabins are laid out on a prime stretch of the Gibson family beach. The spiffiest: Columbia, Frazier, and Shamrock (which has a loft that kids adore). Each cabin comes complete with a full kitchen, grill, Adirondack chairs on the beach (bonfires allowed), and a tremendous view. Also likely: duck-print flannel sheets, flimsy floral curtains, or artwork and furniture probably picked up at a local garage sale. Bring Fido if you'd like. One-week minimum stay July and August, two-day minimum the rest of the year. ■ *1½ miles west of the airport at North Beach Rd, Eastsound; (360)376-2660; PO Box 80, Eastsound, WA 98245; $$; no credit cards; checks OK (closed after Thanksgiving through mid-Feb).*

Orcas Hotel ★ It's a pretty 1904 Victorian just above the ferry terminal, with period pieces, white wicker in the lovely gardens, and a deck overlooking the water (though the gas tanks make for a less-than-perfect view). Best of the dozen accommodations are the two new, larger rooms, which have private balconies and whirlpool tubs. It feels like a small, romantic hotel, with a light breakfast in the adjoining cafe included. The cafe with its grandstand deck is *the* place to wait out the ferry with a beer or a sandwich. The same management rents out a two-bedroom Foxglove Cottage on the water at Deer Harbor. ■ *Orcas ferry landing; (360)376-4300; PO Box 155, Orcas, WA 98280; $$$; beer and wine; AE, DIS, MC, V; checks OK; breakfast, lunch, dinner every day.*

Outlook Inn ★ If you want to stay in the Manhattan of Orcas—that's Eastsound, with its variety of walking-distance restaurants—you'll want to stay at the legendary Outlook Inn. Like the proverbial hippie, it has traded in its countercultural spirit for the luxuries money can buy. Though the old flophouse accommodations with shared bathrooms are still available—and affordable—new swanky suites have bang-up views, decks, whirlpool baths, and heated towel racks, and they command prices a hippie would protest. Perhaps because we remember its humble past, the renovated Outlook Inn feels a little soulless to us. But the bar and restaurant have a loyal local clientele: always a good sign. ■ *On Main St in Eastsound; (360)376-2200; PO Box 210, Eastsound, WA 98245; outlook@pacificrim.net; www.resdesign.com/outlook/; $$–$$$; AE, MC, V; checks OK.* &

Windsong Bed & Breakfast ★ A 1917 schoolhouse-turned-B&B (the first to be registered on Orcas), the Windsong has undergone another renovation and is now a warmly elegant bed-and-breakfast inn. Each of the four rooms is beautifully decorated and amply proportioned, with queen- or king-size beds; each has its own private bath and three have fireplaces. We favor the Rhapsody for its view through the trees to Westsound. A living room for guests offers a big TV and comfy couches; out in the glass-enclosed "Moon Room" a hot tub bubbles. Co-host Sam Haines is big on breakfast: he makes it in four courses. ■ *On Deer Harbor Rd just west of Horseshoe Hwy, Westsound; (360)376-2500 or (800)669-3948; PO Box 32, Orcas, WA 98280; windsong@ pacific rim.net; www.pacificws.com/windsong; $$$; MC, V; checks OK.*

San Juan Island is the most populated in the archipelago; therefore it supports the biggest town, Friday Harbor, though typically nightlife is scarce even here, and the shopping is undistinguished. Attractions include the mid-19th-century sites of the **American** and **English Camps**, established when ownership of the island was under dispute. The conflict led to the infamous Pig War of 1859–60, so called because the sole casualty was a pig. Americans and British shared joint occupation until 1872, when the dispute was settled in favor of the United States. The English camp, toward the island's north end, is wooded and secluded, while the American camp consists of open, windy prairie and beach, inhabited now only by thousands of rabbits. Either makes a fine picnic spot. So does the beautiful **San Juan County Park**, where it's also possible to camp on the dozen often-crowded acres on Smallpox Bay (reservations suggested, (360)378-2992). Another camping option is **Lakedale Resort** (4½ miles from Friday Harbor on Roche Harbor Road, 360-378-2350), a campground on 82 acres with three lakes for swimming and fishing and six new log-cabin suites (make reservations). The best **diving** in the archipelago (some claim it's the best cold-water diving in the world) can be had here; Emerald Seas Diving Center, Friday Harbor (2A Spring Street, (360)378-2772), rents equipment and runs charter boats. It also rents sea kayaks, a wonderful way to see the island's wildlife up close. If you're lucky (your best chance is in late spring), you may even encounter whales that belong to the three native pods of orcas. Or you can join a **guided kayak trip**: Shearwater Adventures, (360)376-4699, offers excursions. Several **charter boats** are also available for whale watching and fishing; try the Western Prince, (360)378-5315 or (800)757-ORCA. Those distrustful of their sea legs can visit the marvelous **Whale Museum** (62 First Street, Friday Harbor, (360)378-4710), with exhibits and excursions devoted to the resident cetaceans; or go to the nation's first official whale-watching park at **Lime Kiln Point State Park** on the island's west side. Bring binoculars and a lot of patience.

▼

San Juan
Islands:
San Juan

▲

The **San Juan Historical Museum** (405 Price Street, Friday Harbor, (360)378-3949) is filled with memorabilia from the island's early days. The 90-year-old-plus founder, a third-generation islander, is there two days a week. Another bit of history is hidden away at the **Roche Harbor Resort** (see review). Here you'll find a mausoleum, a bizarre monument that may tell more about timber tycoon John McMillin than does all the rest of Roche Harbor. The ashes of family members are contained in a set of stone chairs that surround a concrete dining room table. They're ringed by a set of 30-foot-high columns, symbolic of McMillin's adherence to Masonic beliefs.

Oyster fans will be happy to visit **Westcott Bay Sea Farms** off Roche Harbor Road, 2 miles south of Roche Harbor Resort,

(360)378-2489, where you can help yourself to oysters at bargain prices.

Jazz Festival. Throngs of people infest the streets of Friday Harbor for three days of jazz, blues to Dixieland, in mid- to late July; for information, call (360)378-5509.

RESTAURANTS

Duck Soup Inn ★★ Richard and Gretchen Allison are committed to an ambitious reach of the kitchen with local seafoods and seasonal ingredients, and they've succeeded admirably. The wood-paneled dining room, with its stone fireplace, wooden booths, and high windows, is a charmer. The menu is limited to house specialties—succulent sautéed prawns in wild blackberry sauce, applewood-smoked Westcott Bay oysters, and grilled fresh fish. House-baked bread served with tangy anchovy paste (and butter), a small bowl of perfectly seasoned soup, and a large green salad accompany the ample portions. No wonder there's little room left for dessert. ■ *3090 Roche Harbor Rd (4½ miles north of Friday Harbor), Friday Harbor; (360)378-4878; $$; beer and wine; DIS, MC, V; checks OK; dinner Wed–Sun (closed in winter).* ㅤㅤ&

Roberto's ★★ Roberto Carrieri worked in about every restaurant on the island and finally decided to open one himself and do it right. He did. Carrieri and Paul Aiello's tiny Italian restaurant in its little perch above the ferry parking lot has become one of the island's most popular spots. If you want to get in, we suggest the first thing you do upon arriving at Friday Harbor is make reservations. Arrive hungry: portions are huge. And arrive early: the best dishes, like Carrieri's king salmon piccata, disappear fast. But even when they do, the rest of the specials are generally outstanding. Who needs dessert? ■ *205 A St (corner of 1st St), Friday Harbor; (360)378-6333; $$$; beer and wine; MC, V; no checks; dinner every day (variable in winter; closed Jan–Feb.)*

Springtree Cafe ★★ Chef/owner James Boyle garners praise from locals and tourists alike for his consistently excellent Northwest cuisine. Decor is simple—no tablecloths, plain wooden tables graced by a few fresh flowers, some photographs on the walls. But the menu, emphasizing seafood, organics, and local produce, is anything but simple. There's almost always a grilled salmon preparation on the menu. At a recent dinner we were wowed by a spicy Dungeness crab cake and an enormous plate of corkscrew pasta with smoked mussels, prawns, and crabmeat in a basil cream sauce. The best food here is that which is the most adventurous. Vegetarians are well cared for since Boyle eschews meat. Service is folksy and energetic; there's outdoor dining under the elm tree on the patio, weather permitting. ■ *310 Spring St (under the elm on Spring, downtown), Friday Harbor; (360)378-4848; $$; beer and wine; AE, DIS,*

MC, V; local checks only; lunch, dinner every day (Tues–Sat off-season). &

The Place Next to the San Juan Ferry Cafe ★ Behind the unassuming name and the viewy waterside location that typically guarantees mediocrity is this striving concern, garnering much praise from locals. Chef/owner Steven Anderson features a rotating world of cuisines, focusing on fish and shellfish, from BC king salmon to Westcott Bay oysters. On a recent visit we enjoyed a fillet of salmon in a gingery citrus sauce, and a plate of black bean ravioli topped with tiger prawns in a buttery glaze. Servers know exactly how much time you have if your boat's in sight: with luck, enough time to savor the sumptuous crème caramel. ▪ *1 Spring St (on the water, at the foot of Spring St), Friday Harbor; (360)378-8707; $$; beer and wine; MC, V; checks OK; lunch, dinner every day (dinner Tues–Sat in winter).* &

Katrina's Kate Stone has moved her one-woman culinary show from the back of a secondhand store to an airy Victorian with more space for diners. She's doing more seafood now, but by and large look for the same rotating-menu format of simple sensations: her signature spinach-cheese pie and green salad with toasted hazelnuts and garlicky blue cheese dressing are standouts. Check out the breezy deck. ▪ *135 2nd St (corner of West, downtown), Friday Harbor; (360)378-7290; $; beer and wine; MC, V; checks OK; lunch, early dinner Mon–Fri.* &

LODGINGS

Friday Harbor House ★★★ Some shudder at the sore-thumb architecture of San Juan Island's poshest inn, a sister property of the Inn at Langley on Whidbey Island. Others consider this stylish urban outpost a welcome relief from Victorian B&Bs. Regardless, the interior is a bastion of spare and soothing serenity, a mood abetted by the professional management of the place. Each of the 20 rooms is decorated in muted tones, lending a contemporary feel, with gas fireplaces and (noisy) Jacuzzis positioned to absorb both the warmth from the fireplace and the harbor view. Some rooms have tiny standing-room-only balconies, but not all offer a full waterfront view (ask for a room in the main building). Breakfast is homemade continental, with delicious hot scones.

   The dining room, with its knockout harbor view, maintains the spartan cool of the rest of the inn, but warms up considerably under the influence of chef Laurie Paul's (late of Cafe Bissett) cooking. At a recent dinner we savored an appetizer of delectable black bean and garlic mussels, then plunged into a salad of pistachios and baby greens, and then mostly enjoyed our (slightly overcooked) pork tenderloin in apple chutney. Service is warm and efficient. ▪ *130 West St (from ferry, left on Spring, right on 1st, right on West), Friday Harbor; (360)378-8455; PO Box 1385, Friday Harbor, WA 98250; fhhouse@msn.com; $$$;*

full bar; AE, DC, MC, V; checks OK; dinner every day (Thurs–Mon in winter). &

Harrison House Suites ★★ This crisply renovated Craftsman inn, just up the hill from downtown Friday Harbor and run by the effusive Farhad Ghatan, features five impressive suites: all with kitchens and private baths, four with decks, three with whirlpool tubs. It's modern and angular, and those rooms that have views overlook the whole scenic sweep of Friday Harbor. And it's underpriced, for the region; great for families and/or groups of couples. Ghatan also runs a little cafe next door. ■ *235 C St (2 blocks from downtown, at Harrison St), Friday Harbor, WA 98250; (360) 378-3587 or (800) 407-7933; www.rockisland. com/~hhsuites; $$; AE, DIS, MC, V; checks OK.* &

Mariella Inn and Cottages ★★ The moment the organization of this stunning Victorian estate improves, we will award it the three stars its physical splendor warrants. Grandly perched upon the end of a 9-acre point, the 1902 inn with 11 elegant rooms and burnished public spaces features 360-degree views and manicured lawns just begging for wedding ceremonies. Rooms in the inn, each now with private bath, vary: some feel shoehorned in, with considerable noise from the kitchen downstairs; others, like the spendy solarium rooms or the beautiful second-floor deck rooms, are large, with expansive views. In addition, seven pretty little cottages (some, like Foxglove, *very* little) with decks dot the waterside among the madronas. We like the Maple and Ivy cabins, with wood stoves and kitchens; bigger cabins like Kingfisher are great for families. Shifting management over the past year has tended to bring shoddy service and missing amenities, problems one shouldn't encounter in a place this expensive. A large party facility on the grounds, under construction at press time, might further tax the inn's resources. Still, extras abound: robes in the rooms, a cedar hot tub (indoors, alas) for private soaking, sea kayaks and bikes for rent, a 65-foot classic motor yacht for chartering, good continental breakfast (delivered to the cabins) in the morning. And the inn restaurant, open for dinners in-season, is presenting improved (if overpriced) dinners. ■ *630 Turnpoint Rd (left on 1st St, follow signs to Turnpoint Rd), Friday Harbor, WA 98250; (360) 378-6868 or (800) 700-7668; $$$; beer and wine; AE, MC, V; checks OK; dinner every day (variable in winter).*

Olympic Lights ★★ As you approach this isolated bed and breakfast, you may recall the movie *Days of Heaven*: The tall Victorian farmhouse sits lonely as a lighthouse in a sea of open meadow. The renovated interior is more modern and elegant: four upstairs rooms, all with queen beds, furnished with white wicker and bathed in sunlight. The downstairs room is the only one with a private bath, but you shouldn't let that sway you from choosing this retreat. You must remove your shoes to tread the off-white pile carpet. The panorama of Olympic Mountains and Strait of Juan de Fuca from the south rooms adds to the effect. Breakfast includes fresh eggs from the resident hen; the owners also have five cats who roam downstairs. ■ *4531-A Cattle Point Rd (take Argyle Ave out of Friday Harbor to Cattle Point Rd), Friday Harbor, WA 98250; (360)378-3186; $$; no credit cards; checks OK.*

Westwinds Bed & Breakfast ★★ Westwinds commands what may easily be the most magnificent view on all of the San Juan Islands; however, only a few people enjoy the 6 acres of mountainside abundant with deer and quail: This private glass-and-wood paradise is a two-bedroom facility, where guests (one group at a time) have the 1,200-square-foot house to themselves. Look from your cathedral-ceilinged bedroom, private bath, patio, living room, or virtually any seat in the house, and you're likely to feel in possession of a large part of the world (or at least the Strait of Juan de Fuca and the Olympic Mountains). Home-baked continental breakfast is almost as majestic. Particularly popular with honeymoon couples (privacy in this corner of Splurgeville is never an issue), this bed and breakfast now has a sister property just down the road: a cozy, windowy loft home encircled with decks. ■ *4909 H Hannah (2 miles from Lime Kiln Point State Park), Friday Harbor, WA 98250; (360)378-5283; $$$; MC, V; checks OK.*

Duffy House ★ This 1920s farmhouse looking out upon Griffin Bay and the Olympics beyond displays an architectural style (Tudor) that's rare in the islands, in a splendid, isolated site. Decorated with antiques and accented with classic mahogany trim, Duffy House offers five comfy guest rooms, all of which now have private baths. The sunken living room sports a large fireplace and a bounty of information about the islands. Even neophyte bird-watchers won't be able to miss the bald eagles here; they nest just across the street, near the trail to the beach. ■ *760 Pear Point Rd (take Argyle Rd south from town to Pear Point Rd), Friday Harbor, WA 98250; (360)378-5604 or (800)972-2089; www.pacificrim.net/~bydesign/duffy.html; $$; MC, V; checks OK.*

Friday's Historical Inn ★ The former Elite Hotel is living up to its old name. Innkeepers Debbie and Steve Demarest have taken this longtime bunkhouse and given it a completely new life. Eleven rooms are decorated in rich colors of wine, water, and wings. The best room in the place is unquestionably the third-floor perch with its own deck (and water view), kitchen, double shower, and Jacuzzi. Heated floors in the bathrooms and occasional fresh-baked cookies are just two of the thoughtful touches; however, the inn is right in the middle of town and not always the quietest retreat. Downstairs is a bistro with good pizzas and huge salads. ■ *2 blocks up from the ferry on 1st St, Friday*

Harbor; (360)378-5848 or (800)352-2632; PO Box 2023, Friday Harbor, WA 98250; fridays@friday-harbor.com; www.friday harbor.com/~fridays; $$; MC,V; checks OK.

Lonesome Cove Resort ★ Back in 1945, Roy and Neva Durhack sailed their 35-foot yacht here from the Hawaiian Islands. They were getting ready to sail it around the world, but once they saw Lonesome Cove their wanderlust subsided. They're not here anymore, but the resort remains a pretty spot. The six immaculate little cabins set among trees at the water's edge, the manicured lawns, and the domesticated deer that wander the 75-acre woods make the place a favorite for lighthearted honeymooners. The sunsets are spectacular, and there's a fine view of nearby Spieden Island. Cabins have a five-night minimum stay in the summer months (two nights at other times). No pets—too many baby ducks around. ■ *5810 Lonesome Cove Rd (take Roche Harbor Rd 9 miles north to Lonesome Cove Rd), Friday Harbor, WA 98250; (360)378-4477; $$; MC, V; checks OK.* ᕍ

Trumpeter Inn ★ Trumpeter Inn is a contemporary house located amid farmlands about 2 miles outside of Friday Harbor. The pastoral setting is soothing, as are the simply decorated guest rooms with lots of pastels. All rooms have a king- or queen-size bed with crisp cotton sheets and down comforters; five of the six have private baths. We prefer the Bay Laurel Room, a second-floor corner room with a great view of the surrounding meadows and the Olympics in the distance. You may even glimpse the trumpeter swans for whom the inn is named if you visit in winter. Leave your car behind; owners can pick up guests from the ferry. ■ *420 Trumpeter Way (from Friday Harbor, follow Spring St, which runs into San Juan Valley Rd), Friday Harbor, WA 98250; (360)378-3884 or (800)826-7926; $$; MC, V; checks OK.* ᕍ

Wharfside Bed & Breakfast ★ If nothing lulls you to sleep like the gentle lap of the waves, the Wharfside's the B&B for you. It's this region's first realization of the European tradition of floating inns. Two guest rooms on the 60-foot sailboat *Jacquelyn* are both very nicely finished, with full amenities and that compact precision that only living on a boat can inspire. The fore cabin has a double bed and sleeping berths for kids or extras. When the weather's good, enjoy the huge breakfast on deck and watch the yachtsmen head to sea. ■ *On the K dock in Friday Harbor; (360)378-5661; PO Box 1212, Friday Harbor, WA 98250; www.rockisland.com/~pcshop/wharfside.html; $$; AE, MC, V; checks OK.*

Roche Harbor Resort When you walk out of the stately old ivy-clad Hotel de Haro at Roche Harbor and gaze out at the trellised, cobblestoned waterfront and yacht-dotted bay, you'll forget all about the creaky, uneven floorboards, the piecework wallpaper, the sparse furnishings. This faded gem evolved from the company town that John McMillin built a century ago for his lime mill, once the largest west of the Mississippi. It has seen some renovation since Teddy Roosevelt visited, but not so you'd notice. Still, the 111-year-old resort has a terrific view and pretty gardens, plus a few nicely renovated cottages and condos. Between strolling the gardens, swimming, tennis, and visiting the mausoleum (really), there's plenty to do at Roche Harbor. Lately we've even been hearing positive murmurs about the food, a newsworthy development indeed. ■ *In downtown Roche Harbor; (360)378-2155 or (800)451-8910; PO Box 4001, Roche Harbor, WA 98250; roche@rocheharbor.com; www.rocheharbor. com; $$$; AE, MC, V; checks OK.* &

LA CONNER

La Conner was founded in 1867 by John Conner, a trading-post operator, who named the town after his wife, Louisa A. Conner. Much of what you see today was built before the railroads arrived in the late 1880s, when the fishing and farming communities of Puget Sound traded almost entirely by water. In an age of conformity and efficiency, the town became a literal backwater, and something of a haven for nonconformists (Wobblies, WWII COs, McCarthy-era escapees, beatniks, hippies, and bikers), always with a fair smattering of artists and writers, including Mark Tobey, Morris Graves, Guy Anderson, and Tom Robbins.

This long-standing live-and-let-live attitude of the town has allowed the neighboring Native American Swinomish community to contribute to the exceptional cultural richness of La Conner. Even the merchants here have created a unique atmosphere, an American bazaar: Chez la Zoom, Cottons, Nasty Jack's, Two Moons, Organic Matters, and O'Leary's Books, just to name a few.

Tillinghast Seed Co., at the entrance to town, is the oldest operating retail and mail-order seed store in the Northwest (since 1885); in addition to seeds it has a wonderful nursery, a florist shop, and a general store; (360)466-3329. **Go Outside** is a small but choice garden and garden-accessory store; (360)466-4836. If all this shopping leaves you in need of respite, repair to the **Rose and Thistle** tearoom and antique shop, (360)466-3313, for afternoon tea or the stylish **La Conner Brewing Co.** for a fine selection of ales and tasty wood-fired pizzas; 117 S First, (360)466-1415.

Gaches Mansion, on Second Street overlooking the main drag, is a wonderful example of American Victorian architecture, filled with period furnishings and sporting a widow's walk that looks out on the entire Skagit Valley; open weekends, (360)466-4446. The new **Museum of Northwest Art** is worth a visit, especially for its collection of Northwest glass art. Open Tuesday through Sunday, 121 S First, (360)466-4446. If you come into La Conner via the Conway exit off I-5, be sure to stop at **Snow Goose**

Produce on Fir Island Road for one of their ice cream cones in a homemade waffle cone. You can buy tulips here in the spring, and they stock lots of local produce and specialty food items, as well as fresh seafood (including precooked Hood Canal shrimp, a perfect snack for the drive home).

RESTAURANTS

Palmers Restaurant and Pub ★★ Palmers continues to be La Conner's favorite restaurant. Thomas and Danielle Palmer's place is perched on a knoll just behind town at the far end of the La Conner Country Inn. Locals like the hobbitlike pub with wall murals painted by La Conner artists; but for a more elegant atmosphere, climb the stairs. There are two rooms, one with lace curtains on the west-facing windows that draw in the golden evening sun, another with a wood stove to warm winter evenings. The deck is a pleasant spot too. Dinners are reliable; the massive lamb shank bergère is tender and savory with garlic, tomatoes, mushrooms, and herbs. A special prawn dish, with papaya, kiwi, and cilantro, shows the kitchen can work just as successfully with more exotic flavorings. ■ *205 Washington (at 2nd), La Conner; (360) 466-4261; $$; full bar; AE, MC, V; checks OK; lunch, dinner every day.*

Andiamo ★ Andiamo is the Palmers' newest venture, indulging their love of Italian cuisine. The green-sponged walls and rose table linens create an attractive atmosphere; the more intimate tables are in the upstairs dining room, with a view of the Swinomish Channel. The menu features quite a few starters and salads, including a wonderful traditional caesar and a cheesy, garlicky baked gnocchi dish that is really too rich as an appetizer. Oyster saffron bisque is another specialty of the house. Entrees include linguine diavola (gulf prawns in a spicy tomato sauce), vegetarian lasagne, and veal saltimbocca. The lunch menu is more geared to the La Conner browsing scene, featuring mainly salads, pizzas, and pastas. Service is a bit pretentious. ■ *505 S 1st (east side of 1st), La Conner; (360) 466-9111; $$; full bar; AE, MC, V; checks OK; lunch, dinner every day.*

Calico Cupboard ★ It's awfully cute—Laura Ashley meets Laura Ingalls Wilder—but the bakery is the reason to go, turning out excellent carrot muffins, pecan tarts, shortbread, raspberry bars, currant scones, apple Danishes, and much more. Our advice for avoiding the weekend crowds: buy your goodies from the bakery's take-out counter and find a sunny bench by the water. Hearty waffle and omelet breakfasts are offered, but let's face it, most folks come here for the pastries. There are two other Calicos now, one in Anacortes and the other in Mount Vernon. ■ *720 S 1st (south end of 1st), La Conner; (360) 466-4451; $; beer and wine; no credit cards; checks OK; breakfast, lunch, every day.* ⅂ ■ *901 Commercial Ave (on the main drag), Anacortes; (360) 293-7315; $; beer and wine; V, MC; checks OK;*

breakfast, lunch every day. 点 ▪ *120 N 1st (across from Scott's bookstore), Mt Vernon; (360) 336-3107; $; beer and wine; MC, V; checks OK; breakfast, lunch every day, early dinner Thurs–Sat.* 点

La Conner Seafood & Prime Rib House ★ Every weekend, those in the know drop in to get their names on the waiting list and pop out again for another 20 minutes of window-shopping. Their reward is excellent seafood (pasta with fresh Dungeness crab or baby Rock Point oysters sautéed with fresh fennel), and the young are happy with fish 'n' chips. In warm weather, diners flee the split-level dining room of channel-view tables for the ample outdoor seating on the deck. ▪ *614 1st St (on the waterfront), La Conner; (360) 466-4014; $$; full bar; AE, DC, DIS, MC, V; checks OK; lunch, dinner every day.*

LODGINGS

The Heron in La Conner ★★ The Heron is one of the prettiest hostelries in town, with 12 rooms done in jewel-box fashion. Splurge on Room 31, the Bridal Suite, with a Jacuzzi and a gas fireplace, or Room 32, with a gas fireplace, spacious sitting area, and a wonderful view of the Skagit Valley and Cascades. Downstairs is an elegant living room with wing chairs and a formal breakfast/dining room, where a continental breakfast is served. Out back you may have a barbecue in the stone fire pit or slip into the hot tub. ▪ *117 Maple St (on the edge of town), La Conner; (360) 466-4626; PO Box 716, La Conner, WA 98257; $$; AE, MC, V; checks OK.*

La Conner Channel Lodge ★★ At the edge of the Swinomish Channel, the Channel Lodge is an urban version of its more casual cousin, the La Conner Country Inn, a few blocks inland (see review). It's an appealing place, due mainly to its prime waterfront location. Your fireplace (gas) is lit upon your arrival, and some of the rooms have a Jacuzzi with a channel view. (If you're not splurging for a splash, make sure to request a channel-view room away from, or at least not directly underneath, those with potentially noisy waterjets.) The decks are nooks just big enough for a chair and fresh air while you watch the tugs work the waterway. The continental breakfast is rather perfunctory. ▪ *205 N 1st St (on the waterfront at the north end of town), La Conner; (360) 466-1500; PO Box 573, La Conner, WA 98257; laconner@uspan.com; useattle.uspan.com/laconner/; $$$; AE, DC, MC, V; checks OK.*

White Swan Guest House ★★ Poplars line the driveway, Adirondack chairs are placed throughout the garden grounds, wheat and tulip fields stretch beyond. Peter Goldfarb's house is splashed with warm yellow, salmon, evergreen, and peach, and seems to soak up the sunlight—even in the rain. Pamper yourself with a soak in the large claw-footed tub (the three guest rooms share two baths), or curl up on the sofa in front of the wood stove. A charming guest house (one of the few in the valley) out back provides an especially private accommodation, great for families or romantics. Dog lovers enjoy meeting Peter's four friendly canines. Peter serves a country continental breakfast of freshly baked scones or muffins, fruit from his orchard, and coffee; his wonderful chocolate chip cookies are waiting in the afternoons. Bring binoculars for bird-watching and bikes for easy touring around the flat farmlands of Fir Island. ■ *1388 Moore Rd (6 miles southeast of La Conner, call for directions), Mt Vernon, WA 98273; (360) 445-6805; $$; MC, V; checks OK.*

The Wild Iris Inn ★★ This 20-room inn gears itself toward romance with its spacious suites, each featuring a gas fireplace, oversize Jacuzzi, and panoramic view of the Cascades from your balcony or patio. Each room is individually decorated, so specify whether you prefer white wicker and lace or darker, more masculine furnishings. Most of the standard rooms face the parking lot and seem a bit too cramped. If you're here on Friday or Saturday night, do make reservations for dinner (guests only). The dining room has country charm, but the real magic is in the seasonally changing menu, which might include a fresh salmon with peppercorn butter or a grilled duckling breast with mushrooms, sun-dried cherries, and Marsala. The breakfast buffet is also a treat, offering perhaps a delicious hot spiced fruit soup or a vegetable quiche. ■ *121 Maple Ave (on the edge of town), La Conner; (360) 466-1400 or (800) 477-1400; PO Box 696, La Conner, WA 98257; wildiris@ncia.com; www.ncia.com/~wildiris; $$$; AE, MC, V; checks OK.*

La Conner Country Inn ★ Despite its name, the La Conner Country Inn is more of a classy motel than a true country inn. All of the 28 rooms have gas fireplaces; all have been recently updated with country pine furnishings and pretty floral bedspreads and armchairs. The inn is especially accommodating to families; the rooms with two double beds are generously sized. Breakfasts are complimentary and are served in the library, where an enormous fieldstone fireplace and comfy couches beckon you to enjoy a good book. Or check out the cozy Bird's Nest on the second floor, if it's not being used for a meeting. ■ *107 S 2nd St (just off Morris), La Conner; (360) 466-3101; PO Box 573, La Conner, WA 98257; laconner@uspan.com; useattle. uspan.com/laconner/; $$; AE, DC, MC, V; checks OK.*

Rainbow Inn ★ Set amid acres of Skagit Valley flatlands, this turn-of-the-century farmhouse offers sweeping views of lush pastures, Mount Baker, and the Cascades from eight pretty guest rooms (with plenty of Christian accents). Even though one side of the Violet Room faces the road, it's still our favorite, with its grand potbelly stove and access to the second-story porch. Thin cotton robes are provided for a dip in the inn's hot tub. Downstairs there are plenty of lingering zones. New owners Patsy and Tom Squires and their son and daughter-in-law Bruce and Lorene are in the process of updating the guest rooms; the one room they have redone looks great. Bruce is the breakfast chef, and his lemon pancakes are light and flavorful. Breakfast is served on an enchanting glassed-in front porch with tables for two. ■ *1075 Chilberg Rd (½ mile east of town), La Conner; (360)466-4578; PO Box 15, La Conner, WA 98257; $$; MC, V; checks OK.*

Hotel Planter The most famous (and infamous) characters of La Conner's colorful past once inhabited this end of town. Today, owner Don Hoskins has used his connoisseur's eye and artisan's care to create a style that is a tasteful blend of past (original woodwork staircase and entrance) and present (private baths and armoire-hidden TVs in every room). Six rooms face the waterfront (and the often noisy main street); others overlook a Renaissance garden courtyard (with a reserved hot tub). The staff, well versed on the Skagit Valley, is exemplary. ■ *715 S 1st St (end of the line on the south end of 1st St), La Conner; (360)466-4710; PO Box 702, La Conner, WA 98257; $$; AE, MC, V; checks OK.*

MOUNT VERNON

Mount Vernon is a rare working town: one in which there are more good restaurants and bookstores than taverns and churches. It is the Big City to residents of surrounding Skagit and Island Counties, and a college town to a surprising number of local folk, even though Skagit Valley College is but a small school on the very outskirts of town. Browse in **Scott's Bookstore** in the historic Granary Building at the north end, (360)336-6181, then have a pastry at the newest **Calico Cupboard** bakery right next door. Or drop into the **Skagit River Brewing Co.**, (360)336-2884, to sample a glass (or two) of the hearty housebrewed suds.

To travelers on I-5, Mount Vernon is little more than a blur except during the spring, when the lush farmlands are brilliantly swathed in daffodils (mid-March to mid-April), tulips (April through early May), and irises (mid-May to mid-June). The pastoral countryside is flat and ideal for bicyclists, except for the gridlock that occurs on the small farm lanes during the **Tulip Festival** (usually late March to early April; call (360)428-5959 for details). Mount Vernon is really all about fresh food and beautiful flowers, products of surrounding Skagit Valley farms. For information on the many harvest festivals (June is Strawberry Month, September Apple Month, and October Redleaf Month), call the Chamber of Commerce, (360)428-8547.

Little Mountain Park has a terrific picnic spot plus a knockout vista of the valley (look for migratory trumpeter swans in

February). On the other end of the spectrum, the **Chuck Wagon Drive Inn** (800 N Fourth, (360)336-2732) offers 50 different kinds of burgers, electric trains, and the world's largest collection of ceramic whiskey-bottle cowboys.

RESTAURANTS

Wildflowers ★★ Without doubt, chef David Day and owner Michele Kjosen have created a restaurant worthy of attention. And attention is the secret, with the smallest details—in the kitchen and on the plate—being considered. It begins with Kjosen's attentiveness to her guests, which verges on excessive but never crosses the line. Without her help we might have overlooked a marvelous entree: fresh Columbia River sturgeon, marinated and grilled with red wine, garlic, rosemary, and balsamic vinegar, and served with roasted garlic mashed potatoes. Inspirations such as this come on a daily basis. Chef Day has succeeded in nurturing his wildflowers to bloom year-round. An extensive wine list (and expert guidance in choosing a wine to complement your meal) rounds out the experience. ■ *2001 E College Way (from I-5, exit at College Way and head east), Mt Vernon; (360)424-9724; wildflowers@sos.net; $$$; beer and wine; AE, MC, V; checks OK; dinner Tues–Sat.*

Pacioni's Pizzeria ★ Wafts of fresh bread, fresh herbs, and fresh espresso tug at passersby. Those who give in to temptation congregate at the red-and-white-checkered tables, enjoy a friendly glass of red wine, and savor the pungency of pizza. Owners Dave and Paula Alberts have thrown their hearts into this restaurant as impressively as Dave throws the pizza dough into the air (remember the mad Italian baker in *Moonstruck*?). Paula (née Pacioni) is the keeper of family secrets, but we'll let you in on our favorite pie: the tri-color pizza (pesto, ricotta, and Roma tomatoes). Everything is made to order. ■ *606 S 1st St (in old downtown), Mt Vernon; (360)336-3314; $; beer and wine; no credit cards; checks OK; lunch Tues–Sat, dinner Mon–Sat.*

Skagit River Brewing Co. Sitting next to the railroad tracks, the Skagit offers better-than-average pub grub for locals and weary I-5 travelers alike. Once a produce warehouse, this historic building's brick walls and wooden beams now frame hewn-wood tables and comfortable couches. Like a classic English pub, you order at the bar, but you'll find surprisingly un-pub-like touches here, such as fresh flowers on the table. Food ranges from traditional to unexpected: from the Ploughman's Platter and Shepard's Pie to a bleu cheese gardenburger and a turkey melt with Jarlsburg cheese. Soups, sandwiches, and Mexican-inspired dishes round out the menu. Wash it down with one of the craft beers made in-house (try the smooth Steelie-Brown Ale). Live music some weekends. ■ *404 S 3rd (behind the courthouse), Mt Vernon; (360)336-2884; $; beer and wine; AE, MC, V; checks OK; lunch, dinner every day.*

STANWOOD

Stanwood is a sleepy little farm center with a Scandinavian heritage, a Midwestern air, and one good reason for a few minutes' sightseeing. Years ago, local daughter Martha Anderson started working at *rosemaling* (traditional Norwegian flower painting) and teaching it to her fellow Stanwoodians. Now they've embellished many everyday businesses with charming signs decorated in this genre—not for tourist show as in Leavenworth, but out of an authentic impulse to express their heritage and make Main Street pretty.

Pilchuck School. Founded in 1971 by glass artist Dale Chihuly and Seattle art patrons John Hauberg and Anne Gould Hauberg, Pilchuck is an internationally renowned glass art school. Students live and study on this campus, situated in the midst of a country tree farm. An open house twice each summer gives folks a chance to see craftspeople at work; for times and directions, call first, (206)621-8422.

EVERETT

Timber and fishing were once this county seat's raisons d'être, as were the booms and busts that follow the extraction of those natural resources. And though timber still means big business for Everett, the state-of-the-art U.S. naval base now adds even more to the city's growing economy and its ever-increasing population. Everett is experiencing new pride, evident in the revitalization of the downtown core. The redevelopment of the **Hotel Monte Cristo**, a historic landmark boarded up for 20 years, has provided a gorgeous home for the Everett Symphony, the Arts Council, and a stunning display of Pilchuck glass; (206)259-0382.

The **Everett Performing Arts Center**, 2710 Wetmore, hosts a variety of plays, concerts, dance, and other events; call (425)252-2145 or (800)451-5740 for schedule information and tickets.

The **Everett AquaSox** (the single-A short-season farm team for the Seattle Mariners) draw folks away from Seattle to enjoy baseball the old-fashioned way: outdoors. Call (425)258-3673 for tickets and information.

Boeing's South Everett plant offers free 90-minute tours of the world's largest building (measured in volume), where you can watch the assembly of the aviation giant's 747s, 767s, and 777s (strict height requirements for children, tours fill early); call (206)544-1264.

RESTAURANTS

Alligator Soul ★ Casual roadhouse atmosphere—exposed brick, Mardi Gras beads hanging from artwork, hot-pepper lights—and Southern fixings, like heaping portions of smoked ribs with a hot, hot, hot barbecue sauce, give this place its soul. And the sides alone could make a meal: jalapeño cornbread,

▼

Everett

Restaurants

▲

spicy corn relish, cool cole slaw, and a creamy potato salad. Other dishes have even the toughest Yankee longing for a road trip south; try the seafood gumbo, crawfish étouffée, or fried catfish with hush puppies. Great bread pudding is packed with pecans, peaches, and raisins and served with a sweet bourbon sauce. ■ *2013½ Hewitt Ave (near Broadway), Everett; (425) 259-6311; $$; beer and wine; MC, V; checks OK; lunch, dinner every day.*

The Sisters This place is as popular as it is funky. Soups such as mulligatawny, gazpacho, or just plain old beef barley can be outstanding. Sandwiches range from average deli stuff to more healthful concoctions, including a vegetarian burger made with chopped cashews and sunflower seeds. Among the morning fare are some delights: blueberry or pecan hotcakes; granola with yogurt and blueberry sauce; or scrambled eggs with all kinds of extra goodies wrapped in flour tortillas. Fresh-squeezed lemonade and strawberry lemonade quench your thirst, a big slice of blackberry pie cures whatever ails you. ■ *2804 Grand St (8 blocks west of Broadway, in the Everett Public Market), Everett; (425) 252-0480; $; no alcohol; MC, V; checks OK; breakfast, lunch Mon–Fri.*

LODGINGS

Marina Village Inn ★★ Waterfront accommodations are a surprising rarity on Puget Sound, making this 26-room inn on Port Gardner Bay all the more attractive. You get many of the perks expected from a big-city hotel without the parking problems and convention crowds—which explains the place's increasing popularity with corporate executives (so reserve in advance). Rooms are contemporary and stylish, with oak furnishings, tasteful appointments, wet bars, satellite TV, refrigerators, handcrafted ceramic sinks, extension phones in the bathrooms, and trouser presses. Some have notably comfy couches and easy chairs, many have Jacuzzis, and most have telescopes for gazing out over the water. Book a room on the harbor side; sea lions might be lollygagging in the sun on the nearby jetty. ■ *1728 W Marine View Dr (exit 193 off I-5 onto Pacific Ave, turn right on W Marine View Dr to waterfront), Everett, WA 98201; (425) 259-4040 or (800) 281-7037; $$; AE, DC, DIS, MC, V; no checks.*

SNOHOMISH

This small community, formerly an active lumber town, now bills itself as the "Antique Capital of the Northwest." It certainly has plenty of **antique shops** filling the downtown historic district; the Star Center Mall is the largest, with 175 antique dealers from all over the area; 829 Second Street, (360) 568-2131. When you're through taking in the old, get a new perspective of Snohomish from the air. Charter a **scenic flight** at Harvey Field, (360) 568-1541;

take a trip with Airial Hot Air Balloon Company, (360)568-3025; or skydive with the folks at Snohomish Parachute Center, (360)568-5960.

If all this activity works up an appetite, stop into **Jordan's** for lunch, popular with locals for its burgers and baked goods (try the awesome cinnamon rolls), 920 First Street, (360)568-2020. If you just need a slice of something sweet, visit the **Snohomish Pie Company** at 915 First Street, (360)568-3589.

MUKILTEO

Unfortunately, Mukilteo is probably best known for the traffic congestion caused by folks taking the ferry to Clinton on Whidbey Island. Just a block or two south of the ferry terminal there are, however, a small waterfront state park (with picnic tables and barbecue pits) and a historic lighthouse worth seeing. You can also stroll along the waterfront and fish off the docks; for more information call; (425)776-6711.

RESTAURANTS

Charles at Smugglers Cove ★★ Chef Claude Faure and his wife, Janet Kingma, took this landmark building, a 1929 speakeasy and distillery set on a bluff above Possession Sound, and turned it into an elegant restaurant. The atmosphere is country French, with dining rooms both upstairs and down, and a small terrace with views of the Sound. Such dishes as mushroom-sauced veal medallions and poulet aux crevettes (breast of chicken with prawns) appear on the classically French (and somewhat outdated) menu along with the requisite Gruyère-topped onion soup and variations on the escargot theme. Save room for a fancy dessert like crêpes Suzette or Grand Marnier soufflé. ■ *8340 53rd Ave W (at intersection of Hwys 525 and 526), Mukilteo; (425)347-2700; $$$; full bar; AE, DC, DIS, MC, V; local checks only; lunch Tues–Fri, dinner Tues–Sat.*

WHIDBEY ISLAND

Whidbey Island has let just about everyone know that it is officially the longest island in the United States. But they haven't told too many people that Whidbey is only one of eight islands that make up Island County (the others are Camano, Ben Ure, Strawberry, Minor, Baby, Smith, and Deception). Named after Captain Joseph Whidbey, a sailing master for Captain George Vancouver, Whidbey Island was first surveyed and mapped by the two explorers in 1792. More than 200 years later, Whidbey's largest employer is the government (thanks to the navy base in Oak Harbor). The island boasts pretty towns and communities, historical parks, sandy beaches, and some lovely rolling farmland.

Although there are no bike lanes, Whidbey's flat, relatively traffic-free roads make it a good warm-weather biking destination, especially if you stay off the main highway; call (360) 221-6765 for more information on exploring Whidbey. Depart from the mainland at Mukilteo, about 25 miles north of Seattle, for a 25-minute ferry ride to Clinton on the south end of Whidbey Island (and expect long waits in either direction on sunny weekends); **Washington State Ferries**, (360) 355-7308.

WHIDBEY ISLAND: LANGLEY

The nicest town on Whidbey still carries its small-town virtues well, though it may be getting a little too spit-and-polished for some. With the addition of Langley Village on Second Street, it has grown into a two-street town.

Shopping. Swap stories with Josh Hauser at Moonraker Books, (360) 221-6962, then head to the antique- and candy-filled Wayward Son gift shop, (360) 221-3911. For singular shopping, try The Cottage, (360) 221-4747, for heirloom lace and linens; Virginia's Antiques, (360) 221-7797, a repository of Asian and American wares; and Sister, (360) 221-5735, for unusual, attractive women's clothing. Jan Smith's Christmas House has moved to Second Street in Langley from Clinton; it displays handcrafted items including pottery, baby clothing, kitchen wares, and collectibles from more than 200 Whidbey Island artisans; (360) 221-6090.

Art Galleries. Look for original Northwest art, from paintings and pottery to sculpture and glass, at Childers-Proctor Gallery, (360) 221-2978, on First Street. At the Hellebore Glass Studio you can watch glassblower George Springer at work; (360) 221-2067. Museo Piccolo Gallery features glass art and handcrafts from regional and national artists; (360) 221-7737.

JB's Ice Creamery and Espresso, (360) 221-3888, is the place for both java and ice cream. The **Raven Cafe** is another good spot for espresso and light refreshments; (360) 221-3211. Head to **The Dog House**, (360) 221-9996, for a pitcher of microbrew (20 on tap, 100 beers total) after a movie or an evening of live theater at **The Clyde**, (360) 221-5525. The pesto pizza by the slice at **Langley Village Bakery**, (360) 221-3525, is a local favorite. And the **Whidbey Island Winery**, 5237 S Langley Road, (360) 221-2040 (open Thursday–Sunday year-round), has a fine tasting room. Try their rhubarb wine.

RESTAURANTS

Cafe Langley ★★ Owners Shant and Arshavir Gariban have maintained the sparkling consistency that established this downtown storefront cafe as the best bet in town from the moment it opened. Make a reservation (especially on weekends) and prepare for a fine Mediterranean/Greek dining experience. Appetizers range from Indian samosas to crab cakes. Don't overdo on the impossibly delicious hummus served with warm, chewy pita bread. The Greek salad is just the right taste before a feast of Mediterranean seafood stew, a lamb shish kabob, or one of the Land of the Sun-kissed preparations of fresh Northwest salmon or halibut. Split a Russian cream for dessert. ■ *113 1st St (at the south end of town), Langley; (360) 221-3090; $$; beer and wine; AE, MC, V; checks OK; lunch Wed–Mon, dinner every day (closed Tues in winter).*

Star Bistro ★ A steady staple of the Langley bistro scene, the Star (above the Star Store, a steady staple of the Langley shop scene) is a fun and color-splashed place that hops on weekends and after local events. Chef Paul Divina has put together a menu of basic, luscious vacation food—pastry-enclosed French onion soup, creamy oyster stew, spinach and caesar salads, pastas, burgers—along with fancier daily specials, all solid and reliable. There's a kids' menu and a breezy, sun-drenched deck, and you can pull up a stool at the red-topped bar for excellent martinis or margaritas. ■ *201½ 1st St (above the Star Store), Langley; (360) 221-2627; $$; full bar; AE, MC, V; checks OK; lunch, dinner every day (dinner Tues–Sun in winter).*

Trattoria Giuseppe ★ You might not take a second look at Trattoria Giuseppe, located as it is in a little strip mall out on Highway 525. But you'd be making a mistake: locals are raving about the Italian food here. Once inside, the scent of garlic and the country taverna decor make you think you've walked into a little place in the Tuscan countryside. The Penn Cove mussels here are prepared marinara, with fresh tomatoes, garlic, and basil. We like the fusilli alla primavera, with vegetables, prawns, and scallops, and the salmone con spinaci, fresh salmon served over a bed of sautéed spinach with lemon butter sauce. Finish off the meal with a traditional Italian dessert like cannoli or a gelato. ■ *4141 E Hwy 525 (at Langley Rd), Langley; (360) 341-3454; $$; full bar; AE, DIS, MC, V; checks OK; lunch Mon–Fri, dinner every day.*

LODGINGS

Inn at Langley ★★★ It's difficult to conceive of a more idyllic getaway, or one more evocative of the Pacific Northwest, than Paul and Pam Schell's first private venture, built elegantly into the bluff over Saratoga Passage. Architect Alan Grainger designed the building in a marriage of three themes: Frank Lloyd Wright's style, Northwest ruggedness, and Pacific Rim tranquility. Inside this rough-hewn, cedar-shingled building are 24 rooms finely decorated with an eye for pleasing detail: simple Asian furnishings, trimmings of three different woods, and quarry-tiled bathrooms with hooks made from alder twigs. Adjacent is a Jacuzzi, from which you can watch the boat traffic on the Passage and the flicker of your fireplace through the translucent shoji-style screen. We prefer the upper-level rooms. The small conference room, equipped with every business necessity, has the expansive view the country dining room lacks.

In the morning, guests gather in the dining room for a continental spread. Chef Steve Nogal is making waves in his country kitchen with five-course prix-fixe weekend dinners (by reservation only). Diners are met at the door with glasses of sherry, which they sip while Nogal delivers his appetite-whetting spiel. It's an evening-long celebration of Northwest foods, a delightful indulgence that can pay off in a fine if occasionally flawed meal. Portions are very large, so pace yourself. ■ *400 1st St (at the edge of town), Langley; (360) 221-3033; PO Box 835, Langley, WA 98260; $$$; beer and wine; AE, MC, V; local checks only; dinner (by reservation only) Fri–Sun (Fri–Sat Nov–Apr).* &

Boatyard Inn ★★ The industrial look of the green siding and corrugated metal roofs of this inn meshes well with Langley's still-colorful working waterfront. The place is so close to the water that the tide rises up against the first floor. Big windows, pine accents, and back-to-basics Eddie Bauer-esque Northwest furnishings characterize the Boatyard's nine huge, breezy suites (the smallest room is 600 square feet), each endowed with a gas fireplace, galley kitchen, queen-size bed topped with cozy flannel coverlets, sofa bed, cable TV, private deck, and water view. Loft units are suitable for families or small groups. ■ *200 Wharf St (from Cascade Ave, take Wharf St down the hill), Langley; (360) 221-5120; PO Box 866, Langley, WA 98260; $$$; AE, DC, MC, V; local checks only.* &

Chauntecleer House and Dove House ★★ Our only quibble with these two gorgeous cottages on a quiet bluff just north of downtown Langley is that it's just too hard to choose which one to stay in. Decorating these hideaways was a labor of love for transplanted Southerner Bunny Meals, and it shows in every detail. We prefer Chauntecleer House, but only by a nose (or should we say a beak: Chauntecleer is a Chaucerian term for "rooster," and the theme is evident throughout the cottage), for its sunny yellow walls, panoramic view of Saratoga Passage, and open-hearthed wood-burning fireplace. Upstairs in the bedroom, the theme is Northwest nautical. Dove House doesn't share the view, but it is charmingly decorated in the style of a fishing lodge, with a wonderful mixture of Northwest and Southwest art and furniture (the bronze otter was sculpted by Georgia Gerber—you know, the Pike Place Market pig artist). A wood stove adds to the coziness, and there's a second bedroom with bunks if you want to bring the kids. A full breakfast is left in each kitchen. ■ *3557 Saratoga Rd (follow Second St north from town; it becomes Saratoga), Langley; (360) 221-5494 or (800) 637-4436; PO Box 659, Langley, WA 98260; $$$; MC, V; checks OK.*

Galittoire ★★ Galittoire is a sleek, contemporary B&B that's almost sensual in its attention to detail. The decor is spare and deliberate: slanted ceilings, lots of windows, lovely oak trim throughout, and unexpected pleasures, such as silky, snow-white fabric hanging from the ceiling to all corners of the bed. And if a deer wanders through the rolling yard past the gazebo, it may just seem like part of the perfect plan. Amenities abound—hot tub, spa, hors d'oeuvres in the evening—and owner Mahish Massand is an accommodating host. There's a two-night minimum stay on weekends. Galittoire is also a catering company. ■ *5444 S Coles Rd (off Hwy 525), Langley, WA 98260; (360) 221-0548; galittoire@whidbey.com; www.whidbey.com/galittoire; $$$; AE, MC, V; local checks only.*

Villa Isola ★★ Tucked into a pine-studded pastoral landscape, Gwen and Gary Galeotti's version of an Italian country villa goes a long way in re-creating the slow, sweet life of the Old Country. Guests have this inspired space—defined by walls stenciled with grape vines, floor-to-ceiling windows, and modern European furnishings—all to themselves. Three large, sumptuous rooms named after legendary Italian towns continue the Mediterranean motif; each has an oversize bath (one with Jacuzzi), queen-size bed, and down comforter. A new private cottage spoils you further with a Jacuzzi and a wood stove. Espresso and delicacies are served cafe-style in the sunny dining room or on the adjacent deck. Borrow the inn's mountain bikes or engage in a game of bocce (Italian lawn bowling) on the regulation-size court beyond the fruit trees in the big backyard, where local senior citizens compete on Wednesday nights. Gwen keeps the living room flush with CDs and board games and the kitchen stocked with Italian desserts. ■ *5489 S Coles Rd (2 miles southeast of Langley), Langley, WA 98260; (360) 221-5052; www.villaisola.com; $$$; MC, V; checks OK.*

Country Cottage of Langley ★ Innkeepers Kathy and Bob Annecone have spiffed up this collection of three cottages (with five rooms) on 2 acres set behind and overlooking downtown Langley. Our two favorites are the Captain's Cove with its nautical theme, and the Whidbey Rose with a pretty floral look; both have a view of the water, gas fireplaces, and Jacuzzi tubs. All five rooms have private baths, feather beds and down comforters, TV and VCR (with a selection of complimentary videos), refrigerators, and coffee makers. A full breakfast is served in the muraled dining room of the main house, a restored 1920s farmhouse, or may be brought to your room on request. ■ *215 6th (off Langley Rd as you approach downtown from the south), Langley, WA 98260; (360) 221-8709 or (800) 713-3860; $$$; MC, V; checks OK.*

Eagle's Nest Inn Bed and Breakfast ★ Jerry and Joanne Lechner's four-story octagonal getaway is tucked into the forest on a knoll overlooking scenic Saratoga Passage, Camano Island, and Mount Baker. Guests enjoy the view from the four spotless, comfortably appointed upstairs rooms. The best is the Eagle's

▼

Whidbey Island: Langley

Lodgings

▲

Nest, an eight-sided penthouse suite rimmed with windows (and a balcony) offering a 360-degree view. Little touches often missing at other bed and breakfasts, such as hair dryers in the bathrooms and robes to wear to the outdoor hot tub, add to guests' comfort here. The library/lounge is stocked with local art, books, videotapes (each room has a TV and VCR), and CDs. On the main floor, the high-ceilinged living room is dominated by a white wood stove flanked by a baby grand piano, stained-glass windows, and a forest mural, hand-painted by a local artist (look for other hand-painted murals throughout the house). Breakfast is at 9am, but the hot tub and the cookie jar are open all day. ■ *3236 E Saratoga Rd (head out of Langley on 2nd, which becomes Saratoga), Langley, WA 98260; (360)221-5331; eaglnest@whidbey.com; www.pgsi.com/eaglesnest; $$; MC, V; checks OK.*

Garden Path Inn ★ For an island getaway that feels more like an uptown city condo, book a weekend at one of the two upstairs suites above proprietor Linda Lundgren's interior design shop. A brick-and-trellis walkway leads to the tucked-away retreat off First Street. The exquisite back suite is equipped with a full gourmet kitchen, long dining room table, bay window, four-poster bed, and Jacuzzi. Both suites show off Lundgren's decorative flair, an eclectic and intelligent blending of art and crafts, sophistication and comfort, and antique and contemporary pieces—most of which are for sale. ■ *111 1st St (downtown), Langley; (360)221-5121; PO Box 575, Langley, WA 98260; $$–$$$; MC, V; checks OK.*

Island Tyme ★ Newly built Victorian-style inns seem to be all the rage these days: you get the romance of the turrets and gables without the plumbing problems and space limitations inherent in older homes. The Island Tyme is located on a quiet 10 acres about 2 miles from downtown Langley. Innkeepers Lyn and Phil Fauth are raising a young family; as a result, the inn is one of the few bed and breakfasts in the area where kids are welcome (they'll enjoy the resident pygmy goats). But guests without kids enjoy the place too, as the rooms are geared toward romance, most notably the two-room Heirloom Suite, which has a fireplace, a Jacuzzi, and a private deck. All five rooms have TVs and VCRs, with videos available for guests' use. ■ *4940 S Bayview (2 miles from Langley, call for directions), Langley, WA 98260; (360)221-5078 or (800)898-8963; www. traveldata.com/biz/inns/data/isltyme.html; $$; AE, MC, V; checks OK.* ♿

Log Castle ★ This is the house that Jack built—literally. And whenever there's time, U.S. Congressman Jack Metcalf builds on it some more, to his wife, Norma's, newest designs. As a result, the beachside castle has a slightly unfinished air about it, which shouldn't detract in the slightest from what can be a

distinctly unusual experience. Every log tells a story, and the
place can feel quite cozy on a winter evening. The loft suite
comes with an antique ship's stove; two rooms on the other side
of the house are built into an octagonal turret and feature remarkable views. The Metcalfs originally ran the facility as a
Christian retreat center for many years; however, the religious
ambience isn't fanatical. ■ *3273 E Saratoga Rd (1 mile west of Langley), Langley, WA 98260; (360)221-5483; innkeepr@whidbey.
com; www.whidbey.com/logcastle; $$; MC, V; checks OK.*

Lone Lake Cottage and Breakfast ★ Dolores Meeks's place is
still one of the most interesting B&Bs around. The estimable
resort may have outlasted its interior design motifs, but not its
eccentric charm. One of the four lodgings is aboard the tiny
Whidbey Queen, a beamed-ceiling stern-wheeler that's perma-
nently moored on the lake. Guests staying on the *Queen* enjoy
the same extras found in the other lakeside cottages: fireplace,
soaking tub for two, VCR, and CD player. The one-bedroom
Terrace Cottage is the nicest of the landlubber's accommoda-
tions; it looks into the domed top of a stunning aviary housing
some 300 rare birds from around the world. A honeymoon suite
in front of the main house is cool and comfortable and sports
a grand lake view, fireplace, kitchen, and double Jacuzzi. Exotic
ducks, pheasant, quail, peacocks, and swans mingle in an out-
door pen. Each room has a full kitchen stocked with breakfast
makings for the first two days of your stay, plus seasonings for
the barbecue should you get lucky and land a trout or two.
Guests are welcome to use the private beach, canoes, rowboat,
and bikes. ■ *5260 S Bayview Rd (5½ miles from the Clinton ferry,*
*off Hwy 525), Langley, WA 98260; (360)321-5325; www.whidbey.
com/lonelake; $$$; no credit cards; checks OK.*

Saratoga Inn ★ It's a two-minute walk from downtown to the
Saratoga Inn (formerly called the Harrison House), which has
architectural touches reminiscent of New England. Each of the
15 distinctive view rooms is festooned in warm plaids or prints
and furnished with a gas fireplace, an armoire, and an entertainment center. You may choose to have breakfast delivered to
your chamber. Serious solitude seekers can opt for the separate
Carriage House, with a full kitchen, stone fireplace, and king-
size sleigh bed. The Saratoga Inn sometimes hosts small con-
ferences; the richly appointed Library Boardroom is the
meeting room. Everyone's welcome in the tearoom, where you
can socialize over civilized beverages. At press time, the management of this inn was turned over to the prestigious Four Sisters Inn group. We assume that to mean improvements are
imminent. ■ *201 Cascade Ave (take 1st St to Cascade Ave), Langley; (360)221-5801; PO Box 428, Langley, WA 98260; $$$; MC,
V; checks OK.* ⅙

WHIDBEY ISLAND: FREELAND

The unincorporated town of Freeland, population 1,544, is home to Nichols Brothers Boat Builders, manufacturers of cruise boats and stern-wheelers and the town's largest employer. **Freeland Park** on Holmes Harbor has picnic tables, a play area, and a sandy beach.

LODGINGS

Cliff House ★★★ Seattle architect Arne Bystrom designed this dramatic house, which makes for an extraordinary getaway. The striking home on a cliff above Admiralty Inlet is full of light from lofty windows, centering on a 30-foot-high atrium open to the weather and filled with native plants and a sunken living room with a wood-burning fireplace. For a staggering $385 a night for two people, you have use of the entire luxuriously furnished house and its 14 acres of woods. There are hammocks, benches, and a platform deck with a hot tub built high on the cliff. The elfish Sea Cliff Cottage is a more modestly priced option that includes a queen-size feather bed, a kitchenette, and a deck overlooking the water. Peggy Moore sets the country kitchen table (in both houses) with a continental breakfast. ■ *5440 Windmill Rd (Bush Point Rd to Windmill Rd), Freeland, WA 98249; (360)331-1566; www.whidbey.com/cliffhouse; $$$; no credit cards; checks OK.*

WHIDBEY ISLAND: GREENBANK

Here on the narrowest part of the island, stop by **Whidbey's Greenbank Farm**, at one time the largest loganberry farm in the country. Sample their Loganberry Liqueur or Whidbey Port. There are lots of pretty picnicking spots; (360)678-7700.

LODGINGS

Guest House Bed & Breakfast Cottages ★★ We love this place, partly because playing house here fulfills long-lost storybook dreams. Seven varied dwellings are set in a pastoral clearing fringed with woodland. The Farmhouse (closest to the swimming pool and hot tub) is perfect for two couples. The studio Carriage House offers a queen-size feather bed and a whirlpool bath. King-size feather beds and river-rock fireplaces grace the pine-log Emma Jane Tennessee Cottage and the Kentucky Pine Cottage. Comparatively modest and less expensive, but just as cozy, are the Farm Guest Cottage and the funky Hansel and Gretel Log Cabin with kitchen, whirlpool tub, and VCR. (The video library includes 400 flicks.) But everybody's favorite is the Lodge, a $285-a-night custom-built log home for two perched at the edge of a spring-fed wildlife pond with a broad deck and views of the Cascades and the Sound from the loft bedroom. A 24-foot-tall rugged stone fireplace plays center stage in a space that combines the old (a wood stove next to the greenhouse breakfast nook, stuffed animal heads on the walls) with the new (two whirlpool tubs, a dishwasher). Breakfast makings for the first two days of your stay are left in the fully equipped kitchens. ■ *3366 S Hwy 525 (1 mile south of Greenbank off Hwy 525), Greenbank, WA 98253; (360) 678-3115; www.travelassist.com/ reg/wa003s.html; $$$; AE, MC, V; checks OK.*

WHIDBEY ISLAND: COUPEVILLE

The second-oldest incorporated town in the state dates back to the mid-1850s; no wonder the town has a strict agenda of historic preservation. Coupeville's downtown consists of a half-dozen gift and antique shops and several restaurants. A must-see gallery is the **Jan McGregor Studio**, (360) 678-5015, open on weekends throughout the year and every day in summer. McGregor has studied pottery around the world and specializes in rare porcelain techniques. **Toby's 1890 Tavern**, (360) 678-4222, is a good spot for burgers, beer, and a game of pool. Homemade breads, pies, soups, and salads make a memorable meal at **Knead & Feed**, (360) 678-5431, and real coffee lives in Coupeville at **Great Times Espresso**, (360) 678-5358. **Island County Historical Museum**, (360) 678-3310, tells the story of Whidbey Island's early history. Annual community events include the **Coupeville Arts & Crafts Festival**, the second weekend in August, and the **Penn Cove Mussel Festival** in March; for information, call (360) 678-5434.

An extra bike lane follows Engle Road 3 miles south of Coupeville to **Fort Casey**, a decommissioned fort with splendid gun mounts, beaches, and commanding bluffs. Explore the magnificent bluff and beach at the 17,000-acre **Ebey's Landing** and **Fort Ebey State Park**. The **Keystone ferry**, (360) 678-6030, connecting Whidbey to Port Townsend on the Olympic Peninsula, leaves from Admiralty Head, just south.

LODGINGS

Anchorage Inn ★ Another of the "new Victorian" inns, the Anchorage offers moderately priced lodgings on Coupeville's main street. The rooms feel a bit more motel-like than some of the frillier B&Bs, which some folks might prefer. All five rooms have private baths and cable TV; we especially like the waterview room with the four-poster king bed, and the room in the turret. Rates include a full breakfast served in the antique-filled dining room. The "Crow's Nest" at the top of the house is a living area for guests; it has video movies, reading material, and games available. ■ *807 N Main St (take Hwy 20 from Deception Pass or Hwy 525 from the ferry), Coupeville; (360) 678-5581; PO Box 673, Coupeville, WA 98239; anchorag@whidbey.net; www. whidbey.net/-anchorag; $$; DIS, MC, V; checks OK.*

Captain Whidbey Inn ★ Innkeeper John Colby Stone has gone to every effort to make sure that nothing much changes about this old Penn Cove inn, built in 1907 of sturdy and shiny-with-use madrona logs. In such a beloved place, history sometimes outranks comfort and quiet. The walls are so thin they seem to talk, and sniffle, and sneeze; and the sulphur-smelling water from your shower lingers like an unwanted guest. Upstairs, the 12 smallish, almost shiplike original hotel rooms (two of the 12 are suites) have marble sinks in the rooms but share two bathrooms, one for each gender. Stay clear of the rooms above the bar, unless you're planning to be up until closing time. Four sparsely furnished cabins include fireplaces and baths. The best bets are the 13 lagoon rooms, each with private bath and a verandah overlooking two calm inlets. A particularly nice touch is the combination of feather beds and down comforters on all the beds. The public rooms—a lantern-lit dining room with creaky wooden floors that seem to slope toward the sea; the deck (when the weather's warm); a cozy bar festooned with nautical maps, wine bottles, and business cards; a well-stocked library; and a folksy fireplace room—are quite attractive. The restaurant continues to feature, naturally, Penn Cove mussels (you're looking at the mussel beds as you indulge), other fresh seafood preparations, and greens from the inn's elaborate gardens. ■ *2072 W Captain Whidbey Inn Rd (off Madrona Way), Coupeville, WA 98239; (360)678-4097; $$; full bar; AE, MC, V; checks OK; breakfast, lunch, dinner every day (lunch Sat–Sun only in winter).*

Fort Casey Inn ★ Built in 1909 as officers' quarters for nearby Fort Casey, this neat row of nine houses offers tidy, no-frills accommodations with a historical bent. Houses are divided into two-bedroom duplexes, each kitchen stocked with breakfast makings. Decor consists mostly of tied-rag rugs, old military photographs, and renditions of early U.S. presidents. Garrison Hall, with a small reception area and its own private bedroom and bath, can be rented for weddings or private parties. Unlike most B&Bs on Whidbey, Fort Casey Inn welcomes kids and is truly a fun place to explore. Ask the manager anything you need to know about Fort Casey State Park, the bird sanctuary at Crockett Lake, or nearby Ebey's Landing National Historic Reserve. ■ *1124 S Engle Rd (2 miles west of Coupeville), Coupeville, WA 98239; (360)678-8792; $$; AE, MC, V; checks OK.*

Inn at Penn Cove ★ This gracious inn consists of two historic pink homes, the Kineth House (built in 1887, and completely restored to its former grandeur) and the Coupe-Gillespie House (circa 1891, a decidedly more casual affair). The Kineth guest rooms are prettily furnished, if slightly overdecorated. The three rooms in the second house seem best for guests with children (there's a game room with puzzles). Breakfasts are a great send-off, with blueberry and lemon poppyseed muffins, seasonal fruits, cereal, Scandinavian-style breakfast cakes, waffles, or pancakes. ■ *702 N Main St (take Hwy 20 from Deception Pass or Hwy 525 from the ferry), Coupeville, WA 98239; (360)678-8000 or (800)688-COVE; $$; AE, DC, MC, V; checks OK.*

The Old Morris Farm ★ This is no old farmhouse by any means. Owners Mario Chodorowski and Marilyn Randock have successfully transformed their 1909 farmhouse into an elegant countryside B&B. The guest rooms are individual in style and decor yet all reflect the colonial feeling of the house. The Rose Room is done up in paisley, and has a private bath and a deck that leads out to the secluded spa. Enjoy a grand breakfast in the red, red dining room, and evening hors d'oeuvres in the sunwashed living room. Stroll the grounds and enjoy the flower, vegetable, and herb gardens. A small gift shop includes locally made walking sticks. ■ *105 W Morris Rd (take Hwy 20, 3 miles from Coupeville overpass), Coupeville, WA 98239; (360)678-6586; $$; MC, V; checks OK.* ♿

WHIDBEY ISLAND: OAK HARBOR

Named for the thriving Garry oak trees, Oak Harbor is Whidbey's largest city and home to **Whidbey Island Naval Air Station**, a large air base for tactical electronic warfare squadrons. For the most part, Oak Harbor is engulfed in new military and retired military folk.

An interesting stop is Lavender Heart, which manufactures floral gifts on a 12-acre former holly farm. From the gift store, you can peek at the impressive 1,000-square-foot production facility; 3 miles south of Deception Pass at 4233 N DeGraff Road, (360)675-3987. Kids at heart should visit Blue Fox Dri-Vin Theatre and Brattland Go-Karts; 1403 Monroe Landing Road, (360)675-5667.

Deception Pass. The beautiful, treacherous gorge has a lovely, if crowded, state park with 2,300 acres of prime camping land, forests, and beach. **Strom's Shrimp/Fountain and Grill**, just north of the pass, sells fresh seafood for your cookout. They also grill up a mean oysterburger; (360)293-2531.

RESTAURANTS

Kasteel Franssen (Auld Holland Inn) ★ A half mile north of Oak Harbor, this motel with the trademark windmill is just fine, if a shade close to the highway; however, the restaurant is quite delightful. Kasteel Franssen, owned and operated by Joe and Elisa Franssen, has quite a regal, European feel about it and a solid reputation among locals. There's a big gas fireplace and a lively piano bar. Chef and co-owner Scott Fraser of Vancouver, BC, oversees the toque, and the results are pleasing. Dinner offerings include seafood, chicken, and beef, but Fraser also prepares game including caribou and pheasant. Particularly good is the beef tenderloin sautéed and served with a brandy Dijonnaise cream sauce. As for the inn, some upper-story rooms have antiques, and six impressive-looking rooms include hot tubs. There's a tennis court, hot tub, outdoor pool, and children's play area. Rates include a continental breakfast. ■ *33575 SR 20 (8 miles south of Deception Pass), Oak Harbor; (360) 675-0724; $$; full bar; AE, DC, MC, V; local checks only; dinner every day (Mon–Sat in winter).* &

Lucy's Mi Casita It doesn't look like much, lined up along a strip of fast-food joints and automotive stores and decorated with old calendars, beer-bottle-cap curtains, and cutouts of flamenco dancers, but Al and Lucy Enriquez keep locals coming back with their homemade Mexican food and lively atmosphere. Upstairs is a lounge with a balcony (watch out for the 27-ounce Turbo Godzilla margarita). The large menu includes shredded beef tacos, seafood burritos, and Lucy's authentic refried beans; ingredients include chile poblano imported from Mexico, tortillas shipped from California, and homemade hot sauce. Don't miss the *entomatadas*—tortillas topped with tomato sauce, cheese, and onion—a dish from Lucy's hometown of Chihuahua. ■ *1380 W Pioneer Way (on the main drag), Oak Harbor; (360) 675-4800; $; full bar; AE, MC, V; local checks only; lunch, dinner every day.*

VASHON ISLAND

Faintly countercultural, this bucolic isle is a short ferry ride away from downtown Seattle (foot passengers only), West Seattle (take the Fauntleroy ferry), or Tacoma (from the Point Defiance ferry). Call the Washington State Ferries for schedule; (206) 464-6400. It's a wonderful place to explore by bicycle, although the first long hill up from the north-end ferry dock is a killer. Few beaches are open to the public, but there are some public spots where you can take a stroll and enjoy the view.

Vashon Island has many of its own island-based companies that market their goods both locally and nationally; many of these offer tours (it's a good idea to call ahead): **K2 Skis, Inc**, 19215 Vashon Highway SW, (206) 463-3631; **Seattle's Best Coffee** (also known as SBC), Vashon Highway, (206) 463-3932; **Maury Island Farms**, with berries and preserves, at 99th and 204th on Vashon Highway, (206) 463-9659. **Wax Orchards**, on 131st SW north of 232nd, is no longer open for tours, but you can stop by and pick up some fresh preserves, fruit syrups, and apple cider; (206) 463-9735. Island arts are on display at the **Blue Heron Art Center**, Vashon Highway; (206) 463-5131. **The Country Store and Gardens** is an old-fashioned general store stocking most of the island-made products, along with natural-fiber apparel, housewares, gardening supplies, and display gardens you can tour; 20211

Vashon Highway SW, (206)463-3655. **Vashon Island Kayak**
Company offers instruction and day trips, including one to Blake
Island and Tillicum Village; (206)463-9257.

RESTAURANTS

Express Cuisine ★ This storefront restaurant and catering company may not look like much from the outside, but locals line
up for gourmet take-out dinners, or fill up the communal tables
to enjoy dishes like tender prime rib, mouth-watering sirloin
stroganoff, and smoked salmon served over linguine with a
mushroom alfredo sauce. All dinners include an excellent soup
or salad (if they've got seafood chowder on the list, make it your
choice). Service is counter-style. Come early or call ahead for
take-out; otherwise you might have to wait. ■ *17629 Vashon
Hwy SW (near Bank Rd), Vashon Island; (206)463-6626; $; beer
and wine; no credit cards; local checks only; dinner Wed–Sat.* &

Turtle Island Cafe ★ Just off the main drag through downtown
Vashon is Turtle Island Cafe, a small, friendly restaurant that's
a favorite of many islanders. It's no wonder: the food here is
wonderful. Chef Rick Tada puts together a menu with treats
such as angel hair pasta tossed with sun-dried tomatoes and
roasted garlic, oyster stew with polenta, or a hoisin-roasted
chicken. The wine list offers a good selection of reasonably
priced domestic and imported wines, by the bottle or by the
glass. Little things like a perfect, zesty vinaigrette dressing con-
tribute to good meals here. ■ *9924 SW Bank Rd (near intersection of Vashon Hwy and SW Bank Rd), Vashon; (206)463-2125;
$$; beer and wine; MC, V; checks OK; lunch Mon–Fri, dinner ev-
ery day.* &

LODGINGS

Back Bay Inn ★ Although the Back Bay Inn is located on a busy
and potentially noisy corner, the four antique-filled upstairs
rooms are charming. Ask for one of the bigger end-of-the-hall
rooms. Overnight guests play checkers in the downstairs fire-
place library. The inn is no longer serving dinner, although they
are open to the public for breakfast on weekends (and, of course,
every morning for guests). The extensive breakfast menu in-
cludes omelets (smoked salmon or shiitake mushroom, for ex-
ample), challah french toast, and other great waker-uppers. ■
*24007 Vashon Hwy SW (in the community of Burton), Vashon,
WA 98070; (206)463-5355; $$; AE, MC, V; checks OK.*

Harbor Inn and Tramp Harbor Inn ★ Innkeeper Kathy Casper
hosts guests at her modern Tudor-style home on the waterfront
near Burton Acres Park. Best is the showstopping suite with its
king-size four-poster bed, gas fireplace, and spacious bath, featuring both a Jacuzzi tub for two and a separate shower stall.
A full breakfast is served. The Caspers have also renovated the
Tramp Harbor Inn, a 1907 Tudor with beautiful architectural

details and workmanship, which is available as a self-catering house. Located near Tramp Harbor on the island's east side, the house sits on a sometimes-busy corner, but once night settles in, all is quiet. The lovely grounds include a stocked trout pond. There are three bedrooms upstairs. For a taste of what it might be like to live in a beautiful home on Vashon, bring good friends and rent the whole house, with its formal dining room, fully equipped updated kitchen, grand piano, and wood-burning fireplace in the living room. Coffee is provided, but you're on your own for breakfast. ■ *9118 SW Harbor Dr (near Burton), Vashon, WA 98070; (206)463-6794; $$$; no credit cards; checks OK.*

PUYALLUP

At the head of the fertile Puyallup Valley, this frontier farm town serves as a major gateway to Mount Rainier. Much of the bulb, rhubarb, and berry farmland continues to be cultivated, but a great part of it has been strip-malled and auto-row-ravaged around the edges. Avoid the fast-food strip to the south and head east up the valley to Sumner, the White River, Orting, Wilkeson, and Carbonado.

The **Ezra Meeker Mansion** is the finest original pioneer mansion left in Washington. Its builder and first occupant, Ezra Meeker, introduced hops to the Puyallup Valley. The lavish 17-room Italianate house (circa 1890) now stands beautifully restored in the rear parking lot of a Main Street furniture store; 312 Spring Street, (206)848-1770, open Wednesday through Sunday, 1pm to 4pm, mid-March through mid-December.

Puyallup is big on old-time seasonal celebrations, and it's home to two of the biggest in the Northwest: the **Daffodil Festival and Parade** in early April and the **Western Washington Fair**, better known as the Puyallup Fair, in September. It's one of the nation's biggest fairs; call (206)845-1771 for dates and information. **Puyallup Downtown Farmers Market** is held every Saturday, starting at 9am, at Pioneer Park. It runs throughout the growing season, usually late May through September.

LODGINGS

Best Western Park Plaza ★ Don't be deterred by the very average exterior and location of this Best Western, just off Highway 512 and adjacent to South Hill Mall: the interior is surprisingly lovely. The lobby is done up like a fine colonial mansion, complete with wing chairs and a fireplace. Standard rooms are appealing, with dark cherry-wood colonial furniture, but you might want to splurge on a deluxe room with a romantic four-poster canopy bed. Continental breakfast is included, HBO and local calls are free, and there's an outdoor pool. The Park Plaza makes a great base for the South Sound and Mount Rainier; it's very popular for meetings and conventions, so reserve ahead. ▪ *9620 South Hill Park Pl E (off Hwy 512, near South Hill Mall), Puyallup, WA 98373; (253)848-1500 or (800)528-1234; www.bestwestern.com; $$; AE, MC, V; checks OK.*

TACOMA

Flanked by Commencement Bay and the Tacoma Narrows and backed by Mount Rainier, Tacoma is no longer just a blue-collar mill town, but a growing urban center with a thriving cultural core.

The city has fervently embraced the idea of preservation. The historic buildings in the downtown warehouse district are being converted from industrial use to residential and commercial functions, and some of the old warehouses are slated for a University of Washington branch campus. The stately homes and cobblestone streets in the north end are often used as sets for Hollywood's moviemakers, and students still fill the turreted chateau of Stadium High School. **Old City Hall**, 625 Commerce, with its newly coppered roof, Renaissance clock, and bell tower; the Romanesque **First Presbyterian Church**, 20 Tacoma Avenue S, the rococo **Pythian Lodge**, 925½ Broadway; and the one-of-a-kind coppered **Union Station**, 17th and Pacific (now the much praised Federal Courthouse)—all delight history and architecture buffs. The old Union Station rotunda is also graced by some spectacular work by glass artist and Tacoma native Dale Chihuly. This permanent exhibit is actually an annex of the Tacoma Art Museum, open to the public at no charge, so do drop in for a peek. The **Ruston Way Waterfront**, a 6-mile mix of parks and restaurants, is thronged with people in any weather.

▼

Tacoma

▲

The **Broadway Center for the Performing Arts**, 901 Broadway Plaza, often does shows at both the Pantages and Rialto Theatres. Call for tickets and information, (253)591-5894. The restored 1,100-seat **Pantages Theater**, 901 Broadway Plaza, originally designed in 1918 by nationally known movie theater architect B. Marcus Priteca, is the focal point of the reviving downtown cultural life—dance, music, and stage presentations. And the nearby **Rialto Theatre**, 310 S Ninth, has been restored for smaller performance groups. **Tacoma Actors Guild**, Tacoma's popular professional theater—at the Commerce Street level atop the park-covered transit center, (253)272-2145—offers an ambitious and successful blend of American classics and Northwest premieres that draw an audience from throughout the Puget Sound region.

The **Tacoma Art Museum**, 12th and Pacific, (253)272-4258, is housed in a former downtown bank. The small museum has paintings by Renoir, Degas, and Pissarro, as well as a collection of contemporary American prints. The **Washington State Historical Museum**, (888)238-4373, has left its previous home near Stadium High School and is now housed in a handsome new building just south of Union Station at 1911 Pacific Avenue. This new facility not only has many times the previous exhibit space but offers a state-of-the-art museum experience, providing history and innovation under the same roof. From the outside, however, the museum has been carefully designed to blend into its surroundings and complement Union Station, built in 1911.

OTHER THINGS TO DO

Point Defiance Park, situated on the west side of Tacoma, has 500 acres of untouched forest jutting out into Puget Sound and is one of the most dramatically sited and creatively planned city parks in the country. The wooded 5-mile drive and parallel hiking trails open up now and then for sweeping views of the water, Vashon Island, Gig Harbor, and the Olympic Mountains beyond. There are rose, rhododendron, Japanese, and Northwest native gardens, a railroad village with a working steam engine, a reconstruction of Fort Nisqually (originally built in 1833), a museum, a swimming beach, and the much acclaimed **Point Defiance Zoo and Aquarium**. Watching the almost continuous play of seals, sea lions, and the white beluga whale from an underwater vantage point is a rare treat; call (253) 591-5335 for information on the zoo, or (253) 305-1000 for general park information. **Wright Park** at Division and I Streets is a serene in-city park with many trees, a duck-filled pond, and a beautifully maintained, fragrant conservatory, built of glass and steel in 1890. One of the area's largest estates, and the former home of the late Corydon and Eulalie Wagner, is now **Lakewold Gardens** (12317 Gravelly Lake Drive SW, (253) 584-3360), located on a beautiful 10-acre site overlooking Gravelly Lake in Lakewood, just 10 minutes south of Tacoma. Recognized nationally as one of the outstanding gardens in America, Lakewold Gardens is open Thursday through Monday from April through September for guided and nonguided tours (winter tours on Mondays, Thursdays, and Fridays only; call for details). Take exit 124 off I-5 to Gravelly Lake Drive.

The **Tacoma Dome**, the world's largest wooden dome, is the site of many entertainment and trade shows as well as a sports center. The dazzling neon sculpture by Stephen Antonakos provides a dramatic background for events such as the **Tacoma Rockets** hockey games, championship ice-skating competitions, and many other regional activities. Call (253) 272-6817 for ticket information.

Fans who like their baseball played outdoors in a first-class ballpark arrive in enthusiastic droves at **Cheney Stadium** to watch the **Tacoma Rainiers**, the triple-A affiliate of the Seattle Mariners; (253) 752-7707.

Fishing/boating. With the waters of Puget Sound lapping at virtually half of Tacoma's city limits, it is to be expected that many Tacomans and visitors choose to spend their leisure time afloat or on the pier. There are two fishing piers along Ruston Way and public launches and boat rentals at Point Defiance.

Nightlife. Engine House No. 9 near the University of Puget Sound is a friendly, neighborhood beer-lover's dream of a tavern (minus the smoke); 611 N Pine Street, (253) 272-3435. Another fun tavern to check out is The Spar in Old Town, 2121 N 30th, (253) 627-8215.

RESTAURANTS

Altezzo ★★ This attractive restaurant is indeed "lofty" in both space and attitude. Its location at the top of the Sheraton provides a great view of downtown and the surrounding area (request a window table, of course), and some of the best Italian cuisine in Tacoma, courtesy of chef Charlie McManus. His treatment of veal is particularly good (try the scaloppine di vitello marsala). The smoked salmon ravioli with asparagus and a light lemon cream sauce works well too. The tiramisu is the real McCoy. The bar is a great place to kick back with a glass of wine and a plate of antipasti and enjoy the view. ■ *1320 Broadway Plaza (downtown between 13th and 15th, in the Sheraton), Tacoma; (253) 572-3200; $$; full bar; AE, DC, MC, V; checks OK; dinner every day.* ⅄

The Cliff House ★★ Over the years, this restaurant survived on its commanding view of Commencement Bay and Tacoma's north end, and its formal, pretentious airs. Chef Jon Brzycki came on board, however, and established a menu that ensures this place will do more than survive: homemade venison sausage with a wild rice pancake and dried-fruit chutney, a delicious smoked duck salad with a sesame dressing, or pan-roasted pheasant with a light touch of port wine sauce accented with pears and cranberries. Desserts, less noteworthy, are a trip down memory lane, with cherries jubilee and crêpes Suzette flambéed tableside. Maybe just finish off with a brandy and enjoy the view. ■ *6300 Marine View Dr (follow East Side Dr to the top of the hill), Tacoma; (253) 927-0400; $$$; full bar; AE, DC, MC, V; no checks; lunch, dinner every day.* ⅄

Fujiya ★★ Absolute consistency is what attracts a loyal clientele from near and far to Masahiro Endo's stylish downtown Japanese restaurant. For years this has been a favorite spot for the best sushi and sashimi around. Begin your meal with *gyoza* (savory pork-stuffed dumplings). The real test of a Japanese restaurant is the tempura, and Endo makes certain that his is feathery-crisp. And for those who prefer their seafood cooked, the *yosenabe* (seafood stew) is full of delicious things served in a small cast-iron pot. He's a generous and friendly man, Mr. Endo; seldom an evening goes by that he doesn't offer a complimentary tidbit of one kind or another. ■ *1125 Court C (between Broadway and Market), Tacoma; (206) 627-5319; $$; beer and wine; AE, MC, V; checks OK; lunch Mon–Fri, dinner Mon–Sat.*

Stanley and Seaforts Steak, Chop, and Fish House ★★ Every seat in this restaurant has a panoramic view of Tacoma, its busy harbor, and, on a clear day, the Olympic Mountains. But this is one view restaurant that doesn't just rest on its sunsetting laurels. The emphasis is on quality meats and seafood simply grilled over apple wood with flavorings of herbs and fruits. It's the combination of interesting menu selections and dependability that has made Stanley and Seaforts a favorite for almost two decades. The spacious bar features distinctive Scotch whiskeys—and, well, a great sunset to boot. ■ *115 E 34th St (City Center exit off I-5, follow Hwy 7, take 38th west, right on Pacific Ave, right on 34th), Tacoma; (253)473-7300; $$; full bar; AE, DC, DIS, MC, V; local checks only; lunch Mon–Fri, dinner every day.*

Bimbo's ★ Don't be put off by the slightly disreputable name or location: here's a family Italian restaurant that's been attracting regulars for 75 years. Members of the original owner's family are still cooking their native recipes with little regard for today's trends. Rabbit, once the most common source of meat in their region of Tuscany, is served year-round in a hearty, full-bodied tomato sauce. The pork ribs are meaty and luscious, and aficionados of that Italian favorite, tripe, find it judiciously treated here. Their hallmark tomato sauce must cook for hours to reach that thick, rich flavor and deep color; it's a perfect partner for the hearty pasta dishes. ■ *1516 Pacific Ave (at 15th), Tacoma; (253)383-5800; $; full bar; AE, DIS, MC, V; local checks only; lunch Mon–Sat, dinner every day.* &

Cedars III ★ Tacoma is awash with restaurants of various ethnic bents, but Mediterranean cuisine is a rarity. For those babaghanouj and garlic-bathed-chicken cravings, be thankful for Nadim Alawar and his Cedars III restaurant (his first two are in Seattle), not far from the Narrows Bridge. Try the Cedars Delight—a big platter of samplings from the menu, served family-style for two or more. Unfortunately, the pita is the same dry stuff you might find at the grocery store. The wine list consists of only four table reds, from Lebanon, Spain, Morocco, and France. ■ *7104 6th Ave (take 6th Ave exit from Hwy 16, head west), Tacoma; (253)564-0255; $$; full bar; AE, MC, V; checks OK; dinner Tues–Sun.* &

The Dash Point Lobster Shop ■ The Lobster Shop South ★ The Dash Point Lobster Shop could just as well be set next to the moorings of Maine lobster trawlers as it is to the docks of the small public beach on Puget Sound. This sea-weathered restaurant is a welcome change from the number of pricey, slick eateries blossoming along the waterfront. As could be expected, rich, oven-baked lobster (Australian rock lobster) is the house specialty. Large juicy crab cakes, often paired with pan-fried oysters, are another favorite. The place has a full liquor license, too. The larger, swankier **Lobster Shop South** on the Ruston Way waterfront has a distinctly different atmosphere and menu. It provides good seafood dishes, a full bar, and elegant surroundings, but not quite the same charm of the original. There is a small smoking area in the dining room. ■ *6912 Soundview Dr NE (off Dash Point Rd), Tacoma; (253)927-1513; $$; full bar; AE, DIS, MC, V; checks OK; dinner every day.* ♿ ■ *4015 Ruston Way (take Schuster Pkwy to Ruston), Tacoma; (253)759-2165; $$; full bar; AE, DIS, MC, V; checks OK; dinner every day, brunch Sun.* ♿

East & West Cafe ★ What this restaurant lacks in location, it makes up for tenfold in great food and charm. East & West Cafe is a haven of Asian delights on the busy thoroughfare south of the Tacoma Mall. Owner Vien Floyd, a Saigon native, has gained a very loyal following among locals. Her incomparable personality helps make meals here a treat. The emphasis is on Vietnamese and Thai cuisine, a mix that invites you to experiment: the Saigon Crêpe is a large curried crêpe filled with bean sprouts, strips of pork, shrimp, and vegetables, with dipping sauce alongside. The vegetables are always crisp and bright and full of fresh flavor, the sauces have character, meats are tender—you really can't go wrong. For the price, it's hard to have a better meal in Tacoma. ■ *5319 Tacoma Mall Blvd (just west of I-5, take 56th St exit), Tacoma; (253)475-7755; $; beer and wine; MC, V; local checks only; lunch, dinner Mon–Sat.* ♿

Harbor Lights ★ Decor is circa 1950, with glass floats, stuffed prize fish, and a giant lobster, but Tacoma's pioneer Ruston Way waterfront restaurant still packs them in (reserve early). Up-to-the-minute it may not be, but that doesn't seem to bother the seafood fans who regularly crowd into the noisy dining room to consume buckets of steamed clams and mounds of perfectly cooked pan-fried oysters. Grilled fillet of sole is done to perfection; halibut and chips are the best around, as are the crisp hashbrowns. The portions are so gargantuan that only an ace trencherman can dig his way to the bottom of the plate. ■ *2761 Ruston Way (take City Center exit off I-5 and follow Schuster Pkwy onto Ruston Way), Tacoma; (253)752-8600; $$; full bar; AE, DC, MC, V; checks OK; lunch Mon–Sat, dinner every day.* ♿

Katie Downs ★ Katie Downs's Philadelphia-style deep-dish pizza is a winner. You place your own order at the counter for one of their classic combinations. Especially good is the Fearless, which recklessly matches smoked bacon and provolone cheese with white onions, spicy peperoncini—and lots and lots of fresh garlic. Since the pizzas can take close to 30 minutes to make and bake, order some steamer clams to tide you over while you wait and watch the tugs, barges, freighters, and sailboats move across Commencement Bay. This place is noisy, boisterous, and fun, but remember it is a tavern (no minors). ■ *3211 Ruston Way (City Center exit off I-5, follow Schuster Pkwy* onto Ruston Way), Tacoma; (253) 756-0771; $; beer and wine; MC, V; local checks only; lunch, dinner every day. ⎣

Southern Kitchen ★ Calorie counters might pass up this little cafe, but if you have a hankering for the authentic fare of the South, do stop. Abandon all restraint and order up some pork chops smothered with gravy, or liver with lots of lovely onions, all sided by long-cooked collard greens served in their own pot likker, black-eyed peas, or sweet nuggets of yams. The Kitchen also dishes up some mighty fine fried chicken and barbecued ribs. Thin, light corn-batter cakes are served in lieu of rolls, and most folks finish their meal with a slice of homemade sweet potato pie. Breakfasts are great, too: pan-fried butterfish with eggs, buttery grits, home-fries, and genuine Southern biscuits. ■ *1716 6th Ave (at Division), Tacoma; (253) 627-4282; $; no alcohol; AE, MC, V; checks OK; breakfast, lunch, early dinner every day.* ⎣

LODGINGS

Chinaberry Hill ★★ This 1889 mansion (on the National Register of Historic Places) in Tacoma's historic Stadium District has been beautifully restored by Cecil and Yarrow Wayman and turned into a charming, romantic bed and breakfast. Lovers of old homes delight in the attention to detail used in building the house, like the pocket door between the living room and dining room, faced with two different types of wood to match the wood used in each room. There are three rooms in the main house: we prefer the Pantages Suite, with its views of Commencement Bay and its Jacuzzi, or the Manning Suite, which has bay windows overlooking the garden, a fireplace, and a Jacuzzi. Families enjoy the Catchpenny Cottage behind the main house; once the estate's carriage house, it has been made over into a lovely two-story retreat (plans are in the works to make two separate suites out of the upstairs and the downstairs). The Waymans serve a full breakfast in the dining room or, on sunny days, out on the veranda overlooking the water. ■ *302 Tacoma Ave N (City Center exit from I-5, follow Schuster Pkwy exit to Stadium Way, follow Stadium to Tacoma Ave N and turn right), Tacoma, WA 98403; (253) 272-1282; wayman29@ mail.idt.net; www.wa.net/chinaberry; $$$; MC, V; checks OK.*

The Villa Bed & Breakfast ★★ In the heart of Tacoma's historic residential North End is a home that stands out from the crowd. Built for a local businessman in 1925, it was designed with the Mediterranean in mind: open and airy, with high arched windows, tiled roof, and a palm tree out front. This spacious home has been transformed into a gracious bed and breakfast by Becky and Greg Anglemyer. Our favorite room is actually the relatively small Maid's Quarters on the top floor—utterly private, with a grand view of Commencement Bay and the Olympics. Guests have more space in the Bay View Suite, with a fireplace, a sitting area, and a bay-view veranda. A CD player in every room (and a good CD collection downstairs) is music to our ears. ■ *705 N 5th St (City Center exit from I-5, follow Schuster Pkwy exit to Stadium Way, follow Stadium to Tacoma Ave, right on Tacoma to N 5th, go left), Tacoma, WA 98403; (253) 572-1157; villabb@aol.com; www.tribnet.com/bb/villa.htp; $$; MC, V; checks OK.*

Sheraton Tacoma Hotel ★ This is the best hotel in town, but unfortunately that says more about the lack of competition than it does about the quality of the accommodations here. Adjacent to the Tacoma Convention Center, it's quite suitable for conventioneers and corporate travelers, who may not mind that the guest rooms feature bland furnishings, ancient TVs, and those horrible fuzzy nylon blankets. On the plus side, most rooms look out over Commencement Bay or have a view of Mount Rainier. We've come to expect more from a hotel managed by the highly regarded Kimpton Group (affiliated with such fine hotels as the Alexis and the Vintage Park in Seattle). For some of the best Italian food in the area, head up to Altezzo on the top floor (see review). ■ *1320 Broadway Plaza (downtown between 13th and 15th), Tacoma, WA 98402; (253) 572-3200 or (800) 845-9466; $$$; AE, DC, MC, V; checks OK.* ᕶ

PARKLAND

RESTAURANTS

Marzano's ★ The reputation of Lisa Marzano's voluptuous cooking has people arriving from miles away. When the weather turns fair, outside seating on two deck areas is an added plus to this large space. Meals begin with fresh-baked crusty bread, ready to be topped with shredded Parmesan and herbed olive oil. For entrees try the stubby rigatoni, perfect for capturing the extraordinary boscaiola sauce made with mushrooms and ham; the lasagne is sumptuous, as is the elegant chicken piccata pungent with capers and lemons. When all's said and done, we'd go back even if it were just for the many-layered chocolate poppyseed cake floating in whipped cream. Reservations are needed. ■ *516 Garfield S (adjacent to Pacific Lutheran University), Parkland; (253) 537-4191; $$; beer and wine; DIS, MC, V; checks OK; lunch Tues–Fri, dinner Tues–Sat.* ᕶ

GIG HARBOR

Gig Harbor, once an undisturbed fishing village (and still homeport for an active commercial fleet), is now part suburbia, part weekend destination. Boating is still important here, with good anchorage and various moorage docks attracting gunwale-to-gunwale pleasure craft. When the clouds break, Mount Rainier holds court for all.

A variety of interesting shops and galleries line **Harborview Drive**, the single street that almost encircles the harbor. It's a most picturesque spot for browsing and window-shopping.

Gig Harbor was planned for boat traffic, not automobiles (with resulting traffic congestion and limited parking), yet it is still a good place for celebrations. An arts festival in mid-July and a jazz festival in mid-August are two main events. May through October (on Saturdays) the **Gig Harbor Farmers Market** features locally grown produce, plants, and Northwest gifts; at the Pierce Transit Park and Ride, off Highway 16. Call the Chamber of Commerce for more information on any event: (253)851-6865.

Nearby **Kopachuck State Park** is a popular destination (follow signs from Highway 16), as are **Penrose Point** and **Robert F. Kennedy State Parks** on the Key Peninsula, all with numerous beaches for clam digging. (Purdy Spit and Maple Hollow Park are the most accessible spots.) At **Minter Creek State Hatchery** the public can watch the different developmental stages of millions of salmon of various species. About 15 minutes from downtown Gig Harbor, the facilities are open to the public every day, or for group visits by special arrangement. Call (253)857-5077 for directions or more information.

Performance Circle, 6615 38th Avenue NW, (253)851-7529, Gig Harbor's resident theater group, mounts enjoyable productions year-round, with summer shows staged outside in the meadow at 9916 Peacock Hill Avenue NW. Theatergoers bring picnics and blankets, and watch the shows beneath the stars. It's turned into a wonderful small-town custom.

RESTAURANTS

The Green Turtle ★ Mark Wambold of Marco's might be worried about the competition if he didn't own this place as well. Here chef Mimi Wambold gets to spread her wings a bit (she also still oversees Marco's). After a few years of cooking Italian, she's off to the Pacific Rim. Her pan-fried wontons with a vibrant dipping sauce are creating tidal waves in the little harbor community. The spicy seafood sauté is a dressed up phad Thai with mussels, shrimp, scallops, and clams. Although you can get Marco's famed cheesecake here, dessert dances to a different tune than usual, with mango ice cream or a poached pear bathed in chocolate sauce. In fine weather, dine outdoors on the deck overlooking the harbor. ■ *2905 Harborview Dr (past the Tides Tavern), Gig Harbor; (253)851-3167; $$; beer and wine; AE, DIS, MC, V; checks OK; dinner Tues–Sun.* ♿

Marco's Ristorante Italiano ★ Everyone in this area loves what Marco (Mark Wambold) and his wife, Mimi, have done for dining in Gig Harbor. It shows in the busy, crowded bustle of the place (so reserve ahead). Mimi's the star behind the stoves (here as well as at the Green Turtle), her menu ranging from the traditional (spaghetti and meatballs, handmade tortellini in fresh pesto) to the more original specials (a dense, tender piece of tuna sautéed in red wine). Deep-fried olives are an unusual starter. Adjacent to the restaurant is Mimi's Pantry, a retail shop featuring Italian specialty goods. ■ *7707 Pioneer Way (2 blocks up from the harbor), Gig Harbor; (253)858-2899; $$; beer and wine; AE, MC, V; checks OK; lunch, dinner Tues–Sat.* も

Tides Tavern "Meet you at the Tides" has become such a universal invitation that this tavern perched over the harbor often has standing room only, especially on sunny days when the deck is open. And people do come, by boat, seaplane, and car. Originally a general store next to the ferry landing, the Tides doesn't pretend to be anything other than what it is—a self-service tavern (no minors) with pool table, Gig Harbor memorabilia, and live music on weekend nights. Indulge in man-size sandwiches, huge charbroiled burgers, a gargantuan shrimp salad, and highly touted fish and chips (pizzas are only passable). ■ *2925 Harborview Dr (at Soundview), Gig Harbor; (253)858-3982; $; beer and wine; AE, MC, V; checks OK; lunch, dinner every day.*

LODGINGS

The Pillars ★★ From the windows of this landmark house, you can see Colvos Passage, Vashon Island, and Mount Rainier. And from the front door, you're just uphill from the harbor. All three guest rooms are beautifully decorated, with large private baths and separate reading areas furnished with writing desks and telephones. An added bonus is the covered, heated swimming pool and Jacuzzi. The master of the house is also a master baker, so you'll find breakfasts feature particularly tasty home-baked breads and muffins. ■ *6606 Soundview Dr (take the first Gig Harbor exit off Hwy 16), Gig Harbor, WA 98335; (253)851-6644; $$$; MC, V; checks OK.*

The Maritime Inn The Maritime Inn is right in downtown Gig Harbor, albeit across the street from the waterfront. Each of the 15 rooms is comfortably appointed with queen-size beds, gas fireplaces, and TVs; several "specialty rooms" offer themed decor (the Polo Room, the Victorian Room) and a bit more space, including a sun deck, at a slightly higher cost. Space or no, the price is a bit high considering the lack of conversational privacy in the rooms. Avoid the rooms on the front of the inn closest to the street. ■ *3212 Harborview Dr (downtown), Gig Harbor, WA 98335; (253)858-1818; $$; AE, DIS, MC, V; checks OK.* も

Once an Indian village and later Washington Territory's first incorporated town (1854), Steilacoom today is a quiet community of old trees and houses, with no vestige of its heyday, when a trolley line ran from Bair's drugstore to Tacoma. October's **Apple Squeeze Festival** and midsummer's **Salmon Bake**, with canoe and kayak races, are popular; (253)581-1900.

The **Steilacoom Tribal Museum** is located in a turn-of-the-century church overlooking the South Sound islands and the entire Olympic mountain range; (253)584-6308.

Ferries run to bucolic **Anderson Island** (see below), with restricted runs to McNeil Island (a state penitentiary); call Pierce County Ferry Information, (253)596-2766.

RESTAURANTS

▼

Steilacoom

▲

ER Rogers ★ View restaurants on Puget Sound are not novelties, but views like this one are still exceptional, particularly when seen from a restored 100-year-old Queen Anne–style home. Much is noteworthy here, but the Steilacoom special prime rib, first roasted, then sliced and quickly seared, is still tops. You can't beat the huge Sunday buffet brunch, with its large selection of seafood: oysters on the half shell, cold poached salmon, flavorful smoked salmon, cracked crab, pickled herring, steamed clams, and fettuccine with shrimp. There is a beautiful upstairs bar with a widow's walk just wide enough for one row of tables. ■ *1702 Commercial St (corner of Wilkes, off Steilacoom Blvd), Steilacoom; (253)582-0280; $$; full bar; MC, V; checks OK; dinner every day, brunch Sun.* ౹

Bair Drug and Hardware Store Side orders of nostalgia are presented gratis when you step into Bair Drug. Except for the customers, little has changed since it was built—in 1895. Products your grandparents might have used—cigars, washtubs, perfume, and apple peelers—are still on display. Old post office boxes mask the bakery, which turns out pies and pastries such as flaky apple dumplings; the potbelly stove warms customers in the winter. Best of all, there is a 1906 soda fountain, where you can still get a sarsaparilla, a Green River, or a genuine ice cream soda. On weekday afternoons, by reservation only, you can enjoy a traditional high tea, complete with tiny tea sandwiches and tartlets. Friday nights, come to the Bair for a steak or crab-cake dinner. ■ *1617 Lafayette St (at Wilkes), Steilacoom; (253)588-9668; $; beer and wine; MC, V; local checks only; breakfast, lunch every day, dinner Fri.* ౹

LODGINGS

Anderson House on Oro Bay ★★ Anderson Island is a well-kept secret. A short ferry ride from Steilacoom (see Steilacoom introduction) and a few miles from the dock is a large house surrounded by 200 acres of woods. Randy and B. Anderson stay next door at grandfather's home, so guests have exclusive use of the whole house, with its four large bedrooms and antique furnishings. Full farm breakfasts feature breads hot from the oven, fruit pizzas, and other treats. Since this is isolated country with no restaurants, lunch and dinner are also served with advance notice. In addition, the Andersons rent a three-bedroom cedar fishing cabin (wood stove–heated, but updated with full kitchen amenities, right down to a microwave) hidden away on outer Amsterdam Bay with a sweeping view of the Olympics from the deck. A short bike ride from the Anderson House brings you to a mile-long secluded beach. Arrangements can be made to pick up guests at the ferry dock. Boaters and those with seaplanes have their own dock, but check the tides. ■ *12024 Eckenstam-Johnson Rd (call for directions), Anderson Island, WA 98303; (253) 884-4088 or (800) 750-4088; www.non. com//anderson; $$; MC, V; checks OK.*

▼

The capitol's centerpiece is the classic dome of the **Washington State Legislative Building**. Lavishly fitted out with bronze and marble, this striking Romanesque structure houses the offices of the Governor and other state executives. The State Senate and House of Representatives meet here in annual sessions that can be viewed by visitors; (360) 753-5000.

Just opposite the Legislative Building rises the pillared **Temple of Justice**, seat of the State Supreme Court. To the west is the red brick Governor's Mansion, open to visitors on Wednesday afternoons from 1pm to 2:45pm. Reservations must be made in advance; (360) 586-TOUR.

The handsome **Washington State Library**, directly behind the Legislative Building, is open to the public during business hours; (360) 753-2114; it boasts artifacts from the state's early history. At 211 W 21st Avenue, the **State Capitol Museum**, (360) 753-2580, houses a permanent exhibit that includes an outstanding collection of Western Washington Native American baskets.

Downtown, on Seventh Avenue between Washington and Franklin Streets, is the restored **Old Capitol**, whose pointed towers and high-arched windows suggest a late-medieval château. In another part of downtown, just off the Plum Street exit from I-5 and adjacent to City Hall, is the **Yashiro Japanese Garden**, which honors one of Olympia's sister cities.

There is also a triad of colleges here: **The Evergreen State College (TESC)**, west of Olympia, on Cooper Point; **St. Martin's**, a Benedictine monastery and college in adjacent Lacey; and **South Puget Sound Community College**, just across Highway 101. Evergreen State College offers a regular schedule of plays, films, and experimental theater, as well as special events such as its annual February Tribute to Asia. Its library and pool are public; (360)866-6000.

In Olympia proper, the **Washington Center for the Performing Arts** (on Washington Street between Fifth Avenue and Legion Way, (360)753-8586) has brought new life to the downtown. Across Fifth Avenue, the **Capitol Theatre**, (360)754-5378, provides a showcase for the offerings of the active Olympia Film Society as well as for locally produced plays and musicals. Toward the harbor, in a new location near Percival Landing at 700 N Capitol Way, is the lively **Olympia Farmers Market**, which displays produce, flowers, and crafts from all over the South Sound; open Thursday through Sunday during the growing season, (360)352-9096. Increasingly, **Percival Landing** (a waterfront park) is becoming a community focal point, the site of harbor festivals of all kinds. The historic heart of the whole area (Olympia, Lacey, and Tumwater) is **Tumwater Falls**, where the Deschutes River flows into Capitol Lake. A nice walk along the river takes you past several waterfalls. This is the site of the chief local industry, the Tumwater Division of the **Pabst Brewing Company**, which brews Olympia beer, with four free tours Tuesday-Saturday (take exit 103 off I-5, follow signs; (360)754-5000). If you need something sweet after strolling the falls, stop in at **Desserts by Tasha Nicole** in Tumwater at 2822 Capitol Boulevard SE, (360)352-3717: the chocolate-dipped cheesecake on a stick is to die for.

The area's finest nature preserve lies well outside the city limits. This is the relatively unspoiled Nisqually Delta—outlet of the Nisqually River that forms at the foot of a Mount Rainier glacier and enters the Sound just north of Olympia. Take exit 114 off I-5 and follow the signs to the **Nisqually National Wildlife Refuge**. From here, a 5-mile hiking trail follows an old dike around the delta, a wetland alive with bird life. Just south, a rookery of great blue herons occupies the treetops.

RESTAURANTS

Bristol House ★★ Adolf Schmidt (of the Olympia Brewery founding family) is owner and chef at this cheerful place, located south of the Thurston County courthouse. The menu features items such as prawns in a light white-wine sauce with lemon, sun-dried tomatoes, and spinach; and blackened steak salad, served over greens with a caesar-style dressing. Regulars know the popular Bacardi beef is one of the best dishes in town. Go for dinner if you want to take full advantage of the chef's ingenuity; lunches are relatively uninspired. Service is fast and professional. ■ *2401 Bristol Ct SW (off Evergreen Park Dr), Olympia; (360)352-9494; $$; full bar; MC, V; checks OK; dinner Tues–Sat.* &

Capitale ★★ In downtown Olympia, across Sylvester Square from the old courthouse, is a tiny, casual place serving up interesting food in a pleasant atmosphere. The walls are lined with the work of local artists, and jazz music often complements the meals; in good weather a few tables are added outside, giving this place a nice neighborhood feel. The menu is Italianesque, with interesting variations. Consider the tortellini with Brie and avocado, or the sweet-potato gratin appetizer—tender little pieces of sweetness with a sprinkle of Parmesan cheese melted on top. The rectangular pizzas are excellent. Or try the goat cheese and sun-dried tomato tamales. ■ *609 Capitol Way S (at Legion St), Olympia; (360)352-8007; $$; beer and wine; MC, V; checks OK; breakfast Mon–Fri, lunch, dinner Mon–Sat.* &

Gardner's Seafood and Pasta ★★ To loyal fans, Gardner's is the hands-down favorite in Olympia, with very good reason. This homey place with its wood floors and profusion of fresh flowers on all the tables makes you feel as though you're in the home of a good friend who cooks like a dream. Owners Leon and Jane Longan offer good, simple food that always hits the spot. During the right season, you might find the true Puget Sound delicacy of a dozen Calm Cove Olympia oysters, each the size of a quarter, served on the half shell. Pastas can be bland, but the appetizers, such as the roasted rock shrimp with garlic, never are. Connoisseurs of ice cream won't want to pass up Gardner's homemade product. Reservations are important. ■ *111 W Thurston St (north on Capitol Way to Thurston), Olympia; (360)786-8466; $$; beer and wine; AE, MC, V; checks OK; dinner Tues–Sat.*

La Petite Maison ★★ This tiny, converted 1890s farmhouse—overshadowed by a beetling office building—is a quiet, elegant refuge for Olympians seeking imaginative, skillfully prepared Northwest cuisine (the menu changes daily). Among its appetizers are steamed Kamiche clams and mussels, and delicate and flavorful Dungeness crab cakes served with a dill sauce. Entrees include perfectly sautéed medallions of pork with tangy Dijon mustard sauce and fresh poached petrale sole stuffed with salmon mousse. In spring or summer, it's pleasant to sit on the restaurant's glassed-in porch—though the view of overtrafficked Division Street outside may make you long for the days when this place was truly a farm. ■ *101 Division NW (1 block south of Harrison), Olympia; (360)943-8812; $$; beer and wine; DC, MC, V; checks OK; lunch Tues–Fri, dinner Mon–Sat.* &

Louisa ★★ Located just south of downtown Olympia in Tumwater, Louisa is generating quite a buzz. Co-owner Jeff Taylor (formerly of Capitale) and his wife, Connie, have fashioned a pleasantly stylish dining room with lots of blond wood, Oriental rugs, and a few scattered antiques. The cuisine is primarily Italian, with a few Northwest and Pacific Rim influences: main dishes like cheese tortellini and chicken piccata are supplemented by starters such as fresh spring rolls with soy and black vinegar dipping sauce, or local mussels in a coconut-lime-lemongrass sauce. Interestingly, the wine list features only a few wines from Italy; most of the wines listed hail from the Northwest or California. ■ *205 Cleveland Ave (follow Capitol Blvd south to Cleveland), Tumwater; (360)352-3732; $$; beer and wine; MC, V; checks OK; lunch Tues–Fri, dinner Tues–Sat.*

Seven Gables ★★ Visually, this dinner house is the most striking restaurant in Olympia, occupying as it does the fine old Carpenter Gothic residence built by the city's turn-of-the-century mayor, George B. Lane. The site takes full advantage of a splendid Mount Rainier view. Steven and Glenda Taylor are the owners of the delightful spot. Their elegant menu includes such items as a homemade seafood sausage with lobster sauce, red snapper in walnut crust with basil cherry sauce, and beef tenderloin with white mushroom essence. Daily specials include a vegetarian feature. ■ *1205 W Bay Dr NW (¾ mile north of the 4th Ave bridge), Olympia; (360)352-2349; $$; full bar; AE, MC, V; checks OK; dinner Tues–Sun.* ♿

Budd Bay Cafe ★ There's no doubt about it: the Budd Bay Cafe, with its long row of tables looking out across Budd Inlet, is still a preferred after-hours haunt of many of today's legislators, lobbyists, and state government movers and shakers. Restaurateur John Senner is on hand most of the time, seeing that everyone is satisfied. Don't look for elaborate dishes here; the menu (steaks, sandwiches, pasta, salads, seafood) is designed for boaters and people to whom good talk matters more than haute cuisine. The bar is pleasant and lively, with a long list of specialty beers. ■ *525 N Columbia St (between A and B), Olympia; (360)357-6963; $$; full bar; AE, DC, DIS, MC, V; checks OK; lunch Mon–Sat, dinner every day, brunch Sun.* ♿

Sweet Oasis ★ This spot on Capitol Way is particularly informal, but offers some delicious foods of the Mediterranean. Among the daily specials are spanakopita and Lebanese baked vegetables. Friday and Saturday you can get *kibby sineeyah*, a deliciously offbeat dish combining ground lamb with bulgur, pine nuts, and spices, baked in squares. Falafel, meat pies, and other traditional items of Mediterranean fare are available as well. The dessert pastries are house-made and very good. Saturday nights you get a bonus belly-dancing show—a very artful performance—winding casually among the tables. ▪ *507 Capitol Way (at 5th Ave), Olympia; (360)956-0470; $; beer and wine; MC, V; local checks only; lunch, dinner every day (closed Sun–Mon in winter).* &

Urban Onion ★ The site of many a power lunch for Olympia's rising breed of feminist politicians, the Urban Onion (originally called the "Herb and Onion") retains a faint flavor of the counterculture of the '60s. A signature dish is an especially satisfying lentil soup. The Mexican chicken grilled with mushrooms is also outstanding. Breakfasts include a hefty huevos rancheros. The Urban Onion extends into the lobby of the former Olympian Hotel, and meeting space is available. ▪ *116 Legion Way (at Washington), Olympia; (360)943-9242; $$; full bar; AE, DIS, MC, V; checks OK; breakfast, lunch, dinner every day.*

The Fish Bowl Pub and Cafe Aptly named the Fish Bowl, the Fish Tale Ales brewpub is full to the gills with fish paraphernalia, from real specimens swimming around in the large tank to metal salmon sculptures and ceramic fish on the walls. The beers are the draw—all Fish Tale productions are made in the adjoining facilities. The beer's available to go as well. For nibbles (called "Fish Food") consider smoked oysters, cheeses, shrimp cocktail, antipasto, or oyster shooters. There's now an adjacent Fish Bowl cafe, where you can get whole-wheat-crust pizzas from wood-fired ovens. ▪ *515 Jefferson (downtown, corner of Legion), Olympia; (360)943-3650; $; beer and wine; MC, V; checks OK; lunch, dinner every day.* &

The Spar Above the restaurant's old-fashioned booths are blown-up Darius Kinsey photos of teams of old-time loggers beaming over unbelievably mammoth trees they've just brought to earth. Indeed, some 60-odd years ago, the Spar used to be known as a workingman's hangout. Today it's classless, with a mixture of students, attorneys, businesspeople, artists, politicians, fishermen, tourists, and leisured retirees. The Spar's robust milk shakes and homemade bread pudding are locally acclaimed, although much of the menu is purely average. Willapa Bay oysters or fresh salmon from the Farmers Market are sometimes available; the prime rib dinner is popular on weekends. ▪ *114 E 4th Ave (1 block east of Capitol Way), Olympia; (360)357-6444; $; full bar; AE, DC, MC, V; checks OK; breakfast, lunch, dinner every day.* &

LODGINGS

Harbinger Inn ★★ Occupying a restored 1910 mansion, this B&B offers Edwardian furnishings, a fine outlook over Budd Inlet and the distant Olympic Mountains, and five choice guest rooms. Nicest is the Innkeeper's Suite on the top floor, with its king bed, sitting room, gas fireplace, and large bathroom with a soaking tub. Rooms on the front of the house have views, but rooms on the back side are farther from the street, with only the sound of a small artesian-fed waterfall to disturb the tranquillity. All rooms have private baths (although the bath for the Cloisonne Room is downstairs on the main floor, directly below the room). The inn is situated near excellent routes for bicycle riding, and Priest Point Park is close by. A light breakfast (perhaps fresh fruit, followed by oatmeal) is served. The Harbinger is popular with lobbyists, so reserve well ahead during the legislative session. ■ *1136 E Bay Dr (1 mile north of State St), Olympia, WA 98506; (360) 754-0389; $$; AE, MC, V; checks OK.*

Holiday Inn Select Few urban hotels around Puget Sound take such striking advantage of the Northwest's natural beauty as this one, dramatically perched on a high bluff above Capitol Lake, with much greenery in view, and the Capitol dome—illuminated by night—rising to the north. There are fairly large rooms, a heated outdoor pool (seasonal), a year-round Jacuzzi, and occasionally music in the lounge. Some rooms can be noisy, so it's advisable to request one on the water side. ■ *2300 Evergreen Park Dr (exit 104 from I-5), Olympia, WA 98802; (360) 943-4000 or (800) 551-8500; $$; AE, DC, MC, V; no checks.* &

TENINO

Wolf Haven, 3111 Offut Lake Road, (360) 264-4695, is an educational research facility that teaches wolf appreciation and studies the question of whether to reintroduce wolves into the wild. The public is invited to see the wolves or join them in a howl-in.

RESTAURANTS

Alice's Restaurant ★ Located in a fine turn-of-the-century farmhouse on a lively little creek, Alice's serves hearty dinners, all including cream of peanut soup, a Waldorf salad, trout, an entree (baked ham with pineapple glaze, fresh oysters, a selection of game dishes, perhaps quail, and even catfish), and choice of dessert. In conjunction with the restaurant, Vincent de Bellis operates the Johnson Creek Winery, whose wines make up the wine list offering. Advance reservations are required. ■ *19248 Johnson Creek Rd SE (call for directions), Tenino; (360) 264-2887; $$; beer and wine; AE, DC, MC, V; checks OK; dinner Wed–Sun.* &

YELM

RESTAURANTS

Arnold's Country Inn ★ Long known as one of Olympia's most accomplished chefs, Arnold Ball established his latest restaurant just outside Yelm on the road to Mount Rainier. Steaks and meat dishes dominate here. But besides steak Diane, there are

familiar Arnold's specialties such as chicken sautéed with raspberry brandy, roast duckling à l'orange, and traditional escargots. Arnold is careful with small details: his rolls baked on the
premises are warm and delicious, as are his fine pies. His wine
list is adequate, but many patrons are happy to drive all the way
from Olympia just for the food. ■ *717 Yelm Ave E (across
from Thriftway Shopping Center), Yelm; (360) 458-3977; $$; full
bar; AE, MC, V; local checks only; breakfast, lunch, dinner
Tues–Sun.* ⑤

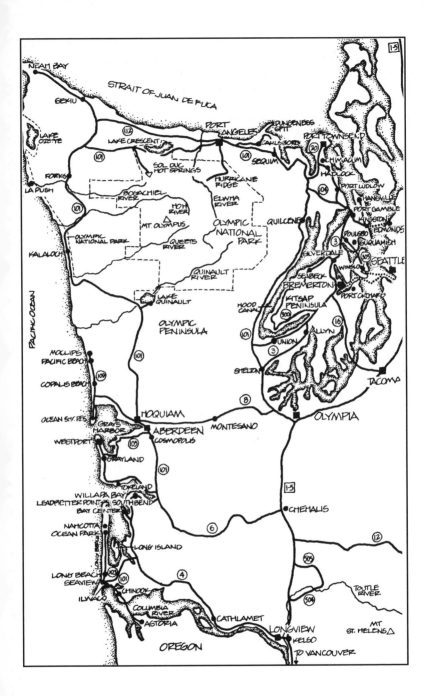

Olympic Peninsula

The Kitsap Peninsula north to Hansville and Foulweather Bluff, angling west across Hood Canal to Port Townsend, continuing westward along the Strait of Juan de Fuca shore to Cape Flattery, then southward along the Pacific coast to Ocean Shores. The southern boundary angles eastward to Shelton and northeast to Kitsap County.

PORT ORCHARD

The center of this small town hugs the southern shoreline of one of Puget Sound's many fingers of water—Sinclair Inlet. With its boardwalk and beach access, the waterfront area is a true gathering place. On Saturdays, from the end of April through October, the **Port Orchard Farmers Market** (Marina Park, one block from Bay Street) offers a tantalizing selection of cut flowers, fresh vegetables, baked goods, and crafts. Take home some Hood Canal oysters or ask the oyster lady to cook a few on her grill. There are numerous antique shops, and **Sidney Art Gallery and Museum** displays Northwest art on the first floor of the Masonic Lodge Building; (360)876-3693.

Horluck Transportation, a privately owned foot ferry that runs every half hour, seven days a week, provides an economical means of travel between the main ferry terminal at Bremerton and downtown Port Orchard; (360)876-2300.

LODGINGS

Reflections Bed and Breakfast Inn ★★ Every cliché that's used to describe an excellent Northwest bed and breakfast applies to this sprawling B&B set on a hillside overlooking Sinclair Inlet, with the Olympic Mountains as backdrop. Former New Englanders Jim and Cathy Hall extend warm hospitality to their guests—complete with a hearty breakfast of regional dishes that everyone plans the night before. The Halls furnish the four guest rooms with family antiques, including heirloom quilts. The largest room has a private porch and Jacuzzi tub. The well-tended grounds include a hot tub, a gazebo, and always a multitude of birds eating and preening at various feeders. ■ *3878 Reflections Lane E (east of Port Orchard off Beach Dr), Port Orchard, WA 98366; (360)871-5582; jimreflect@hurricane.net; www.cimarron.net/reflections; $$; MC, V; checks OK.*

BREMERTON

Bremerton and its naval station have been entwined since the early 1890s, when a young German, one William Bremer, sold close to 200 acres of bay front to the U.S. Navy for $9,587. Today, the navy shipyards are still right downtown, and rows of moth-gray ghost ships—all silent reminders of past naval battles—loom offshore. Only the destroyer USS *Turner Joy*, which saw action off Vietnam, is open for self-guided tours, Thursday through Monday. Adjacent to both the ferry terminal and the *Turner Joy*, the **Bremerton Naval Museum** depicts the region's shipbuilding history back to bowsprit-and-sail days; (360)479-7447; open daily in summer, closed Mondays Labor Day through Memorial Day.

Farther north on Kitsap Peninsula is the **Trident Nuclear Submarine Base** at Bangor. Occasionally a pod of orcas can be glimpsed escorting one of the mammoth submarines through the local waters to deep-sea duty. Since 1915, Keyport has been the major U.S. site for undersea torpedo testing. Now it also is home to an extraordinary **Naval Underseas Museum**, housing the first Revolutionary War submarine. Open daily (closed Tuesdays November through April); (360)396-4148.

Washington State Ferries provide transportation to the Kitsap Peninsula and highway access to the Olympic Peninsula. They run regularly between downtown Seattle and Bremerton, and between Fauntleroy in West Seattle and Southworth near Port Orchard; (206)464-6400 or (800)84-FERRY.

RESTAURANTS

Boat Shed ★ This casual seafood restaurant overhanging the Port Washington Narrows is aptly named. Rough wood panels the walls inside and out, and a solitary fish tank serves as decor. Scaups and scoters run and patter along the water while boats of every size pass by. Whenever possible, hit the deck and enjoy a pint of ale, a gigantic serving of tangled Cajun onion strings, and a cup of rich clam chowder, or the knockwurst piled with red onions and cheese on sourdough. A sesame seed-coated piece of tuna is topped with a pat of wasabe butter; lime enlivens the Dungeness crab cakes. Even most of the pasta dishes showcase the bounty of the local waters. ■ *101 Shore Dr (east side of Manette Bridge, on the water), Bremerton; (360)377-2600; $; full bar; MC, V; local checks only; lunch, dinner every day, brunch Sun.* &

SEABECK

LODGINGS

Willcox House ★★★ Colonel Julian Willcox and his wife, Constance, once played host to such famous guests as Clark Gable at this copper-roofed, art deco, 10,000-square-foot manse on the east side of the Hood Canal. Oak parquet floors, walnut-paneled walls, and a copper-framed marble fireplace—one of five throughout the house—grace the front rooms. Downstairs is a bar, a game room, and a clubby library, where you can look out over the canal, the impressive gardens, and a saltwater lap pool. Comb the beach for oysters, fish from the dock, or hike the hillside trails. A hearty breakfast is served, and lunch is offered to multinight guests, as is a prix-fixe dinner (open to nonguests on weekends by reservation). On Friday nights in summer there's a salmon barbecue served on the dusky terrace. It's about a half-hour drive from the Bremerton ferry, though some guests opt to arrive by boat or floatplane. ■ *2390 Tekiu Rd (9 miles south of Seabeck, call or write for directions), Seabeck, WA 98380; (360) 830-4492 or (800) 725-2600; $$$; DIS, MC, V; checks OK.* &

SILVERDALE

RESTAURANTS

Bahn Thai ★★ Equally as good as (and arguably even better than) the highly esteemed Seattle Bahn Thai (which his wife and brother still run) is Benchai (Benny) Sunti's newer version—which has the same name, the same personal service, and a similar menu, but a much different look. This is a place to come with a group of hungry eaters to share a wide variety of the brightly flavored dishes of Thailand. *Tod mun*—spicy, crisp patties of minced fish, green beans, and lime leaves—is served with a contrasting fresh cucumber relish, making an excellent starter before *tom yum goong*, a favorite Thai soup of prawns and lemongrass. Try one of six different exotic curries, including mussamun—beef and potatoes sauced with a mildly hot curry infused with coconut milk and cloves, nutmeg, and cinnamon: not your everyday plate of meat and potatoes. ■ *98811 Mickelberry Rd (½ block north of Bucklin Hill Rd), Silverdale; (360) 698-3663; $; full bar; AE, MC, V; local checks only; lunch, dinner every day.* &

Hakata ★ For those searching for sushi with a difference, chef Yoshiyuki Sugimoto offers some intriguing selections in his own immaculate restaurant in an out-of-the-way shopping plaza. Tobiko (flying fish roe) and wasabe (pungent Japanese horseradish) explode with flavor when you bite through a hand roll. A tangy leaf of shiso adds a subtle surprise to a delicate nigiri sushi of flounder, and the spider roll—made with crunchy softshell crab—is a house favorite. In a class by itself is the fat, fancy futomaki roll with its pinwheel of contrasting ingredients. For lunch, try one of the popular meal-in-one dishes like donburi (big bowls of rice heaped with such delights as shrimp and vegetable tempura). ■ *10876 Myhre Pl #108 (take Kitsap Mall exit off Hwy 3, behind the post office in Pacific Linen Plaza), Silverdale; (360) 698-0929; $; beer and wine; MC, V; local checks only; lunch Tues–Sat, dinner Tues–Sun.* &

Yacht Club Broiler ★ This is a simple restaurant with some elegant touches and a water view: copper-covered tables, walls lined with delicate rice-paper fish prints, and bare wood floors softened by Oriental-style rugs. As you might expect from its name and its location (on Dyes Inlet), seafood is a major menu item here. What is unexpected is the excellent quality of that seafood (as the commercial fishermen who eat here will attest), be it the sweet, moist Dungeness crab cakes or a bucket of plump steamed clams. ■ *9226 Bayshore Dr (from Hwy 305, take Silverdale exit, first right into town, then left on Bayshore), Silverdale; (360) 698-1601; $$; full bar; AE, DC, MC, V; checks OK; lunch, dinner every day, brunch Sun.* &

LODGINGS

Silverdale on the Bay ★ This tastefully designed resort hotel serves equally well as a conference site or a getaway destination, although the encroaching shopping malls are a distraction. Many rooms have balconies with views over Dyes Inlet; minisuites are the best. Extras establish it as the resort it aspires to be, with an indoor lap pool, large brick sun deck, sauna, weight room, video game room, and dock. The Mariner Restaurant offers white-linened tables, professional service, and nicely prepared meals that aren't too pricey. Enjoy breakfast par excellence, with boardinghouse-style biscuits and gravy or Belgian waffles piled with strawberries and cream. ■ *3073 Bucklin Hill Rd (turn east at the intersection of Silverdale Way and Bucklin Hill Rd), Silverdale, WA 98383; (360) 698-1000 or (800) 544-9799; $$; full bar; AE, DC, MC, V; checks OK; breakfast, lunch, dinner every day.*

POULSBO

Poulsbo was once a community of fishermen and loggers, primarily Scandinavian. Today, it's full of gift shops and its snug harbor is full of yachts. The Scandinavian heritage, however, is still going strong—Front Street sports its *"Velkommen til Poulsbo"* signs, and the architecture is a dolled-up version of the fjord villages of Norway. Once you've seen the town, be sure to stroll the boardwalk along Liberty Bay. **Olympic Outdoor Center** rents canoes and kayaks for those who yearn to get out on the water; (360) 697-6095.

The **Poulsbo Country Deli**, (360) 779-2763, makes good sandwiches, soups, quiche, and desserts (the park along the waterfront is a perfect spot for a picnic). Or select something from the overwhelming choices at the famed **Sluy's Bakery** (18924 Front Street NE, (360) 779-2798). Too crowded? Walk south one block to **Liberty Bay Bakery** (18996 Front Street NE, (360) 779-2828), with tables and coffee and, some think, superior treats. Finally, **Boehm's Chocolates** has an outpost here (18864 Front

Street, (360)697-3318); it's worth walking into its quiet, dark interior just for the wonderful smell.

RESTAURANTS

Molly Ward's Gardens ★★ Sam and Lynn Ward's homespun establishment (which doubles as a dried-flower shop, with the latest pickings hanging above you) shines best when the sun does—when the open French doors welcome the garden scents, when the chefs can forage in the organic garden, and when you and your friends have time to savor the entire experience, maybe even wander through the garden between courses. Lunch might take up the entire afternoon (hold out for a sunny day and reserve one of the four garden tables). Dinners are a bit more elaborate, maybe a Copper River salmon with balsamic vinegar or pork tenderloin with rhubarb chutney. Whatever it is (decided at the whim of Sam Ward), it is accompanied by delicate garden soup or salad. ■ *27462 Big Valley Rd (just past Manor Farm Inn), Poulsbo; (360)779-4471; $$; beer and wine; MC, V; checks OK; lunch, dinner Tues–Sun.*

Cafe Internationalé ★ African music may be bopping at lunch, classical French at dinner—music and food, it all depends on the mood of either chef, and their inspirations might come from any corner of the world. There really isn't a menu; the only entree choices (usually about four) are on the board when you walk in. Make your decision then—or let your waitress decide. She knows what's best of the lot on each particular day. The decor is somewhat miscellaneous: Victorian gilt-framed paintings and mirrors, iron garden-style chairs, and a terra-cotta tile floor. The deck overlooking Liberty Bay is great when the weather is. ■ *9043 Front St (south end of town on the main street), Poulsbo; (360)779-2262; $$; beer and wine; MC, V; checks OK; lunch, dinner Tues–Sun.* ⅃

LODGINGS

Manor Farm Inn ★★ A lavish retreat in the middle of nowhere, Manor Farm is a small gentleman's farm with horses, pigs, sheep, cows, chickens, and a trout pond—a beguiling mix of the raw and the cultivated that succeeds in spoiling even the city-bred. Jill Hughes, a Los Angeles native, is the proprietor, who runs a superlative accommodation. There are seven bright guest rooms (two have fireplaces) and a hot tub. Breakfast happens twice at Manor Farm: first a tray of hot scones and orange juice is left at your door; then at 9am (for nonguests as well), there are fresh fruit, porridge folded with whipped cream, eggs from the farm chickens, and rashers of bacon. Three-course dinners ($29.95) are served on Friday and Saturday nights only (you'll be asked to choose your entree upon reservation). Reservations are necessary; no kids (under 16) are allowed at the inn or restaurant. ■ *26069 Big Valley Rd NE (off Hwy 305, ½ hour*

▼

Poulsbo

Lodgings

▲

from Winslow ferry dock), Poulsbo, WA 98370; (360) 779-4628; $$$; MC, V; checks OK; breakfast every day (May–Oct), dinner Fri–Sat.

SUQUAMISH

In Suquamish on the Port Madison Indian Reservation (follow the signs past Agate Pass), the **Suquamish Museum** in the Tribal Center is devoted to studying and displaying Puget Sound Salish Indian culture; (360) 598-3311. **Chief Sealth's grave** can be found nearby, on the grounds of St. Peter's Catholic Mission Church. Twin dugout canoes rest on a log frame over the stone, which reads, "The firm friend of the whites, and for him the city of Seattle was named."

KINGSTON

RESTAURANTS

Kingston Hotel Cafe ★★ If every town had a spot like this, the world would be a better place. Judith Weinstock (formerly of Bainbridge Island's famed Streamliner Diner) adopted this two-story, Western-front building overlooking the Sound and turned it into one of the most inviting eateries (with some of the most enticing food) on the peninsula. In winter, cozy up to the wood stove and a bowl of rich and unusual Roasted Apple-Ginger Bisque; seafood is a good choice year-round, with offerings like Indian Halibut Cakes topped with fresh mango chutney or a braid of salmon and halibut served with a savory Brandied Wild Blackberry Sauce. Baked goods are always warm and fresh. When the mood's right, there may be some local live music. It's so much more than a cafe—it's a meeting place. Bring the kids and let them play in the garden while you sit on the deck and enjoy another latte with your breakfast. Upstairs you'll find David Weinstock's custom jewelry studio. ■ *25931 Washington Blvd (at 1st Ave, 1 block north of the ferry terminal), Kingston; (360) 297-8100; $; beer and wine; MC, V; checks OK; breakfast, lunch, dinner (seasonal hours, call ahead).*

PORT GAMBLE

Built in the mid-19th century by the Pope & Talbot timber people, who traveled here by clipper ship from Maine, this is the essence of the company town. Everything is still company-owned and company-maintained—though the company is now Olympic Resource Management, not Pope & Talbot—and the dozen or so Victorian houses are beauties and in splendid repair. The town, which was modeled on a New England village, also boasts a lovely church and a vital and well-stocked company store. The historical museum, (360) 297-8074, is a gem, too, with an ideal presentation of a community's society and industrial heritage, designed by Alec James, a designer for the displays for the Royal Provincial Museum in Victoria. The lumber mill is no longer in operation.

HANSVILLE

Just beyond the unassuming fishing town of Hansville are a couple of the prettiest, most accessible, and least explored beaches on the peninsula. To the east is **Point No Point**, marked by a lighthouse and great for families with kids. Follow the road from Hansville to the west and you'll come across **Cape Foulweather**. The short trail through the woods is tough to find, so look for a The Nature Conservancy sign on the south side of the road.

SHELTON AND HOOD CANAL

The logging community of Shelton sells thousands upon thousands of Christmas trees nationwide each year. In the nearby bays and inlets, the oyster and clam populations are making a comeback, and vacation homes line the miles of scenic shoreline. Traveling on Highway 101, which hugs the west side of Hood Canal through tiny towns with names like Duckabush, Lilliwaup, Dosewallips, and Hamma Hamma, you should stop at any roadside stand or store for fresh crab and oysters. Sample **Hoodsport Winery**'s selection at their cottage tasting room (N 23501 Highway 101, (360)877-9894).

This stretch of highway serves as the jumping-off spot for many recreational areas in the **Olympic National Forest**, including Lake Cushman and its state park. Numerous hiking trails lead to remote, cloud-draped alpine lakes and meadows. Every summer weekend, concerts are given by the internationally acclaimed Seattle-based Philadelphia String Quartet and world-class guest artists at the **Olympic Music Festival**, where music lovers sit on hay bales in an 80-year-old Dutch colonial barn or stretch out on the gentle hillside while listening to chamber music. (Directions: 11 miles west of the Hood Canal Bridge on Highway 104, then a quarter mile south from the Quilcene exit; (360)732-4000.)

RESTAURANTS

Xinh's Clam & Oyster House ★★ Chef Xinh Dwelley knows how to choose fresh bivalves. She's been the quality control manager (and done her fair share of shucking) at Taylor United Inc. (a Shelton shellfish company) for almost two decades. And it was there that she won the attention of many people-in-the-right-places when she began cooking elaborate lunches for visiting shellfish buyers. Today, Xinh (with the financial backing of Taylor United) runs not only Shelton's finest seafood restaurant (with an Asian twist) but one of the best (and freshest) little clam and oyster houses on the peninsula. Xinh herself picks out the best of each day's haul. Slide down a few Olympias or

Steamboat Island Pacifics on the half shell and then see what Xinh can do with a sauce. You'll not find a better heaping plate of mussel meats in a Vietnamese curry sauce around. ■ *221 W Railroad Ave, Suite D (at 3rd St), Shelton; (360)427-8709; www.taylorunited.com/xinhs; $$; beer and wine; MC, V; checks OK; dinner Tues–Sat.* &

UNION

RESTAURANTS

Victoria's ★★ There is a stone-and-log structure on the east bank of Hood Canal that has been a stopover spot since the early 1930s. Locals remember it as a lively dance hall and tavern, but in the last decade it has evolved into one of the better eateries on the Canal. High beamed ceilings, a fireplace, and large windows that look out upon a nearby brook and sheltering trees set the scene for equally appealing food. The seafood can be exceptional, and the ample portions of prime rib make for good eating. Desserts are imaginative—and rich. ■ *E 6791 Hwy 106 (1 mile west of Alderbrook Inn), Union; (360)898-4400; $$; full bar; MC, V; checks OK; breakfast Sun, lunch, dinner every day (seasonal hours in winter).* &

BRINNON

RESTAURANTS

Half-Way House Restaurant ★ Brinnon is a town you can miss if you blink, but keep your eyes open for the Half-Way House, especially on Tuesday around dinnertime. That's the night that chef Joseph Day puts on a gourmet five-course champagne dinner. The tiny cinder-block cafe is packed with loggers and others in the know who come for his escargots in mushroom caps and lobster with wild rice (lobster is served every third Tuesday). The meal ends, properly, with a cheese plate and sinfully rich desserts. If you can't get a table on Tuesday, the food is still good the rest of the week, especially the homemade soups and pies. Reservations are required on Tuesday nights only. ■ *Hwy 101 and Brinnon Lane (on the west side of Hwy 101, next to post office), Brinnon; (360)796-4715; $ ($$ on Tues); full bar; AE, MC, V; local checks only; breakfast, lunch, dinner every day.* &

QUILCENE

RESTAURANTS

Timber House Surrounded by cedar and hemlock, the Timber House resembles nothing so much as a hunting lodge gussied up to make it comfortable for the womenfolk. Descriptive logging scenes are painted on the hand-carved tables and counter ledges: a nice touch. The local seafood is the main reason to eat here. Quilcene oysters come from right down the road, and there's much more from the waters around the Sound. Dungeness crab is a winner: sautéed, as a sandwich filling, in an omelet or in a salad. Locals swear by the roast beef dinners. ■ *Hwy 101 S (about ½ mile south of Quilcene), Quilcene; (360) 765-3339; $$; full bar; MC, V; checks OK; lunch, dinner Wed–Mon.* &

PORT LUDLOW

LODGINGS

Inn at Ludlow Bay ★★ The Inn (a sister establishment of Pam and Paul Schell's Inn at Langley and Friday Harbor House) guards the entry to Hood Canal. It exudes the atmosphere of a New England estate all crammed onto one small point of land (near the harbor to the Port Ludlow Resort), but inside is a gorgeous, peaceful retreat with 37 big, well-appointed rooms—with fireplaces, great views, and deep tubs. You can play chess in the common room, or hold your own private wine-tasting in front of a blazing fire. The Inn's restaurant is a pretty room, but the food is all dressed up with nowhere to go—just like lumber company Pope & Talbot's planned development that surrounds the bay. ■ *1 Heron Rd (6 miles north of Hood Canal Bridge, on west side), Port Ludlow, WA 98365; (360) 437-0411; $$$; AE, DC, DIS, MC, V; checks OK.* &

Nantucket Manor ★★ This place is a gleaming white eye-catcher, complete with clipped lawn, carefully tended flower gardens, and a mountainous view. A balcony over the terrace gives water-facing rooms upstairs their own private sunning and relaxing spot. Seals, otters, and eagles disport themselves in or over the bay. Owners Peggy and Peter Conrardy's tidelands are there for guests to harvest clams; or you can have a beach picnic or an evening bonfire. The five guest rooms are comfortable and spacious; the four-poster beds are loaded with pretty pillows. Hot tub and breakfasts are both very special. ■ *941 Shine Rd (left on Shine Rd just west of Hood Canal Bridge), Port Ludlow, WA 98265; (360) 437-2676; www.olympus.net/ biz/nantucket/; $$; AE, DC, MC, V; checks OK.*

Port Ludlow Resort and Conference Center ★ Pope & Talbot's legendary 1880s sawmill manager's "biggest damn cabin on the Sound" (actually a splendid Victorian home) once shared this site—overlooking the teardrop bay—with the busy Port Ludlow mill. It is now a popular resort facility, catering especially to groups, with a marina, tennis courts, 27-hole championship golf course, hiking and cycling trails, and year-round swimming pool on 1,500 developed acres. The individually decorated suites—all privately owned as second homes by out-of-town families—are very livable, with fireplaces, kitchens, and private decks, many with views of the harbor. But stay away from the standard rooms, which resemble a budget motel, complete with paper-thin walls and noisy heaters. The Harbormaster Restaurant has a pleasant bar and a delightful deck. ■ *200 Olympic Pl (6 miles north of Hood Canal Bridge on west side), Port Ludlow, WA 98365; (360) 437-2222 or (800) 732-1239; $$$; AE, MC, V; checks OK.*

PORT HADLOCK

The false-front, Old West–style buildings in Port Hadlock have been painted with the same hot pinks, blues, and purples that some supermarkets use to ice cakes—a new take on "local color." South of Hadlock on Highway 19, the **Chimacum Cafe**, (360) 732-4631, serves a great piece of homemade pie. North of Hadlock, at the Shold Business Park off Highway 19, buy a bag of superb fresh bagels (baked daily) and toppings to go at **Bagel Haven Bakery & Cafe**, 227 W Patison, (360) 385-6788.

RESTAURANTS

Ajax Cafe ★ When we first found this place 20 years ago on the abandoned Hadlock waterfront, a disheveled row of cabins was for rent next door, a ramshackle building and pier were for sale, and the *Comet*, a huge wooden fishing vessel, was sinking in the bay. The Ajax Cafe, in a forgotten hardware storefront, was funky and riotous fun. In those days, even the local magistrate ordered the red wine that was listed as "special coffee" on the menu (because the cafe had no liquor license). Not much has changed, except the Ajax, which has been cleaned up without losing its character (and now has a liquor license). The new owners, from Maine, serve up big plates of seafood with fresh vegetables. The signature dish is a flavorful fishermen's stew: poached fish swimming in leek and saffron broth and served with garlic aioli. There's live music (jazz, blues, folk) most nights. ■ *271 Water St (in lower Hadlock on the waterfront, off Oak Bay Rd), Port Hadlock; (360) 385-3450; $$; beer and wine; MC, V; local checks only; dinner Tues–Sun.*

MARROWSTONE ISLAND

Marrowstone Island faces Port Townsend across the bay. To get there from Port Ludlow or Hadlock, watch for signs directing you to Indian Island, Fort Flagler State Park, and Marrowstone from Oak Bay Road. **Fort Flagler State Park**, an old coastal fortification, has acres of trails, grassy fields, and miles of beaches to walk on, with RV and tent camping. A large group of seals hangs out at the end of a sand spit and often surround kayakers paddling by, as do nesting gulls. Marrowstone's enterprise long ago was turkey farming; today several locals farm oysters and harvest clams. At the historic (oiled floors, covered porch) **Nordland General Store**, you can pick up a bag of oysters—great picnic stuff—and, summers, even rent a small boat to paddle on Mystery Bay. In winter, locals gather around the wood stove in the back of the store with their espresso.

LODGINGS

The Ecologic Place A great spot for families who'd rather spend more time out than in, this is your basic gathering of rustic cabins in a natural setting. And what a setting. The Ecologic Place borders on a tidal estuary that flows into Oak Bay and then Puget Sound, and offers a view of the Olympics and Mount Rainier, conditions permitting. The cabins, each with its own character, have never been acquainted with an interior decorator, but have everything you need to enjoy the simple beauty of the place—wood stoves, equipped kitchens, comfortable mattresses on the queen-size beds, and fine-for-the-children bunks and twin beds. Bring bikes, boats, books, bathing suits, binoculars, children, and groceries too. ■ *10 Beach Dr (turn right at "Welcome to Marrowstone" sign), Nordland, WA 98358; (360)385-3077; www.seattle2000.com/seattle2000; $$; MC, V; checks OK.*

▼

PORT TOWNSEND

During the early days of the clipper ships, Port Townsend was the official point of entry to Puget Sound. Vessels from around the globe landed, and the foreign consuls added a cosmopolitan flavor to the social life of the wealthy folk who settled here. This early prosperity gave rise to the construction of more than 200 Victorian homes, reflecting the reign of Queen You-know-who. When the mineral deposits petered out, the railroad never came, and the elite investors left, Port Townsend became a land of vanished dreams and vacant mansions. The restored buildings, now forming a National Historical Landmark District, and the wraparound views lie at the heart of the town's charm.

Chetzemoka Park, a memorial to the S'Klallam Indian chief who became a friend of the first white settlers, in the northeast corner of town, has a charming gazebo, picnic tables, tall Douglas firs, and a grassy slope down to the beach. **Fort Worden**, along with sister forts on Marrowstone and Whidbey Islands, was part of the defense system established to protect Puget Sound a century ago. The 433-acre complex overlooking Admiralty Inlet now incorporates turn-of-the-century officers' quarters, campgrounds, gardens, a theater, and a concert hall (see Fort Worden lodging review). A huge central field, formerly the parade ground, is perfect for games or kite flying. The setting may look familiar to those who saw the movie *An Officer and a Gentleman*, most of which was filmed here. At the water's edge, an enormous pier juts into the bay—it's the summer home to the **Marine Science Center**, (360)385-5582, with touch tanks, displays of sea creatures, and cruises to nearby Protection Island, the largest seabird rookery in the region. There's a safe, protected swimming beach on one side of the pier, and access to miles of beaches. Above on the hillside you can spend hours exploring the deserted concrete bunkers.

Fort Worden is also home to **Centrum**, a sponsor of concerts, workshops, and festivals throughout the year. Many of these take place in the old balloon hangar, reborn as McCurdy Pavilion. The **Centrum Summer Arts Festival**, one of the most successful cultural programs in the state—with dance, fiddle tunes, chamber music, a writers conference, jazz, blues, and theater performances— runs from June to September; (360)385-3102.

A historic-homes tour happens the first weekend in May and again the third weekend in September. The **Rhododendron Festival** in May, with a parade and crowning of the queen, is the oldest festival in town. The Wooden Boat Foundation, (360)385-3628, presents the **Wooden Boat Festival,** (360)385-4742 (festival line), at Point Hudson Marina on the weekend after Labor Day: a celebration of traditional crafts and a showcase for everything from prams to kayaks to yachts to tugboats.

▼

**Port
Townsend**

▲

The Jefferson County Historical Society has a fascinating museum at 210 Madison Street, (360)385-1003, in the original city hall, with old jail cells. Colorful shops line Water Street: **Northwest Native Expressions** (637 Water Street, (360)385-4770), owned by the Jamestown S'Klallam tribe, has a wide selection of Puget Sound, British Columbia, and Southeast Alaska prints, jewelry, and related books. **Melville and Co.** (914 Water Street, (360)385-7127) offers an extensive selection of English mysteries, old comics, and rare books. **William James Bookseller** (829 Water Street, (360)835-7313) has a vast and well-organized inventory of used books. **Earthen Works** (702 Water Street, (360)385-0328) specializes in high-quality Washington craft items. The best ice cream cones can be had at **Elevated Ice Cream** (627 Water Street, (360)385-1156); the best antique selection is at **Port Townsend Antique Mall** (802 Washington Street, (360)385-2590), where about 40 antique merchants have convened under one roof. You'll find the best pastries at **Bread and Roses Bakery** (230 Quincy Street, (360)385-1044), while great picnic food can be found at **Twyla's Take Out** (1933 Sims Way, (360)385-8646), a bright yellow house just on the south end of town. At **Riley's General Store** (1020 Water Street, (360)385-3961) you can buy incredible chocolates. For wines, try **The Wine Seller** (940 Water Street, (360)385-7673), a place to pick up a few gourmet snacks for a picnic. For live music and local color, check out the historic **Town Tavern** (Water and Quincy Streets), where the enormous historical back bar, pool tables, and the owner's great taste in music draw an interesting assortment of people. **Sirens**

(823 Water Street, (360)379-0776), hidden way up three flights of stairs in the historic Bartlett Building, is a delightful place to enjoy a glass of wine, have a snack, and listen to music from the Bay View deck. Don't overlook the revitalization of uptown, especially **Aldrich's** (Lawrence and Tyler Streets, (360)395-0500), an authentic 1890s general store with an upscale twist; upstairs is the **Abundant Life Seed Foundation,** a clearinghouse for collectors of heirloom and vegetable seeds; (360)385-5660.

Washington State Ferries make daily trips to Whidbey Island; (206)464-6400 or (800)84-FERRY. The Puget Sound Express (431 Water Street, (360)385-5288) runs a daily ferry summers to Friday Harbor on San Juan Island.

RESTAURANTS

Lonny's Restaurant ★★★ The film *Big Night* comes to mind, not because of the decor (warmly tinted walls, arches, and 17th-century botanical prints), but because of the partnership of Lonny Ritter, who has opened some of the Olympic Peninsula's best restaurants, and Tim Roth, most recently of Seattle's highly regarded Al Boccalino. Both are demonstrative guys who could easily play the part of the fictitious brothers. In fact, when *Big Night* opened at the Rose Theater, the two chefs replicated its outrageous dinner, complete with suckling pig (tickets sold out in 12 minutes). The film's signature dish, timpano, a huge creation with layers of meats and cooked eggs wrapped in a rich crust and slowly baked, is frequently served as a special appetizer. If you're used to a low-fat, salt-free diet, forget about it for one night and try the oyster stew, made with sweet cream, fennel, and diced pancetta; or the Dungeness crab and mushrooms bathed in cream and imported Italian Gorgonzola. Waitstaff work the room nicely, filling it with self-confident chatter, as do the patrons who make the trip from Seattle just to eat here. ■ *2330 Washington St (adjacent to Port Townsend harbor), Port Townsend; (360)385-0700; $$; beer and wine; MC, V, checks OK; dinner only Wed–Mon.* &

Belmont ★★ In a town where good seafood is almost ho-hum, the Belmont is a special treasure. And in a town where sweeping water views are as common as seagulls, the Belmont stands out. The ideal place to be seated in this three-level restaurant is up the stairs to the back or out on the deck overlooking the bay. And the ideal dish to order is an exquisite fillet of Northwest salmon, broiled exactly right. Taking further advantage of the availability of impeccably fresh seafood, chef Bill Severin now offers an appetizer of sushi. Excellent lunch salads include a very large and distinctively Asian-influenced chicken salad. Ask about staying in one of the renovated Victorian-era hotel rooms (two overlook the water). ■ *925 Water St (center of town, waterside), Port Townsend, WA 98368; (360)385-3007; $$; full bar; AE, DC, MC, V; local checks only; lunch, dinner every day.*

Lanza's ★★ Lori, the youngest Lanza sister (of five siblings), and her husband, Steve, have reclaimed the family's pizzeria. The restaurant was out of family hands (it's been passed from sibling to sibling) for only a few years—and now the menu is back to its old best. Family recipes include homemade sausage, gnocchi, and big calzones stuffed with smoked salmon, fat prawns, and pesto. As always, organically grown local herbs and vegetables are used. Pizza can be ordered to go. There's live music on Friday and Saturday nights. ■ *1020 Lawrence (in upper town, above bluffs), Port Townsend; (360)379-1900; $$; beer and wine; MC, V; checks OK; dinner Mon–Sat.*

Blackberries ★ Of its two locations in Port Townsend, we favor the one attached to the conference center dining hall in Fort Worden State Park (open only from May to October). It's as fresh as a sun porch with Adirondack-style touches—artist Martha Worthley's lovely stenciled walls and curtains (crows and blackberry vines) and pieced wooden frames around historic photographs. The restaurant downtown on Water Street is a fussy pink and green to match the adjacent Palace Hotel (a former brothel) and is open year-round for lunch, dinner, and Sunday brunch. Blackberries has had one of the more creative menus in town, favoring fruity sauces over fish and meats: red grape and champagne over scallops, red currants over chicken, roasted garlic and pear/mint relish with lamb. A halibut-salmon braid with salal beurre rouge is both beautiful and delicious and, we hope, a keeper when the new chef revises the menu. ■ *200 Battery Way, Building 210 (Fort Worden State Park Conference Center, 1 mile north of downtown), Port Townsend; (360)385-9950; $$; beer and wine; MC,V; checks OK; lunch, dinner Wed–Sun.* ■ *1002 Water St (adjacent to the Victorian Palace Hotel), Port Townsend; (360)379-1200; $$; beer and wine; MC, V; checks OK; lunch, dinner days vary (call ahead for hours); brunch Sun.*

Coho Cafe ★ It's a favorite place to wake up, and no wonder: the coffee is strong and refills are free, sun streams through the old storefront windows, walls are warmly painted deep orange with a dark purple ceiling, and tables are playfully set with mismatched silverware, bandanna napkins, and fresh flowers. Healthy breakfasts are served all day: homemade seafood sausage, or chunks of smoked salmon, spuds, and red onions in the salmon hash. French toast is soaked in a hazelnut egg custard and served with yogurt and bananas. Toss it down with freshly squeezed juice combos or smoothies with a dose of spirulina, bee pollen, ginseng, ginger, or wheat grass, and blast into the day. There are lunches too, with miso-based soups and lots of veggies. ■ *1044 Lawrence St (across from Uptown Theater), Port Townsend; (360)379-1030; $; no alcohol; no credit cards; checks OK; breakfast, lunch Wed–Sun.*

Fountain Cafe ★ Some grouchy locals complain about the service, the sauces, and even the paint, but they still bring their out-of-town guests here. And they come in droves, crowding the door of this tiny storefront dining room to inspect the art on the spring-green walls while waiting for a table. New owners wisely didn't change the old favorites on the menu, including the vegetarian pasta with artichokes, olives, and feta that's been in place for at least 10 years. The dinner salad is an impressive heap of fresh field greens on a platter (a big improvement); the wine list is short but includes some good selections. Save room for the loganberry fool, a wondrous blend of custard, fruit, and whipped cream. ■ *920 Washington St (at foot of Port Townsend fountain steps), Port Townsend; (360)385-1364; $$; beer and wine; MC, V; checks OK; lunch, dinner every day.*

Khu Larb Thai ★ This gracious restaurant with its muted cool greens is a welcome balance to the tingling heat and vibrant flavors that unmistakably identify the food as Thai. One of the best of the aromatic curries is a gently steamed salmon fillet with cabbage and a slightly sweet but still spicy sauce. Delicious chicken wings stuffed with ground pork and shrimp look like fat, crisp lollipops, with a liberal use of pineapple. There's now a sister restaurant in Sequim (see review). ■ *225 Adams St (off Water St), Port Townsend; (360)385-5023; $$; beer and wine; MC, V; local checks only; lunch, dinner every day (closed Wed Oct–May).* &

The Public House ★ The Public House is a large space with soaring ceilings, brought into human scale by clever interior design. It's both comfortable (with antique light fixtures, wood floors, dark green wainscoting, and a nonsmoking bar that's a marvel of the cabinetmaker's art) and casual (a great place for a big spicy bowl of gumbo, a Vermont cheddar burger, or a salmon, black bean, and goat cheese burrito with a light cucumber salsa). Select a beer from the impressive list of drafts and watch the world go by through the big front windows. There's live music at night. ■ *1038 Water St (on north side of street), Port Townsend; (360)385-9708; $; full bar; AE, DIS, MC, V; local checks only; lunch, dinner every day.* &

Salal Cafe ★ Breakfasts are justly famous here, with a couple of morning newspapers circulating and locals trading stories back in the solarium. The omelets are legendary—both in quality and in variety (we like the Greek, with basil, spinach, and feta). Other morning starters, such as cheese blintzes, honey crêpes, or an occasional smoked salmon frittata, are equally satisfying. This light, cheerful spot serves lunch, with a smattering of basic Mexican plates, but breakfast is where the Salal Cafe really shines. ■ *634 Water St (at Quincy), Port Townsend;*

*(360)385-6532; $; beer and wine; MC, V; checks OK; breakfast
all day Sat, breakfast, lunch Wed–Mon, dinner Thurs–Mon.* ♿

Silverwater Cafe ★ Owners David and Alison Hero—he's a carpenter, potter, and baker, while she's a gardener and cook—
have created the restaurant of their dreams on the first floor of
the town's historic Elks Club building. It's a warm, lovely gathering place combining last-century architecture with satisfying
food served on David's handmade plates and a carefully selected wine list. All dinners begin with a basket of fresh rosemary bread. For starters, try the artichoke pâté, fresh sautéed
oysters, or a big spinach salad; lunches include filling salmon
salad sandwiches and hearty homemade soups; local raves for
dinner are the green-peppercorn steaks, the amaretto chicken
in a tart and spicy lemon and curry sauce, and a seafood pasta
loaded with prawns and wild mushrooms and doused with
brandy. If you time things right, you can come back after the
early movie for a piece of David's lemon poppyseed cake and a
cup of chamomile tea. ■ *237 Taylor St (next to Rose Theater),
Port Townsend; (360)385-6448; $$; beer and wine; MC, V; checks
OK; lunch, dinner every day.*

▼

LODGINGS

The James House ★★★ The first bed and breakfast in the
Northwest (1889) is still in great shape, though when a gale
blows off the strait and hits the high bluff, you are glad to be in
one of the three rooms that have a fireplace or a wood-burning
stove. This fine B&B rests in the competent hands of Carol Mc-
Gough, who is still improving it, continually freshening the 12
rooms and the delightful garden. Rooms in the front of the
house have the best views across the water. Not all rooms have
private baths, but the shared facilities are spacious and well
equipped. The main floor offers two comfortable parlors, each
with a fireplace and plenty of reading material. Breakfast is
served either at the big dining room table or in the kitchen with
its antique cookstove. Ask about the bungalow on the bluff. ■
*1238 Washington St (corner of Harrison), Port Townsend, WA
98368; (360)385-1238 or (800)385-1238; www.jameshouse.com;
$$; AE, MC, V; checks OK.*

Ann Starrett Mansion ★★ The most opulent Victorian in Port
Townsend, this multigabled Queen Anne hybrid was built in
1885 by a local contractor who just had to have himself a home
with more of everything than his neighbors' homes. He succeeded. The spiral stairway, octagonal tower, and "scandalous"
ceiling fresco are visually stunning. All rooms are furnished
with antiques and have lovely decorative touches—although
some guests may find the florid color scheme (appropriate to
the rococo decor) a bit unsettling. The Drawing Room (with a
tin claw-footed bathtub) opens to views of the Sound and Mount
Baker, while the newer, romantic Gable Suite, which occupies

the whole third floor, has a skylight (also with a knockout view) and a spacious seating area. Breakfasts are ample. The house is open for public tours from 1pm to 3pm, when any unoccupied bedrooms are cordoned off for viewing (this creates something of a "living museum" atmosphere). ■ *744 Clay St (corner of Adams), Port Townsend, WA 98368; (360)385-3205; $$; AE, MC, V; checks OK.*

Bay Cottage ★★ Susan Atkins has turned a cluster of cottages on the shore of Discovery Bay into a delightful retreat. The cottages have good stoves and refrigerators, a tasteful mix of antique furniture, and comfy mattresses covered with feather beds. There's direct access to a private sandy beach—marvelous for swimming, bonfires, and beachcombing. Susan stocks the kitchens with basic breakfast necessities, and when the mood strikes she has been known to bake cookies for guests. Each cottage has its own picnic basket, binoculars, and library. The rose garden is an enchantment. It's an ideal retreat for romantics or, as some say, a great girl getaway. No pets. ■ *4346 S Discovery Rd (½ mile west of Four Corners Grocery), Port Townsend, WA 98368; (360)385-2035; $$; no credit cards; checks OK.*

Hastings House/Old Consulate Inn ★★ This ornately turreted red Victorian on the hill is one of the most frequently photographed of Port Townsend's "Painted Ladies." It is also one of its most comfortable. A large collection of antique dolls is displayed in the entryway, and new arrivals are often greeted by the aroma of freshly baked cookies, to be nibbled later at afternoon tea. All of the immaculate rooms have closet-size private baths, but guests in the enormous Master Suite can soak in a claw-footed bathtub, later warming themselves in front of their own antique fireplace. The third-floor Tower Suite, with a sweeping bay view and swathed in lace, is the essence of a Victorian-style romantic valentine. There's also a hot tub for guest use. Owners Rob and Joanna Jackson serve a mammoth seven-course breakfast—over which Joanna is more than delighted to wittily recount the inn's history. ■ *313 Walker St (on the bluff, at Washington), Port Townsend, WA 98368; (360)385-6753 or (800)300-6753; www.oldconsulateinn.com; $$$; AE, MC, V; checks OK.*

Quimper Inn ★★ The light from all the windows plays across richly hued walls, suffusing every corner of the house with a mellow glow. A first-floor bedroom resembles a library with a comfortable bed and bath, and upstairs there is a lovely suite with period decor and private bath. The room with bay windows and a brass bed also has its own commodious bath with a 6-foot-long tub, a pedestal sink, and wicker furniture. Sue and Ron Ramage treat their inn and their guests with thoughtful care. Breakfasts are well executed. ■ *1306 Franklin St (corner of Harrison), Port Townsend, WA 98368; (360)385-1060 or*

(800) 557-1060; www.olympus.net/biz/quimper/quimper.html; $$; MC, V; checks OK.

Ravenscroft Inn ★★ A nonconformist among the surrounding Victorians, Ravenscroft Inn was built in 1987, with a design borrowed from historic South Carolina. The structure is large and impressive, with a long front porch, redwood-stained clapboards, and a graceful end chimney. A suite on the third floor sports dormer windows that overlook the town and harbor. Thick, warm carpeting throughout the house deadens sound and creates immediate coziness. The color scheme in every room is unique; each has wicker or antique-reproduction furniture and custom upholstery (and one romantic room on the second floor has its own fireplace). Breakfast is the high point of a stay here, when guests enjoy a gourmet meal from the immense open-style kitchen, often with a piano accompaniment. ■ *533 Quincy St (on the bluff, at Clay), Port Townsend, WA 98368; (360) 385-2784; $$; AE, DC, DIS, MC, V; checks OK.*

Fort Worden ★ Fort Worden was one of three artillery posts built at the turn of the century to guard the entrances of Puget Sound. The troops are long gone, and the massive gun mounts on the bluff have been stripped of their iron, but the beautifully situated fort now is a state park, a conference center, a youth hostel (especially for teenagers biking the Peninsula), the site of the splendid Centrum Arts Festival, and an unusual place to stay. Twenty-four former officers' quarters—nobly proportioned structures dating back to 1904—front the old parade ground. These two-story houses have been made into spacious lodgings, each with a complete kitchen, at bargain rates (great for family reunions, but there are a few smaller homes for couples, too). The most coveted of the one-bedroom lodgings is Bliss Vista, perched on the bluff, with a fireplace and plenty of romantic appeal. The three-story brick turret called Alexander's Castle, built in the 1890s, is lots of fun. RV sites are near the beach and tucked into the woods. Reservations should be made at least a year in advance. ■ *200 Battery Way (1 mile north of downtown, in Fort Worden State Park), Port Townsend, WA 98368; (360) 385-4730; $$; no credit cards; checks OK.*

Heritage House ★ Visitors to this hillcrest Victorian bed and breakfast find a sprightly variety of refinished antiques, complementing guest rooms with names like Lilac and Morning Glory. Five of the seven rooms have private baths; the Peach Blossom has an oak-and-tin claw-footed bathtub that folds away when not in use. Relax in the evenings on the porch swing; in the mornings, perhaps, over a breakfast of decadent French toast. The views over the north Sound and the business district come close to rivaling those of Heritage's venerable neighbor, the James House. Children over eight years are permitted, but pets are not. ■ *305 Pierce St (corner of Washington), Port*

Townsend, WA 98368; (360)385-6800 or (800)385-6867; $$; AE, MC, V; checks OK. &

Lizzie's ★ Lizzie, the wife of a tugboat captain, put the deed of this model of Victorian excess in her own name; her name now also graces a line of bath lotions created by owners Patti and Bill Wickline. Breakfast, served around an old oak table in the cheerful kitchen, can turn into a friendly kaffeeklatsch; a soak in the tub in the black-and-white corner bathroom—especially if the sun is slanting in—is a Victorian treat. There are views from several of the seven bedrooms, all of which have private baths and flowered decor. Lizzie's Room comes with its own fireplace. Two parlors seem to have been plucked from the past; in one you'll even find a vintage stereoscope. ■ *731 Pierce St (near corner of Lincoln), Port Townsend, WA 98368; (360)385-4168 or (800)700-4168; $$; DC, MC, V; checks OK.*

Palace Hotel ★ The 1889 Romanesque-style Palace places visitors in the midst of Port Townsend's shopping and gawking district. The 15 rooms retain the building's ex-bordello atmosphere; Marie's (the venerable madame of the house until the mid-1930s) Room is decorated in original shades of burgundy and forest green. Warning: Long flights of stairs, though handsome reminders of another era, can be a challenge, and nightlife noises from a nearby tavern can make for a restless sleep. Still, it's worth a venture. There's complimentary breakfast, and off-street parking is available. Blackberries restaurant is located off the front lobby. ■ *1004 Water St (corner of Tyler), Port Townsend, WA 98368; (360)385-0773 or (800)962-0741; palace@olympus. net;www.olympus.net/palace; $$; AE, DIS, MC, V; checks OK.*

SEQUIM AND DUNGENESS VALLEY

Sequim (pronounced *skwim*) was once a carefully kept secret. The town sits smack in the middle of the "rain shadow" cast by the Olympic Mountains: the sun shines 306 days a year, and annual rainfall is only 16 inches. Now Sequim's been discovered, especially by the retiree population, and is growing fast. Farms have become subdivisions, and golf courses sprout in what used to be pastures. But there is still lots to do and see nearby.

On Sequim Bay, near Blyn, the S'Klallam Indians operate the unique **Northwest Native Expressions** art gallery (1033 Old Blyn Highway, (360)681-4640). Across the highway stands the **7 Cedars**, a truly mammoth gambling casino with valet parking and good food (270756 Highway 101, (800)4LUCKY7). **Cedarbrook Herb Farm** (open daily March through December 23), Washington's oldest herb farm, has a vast range of plants—including scented geraniums—fresh-cut herbs, and a pleasant gift shop; 1 mile toward the mountains off Highway 101 (1345 Sequim Avenue S, (360)683-7733). **Olympic Game Farm** breeds endangered species and raises a few animals for Hollywood roles. An hour-long guided walking tour is available mid-May through Labor Day, with a driving tour available year-round; 5 miles north of Sequim (1423 Ward Road, (360)683-4295).

Dungeness Spit, 6 miles northwest of Sequim, is a national wildlife refuge for birds (more than 275 species have been sighted) and one of the longest natural sand spits in the world; (360)457-8451. The driftwood is extraordinary, the winds are often good for kite flying, and a long walk down the narrow 5½-mile beach takes you to a remote lighthouse (check a tide table before planning your walk). Two small but notable wineries are in the vicinity: **Lost Mountain Winery** (3174 Lost Mountain Road, (360)683-5229) offers tastings, mainly by arrangement or chance; **Neuharth Winery** (885 S Still Road, (360)683-9652) is open daily for tastings in summer (Wednesday through Sunday in winter).

RESTAURANTS

The Buckhorn Grill ★★ It may be a motel restaurant, but the Buckhorn Grill—which shares 17 wooded acres with the Best Western Sequim Bay Lodge—brings in hungry eaters from Sequim and Port Angeles. Chef Teruo Kinoshita makes sure the food is well presented and served quickly and politely. The menu may not run to the rare and exotic; but it's one of the most consistent on this end of the Peninsula. You can count on such dishes as the braised lamb shank and the Dungeness crab cakes (just minutes from the namesake home of the Dungeness crab). Vegetables and salads are handled with finesse; the wine list is comprehensive. Window booths are for smokers, but that's okay because the best seats are those within the warmth of the gas fireplace. The adjacent Sequim Bay Lodge is an attractive 54-unit roadside resort with a putting course, outdoor heated pool, hot tub, and fireplace suites; (360)683-0691 or (800)622-0691. ■ *268522 Hwy 101 (east of town), Sequim; (360)683-9010; $$; full bar; MC, V; checks OK; breakfast, lunch, dinner Thurs–Tues.* &

Eclipse ★ Tom Wells, a former physicist and now co-owner, host, and sole waiter, and his wife, Cambodian-born Lay Yin, start cooking and serving at 8am and close by 3pm—and many or all of the dishes on the menu may disappear even before noon. (In-the-know locals phone ahead and have Yin set aside their orders.) Diners enter through the back door of this tract home, sit at a minuscule counter or at one of the two tables, and consider themselves blessed to eat whatever is available from the predominantly Southeast Asian menu: perhaps chicken congee (a thick and savory rice soup, and a breakfast favorite) or that universal snack, the spring roll—here delicate and delicious. Good-value group dinners, with 20 or more dishes, can be arranged. ■ *139 W Alder (½ block west of Sequim Ave, cor-*

ner of 3rd), Sequim; (360)683-2760; $; no alcohol; no credit cards; checks OK; breakfast, lunch Sat–Tues. ♿

Khu Larb Thai II ★ Ever since the Itti family opened their second establishment, Sequim residents are thrilled that they don't have to drive to Port Townsend anymore to savor the vibrant flavors of Thailand. This gracious restaurant, prettied with an elegant rose (the restaurant's namesake) on every table, has quickly become locals' first choice for, well, something different. Indeed, Thai food stands out in the land of the logger burger, and the Ittis have perfected this aromatic cuisine. Newcomers to Thai food should request the tried-and-true *tum kah gai* (a chicken soup with a coconut and lime broth), the phad Thai (sweet, spicy noodles stir-fried with egg, bean-cake, and vegetables), or the garlic pork. The more adventurous should pick any of the aromatic curries. ▪ *120 W Bell St (1 block north of the main street, at Sequim Ave), Sequim; (360)681-8550; $; beer and wine; MC, V; local checks only; lunch, dinner every day (call ahead in winter).* ♿

Oak Table Cafe ★ Breakfast (served until 3pm) is the thing at this cafe. And a feast it is: huge omelets, fruit crêpes, or the legendary puffy apple pancakes. Service is friendly and efficient—the coffee keeps coming—and the cream is the real thing. The place is noisy and boisterous and chatty. Good, old-fashioned lunches (turkey sandwiches, soothing—but unexciting—soups) with a few enlightened salads (chicken sesame salad) are the midday specialties of this cafe (owned by one of the Nagler family, who also own the Chestnut Cottage and First Street Haven in Port Angeles). ▪ *292 W Bell St (1 block south of Hwy 101, at 3rd), Sequim; (360)683-2179; $$; no alcohol; no credit cards; checks OK; breakfast every day, lunch Mon–Sat.*

Jean's Deli Jean's Deli, which made a name for itself in an old corner minimart at the corner of Highway 101 and Carlsborg Road, has moved up (and into town). Jean Klahn has scored in her new location (in a wonderful renovated 102-year-old church). Her soups are as delightful as ever, and her carrot cake and "lemon lush" desserts are absolutely heavenly. Good muffins, honeybuns, and cinnamon rolls are offered as early as 5am. ▪ *134 S 2nd Ave (at Bell), Sequim; (360)683-6727; $; no alcohol; no credit cards; checks OK; breakfast, lunch Mon–Sat.*

LODGINGS

Greywolf Inn ★ In a peaceful gray home on the east side of Sequim, transplanted Southerners Bill and Peggy Melang built this modest B&B offering six tasteful guest rooms. Their hospitality is always evident (especially at the hearty breakfasts, which often feature North Carolina country ham). The wooded hillside has a trail for walkers and bird-watchers. A small courtyard with an enclosed hot tub is right next door, along with

▼

Sequim and Dungeness Valley

Lodgings

▲

various exercise machines for the more ambitious. ■ *395 Keeler Rd (1 mile east of Sequim), Sequim, WA 98382; (360)683-5889 or (800)914-WOLF; $$; AE, DIS, MC, V; checks OK.*

Groveland Cottage ★ At the turn of the century, this was a family home in Dungeness—a wide spot in the road, a short drive from the beach. Now, the place has the comfortable salty-air feel of an old summer house, with four cheerful rooms, all with private baths. A one-room cottage out back may not be as special, but many folks like having their own cooking space. The place fills up in the summer with guests addicted to owner Simone Nichols's little luxuries—such as receiving the newspaper and coffee in your room before sitting down to her four-course breakfast. ■ *4861 Sequim-Dungeness Way (follow signs from Sequim toward Three Crabs), Dungeness, WA 98382; (360)683-3565; $$; AE, DIS, MC, V; checks OK.*

Juan de Fuca Cottages ★ Any of these five comfortable cottages—either overlooking Dungeness Spit or with a view of the Olympics—is a special hideout, whether for a winter weekend or a longer summertime sojourn. (A two-bedroom suite has both views and a welcoming fireplace.) All are equipped with a Jacuzzi, kitchen utensils, games, and reading material, as well as cable TV and VCR, and there's a 250-film library from which to choose. Outside is the spit, begging for beach walks and clam digging. Two-night minimum stay July and August (and weekends year-round). ■ *182 Marine Dr (7 miles north of Sequim), Sequim, WA 98382; (360)683-4433; $$; DIS, MC, V; checks OK.*

PORT ANGELES

The north shore of the Olympic Peninsula was home to several thriving Native American tribes long before outside explorers laid claim to the area. Today this blue-collar mill town is known as Port Angeles, "where the Olympics greet the sea." **Port Angeles Harbor**, protected against wind and waves by Ediz Hook sand spit, is the largest natural deep-water harbor north of San Francisco. It is also a jumping-off point to **Victoria**, 17 miles across the straits on Canada's Vancouver Island, via the ferry *Coho*, operated by Black Ball Transportation, (360)457-4491; or the much quicker *Victoria Express*, a foot-passenger ferry that runs two or three times daily during summer and early fall; (360)452-8088 or (800)633-1589.

Port Angeles is also at the northern (and most popular) end of **Olympic National Park**. The park, as big as Rhode Island, with a buffer zone of national forest surrounding it, contains the largest remaining herd of the huge Roosevelt elk, which occasionally create "elk jams" along Highway 101. Follow the signs to the visitors center; (360)452-0330. Then drive 17 miles along winding precipices to mile-high **Hurricane Ridge** and breathtaking views that mountains with twice the altitude seldom offer. Rest rooms and snack facilities are available. There are many hiking trails; (360)452-0330. In winter there is good cross-country skiing, a poma-lift downhill-skiing-and-tubing area (weekends only), and snowshoe rental and guided snowshoe nature walks through March. Check current road conditions by calling a 24-hour recorded message, (360)452-0329, before you set out. Olympic Raft and Guide Service offers easy Class I and Class II floats (and sea kayaking and fishing ventures to boot) on the Elwha and Hoh Rivers; (360)452-1443 or (888)452-1443.

Downtown, **Port Book and News** (104 E First, (360)452-6367) sells a wide selection of magazines and the daily *New York Times* and *Wall Street Journal*. **Mombasa Coffee Company** (113 W First, (360)452-3238) serves excellent fresh-roasted coffee. **Bonny's Bakery** (215 S Lincoln, (360)457-3585), near the library, is a good place to stock up for picnic and ferry-ride food, especially cinnamon rolls and freshly made sandwiches. Browse **Swain's General Store** (602 E First, (360)452-2357), which sells virtually everything.

RESTAURANTS

C'est Si Bon ★★ Yes, it *is* good—especially if you're yearning for classic pre-nouvelle French cooking with its splendid sauces. Dine leisurely in an attractive setting (the best tables, in window bays, overlook the rose garden). If the food is slow in coming, host Juhasz Norbert regales waiting guests with tales of his musical experiences in France and Hollywood (and others who've heard him beg him to bring out his violin). A big bowl of onion soup, bubbling under a brown crust of cheese, can serve as a meal in itself for those easily sated, particularly when followed by a refreshing salad. Preparations have been uneven lately, as if the chef is not taking enough time with the time-consuming sauces; however, if you stick to the simpler preparations such as the braised lamb, the classic steak au poivre, or the fresh halibut and salmon served in season, you'll leave nodding to your dinner partner *"Oui, c'est si bon."* The chocolate mousse is wickedly rich, and the wine list has good choices for those who aren't. ■ *23 Cedar Park Dr (4 miles east of Port Angeles on Hwy 101 E), Port Angeles; (360)452-8888; $$$; full bar; AE, MC, V; checks OK; dinner Tues–Sun.*

Bella Italia ★ Everyone on the north end of the peninsula seems to be talking about Bella Italia. Not bad press for a restaurant in the woody basement of the Country Aire health food store. Here's an Italian restaurant that uses organic and local produce (and freshly baked breads) as much as possible. Trouble is, it's not always possible (which makes for inconsistent preparations), especially in the dead of winter. So if you really want to see the chefs do their thing, wait until local goods can be harvested. Other times of the year, stick to the pastas tossed with seasonless treasures such as pesto or sun-dried tomatoes. ▪ *117-B E 1st St (basement of Country Aire store at 1st and Lincoln); Port Angeles; (360)457-5442; $$; full bar; AE, MC, V; local checks only; lunch, dinner every day.*

Chestnut Cottage ★ Owners Diane Nagler and Ken Nemirow (who also run First Street Haven) are very particular when it comes to quality food and service. It definitely shows. Their Chestnut Cottage is *the* place to go for an exceptional breakfast in delightful country Victorian–style surroundings smack in the middle of downtown P.A. A custardy apple and walnut French toast is only one of several morning treats; others include Belgian waffles, pancakes, quiches, frittatas, or lemon blintzes drizzled with raspberry purée. On the simpler side, a bowl of porridge and berries will surely satisfy. Or go exotic with a breakfast pizza (ham and eggs on pita). ▪ *929 E Front St (on Hwy 101, east of center of town), Port Angeles; (360)452-8344; $$; beer and wine; DIS, MC, V; checks OK; breakfast, lunch every day.* ♿

Chihuahua ★ Like small towns all across the country, Port Angeles has its share of Mexican restaurants. A notch or two above most is the Chihuahua—a small, busy spot en route to Hurricane Ridge that specializes in the foods of northern Mexico. Although most of the dishes cater to Tex-Mex tastes, owners Raphael and Juan Hernandez offer other more regional dishes, such as chile Colorado—a comforting pork stew, thick with chiles, herbs, and spices—or machaca con huevos— shredded beef scrambled with eggs, onions, and tomatoes. Occasionally, wonderful soups are bubbling away in the kitchen. On Sunday, ask for the menudo, a hearty soup of tender tripe in a well-flavored broth (especially recommended for hangovers). ▪ *408 S Lincoln (1 block south of old Clallam County Courthouse, between 4th and 5th), Port Angeles; (360)452-8174; $; beer and wine; DIS, MC, V; checks OK; lunch, dinner every day.*

▼

First Street Haven ★ It's just a skinny slot of a restaurant, easily missed among the storefronts if you're not paying attention. The cinnamon rolls are what draw the locals—in addition to the socializing on Saturday or Sunday morning. Fresh and unusual salads with homemade dressings, hearty sandwiches, pastas, and quiche dominate the menu, and the chili is great on a cold winter day. Expertly made espresso and their own coffee blend are fine jump-starters, especially with a fresh blueberry muffin or sour cream coffee cake. Prices are reasonable, and service is friendly and attentive. ▪ *107 E 1st St (at Laurel, next to the Toggery), Port Angeles; (360)457-0352; $; no alcohol; no credit cards; checks OK; breakfast, lunch Mon–Sat, brunch Sun.*

Toga's International ★ Ambitious young owner/chef Toga Hertzog trained in the Black Forest—so it's no surprise that his sauerbraten is a hit. But you might be surprised at his

"Jägerstein" meal (you cook it yourself at the table on a hot stone) and his upscale restaurant aspirations. He's doing a splendid job (and his prices reflect his ambitions). Creamy-smooth Hungarian mushroom soup, tinged with paprika, is heavenly. Lamb shanks are a favorite, as is the chicken Florentine. Service can be interrupted by long pauses; this is a family-run enterprise, and the family is small. ▪ *122 W Lauridsen Blvd (on Hwy 101 just west of Port Angeles), Port Angeles; (360)452-1952; $$; beer and wine; MC, V; checks OK; dinner Tues–Sun.*

LODGINGS

Domaine Madeleine ★★★ Set on a bluff overlooking the Strait of Juan de Fuca among tall firs, lawns, and gardens, this home is an ideal spot to get away and relax. It's the location, location, location, yes; but even more, it's the Chamberses—Madeleine and John—whose infectious *joie de vivre* loosens up even the most rigid travelers. Of the five sleeping areas, the spacious upstairs Ming Suite with its own large balcony and antique Oriental furnishings is our favorite. Next comes, believe it or not, the Renoir Room (the only one without a Jacuzzi), which is the smallest of the choices, except at night, when the living room belongs to you. The other areas are more private, with separate entrances (two are in another building), but all have the same deluxe amenities (Jacuzzi, fireplace, VCR, CD player, phone). The living room is dominated by a mighty basalt fireplace and views of distant Victoria, the Canadian coastal range, and Mount Baker. Soft sofas, antique and Oriental furnishings, and a harpsichord fill the room. Breakfast is a thorough five-course indulgence, always starting with baskets of John's freshly baked tiny French rolls, followed by Washington cheeses and fresh fruit and featuring a rich egg or salmon dish elegantly prepared by the hosts. ▪ *146 Wildflower Lane (north of Hwy 101 between Sequim and Port Angeles; call for directions), Port Angeles, WA 98362; (360)457-4174; domm@olypen.com; www.northolympic. com/dm; $$$; AE, DIS, MC, V; checks OK.*

Tudor Inn ★★ One of the best-looking buildings in town, a completely restored Tudor-style bed and breakfast, is located 12 blocks from the ferry terminal in a quiet residential neighborhood. Owners Jane Glass and her daughter Katy are friendly hosts, well versed in Port Angeles political and cultural life. Their house boasts a library, a fireplace, crisp linens, and antique touches here and there. The five rooms have been spruced up, and the best one has a balcony with wonderful views, a fireplace, and a claw-footed bathtub, as well as a shower. Jane serves a traditional full breakfast with none of the forced conviviality around the dining table that sometimes afflicts other B&Bs. She will gladly arrange for fishing charters, horseback rides, winter ski packages, and scenic flights. ▪ *1108 S Oak St* *(at 11th), Port Angeles, WA 98362; (360) 452-3138; tudor-info@ aol.com; www.northolympic.com/tudorinn; $$; AE, DIS, MC, V; checks OK.*

Olympic Lodge ★ If you don't have the time to hike the back-country, just walk the halls of this lodge to see what you are missing: Sequim photographer Ross Hamilton has a large collection of work on permanent display. The 106 rooms are spacious and well appointed with cherry furniture; many have views of the mountains. There is a large heated swimming pool as well as a Jacuzzi spa. If you want a priceless view, reserve an affordable bluff room of the Uptown Motel just west of this lodge; however, view aside, this Best Western hotel seems to offer the right combination of comfort and rustic atmosphere that fits in Port Angeles. ■ *140 Del Guzzi Dr (on Hwy 101, east side of Port Angeles), Port Angeles, WA 98362; (360) 452-2993 or (800) 600-2993; $$–$$$; AE, DC, MC, V; no checks.* &

LAKE CRESCENT

Highway 101 skirts the south shore of 600-foot-deep Lake Crescent with numerous scenic pullouts. The Fairholm store and boat launch are on the far west end of the lake, with East Beach 10 miles away on the other end. Lake Crescent is home to rainbow trout and steelhead, to Beardslee and the famous crescenti trout, which lurk in its depths. Rental boats are available. Ask at Lake Crescent Lodge about the easy 1-mile hike that takes you to the 90-foot Marymere Falls.

LODGINGS

Lake Crescent Lodge ★ Built over 80 years ago, the well-maintained Lake Crescent Lodge has also been well worn since the days when it was known as Singer's Tavern. The historic main building has a grand veranda that overlooks the deep, crystal blue waters of Lake Crescent, a so-so restaurant, and a very comfortable bar. The upstairs rooms are noisy and rustic—a euphemism that means, among other things, that the bathroom is down the hall. The motel rooms are the best for the money, but the clutter of tiny basic cabins, with their porches and fireplaces, can be fun (if you bear in mind that they were built in 1937, back when President Franklin Roosevelt came to visit Olympic Park). The service is just fine—mainly enthusiastic college kids having a nice summer. It's true this side of the lake sees less sun than the north side, but then, you don't really come to the rain forest to see the sun, do you? ■ *416 Lake Crescent Rd (20 miles west of Port Angeles on Hwy 101), Port Angeles, WA 98363; (360) 928-3211; $$; AE, DC, MC, V; checks OK (closed Nov–Apr).*

SOL DUC HOT SPRINGS

Whether you arrive by car after an impressive 12-mile drive through old-growth forests, or on foot after days of hiking mountain ridges, these hot springs are the ideal trail's end. The Quileute Indians called the area "Sol Duc"—"sparkling water." In the early 1900s, Sol Duc became a mecca for travelers seeking relief from their aches and pains. For about $6, you can have a hot soak, followed by a swim in a cold pool. You can also opt for a lengthy massage. Open daily mid-May through end of September, weekends only mid-March through mid-May; closed October through mid-March; (360)327-3583. The hike to nearby Sol Duc Falls passes through one of the loveliest stands of old-growth forest anywhere.

LODGINGS

Sol Duc Hot Springs Resort Surrounded by forest, 32 small cedar-roofed sleeping cabins are clustered in the grassy meadow. The favorites are those with their porches facing the river. Up to four adults and two kids can share a cabin (though it'll be a pretty cozy fit). The duplex units have kitchens, and in keeping with the natural serenity, there are no TVs anywhere (and there's a no-smoking policy everywhere). Camping and RV sites are available. The Springs Restaurant is open for breakfast, lunch, and dinner, and a snack deli is open midday. Use of the hot springs and the pool is included in the cabin rental fee. ■ *Turnoff a few miles west of Lake Crescent, then 12 miles south of Hwy 101; (360)327-3583; PO Box 2169, Port Angeles, WA 98362; $$; AE, DIS, MC, V; checks OK (open mid-May–Sept, weekends only in Apr and Oct).*

CLALLAM BAY/SEKIU

Twenty-one miles south on Hoko-Ozette Road from Sekiu is **Lake Ozette**, the largest natural body of fresh water in the state. At the north end of the lake there is a campground and trails leading to several beaches where you can see the eerie eroded coastal cliffs looming out of the water. It was near here that tidal erosion exposed a 500-year-old village, with homes perfectly preserved. The archaeological dig was closed in 1981 after 11 years of excavation; artifacts are on display at the Makah Museum in Neah Bay.

LODGINGS

Winters' Summer Inn ★★ Few would guess at the richness of the views from the back of this modest-looking house on Highway 112. And, indeed, the overlook of the Clallam River, the strait, and Vancouver Island is its biggest asset. There's a broad deck off the first floor, jutting out almost over the river, furnished with tables and potted plants and flanked by flower and herb gardens. Stairs lead up to another deck, the private domain of guests in the second-floor apartment (the place to choose for maximum space and seclusion). The apartment's decor is 1950s family room, but it has a complete kitchen and, what with trundle beds and hideabeds, cozily sleeps eight; it also has a fireplace and a pool table. The two downstairs rooms are more stylishly furnished; one has a Jacuzzi. Note the art on the walls, including some striking paintings by owner K. C. Winters herself. Hospitality is informal here; you're welcome to use the Winterses' kitchen, and say kind words to the family dog. ■ *16651 Hwy 112 (on the right as you leave town west-bound), Clallam Bay; (360) 963-2264; PO Box 54, Clallam Bay, WA 98326; $–$$; no credit cards; checks OK.*

NEAH BAY

This is literally the end of the road: Highway 112 ends at this small waterside town on the northern edge of the **Makah Indian Reservation**. Ten miles of unimproved road, known as the End of the World Loop, continues to **Cape Flattery**. The Makah allow public access across their ancestral lands—a half-mile walk on what is usually a muddy trail—to Land's End, the far northwestern corner of Washington's seacoast. From these high-cliffed headlands, cow-calf pairs of gray whales can often be seen migrating north in April and May. Salmon-fishing charters are available. Sandy **Hobuck Beach** is open for picnics (no fires), surfing, and horseback riding, and farther on, the Tsoo-Yas (Sooes) Beach is accessible (if you pay the landowners a parking fee). Call the visitors center in Port Angeles for coastal access information; (360) 452-0330.

See artifacts from a 500-year-old village in the **Makah Cultural and Research Center** (Front Street, (360) 645-2711).

FORKS

From this little town on the west end of the Olympic Peninsula, you can explore the wild coastal beaches, hook a steelhead, or go mountain biking, camping, or hiking. The pristine waters of the Hoh, Bogachiel, Calawah, and Sol Duc Rivers all flow near Forks, making it a key destination for fishermen. Ask your innkeeper, the informative Forks Visitors Center, (360) 374-2531 or (800) 44-FORKS, or inquire at **Olympic Sporting Goods**, (360) 374-6330, next to the liquor store, for information on recommended fishing guides, licenses, or where best to land the Big One. On the outskirts of town, the **Timber Museum** tells the story of the West End's logging heritage. Next door is the Visitors Center, where you can pick up a list and a map of **Arttrek**, a self-guided tour of nearly two dozen local studios and galleries; most are in the artists' own homes, but when the Arttrek sign is out, you're welcome in.

The **Hoh Rain Forest**, 30 miles south of Forks, is the wettest location in the contiguous United States, with an average yearly rainfall of 133.58 inches. This steady moisture nurtures the dense vegetation—more than 3,000 species of plant life—including the **Rain Forest Monarch**, a giant Sitka spruce over 500 years old towering close to 300 feet over the moss- and fern-carpeted forest floor. Take the spur road off Highway 101, 13⅕ miles south of Forks, to the Visitors Center; (360)374-6925. For those with more time, one- to three-day round-trip hikes up Mount Olympus provide some of the best hiking experiences in the world. The longer trip to Glacier Meadows is best mid-July through October. Be sure to stop in at Peak 6 Adventure Store, about 5 miles up the road to the Hoh, (360)374-5254, a veritable miniature REI right where you need it most.

LODGINGS

Eagle Point Inn ★★ Cradled on 5 acres in a bend of the Sol Duc River, this spacious log lodge was especially designed by Chris and Dan Christensen to provide a perfect combination of comfort and style. And it has become one of the most impressive places to stay near the rain forest. The two downstairs bedrooms, each with queen-size beds covered with a thick down comforter, have commodious bathrooms. The open two-story common living quarters house Chris's collection of kerosene lamps and other interesting antiques, but there's still plenty of room for guests to spread out and relax in front of the fireplace, made of rocks from the Sol Duc River. The Christensens live nearby in what was the original lodge, leaving you just the right amount of privacy. Even if you need to get up before dawn to fish, a hearty breakfast will be ready when you are. A covered outdoor kitchen down near the river is ideal for barbecuing your own meal at night. ■ *384 Stormin' Norman Rd (10 miles north of Forks on Hwy 101; go east on Stormin' Norman Rd at milepost 202), Beaver; (360)327-3236; PO Box 546, Beaver, WA 98305; $$; no credit cards; checks OK.*

Huckleberry Lodge ★ Two avid outdoors enthusiasts, Kitty and Bill Speery, own Forks' most fun adventure lodge, but during the week they leave it in the capable hands of budding innkeeper Erin Piggott—who works hard to please everyone, whether it's a 4:30am breakfast, a four-course dinner, or arrangements for a full day of fly-fishing or ATV adventures. You're well taken care of at this new lodge. The owners have remembered all the niceties (robes, slippers, toiletries) and the naughties (poker chips, cigars—complete with a heated outdoor smoking canopy—a hot tub under the evergreens, and a sauna). You could just spend the night, have breakfast, and do your own thing, but this place really works best if you and friends come with a mission for the weekend (ask Erin to suggest an outing) and dine on a home-cooked meal of salmon or elk. The pool table in the family room, the buffalo head (among numerous others) in the living room, and the display of Native

American artifacts give you a little insight into the spirit of the place. A new cabin (complete with a kitchen) is a good choice for the more independently minded (or for longer stays). And there are a couple of RV hookups on the premises for those who want to get away from the hubbub of the busy RV parks. It's a place with loads of potential, and we look forward to watching this relative newcomer develop. ■ *1171 Big Pine Way (at north end of Forks, east on Olympic Dr, to Huckleberry Lane which becomes Big Pine), Forks, WA 98331; (360)374-6008; $$; MC, V; checks OK.*

Miller Tree Inn ★ Set back from the road in a cluster of large trees encircled by pastures and wooded hills, the stately Miller Tree Inn, just a few blocks east of Highway 101, is not what you'd expect in this rugged territory. One of the original homesteads in Forks is run by Ted and Prue Miller, a retired logger and his wife. The atmosphere is relaxed; fresh lemonade is served on the lawn in summer, and the kitchen is not off-limits if you just ask. Though very comfortably furnished, some of the bedrooms may prove a bit small (best is the old sleeping porch). Fisherfolk appreciate the pre-dawn breakfasts, the Millers' knowledge of local river conditions, the room set aside for cleaning and freezing your catch, and the hot tub to relax in after a day on the river. Kids and well-mannered pets are welcome. The Millers have hired an accomplished chef to prepare dinner for you (with advance notice), and since the dining options in Forks are limited, he is a welcome sight for most guests. ■ *654 E Division St (at 6th St, next to City Hall), Forks; (360)374-6806; PO Box 953, Forks, WA 98331; $; MC, V; checks OK.*

LA PUSH AND OCEAN BEACHES

The Dickey, Quillayute, Calawah, and Sol Duc rivers all merge and enter the ocean near La Push. To the north and south extend miles of wilderness coastline—the last such stretch remaining in the United States outside of Alaska. It is home to the Quileute Indians, and today the small community still revolves around its fishing heritage, although plans are afoot to bring in a gambling casino. The lure of wild ocean beaches, with their jagged offshore rocks and teeming tide pools, bring those seeking adventurous solitude. The only nearby lodging is the **Ocean Park Resort** in La Push, (360)374-5267, which is too worn to recommend.

Several miles to the north, Mora Road leads to Rialto Beach and a three-day wilderness beach hike to **Cape Alava** off Lake Ozette. A shorter but more strenuous hike leads from Third Beach, south of La Push, 16 miles to the Hoh River (an extraordinarily dramatic stretch). Warning: All ocean beaches can be extremely dangerous due to fluctuating tides and unfordable creeks during periods of heavy rain. Be sure to stop in at the ranger station in nearby Mora to get a use permit and tide tables; (360)374-5460.

Along Highway 101, just south, is the wide stretch named **Ruby Beach** for the tiny garnet crystals that compose much of its sand, ideal for walking. A mile farther is the viewpoint for **Destruction Island**, a wildlife sanctuary topped by a lighthouse. Nearby, a trail leads to the world's largest Western red cedar. There are several more beaches to explore as you continue south—particularly at **Kalaloch**, which has a campground and a fine clamming beach.

KALALOCH

Kalaloch Lodge (157151 Highway 101, Forks, (360)962-2271) is one of the most isolated beachside resorts in Washington. Unfortunately, the accommodations are quite rudimentary and the food in the restaurant standard at best. If you're looking for a view, you can't beat it. Those in the know, camp.

LAKE QUINAULT

Lake Quinault, at the inland apex of the Quinault Indian Reservation, is usually the first or the last stop on Highway 101's scenic loop around the Peninsula's Olympic National Park and Forests. The glacier-carved lake is surrounded by cathedral-like fir forests, the fishing is memorable, and there are several easy trails, including one to **Campbell Grove** with its enormous old-growth trees. The ranger station provides information on other more strenuous hikes up the North Fork of the Quinault River or to **Enchanted Valley**, a glorious several-day round-trip journey. A large 1930s log chalet at the end of the trail can accommodate 50 to 60 hikers overnight.

LODGINGS

Lake Quinault Lodge ★ A massive cedar-shingled structure, this grand old lodge was built in 1926 in a gentle arc around the sweeping lawns that descend to the lake. The rustic public rooms are done up like Grandma's sun porch in wicker and antiques, with a massive stone fireplace in the heart of the lobby; the dining room overlooks the lawns, and the bar is lively at night. Rooms in the main building are small but perfectly nice; half have lake views. The choice lodgings are the 36 newer lakeside rooms a short walk from the lodge. Amenities consist of a sauna, an indoor heated pool, a Jacuzzi, a game room, canoes and rowboats, and well-maintained trails for hiking or running. Summer reservations take about four to five months' advance notice (but winter reservations are wide open—and a great time to experience the rain forest). The dining room puts up a classy front (especially compared to Kalaloch or Lake Crescent Lodges). Lunches are classic National Park (read: Monte Cristos and logger burgers), but dinners are a bit more creative, with entrees such as grilled salmon with lingonberry sauce or roast lamb with Madeira sauce. On occasion there are convention-eers around, drawn by the spalike features of the resort, but somehow the old place still exudes the quiet elegance of its past. ■ *South Shore Rd, Quinault; (360) 288-2900 or (800) 562-6672 (from WA and OR); PO Box 7, Quinault, WA 98575; $$–$$$; AE, MC, V; checks OK.*

MOCLIPS

LODGINGS

Ocean Crest Resort ★ Nestled in a magnificent stand of spruce on a bluff high above one of the nicest stretches of beach on the Olympic Peninsula, the Ocean Crest has always offered rooms with memorable views. The best views now are those from the modern units—done up in cedar paneling with fireplaces and European-style showers—and the best of the best are in build-ing 5. A recreation center is just across the road, with a swim-ming pool, sauna, Jacuzzi, and weight room, and there's access to the beach along a winding walkway through a lovely wooded ravine. An annex a quarter mile down the road offers two apart-ments, each with complete kitchen, porch, and two bedrooms. Unfortunately, maids are hard-pressed to trek the extra dis-tance, and you may need to request their services. In fact, at-tention to detail and housekeeping at the resort have been a bit of a problem lately. There are few views on the Northwest Coast that can rival the panorama from the dining room at the Ocean Crest, but the furnishings are old and the food and service in-consistent. Upstairs is a cozy bar, furnished with Northwest Coast Indian artifacts. ■ *SR 109 N (18 miles north of Ocean Shores), Moclips; (360) 276-4465; PO Box 7, Moclips, WA 98562; $$$; AE, DIS, MC, V; checks OK.*

PACIFIC BEACH

LODGINGS

Sandpiper ★★ Here's the place to vacation with four other cou-ples, or to bring the kids, the grandparents, and the family dog: miles of beach, a fleet of kites, and volleyball players. The spot-less resort consists of two four-story complexes containing large, fully equipped suites—usually a sitting room with a din-ing area and a fireplace, a compact kitchen, a small porch, and a bedroom and bath. There are splendid views of the beach (and a childrens' play area) from every deck. Penthouse units have an extra bedroom and cathedral ceilings. The rooms in the older complex are a tad larger than the others. There are also cottages and one-room studios. This resort knows enough not to try to compete with the draws of the Pacific: there's no pool, no TV, no restaurant, no in-room telephones, no video ma-chines—but the large gift shop does sell board games, kites, and sand buckets, plus condiments and sweatshirts. Prices are reasonable and the staff is very hospitable. Minimum stays are imposed on weekends and summers, and reservations are best made months in advance. Housekeeping drops by every day to see if you need anything (but you'll need to pay extra for logs for the fireplace); otherwise, you're on your own—just like home. ■ *4159 Hwy 109 (1½ miles south of town), Pacific Beach; (360) 276-4580; PO Box A, Pacific Beach, WA 98571; $$; MC, V; checks OK.*

OCEAN SHORES

Ocean Shores is finally outgrowing its schlocky past. The push for big-time gambling has waned, and the convention center is busy year-round with trade shows, collectors' fairs, and art exhibits. There's an annual jazz festival, a photography show with a statewide following, and sand castle and kite-flying competitions. McDonald's put up its golden arches in 1994, and building is booming.

To get away from it all, and avoid downtown altogether, re-serve one of the private beach houses that owners occasionally rent. Reservations need to be made weeks in advance; (360) 289-2430 or (800) 562-8612 in Washington only. The same numbers can also take motel reservations. Ocean Shores has never been a restaurant town, but two merit mentions.

RESTAURANTS

Alec's by the Sea ★ Alec's by the Sea does a lot of things well, including grilled razor clams, chicken fettuccine, and steaks. The delicious Philadelphia Prime Sandwich features sliced prime rib, grilled with onions and juicy bell peppers, topped with Swiss cheese, and served on a toasted French roll. A large menu, generous portions, efficient waitstaff, and crayons for the kids add up to a high-quality, friendly family restaurant. ■ *131 E Chance a la Mer Blvd NE (Point Brown Rd, left onto Chance a la Mer Blvd), Ocean Shores; (360) 289-4026; $$; full bar; AE, DC, DIS, MC, V; local checks only; lunch, dinner every day.*

Galway Bay Restaurant & Pub Guinness on tap (which every-one knows is good for you) and authentic Irish stew, with lamb, potatoes, carrots, and succulent sautéed onions, plus soda bread and real butter. Need we say more? This is surely the best way to warm up after a day of beachcombing. ■ *676 Ocean Shores Blvd NW (in town, ½ block from Shilo Inn), Ocean Shores; (360) 289-2300; $$; full bar; AE, DIS, MC, V; checks OK; lunch, dinner every day.* ⅅ

LODGINGS

Shilo Inn ★★ Hands down, this is the best place on the beach. Mark Hemstreet, owner of the nation's largest privately owned hotel chain, really knows his industry, and this particular inn shows it off the best. The service is first class at the area's newest, $10 million, 113-suite convention resort. And it's one of the few ocean-front establishments to have lived up to all of its PR hoo-ha. Each of its suites (*all* the rooms are junior suites) features a beachfront balcony (*all* face the ocean), fireplace, microwave, refrigerator, wet bar—you name it, everything, right down to an iron and ironing board. Facilities include an indoor pool, sauna, steam room, and fitness center. Even the restaurant is a find, with individual pizzas and fresh seafood. Weekend brunches are knockouts. ■ *707 Ocean Shores Blvd NW (in town), Ocean Shores, WA 98569; (360) 289-4600 or (800) 222-2244; $$$; AE, DC, MC, V; checks OK.* &

The Best Western Lighthouse Suites Inn ★ This handsome, hospitable hotel is one of the better places to stay on the beach. Each tastefully decorated, spacious room features a fireplace, wet bar, microwave, refrigerator, and coffeepot, plus cable TV and VCR. Sixty of the 76 rooms have a full ocean view. There's an indoor pool and spa and a cozy library. No restaurant, but a continental breakfast is free. ■ *491 Damon Rd NW (at north city limits), Ocean Shores; (360) 289-2311 or (800) 757-SURF; PO Box 879, Ocean Shores, WA 98569; 1757surf@techline.com; www.oceanshores.com/lodging/lighthouse; $$$; AE, DC, MC, V; checks OK.* &

▼
Ocean Shores

Lodgings

▲

The Grey Gull ★ This condominium-resort looks like a ski lodge (a rather odd style here on the beach), with jagged angles, handsome cladding, and a front door to strain the mightiest triceps. There are 36 condominium units, facing the ocean on a broad stretch of the beach (although not all have views; prices are calibrated accordingly), each outfitted with a balcony, fireplace, kitchen, TV, VCR, and attractive furnishings. The resort has a pool, a sauna, and a spa. You are right on the beach—the main plus—and the lodge has been built with an eye for good Northwest architecture. Prices for the suites get fairly steep, but there are smaller units too, and you can save money by doing your own cooking in the full kitchen. ■ *651 Ocean Shores Blvd SW (in town), Ocean Shores; (360) 289-3381; PO Box 1417, Ocean Shores, WA 98569; $$$; AE, DC, MC, V; checks OK.*

Southwest Washington

A clockwise route: southward on the southern half of I-5, west along the Columbia River, north along the Long Beach Peninsula and the south coast, and eastward at Grays Harbor.

CENTRALIA

The Chehalis-Centralia Railroad offers round-trip steam-train rides between these twin cities weekends from Memorial Day through September. Shoppers find a bargain mine of factory outlet stores along I-5 outside Centralia, and the 80 antique dealers who work the downtown area offer good finds too. The Kulien Shoe Factory (611 N Tower, (360)736-6943) is a tiny company that crafts handmade shoes. Train buffs love the Lewis County Historical Museum, open Tuesday through Sunday (599 NW Front Street, Chehalis, (360)748-0831).

RESTAURANTS

Winter Kitchen ★ Julie Norman owns this little green house decorated year-round in tasteful Christmas attire. The lunch menu is short and sweet—cheap, too, with sandwiches, salads, and an oyster stew, all (except a seafood salad) less than $5. Red floats, green floats, apple cider, and hot chocolate make this a fun spot to stop on a wearying highway drive. Friday-night candlelight dinners (until 8pm) come complete with a candle on your plate. ■ *827 Marsh St (2 blocks east of exit 81 off I-5), Centralia; (360)736-2916; $; no alcohol; no credit cards; checks OK; lunch Mon–Fri, early dinner Fri.*

CHEHALIS

RESTAURANTS

Mary McCrank's Good, homemade value. This 1935 dinner house occupies a large home, with fireplaces in some of the dining rooms; windows overlooking the garden, lawns, and stream; and armchairs scattered around the comfy rooms. Dinner starts with breads, jams, and a tray of homemade relishes (soups and salads, however, are perfunctory). Offerings include chicken with dumplings, pork chops, and other country fixings. A glorious pie comes for dessert: we never turn down the sour-cream raisin. ■ *2923 Jackson Hwy (4 miles east of I-5 on Jackson Hwy,*

4 miles south of Chehalis), Chehalis; (360) 748-3662; $; beer and wine; MC, V; checks OK; lunch Tues–Sat, dinner Tues–Sun.

LONGVIEW

RESTAURANTS

Henri's The Longview big shots all come here for lunch, when the large place can be fun and reliable; at dinner, when the pretension level rises and the number of customers dips, things can be rather lonely. Still, the steaks are perfectly good, you can have some nice seafood bisques, and the rack of lamb with béarnaise is quite tasty. There is a fancy wine room, into which guests are escorted by owner Henry Paul, who learned how to do this kind of thing years ago at Seattle's Golden Lion. ■ *4545 Ocean Beach Hwy (at 45th), Longview; (360) 425-7970; $$; full bar; AE, MC, V; local checks only; lunch Mon–Fri, dinner Mon–Sat.*

LODGINGS

Monticello Hotel This 75-year-old edifice has suffered a loss of confidence over the years, but we're happy to report that new owners have begun extensive repairs and upgrades, so the place is slowly coming around. It fronts on Civic Center Park with an impressive facade of brick and terra-cotta. There are now four executive suites in the hotel (some rooms are still rented out as senior housing); or you can stay in the motel-like wing, with its very standard but fairly priced rooms. ■ *1405 17th Ave (at Larch), Longview, WA 98632; (360) 425-9900; $$; AE, DC, MC, V; local checks only.*

VANCOUVER

Vancouver, long known as a bedroom community of Portland, is coming into its own with new industry and fast growth, including a number of up-and-coming restaurants.

Fort Vancouver was the major settlement of the Hudson's Bay Company until the 1860s, when it passed to the Americans. The stockade wall and some of the buildings have been reconstructed, and the visitors center has a decent museum and a notable heirloom garden; 1501 E Evergreen Boulevard, (360) 696-7655. On your way to Officers Row, you'll pass the active military post, **Vancouver Barracks**. The Heritage Trust of Clark County gives tours of the restored officers' quarters nearby; (360) 737-6066. The Grant House on Officers Row now houses the **Folk Art Center**, a tribute to regional art. It's open Tuesday through Saturday; (360) 694-5252. (Sheldon's Cafe, a pleasant place to dine, is housed there too.) **The Clark County Historical Museum** reconstructs pioneer stores and businesses and is open 1 to 5pm Tuesday though Saturday; 1511 Main Street at 16th, (360) 695-4681.

Covington House is the oldest log house (1846) in the state; 4201 Main Street, (360)695-6750. (Call to make arrangements for a tour.) Among the modest tourist attractions is the Northwest's **oldest apple tree** (in Old Apple Tree Park, east of I-5 on Columbia Way). The **Vancouver Farmers Market**, with local produce, flowers, and food vendors, sprawls over several blocks at the south end of Main Street from 9am to 3pm Saturdays, April through October. The **Water Resources Center**, with exhibits and a superb view of the Columbia River, is open 9am to 5pm Monday through Saturday at the east end of Columbia Way on the edge of Marine Park; (360)696-8478. **Ridgefield National Wildlife Refuge**, 3 miles west of I-5 exit 14, has nature trails leading to the bird refuge on the lowlands of the Columbia River; (360)887-3883. **Moulton Falls**, Northwest Lucia Falls Road near County Road 16, has a three-story-high arched bridge spanning the East Fork of the Lewis River, a 387-acre park, and two waterfalls. It's 2 miles south of Yacolt and 9 miles east of Battle Ground. Lacamas Park, at 300 acres and a half mile north of Camas on State Highway 500, features **Round Lake**, a 32-acre haven for bass and bluegill, along with trails and wild camas lilies that bloom in mid-April.

RESTAURANTS

Beaches Restaurant & Bar ★★ Perched above the Columbia, with an open view and a contemporary interior, this young spot has become Everybody's Eatery, pleasing suits and shorts and kids with its easygoing casualness and simple menu of wood-oven specialties, whole-meal salads, pastas, steamed mussels, and half-pound burgers. It offers a few comfort-food signatures such as the popular Jack Daniel's Flamin' Wings, seafood cioppino, and hot berry cobbler. The swinging bar fills up seven nights a week, and there's a growing, reasonably priced wine list. ■ *1919 SE Columbia River Dr (take Camas (Hwy 14) exit off I-5, go east 1½ miles, turn right at upside-down Beaches sign), Vancouver; (360)699-1592; $$; beer and wine; AE, DC, MC, V; no checks; lunch, dinner every day.*

Sheldon's Cafe at the Grant House ★★ The 1849 Grant House, named for Ulysses S. Grant, doubles as a folk art museum and cafe. Its location, with veranda and herb garden, is quite charming. For lunch, soups, salads, quiches, seafood, sandwiches, and regional specialties, including the favorite deviled eggs and house-smoked meats, are the bill of fare; for dinner, a Northwest bistro menu tempts with pasta, salmon, Willapa Bay oysters, and grilled duck breast, with apple crisp or praline gingerbread for dessert. American cuisine is the emphasis. We'd come back any time for the free regional folk art exhibit. ■ *1101 Officers Row (midtown Vancouver, off Evergreen Blvd), Vancouver; (360)699-1213; $$; beer and wine; MC, V; checks OK; lunch, dinner Tues–Sat.*

Andrew's Restaurant and Catering ★ Some come here for the almond biscotti and good coffee. Others like the outdoor seating that lends this little cafe in Vancouver a somewhat European air, although there is a decidedly Northwest flavor to the menu and a small-time feel to the cafe. Lunch is refreshingly unpretentious: polenta with pesto or marinara sauce; smoked salmon pasta or spinach lasagne; a focaccia sandwich; an array of fresh, imaginative salads (from roasted eggplant to an Asian noodle variation). Best of all, nothing exceeds $7.50. ■ *611 W 11th St (between Grant and Franklin, across from the courthouse), Vancouver; (360) 693-3252; $; no alcohol; MC, V; checks OK; breakfast, lunch Mon–Fri.*

Hidden House ★ The Hiddens, a leading family in these parts since 1870, made their money with a brick factory. Their handsome brick home was opened by Susan Courtney as a restaurant in 1976, and she has succeeded in turning it into a reliable—if old-fashioned—place for an intimate dinner or a comforting lunch. The "complete dinner" menu offers about a dozen slightly dated small-city standards (Swiss almond chicken, garlic roasted tenderloin, roast pork tenderloin with peach salsa). A "beggar's banquet" of soup, salad, and homemade poppyseed or pumpkin bread is a midday favorite, as is the "BBFGT," bacon, basil and fried green tomato sandwich. There's a fairly inclusive Northwest wine list. A satellite cafe, the Paradise Cafe, is open for breakfast and lunch next door; 304 Main Street, (360) 696-1612. ■ *100 W 13th St (corner of Main, downtown), Vancouver; (360) 696-2847; $$–$$$; beer and wine; AE, DC, MC, V; checks OK; lunch Mon–Fri, dinner Tues–Sun.*

Nature's Marketplace ★ This is a 21st-century supermarket that has updated the food scene in southwest Washington, with a wide selection of organic produce and hormone-free meat, cooking classes, and hip, ready-prepared and ready-to-cook foods. Take away or eat your food here in the bright and ecologically correct Cafe Court. Find ethnic dips, casseroles, salads, pizzas, baked potato bar, marinated meats, European breads, rich desserts, and even breakfast. ■ *8024 E Mill Plain Blvd (from I-205, head east on Hwy 14 to Lieser St exit, left on Mill Plain), Vancouver; (360) 695-8878; $; beer and wine; AE, DIS, MC, V; checks OK; open every day.*

Pinot Ganache ★ Downtown Vancouver, forever struggling to brush up its image, shows off a glimmer of panache at Pinot Ganache, though ownership has changed three times in five years. The interior lacks liveliness, but is slick enough, with well-spaced tables and live jazz on Tuesday and Thursday nights. The ever-changing multiethnic meals, such as Asian-style roast duck, Arabic falafel pita, and Mongolian lamb chops, are well presented. Desserts are very fancy: chocolate cappuccino coffee cake and double-lemon cheesecake. The place brightens in summer, when pink geraniums bloom in the sidewalk cafe. ■ *1004 Washington St (corner of Evergreen), Vancouver; (360) 695-7786; $$$; beer and wine; AE, MC, V; checks OK; lunch Mon–Sat, dinner Tues–Sat.*

Thai Little Home ★ It's not as fancy as similar joints across the river in Portland, but Serm Pong and his family prepare fresh, home-cooked Thai food that locals think is just fine. *Yum nuer* (sliced beef salad with cucumber, seasoned with chile and lime juice) rivals the popular *pra koong* (shrimp with chile paste, lemongrass, and lime juice); we've enjoyed both *mee krob* (crisp Thai noodles) and chicken satay at the beginning of meals. Service is friendly, informed, and fast. ■ *3214 E Fourth Plain Blvd (just north of downtown Vancouver and Clark College), Vancouver; (360) 693-4061; $; beer and wine; AE, MC, V; local checks only; lunch, dinner Mon–Sat.*

Dante's Ristorante From the outside, you won't notice the hunkered-down gray building, but inside, the gregarious Caltagirone family serves up good-value Italian specialties such as spaghetti all'Amatriciana with a light garlic-pancetta sauce, prawns Mediterranean, and predictable but generous full-meal-deal raviolis, manicottis, and cannellonis. Pizzas are popular with kids, and the revamped interior brings a touch of the trattoria to this small but growing town. Desserts include a locally loved tiramisu. The food is hearty; the wine list is by the glass. ■ *111 E Main St (about 8 miles off I-5, take Battle Ground–Orchards exit off I-5), Battle Ground; (360) 687-4373; $, beer and wine; MC, V; checks OK; dinner Mon–Sat.*

▼

Vancouver

Restaurants

▲

Fa Fa Gourmet It's in the 'burbs on the edge of a shopping center, but the Chia family makes this sprawling restaurant as authentic Chinese as you'll find in the area. Chef/owner Tseng Chia has a skilled hand with spices and prepares Sichuan and Hunan dishes. The menu is also popular with Japanese customers, and for good reason: a seaweed salad is on the menu, as are drunk chicken, five-spice duck, Bird's Nest Deluxe, crisp prawns in red chile sauce, and the more routine family-style dinners. ■ *11712 NE Fourth Plain Rd (take I-5 to Fourth Plain exit, head east), Vancouver; (360) 260-1378; $$; beer and wine; MC, V; checks OK (with debit card); lunch, dinner every day.*

New York Richie's You'll get East Coast lip here (owner Richie Brose doubles as Hercules at Hollywood's Universal Studios) as well as the "elbow-dripper" (Philly cheese steak) in this eat-in/take-out joint with an attitude. Richie's specializes in wood-oven pizzas, hot pastrami sandwiches, Italian subs, imported hot dogs, fresh chili, pastas and sauces, and cheesecake. ■ *8086 E Mill Plain Blvd (from I-205, head east on Hwy 14 to Lieser St exit, left on Mill Plain), Vancouver; (360) 696-4001; $; beer only; no credit cards; checks OK; lunch, dinner Mon–Sat.*

CATHLAMET

Cathlamet, the county seat of Wahkiakum County, is an old-style river town, tied almost as closely to the Columbia as Mark Twain's Hannibal, Missouri, was to the Mississippi. Fishing is everyone's recreation—in season, for trout, salmon, and steelhead; all year round for the Columbia's mammoth, caviar-bearing sturgeon. Nearby **Puget Island**, reachable by bridge, is flat dairyland, ideal for cycling; a tiny ferry can take you from there directly across to Oregon. Wahkiakum County is the sort of place where nostalgia buffs discover round barns and covered bridges. You can camp right on the river beach at **Skamokawa** (say ska-MOCK-away) **Vista Park**.

LODGINGS

The Bradley House/Country Keeper ★ It's not exactly in the country (Main Street, Cathlamet, is more exact), but it's certainly a keeper. This former town library is an immaculate 1907 mansion—original decorative hardwood floors, Oriental rugs, light fixtures, and all. It's handsomely furnished with period pieces. As a tribute to the mansion's former incarnation, the comfortable bedrooms are filled with books. A porch with a distant view of the Columbia invites long afternoon visits in summer. ■ *61 Main St (just off SR 4, at the north end of town), Cathlamet, WA 98612; (360) 795-3030; $$; MC, V; checks OK.*

CHINOOK

Nestled on the shores of Baker Bay, part of the broad Columbia River estuary, Chinook was formerly a profitable salmon fish-trapping center. The too-efficient fish traps were outlawed earlier this century; today, most of the thousands of wooden pilings visible in the bay at low tide are all that remain of these harvesting contraptions.

Nearby, on Scarborough Hill, **Fort Columbia State Park** is a collection of restored turn-of-the-century wooden buildings that once housed soldiers guarding the mouth of the Columbia River from the threat of foreign invasion. The former commander's house is now a military museum (nearby is the youth hostel); foreboding concrete bunkers once held huge cannons. The park also claims some of the area's largest rhododendron bushes. Open daily mid-May to September, but hours vary; (360) 777-8221.

RESTAURANTS

The Sanctuary ★ You dine in a sanctified setting, an old Methodist church complete with pump organ, stained-glass windows, statues of angelic cherubs—even pews to sit in, for God's sake. Amid the finery, owner/chef Joanne Leech serves an eclectic array of food, from fresh seafood to *svenska kottbullar* (Swedish meatballs) and *fiskekaker* (Scandinavian fish cakes)—

both of which can be sampled as appetizers. She also purveys the area's best fresh-baked bread. Innovative preparations include fresh snapper fillet coated with a crunchy, potato-pancake crust; or a filet mignon served with a zingy Jack Daniel's mustard sauce. For dessert, homemade sherbet—blackberry one time, lemon another—is, er, heavenly. Ditto for the "sinful sundae." Light lunches are served in the herb house. ■ *794 Hwy 101 (at Hazel), Chinook; (360) 777-8380; $$; full bar; AE, DC, MC, V; checks OK; dinner Wed–Sun (winter hours vary).* &

LONG BEACH PENINSULA

The slender finger of land dividing Willapa Bay from the Pacific is famous for its 37-mile-long flat stretch of public beach (reputedly the longest such stretch worldwide); its gentle marine climate; its exhibition kite flying; its cranberry bogs, clamming, and rhododendrons; and its food, which is unequaled by any like-size area on the Northwest Coast.

Willapa Bay's **Long Island**, reachable only by boat, harbors a 274-acre old-growth cedar grove. Some trees are over 200 feet tall, with trunks 11 feet in diameter. Campsites are available. The island is part of the **Willapa National Wildlife Refuge**, with headquarters on Highway 101, back on the mainland and 10 miles north of Seaview; (360) 484-3482.

LONG BEACH PENINSULA: ILWACO

Named after a Chinook Indian chief, Ilwaco is best known as the sport-fishing hub of the lower Columbia River. Two popular **sportfishing** operators, both located at the port docks, are Sea Breeze Charters, (360) 642-2300, and Coho Charters, (360) 642-3333. Because of intermittent ocean closures for sport fishing, many charter operators are now offering eco-tours. Phone ahead for information.

The **Ilwaco Heritage Museum** is a fine example of a small-town museum. It not only offers a look at southwest Washington history (including Native American artifacts and a scale-model glimpse of the peninsula in the 1920s) but also contains an excellent research library, art gallery, and a whole separate building of train memorabilia; 115 SE Lake Street, (360) 642-3446.

Fort Canby State Park covers 2,000 acres stretching from North Head south to Cape Disappointment at the Columbia's mouth. Good surf fishing and wave watching can be had from the North Jetty, 2 miles of massive boulders separating the ocean and river, with an observation platform for good views. The park also includes hiking and biking trails and 250 campsites, open all year; (800) 233-0321 or (360) 642-3078.

Also in the park is the **Lewis and Clark Interpretive Center**, which depicts the explorers' journey from St. Louis to the

Pacific, explains the history of the Cape Disappointment and North Head lighthouses, and enjoys the best view of the Columbia River bar—a great storm-watching spot. North Head is open for tours in summer, but Cape Disappointment remains a working lighthouse closed to the public. Both may be approached on foot; (360)642-3029.

LODGINGS

Chick-a-Dee Inn at Ilwaco ★ Located on a quiet, dead-end street overlooking the town, this bed and breakfast is housed in the 75-year-old former Ilwaco Presbyterian Church. You enter through a vestibule-turned-gift-shop and past rows of intact pews. A full breakfast is served in the former sanctuary, which has been transformed into a spacious dining area backed by a fireplace. Innkeepers Chick and Dee Hinkle have decorated all nine guest units (some tucked into upstairs eaves and dormers) in shades of blue and white, with plush bedding, lacy curtains, and handsome furnishings. The two-bedroom Captain's Suite features a fireplace, a refrigerator, and a massive captain's bed from the Hamburg-American ship line. A roomy parlor has myriad comfy chairs and couches, watercolor seascapes, sea charts, and a ship's binnacle. Three acres of grounds include a tree-sheltered picnic and sitting area. On warm-weather evenings, Chick revs up his 1940-vintage Cadillac limo and gives guests a spin. ■ *120 Williams St NE (off 4th), Ilwaco; (360)642-8686; PO Box 922, Ilwaco, WA 98624; $$; AE, MC, V; checks OK.*

LONG BEACH PENINSULA: SEAVIEW

Some of the peninsula's prettiest stretches (and a couple of its finest restaurants and lodgings) are tucked into this small, beach-front, bedroom community. Almost every westward road leads to the beach, where you can park your car to stroll the quaint neighborhoods and traverse the rolling dunes. The Charles Mulvey Gallery displays quintessential peninsula watercolors of ocean, beach, and bay (call to check winter hours); 46th Place and L Street, (360)642-2189. Campiche Studios, 3100 S Pacific Way, (360)642-2264, features watercolors, sculptures, and photography.

RESTAURANTS

The Shoalwater (at The Shelburne Inn) ★★★ Like swallows returning to Capistrano, food-savvy travelers and locals celebrating life's big occasions continue to return to the Shoalwater for a fussy, Northwest-inspired dining experience in a resort area more inclined to casual culinary pursuits. Longtime owners Ann and Tony Kischner's devotion to fine foodstuffs and fabulous wine continues to make the Shoalwater the Northwest Coast's most beloved destination dining spot. The main salon—with tongue-and-groove walls and ceiling, brass light fixtures, grandfather clock, and lovely antique wine closet—resembles a first-class captain's cabin. Back in the kitchen, chef Terry Riley takes the helm, offering native ingredients that bow to the season. Willapa Bay oysters (none fresher), wild mushrooms (Long Beach is a forager's dream), and tart salal berries (flavoring a vinaigrette that may be bought by the bottle) highlight a seafood-heavy menu that pays due homage to meat and chicken. Those with a sweet tooth can thank pastry chef Ann Kischner, whose professional hand with desserts deserves applause. Engaging, well-meaning service isn't as polished as one might expect. ■ *4415 Pacific Hwy (Pacific Hwy 103 and N 45th), Seaview; (360) 642-4142; $$$; full bar; AE, DC, MC, V; checks OK; lunch, dinner every day, brunch Sun.* &

Cheri Walker's 42nd Street Cafe ★★ Cheri and Blaine Walker, once of Shoalwater restaurant fame (she ran the kitchen, he was the manager), preside over this popular dinner house just down the highway from the Shelburne Inn. Cheri has transformed the kitchen, slowly but surely. Americana fare shares the spotlight with a more imaginative menu of pasta and less-than-usual sauces (port wine and cranberry, for one). You can count on comfy-cozy decor, cheerful waitresses, and hearty portions of home cooking (berry conserves and corn relish, chicken fried in an iron skillet). Only the freshest fish is used (and it won't be breaded). Local oysters are featured in a number of creations, and desserts (plum almond crisp) are terrific. The Walkers have found their niche: comfort food with lots of flair. ■ *4201 Pacific Hwy (corner of 42nd St), Seaview; (360) 642-2323; $$; beer and wine; MC, V; checks OK; lunch Wed–Sun, dinner every day (winter hours vary).* &

The Heron and Beaver Pub ★★ While the adjoining-and-much-fussier Shoalwater gets all the acclaim (same owners, same kitchen, a great deal of menu overlap), the Heron and Beaver remains a pint-size destination in its own right. In this cozy, crowded, slip of a bar you might slurp down Willapa Bay oyster shooters doused with a vodka-and-pepper-kicking cocktail sauce and then chase it with a microbrew. Or indulge in a "light meal"—perhaps a splendid mess of spicy blackened oysters, or an Asian-inspired Dungeness crab cake. Explore the extensive wine list, sample a trio of single-malt Scotches from the carefully stocked bar, or just hunker down over such Silver Palate–style sandwiches as a BLT with Canadian bacon and basil-pesto mayo or a burger anointed with homemade cranberry-blueberry mustard. Psssst: Ask nice, and they'll even let you order off the Shoalwater's menu without changing out of your jeans. ■ *4415 Pacific Hwy (in the Shelburne Inn, Pacific Hwy 103 and N 45th), Seaview; (360) 642-4142; $$; full bar; AE, DC, MC, V; checks OK; lunch Mon–Sat, dinner every day, brunch Sun.* &

My Mom's Pie Kitchen The name says it all—and it's even more appropriate now that Mom's has moved from a mobile home in Long Beach to a quaint old home in Seaview. This is a small establishment that serves a host of homemade pies. Banana cream, pecan, sour cream, chocolate-almond, raisin, rhubarb, raspberry, and myriad other concoctions are offered, depending on the time of year and, in some cases, the time of day. Arrive too late (especially in summer), and this sweetnik's haven might be sold out of your favorite (but it's easy enough to find a satisfying replacement). Before savoring a slice, satisfy yourself with a steamy bowl of chowder or a silky Dungeness crab quiche. ■ *4316 S Pacific Hwy (Pacific Hwy and 43rd St), Seaview; (360)642-2342; $; no alcohol; MC, V; checks OK; lunch Wed–Sun.*

LODGINGS

The Shelburne Inn ★★★ You can't see the ocean from here, but you most definitely can feel its allure throughout the historic Shelburne, a creaky but dignified century-old structure. Trouble is, there's a busy highway out front, with a well-lit supermarket across the way. Request a west-facing room to assure peace and quiet. They're bright and cheerful, with antiqued interiors, private baths, and cozy homespun quilts covering queen-size beds. Don't expect the modern amenities (saunas, Jacuzzis) that have become de rigueur at so many chic hideaways. The third floor offers the best buys, lots of tongue-and-groove woodwork, and gently slanted floors (the entire building was pulled across the street by a team of horses in 1911). Breakfasts are superb: innkeepers David Campiche and Laurie Anderson whip up satisfying eye-openers of razor-clam cakes or scrambled eggs with smoked salmon, chives (from the herb garden out front), and Gruyère cheese—not to mention the pastries. The separately owned Shoalwater (see review) is the dinner restaurant. ■ *Pacific Hwy 103 and N 45th, Seaview; (360)642-2442; PO Box 250, Seaview, WA 98644; shelinn@ aone.com; $$$; AE, MC, V; checks OK.* &

Sou'wester Lodge ★ This place is definitely not for everyone, but those who appreciate good conversation, a sense of humor, and rambling lodgings on the beach find Leonard and Miriam Atkins's humble, old-fashioned resort just what the doctor ordered. The main structure was built in 1892 as a summer home for U.S. Senator Henry Winslow Corbett; you can also stay in fully equipped cabins or a collection of classic trailers. The hosts are as much a draw as the lodgings. Originally from South Africa, they came to Long Beach by way of Israel and Chicago. The view from the lodge's balcony—across windswept, grassy dunes to the sea—is enough to keep them here permanently. Interesting books and periodicals clutter the living room, which also occasionally hosts lectures, chamber music concerts, and informal (but stimulating) conversations. Leonard has deemed this joint the official outpost of the "B & (MYOD)B club"—Bed and (Make Your Own Damn) Breakfast. ■ *1½ blocks southwest of the traffic light on Beach Access Rd (38th Pl), Seaview; (360)642-2542; PO Box 102, Seaview, WA 98644; $; MC, V; checks OK.*

LONG BEACH PENINSULA: LONG BEACH

Long Beach is bustling with tourists, so if you visit during the summer, prepare for the onslaught. A popular hangout is the half-mile-long elevated boardwalk (with night lighting) stretching between S 10th and Bolstad Streets, accessible by wheelchairs, baby strollers, and, of course, feet.

Kite lovers can visit the **Long Beach World Kite Museum and Hall of Fame**, Third and N Pacific Highway, (360)642-4020, or buy their own at Long Beach Kites, at the stoplight, (360)642-2202, or at Stormin' Norman's, one block south, (800)4-STORMIN. August's **International Kite Festival** brings thousands of soaring creations to the skies. The entire peninsula swells with visitors for this event, so plan ahead; (360)642-2400. Milton York Candy Company, (360)642-2352, on the main drag, purveys chocolates and ice cream, while nearby Plain Jane's, (360)642-4933, offers tasty chocolate chip cookies and other sweets. Farther out, Clark's Nursery, (360)642-2241, grows fields of rhododendrons.

RESTAURANTS

Max's ★ This diminutive, elongated eatery purveys upwards of 100 menu choices, including lots of seafood dishes; many offer a rush of exceedingly rich ingredients. Appetizers include fried artichoke hearts wrapped with bacon, escargots baked in a mornay sauce, and a baked crab dip accompanied by tiny baguettes. Entrees such as cashew prawns and salmon stuffed with cream cheese and shrimp look, and taste, elegant. Steamed clams and mussels are straightforward, but steaks are available either grilled simply or served with a peppercorn demiglace. For breakfast, the North Pacific omelet—filled with Dungeness crab, bay shrimp, veggies, Swiss and Jack cheeses, then topped with avocado and served with hollandaise—sizzles with a half-dozen different flavors. Service is beach-town friendly. ■ *111 S Pacific Hwy (on main drag), Long Beach; (360)642-5600; $$; full bar; AE, DC, DIS, MC, V; checks OK; breakfast, lunch, dinner every day.*

Pastimes What began as a hip espresso house with lots of books and board games is now a restaurant too. Actually, this place with the glassed-in eating (and sipping) area and the gift shop up front is a pocket of serenity in bustling downtown Long Beach. The ambience is laid back, the soups and salads (try the wild rice with hazelnuts in an orange-fennel vinaigrette) and quiches are super, and the coffee-drink selection is the best around. Luscious scones, fresh bagels, and gooey, thick cinnamon rolls are baked daily, and there's even a quote du jour to keep you thinking. An outside espresso garden invites you to enjoy a gourmet sipping concoction in the warmer air of summer. ■ *504 Pacific Hwy S (at 5th), Long Beach; (360) 642-8303; $; wine and beer; MC, V; checks OK; breakfast, lunch every day.*

LODGINGS

Boreas Bed & Breakfast ★ Boreas is a picturesque lodging in a postcard-perfect setting. A remodeled 1920s beach house, it's tastefully decorated with art and antiques and appointed with handsome furnishings. Presently, two bedrooms share a bath and both sport views (one of the water, the other of the mountains). Two suites open onto decks and gardens; a third is upstairs with an ocean view. All rooms have "extra" sleeping arrangements—with feather beds, futons, or a spare bed—which give families options. A favorite retreat of guests is the fully enclosed, heated gazebo with a state-of-the-art spa overlooking the dunes. Everything is just a short walk from the beach. At press time, new owners Susie Goldsmith and Bill Verner were planning a remodel. ■ *607 North Blvd (1 block west of the main drag), Long Beach; (360) 642-8069; PO Box 1344, Long Beach, WA 98631; boreas@aone.com; www.europa.com/ ~boreas; $$; AE, DC, MC, V; checks OK.*

Scandinavian Gardens Inn Bed & Breakfast ★ There really is a touch of Scandinavia here. Each of five guest rooms (on two floors) is decorated in a different theme, from Icelandic to Norwegian (even the teddy bears wear national costumes), with an eye-pleasing mix of modern and antique furnishings and bright, cheery colors. In the Scandinavian tradition, guests remove their shoes at the entranceway and roam the lushly carpeted floors in socks or slippers. The Swedish Suite is the roomiest, with a skylit bathroom and a separate, two-person tub; the Norwegian Room, with green-and-gold decor and a lovely pine bed, has its bathroom across the hall. All guests can enjoy the indoor spa, cedar sauna, and exercise equipment. In addition to egg dishes, breakfast might include blueberry crêpes, rice pudding with a strawberry-rhubarb sauce, and lots of baked goodies, such as almond bread and ginger muffins. Hosts Marilyn and Rod Dakan (who serve breakfast wearing Scandinavian attire) accommodate any special dietary requirements, and fruit juices and cider are available anytime. The beach is a short distance away, but out of view. ■ *1610 California Ave S (1 block off the main street), Long Beach; (360) 642-8877 or (800) 988-9277; Rt 1, Box 36, Long Beach, WA 98631; $$; MC, V; checks OK.*

Ocean Park, founded as a religious settlement, is now a tranquil retirement community with a quiet beach—except in June, when the **Garlic Festival** takes over the town. Needless to say, there's lots of stinkin' good food at this event; (800)451-2542. The Wiegardt Watercolors Gallery, 2607 Bay Avenue, (360)665-5976, displays Eric Wiegardt seascapes in a restored Victorian house. Nearby, at 25712 Sandridge Road, (360)665-4382, the Shoalwater Cove Gallery exhibits nature scenes in soft pastels.

LODGINGS

Caswell's on the Bay Bed & Breakfast ★★ Sequestered off quiet, rural Sandridge Road—where cows, cranberry bogs, and rhodie farms dominate the landscape—this immense (6,500-square-foot) neo-Victorian mansion enjoys a serene Willapa Bay setting where the outside world seems nonexistent. Ex-Seattleites Bob and Marilyn Caswell designed and built their B&B dream house with five spacious guest rooms, all with private baths and a sprinkling of 19th-century American, English, and French antiques. Three bedrooms look out over the forested grounds and a garden awash with rhododendrons blooming much of the year; the Shoalwater Room and Terrace Suite enjoy bay vistas (and the latter has an outside balcony). Lovely ground-floor living, dining, and library areas are highlighted by both plush carpeting and exposed oak floors. A windowed sun room (with spyglass and binoculars) and a back veranda are just right for reading, relaxing, and gazing out at the Willapa Bay oyster beds and blue herons. In addition to a full breakfast, the Caswells serve afternoon tea complete with treats. ■ *25204 Sandridge Rd (½ mile south of the Nahcotta intersection), Ocean Park; (360)665-6535; PO Box 1390, Ocean Park, WA 98640; $$$; MC, V; checks OK.*

▼

**Long Beach
Peninsula:
Ocean Park**

Lodgings

▲

Klipsan Beach Cottages ★ This cozy operation, a row of nine small, separate, well-maintained older cottages, stands facing the ocean in a parklike setting of pine trees and clipped lawns. Since these are individually owned condominiums, interior decoration schemes can vary widely, but all of the units feature fireplaces (or wood stoves), full kitchens, and ocean-facing decks just a couple of hundred feet from the beach. Children are fine, but pets are not. All units are nonsmoking. ■ *22617 Pacific Hwy (Hwy 103, 2 miles south of Ocean Park), Ocean Park, WA 98640; (360)665-4888; $$–$$$; MC, V; checks OK.* &

Shakti Cove Cottages ★ Now under new ownership, this formerly ragtag clutch of old cabins—set on 3 forested acres just off the beaten track and within earshot of the thundering Pacific—has been treated to an extensive upgrade by "cove-keepers" Celia and Liz Cavalli. The former Seattleites cater unobtrusively to the needs of happy campers at this priced-right getaway. If "have pets, will travel" is your motto, this is your place. Even oversize canines receive an open-armed welcome—as do a largely gay and lesbian clientele (homophobes will be far more comfortable elsewhere). Each spotlessly clean, funky-but-comfortable cabin offers complete kitchen facilities, private bath with shower, cable TV (no phone), and private carport, to say nothing of easy access to a stunning stretch of beach. Don't expect daily maid service, and don't bother bringing provisions: Jack's Country Store (if they don't have it, you don't need it) is a just short walk away. ■ *On 253rd Pl (1 block west of Pacific Hwy 103), Ocean Park; (360)665-4000; PO Box 385, Ocean Park, WA 98040; $$; MC, V; checks OK.*

LONG BEACH PENINSULA: NAHCOTTA

Nahcotta has become almost synonymous with **oysters**. At the Nahcotta Oyster Farm, 270th and Sandridge Road, on the old rail line, you can pick up some pesticide-free 'sters (or gather your own for half price); Jolly Roger Seafoods, across from The Ark, (360)665-4111, is also a good bet. The Nahcotta Natural Store, at 270th and Sandridge Road, (360)665-4449, is a pleasant stop for beverages and grub. Two places help explain the oyster story: the **Willapa Field Station** (267 Sandridge Road, (360)665-4166) has outdoor interpretive signs, maps, and info; **Willapa Bay Interpretive Center** (on the Nahcotta pier, open in summer only) features a viewing deck and indoor exhibits.

RESTAURANTS

The Ark ★★ For a half century the Ark has sat among the canneries at the end of the old Nahcotta dock overlooking Willapa Bay and its beds of oysters. Years ago, the restaurant gained legendary status after winning praise from the late James Beard. It's true, you can't get seafood much fresher, and the Ark oyster feed (the record is 110) of Willapa Bay bivalves lightly breaded and pan-fried continues to receive accolades; however, not everything here deserves raves. Someone in the kitchen has a heavy hand with the cream (you'll find it overwhelming many items, from their famed Oysters Italian to their heavenly—in moderation—calamari Dijonnaise to the house salad dressing). Our advice? Order simply (and try not to fill up on the exceptional herb-spiked rolls): a silky appetizer of Asian-style grilled Japanese eggplant, two honest-to-God scampi kindly sautéed with tomatoes, mushrooms, and onions, or Willapa Bay sturgeon with mushrooms, sun-dried tomatoes, and balsamic vinegar. Of course, don't miss the oyster feed; but do wonder why raw oysters on the half shell are nowhere in sight. ■ *273rd and Sandridge Rd (on the old Nahcotta dock, next to the oyster fleet), Nahcotta; (360)665-4133; $$$; full bar; AE,*

MC, V; checks OK; dinner Tues–Sun (Thurs–Sun in winter), brunch Sun.

LODGINGS

Moby Dick Hotel ★ Although it looks fairly institutional at first glance, this friendly place is one of those that grows on you. Originally built in 1929 by a railroad conductor with his gold-prospecting money, the hotel is under the careful ownership of Fritzie and Edward Cohen (of the Tabard Inn in Washington, DC). It's quite beachy (without really having a beach), with an extravagant garden, a couple of chairs outside for bayside lounging, a couple of spacious public rooms, nine small and modest bedrooms (most with shared bath), and a rambling bay front (loaded with oysters). In the afternoon, join the innkeepers for a few Pacific oysters on the half shell. A very private sauna pavilion is tucked away in a cedar grove overlooking the bay. Full breakfasts (included) make use of the hotel's own garden produce. Pets are welcome. Dinners are offered (for guests and others) off and on depending on whether the chef is in residence; call ahead to find out. ■ *South of Bay Ave on Sandridge Rd, Nahcotta; (360) 665-4543; PO Box 82, Nahcotta, WA 98637; mobydick@aone.com; www.aone.com/~mobydick; $$; MC, V; checks OK.*

LONG BEACH PENINSULA: OYSTERVILLE

Oysterville dates to 1854 and was the county seat until (legend has it) a group from South Bend stole the county records in 1893. South Bend remains the county seat to this day, but Oysterville has its own charm. It's listed on the National Register of Historic Places and features a distinctive row of shoreside homes, surrounded by stately cedars and spruce trees. (Follow Sandridge Road north to the Oysterville sign.)

Oysterville is, of course, known for its bivalves, and Oysterville Sea Farms, at the old cannery in Oysterville, sells 'em by the dozen (open weekends, year-round).

Leadbetter Point State Park, on the northern tip of the peninsula, is a stopover site for over 100 species of birds, and a nature-lover's paradise with miles of sandy trails as well as untrampled ocean beaches. Hiking trails abound (3 miles north of Oysterville on Stackpole Road).

TOKELAND

Set on the long peninsula reaching into northern Willapa Bay, this crabbing community, named after 19th-century Chief Toke, is the loneliest part of the southwest Washington coast, where the omnipresent tackiness of contemporary resort life is least apparent. In the meantime, pick up a container of crabmeat and some cocktail sauce from Nelson Crab (open daily 9am–5pm) to enjoy while sitting on a driftwood log at the beach across the street; (360) 267-2911.

LODGINGS

Tokeland Hotel ★ This chaste, century-old structure teetered for several years on the edge of genteel collapse before a series of rescues. A Seattle couple bought "the oldest resort hotel in Washington" and made major improvements in both the food and the plumbing. The remodeling will probably never be complete, but all 18 rooms are open. Some offer views of pristine Willapa Bay. Mind you, they're somewhat spartan, and bathrooms are shared, but the rooms have an old-fashioned charm that doesn't include a lumpy mattress. The creaky-floored restaurant is often filled with folks from the surrounding community who take advantage of large helpings of good food at reasonable prices. Breakfast is included in the price of a room (kids love the pigs in a blanket). ■ *100 Hotel Rd (at Kindred Ave), Tokeland, WA 98590; (360) 267-7006; $$; beer and wine; DC, MC, V; local checks only; breakfast, dinner every day, lunch Mon–Sat (soup and dessert only on Sun; winter hours vary).*

GRAYLAND

RESTAURANTS

The Dunes ★ Turn off Highway 105 at the sign of the giant razor clam and follow the bumpy gravel road a quarter mile down to the dunes. You will discover a funky kind of place that's as comfortable as an old windbreaker: a beachcomber's hideaway, decorated with shells, ship models, stained glass, and, most recently, a greenhouse at the entry. With a fireplace in the middle and linen-draped oak tables, the main dining room is warm and enticing after a walk on the beach. The aptly named restaurant offers a front-row seat on the ocean just beyond the dunes. Quality control isn't what it was when the moderately eccentric owners were in their prime, but most of the time you won't find fresher seafood. ■ *783 Dunes Rd (off Hwy 105), Grayland; (360) 267-1441; $$; beer and wine; AE, DC, MC, V; checks OK; breakfast, lunch, dinner every day (winter hours vary).*

GRAYS HARBOR

The debate over the spotted owl and widespread negative publicity in the wake of native son Kurt Cobain's suicide ("Aberdeen is not Nirvana!" was the refrain) left the locals in a temporary funk. But this county, with natural resources to match its natural beauty and real estate bargains galore, has rebounded. The wild beauty of the expansive bay and the obvious attractions of the coastal beaches draw retirees, tourists, surfers, and migrating shorebirds.

A half million Arctic-bound shorebirds migrate from as far south as Argentina and congregate on the tidal mud flats at the wildlife refuge of **Bowerman Basin** each spring from about mid-April through the first week of May. At high tide, the birds rise in unison in thick flocks that shimmer through the air, twisting and turning, before settling back onto their feeding grounds. There are trails through the marsh (located just beyond the Hoquiam airport). Be sure to wear boots. For more information and peak migratory days, call the Grays Harbor National Wildlife Refuge, (360)753-9467.

WESTPORT

For a small coastal town that regularly endures flood tides of tourists, Westport remains surprisingly friendly, scenic, and uncondominiumed. Most "fishers" rise early and join the almost comically hasty 6am exodus from the breakwater to cross the bumpy bar and head for the open sea. (Breakfast cafes are open by 5am, some much earlier, especially those down by the docks.) The unpredictable **salmon fishing** seasons of recent years have changed charter-boat marketing. Bottom-fishing trips for halibut, lingcod, and rockfish are increasingly popular, and many charter operators now feature whale-watching cruises as well. **Gray whales** migrate off the coast March through May on their way toward Arctic feeding waters, where they fatten up for the trip back down to their breeding lagoons in Baja come fall.

Charter rates vary little from company to company. Some of the best **charters** include Cachalot, (360)268-0323; Deep Sea, (800)562-0151 or (360)268-9300; Westport, (800)562-0157 or (360)268-9120; Islander, (800)322-1740 or (360)268-9166; Washington Charters, (800)562-0173 or (360)268-0900; Travis, (360)268-9140. (Toll-free numbers are often in operation only during the season.)

You can drop by and pick up a bushel of Brady's Oysters (a shack at water's edge), (360)268-0077, or take home some great chorizo, kielbasa, or beef jerky, all made on the premises of Bay City Sausage Company, (360)648-2344. Both are located near Westport on the Aberdeen-Westport Highway.

Things quiet down until the 3:30pm return of the fleets. You can explore the town during this lull, or head for the expansive beaches—open for driving, jogging, clamming, or picnicking—along the coast from Grayland to Westport. Wet-suited surfers can be found year-round hoping to catch their own Big One along the jetty at Westhaven State Park, where there's a new concrete walkway cresting the dunes all the way to the historic **Westport Lighthouse**.

RESTAURANTS

Constantin's ★★ Constantin "Dino" Kontogonis, who came to Westport in 1987 to get away from Seattle, is a gregarious Greek with a gift for cooking. Dino's place is only a stone's throw from the Westport docks, so there's fresh seafood galore, including salmon, oysters, crab, and squid. Just park alongside the charter boats and follow your nose to the tiny cafe with a big heart. Olive oil, garlic, shallots, onions, and fresh herbs mingle in the saucepan with tomatoes, mushrooms, and wine; pasta comes with seafood, fresh veggies, or a from-scratch basil pesto, ensuring that the aromas wafting past the plastic grapes are heavenly. The menu changes as often as the fresh seasonal ingredients Dino insists on using, and the wine list is one of the most ambitious on the Olympic Peninsula. Locals might complain of high prices, but by city standards they're really quite reasonable. And no one ever leaves hungry. ■ *320 E Dock St (½ block from the dock), Westport; (360)268-0550; $$; beer and wine; AE, MC, V; local checks only; lunch, dinner every day (call for winter hours).* &

LODGINGS

The Chateau Westport ★ This is considered the fanciest motel lodging in Westport—though it bears no resemblance to any chateau we know. Prices for the 108 units are moderate, especially in the off season when beachcombing is best; indoor pool and hot tub are available. Studio units have fireplaces and can be rented alone (with a queen-size hideabed) or in conjunction with adjoining bedrooms to form a suite. It's not the quietest place, and the continental breakfast is nothing to get excited about, but the ocean views are magnificent; those from the third and fourth floors are best. ■ *710 W Hancock (at S Forest St), Westport; (360)268-9101; PO Box 349, Westport, WA 98595; $$; AE, DC, MC, V; no checks.* &

COSMOPOLIS

LODGINGS

Cooney Mansion ★★ For many years this 1908 manse housed timber tycoon Neil Cooney, his servants, and his out-of-town guests. There's a very masculine feel to the place (Cooney was a bachelor and a J. Edgar Hoover–style taskmaster who had 1,200 workers under his thumb): spruce wainscoting in the living room, large windows with dark wooden frames, heavy Craftsman furniture throughout. A clubby feel prevails and, from the deck on the second floor, you can sit and watch golfers on the 18-hole public course next door. Tennis courts are visible as you head up the driveway (they are part of Mill Creek Park, but are available for guests' use). Jim and Judi Lohr are fastidious hosts, offering eight guest rooms and a bounteous "Lumber Baron's Breakfast." Kids clearly are discouraged here. ■ *1705 5th St (follow C St to 5th), Cosmopolis; (360)533-0602; PO Box 54, Cosmopolis, WA 98537; cooney@techline.com; www.techline.com/~cooney; $$; AE, DC, MC, V; no checks.*

With the timber industry in decline, these old Siamese-twin lumber towns are in transition, as they have been since the sawmilling and shipping glory days of the early 1900s. The **Grays Harbor Historical Seaport**, east side of Aberdeen, (360)532-8611, provides tours of a splendid replica of Captain Robert Gray's *Lady Washington*, a 105-foot floating museum. The ship is often on tour to other ports of call, so be sure to phone ahead.

RESTAURANTS

Parma ★★★ In Aberdeen, the closest thing to heaven is when Pierre Gabelli's mother brings you a plate of his gnocchi. The dimpled potato dumplings melt in your mouth, and the French-Italian chef is always experimenting. One night it's a spicy arrabbiata, the next it's spinach gnocchi expertly sauced with Gorgonzola. The nightly specials are often adventurous and never disappointing: wild boar with polenta; mussels, clams, and saffron with spinach fettuccine. The pasta is house-made, and a charcoal grill produces succulent steaks, chops, and sausages. In between courses, Gabelli's papa, a retired electronics engineer, brings you up to date on Ferrari's wind tunnel tests. Mama, meanwhile, keeps busy baking bread so rich it could be dessert and desserts so rich you'll wish you hadn't eaten all that rigatoni. ■ *116 W Heron St (1 block west of Broadway), Aberdeen; (360)532-3166; $$; beer and wine; AE, MC, V; checks OK; dinner Tues–Sat.* ♿

Billy's Bar and Grill ★ The best little whorehouse in town used to be right across the street from this historic pub, and the walls at Billy's sport some original artwork that recalls Aberdeen's bawdy past. The place is named after the infamous Billy Gohl, who terrorized the Aberdeen waterfront in 1907. Billy shanghaied sailors and robbed loggers, consigning their bodies to the murky Wishkah River through a trapdoor in a saloon only a block away from the present-day Billy's—where you get a square-deal meal (thick burgers and seasoned fries) and an honest drink, without much damage to your pocketbook. ■ *322 E Heron St (corner of G St), Aberdeen; (360)533-7144; $; full bar; AE, DC, MC, V; local checks only; breakfast, lunch, dinner every day.* ♿

Bridges ★ Sonny Bridges started out with a corner cafe over 30 years ago and kept expanding his horizons—both in space and in taste. The current incarnation is an airy, pastel-hued setting with casual class. The diverse menu contains few surprises, but Sonny owns a piece of the best seafood market in town, and the clams and salmon can't be beat. There's also prime rib that's really prime and pasta that hasn't been overcooked. The busy bar is first-class, with espresso drinks and Northwest wines and

▼

Aberdeen/ Hoquiam

Restaurants

▲

beers. The staff, as always, is extraordinarily professional. ■ *112
N G St (1st and G), Aberdeen; (360)532-6563; $$; full bar; AE,
DC, MC, V; local checks only; lunch Mon–Sat, dinner every day.* ⅃

The Levee Street ★ We're talking ambience here: plum-colored
carpets, soft music, and a great view of tugboats and seabirds.
And this is one of the few nonsmoking restaurants in timber
country. The extensive and eclectic menu offers everything
from the "Raging Bull"—a logger's portion of medium-rare
prime rib coated with a port and peppercorn sauce—to fresh
salmon and bouillabaisse. They have great, chewy bread sticks.
■ *709 Levee St (7th and Levee), Hoquiam; (360)532-1959; $$;
full bar; AE, DC, MC, V; checks OK; lunch Tues–Fri, dinner
Tues–Sat.* ⅃

LODGINGS

Aberdeen Mansion Inn ★★ It's a bit of a tourist attraction, what
with street signs leading from downtown to this "historic Aberdeen mansion," and gawking visitors are asked to pay a fee
for a tour; but if you get beyond that and actually make a reservation, your stay will be pleasant, peaceful, and private (restrictions are on the visitors, not you). Mitchell and Karen Pavletich
turned the local landmark into a four-room (and one suite) bed-
and-breakfast inn. And if you've got a reason to spend the day
in Aberdeen, this former lumber baron's mansion gives you
a reason to spend the night. No children, period. ■ *807 N M
St (corner of 5th), Aberdeen, WA 98520; (360)533-7079 or
(888)533-7079; $$; AE, MC, V; checks OK.*

Lytle House Bed & Breakfast ★ In 1897, when timber baron
Robert Lytle built what was to become Hoquiam's architectural
landmark, Hoquiam's Castle, his brother Joseph erected a
smaller version next door. This has become Lytle House, dec-
orated throughout with the almost-requisite Victorian embel-
lishments (don't miss the magnificent square grand piano). The
front parlor feels too formal for anyone to hunker down in a big
chair for reading, but there are more than enough parlors for
all, and the eight guest rooms are quite spacious. On the sec-
ond floor, the Windsor Room has a small library, an antique
wood stove, and a balcony overlooking the town. Of the eight
rooms, six have private baths, including one Japanese-style with
soaking tub, and four have water views. Breakfasts are excel-
lent. Owners Robert and Dayna Bencala—two young refugees
from California—are B&B hosts of the best kind: genuinely
hospitable yet unobtrusive. ■ *509 Chenault (west on Emerson,
right on Garfield, up hill to Chenault), Hoquiam, WA 98550;
(360)533-2320 or (800)677-2320; benchmark@techline; $$;
AE, DC MC, V; checks OK.*

RESTAURANTS

Savory Faire ★★ Savory Faire grew out of Candi Bachtell's popular cooking classes at Montesano's award-winning Community School. Today, marvelous aromas come wafting out of Candi and Randy Bachtell's charming place just a block away from the handsome and historic Grays Harbor County Courthouse. Breakfasts feature flawlessly cooked omelets, country-fried potatoes, fresh-baked breads, and wonderful cinnamon rolls. The coffee is as good as you'll find anywhere in Seattle. At lunchtime, try the turkey pesto sandwich or an exceptional French dip. There is now a wine boutique on the premises, as well as specialty coffees, cookbooks, condiments, and kitchenware. ■ *135 S Main St (take Montesano exit off Hwy 12), Montesano; (360)249-3701; $; beer and wine; AE, DC, MC, V; checks OK; breakfast, lunch Mon–Sat, dinner Tues–Sat.*

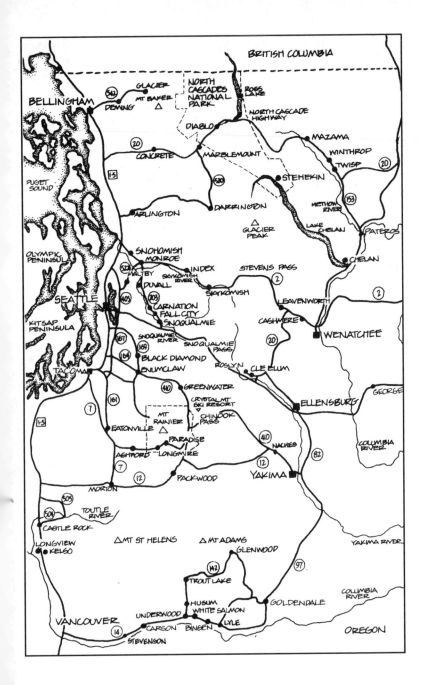

Washington Cascades

*Easterly crossings, starting in the north from Deming
to Mount Baker, then to the Methow Valley along the
North Cascades Highway. Farther south in the Cascade Loop:
eastward along Highway 2 to Cashmere, south to Cle Elum on
Highway 97, westward again on I-90, then north through dairy
country to Duvall. The two Mount Rainier approaches—Maple
Valley to Chinook Pass; Eatonville to Paradise—followed by
a southward route through the heart of the Cascades, past
Mount St. Helens, and a short easterly jog along the
Columbia River (including Mount Adams).*

DEMING

RESTAURANTS

Deming Restaurant and Lounge ★ In operation since 1922, this
is one of the few real steak houses left hereabouts. It's not a
fancy place, but everyone comes for the steak. You can get a
tender, well-aged 6-ounce tenderloin for $9.95, a 16-ouncer for
$16.95. The ultimate challenge here: you can have a 72-ounce
steak, with a baked potato and spaghetti, for free—provided
you can eat the whole thing in a half hour. If you can't, it's $44.95.
So far, everyone has paid up. ■ *5016 Deming Rd (off Mount
Baker Hwy, at 1st St), Deming; (360)592-5282; $$; full bar; MC,
V; checks OK; lunch, dinner every day.*

Carol's Coffee Cup Carol's is a local institution: a pleasant little
hamburger joint/bakery/cafe, long a favorite with loggers,
skiers, and hikers. The hamburgers are fine, but the big cin-
namon rolls and homemade pies are best. Be prepared for a
long wait on summer weekends and during the peak of the
Mount Baker ski season. ■ *5415 Mt Baker Hwy (1½ miles east
of Deming), Deming; (360)592-5641; $; no alcohol; DIS, MC, V;
checks OK; breakfast, lunch, dinner every day.* ⑤

LODGINGS

The Logs Resort ★ Five log cabins nestled among dense stands
of alder and fir at the confluence of the Nooksack River and
Canyon Creek compose this rustic retreat. Cabins are com-
fortable, not luxurious: they sleep up to eight people in bunk-
bedded rooms and on pull-out couches. The centerpoint of each
cabin is the large fireplace (built from river cobbles and slabs
of Nooksack stone), stocked with firewood. Each cabin has a

fully equipped kitchen and a charcoal grill. There's a pool and a volleyball court for summer. This is a great place to bring the kids and the family dog. ■ *Milepost 30.5 Mt Baker Hwy (30 miles east of Bellingham, 2½ miles west of Glacier), Deming; (360)599-2711; 9002 Mt Baker Hwy, Deming, WA 98244; $$; no credit cards; checks OK.*

GLACIER

RESTAURANTS

Milano's Restaurant and Deli ★ After a day in the mountains, this place is exactly what you want: casual carbos. Popular with locals and carbo-loading hikers and skiers alike, this tiny, clean restaurant is really three: a deli (with meats and sandwiches), an informal Italian restaurant (with hearty pastas and a well-priced wine selection), and a nice place for dessert and coffee. The pasta, made fresh daily, stars in two different lasagnes, a filling chicken Gorgonzola, and a slew of wonderful raviolis. ■ *9990 Mt Baker Hwy (right on the highway), Glacier; (360)599-2863; $$; beer and wine; MC, V; checks OK; breakfast Sat–Sun, lunch, dinner every day.*

MOUNT BAKER

Mount Baker Ski Area, 56 miles east of Bellingham, has gained quite a reputation with snowboarders. It's open mid-November through April (the longest season in the state). The mountain never lacks for snow, and runs are predominantly intermediate, with bowls, meadows, and trails. Call (360)734-6771.

MARBLEMOUNT

Hundreds of bald eagles perch along the Skagit River from December through March, scavenging on spawned-out salmon. You'll be able to spy a number of them from the road, along Route 20 between Rockport and Marblemount (bring your binoculars). However, the best way to view them is from the river; call **Downstream River Runners**, (425)486-0220; **Northern Wilderness River Riders**, (206)448-RAFT; or **Orion Expeditions**, (206)547-6715. The adventuresome may want to canoe downriver from Marblemount to Rockport (an easy 8 miles); the river appears tame but can be deceptively swift.

DIABLO

Since the only road access to Ross Lake is south from Hope, BC, the best way to get to the southern end of the lake—save by a 3½-mile hike—is on the **Seattle City Light** tugboat from Diablo. Here Seattle City Light built an outpost for crews constructing and servicing the dams on the river. The tugboat leaves twice daily

(8:30am and 3pm), running from mid-June through the end of October, and the ride costs $2.50; (206)386-4393.

Skagit Tours. Worth visiting are the dams themselves, built by a visionary engineer named James Delmage Ross. Skagit tours are 4-hour journeys through the Skagit Project, including a slide presentation, a ride up an antique incline railway to **Diablo Dam**, and then a boat ride through the gorge of the Skagit to Ross Dam—a construction of daring engineering in its day. Afterward there is a lavish chicken dinner back in Diablo. There are also 90-minute minitours available. Six miles down the road in Newhalem are inspirational walks to the grave of Ross and to Ladder Creek Falls, with plantings gathered from around the world. Tours are arranged through Seattle City Light, 1015 Third Avenue, Seattle, WA 98104, (360)684-3030; summer only; reserve well in advance.

MAZAMA

With a sociable soup-and-espresso counter, products that range from Tim's chips to Patagonia shirts, a clever goat logo on everything from water bottles to T-shirts, and a picnic area (complete with grillmeister in the summer), **Mazama Country Store** has become a favorite hangout for valley locals and travelers alike; (509)996-2855. Mazama itself seems to be becoming a little high-end mecca for fishing (a fly-fishing shop sells Sage products) and climbing enthusiasts (a mountaineering store supports its own climbing wall).

LODGINGS

Freestone Inn and Early Winters Cabins ★★ The 12-room log lodge is phase one of Arrowleaf Development's much bigger plans, which include an 18-hole golf course, a second, larger lodge, and 450 homes; however, even in its embryonic stage the inn sets an elegantly rustic tone for the entire 1,200-acre Wilson Ranch. The two-story lodge, with its use of dark, old-looking logs, blends into the landscape well, and gentle touches lend an environmental appeal. A massive river-rock fireplace centers the lobby, and there's a tiny library nook nearby. The earth-toned rooms, each trimmed in pine and showcasing a stone fireplace, are subdued and classy. The ground-floor rooms are our favorites, opening onto the lakefront lawn or snowy banks. An outdoor hot tub is just between the lake (for swimming in or skiing on) and the lodge. Although the views from the inn are more territorial than grand, the activities are as vast as the Methow Valley itself, with Jack's Hut serving as base camp for virtually anything you can dream of doing—from skiing to whitewater rafting, fly-fishing to hunting. In addition to rooms at the inn, you'll find two luxurious Lakeside Lodges (complete with kitchens and lots of room for families or friends) and six smaller Early Winters Cabins. Nestled in the woods beside Early Winters Creek, these look dark and rustic, but inside, they've been touched with the same sensitivity of style as the inn. In sum, the whole place is probably worthy of three or more stars; however, we will let time be the test and watch how the rest of the project progresses. In the restaurant, chef Todd Brown uses local ingredients such as wild mushrooms, game, and lake trout at dinner. Some guests lunch in town, but most elect to have the kitchen prepare a backpacker's lunch stuffed with good energy. Continental breakfast is complimentary for those at the inn (not in the cabins). ■ *17798 Hwy 20 (1½ miles west of Mazama, just off Hwy 20), Mazama; (509) 996-3906 or (800) 639-3809; Box 11, Mazama, WA 98833; $$$; AE, DC, DIS, MC, V; local checks only; dinner Tues–Sun.*

Mazama Country Inn ★★ With a view of the North Cascades from nearly every window, this spacious 6,000-square-foot lodge makes a splendid year-round destination (especially for horseback riders and cross-country skiers), with 14 good-sized rooms of wooden construction with cedar beams. Some of the guest rooms (all fairly standard) have air conditioning, nice on hot summer Eastern Washington nights. Each room has a private bath, thick comforters on the beds, and futonlike pads that can be rolled out for extra guests. The four rooms behind the sauna have individual decks, two with views of Goat Peak and two looking out into the woods. Winter packages include three family-style meals, but summers are à la carte (best are the meat selections such as beef tenderloin or the spicy ribs). Reservations for meals are suggested. Five cabins with kitchen and bath are available for families or groups of up to 14. ■ *14 miles west of Winthrop, just off Hwy 20, in Mazama; (509) 996-2681 or (800) 843-7951; HRC 74, Box B9, Mazama, WA 98833; mazama@methow.com; www.mazamainn.com; $$; beer and wine; DIS, MC, V; checks OK; breakfast, lunch, dinner every day.*

Mazama Ranch House ★ What was once the original house at the Mazama ranch is no longer part of the Mazama Country Inn. Owners Steve and Kristin Devin now run the ranch house (which sleeps up to 13 guests) and the eight-room motel-style addition. The back door of each room opens to a sunny deck, which is literally on the valley's trail system (so's the under-the-big-sky hot tub). An additional cabin, the rustic Longhorn cabin, has its own sleeping loft and wood stove. There's no restaurant (that's over at the Country Inn) and no common area, but when you've got hundreds of miles of skiing (the old chicken coop is now a waxing room), mountain-biking, or horseback-riding trails just one step from your room, who needs anything but a firm bed and a kitchenette for your Gatorade and PB&Js? The barn, corral, and arena are available for free to any overnighter who arrives with a horse (no pets under 1,000 pounds). For those who don't have their own horse, there's an excellent outfitter just down the road. ■ *42 Lost River Rd (just south of the Mazama*

▼

Mazama

Lodgings

▲

Country Inn, same entrance), Mazama; (509)996-2040; HCR 74, Box A-6, Mazama, WA 98833; devin@methow.com; www.methow. com/~devin/ranch/; $$; MC, V; checks OK. &

WINTHROP

Stroll through this Western-motif town and stop in at the **Shafer Museum**, housed in pioneer Guy Waring's 1897 log cabin on the hill behind the main street. Exhibits tell of the area's early history and include old cars, a stagecoach, and horse-drawn vehicles. It is said that Waring's Harvard classmate Owen Wister came to visit in the 1880s and found some of the material for *The Virginian* here.

The valley offers fine whitewater rafting, spectacular hiking in the North Cascades, horseback riding, mountain biking, fishing, and cross-country or helicopter skiing. An excellent blues festival in the summer brings in such talents as John Mayall and the Bluesbreakers and Mick Taylor. And after you've had a big day outside, quaff a beer at the **Winthrop Brew Pub**, (509)996-3174, in an old schoolhouse in downtown Westernville, a favorite local hangout. **Winthrop Mountain Sports** (257 Riverside Avenue, (509)996-3388) is a good stop for sporting supplies and clothes. **Purple Sage** (245 Riverside Avenue, (509)996-3600) has a load of contemporary Westernalia, and the **Tenderfoot General Store** (at the corner of Riverside Avenue and Highway 20) has anything else you might have forgotten.

Methow Valley Central Reservations is a booking service for the whole valley—Mazama to Pateros—as well as a good source of information on things to see and do and on current ski conditions. Write PO Box 505, Winthrop, WA 98862, or call (800)422-3048 or (509)996-2148.

The Methow Valley Sports Trail Association keeps the valley's excellent cross-country ski trails—150 miles—groomed and available to visitors; PO Box 327, Winthrop, WA, 98862, (509)996-3287; or phone Central Reservations for conditions (see above).

Hut-to-Hut Skiing offers miles of cross-country ski trails connecting with three spartan huts in the Rendezvous Hills. Each hut bunks up to eight people and comes equipped with a wood stove and a propane cookstove. Open for day skiers—a warm, dry lunch stop. For Rendezvous Huts information, call the Central Reservations office listed above.

RESTAURANTS

Duck Brand Cantina, Bakery, and Hotel Built to replicate a frontier-style hotel, Duck Brand is a Winthrop standby for good, filling meals at decent prices—from bulging burritos to fettuccine to sprout-laden sandwiches on whole-grain breads. American-style breakfasts feature wonderful cheesy Spanish potatoes and billowing omelets. The in-house bakery produces delicious baked goods, from biscotti to giant cinnamon rolls to 3-inch-thick berry pie. When you're not in the mood for painfully slow service, just take the sweets to go. Upstairs, the Duck Brand Hotel has six sparsely furnished rooms, priced right. ■ *248 Riverside Ave (on the main street through town), Winthrop; (509) 996-2192; $; beer and wine; AE, MC, V; local checks only; breakfast, lunch, dinner every day.*

LODGINGS

Sun Mountain Lodge ★★★ Here's a spot that has not only stood the test of time, but overcome it—every year the place just seems to be getting better and better. And this year, with the addition of the stunning Mount Robinson rooms, they've outdone themselves. The location has always been dramatic, set on a hill high above the pristine Methow Valley and backed by the North Cascades. Now the massive timber-and-stone resort is equally impressive. It's an urban-cowboy kind of place. Everything's big, from the fireplaces (and their logs) to the views (and every space has a view). Inside, it's styled like the finest Montana ranch, with log furniture, wrought-iron sconces, glass coffee tables. The furnishings vary from building to building: the finest are the eight Mount Robinson rooms (reserve early and get a towering view from the bathtub *and* the shower), but even the older lodge rooms are a few notches above most hotel rooms. In addition, there are 13 appealing cabins available just down the hill at Patterson Lake (good for families—there's a children's play area both here and at the main lodge). The best cabins are the four with the lofts. In summer, there's tennis (two sets of courts), horseback riding (new barn for the horses too), swimming (two heated pools, seasonal), volleyball—along with myriad other lounge sports—fly-fishing trips, golf (nearby), mountain biking, and more. Child care/activity programs are available too. In winter, about 150 miles of well-groomed cross-country trails make this a haven for Nordic skiers. Any time of year you can soak in one of the three outdoor hot tubs (the one nearest the Mount Robinson unit is breathtaking). The restaurant offers an unbeatable table to every guest. Chef Jeff James features locally grown ingredients whenever possible (one appetizer sums it up: Sally Jackson goat cheese wrapped in grilled zucchini, toasted Oregon hazelnuts, and organic baby greens). Lunches and breakfasts are a lot simpler, just the way you expect them to be. The wine list is well chosen. ■ *Patterson Lake Rd, 9 miles southwest of Winthrop; (509) 996-2211 or (800) 572-0493; PO Box 1000, Winthrop, WA 98862; smtnsale@methow.com; www.travel-in-wa.com/ADS/sun_mtn.html; $$$; full bar; AE, MC, V; checks OK; breakfast, lunch, dinner every day.*

WolfRidge Resort ★ The resort (four log buildings with a combination of two-bedroom townhouses, one-bedroom suites, and basic hotel-style rooms) sits—both literally and metaphorically—somewhere between the home-style Mazama Country

Inn and the more showy Sun Mountain Lodge. The lodgings are tastefully, if simply, furnished and provide families and small groups with a full kitchen. In addition, there's one separate cabin for groups of up to six. The 50-acre setting includes an outdoor pool, a Jacuzzi in a river-rock setting, a playground, and a barbecue area (and in winter, a warming hut for skiers). Horseback riders are referred to the local outfitters. ■ *Wolf Creek Rd, 5 miles northwest of Winthrop; (509) 996-2828; Rt 2, Box 655, Winthrop, WA 98862; $$–$$$; MC, V; checks OK.* ⅄

River Run Inn Craig and Carol Lints took a longtime rental house on the banks of the Methow River, built a six-bedroom motel-style addition, connected the two with a modest indoor-pool atrium, and called it an inn. Just a half-mile stroll west of Winthrop, this board-and-batten complex makes a pleasant alternative to the more standard motels in town. The Mountain House rooms open out to the river and are larger than usual. The fairly plain but comfortable house (which sometimes operates as a B&B) is best when you rent the whole thing with a group of friends. Woods and a long dirt driveway keep the highway and its business at bay. ■ *27 Rader Rd (½ mile west of Winthrop on Hwy 20), Winthrop, WA 98862; (509) 996-2173 or (800) 757-2709; $$; MC, V; checks OK.* ⅄

PATEROS

LODGINGS

Amy's Manor ★★ Built in 1928, this enchanting manor is dramatically situated at the foot of the Cascades overlooking the Methow River. The rooms are country-quaint, with patchwork quilts tossed over rocking chairs and comfortable beds. The 170-acre estate includes a small farm with chickens and rabbits. When you combine a harvest from the organic garden with a former Bay Area chef, the table's bounty, be it breakfast or dinner, never disappoints. This is your best bet for miles. ■ *435 Hwy 153 (5 miles north of Pateros), Pateros, WA 98846; (509) 923-2334 or (888) 923-2334; $$; MC, V; checks OK.*

INDEX

Here's where rock climbers go to climb "The Wall." Challenging cliffs loom just behind this tiny town. **The Bush House** (a modest inn first established during the mining boom of 1889) now has 11 pretty (and simple) sleeping rooms. The pub garden out back makes a delightful summertime diversion; 300 Fifth Street, Index; (360) 793-2312.

LAKE WENATCHEE

Lake Wenatchee, just a few miles northwest of Leavenworth, has a state park at one end, with a large, sandy public swimming beach, and campsites in the woods closer to the river. The only lakeside campsites are on the south shore, where you'll also find the trailhead to Hidden Lake (a short family hike to an alpine lake). Ask at the ranger station on the north side of the lake about other great day hikes in the area; (509)548-6977. Wring yourself dry and go play some golf or tennis at the new (and still a bit raw) **Kahler Glen Golf and Ski Resort**; 20890 Kahler Drive, Leavenworth; (509)763-2121 or (800)440-2994 or www.kahlerglen.com for condo reservations.

PLAIN

LODGINGS

Natapoc Lodging ★★★ For any city dweller who has ever dreamed of a weekend home on the Wenatchee River, Natapoc is the next best thing. Each log house claims 1 to 5 piney acres and at least 200 feet of riverfront. All are stocked with everything from a VCR to a microwave oven. And they come in all sizes, from an utterly romantic twosome to a rambling twentysomething. The bigger homes are particularly well thought out, especially for groups (extra bedding, loads of silverware, two living areas, and a large out-of-the-way hot tub). There are lots of outdoorsy things to do, from fly-fishing to cross-country skiing, but frankly, all we really want to do is soak in the cabin's hot tub and make angels in the snow. ■ *4 miles south of Lake Wenatchee, on Beaver Valley Rd, Leavenworth; (509)763-3313 or (888)NATAPOC; 12338 Bretz Rd, Leavenworth, WA 98826; info@ natapoc.com; www.natapoc.com; $$$; AE, MC, V; checks OK.*

Mountain Springs Lodge ★★ This is a big mountain retreat that lets the sun in—any season. Two 20-person-plus lodges and two smaller A-frame chalets face a sprawling lawn. And you'll find yourself pouring out to that lawn too—for volleyball, croquet, or a cartwheel or two. Follow the brook to the barn, where events as special as weddings or as down-home as a family reunion chuck-wagon barbecue take place. A special place for anyone, anytime, but best when you've got an energetic group and rent one of the big lodges (Pine or Ponderosa) or the entire place (great for conferences, reunions, and weddings up to 60). Pine is our favorite, if only because it's not attached to the office. Hot tubs and massive rock fireplaces become the hot spots after a day of snowmobiling (available here) or in the saddle (horses for rent nearby). At press time, a new Beaver Creek Lodge with two suites and a restaurant was in the works. Until then, meals are available with advance reservation. ■ *19115 Chiwawa Loop Rd (½ mile north of Plain), Leavenworth, WA 98826;*

Featherwind's B&B and Country Garden Guest Lodge ★ Romantics favor this floral-and-quilt hideaway in the woods. B&B guests share morning coffee, breakfast, and fresh evening treats, and are well cared for. There's a hot tub and a pool (summers only) to cool the dry summer heat. Those wanting more independence might request one of the two additional houses just down the road. The piney Garden Guest Lodge is great for weddings, and the Cascade Berry bunkhouse is a good place to stash a bunch of friends—it's clean, fresh, and new. The yard—although portions of it are immaculate, just enough for the wedding album—could use a little sprucing up here and there, but this place is quickly becoming a favorite hideaway in the Plain Valley. ■ *17033 River Rd (3 miles from Plain), Leavenworth, WA 98826; (509) 763-2011; $$; MC, V; checks OK.*

LEAVENWORTH

A stunning alpine setting in the Cascade Range, Leavenworth, once a railroad yard and sawmill town, decided years ago to recast itself as a Bavarian-style town with tourism as its primary industry. The architecture sets the tone, and while some cringe at the dirndls-and-lederhosen decor, beyond the facade, most find a very appealing town. Popular festivals are the **Autumn Leaf Festival** the last weekend in September and the first weekend in October, the **Christmas Lighting Festival** the first two Saturdays in December, and **Maifest** the second weekend in May.

▼

Leavenworth

▲

Shopping. We recommend browsers head to the Gingerbread Factory (828 Commercial Street) for authentic decorated gingerbread cookies and a delightful village of gingerbread houses; Images and Sounds (Ninth and Commercial) for distinctly non-Bavarian posters, prints, and notecards; Die Musik Box (837 Front Street) for a dazzling (and sometimes rather noisy) array of music boxes; the Alpen Haus (downstairs at 807 Front Street) for a fascinating collection of dollhouse furniture and miniatures; Cabin Fever Rustics (923 Commercial Street) for help in creating the Western bungalow; and A Country Heart (821 Front Street) for country touches for the urban home.

Other attractions include **Homefires Bakery**, where visitors can see the German-style wood-fired oven (the nine-grain bread is the thing to get) and during fair weather can sit at the picnic table on the lawn and have cinnamon rolls and coffee (an easy mile southwest of town, 13013 Bayne Road, off Icicle Road, (509) 548-7362). There's also the **Leavenworth Brewery** (636 Front Street, (509) 548-4545), which has on tap nine beers made on the premises (the types rotate with the seasons), and offers daily tours of the small brewery itself.

Outdoor activities abound in this area year-round; check with the Leavenworth Ranger Station (on the eastern edge of town, (509)782-1413) or visitors center for information and maps on hiking, fishing, skiing, mountain biking, rafting, and horseback riding. Tour the **fish hatchery** on Icicle Creek (12790 Fish Hatchery Road, off Icicle Road, (509)548-7641) to watch the chinook salmon run (June and July) and spawn (August and September); golf at the scenic 18-hole Leavenworth Golf Club, (509)548-7267.

Scottish Lakes Back Country Cabins, 8 miles into the backcountry west of Leavenworth, is a cluster of primitive plywood cabins at the edge of one of the nation's finest wilderness areas. You can ski the 8 miles or be carted up in a heated 12-seat snowcat and ski the 3,800-foot descent home; High Country Adventures, PO Box 2023, Snohomish, WA 98291-2023, (206)844-2000 or (888)9-HICAMP, by reservation only.

RESTAURANTS

Restaurant Osterreich (Tyrolean Ritz Hotel) ★★ Find your way down to the cellar of the Ritz, and you'll find yourself in one of Leavenworth's finest Austrian restaurants. It's a dim place, void of windows, but gently flickering candlelight warms the room. Alpine illustrations fill the walls and big bouquets of flowers divide the restaurant from the bar. The Austrian chefs show their talent here; if it's hearty German fare you crave, this is your best bet in town. Come hungry. Appetizers, especially the crawfish strudel with a tart sorrel salad, are outstanding. Still, many appetites have been satisfied just by one of the entrees, such as the robust braised lamb shank or the duck. Desserts are excellent, but we doubt you'll have room. Upstairs, the friendly hotel offers 16 standard, streetfront rooms. ■ *633 Front St (in basement of Tyrolean Ritz Hotel, on the main street), Leavenworth; (509)548-4031; $$; full bar; AE, MC, V; checks OK; lunch, dinner every day.* &

Lorraine's Edel Haus Inn ★ Edel Haus got its start as a bed and breakfast; today it's a quiet, pleasant restaurant with an international menu, and one of the few places in town where vegetarians find reprieve from the schnitzel. Here you'll find plump portobello mushrooms with goat cheese and garlic pâté on crostini, a rich apple-and-beet polenta laced with Gorgonzola and a basil/walnut vinaigrette, or a perfect puttanesca. The ambitious menu changes about once a month. You can always find a schnitzel at the Edel Haus, but those who prefer calling it "Lorraine's" know that the chef has a lot more fun elsewhere on the menu. Upstairs, there are several pretty guest rooms, and next door there's a cottage suite with a Jacuzzi and gas fireplace. Lorraine's doesn't serve breakfast, but does offer its overnight guests a 50 percent discount on the other meals. ■ *320 9th St (between Commercial and the river), Leavenworth;*

(509)548-4412; $$; beer and wine; MC, V; local checks only; lunch, dinner every day (dinners only in winter).

LODGINGS

Abendblume Pension ★★★ This is the place where you come to leave everything behind (especially the kids). It's one of the most elegant, sophisticated inns in town, run by the most gracious host. A sweeping staircase, beautifully adorned, leads upstairs. The two best rooms have wood-burning fireplaces, Italian marble bathrooms with whirlpool tubs that discreetly open to the room (including a shower with two heads and four body sprays), and sun-drenched window seats. But, trust us, every room (each with its own VCR) is an escape here, regardless of the size. There's a grand piano in the parlor, and outside on the patio a hot tub that cascades into a garden waterfall. In the morning, breakfast at your own table in the pine-trimmed breakfast room when you are ready. ■ *12570 Ranger Rd (north on Ski Hill Dr at west end of town, then west on Ranger Rd), Leavenworth; (509)548-4059 or (800)669-7634; PO Box 981, Leavenworth, WA 98826; $$$; MC, V; checks OK.*

Run of the River ★★★ Here's a place that just keeps getting better and better. Monty and Karen Turner built this log inn on the bank of the Icicle River, and it boasts such solitude, comfort, and exquisite attention to detail that you may want to spend the entire day on the deck, reading or watching the wildlife in the refuge across the river with the binoculars provided. There are six rooms, each with hand-hewn log bed, private bath, TV (cable), deck, complimentary robes, and even your own bubble kit, in case stargazing from the hot tub isn't enough entertainment. Best rooms face the river. Our favorite, the Aspens Room, warmed by a wood stove (already lit upon your arrival), has perhaps the best river view and is closest to the well-planned (and quiet) outdoor Jacuzzi. But others prefer to be upstairs in a room with a reading loft. Hearty breakfasts emphasize the seasonal discoveries from a local organic farmer and the Turners' own herb garden. Mountain bikes are available for off-road explorations (ask the Turners for where-to-go tips—they've published an excellent array of area-specific activity guides). ■ *9308 E Leavenworth Rd (1 mile east of Hwy 2), Leavenworth; (509)548-7171 or (800)288-6491; PO Box 285, Leavenworth, WA 98826; $$; AE, MC, V; checks OK.*

▼

Leavenworth

Lodgings

▲

Sleeping Lady ★★★ This is exactly the kind of place Leavenworth needed—a quintessential Northwest retreat with an acute awareness of the environment. It was built from the remnants of a 1930s CCC camp into a place where people come to be together—sometimes with a group (the place is particularly well set up for conferences), and sometimes with a friend for an evening musical performance (it's the only resort in the Northwest to have a resident string ensemble). The rooms (log beds with additional beds in alcoves or lofts, and their own baths) are set in four different clusters, each with its own courtyard. Best for small groups is the Eyrie, a secluded cabin on the hill with its own wood stove, whirlpool bath, and (our favorite touch) a sleeping porch. There are also a couple of more economical bunkhouses. Numerous conference buildings (from a dance studio to a spacious 60-person meeting house) are comfortably elegant, with touches such as Oriental rugs and wood stoves; however, all spaces are well set up for high-tech compatibility. The original fieldstone chapel is now a spectacular 200-seat performing arts theater (and the home of the Icicle Creek Music Center). The grotto with its rocky firepit makes a great gathering spot. Although conferences have first dibs here, there is flexibility for other guests on a space-available basis. Chef Damiane Brown serves an excellent meal in a (slightly disconcerting) buffet-style. All in all, a superb place to rest your soul and awaken your senses. ■ *7375 Icicle Rd (2½ miles south of Leavenworth), Leavenworth; (509)548-6344 or (800)574-2123; PO Box 1060, Leavenworth, WA 98826; sleepingla@aol. com; www.sleepingladyresort.com; $$; MC, V; checks OK.* &

Haus Lorelei Inn ★ Here's a rarity: a bed and breakfast that welcomes kids. There are 10 comfortable European-style rooms (not indestructible, but not overly precious either), and each is large enough to set up a spare bed here and there (the Nussknacker even has room enough for two beds in the bathroom, of all places). Those who don't want the kids so close by could stash them in the clubby little Hansel and Gretel Room. (Remember how you always used to make a fort in the closet? Well, here it is, in real life.) The Prinzessin, an octagonal room with a canopy bed, overlooking the river on the main floor, is stunning. The 2-acre site, surrounded by towering pines and fronting the Wenatchee River, is only two blocks from Leavenworth's main street. Each of Elisabeth Saunders' rooms affords gorgeous views of the Cascades; at night you can hear the river rushing over the boulders. Guests may use the private tennis court. There's a hot tub overlooking the river, and a sandy swimming beach on the river isn't far. ■ *347 Division St (1 block off Commercial), Leavenworth, WA 98826; (509)548-5726 or (800)514-8868; www.hauslorelei.com; $$; no credit cards; checks OK.*

Mountain Home Lodge ★ Although you can drive to this lodge in the summer (over 3 miles of rough dirt road), in the winter a heated snow-cat picks you up from the parking lot at the bottom of Mountain Home Road. Miles of tracked cross-country ski trails leave from the back door; you can snowshoe and sled, and there's a 1,700-foot toboggan run. Complimentary cross-country ski equipment is available on loan at the lodge. There's a Jacuzzi on the deck looking out to a broad meadow and the mountains across the valley. Summer activities include hiking, horseshoe pitching, badminton, swimming, and tennis, but there aren't many places to gather when the weather's not co-operating. The nine rooms themselves are very plain (almost motelish), and noise travels from bedroom to bedroom. No kids. Simple meals are included in the price during the winter. ■ *8201-9 Mountain Home Rd (off E Leavenworth Rd and Hwy 2), Leavenworth; (509)548-7077 or (800)414-2378; PO Box 687, Leavenworth, WA 98826; $$$; DIS, MC, V; checks OK.*

Mrs. Anderson's Lodging House ★ This nine-room inn attached to an excellent quilt shop right in Leavenworth has charm to spare and very friendly operators. Although it originally opened in 1903 as a boardinghouse for sawmill workers, it's now the perfect restover for traveling women (though some men like it too). Rooms are minimally, crisply furnished, boardinghouse-style—but sparkling clean. And it's a bargain. (All prices include breakfast of muffins, cereal, juice, tea, and coffee.) We fancy the room upstairs with the deck facing town, or the room with the splendid view of the North Cascades. ■ *917 Commercial St (near center of town), Leavenworth, WA 98826; (509)548-6173 or (800)253-8990; $; AE, MC, V; checks OK.*

River Chalet ★ An ideal vacation spot for groups of couples, this contemporary guest house on the east side of Leavenworth gives the visitor a real feel for the Northwest. It's right on the Wenatchee River, and large windows look out toward the mountains. Four bedrooms sleep 10 comfortably (but slumber parties of 22 sleeping-baggers have occurred); wood stoves keep you warm. Outside there's a hot tub. A large kitchen makes gourmet collaborations a pleasure. Cost is $200 for four, $25 for each additional person. Catering can be arranged on request. ■ *1131 Monroe St (4 miles east of Leavenworth, off Hwy 2), Wenatchee, WA 98801; (509)663-7676; $$$; no credit cards; checks OK.*

Enzian Motor Inn This is the best hotel/motel place in town (and the price includes your breakfast). Built by former contractor Bob Johnson and his son Rob, it is now owned and operated by Rob and his wife, Nancy. The Johnsons were meticulous about detail throughout. Stair rails and ceiling beams are hand-carved by a true Bavarian woodworker. The suites offer in-room spas and fireplaces; even the standard rooms are tasteful and a cut above most "motor inns." During the summer Rob plays the alpenhorn on the balcony. ■ *590 Hwy 2 (on north side of Hwy 2, in center of town), Leavenworth, WA 98826; (509)548-5269 or (800)223-8511; $$; AE, DC, DIS, MC, V; checks OK.* &

CASHMERE

This little orchard town gives cross-mountain travelers who aren't in a Bavarian mood an alternative to stopping in Leavenworth. The main street has put up Western storefronts; the town's bordered by river and railroad.

Chelan County Historical Society and Pioneer Village (600 Cottage Avenue, (509)782-3230) has an extensive collection of Indian artifacts and archaeological material; the adjoining pioneer village puts 19 old buildings, carefully restored and equipped, into a nostalgic grouping.

Aplets and Cotlets, confections made with local fruit and walnuts from an old Armenian recipe, have been produced in Cashmere for decades. You can tour the plant at Liberty Orchards and (of course) consume a few samples (117 Mission Street, (509)782-2191).

RESTAURANTS

The Pewter Pot Here you can get Early American food such as apple country chicken topped with owner Kristi Biornstad's own apple cider sauce, Plymouth turkey dinner, and New England boiled dinner. Desserts are tasty. The restaurant, short on atmosphere, has been prettied with lace-curtain dividers that help soften the lone room. Biornstad works hard to serve dishes that reflect the area, using local ingredients. Try one of the daily specials. But if you want dinner, arrive early; the place closes promptly at 8pm even on Saturdays. ■ *124½ Cottage Ave (downtown, in business district), Cashmere; (509) 782-2036; $$; beer and wine; MC, V; checks OK; lunch, dinner Tues–Sat.* ⑥

LODGINGS

Cashmere Country Inn ★★ This is a first-class inn in the middle of Aplet-and-Cotlet country. The farmhouse and its gardens are fitted out with a keen eye for aesthetics. The five guest rooms are a bit smaller than you might expect for a place of such ambitions, but we'll trade extra dimension for such attention to details any day (a lit fire in the fireplace, complimentary Saturday night dessert). One room, with French doors opening to the swimming pool and hot tub area, is also available. Breakfasts are an accomplished cook's delight. Take advantage of this place any time of the year: in summer for poolside lounging, in fall for apple picking (and fresh cider). ■ *5801 Pioneer Dr (off Hwy 2, follow Division to Pioneer), Cashmere, WA 98815; (509) 782-4212 or (800) 291-9144; $$; AE, MC, V; checks OK.*

THORP

LODGINGS

Circle H Holiday Ranch ★★ Sweeping views of the Kittitas Valley and the Cascade foothills and a small herd of horses are the big draws to the Circle H, located an easy hour and a half from Seattle. The sprawling, modern ranch house was bought out of bankruptcy from an agriculture baron who had hit hard times; Betsy Ogden converted the bunkhouses into two-room suites, decorated with the overflow from her collection of Westernalia. Each sleeps four and contains a kitchenette and bath; books, puzzles, and playing cards fill the shelves, but no phones or TVs (there's a big-screen TV in the day room). Meals, included in the price of your stay, are served family-style (breakfast only in winter). The corral supports a small menagerie, from rabbits to burros. Oliver, the ranch collie, playfully herds guests around the landscaped grounds. The Ogdens welcome young hands to help with ranch chores, while others opt for a trail ride on one of the horses. The 100,000-acre L. T. Murray Wildlife Area backs up to the ranch and is prime for hiking, biking, and riding, and the nearby Yakima River provides quality fly-fishing and lazy-day river rafting. ■ *810 Watt Canyon Rd (exit 101 off I-90), Thorp, WA 98946; (509)964-2000; $$$; MC, V; checks OK.*

CLE ELUM

Cle Elum Bakery is a longtime local institution, doing as much business these days with travelers as with locals. From one of the last brick-hearth ovens in the Northwest come delicious torcetti, cinnamon rolls, and great old-fashioned cake doughnuts (closed Sundays; First and Peoh, (509)674-2233). **Owen's Meats** across the street is an excellent stop for fresh meats and outstanding beef and turkey jerky; (509)674-2530.

RESTAURANTS

Mama Vallone's Steak House & Inn ★ Talk to the regulars and they'll tell you about the warm welcomes, great steaks, and good homemade pasta at Mama Vallone's. One of the biggest deals is bagna cauda, a "hot bath" of garlic, anchovy, olive oil, and butter into which you dip strips of steak, chicken breast, vegetables, or your favorite seafood. Also recommended are the hearty Tuscany dinner and the pan-fried Veal Vallone, in a bourbon sauce with mushrooms, capers, and much more. Wines are okay; service is exceptional. Upstairs, there are two bedrooms with private baths and antique reproductions. ■ *302 W 1st St (on main drag at west end of town), Cle Elum; (509)674-5174; $$; full bar; AE, DC, MC, V; checks OK; dinner every day.*

LODGINGS

Hidden Valley Guest Ranch ★ A short hour from Seattle is the state's oldest dude ranch on a very private, very beautiful 700 acres. Bruce and Kim Coe have spruced up some of the old cabins: the floors may still be a bit uneven, but the cabins have nice touches like homemade quilts and potbelly stoves. Of the 13 cabins (and a couple of rooms) our favorites are the older ones, particularly Apple Tree and Spruce number 5. The new ones, though fine, trade some charm for separate bedrooms and kitchenettes. Miles of wildflower-lined trails, horseback riding, nearby trout fishing, a pool, a hot tub, and a basketball hoop make up for the basic accommodations. Kids love this place. Indoor fun can be found in the ranch house (table tennis, pool table, and all sorts of fireside games). All meals (included in the price) are taken in the cookhouse, a dining room serving country-style buffets. Some mornings they load up the chuck wagon with wrangler-style breakfasts. Winters are quiet (only breakfast is served), but cross-country skiers and snowmobilers are welcome to use the cabins (best to reserve one with a wood stove, of course). ■ *3942 Hidden Valley Rd (off SR 970 at milepost 8), Cle Elum, WA 98922; (509)857-2322 or (800)5-COWBOY; brucecoe@televar.com; $$; MC, V; checks OK.*

The Moore House ★ This bed and breakfast was originally built in 1913 to house employees of the Chicago, Milwaukee, St. Paul & Pacific Railroad. Now on the National Register of Historic Places, the bunkhouse, with 10 guest rooms and a honeymoon suite, is light, airy, and pleasantly furnished with reproduction antiques. Railroad memorabilia—vintage photographs, model trains, schedules, and other artifacts—are displayed in the hallways and the public rooms. Two cabooses in the side yard are fully equipped with baths, fridges, queen-size beds, and private sun decks. Unfortunately, the current owners aren't the railroad buffs the former owners aimed to be. There's an outdoor hot tub that the proprietors will rev up for your use. ■ *526 Marie St (adjacent to Iron Horse State Park Trail), Cle Elum; (509)674-5939 or (800)2-2-TWAIN; PO Box 629, South Cle Elum, WA 98943; $$; AE, DIS, MC, V; checks OK.*

ROSLYN

Modest turn-of-the-century homes in this former coal-mining town have become weekend places for city folk, and the former mortuary is now a video store and movie theater, but the main intersection (once the stage set for the hit TV series *Northern Exposure*) still offers a cross section of the town's character.

Northern Exposure fans will recognize the old stone tavern, inexplicably called **The Brick**, which has a water-fed brass spittoon running the length of the bar; (509)649-2643. Down the road, behind the town's junkyard, you'll find **Carek's Market**, one of the state's better purveyors of fine meats and sausages; 4 South A Street, (509) 649-2930.

RESTAURANTS

Roslyn Cafe ★ The Roslyn Cafe remains the kind of funky eatery that every picturesque, slightly chic town like Roslyn should have. It's an old building with high ceilings, a short bar that is now a counter, neon in the window, hard chairs, a jukebox with original 78s—full of a sense of different types belonging. Dinners try to be a bit fancier—grilled halibut with dill sauce, Chinese pepper steak. But it's best at lunch, when you can get really good burgers, a fine corn chowder, or a super Philadelphia steak sandwich. Breakfast is also worth the side trip. ■ *28 Pennsylvania Ave (at 2nd), Roslyn; (509) 649-2763; $; beer and wine; MC, V; local checks only; breakfast, lunch every day, dinner Fri–Mon.*

SNOQUALMIE

The lovely Snoqualmie Valley, where the dairyland folds into the mountains, is best known for its falls and its scenery, once the setting for the TV series *Twin Peaks*. The series is long since over, but Peakers can still purchase a T-shirt almost anywhere (even at the bank). The 268-foot **Snoqualmie Falls** just up the road is, as it has always been, a thundering spectacle. There is an observation deck; better is to take a picnic down the 1-mile trail to the base of the falls.

Puget Sound Railway runs a scenic tour up to Snoqualmie Falls gorge most Saturdays and Sundays from April through October. There's also a good railroad museum. Call Snoqualmie Depot for schedule; (206) 746-4025.

The **Snoqualmie Winery**, under the ownership of Stimson Lane, is a splendid stop on the way through the Cascades, with tours, tastings, and a marvelous view; 37444 SE Winery Road, (206) 888-4000.

Snoqualmie Pass. These four ski areas, (206) 236-7277, offer the closest downhill and cross-country skiing for Seattle buffs. Alpental is the most challenging; Snoqualmie has one of the largest ski schools in the country; Ski Acres has some challenging bump runs; and the smallest, Hyak, is a favored spot for downhill telemark skiers, with lighted, groomed cross-country tracks and many miles of trails. In summer, the relatively low-lying trans-mountain route is a good starting point for many hikes. At present, the **Summit Inn** at Snoqualmie Pass (a simple hotel, tastefully done) is your only choice for year-round lodging at the pass; (206) 434-6300 or (800) 557-STAY. Recently, however, the Colorado-based Booth Creek Ski Holdings, Inc. purchased the entire Pass area for development. Look for big changes in 1998.

LODGINGS

The Salish Lodge ★★★ The falls may be the initial draw. But since you really can't see much of them from many of the rooms, it's a good thing the rooms are as much a selling point as the falls themselves. Each room is designed in a tempered country motif: light, clean-lined wooden furnishings, pillowed window seats (or balconies in some), flagstone fireplaces (with a woodbox full of split wood and kindling), and a cedar armoire. The little things are covered here: TV cleverly concealed, bathrobes, and even a telephone in the bathroom. Jacuzzis are separated from the bedrooms with a swinging window. The rooftop

open-ceiling hot tub is another nice feature. There are five banquet rooms downstairs and every detail is well attended to.

The excessive multicourse brunch lives on—though we can
live without it, opting instead for dinner and praying for a table
with a view of the falls. Chef Dean Ecker lends a light touch to
the Northwest-inspired menu. The wine list is almost legendary. ■ *6501 Railroad Ave SE (exit 27 off I-90, follow signs to
Snoqualmie Falls), Snoqualmie, WA 98065; (206)888-2556;
www.salish.com; $$$; full bar; AE, DC, MC, V; checks OK; break-
fast every day, lunch Mon–Fri, dinner every day.* &

FALL CITY

RESTAURANTS

The Herbfarm [*unrated*] This legendary four-star restaurant in
the foothills of the Cascades (which began as a front-yard
wheelbarrow filled with a few extra herbs) went up in flames in
1996; however, plans to rebuild are underway. Look for a re-
opening in late 1998. We expect the new incarnation of owner
Ron Zimmerman and chef Jerry Traunfeld's internationally
renowned restaurant to be just as dramatic as it was before the
fire (and maybe we'll even get a few extra seats out of the
tragedy). What The Herbfarm presents is not simply a meal, but
an opportunity for tasting, learning, and talking about what you
have eaten. Meals generally begin with a short tour of the
herbal gardens, and the education continues throughout the
progression of courses. The gardens and gift shop remain open.
■ *32804 Issaquah–Fall City Rd (3½ miles off I-90 from exit 22),
Fall City; (425)222-7103; herborder@aol.com; open every day.* &

CARNATION

Carnation is a lovely stretch of cow country nestled in the Sno-
qualmie Valley, where a stop for a giant cinnamon roll at **The
River Run Cafe** is practically mandatory; 4366 Tolt Avenue,
(206)333-6100.

At **MacDonald Memorial Park**, meandering trails and an
old-fashioned suspension bridge across the Tolt River provide a
great family picnic setting; Fall City Road and NE 40th Street.

Remlinger Farms. The sky's the limit for your favorite fruits
and vegetables at this U-pick farm. The Strawberry Festival in
mid-June starts off the season. Throughout the summer you can
choose from the best in raspberries, apples, corn, and grapes. The
kids, young and old alike, love tromping through the fields in
search of the perfect jack-o'-lantern-to-be in October; (206)333-
4135 or (206)451-8740.

BLACK DIAMOND

Black Diamond Bakery, now much more than just a bakery, boasts the last wood-fired brick oven in the area. The bread that comes out of it is excellent: 26 different kinds, including raisin, cinnamon, sour rye, potato, seven-grain, honey-wheat, and garlic French. To get there, take the Maple Valley exit from I-405; at Black Diamond, turn right at the big, white Old Town sign; at the next stop sign, veer left; the bakery is on the right; 32805 Railroad Avenue, (360)886-2741.

GREENWATER

RESTAURANTS

Naches Tavern Now this is the way to do a country tavern. The fireplace is as long as a wall and roars all winter long to warm the Crystal Mountain après-ski crowd. The group assembled is a peaceable mix of skiers, hunters, loggers, and locals. The food is homemade and modestly priced—deep-fried mushrooms, chili, burgers, pizza, four-scoop milk shakes. There's a coun-trified jukebox, pool tables, a lending library (take a book, leave a book) of yellowing paperbacks, and furniture so comfortable that the stuffing is coming out. Play a little cribbage, stroke the roving house pets, nod off in front of the hearth. ■ *58411 SR 410E (north side of Hwy 410), Greenwater; (360)663-2267; $; beer and wine; no credit cards; no checks; lunch, dinner every day.*

▼
Crystal
Mountain
Lodgings
▲

CRYSTAL MOUNTAIN

Crystal Mountain Ski Resort is the best in the state, with runs for beginners and experts, plus fine cross-country touring; (360)663-2262. Less well known and less used are the summer facilities. You can ride the chairlift and catch a grand view of Mount Rainier and other peaks; rent condominiums with full kitchens, balconies, or other facilities from **Crystal Mountain Reservations**, (360)663-2558; and play tennis. Other than that, there's just a grocery store, a sports shop, and Rafters, the bar-and-buffet restaurant atop Crystal's lodge. In summer, the Summit House on the mountain offers weekend dinners. Off Highway 410 just west of Chinook Pass.

LODGINGS

Silver Skis Chalet ★ These condominiums are your best bet if you want to stay right on the mountain. They've all got kitchens, and you can pick or choose whether you want a fireplace or what from the 60-or-so options. Great for families, especially with the perk of a pool heated to 90 degrees. ■ *Crystal Mountain Ski Resort; (360)663-2558; 1 Crystal Mt Blvd, Crystal Mt, WA 98022; $$; AE, MC, V; checks OK.* 占

EATONVILLE

Northwest Trek is a "zoo" where animals roam free while people tour the 600-acre grounds in small open-air trams. The buffalo herd steals the show. You can also combine your visit with breakfast at the in-park food service concession, the Fir Bough. Open daily February through October, weekends only the rest of the year; group rates available; 17 miles south of Puyallup on Route 161, (360)832-6116. &

ELBE

The advent of an Elbe dinner train (and an enterprising restaurateur) has turned this onetime sawmill town into more of a museum (some say a graveyard) for antique cabooses. The **Cascadian Dinner Train**—$55 per person, (888)RRDINER—is a 4-hour, 40-mile round-trip train ride from Elbe to Mineral Lake and back. The seven-course dinner (shrimp cocktail, prime rib, and the works) is surprisingly good, and the conductor is well versed in the area's lore. You don't get dinner on the hour-long **Mount Rainier Scenic Railroad**—summers only, (360)569-2588—but the scenery (to Mineral and back) is equally attractive.

ASHFORD

If Ashford is the gateway to Paradise, then **Whittaker's Bunkhouse** (30205 State Route 706 E; (360)569-2439) is the place to stop on the way to the very top—of Mount Rainier, that is. A good place to meet the guides, climbers, hikers, and skiers of The Mountain, it's also the headquarters for the **Mount Tahoma Trails Association** (MTTA). Rooms are basic and cheap (bunks available) but plush compared to a camping pad.

Mount Tahoma Ski Huts, run by MTTA, is Western Washington's first hut-to-hut ski trail system. There are more than 90 miles of trails, three huts, and one yurt in a spectacular area south and west of Mount Rainier National Park. Inquire at Whittaker's Bunkhouse, or contact Mount Tahoma Trails Association, PO Box 206, Ashford, WA 98304; (360)569-2451.

LODGINGS

Wellspring ★★ For more than a decade, Wellspring has quietly greeted outdoor enthusiasts with two spas nestled in a sylvan glade surrounded by evergreens. A soothing hour or two at Wellspring has become almost de rigueur for folks coming off Mount Rainier. Trouble is, no one wanted to leave. Now, that's okay. There are three log cabins with a very in-the-woods feel (no kitchens, no TVs, no phones, just wood stoves and down comforters). A fourth board-and-batten building holds our two favorite lodging options: Tatoosh, with a barn-wood kitchen, river-stone fireplace, and waterfall-like shower, and The Nest, the tiniest of rooms, with a swinging bed below a skylight that will make any bird happy. Pick up a basketful of breakfast when you check in, make an appointment for an hour's massage, and you'll tuck in just perfectly here. ■ *54922 Kernahan Rd (2¼ miles east of Ashford), Ashford, WA 98304; (360)569-2514; $$; MC, V; checks OK.*

Alexander's Country Inn ★ This quaint country inn (circa 1912) just east of Ashford has a somewhat garish blue exterior, and guests enter through a teacup-and-potpourri gift shop. Still, once you're inside, and upstairs (where there's a large common area for guests), the mood mellows. Best is the Tower Room, a small suite in the turret of the manor. A large wheelchair-accessible suite has been added on the second floor—very private, with its own deck. Indeed, this blending of old and new is the real genius here; it feels turn-of-the-century, but the comforts are 1990s. Complimentary wine is served in the parlor in the evening, and there's an outdoor Jacuzzi. There's nothing particularly noteworthy about the two cabins in the corner of the property. The dining room is your best bet in these parts for a fine meal that includes a perfectly pan-fried trout—caught out back in the holding pond. During the summer, get a table on the brick patio. ■ *37515 Rt 706 E (4 miles east of Ashford), Ashford, WA 98304; (360)569-2300 or (800)654-7615; $$; beer and wine; MC, V; checks OK; breakfast (summer only), lunch, dinner every day (weekends only in winter).*

Mountain Meadows Inn and B&B ★ If seclusion near the base of one of Washington's busiest tourist destinations is what you're looking for, you'll find it at Mountain Meadows Inn. Just off the main road, the place is privately situated on 11 landscaped acres (complete with trout pond, nature trails, and an outdoor fire pit for starlit conversation). Five large guest rooms are filled with a hodgepodge of antiques. There's nothing kitschy here; just a tasteful home filled with some Native American baskets. If you need more space, ask about the guest house with two studio apartments. Full breakfasts fuel a day of exploration. ■ *28912 SR 706 E (¼ mile west of Ashford), Ashford; (360)569-2788; PO Box 291, Ashford, WA 98304; $$; MC, V; checks OK.*

Nisqually Lodge ★ Reasonably priced and clean, this standard hotel-like lodge just a few miles before the west entrance to Mount Rainier National Park offers welcome respite to those willing to trade some charm for a phone, TV, and air conditioning. The 24-room, two-story lodge is well visited—returnees like the stone fireplace in the lobby, and the hot tub outside (though the walls are somewhat thin). Coffee and pastries are served for breakfast. ■ *31609 Rt 706 (Hwy 7 to Rt 706, 5 miles from park entrance), Ashford, WA 98304; (360)569-8804; $$; AE, DC, MC, V; no checks.* ♿

The majestic mountain is the abiding symbol of natural grandeur in the Northwest and one of the most awesome mountains in the world. Its cone rises 14,411 feet above sea level, thousands of feet higher than the other peaks in the Cascade Range. The best way to appreciate the mountain is to explore its flanks: 300 miles of backcountry and self-guiding nature trails lead to ancient forests, dozens of massive glaciers, waterfalls, and alpine meadows lush with wildflowers during its short summer. Chinook and Cayuse Passes are closed in winter; you can take the loop trip or the road to Sunrise only between late May and October. The road from Longmire to Paradise remains open during daylight hours in winter. It is advisable to carry tire chains and a shovel during winter, and it is always wise to check current road and weather conditions by calling a 24-hour information service, (360)569-2211. Obligatory backcountry-use permits for overnight stays can be obtained from any of the ranger stations.

Longmire. A few miles inside the southwestern border of the park, the little village of Longmire has the simple **National Park Inn**, (360)569-2275, which also holds a small wildlife museum with plant and animal displays, a hiking information center, and a cross-country skiing rental outlet. The Inn is open year-round.

▼

**Mount
Rainier**

▲

Paradise. At 5,400 feet, Paradise is the most popular destination on the mountain. On the way to this paved parking lot and visitors center, you'll catch wonderful views of Narada Falls and Nisqually Glacier. The visitors center, housed in a flying saucer-like building, has a standard cafeteria and gift shop, extensive nature exhibits and films, and a superb view of the mountain from its observation deck. Depending on the season, you could picnic (our advice is to bring your own) among the wildflowers, explore some of the trails (the rangers offer guided walks), let the kids slide on inner tubes in the snow-play area, try a little cross-country skiing, or even take a guided snowshoe tromp. **Paradise Inn**, (360)569-2275, is a massive 1917 lodge with 126 bare-bones rooms.

Sunrise. Open only during the summer months, the visitors center at Sunrise (6,400 feet) is the closest you can drive to the peak. The old lodge here has no overnight accommodations, but it does offer a snack bar and exhibits about the mountain. Dozens of trails lead from here, such as the short one leading to a magnificent viewpoint of Emmons Glacier Canyon.

Climbing the Mountain. There are two ways to do this: with Rainier Mountaineering, the concessionaire guide service, or in your own party. Unless you are qualified to do it on your own—and this is a big, difficult, and dangerous mountain on which many people have been killed—you must climb with the guide service; call Paradise, (360)569-2227, in the summer; Tacoma, (253)627-6242, in the winter. If you plan to climb with your own party, you must register at one of the ranger stations in Mount Rainier Na-

tional Park, (360)569-2211. Generally, the best time to climb the
mountain is from late June through early September.

PACKWOOD

LODGINGS

Hotel Packwood Just 10 miles west of White Pass Ski Area,
Packwood makes a good base camp for wintertime skiers and
summer hikers into the Goat Rocks Wilderness. A couple of
motels in town may have more modern appliances, but this
spartan lodge (open since 1912) remains a favorite. The woody
aroma from the wood stove in the lobby permeates the place
just enough to make you feel as if you're really in the middle of
the mountains, even though you're really in downtown Packwood. A small, narrow staircase climbs up to the simple shared-
bath rooms. ■ *104 Main St (right downtown), Packwood;
(360)494-5431; PO Box 130, Packwood, WA 98361; $; no credit
cards; checks OK.*

MOUNT ST. HELENS

The temperamental Mount St. Helens simmers about 2 hours
south of Seattle off I-5. On a clear day, it is well worth the trip to
see the 8,365-foot remains, as well as the mountain's regrowth
since the incredible eruption of May 18, 1980 (it's 1,300 feet shorter
than before the blast).

Close to the freeway, before you begin the ascent to the ridge,
you can stop in to see the Academy Award–nominated film *The
Eruption of Mount St. Helens* projected onto the Cinedome's three-
story-high, 55-foot-wide screen. The rumble alone, which rattles
your theater seat, is worth the price of admission (shows every 45
minutes). It's just off I-5 at the Castle Rock exit; (360)274-8000.

There are numerous other viewpoints (via Cougar from the
south, or Randle from the north), but all the visitors centers are
on Highway 504. Those who enter from Randle will get a dramatic
view of the blowdown destruction.

There are now five places to stop along Highway 504 (also
called the Spirit Lake Memorial Highway), and they all complement each other. The US government requires an $8-per-person
fee to visit any of the three Forest Service's visitors centers in the
region (the fee covers all three). The first is the US Forest Service's
Mount St. Helens Visitors Center, (360)274-2100, just 5 miles
east of I-5 at Castle Rock. Built shortly after the eruption, it com-
memorates the blast with excellent exhibits, a walk-through vol-
cano, hundreds of historical and modern photos, geological and
anthropological surveys, and a film documenting the mountain's
destruction and rebirth. This is a good place to get a broad perspective of volcanoes. The second stop is the **Hoffstadt Bluff Rest
Area and Viewpoint** (milepost 27 on the Spirit Lake Memorial
Highway; (360)274-7750), run by Cowlitz County, which explores

the lives and deaths of those most directly affected by the blast. There's also a restaurant and gift store, and helicopter tours are available here. The third stop, operated by Weyerhauser, is the **Forest Learning Center** at North Fork Ridge (at milepost 33.5; (360)414-3439), which focuses on how the tree farms were affected and the wood was salvaged in the wake of the eruption. The fourth stop, 43 miles east of I-5, is **Coldwater Ridge**, (360)274-2131. It's a multimillion-dollar facility with a million-dollar view— of the black dome that rests in the 2-mile-wide steaming crater and of Coldwater and Castle Lakes, both formed by massive mudslides. This second US Forest Service center focuses on the astounding biological recovery of the landscape. The fifth stop up Highway 504, and the third facility run by the Forest Service, is the **Johnston Ridge Observatory** (milepost 52, (360)274-2140), which offers a bird's-eye view directly into the crater itself. The focus here (9 miles closer to the mountain than Coldwater) is on the May 18, 1980, eruption itself, how geologists monitor volcanoes, and what we have learned about volcanoes since the eruption.

For those interested in climbing the mountain, plan on about four hours up and two hours down; but the registration procedure often adds an extra day. You need to get a permit ($15 per person) well ahead of time (call the monument headquarters at (360)247-3900 for the procedure) and you must then register at Jack's Store just west of Cougar. Best times to climb are May and June (there's still enough snow to tame the ash). Be sure to bring a good pair of hiking boots, drinking water, sunscreen, sunglasses, and an ice axe.

TROUT LAKE

Mount Adams and its surrounding area offer natural splendor largely overlooked by visitors, who seldom venture in from the Columbia Gorge. Besides climbing to the summit of the 12,276-foot mountain—greater in mass than any of the five other major volcanic peaks in the Northwest—hikers and skiers can explore miles of wilderness trails in the Mount Adams Wilderness Area and the Gifford Pinchot National Forest.

Volcanic activity long ago left the area honeycombed with caves and lava tubes, including the **Ice Caves** near Trout Lake, with stalactites and stalagmites formed by dripping ice. To the southwest of Trout Lake is **Big Lava Bed**, a 12,500-acre lava field filled with cracks, crevasses, rock piles, and unusual lava formations. Contact the Mount Adams Ranger Station in Trout Lake, (509)395-2501, to register for ascents and for information on area activities.

In the warm months, Klickitat County is a land of abundance: morel mushrooms in the Simcoe Mountains (April through June), wildflowers in the Bird Creek Meadows (part of the only area of the Yakama Indian Reservation open to the public) in late July, and wild huckleberries—reputedly the best in the state—in and around the Indian Heaven Wilderness (mid-August to mid-September).

Serenity's Village ★ There are only a handful of places to stay in the Trout Lake Valley at the base of Mount Adams, and these four new chalet-style cabins on the Mount Adams Highway are your best bet. They're just off Highway 141, with a snapshot view of Mount Adams. The biggest ones have lofts and Jacuzzis, but the two smaller lodges are slightly more private. All are tastefully finished, warmed by gas fireplaces, and equipped with basic kitchen facilities. And kids are easily accommodated. Serenity's restaurant right next door is the best of the few choices in this neck of the woods (but hours are erratic). No pets. ▪ *Milepost 23, Hwy 141 (23 miles north of White Salmon), Trout Lake; (509)395-2500 or (800)276-7993; PO Box 217, Trout Lake, WA 98650; $$; MC, V; checks preferred.* ᕫ

GLENWOOD

LODGINGS

Flying L Ranch ★ We love the Flying L: this 160-acre ranch is like a big kids' camp in some of the most spectacular country around. Except that here, you're on your own. Bicycle the backroads, hike the trails, observe the birds in the Conboy Wildlife Refuge, or ski Mount Adams. We can only hope that the new owners (scheduled to move in at press time) are as knowledgeable about the area as the Lloyd brothers, who originally ran this place. The pace here is relaxed. You'll feel quite comfortable putting on some classical music and curling up with an old issue of National Geographic by the fireplace in the main lodge's spacious living room or watching evening fall over Mount Adams from the hot tub in the gazebo. The bedrooms are nothing fancy—but we like 'em that way. The Charles Russell Room, the George Fletcher Room, and the Mount Adams Suite have fireplaces. There are two basic cabins back in the woods. You might have huckleberry pancakes for breakfast; lunch and dinner you'll have to do yourself in one of the two well-equipped community kitchens. Dinners for large groups can be prepared with advance notice. ▪ *25 Flying L Lane (½ mile off Glenwood-Goldendale Hwy), Glenwood, WA 98619; (509)364-3488 or (888)MT-ADAMS; $$; AE, MC, V; checks OK.* ᕫ

▼

Stevenson

▲

STEVENSON

Stop by the **Columbia Gorge Interpretive Center** for a history of the Gorge, including a nine-projector slide show that re-creates the Gorge's cataclysmic formation, Native American fishing platforms, and a 37-foot-high replica of a 19th-century fish wheel. Just west of Stevenson off Highway 14, (509)427-8211.

LODGINGS

Skamania Lodge ★★ The grandest lodge in the Gorge was constructed to spark economic development on the forgotten Washington side of the Columbia River. Although it has an 18-hole golf course, is situated just above a prime bend in the Columbia River, and is managed by the company that runs the upscale Salishan and Salish Lodges, this was never intended to be a luxury resort: there's no solicitous concierge or nightly bed turndown, and service can be a bit impersonal. Given that the building resembles (from the outside) a deluxe college dormitory, think of the Skamania Lodge as a park resort and a conference center (which it is). Inside, the massive stone-and-wood lobby, with its grand fireplace, takes full advantage of a spectacular natural setting. With 195 tastefully decorated rooms, this place can handle lots of people. The best rooms are the ones with fireplaces on the river-view side. The forest view includes the parking lot, and the ground-floor rooms are the least private. Guests have use of the golf course, hiking trails, two tennis courts, a lap pool, saunas, indoor and highly appealing outdoor hot tubs, fitness machines, and an electronic games room. Executive chef Emmanuel Afentoulis earns praise for his interpretation of Northwest cuisine, including the Friday-night seafood buffet and a very popular Sunday brunch. This is certainly the grandest restaurant on this side of the Gorge. A less-expensive cafe also serves three meals. ■ *1131 Skamania Lodge Way (just west of Stevenson); (509) 427-7700 or (800) 221-7117; PO Box 189, Stevenson, WA 98648; www.skamania.com; $$$; full bar; AE, DC, MC, V; checks OK; breakfast every day, lunch Mon–Sat, dinner every day, brunch Sun.* &

CARSON

The eccentric 1897 **Carson Hot Springs**—PO Box 1169, Carson, WA 98610, (509) 427-8292—reminiscent of days when the sickly "took the waters" to improve their health, is today a bit worn; but we still recommend the hot mineral bath ($10), after which you're swathed in towels and blankets for a short rest. The women's side is much more crowded than the men's, so if you go in a mixed group, the men will finish sooner. To avoid this problem, you can reserve a massage in advance ($40 per hour), and a bath time will also be reserved for you. Don't expect as healthy a treatment from the restaurant.

BINGEN

RESTAURANTS

Fidel's ★ This Mexican restaurant seems transplanted straight from California; in fact, Fidel and Martha Montañez brought their family recipes from San Diego. Lively Mexican music sets the mood. Enormous margaritas go with the warm chips and salsa. The menu offers carne asada, a chile verde, a chile colorado, and omelets machaca (with shredded beef, chicken, or pork). Portions are generous (often big enough for two), and the chile relleno—encased in a thick layer of egg whites so that it resembles a big pillow—is *muy sabroso.* ■ *120 E Stuben St (1 mile east of Hood River toll bridge on Hwy 14), Bingen; (509) 493-1017; $; full bar; MC, V; checks OK; lunch, dinner every day (call ahead in winter).* &

GOLDENDALE

Maryhill Museum, a stately Palladian mansion, perches rather obtrusively upon the barren Columbia River benchlands. Constructed in 1917 by the eccentric Sam Hill, son-in-law of railroad tycoon James J. Hill, Maryhill began as the European-inspired dream home for Hill and his wife, Mary, but became instead what it is today: a fine-art museum. With one of the largest collections of Rodin sculptures in the world, a whole floor of classic French and American paintings and glasswork, unique exhibitions such as chess sets and Romanian folk textiles, and splendid Northwest tribal art, the museum makes for quite an interesting visit. A cafe serves espresso, pastries, and sandwiches, and peacocks roam the lovely landscaped grounds; Highway 14, 13 miles south of Goldendale, (509) 773-3733 or maryhill@gorge.net. Up the road is another of Sam Hill's bizarre creations: a not-quite-life-size replica of **Stonehenge**, built to honor local World War I veterans.

Goldendale Public Observatory, on a hill overlooking town (20 minutes north of Goldendale on US 97), was a popular spot when Halley's comet dropped in. High-powered telescopes give incredible celestial views through unpolluted skies. Open Wednesday through Sunday, April through September; in winter, open weekend afternoons and Saturday evenings; (509) 773-3141.

LODGINGS

Highland Creeks Resort ★★ This sheltered, backwoods resort is nestled in the Simcoe Mountains. All rooms have skylights, carpeting, locally made ponderosa pine furniture, insulation for quietness, and private hot tubs—the most romantic are on private porches overlooking the river. Guests take advantage of the wilderness—hiking and fishing in summer, cross-country skiing and sleigh rides in winter. The dining room in the main lodge makes splendid use of its situation at the confluence of three creeks, with glass and cedar walls that seem to bring the trees inside. Salmon is cooked on a cedar plank; soups are made from scratch every day. ■ *2120 Hwy 97 (18 miles north of the Columbia), Goldendale, WA 98620; (509) 773-4026 or (800) 458-0174; $$; full bar; AE, MC, V; checks OK; breakfast, lunch, dinner every day (call ahead in winter).* &

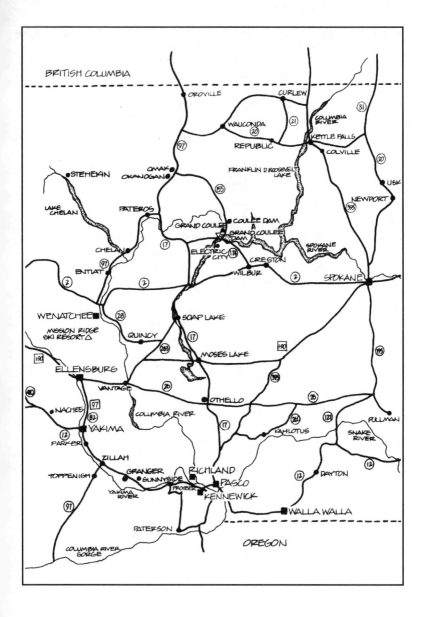

Eastern Washington

An eastward route along I-90, Ellensburg to Spokane, then a northwesterly arc through the northeast corner of the state to the Okanogan and Colville National Forests. The Wenatchee loop begins in Okanogan and continues clockwise through Grand Coulee, Soap Lake, and north again to Wenatchee and Chelan (and Stehekin, accessible from Chelan). Finally, an eastward drive along the bottom of the state—Yakima to Pullman.

ELLENSBURG

If you get away from the tourist ghetto next to the freeway, as you should, this college-and-cowboy town projects a pleasant ease. Its famous Labor Day rodeo draws many for its slice-of-life view of rural America.

Central Washington University. The campus makes for a wonderful stroll, especially through the serene Japanese Garden, designed by Masa Mizuno. The curious should call ahead and arrange a Saturday or Sunday workshop with the Chimpanzee and Human Communication Institute (at 14th and D at the north end of campus). Here you can observe humans and chimps communicating through American Sign Language. Call in advance for workshop times and prices; (800) 752-4380.

Art. Sarah Spurgeon Gallery, on 14th Street in the fine-arts complex at Central, presents regional and national exhibits in all media, Monday through Friday (closed in September); (509) 963-2665. The Clymer Museum and Gallery, at 416 N Pearl Street, honors Ellensburg's own chronicler of the Western frontier, John Clymer, whose work appeared in several editions of the *Saturday Evening Post;* (509) 962-6416. Gallery One, 408½ N Pearl, (509) 925-2670, has nice quarters in an old building, displays good contemporary art, and sells regional crafts; it's open 11am to 5pm Monday through Saturday.

Theater. Central Washington's only professional repertory theater presents over 35 performances by the energetic Laughing Horse Company during July and August (Wednesday through Saturday at 8pm); for reservations, call (509) 963-3400. Plays are staged in the architecturally stunning Tower Theater on the Central campus.

Ellensburg Oddities. Close to the Central campus along Ninth Street are tree-lined blocks of attractive turn-of-the-century homes. For something a bit out of the ordinary, check out the "Ellensburg Bull" statue by Richard Beyer, located in the historic downtown business district, or the cowboy sculpture by Dan Klennard that guards the corner of Fifth and Pearl; or stop by 101 N Pearl for a gander at Dick & Jane's Spot, a blend of unusual yard art, including reflector gyros, statues, and other unique offerings. Treat the kids to an ice cream straight from the dairy at Winegar Family Dairy, Seventh and Main, (509)933-1821 (Monday through Saturday 7am to 7pm, Sunday 11am to 6pm). Or down an espresso while sitting in the saddle at the Cowboy Espresso Bar in Jaguar's clothing store, 423 N Pearl, (509)962-6081.

The hills surrounding Ellensburg are speckled with blue agates found nowhere else in the world but here in the Kittitas Valley. If you don't stumble upon any, you can purchase some at any of the local gem shops, particularly the Ellensburg Agate Shop, 201 S Main, (509)925-4998.

Olmstead Place, 4 miles east of town on Squaw Creek Trail Road (off I-90), is a cottonwood log cabin from an 1875 cattle ranch that's now coming back to life; tours Saturday and Sunday noon to 4pm, and by appointment; (509)925-1943. Not too far from Ellensburg is the Thorp Mill, an 1883 gristmill still in mint condition after 114 years. It's open for tours by appointment; (509)964-9640, or write PO Box 7, Thorp, WA 98946.

The big event in Ellensburg is the **Ellensburg Rodeo**, held Thursday through Monday of every Labor Day weekend at the fairgrounds; (509)962-7639.

Yakima River. There are fine canoe and raft trips to be made through the Yakima River's deep gorges. Fly fishermen know this to be one of the finest trout streams in the country. Highway 821, south of town, follows the gorge. Information about floats and river trips: (509)925-3137.

RESTAURANTS

Austin's Roadside Eats & Entertainment ★★ Chef Austin Smith went west from Boston and found his niche in Ellensburg. His cafe shares a long, narrow space with Croweye Bead Co.—a complementary pairing in that the college crowd that hangs out here enjoys browsing through the beads while waiting for a stool at the counter or one of the few tables. Austin's menu leans toward (but is not restricted to) vegetarian. Throughout the menu are fresh and high-quality ingredients, ranging from the organic eggs and vegetables from local farms to fresh breads from a local bakery to mayonnaise and croutons made on the premises. Smith mixes a breakfast granola of organic oats, wheat germ, and nuts sweetened with molasses; the French toast is served with yogurt and real maple or huckleberry syrup. Deli sandwiches, burritos, salads, and soups round out the lunch menu. When black bean soup, seasoned with fennel, is the soup of the day, make the trip across town for it. ■ *311 N Main St* *(downtown), Ellensburg; (509)925-3012; $; beer only; no credit cards; checks OK; breakfast, lunch every day (Mon–Fri Nov–Mar).*

The Valley Cafe ★★ This 1930s-built bistro, with mahogany booths and back bar, would be an oasis anywhere—but is especially so in cow country. People traveling to Ellensburg arrange to arrive around lunchtime just to eat at this airy art deco spot. Salads, or one of the deli sandwiches, are the choice at lunch. Eclectic concoctions, fresh seafood, and Ellensburg lamb compose most of the dinner menu. There's a well-thought-out list of Washington wines, and some bracing espresso drinks. If you require faster service, want pastries with a latte for breakfast, or need a box lunch, a take-out branch is next door. ■ *105 W 3rd (near corner of Main), Ellensburg; (509)925-3050; $$; beer and wine; AE, DC, DIS, MC, V; checks OK; lunch, dinner every day (breakfast, lunch every day at take-out branch).*

VANTAGE

Situated on a splendid stretch of the Columbia, Vantage has nothing much in the way of food, but the view from the parking lot of the A&W surpasses that of all other known root-beer stands. Nearby **Ginkgo Petrified Forest State Park** has an interpretive center—open daily in summer 10am to 6pm (by appointment only otherwise), (509)856-2700—that takes you back to the age of dinosaurs; then you can go prospecting for your own finds. It's a great spot for a picnic.

▼

Spokane

▲

GEORGE

A naturally terraced amphitheater looking west over the Columbia Gorge offers a spectacular summer-evening setting for musical events, attracting thousands of people with big-name artists and performances from Lollapalooza to Boyz 2 Men, Def Leppard to Metallica, Bonnie Raitt to Tina Turner. You can bring a picnic, but no booze (they'll search your packs and toss it, so don't bother). Arrive early; the one country road leading to George is not fit for crowds of this kind. For tickets, call Ticketmaster in Seattle, (206)628-0888. George is a 3-hour drive from Seattle, 2 hours from Spokane; although you may find camping nearby, the closest lodgings are found in Ellensburg, Vantage, or Ephrata.

SPOKANE

The friendly city by Spokane Falls is far more attractive to visit than is generally recognized. It is full of old buildings of note, marvelous parks, and splendid vistas, and the compact downtown is most pleasant for strolling. The Gold Rush of the 1880s brought it wealth, and railroads brought it people. The centennial for many of Spokane's older buildings is 1998; look for the free brochure of historical walking tours at the The Spokane Visitors Center (201 W Main, (800)248-3230 or (509)747-3230).

Parks. Riverfront Park is the pleasant green heart of the old city. Developed from old railroad yards for Expo '74, the park is now an airy place full of meandering paved paths, with entertainments ranging from ice-skating to an IMAX theater. The 1909 carousel is a local landmark, hand-carved by master builder Charles Looff. The music is too loud for children under about 4 (and most adults), but older kids love riding the menagerie. Manito Park, at Grand Boulevard and 18th, has a splendidly splashable duck pond, a conservatory, and theme gardens. Finch Arboretum (west of downtown Spokane), a pleasant picnic site, hosts a modest but attractive collection of trees and shrubs among ravines and a stream. For a panoramic vista of Spokane, visit Cliff Park at 13th and Grove.

Nature. Two natural areas just a couple of miles outside Spokane's city limits offer excellent places to hike and see birds and wildlife: the Little Spokane Natural Area, (509)456-3964, and the Spokane Fish Hatchery, (509)625-5169. The fishery is at 2927 W Waikiki Road; for the Natural Area, look for the Indian Rock Paintings parking lot on Rutter Parkway. The Dishman Hills Natural Area, a 460-acre preserve in the Spokane Valley, has a network of trails with mixed wildlife habitats; take I-90 east to Sprague Avenue exit, go east 1½ miles to Sargent Road, turn right half a mile to the parking area. Just 25 miles south of Spokane you'll find the 15,000-acre Turnbull National Wildlife Refuge, (509)235-4723, especially interesting during fall and spring bird migration. Take I-90 west, exit at Cheney, go through the town, and turn left on Smith Road.

Culture. Brazilian-born Fabio Machetti is the conductor of the Spokane Symphony, and programs, including a pops series, are lively and innovative. An annual free Labor Day concert in Comstock Park draws thousands of picnicking spectators; (509)326-3136. The Spokane Civic Theatre, 1020 N Howard, (509)325-2507, offers a mixed bag of amateur performances each season; the Interplayers Ensemble Theatre, 174 S Howard, (509)455-7529, is a professional company with a full season. Riverfront Park often hosts concerts of jazz, bluegrass, and popular music during the summer; call (509)456-4386 for information. The 12,000-seat Spokane Veterans Arena is big enough to attract major entertainers and bands to the city; most of the tickets are sold through a local ticket agency, G&B Select-a-Seat, (509)325-7328 or (800)325-7328. A "Best of Broadway" touring performance series is held at the Opera House, at the south edge of Riverfront Park; (509)325-7328.

Museums. Cheney Cowles Museum displays pioneer and mining relics; 2316 W First, (509)456-3931.

Sports. Golf is very good here. Indian Canyon, (509)747-5353, and Downriver, (509)327-5269, are two of the most beautiful public courses in the nation. The Creek at Qualchan, (509)448-9317, is the newest and most challenging of the public courses.

There are no fewer than nine others. Several privately owned courses are also open to the public; among those, Wandermere, (509)466-8023, is considered by local golfers to be the most scenic, with plenty of terrain variety. Spokane's parks and hilly roads and the Centennial Trail (flanking the river from Riverside State Park to Coeur d'Alene) offer great bicycle riding. Runners find themselves in good company, especially in May during Spokane's annual Bloomsday Run; (509)838-1579. The Spokane Veterans Arena (see Culture, above) is the home of the Western Hockey League Spokane Chiefs. The good ski areas nearby are 49 Degrees North, 58 miles north of Spokane near Chewelah, (509)935-6649, a good place for beginners; Mount Spokane, 31 miles north on Highway 206, (509)238-6281, with fair facilities, some challenging runs, and 17 kilometers of groomed cross-country ski trails with two warming huts (a SnoPark pass is required); Schweitzer Mountain Resort in Sandpoint, Idaho, (208) 263-9555, with excellent facilities for family skiing; and Silver Mountain at Kellogg, Idaho, (208)783-1111, where skiers ride the world's longest single-span gondola from the parking area in downtown Kellogg to the mountainside lodge, about a 20-minute ride. (Summers, mountain bikers flock to Silver Mountain and can take their bikes up the mountain on the gondola.) Also in summers, Mount Spokane State Park, (509)456-4169, is prime huckleberry terrain.

Brewery Tour. Hale's Ales, which now has breweries in Spokane and Seattle, is a microbrewery that welcomes visitors— when the day's brewing work is done. Call ahead for a reservation for a tour and a taste of their pale ale, bitter, porter, Moss Bay ale, and seasonal specialties: E 5634 Commerce Street, (509)534-7553.

RESTAURANTS

Luna ★★★ Local diners flock to this restaurant any night of the week, but on weekends, it's downright tough to get in (a novelty in Spokane), especially for dinner or Sunday brunch. The eclectic menu, which changes seasonally, crosses the boundaries of ethnic cuisine, with the emphasis on fresh herbs and seasonal fruits and vegetables. The restaurant is in a renovated one-story former produce market that features an open kitchen and booths with marble-top tables. The food is innovative, delicious, and beautifully presented. One of our favorites is the grilled prawns with Parmesan-flavored polenta, surrounded by a showy ring of red pepper sauce. A fair-weather patio awaits summer. Reservations are recommended. ■ *5620 S Perry (south on High Dr to 56th, left 1 block to Perry), Spokane; (509)448-2383; $$; AE, MC, V; beer and wine; checks OK; lunch, dinner every day, brunch Sun.*

Milford's Fish House and Oyster Bar ★★★ With recent updates to the decor and the menu, Spokane's oldest fish house is better than ever. The exposed brick, pressed-tin ceiling, and terra-cotta tile terrazzo floor remain; gone are the checkered tablecloths and the fern bar ambience. Booths are separated by leaded glass windows, and dark wood and brass reign here now. It's a downright cozy place with a long history. The lobby and bar were once the New Transfer Market, where crowds transferred just outside from trolley to trolley; the executive dining room was a barbershop for six decades; the main dining room was the William Quick Cigar Store. Diners are encouraged to browse the many historical photos throughout the restaurant. The entire menu at Milford's is now a fresh sheet, heavy on the seafood, although Angus beef and free-range chicken entrees are available. Puget Sound is the source of much of the fish, from Eastern Maine mussels (farmed in Penn Cove) to Atlantic salmon (also raised in Puget Sound). Canadian halibut and Alaskan cod also make frequent appearances on the fresh sheet. The entrees arrive beautifully presented: the salmon fillet is topped with dill, the halibut fillet sports a ribbon of marionberry mustard sauce, all flanked by crisp new potatoes and a fresh vegetable of the day. Reservations are highly recommended, especially on weekends. ▪ *719 N Monroe St (corner of Broadway), Spokane; (509)326-7251; $$; full bar; MC, V; checks OK; dinner every day.* &

Fugazzi Restaurant ★★ When it first opened, Fugazzi was the place to be seen in Spokane, especially at lunchtime, when the business crowd gathered to wheel and deal over a salad and freshly baked bread. Soon it settled into simply one of the better places in Spokane to eat innovatively prepared cuisine. The eatery changed hands and at press time, the bakery is splitting off and moving across the river, but the eclectic fare has remained consistently delicious and surprising. A Thai salad might join Southwest black-bean ravioli on the menu. The freshly baked rustic breads that arrive at the table first shouldn't be passed up—and can now be bought in bulk at Fugazzi Bread (810 N Monroe), along with pastries. The ambience is as eclectic as the food, borrowing heavily from the industrial warehouse movement in restaurant decor, overlaid with primary colors. With lights dimmed at night, though, it can appear warmly intimate. ▪ *1 N Post St (at Sprague, downtown), Spokane; (509)624-1133; $$; beer and wine; AE, MC, V; checks OK; lunch, dinner Tues–Sat.*

Clinkerdagger's ★ Clinkerdagger's has more on its menu than basic chicken and steak selections (such as a few fussy Northwest-oriented dishes), but when push comes to shove, it's those basics—well handled and attractively presented—that win us over. Service here is notoriously slow. Reservations are recommended; request the coveted window seats (but there are no guarantees) in the spring, when the Spokane River is rushing over the falls out front. ▪ *621 W Mallon Ave (east of Monroe, in*

Flour Mill), Spokane; (509)328-5965; $$; full bar; AE, DC, MC, V; local checks only; lunch Mon–Sat, dinner every day.

The Downtown Onion ★ The magnificent old bar is a relic of the days when the building that houses this eatery was a fine hotel, the St. Regis. Some of the architectural details—the pressed-tin ceiling, the wooden dividers—are from the original hotel. The Onion set the standard in Spokane for gourmet hamburgers, and they're still local classics. The beer selection would be outstanding anywhere; fruit daiquiris (especially the huckleberry) are a specialty. A young, informal crowd dominates on most nights, especially on Monday nights during NFL season. Being part of the chaos is part of the fun of this place, so don't take a table in the sun room. The same menu is served at the North Onion at 7522 N Division, (509)482-6100. ■ *302 W Riverside Ave (at Bernard), Spokane; (509)747-3852; $; full bar; AE, MC, V; checks OK; lunch, dinner every day.* &

Knight's Diner ★ Eggs the way you want them and crisp hashbrowns have been served up in this renovated circa-1900 railroad car for four decades, with only a brief interruption when the diner was moved to its new site at the south end of the Hillyard neighborhood. Those seeking an old-fashioned breakfast flock to this former Pullman passenger car, where they sit on stools and eat at a mahogany counter that runs the length of the car. Those on grill-front stools get to watch the cook keep the dozens of orders all cooking at once. Hungry diners can order the 24 dollar-size pancakes. Few bother with the lunch menu. ■ *2909 N Market (at Green St), Spokane; (509)484-0015; $; no alcohol; no credit cards; checks OK; breakfast, lunch Tues–Sun.*

Marrakesh ★ This Moroccan restaurant (in a former used-appliance store) does much to broaden Spokane's ethnic offerings. Diners sit on benches along the walls or on tippy hammocks. The meal begins with a traditional finger-washing routine and ends with the sprinkling of fragrant rose water over your hands—practical since your fingers are your utensils. A set price of $15.50 buys a five-course meal in which you choose only the entree. The execution of the food is never quite as good as the dining ceremony itself. Plan to go with at least a group of four; if it's crowded and there are only two of you, you may be seated with another couple or a larger group. ■ *2208 Northwest Blvd (west of Monroe), Spokane; (509)328-9733; $$; beer and wine; MC, V; checks OK; dinner Tues–Sun.*

Niko's Greek & Middle Eastern Restaurant ★ Niko's is deservedly popular locally for traditional Greek food, much of which is homemade in this modest taverna-style restaurant. Lamb is well treated here, and the garlicky, smooth hummus can be ordered as an entree at lunch with a plate of vegetables or pita. Niko's Favorite—chicken, tomatoes, and vegetables over rice with tahini sauce—is ours, too. The Greek salads have plenty of salty, strong feta and Greek olives; the baklava is loaded. Thursday is belly-dancing night. Niko II, downtown at W 725 Riverside Avenue, (509)624-7444, is a popular lunch spot. ■ *321 S Dishman-Mica Rd (2 blocks off Sprague), Spokane; (509)928-9590; $; beer and wine; no credit cards; checks OK; lunch Mon–Fri, dinner Mon–Sat.*

Patsy Clark's ★ Patrick F. Clark, "Patsy" to his friends, arrived in America in 1870 at the age of 20, and by the time he was 40 he was a millionaire many times over, thanks to the success of Montana's Anaconda Mine. Naturally anxious to display his success, he instructed architect Kirtland Cutter to build him the finest mansion he could conceive—never mind the cost. Marble was shipped in from Italy, wood carvings and clocks from England, a mural from France, and a spectacular stained-glass window (with more than 4,000 pieces) from Tiffany's of New York. Locals like to show off Patsy's, but not so much for its dinners. An elegant spot it is, and you should find some excuse to stop by, even if it's only for a drink (the wine list is one of the best in the area). Sunday brunch—a memorable experience in terms of sheer quantity—requires reservations. ■ *2208 W 2nd Ave (15 blocks west of downtown, at 2nd and Hemlock), Spokane; (509)838-8300; $$$; full bar; AE, DC, DIS, MC, V; local checks only; lunch Mon–Fri, dinner every day, brunch Sun.* ಈ

Thai Cafe ★ This ethnic oasis in the Eastern Washington desert is well off the beaten track, so you're not likely to just stumble into it. A waft of curry greets patrons at the door, and you'll find such seasonings, along with coconut milk and peanuts, in most of the entrees. We've yet to be disappointed with any of the chicken selections. Try the *pra ram long song*—chicken with peanut sauce, served on a bed of fresh spinach—or the squid. And don't miss the desserts—black rice pudding over ice cream, or warm bananas in coconut milk. ■ *410 W Sprague Ave (at Washington), Spokane; (509)838-4783; $; Thai beer only; no credit cards; local checks only; lunch Mon–Fri, dinner Mon–Sat.* ಈ

Europa Pizzeria Restaurant Exposed brick walls and bare wood give this place a certain Old World charm, and the relaxed atmosphere attracts good-tempered students from downtown college branch campuses. With the expansion into the adjacent former antique shop, the bar area is one of the best in town. Couches and wing chairs divide the space into conversation areas, and generous portions of baked pasta entrees and calzone are served by a cheerful staff. Bar-side advice is reliable and the pace relaxed (sometimes too much so for those on a lunch hour). ■ *125 S Wall St (north side of the railroad trestle downtown, next to Magic Lantern Theater), Spokane; (509)455-4051; $; beer and wine; MC, V; checks OK; lunch, dinner Mon–Sat.*

Fotheringham House ★★ Owners Graham and Jackie Johnson restored this quintessential Victorian house to the grandeur intended by its builder, David B. Fotheringham, the first mayor of Spokane. The details inside and out—pressed-tin ceilings, brass feet on a big claw-footed tub, Americana quilts, hundreds of daffodils in the lawn, Victorian-style perennial gardens—make all the difference in this 1891 Browne's Addition house. Its location next to Patsy Clark's mansion doesn't hurt either. The former mayor's bedroom has views of Coeur d'Alene Park. The Museum and Mansion Rooms are smaller and share a bath. Restoration of the original turret on the house earned awards from the local historical society. Summers, guests can relax in the wicker swing on the wraparound porch, stroll the cobblestone paths through the butterfly and bird gardens, or play tennis on the courts in the park. ■ *2128 W 2nd Ave (Maple St exit from I-90, north to 2nd, turn west, stay in right lane), Spokane, WA 99204; (509)838-1891; $$; MC, V; checks OK.*

Waverly Place ★★ Across the street from what was a racetrack, Waverly Place retains the elegance of the Victorian era, inside and out. The track is now Corbin Park, a lovely oval with a couple of tennis courts, a shady tree canopy, and walking trails. Add Waverly Place's own pool and a tall glass of lemonade and call it vacation. There are four guest rooms. The Skinner Suite is decorated with oak furnishings—including a sleigh bed—and is one of two suites, each with private bath. The stairs from the former Garden Room to the third floor have been opened, and this two-level suite includes a 700-square-foot sitting room with window seats affording views of the park and the pool. The bath has a shower room and an iron claw-footed tub. Of the other two rooms, which share a bath, Anna's Room has a window seat that overlooks the park. Fresh fruit, Swedish pancakes with huckleberry sauce, sausages, and coffee are breakfast samplings. ■ *709 W Waverly Pl (exit I-90 at Division St, north on Division and Ruby to N Foothills Dr, west to Washington, north to Waverly), Spokane, WA 99205; (509)328-1856; $$; AE, DC, MC, V; checks OK.*

Cavanaugh's Inn at the Park ★ This hotel on the bank of the river across from Riverfront Park has 402 rooms, many with southern views of downtown Spokane (and a few, of the hydropower weir). All seven stories of rooms open out to the spacious lobby; it can be noisy, so specify a quiet corner room or perhaps one in the wing at the east end of the hotel, away from the lobby and busy Washington Street, or in the tower at the west end of the complex. The attractive Windows on the Seasons restaurant overlooks the river. ■ *303 W North River Dr (Division St exit from I-90, north to North River Dr), Spokane, WA 99201; (509)326-8000 or (800)843-4667; www.cavanaughs.com, $$; AE, DC, MC, V; checks OK.* ♿

Marianna Stoltz House ★ A traditional 1908 American four-square house, the Marianna Stoltz House is in one of the older Spokane neighborhoods that hasn't quite gentrified, which makes it a gem among the other old homes in the area. Maple and fir floors, wainscoting throughout, and even much of the wallpaper dates to the first owner, a railroad contractor. The house is filled with antique furniture. Of the four guest rooms, one has a private bath (which includes a 6-foot claw-footed tub), and all have cable TV, but in summer many guests opt to spend the evening out on the wraparound porch, surrounded by the century-old trees. The traffic on the four-lane street out front can be intrusive, so light sleepers might request a back room. The Gonzaga University campus is five blocks south, and the Centennial Trail, popular with cyclists, joggers, and walkers, runs through the campus adjacent to the Spokane River. ■ *427 E Indiana St (1 mile north of downtown and 5 blocks east of Division St), Spokane, WA 99207; (509) 483-4316; $$; AE, DC, DIS, MC, V; checks OK.*

West Coast Ridpath Hotel ★ The 340 rooms, renovated and updated in late 1996, are pleasant and spacious, and those in the tower overlook the city. The downtown location is convenient. This place is popular with conventioneers and tourists, and some of the public areas can be crowded, but the mood here is always convivial. The rooftop restaurant, a predictable Ankeny's, boasts a grand view of Spokane. At night, the town glitters through the wall-to-wall windows. ■ *515 W Sprague Ave (downtown), Spokane, WA 99204; (509) 838-2711 or (800) 426-0670; $$; AE, DC, MC, V; checks OK.*

KETTLE FALLS

The Colville River valley has tiny farming communities, but outdoor recreation—fishing and cross-country skiing, primarily—is beginning to draw many to the pristine area. Highway 20 from Colville to Tonasket is a National Scenic Byway. It climbs over **Sherman Pass**—amazingly, the highest paved pass in Washington.

LODGINGS

My Parent's Estate ★ This 125-year-old house has been a mission school, an abbess's home for a Dominican convent, a home for troubled boys, and a private residence; it's now a quiet haven in the woods. The 49-acre estate on the Colville River boasts a gym, a barn, a caretaker's house, and a cemetery. Hosts Al and Bev Parent are proud of their home; Bev's Arts and Crafts collection is displayed around the house. The three guest rooms encourage quiet country relaxation, with comforters on the queen-size beds, refinished vanities, and antique washbasins and private baths. The lofty living room is dominated by a floor-to-ceiling stone fireplace. A two-bedroom cottage has a Western theme, and amenities include laundry facilities, a full kitchen, and a suite in which guests can soak in an old-fashioned claw-footed tub. What to do? Cross-country ski in the winter; in summer, float the Colville River, hike, or play in the water at nearby Franklin D. Roosevelt Lake. ■ *7 miles past downtown Colville on Hwy 395, Kettle Falls; (509) 738-6220; PO Box 724, Kettle Falls, WA 99141; $$; MC, V; checks OK.*

CURLEW

RESTAURANTS

The Riverside Restaurant and Lounge ★ This is an oasis in Washington's northeastern corner. The setting is pleasant: wooden tables and chairs and a wooden bar. The dining room has a large wood stove. There's a view of the Kettle River, the produce is fresh, and the food is fairly simple but always good. You can get the all-American thick sirloins, but there's also good Mexican fare, and where else in this territory can you get a shredded beef enchilada sided by gently steamed asparagus? ■ *813 River St (on the main drag), Curlew; (509) 779-4813; $$; full bar; MC, V; checks OK; dinner Wed–Sun.*

WAUCONDA

RESTAURANTS

The Wauconda Cafe, General Store, and Post Office If you want atmosphere, here it is in this small general store cum gas station cum post office cum restaurant. A lunch counter with a few booths is squeezed between the general store and the dining room. It's a popular hangout for the local folk, both rancher types and counterculturalists. The view is out across the rolling meadows so typical of the Okanogan Highlands, with a few weatherbeaten barns enhancing the horizon, and wildflowers in the spring. The food is fresh and simple: tasty burgers, milk shakes, sandwiches, and homemade soups for lunch; sautéed prawns, prime rib, and big salads for dinner. Owners Dennis and Lucy Smith have added Chinese food to the menu on weekend nights. Breads and desserts are homemade. ■ *2432 Hwy 20 (the only building in "town"), Wauconda; (509) 486-4010; $; beer and wine; MC, V; local checks only; breakfast, lunch, dinner every day.*

OMAK

The famous—and controversial—Suicide Race is the climax of the **Omak Stampede** the second weekend of August; (509) 826-1002 or (800) 933-6625, Stampede@televar.com.

RESTAURANTS

Breadline Cafe ★ Here in the heart of steak and Stampede country, the Breadline offers a choice of fare. In the front of an old bottling-works building, owner Paula Chambers' eatery features a low-tech bistro/nightclub offering full dinners and live music—from small folk bands to big-name blues artists like Charlie Musselwhite. The country-style menu includes steak and scampi, Cajun chicken, and pasta. We like the big, informal market in the back, with fresh-baked breads, pastries, and deli items. Watch the whole-grain bread come out of the oven as your hearty sandwich or salad is prepared. Hot apple fritters with cream maple sauce finish you off. ■ *102 S Ash St (Ash and 1st), Omak; (509)826-5836; $; full bar; AE, MC, V; checks OK; lunch Mon–Sat, dinner Tues–Sat, brunch Sun.*

OKANOGAN

LODGINGS

U and I Motel The name suits this family-run place's folksiness. It's not much to look at from its front on the old backroad between Okanogan and Omak, but a closer look uncovers a pleasant little nook for hiding away from it all. The two-room cabinettes are less than spacious, but they're clean and cozily done up in rustic paneling. They are a deal, too. Best of all, the whole backyard of the motel is a grassy lawn and flower garden fronting the tranquil Okanogan River. Grab a deck chair, cast a fishing line, and watch the river flow. Pets OK. ■ *838 2nd Ave N (off Hwy 97 on old 97 at 2nd Ave N), Okanogan, WA 98840; (509)422-2920; $; MC, V; local checks only.*

COULEE DAM

LODGINGS

Coulee House Motel Dam good view and decent amenities—a pool, Jacuzzi, and refrigerators in some of the 61 large, clean rooms, to name a few—earn our favor. At night you can sit on the tiny lanai outside your room (smoking or non) and watch the animated laser light show (summers only) over one of the largest dams on earth as the water cascades past. ■ *110 Roosevelt Way (at Birch), Coulee Dam, WA 99116; (509)633-1101; $$; AE, DC, MC, V; no checks.*

Four Winds Once a dormitory for dam engineers, the Four Winds is now Coulee Dam's most personable bed-and-breakfast inn, and it's within walking distance of the dam itself. There are 11 spotlessly clean rooms with many combinations of baths (private, shared with one other room, down the hall, etc.). At one end of the building is a foyer for reading, conversation, or board games. Nothing fancy here, but everything is competently overseen by Richard and Fe Taylor, who at 8:30am serve a virtual smorgasbord. ■ *301 Lincoln St (across from Coulee Dam City Hall), Coulee Dam, WA 99116; (509) 633-3146 or (800) 786-3146; $$; AE, DIS, MC, V; checks OK.*

GRAND COULEE

Grand, yes—this is a wonderful area from which to appreciate the outsize dimensions of the landscape and the geological forces that made it. The Columbia River slices through central Washington with an eerie power, as the water rushes by in silky strength through enormous chasms. In prehistoric times, glacier-fed water created a river with the largest flow of water ever known. Today it's the second-largest river in the nation, traversing a valley of an equally staggering scale.

Grand Coulee Dam is one of the largest structures on the earth—tall as a 46-story building, with a spillway twice the height of Niagara and a length as great as a dozen city blocks. The dam, completed in 1941, was originally intended more to irrigate the desert than to produce electricity; so much power was generated, however, that the dam became a magnet for the nation's aluminum industry. The north-face extension (completed in 1975) was designed by Marcel Breuer, a great practitioner of the International Style, and the heroic scale of the concrete is quite magnificent, especially when illuminated by the inspirational nighttime laser light show. There are daily self-guided tours of the dam; hours vary according to season: (509) 633-3838.

Eccentric inventor Emil Gehrke amassed an oddly compelling **windmill collection** at North Dam Park on Highway 155, between Electric City and Grand Coulee. Four hard hats tilted sideways catch the wind, cups and saucers twirl around a central teapot—it's whimsical and fascinating.

Houseboating. For many years, Lake Roosevelt was untapped by the RV-on-pontoons fleet. Now there are 40 houseboats available to explore the 150-mile-long lake formed by Grand Coulee Dam, and most book up early for the summer. The sun's almost guaranteed, and all you need to bring is food, bed linens, towels, and your bathing suit; boats are moored at Keller Ferry Marina, 14 miles north of Wilbur, (800) 648-5253.

SOAP LAKE

Early settlers named the lake for its unusually high alkali content, which gives the water a soapy feel.

Dry Falls, off Route 17 north of town, is the place where the prehistoric torrential Columbia once crashed over falls 3 miles wide and 400 feet high; an interpretive center (Friday through Monday, 10am to 5pm, summer) explains the local geology, which has been compared to surface features of Mars. From this lookout, you can also see the **Sun Lakes**, puddles left behind by the ancient Columbia. It's RV territory, but the waters are prime spots for swimming and fishing; (509) 632-5583.

LODGINGS

Notaras Lodge On the shores of Soap Lake, you can stay in the Norma Zimmer Room (the bubble lady on the "Lawrence Welk Show") or the Bonnie Guitar Honeymoon Suite (named for a local country western celeb whose own guitar is memorialized in an epoxied table along with other souvenirs of the singer's career). Such memorabilia are owner Marina Romary's passion; the Western Nostalgia Room boasts a pool table as well as a whirlpool. The healing waters of Soap Lake are on tap in the bathrooms (eight of which have Jacuzzis). Romary also owns nearby Don's Restaurant, 14 Canna Street, (509) 246-1217, a popular steak-and-seafood-and-Greek eatery, where macho meals are served in a dark, slightly seamy interior. ■ *236 E Main St (4 miles north of Ephrata on Hwy 28, 1 block west on Main St), Soap Lake; (509) 246-0462; PO Box 987, Soap Lake, WA 98851; $$; MC, V; checks OK.* ♿

WENATCHEE

You're in the heart of apple country, with an Apple Blossom Festival the first part of May. **Ohme Gardens**, 3 miles north on Route 97A, is a 600-foot-high promontory transformed into an Edenic retreat, with a fastidiously created natural alpine ecosystem patterned after high mountain country. There are splendid views of the valley and the Columbia River; (509) 662-5785. The **Riverfront Loop Trail** on the banks of the Columbia River makes for a pleasant evening stroll—or an easy bike ride for those who want to pedal the whole 11-mile loop, which traverses both sides of the river (and crosses two bridges) from Wenatchee to East Wenatchee. Best place to hook onto the trail is at the east end of Fifth Street; or call Wenatchee Chamber of Commerce, (509) 662-4774.

Mission Ridge, 13 miles southwest on Squilchuck Road, offers some of the best powder snow in the region, served by four chairlifts (cross-country skiing, too); (509) 663-7631. On the third Sunday in April, the Ridge-to-River Pentathlon is an impressive sporting event.

Rocky Reach Dam, 6 miles north on Route 97, offers a beautiful picnic and playground area (locals marry on the well-kept grounds), plus a fish-viewing room. Inside the dam are two large galleries devoted to the history of the region.

RESTAURANTS

John Horan's Steak & Seafood House ★★ Many of the orchards that once surrounded this turn-of-the-century home, built by Wenatchee pioneer Mike Horan, are gone. Yet the roundabout drive to the house near the confluence of the Wenatchee and

Columbia Rivers sets the tone for an evening that harkens back to more gracious times; and on a warm summer's eve the place can't be beat for ambience. The feel of the early 1900s remains in the dark floral wallpaper, the lace-draped windows, and the original Horan family furnishings and photographs. Proprietors Inga and John Peters offer country hospitality; their chef makes his mark with fresh fish and meat dishes, including a marvelous Columbia River sturgeon in season, but you'll be equally impressed with the beef tips—a flavorful combination of sautéed beef, mushrooms, and bell pepper, with hints of garlic and red wine. The lemon swirl cheesecake proves refreshing and light. The Carriage Pub and Cafe next door to the Peters' main restaurant offers similar but lighter fare in a publike atmosphere. This is a friendly stop for those seeking a glass of wine, a Northwest microbrew, or a game of cribbage. ■ *2 Horan Rd (just south of K-Mart plaza along the Wenatchee River), Wenatchee; (509)663-0018; $$$; full bar; AE, MC, V; checks OK; dinner Mon–Sat (lunch Mon–Fri at pub).* ♿

Steven's at Mission Square ★★ Steven's is a handsome place where chef Jeff Seal (who worked closely under Wenatchee's premier chef, Steve Gordon, before Gordon departed to wetter climes) serves Northwest cuisine with a few international excursions. The split-level dining room with potted plants is trendy; full-length mirrors reflect the well-dressed clientele. Pasta and seafood dishes are served here with pride and a flourish, from fettuccine with asparagus and prosciutto to apricot-honey-mustard chicken with sweet basil on a bed of spinach, pecans, and Bermuda onions. The lunch menu is highlighted by a grilled prawn sandwich and a red Thai curry. Bread is freshly baked and warm, and desserts are first-rate. ■ *218 N Mission St (1 block off Wenatchee at 2nd), Wenatchee; (509)663-6573; $$; full bar; AE, MC, V; checks OK; lunch Mon–Fri, dinner Mon–Sat.* ♿

The Windmill ★★ A constantly changing number on a blackboard has kept track of the steaks sold at this celebrated steak house since Mary Ann and Greg Johnson started running it in early 1997. The place looks like a wreck from the outside, but a better tenderloin we've never tasted in Wenatchee. Although the owners have changed here once (in the past dozen years), the waitresses here stay and stay, sporting pins that proudly declare the number of years they've served. The meals, too, are time-tested and classic. There are seafood and pork chops at this venerable steak house, but don't be a fool. Ritual dictates that you finish with a piece of one of the magnificent pies. ■ *1501 N Wenatchee Ave (1½ blocks west of Miller, on the main thoroughfare), Wenatchee; (509)665-9529; $$; beer and wine; AE, MC, V; checks OK; dinner Mon–Sat.*

Garlini's Ristorante Italiano ★ There's nothing fancy about the outside of this niche restaurant tucked away on one of the main streets in East Wenatchee. But inside, the dark, heavy wood, dim lighting, and festive music bring Italy to the senses. Craig Still makes sure all the old Garlini family Italian favorites are cooked as expected: seafood fettuccine, chicken and veal parmigiana, and lasagne just like Mamma's. Large, round tables and ample space accommodate families and large parties. Expect to wait a little longer for your meals on busy weekends. Busy or not, the servers keep a ready smile. ■ *810 Valley Mall Pkwy (1 block north of Wenatchee Valley Mall), East Wenatchee; (509)884-1707; $; beer and wine; AE, MC, V; checks OK; dinner Tues–Sun.*

Mickey O'Reilly's Sports Bar & Grill ★ Modeled after Seattle's Jake O'Shaughnessey's, this sports bar doubles as a family restaurant and gathering place. It's a take-me-out-to-the-ball-game kind of spot. The bar is separate from the main dining area, but TV screens with the hottest sporting events are visible from any perch. The courteous young waitstaff trot around in shorts and T-shirts, while the menu runs from a multitude of burgers to a mixed grill—which taste best when eaten out on the deck, with its great view. Don't blow your chance to try an Ice Cream Potato, spud-shaped vanilla ice cream rolled in powdered chocolate "peel." ■ *560 Valley Mall Pkwy (across from Wenatchee Valley Mall), East Wenatchee; (509)884-6299; $; full bar; AE, MC, V; checks OK; breakfast buffet Sat–Sun, lunch, dinner every day.*

LODGINGS

The Warm Springs Inn ★ The Wenatchee River is a perfect backdrop, and the pillared entrance and dark-green-and-rustic-brick exterior lend a certain majesty to Janice and Dennis Whiting's B&B. Four guest rooms with private baths are dressed in floral accents. A path behind the two-story inn (which served as a hospital in the 1920s) leads through a wooded area to the river's edge. Guests can relax in the naturally lit sitting room or enjoy the company of others on the veranda. Janice keeps coffee brewed at all times. ■ *1611 Love Lane (head toward Cashmere and turn left off Hwy 2 onto Lower Sunnyslope Rd), Wenatchee, WA 98801; (509)662-8365 or (800)543-3645; www.wsi.jpg@ ww.gopages.com; $$; MC, V; local checks only.*

The Chieftain The motels all line up along Wenatchee Avenue, but this one has been around since 1928. It may need a new paint job, but it's popular with the locals who come to its restaurant for the famous prime rib evenings. The rooms themselves are larger than those of the Chieftain's cousins down the pike. Ask for a room in the executive section, surprisingly spacious quarters for a very reasonable price. There's a swimming pool, a hot tub, and a helicopter pad (that is used more often as a basketball court). You can bring your pet with advance notice. Expect no view. ■ *1005 N Wenatchee Ave (off 9th), Wenatchee; (509)663-8141 or (800)572-4456; PO Box 1905, Wenatchee, WA 98807; $$; full bar; AE, DC, MC, V; checks OK; breakfast, lunch, dinner every day.* &

West Coast Wenatchee Center Hotel This is the nicest hotel on the strip (a very plain strip, mind you), with its view of the city and the Columbia River. The nine-story hotel has only three nonsmoking levels, and the rooms themselves are nothing out of the ordinary. Rates may rise if most rooms are already booked the day you call, so do make advance reservations and be sure to ask about package rates. The Wenatchee Roaster and Ale House is on the top floor, and the city's convention center is next door, connected by a skybridge. The outdoor pool is great under the hot Wenatchee sun (the indoor pool's for the other season). ■ *201 N Wenatchee Ave (center of town), Wenatchee, WA 98801; (509)662-1234 or (800)426-0670; $$; AE, DC, MC, V; checks OK; breakfast, lunch, dinner every day.* &

CHELAN

This resort area is blessed with the springtime perfume of apple blossoms, a 55-mile lake thrusting like a fjord into tall mountains, 300 days of sunshine a year, and good skiing, hunting, fishing, hiking, and sailing. It has been trying to live up to its touristic potential since C. C. Campbell built his hotel here in 1901, but with mixed success. Now that time-share condos have sprung up near the golf course and B&Bs have bloomed near the cross-country trails, though, the amenities have greatly improved. No one need improve the scenery.

The top attraction is the cruise up Lake Chelan on an old-fashioned tour boat, *The Lady of the Lake,* or the newer *Lady Express.* The lake is never more than 2 miles wide (it's also one of the deepest in the world), so you have a sense of slicing right into the Cascades. At **Stehekin** (see also Stehekin, below), located at the head of the lake, you can visit craft shops, take a bus tour, eat a barbecue lunch, and get back on board for the return voyage. The tour boat departs Chelan at 8:30am daily in summer, three or four days a week off-season, and returns in the late afternoon; rates are $22 per person round-trip; kids 6 to 11 years old travel half-price. No reservations are needed. The faster *Lady Express* shortens the daily trip to just over 2 hours, with a 1-hour stop in Stehekin before heading back; round-trip tickets are $41, and reservations are suggested (daily from mid-April to mid-October, less frequently in winter). More info: The Lake Chelan Boat Company, (509)682-2224 (information) or (509)682-4584. Or fly up to Stehekin, tour the valley, and be back the same day via Chelan Airways, (509)682-5555.

Condominium Rentals. The best reason for going to Chelan is Lake Chelan itself. And some of the best accommodations are the condominiums on its shores. If you would like to rent a condo, call **Chelan Vacation Rentals,** which is a rental clearinghouse for many of the condos on the lake at Spader Bay, Lake Chelan Shores, and Lakeside Villa, and for numerous privately owned homes; (509)682-4011 or (800)356-9756. Each condo is privately owned, so be aware that furnishings and taste vary greatly. **Wapato Point** condominiums are rented directly through their office; (509)687-9511.

Chelan Butte Lookout, 9 miles west of Chelan, provides a view of the lake, the Columbia River, and the orchard-blanketed countryside.

Sports. Lake Chelan Golf Course is an attractive course near town (call (509)682-8026 for tee times); fishing for steelhead, rainbow, cutthroats, and chinooks is very good in Lake Chelan, with remote, smaller lakes particularly desirable.

RESTAURANTS

Goochi's Restaurant ★ After years of abuse as a tavern in the historic Lakeview Hotel building, this pretty space with its huge antique cherry-wood back bar is now a smart dinner stop. Classic rock 'n' roll plays on CDs, and neon sculpture decorates the cedar-planked walls. Burgers and pasta selections are popular with children; for the adults, however, the restaurant strives for a slight twist on the usual, offering black-eyed peas in lieu of potatoes or rice pilaf. A moist chicken breast may come with a tart lemon-thyme cream sauce. Soups (such as Southwestern beef) are often spicy and flavorful. Chelan's Riverfront Park, just around the corner, is good for a postprandial stroll. ▪ *104 E Woodin (across from Campbell's Lodge), Chelan; (509)682-2436; $; full bar; AE, MC, V; local checks only; lunch, dinner every day, brunch Sat–Sun.* &

LODGINGS

Campbell's Lodge ★★ Chelan's venerable resort (whose history goes back to 1901) continues to be the most popular place for visitors, with prime lakeside property and 170 rooms, many with kitchenettes. As buildings are being added, the old ones are beginning to feel a bit dowdy. So reserve early and request one of the rooms in either building 1 (the newest) or building 3. Among the facilities, you'll find two heated pools, a sandy beach, an outdoor Jacuzzi, and moorage should you bring your boat. The convention center services up to 250 people. Campbell House, the most dependable restaurant at the lake (but still rather unexciting), is here. It has great service. Reservations can be scarce at both restaurant and lodge in high season. ▪ *104 W Woodin (on the lake at the end of the main street through*

▼
Chelan
▲

Chelan), Chelan; (509)682-2561 or (800)553-8225; PO Box 278, Chelan, WA 98816; campbell@cascade.net; www.campbellsresort. com; $$$; full bar; AE, MC, V; checks OK; breakfast, lunch, dinner every day. &

Kelly's Resort ★ Kelly-owned for almost a half century, this resort is a favorite among families who prefer the location on the shore and away from town. The original 10 fully equipped cabins are set back in the woods; they're dark and rustic, but they're great for those on a budget and families seeking a playground. We prefer one of the four condo units on the lake (from the lower units you can walk right off the deck into the water). There's also a nice deck near the grocery store (a good spot to have a beer) and a knotty pine common area with table tennis and a fireplace. ■ *14 miles uplake, on the south shore, Chelan; (509)687-3220; Rt 1, Box 119, Chelan, WA 98816; $$–$$$; MC, V; checks OK.*

Darnell's Resort Motel Situated right on the shore of the lake, this is a resort especially suited to families. Suites are large and have views (but price seems steep for a place that deserves a bit of TLC after so much use). Lots of amenities are included with the price of the room: putting green, heated swimming pool, sauna, hot tub, exercise room, shuffleboard, volleyball, badminton, tennis, barbecues, bicycles, rowboats, and canoes. Down the road from Campbell's and the center of town, Darnell's is slightly removed from the seasonal hurly-burly. ■ *901 Spader Bay Rd (off Manson Hwy), Chelan; (509)682-2015 or (800)967-8149; PO Box 506, Chelan, WA 98816; $$$; AE, MC, V; checks OK.*

STEHEKIN

A passage to Stehekin, a little community at the head of Lake Chelan, is like traveling back in time. This jumping-off point for exploring the rugged and remote North Cascades National Park can be reached only by a 4-hour *Lady of the Lake* boat trip or the faster *Lady Express,* (509)682-2224 or (509)682-4584; by Chelan Airways floatplane, (509)682-5555; by hiking (write Chelan Ranger District, PO Box 189, Chelan, WA 98816); or by private boat. The boat and the plane take you to Stehekin from Chelan. For a shorter boat ride, catch the *Lady Express* uplake at Field's Point. (See Chelan introduction, above, for more information.)

Exploration is the prime reason for coming here. There are several day hikes, including a lovely one along the lakeshore and another along a stream through the Buckner Orchard, and many more splendid backcountry trails for the serious backpacker. In winter there are some fine touring opportunities for cross-country skiers or snowshoe enthusiasts, although the town pretty much shuts down then. The ranger station at Chelan (open year-round),

▼
Stehekin
▲

(509) 682-2576, is an excellent source of information for these activities. A National Park Service shuttle bus provides transportation from Stehekin to trailheads, campgrounds, fishing holes, and scenic areas mid-May to mid-October; for information, call (509) 682-2549. Rent bikes or boats at the North Cascades Lodge; (509) 682-4494.

Stehekin Valley Ranch. The Courtney family picks you up at Stehekin in an old bus and takes you to the farthest end of the valley for seclusion and hearty family-style meals at their ranch. Open in the summer months, their rustic tent-cabins offer a place to bunk and just the basics (a kerosene lamp, showers in the main building), plus hearty, simple food at a decent price ($60 per night per person). **Cascade Corrals**, also run by the family, arranges horseback rides and mountain pack trips; (509) 682-4677, or write Stehekin Valley Ranch, Box 36, Stehekin, WA 98852.

The **Stehekin Pastry Company** is a local favorite for sweet desserts and rich conversation (summers only), a short stroll from the boat landing.

LODGINGS

Silver Bay Inn ★★ The Silver Bay Inn, located where the Stehekin River flows into Lake Chelan, is a wonderful retreat for those who want to explore the Stehekin Valley. Friendly Kathy and Randall Dinwiddie welcome their guests to this passive solar home with hikes and stories only the locals know. Guests get a continental breakfast. The setting is spectacular: 700 feet of waterfront with a broad green lawn rolling down to the lake. The main house has a master suite (with a two-night minimum stay to ensure you'll take time to enjoy yourself) decorated in antiques, with a separate sitting room, two view decks, a soaking tub, and a faraway view, as well as two other smaller rooms. Two separate lakeside cabins are remarkably convenient (dishwasher, microwave, all linens) and sleep four and six. Bicycles, canoes, croquet, and (for the less active) hammocks are available. A hot tub has a 360-degree view of the lake and surrounding mountains. In July, August, and September, Silver Bay is a perfect place for families with kids over 8 (younger kids welcome other months). ■ *Take* Lady of the Lake *to Stehekin; (509) 682-2212 or (800) 555-7781; PO Box 85, Stehekin, WA 98852; www.seattlesquare/silverbay.com; $$; MC, V; checks OK.*

NACHES

LODGINGS

Whistlin' Jack Lodge ★★ There are a number of fishing lodges nestled in the pines on the Naches River, but this one, just on the east side of Mount Rainier's Chinook Pass, is our favorite. Ideal for all manner of outdoor activity, from hiking and fishing to alpine and cross-country skiing, this mountain hideaway (originally built in 1957) has all the comforts of home and then some. There are six cabins, two bungalows, and eight motel units here, but best are the cabins—specifically, the Naches (with a riverfront lawn and hot tub on the deck) or the Grandview (so close to the rushing river you could almost fish from your deck). If you book a bungalow or room without a kitchenette, try the pan-fried trout in the restaurant. Access via Chinook Pass near Mount Rainier is restricted almost seven months a year, but lodge patrons (many of them families) are used to driving the winding road from Yakima instead. ■ *20800 SR 410 (40 miles west of Yakima), Naches, WA 98937; (509) 658-2433 or (800) 827-2299; $$; DIS, MC, V; checks OK.*

YAKIMA WINE COUNTRY

If your last visit to the Napa Valley recalled rush-hour traffic on the freeway to Disneyland, you may be ready for the less-traveled, more organic pleasures of Washington's Yakima wine country. Get off the freeway at virtually any point between Union Gap and the Tri-Cities and you'll find a scene of unspoiled pastoral splendor. (See also Tri-Cities Wine Country.) Vineyards and orchards follow the meandering Yakima River. Cattle graze the pastures. And the small towns scattered here and there provide constant surprises and unexpected small pleasures. The burgeoning wine industry (there are just over two dozen wineries in the valley, and more on the way) has encouraged small businesses to go after the tourist trade. Warm welcomes in the shops and tasting rooms are genuine; they really are glad to see you.

▼

**Yakima Wine
Country**

▲

The Yakima Valley Wine Growers Association (PO Box 39, Grandview, WA 98930; (509) 786-2163) publishes a useful brochure that lists member wineries along with tasting-room hours, easy-to-follow maps, and a bit of history. Big or small, all the wineries offer a taste of what's new and a chance to chat about the vintage in the most relaxed circumstances. Here's a quick rundown, as you head east from Yakima. **Staton Hills**, 71 Gangl Road, Wapato, (509) 877-2112, in an attractive building, has a view of the Yakima Valley and Mount Adams, and picnic grounds. **Bonair Winery**, 500 S Bonair Road, Zillah, (509) 829-6027, is a small, friendly, family-run winery, with a flair for chardonnay. **Hyatt Vineyards Winery**, 2020 Gilbert Road, Zillah, (509) 829-6333, features fine dry white wines and a lovely view of the vineyard, the east slopes of the Cascades, and Mount Adams; there's a picnic area. **Zillah Oakes Winery**, facing Highway 82, Zillah, (509) 829-6990, has off-dry white wines, a gift shop, and a tasting room with a Victorian motif. **Covey Run**, 1500 Vintage Road, Zillah, (509) 829-6235, is one of the larger wineries, with an expansive tasting room, picnic grounds, views of Zillah and the Yakima Valley, and a full line of well-made wines; check out the line of Reserve and Vineyard Designated wines. **Portteus Vineyards**, 5201 Highland Drive,

Zillah, (509)829-6970, is new, family-owned, with estate-bottled reds—cabernet, merlot, syrah, zinfandel, cabernet franc—as well as chardonnay. **Horizon's Edge Winery**, 4530 E Zillah Drive, Zillah, (509)829-6401, offers yet another spectacular view, and a good lineup of wine—muscat canelli, chardonnay, cabernet savignon, merlot, and pinot noir. **Washington Hills Cellars**, 111 E Lincoln Avenue, Sunnyside, (509)839-9463, has a large selection of pleasant wines in a no-frills facility. **Eaton Hill Winery**, 530 Gurley Road, Granger, (509)854-2508, serves winemaker's dinners in a restored homestead and cannery, and offers six cabernets as well as white wines. **Stewart Vineyards**, 1711 Cherry Hill Road, Granger, (509)854-1882, is one of the oldest vineyards in the state, whose rieslings and cabernets are worth noting. **Tefft Cellars**, Outlook, (509)837-7651, produces medal-winning cabernets and merlots, as well as Italian varietals and a small number of hand-crafted wines. **Tucker Cellars**, Sunnyside, (509)837-8701, is a family enterprise offering an extensive selection of Yakima valley fruit and produce as well as wines. Excellent tours can be had at **Chateau Ste. Michelle**, W Fifth and Avenue B, Grandview, (509)882-3928, where the state's biggest winery set up shop in the late '60s, and the highly regarded reds are still made in a facility dating back to the repeal of Prohibition. **Yakima River Winery**,

Prosser, (509)786-2805, has a riverside location, with full-blown reds and superb dessert wines. **Pontin del Roza**, Prosser, (509)786-4449, is family-owned and -operated. **Hinzerling Winery**, 1520 Sheridan, Prosser, (509)786-2163, was one of the state's pioneering wineries; look for tannic reds and fine late-harvest "Die Sonne" gewürztraminer. **Chinook Wines**, Prosser, (509)786-2725, offers a charming, intimate setting in which small quantities of some of Washington's best wines are produced; don't miss the merlot. **The Hogue Cellars**, Wine Country Road, Prosser, (509)786-4557, is a spectacularly successful family enterprise making superb whites and cellar-worthy reds; look for "Reserve" wines. **Oakwood Cellars**, Benton City, (509)588-5332, specializes in lemberger, merlot, and cabernet, and resides in the vicinity of Red Mountain. **Kiona Vineyards Winery**, Benton City, (509)588-6716, a small estate winery, was the first to plant on Red Mountain, making remarkable cabernet, lemberger, and dry and sweet rieslings. **Seth Ryan Winery**, Benton City, (509)588-6780, is a winery whose first bottlings of riesling and chardonnay gained recognition. **Blackwood Canyon**, Benton City, (509)588-6249, just up the road from Kiona, is a no-frills facility making controversial but distinctive wines; the late-harvest wines are excellent. **Columbia Crest Winery**, Paterson, (509)875-2061, is off the beaten track a half hour south of Prosser; this impressive facility showcases sophisticated winemaking on a grand scale.

Irrigation (first tried by the Indians and missionaries here in the 1850s) has made this desert bloom with grapes, apples, mint, asparagus, stone fruit, and hops. The town also blooms with small conventions.

Front Street Historical District includes a 22-car train, which houses shops and restaurants, and the renovated Pacific Fruit Exchange Building, which holds a local farmers market.

The Greenway Bike Path winds along the Yakima River for 7 miles. Start out in Sherman Park on Nob Hill and go north to the Selah Gap. Along the way, look for bald eagles and blue herons, or pick out a fishing hole; (509) 453-8280.

The Wine Cellar is a fine place to sample local vintages and orient yourself for a more extended foray into the wine country. Food products are available; 25 N Front Street, (209) 248-3590.

Interurban Trolley. A restored 1906 trolley provides summer-evening and weekend rides around Yakima. Call (509) 575-1700 for schedules.

Horse racing. Yakima Meadows has live races November through March. It's a dandy place to see small-town, Old West racing; 1301 S 10th, (509) 248-3920.

Yakima Valley Museum has handsome pioneer pieces, a collection from Yakima's most famous native son, Supreme Court Justice William O. Douglas, plus a children's "underground" museum and an old-fashioned soda fountain. Open every day; 2105 Tieton Drive, (509) 248-0747.

RESTAURANTS

Birchfield Manor ★★ Birchfield Manor offers elegant French country dining. When you arrive for your appointed seating, owners Wil and Sandy Masset greet you at the door and show you to your table in the large living room of their antique-filled historic home. Meals here are preceded by their reputation, which is taken very seriously. Trained in Europe, Wil produces an ambitious, imaginative meal, letting the food set the mood for a formal evening, and offering a one-of-a-kind experience here in central Washington. You may choose from one of six entrees, perhaps a double breast of chicken Florentine or a very authentic bouillabaisse. Washington wines are featured, and the courses—dutifully explained by a friendly waitperson—are both individualistic and complementary. There are five B&B rooms upstairs ($80 to $175) and four fireplace and whirlpool suites for a chunk more change. An outdoor pool is for guests only. ■ *2018 Birchfield Rd (exit 34 off I-82 onto Hwy 24, head east 2 miles, then south on Birchfield), Yakima; (509) 452-1960; $$$; beer and wine; AE, DC, MC, V; checks OK; dinner Thurs–Sat.* ⅙

El Pastor ★★ From the first bite of chips and salsa, you're in for one of those rare dining experiences, the kind usually serendipitously unearthed on side streets of major cities. For less than you'd shell out at a fast-food drive-through window, you can enjoy flavorful Mexican fare (try the chicken taquitos rancheros or the arroz con pollo) made with the freshest ingredients and served with baseball-sized bowls of cilantro-laden salsa and palate-pleasing guacamole. The Garcia family's restaurant—patriarch Luciano, sons Sergio and Hector, daughter Emma—has become one of Yakima's best-kept secrets. You'll leave El Pastor feeling like a very happy insider. ■ *315 W Walnut (corner of 4th Ave), Yakima; (509) 453-5159; $; beer; MC, V; checks OK, lunch, dinner Mon–Sat.*

Deli de Pasta ★ The North Front Street area is a comfortable blend of the old, the funky, and the hip. A half-block south of Grant's Brewery Pub, this intimate Italian cafe is quite popular with the locals. Owners Bob and Diane Traner have a flair for decor, making simple touches (red wooden chairs, red tablecloths, white linen napkins) seem somehow extraordinary. Fresh pastas and sauces, made on the premises, can be mixed and matched to suit your mood. The service is friendly, the coffee's fine, and the congenial atmosphere encourages many happy returnees. ■ *7 N Front St (½ block off Yakima Ave), Yakima; (509) 453-0571; $; beer and wine; AE, MC, V; checks OK; lunch, dinner Mon–Sat.*

Gasperetti's Restaurant ★ A somewhat formal dining room is set with elegant banquettes, linen-covered tables, and low lights. In the Bar Giovanni, palms nestled in Italian terra-cotta provide privacy between tables covered with wine-bottle-motif brocade and glass tops. Appetizers of note include roasted garlic and Rollingstone chèvre and calamari with spicy oil. Among a listing of pastas and meats, tender fresh Dungeness crab comes wrapped in cannelloni and sauced with mornay and marinara. Desserts are expertly prepared, and the expansive wine list offers excellent bottlings of Washington wines, including many hard-to-find reds, in addition to a solid selection of Italian labels. It's too bad the service ruins all by giving too much attention to regulars and no attention to others. ■ *1013 N 1st St (6 blocks south of the N Front St exit off I-82), Yakima; (509) 248-0628; $$; full bar; AE, MC, V; checks OK; lunch Tues–Fri, dinner Tues–Sat.* ᵫ

Grant's Brewery Pub ★ Bert Grant is one of the creators of the Northwest's boom in microbreweries, which brought back full-flavored, fresh, locally made ales and stouts. His namesake pub is in the old train station, where small experimental batches are brewed; the bulk of the beer is made 2 miles south (tours by reservation only). It's a popular place that serves up a British pub menu to accompany Grant's brews. Homemade soups and

Mexican food occasionally appear at lunch. This is a good place to meet friendly residents. ■ *32 N Front St (head west on Yakima Ave, turn right on Front), Yakima; (509) 575-2922; $; beer and wine; MC, V; checks OK; lunch, dinner every day.*

Santiago's ★ The high ceiling, dramatic brick walls, huge mural in the bar, and Southwestern art are festive, while the enormous skylight creates the exotic atmosphere of a Mexican courtyard (albeit in downtown Yakima). The chalupas and the tacos Santiago (with beef, guacamole, and two kinds of cheese) are especially popular. Steak picado (their version of fajitas) was on the menu long before the sizzling sirloin strips became chic at every other Mexican restaurant. ■ *111 E Yakima Ave (close to the intersection of 1st and Yakima), Yakima; (509) 453-1644; $; full bar; MC, V; checks OK; lunch, dinner Mon–Sat.*

LODGINGS

Rio Mirada Motor Inn ★ This Best Western motel, just off the I-82 freeway and right next to the shimmering Yakima River, doesn't look like much from the road. But once inside, you'll find 96 attractive, moderately priced rooms, each with a small balcony and a view of the river (second-story rooms are the best). Most rooms have tiny refigerators and a few have kitchenettes. For exercise there's an indoor heated pool and the pleasant 7-mile Greenway Bike Path that runs along the riverbank. ■ *1603 Terrace Heights Dr (exit 33 off I-82), Yakima, WA 98901; (509) 457-4444; $$; AE, DC, MC, V; Washington State checks only.* ₺

▼

▲

TOPPENISH

Western artist Fred Oldfield was raised here and returns occasionally at the request of the Toppenish Mural Society, (509) 865-6516, to lead a mural-painting posse. As a result, the whole town is an art gallery, with large walls covered in murals. Clusters of Western shops, antique stores, and galleries make strolling and shopping pleasant, and there are rodeos scheduled throughout the summer months.

Yakama Nation Cultural Heritage Center, located on ancestral grounds, houses an Indian museum and reference library, plus a gift shop, a Native American restaurant, a commercial movie/performing arts theater, and the 76-foot-tall Winter Lodge, for conventions and banquets. Open every day, about a half-mile west of Toppenish on Highway 97, (509) 865-2800. **Fort Simcoe** was built in 1856, and its gothic revival officers' quarters still stand in desolate grandeur; 28 miles west of Toppenish on Route 220.

ZILLAH

RESTAURANTS

El Ranchito ★★ Here in hops- and fruit-growing country, home to many Mexican-Americans, is a jolly tortilla-factory-cum-cafeteria that makes a perfect midday stop. You eat in the large dining area or in the cool, flower-shaded patio during the summer. After lunch you can browse in the gift shop, a mini-mercado with Mexican pottery, rugs, and hard-to-find Mexican peppers, spices, canned goods, fresh tortilla chips, and even south-of-the-border medicines. The authentic food is ordered à la carte. The smooth burritos, tasty nachos, and especially the barbacoa, a mild, slow-barbecued mound of beef served in a tortilla shell or a burrito, are generous and recommended. There is a Mexican bakery on the premises, but no cerveza. ■ *1319 E 1st Ave (exit 54 off I-82, follow the signs), Zillah; (509)829-5880; $; no alcohol; no credit cards; checks OK; breakfast, lunch, dinner every day*

SUNNYSIDE

RESTAURANTS

Taqueria la Fogata A small, simple roadside Mexican taqueria doing a lot of things right. The clientele is clearly local, the help clearly Mexican, and the menu expansive enough to include specialties such as *pozole* (Michoacán stew of pork back and feet and hominy) and *menudo* (Michoacán tripe and cow's-feet stew in a spicy sauce) along with all the usual tacos and burritos. The service is friendly and prices prehistoric. ■ *1204 Yakima Valley Hwy (in middle of town), Sunnyside; (509)839-9019; $; no alcohol; MC, V; checks OK; breakfast, lunch, dinner every day*

LODGINGS

Sunnyside Inn Bed and Breakfast ★ The 10 bedrooms in this 1919 home are huge (so big they sometimes feel empty). Four have outside entrances, and all come with phones, cable TV, air conditioning, and enormous private baths with Jacuzzi tubs. On the main floor, ask for the Jean Room (king-size bed, outside entrance) or the Karen Room (gas fireplace). Upstairs, the cheerful Viola Room is decorated in peach, and the Lola Room features a pleasant sun porch. For those who like the friendliness of B&Bs but need their fair share of privacy, this place is a godsend. Breakfast is a bountiful affair of blueberry pancakes, warmed syrups, fruit, and classical music. ■ *800 E Edison Ave (exit 63 or 69 off I-82), Sunnyside, WA 98944; (509)839-5557 or (800)221-4195; $; AE, MC, V; checks OK.* ⌖

GRANDVIEW

RESTAURANTS

Dykstra House Restaurant Who can resist a restaurant that features bread made from hand-ground whole wheat grown in the Horse Heaven Hills? Rich desserts and a few choice Washington State wines complement this mansion's simple menu (Friday-night dinners are Italian, and Saturday nights you always have an option of beef, chicken, or fish). If you come here with an open mind, you won't be disappointed. Proprietor Linda Hartshorn takes the time to make visitors feel at home in the gray stone 1914 home of Grandview's former mayor and in the town at large. Local groups often reserve the upstairs for meetings or parties. Reservations are required for Saturday dinner. ■ *114 Birch Ave (exit 73 off I-82, 1½ miles on Wine Country Rd), Grandview; (509) 882-2082; $$; beer and wine; AE, DC, MC, V; checks OK; lunch Tues–Sat, dinner Fri–Sat.*

PROSSER

Cherries have always grown well in the Yakima Valley, except when the weather doesn't cooperate. Too much rain cracks cherries, too little leaves them small. **Chukar Cherries** turns imperfect cherries into a year-round delicacy—dried cherries. In the showroom of their production center you'll also see chocolate-covered cherries, cherry poultry sauce, and even cherry waffle mix; 306 Wine Country Road, Prosser, (509) 786-2055.

LODGINGS

Wine Country Inn Bed & Breakfast A welcome addition to the limited overnight options in Prosser, this riverside home has three rooms upstairs and one down. The river winds lazily by the front door and the adjoining restaurant, from which owners/innkeepers Chris Flodin and Audrey Zuniga turn out terrific country breakfasts, lunches, and ample, hearty dinners. The thin-walled rooms are clean and comfortable. A deck and a gazebo open onto the river, with outside restaurant seating on warm summer nights. ■ *1106 Wine Country Rd (exit 80 off I-82, near bridge in Prosser), Prosser, WA 99350; (509) 786-2855; $; beer and wine; AE, MC, V; checks OK; lunch Mon–Sat, dinner Wed–Sat, brunch Sun.* ᕗ

TRI-CITIES WINE COUNTRY

The Tri-Cities wine country is the hub of the huge Columbia Valley viticultural appellation, which includes both the Yakima Valley and Walla Walla Valley appellations within its borders. Here its three principal rivers (Columbia, Snake, and Yakima) converge. A few miles to the west, at Red Mountain, the Yakima Valley wineries begin (see Yakima Wine Country); and a few miles to the east is the small cluster of Walla Walla Valley wineries. The Tri-Cities Visitor and Convention Bureau, (509)735-8486, provides up-to-date wine-touring maps and tasting-room schedules, and visitors find some of the state's oldest wineries and vineyards located nearby (90 percent of the state's vineyards are reportedly located within a 50-mile radius of Red Mountain). In the immediate area are **Bookwalter Winery**, 2708 Commercial Avenue, Pasco, (509)627-5000, a small facility located just off the cloverleaf joining Highway 395 and I-82; **Gordon Brothers Cellars**, 531 Levey Road, Pasco, (509)547-6224, one of the state's best vineyards, with a special flair for merlot and a nice view of the Snake River; and **Preston Wine Cellars**, 502 E Vineyard Drive, Pasco, (509)545-1990, a large, family-owned enterprise with an expansive tasting room and park. Southwest of Tri-Cities is Stimson Lane's $25 million showcase **Columbia Crest Winery**, Highway 221, Paterson, (509)875-2061.

TRI-CITIES: RICHLAND

Richland was once a secret city, hidden away while the atomic bomb workers did their thing in the 1940s; now "the Atomic City" is the second largest of the Tri-Cities. Interestingly, Hanford now employs more people to dismantle the site than it ever did in its heyday. However, as nuclear reactors close and the controversy over hazardous waste continues, civic leaders are working hard on industrial diversification. **Columbia River Exhibition of History, Science, and Technology** (CREHST), formerly known as the Hanford Science Center, is under development and will be opening to the public by the end of 1997. The extensive new center will be located above Howard Amon Park; call for more information; (509)376-6374.

Howard Amon Park, along the bank of the Columbia, is a great spot for picnics, tennis, golf, jogging, or just ambling. Allied Arts, 89 Lee Boulevard, (509)943-9815, located at the edge of the park, displays the work of mostly local artists in the oldest building in Richland.

RESTAURANTS

The Emerald of Siam ★★ One of the most authentic Thai restaurants in Eastern Washington is improbably located in a converted drugstore in a Richland shopping center. Thai-born Ravadi Quinn and her family run a cultural center for visiting school groups, a display of Thai handicrafts for sale, and an Oriental grocery. In the small restaurant, delicious native recipes include curries, satays, and noodles. All get high marks. Quinn's many projects include occasional cooking classes and her own cookbook, *The Joy of Thai Cooking*. ■ *1314 Jadwin Ave (at William), Richland; (509)946-9328; $; beer and wine; DIS, MC, V; local checks only; lunch Mon–Fri, dinner Mon–Sat.*

Vannini's Italian Restaurant ★★ This is a culinary jewel in an unlikely setting. If you knew Vannini's in Yakima, you'll recognize Vannini's in Richland. Devin and Aaron Burks partnered with Lesley Vannini to offer exquisite Northern Italian and Southern Italian cuisine in an intimate setting: a renovated railroad dining car in which some of the windows have been replaced with stained glass and tables are small (naturally) and candlelit. The tortellini Oreste, a three-cheese tortellini smothered in pesto sauce and tossed with sun-dried tomatoes and walnuts, is a standout. Local and Italian wines are available, and kids get a discount on real Italian sodas. ■ *1026 Lee Blvd (George Washington Way exit from I-82, follow George Washington Way to Lee Blvd and turn left), Richland; (509) 946-4525; $$; beer and wine; AE, MC, V; local checks only; lunch Mon–Sat, dinner every day.* ᣑ

Giacci's ★ In Richland's oldest building (1906), wonderful aromas waft from the busy kitchen and Puccini arias float through the air. Good salads and Italian sandwiches compose the lunch menu at this attractive deli/restaurant. A similar menu makes for a rather ordinary dinner. Still, you'll finish on a fine note if you add a glass of Chianti and one of their excellent desserts. There are outdoor tables in summer. ■ *94 Lee Blvd (corner of George Washington), Richland; (509) 946-4855; $; beer and wine; MC, V; local checks only; lunch, dinner Mon–Sat.* ᣑ

LODGINGS

Red Lion Hanford House ★ Location, location, location. For conventions you might do better at the Best Western Tower Inn down the street, but the Hanford House has secured Richland's finest piece of real estate right on the Columbia (aka Lake Wallula), fronting more miles of park than most guests can manage in an afternoon jog. Because of the unusual shape of the hotel, not many of the 150 rooms are riverfront (best bets are 175 to 187 and 275 to 287). Or ask for one of the large rooms facing the attractive grassy courtyard and the dandy pool area (a must on the broiling Tri-Cities summer days). This is *the* place to stay in the Tri-Cities. ■ *802 George Washington Way (take Richland exit off I-82 to George Washington Way), Richland, WA 99352; (509) 946-7611 or (800) 733-5466; $$; AE, DC, DIS, MC, V; checks OK.*

TRI-CITIES: PASCO

LODGINGS

Red Lion Inn ★ This large, sprawling motel (279 rooms) in half-timbered style has several notable attractions. There are two outdoor pools, an exercise facility, and an 18-hole municipal golf course that runs right alongside the motel, making it appear to be set in a park even though it's right on the freeway. The Red

▼

Tri-Cities: Pasco

Lodgings

▲

Lion is exceptionally convenient to the Tri-Cities airport and Columbia Basin Community College. Local residents like the restaurant here for "dressy" occasions, where the blue flaming desserts and coffees can be seen clear across the dining room. This is one of the few restaurants in Eastern Washington that really knows how to cook seafood and beef. The service is unpolished but eager to please. ■ *2525 N 20th St (take 20th St exit off Hwy 395), Pasco, WA 99301; (509) 547-0701; $$; full bar; AE, DC, DIS, MC, V; checks OK; breakfast, lunch, dinner every day.*

TRI-CITIES: KENNEWICK

RESTAURANTS

Chez Chaz ★ A fun collection of salt shakers sits on the counter and every table has its own sodium centerpiece, but that's as whimsical as this restaurant in an office building on Clearwater Avenue gets. The dinner menu is quite limited, probably because most people choose to do Chez Chaz for a well-executed lunch. There is a long list of sandwiches, like a great hot version of the Smoky Tom (turkey, cream cheese, provolone, and barbecue sauce on sourdough). But chef Chaz can do so much more—as evidenced by the specials: a spicy, peanutty Thai beef sauté on gently cooked vegetables or a linguine with a light tomato and basil cream sauce. ■ *5001 Clearwater Ave (between Edison and Union), Kennewick; (509) 735-2138; $$; beer and wine; no credit cards; checks OK; lunch Mon–Sat, dinner Tues–Sat.*

Casa Chapala Tri-Cities' most endeared Mexican eatery is run by a couple so young that when they opened, they couldn't legally get a liquor license. They're old enough now, and have maintained this very festive place where the help speak little English. Come Wednesday through Saturday between 5pm and 8:30pm and request a seat near the tortilla factory. Tortillas are that fresh, and you can be sure anything inside of them is too. ■ *107 E Columbia Dr (at Washington), Kennewick; (509) 586-4224; $; full bar; AE, MC, V; checks OK; lunch, dinner every day.*

WALLA WALLA

The Walla Walla Valley is an important historical area: the Lewis and Clark expedition passed through in 1805, fur trappers began traveling up the Columbia River from Fort Astoria in 1811 and set up a fort in 1818, and in 1836 missionary Marcus Whitman built a medical mission west of the present town. But when a virulent attack of measles hit the tribes in November 1847, a group of enraged Cayuse men killed the missionaries. The incident came to be called the Whitman Massacre.

Walla Walla has grown into a pleasant vale of 26,000, with fecund wheatlands all around, and **Whitman College**, a pretty private college anchoring the city (the campus is a nice place to stroll, (509)527-5176). The community boasts the oldest symphony orchestra west of the Mississippi River, which performs a season of winter concerts; call for more information: (509)529-8020.

Whitman Mission, (509)529-2761, 7 miles west of town off Highway 12, sketches out the story of the mission and the massacre; there aren't any historic buildings, but the simple outline of the mission in the ground is strangely affecting. A hike up an adjacent hill to an overlook offers the best impression of what the area looked like to the Whitmans and their fellow settlers. The mission became an important station on the Oregon Trail, and Narcissa Whitman's arrival was notable in that she and Eliza Spalding, also with the Whitman party, were the first white women to cross the continent overland.

Fort Walla Walla Museum in Fort Walla Walla Park on the west edge of town has a collection of 14 historic buildings and pioneer artifacts. Call (509)525-7703 for hours; camping and picnicking are available at the park adjacent to the museum. Summers only.

Onions. Walla Walla Sweets are splendid, truly sweet onions, great for sandwiches; here you can get the "number ones," with thin skins (usually mid-June through mid-July); (509)525-0850.

Wines. The Walla Walla region is home to some of the state's most brilliant wineries. Most notable are Leonetti Cellars (Walla Walla, (509)525-1428) for their cabernets and merlots and Woodward Canyon (Lowden, (509)525-4129) for their cabernets. Both wineries have been recently top-rated by *Wine Spectator*. Others are L'Ecole No. 41, Lowden, (509)525-0940; Waterbrook Winery, Lowden, (509)522-1918; and Seven Hills Winery, with production facilities over the state line in Milton-Freewater, Oregon, (509)938-7710 (open by appointment only). Most are open seasonally and with limited hours, or by appointment.

Juniper Dunes Wilderness. This 7,140-acre wilderness, protected under the 1984 Washington Wilderness Act, includes some of the biggest sand dunes—up to 130 feet high and a quarter mile wide—and the largest natural groves of western juniper, some 150 years old, in the state. This pocket of wilderness is all that remains of an ecosystem that once stretched over nearly 400 square miles south to the Snake and Columbia Rivers. Getting to the parking area, which is 15 miles northeast of nearby Pasco, involves driving some unmarked backroads through farmland; for directions to the parking area, call the Bureau of Land Management, (509)536-1200.

▼

Restaurants

▲

RESTAURANTS

Merchants Ltd. ★ It's a cluttered New York–style deli, with culinary merchandise piled ceiling-high on broad shelves, a deli counter loaded with breads, cheeses, sausages, salads, and caviars, and a glass-fronted bakery. The homemade soups are deservedly popular, but you won't be disappointed in the chicken salad or the tabbouleh. There are tables inside, or you can sit out front under the awning at a sidewalk table and watch Walla Walla waltz by. Upstairs is a more sedate dining room where the food is quite good. Lunch is served buffet-style Tuesday through Friday (as is a Wednesday spaghetti dinner). Excellent wine list. ■ *21 E Main St (take 2nd St exit off Hwy 12, turn left on Main), Walla Walla; (509)525-0900; $$; beer and wine; MC, V; checks OK; breakfast, lunch Mon–Sat, early dinner Wed.*

Jacobi's For dining with a historic ambience, head for the former Northern Pacific Railroad depot, home to Jacobi's, a cafe partially located in a former railroad dining car and otherwise expanded in 1996 to include the entire depot. The college crowd hangs out here, where they talk over espresso and beer from regional microbreweries. For a more elegant ambience, ask for a table in the railroad dining car. The cafe boasts "specialties from the Walla Walla Valley and beyond," and lives up to its promise. The 20-page menu includes local offerings such as Washington apples with Jacobi's caramelized dip (an appetizer), stuffed potatoes, an eggplant sandwich, steak, seafood—the works. The eatery offers an impressive array of Northwest wines and beers. ■ *416 N 2nd St (take 2nd St exit off Hwy 12 to the old Northern Pacific depot), Walla Walla; (509)525-2677; $; beer and wine; MC, V; checks OK; lunch, dinner every day.*

Paisanos [*unrated*] One of the newest entries on the Walla Walla culinary scene, Paisanos' chef Jennifer Parent serves up Italian fare that has locals raving about, and flocking to, the downtown restaurant. Parent incorporates as many fresh, local vegetables into the dishes as possible, which makes for inventive combinations. Early reports recommend the smoked duck cappellini, the scampi Paisanos, or the utterly simple angel hair pasta tossed with extra virgin olive oil, fresh herbs, and shallots. We look forward to watching this place develop. ■ *26 E Main (take 2nd St exit off Hwy 12, turn left on Main), Walla Walla; (509)527-3511; $$; beer and wine, AE, DC, MC, V; checks OK; lunch, dinner Mon–Sat.* &

LODGINGS

Green Gables Inn ★★ Margaret Buchan and husband, Jim, the sports editor at the local newspaper, converted this Arts and Crafts–style mansion to a bed and breakfast and reception facility close to Whitman College. True to the architectural style, a broad covered porch sweeps across the front of the mansion and around one side, an ideal setting for relaxing on a warm afternoon, lemonade and book in hand. Inside, the large foyer is flanked by two sitting areas, both with fireplaces and one with a TV where guests can watch ball games with Jim. Names for the five guest rooms are from the L. M. Montgomery book *Anne of Green Gables*. A favorite is Idlewild, the only one with a fireplace, private deck, and Jacuzzi. Another is Dryad's Bubble, a spacious room with a comfortable reading area and French doors that open to a small balcony. A remodeled Carriage House with tiled bath, queen-size hideabed, and day bed in addition to the separate bedroom is a good family option complete with a kitchen (full breakfast is included in the lodging price, though). ■ *922 Bonsella (take Clinton exit off Hwy 12 to Bonsella), Walla Walla, WA 99362; (509)525-5501 or (888)525-5501; greengables@wwics.com; $$; AE, DC, MC, V; checks OK.*

Stone Creek Inn ★ When it was built by Miles Moore in 1883, the Moore mansion was a home in the country. Now it's a 4-acre oasis surrounded by a modest residential neighborhood on a busy arterial. It is notable as the home of the last governor of Washington Territory. The mansion has four guest rooms, including a bright first-floor room with an opulent bath and a second-floor room with a fireplace and a screened porch. ■ *720 Bryant (call ahead for directions), Walla Walla, WA 99362; (509)529-8120; $$; no credit cards; checks OK.*

DAYTON

An impressive 88 Victorian buildings on the National Register of Historic Places make Dayton worthy of a stop, although don't expect to find all of the buildings restored. The town profited from a gold rush in 1861 in Idaho, as Dayton was on the main stage route between Walla Walla and Lewiston. Merchants and farmers built lavish houses during the boom years.

Skiing. In season, skiers can head for the Blue Mountains and Ski Bluewood, (509)382-4725, 21 miles southeast of Dayton (52 miles from Walla Walla), for cross-country and downhill skiing. The area, with the highest base elevation in the state, gets more than 300 inches of snow a year on its 26 runs.

RESTAURANTS

Patit Creek Restaurant ★★★ Bruce and Heather Hiebert have achieved the seemingly impossible: they've turned a small rural cafe into an excellent regional restaurant. Serving good food to the locals (both conservative farmers and more liberal college types) has been an experience—at times frustrating and educational—but the effort has paid off. There is now a steady and very appreciative clientele who don't mind driving long distances to eat superbly roasted meat at Patit Creek, located in what was a service station in the 1920s and later a soda fountain. Appetizers are notable, particularly the smoked salmon cheesecake (nonsweet) and the chèvre-stuffed dates wrapped in bacon and broiled. Bruce uses only the freshest vegetables and herbs. In the spring, fresh morel mushrooms are offered in a different entree each night. A little later in the season, he'll wander into the hills in search of extraordinarily sweet wild onions to use in some of his sauces. The wine list is short but includes the finest Walla Walla–area vintages. Heather's homemade pies and desserts provide a proper conclusion to such delightful dinners. Urbanites may sneer at fine food being served in a room with such folksy decor, a small gripe that easily disappears shortly after the first bite. Call for reservations, crucial on weekends. ■ *725 E Dayton Ave (on Hwy 12 at north end of town), Dayton; (509)382-2625; $$; beer and wine; MC, V; local checks only; dinner Tues–Sat.* ⟐

LODGINGS

The Weinhard Hotel ★ Dayton's loaded with restored Victorian buildings, but the Weinhard Hotel stands out as the quintessence of the era. Yes, a Weinhard—the nephew of the Henry of beer fame—actually built the Weinhard Building as a saloon and lodge hall in the late 1800s. Dan and Ginny Butler restored the building and converted it to a modest hotel just a few years ago. All of the 15 rooms are furnished with Victorian-era antiques. The roof garden is pleasant except during the heat of summer. Guests are served a complimentary continental breakfast in the lobby; or those a bit hungrier can order a full breakfast later in the morning in the hotel's modest dining room, which is open from midmorning through dinner (closed Tuesday–Wednesday). ■ *235 E Main St (downtown), Dayton, WA 99328; (509)382-4032 or (509)382-1681 (restaurant); $$; AE, MC, V; checks OK.*

The Purple House B&B A native of Southern Germany, owner Christine Williscroft brought her passion for Chinese antiques and Oriental rugs to her bed and breakfast. Breakfasts reflect Williscroft's European heritage: strudel or huckleberry crêpes. She can pack a picnic lunch for explorers, and on request will cook a European dinner, served family style. A typical dinner (guests only) would be Hungarian goulash, or trout in season when Williscroft goes fishing in the Touchet River. French doors in the first-floor guest room (decidedly feminine) open to a patio and swimming pool. The two upstairs rooms get quite hot in summer (at least the south-facing room has a ceiling fan). Small pets are allowed with advance warning. A studio bedroom above the garage is cozy but dark; however, it has a freestanding fireplace and a kitchenette. ■ *415 E Clay (1 block off Hwy 12, downtown), Dayton, WA 99328; (509)382-3159; $$$; MC, V; checks OK (closed Oct).*

PULLMAN

Pullman's population swells in the fall with Washington State University students, while the permanent residents are a mix of wheat farmers and university faculty. The largest of the Palouse towns, Pullman retains some of its cowpoke image, but covets an international reputation as a university town. The central business district consists mostly of one main street crowded with shops and some restaurants. There is abundant free parking just off the main street. Browsers might visit the Nica Gallery for an excellent representation of Eastern Washington artists, 246 E Main Street, (509)334-1213, and Bruised Books for used books that sometimes include hard-to-find first editions, 105 N Grand, (509)334-7898.

Washington State University. The campus is expanding constantly. The Fine Arts Center is a showcase with a spacious gallery that attracts exhibits by notable artists. Martin Stadium, home of the WSU Cougar football team, holds Pac 10 Conference–size crowds; the baseball team plays on Bailey Field near the 12,000-seat Beasley Performing Arts Coliseum, which houses both the basketball team and frequent rock concerts; (800)325-SEAT for tickets and an events calendar. Visitors might want to drop by Ferdinand's, (509)335-2041, located in the Agricultural Science Building and open weekdays only, which offers ice cream, milk shakes, and Cougar Gold cheese, made from milk and cream from WSU's own dairy herd. Tours of the university, (509)335-4527, leave French Administration Building at 1pm Monday through Friday year-round.

Kamiak Butte, 13 miles north on Route 24, offers a good place for a picnic and nice overlooks of the rolling wheat country. About 30 miles north of Pullman on Highway 195, **Steptoe Butte** towers above the Palouse and affords an impressive panoramic view as well as unobstructed stargazing. There's a picnic area at the top, but plan for wind, which is constant. History buffs find Steptoe Battlefield near Rosalia interesting; as at the Little Bighorn, the U.S. Cavalry lost this one, too.

Palouse Falls. Just north of its confluence with the Snake River, the Palouse River gushes over a basalt cliff higher than Niagara Falls and drops 198 feet into a steep-walled basin. Hiking trails lead to an overlook above the falls and to streamside below the falls. The falls are best during spring runoff, starting in late March. Camping is allowed. Just downstream from the falls is the Marmes Rock Shelter, where remains of the earliest known inhabitants of North America, dating back 10,000 years, were discovered by archaeologists in the late '60s. At the confluence of the Snake and Palouse Rivers, there is a public boat launch at Lyons Ferry State Park. The Marmes site is accessible via a 2½-mile unmaintained trail from Lyons Ferry State Park and by canoe. Much of the actual shelter area is flooded by the backwaters of Lower Monumental Dam, but the area is still popular with canoeists. Call Lyons Ferry Marina for more information; (509)399-2001.

RESTAURANTS

The Seasons ★★ No doubt Pullman's finest dining experience, this elegant eatery occupies a renovated old house atop a flower-covered cliff. Dinner is presented in a proper and elegant fashion; chicken and seafood are good choices. Salad dressings are made on the premises, and salads are served with scrumptious homemade breads such as whole-wheat with cornmeal, poppy seeds, and sesame seeds. ■ *215 SE Paradise St (on the hill about ½ block off Grand), Pullman; (509)334-1410; $$; beer and wine; AE, DC, MC, V; checks OK; dinner Tues–Sun.*

Swilly's ★★ Located in what was a 1920s photography studio, Swilly's borders the Palouse River and sports a small outdoor cafe. Across the street is one of the 20 artesian wells, drilled between 1890 and 1909, that were the deciding factor in locating a state college in Pullman. Inside, the warmth of the hardwood floors, the exposed brick walls, and the rich smell of espresso invite lingering. Works by area artists decorate the walls. The eatery boasts fresh local ingredients, right down to cream from a nearby dairy and bread from a local bakery. A separate calzone menu is billed as "the freshest and finest in the Palouse." The regular seasonal menu offers pastas with tempting ingredients such as marinated artichoke hearts, a lemon-caper combination, or an Oriental fish sauce. Swilly's has a modest selection of imported beers and a wine list with a good representation of Washington wines. ■ *200 NE Kamiaken St (1 block east of Grand), Pullman; (509)334-3395; $$; beer and wine; AE, MC, V; checks OK; lunch, dinner Mon–Sat.*

Hilltop Steakhouse This motel and restaurant has probably the best steaks in Pullman, Sunday brunch, and a wonderful view of the university and surrounding hills. The decades-old motel has been demolished and a new three-story, 60-room Best Western Heritage Inn has been built in its place, opened in mid-1997. The food is consistently good, albeit predictable, fare. ■ *928 Olsen (at city limits off Hwy 195, between Olsen and Davis Way), Pullman; (509)334-2555; $$; full bar; AE, DC, MC, V; checks OK; lunch Mon–Fri, dinner every day, brunch Sun.*

LODGINGS

Paradise Creek Quality Inn Just far enough off Route 270 to afford guests quiet nights away from traffic noise, this 66-room motel is also within easy walking distance of the WSU campus. It's situated literally over the meandering creek for which it's named. ■ *SE 1050 Bishop Blvd (¼ mile east of the WSU campus, near the junction of Hwy 270 and Bishop), Pullman, WA 99163; (509)332-0500 or (800)669-3212; $$; AE, DC, DIS, MC, V; checks OK.*

BRITISH COLUMBIA

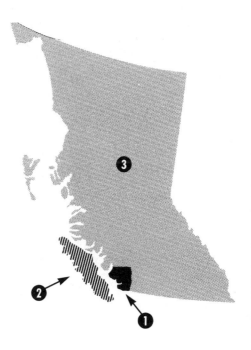

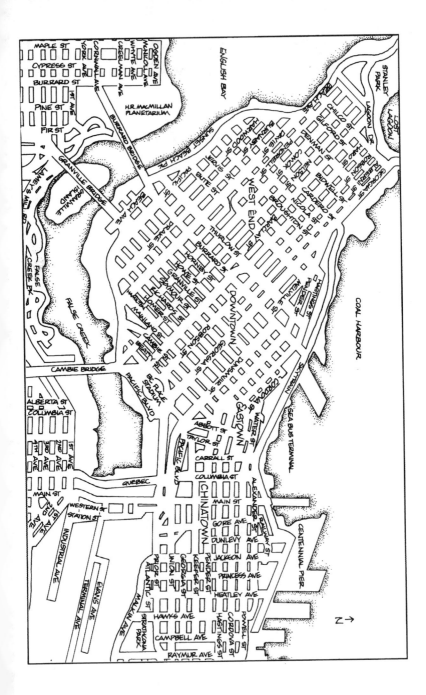

Vancouver and Environs

*Vancouver restaurants and lodgings,
including Greater Vancouver (Burnaby, Richmond,
West Vancouver, North Vancouver, and Ladner).*

VANCOUVER

Vancouver is Canada's fastest-growing metropolis and a city of magical contradictions—from rough-and-tumble Hastings Street, where timeworn brickwork still exudes a wild, beer-for-a-dime seaport-town atmosphere, to trendy Robson Street, with its futuristic Japanese noodle houses and haute couture. Lotus land, la la land, supernatural, astrological, New Age, old age, every age— it all culminates in this city nestled between mountains and ocean.

Vancouver has long touted itself as Canada's gateway to the Pacific Rim, and British Columbia is fortunate to be plugged into the world's fastest-growing economy. In fact, Vancouver has always accepted the waves of immigrants that have broken on its shore. The city seems living proof that a benign environment will produce an easygoing disposition.

The main branch of the Vancouver Public Library is now located in the dramatic Library Square complex (Robson and Homer Streets, (604)331-4000). Designed by world-renowned architect Moshe Safdie (he's also responsible for the Ford Centre across the street), the Library is a marvel. As they did to the Roman Coliseum that inspired it, people come by the thousands daily—instead of gladiators, it is books, magazines, audio and video tapes, and multimedia tools that await the curious.

Robson is still the city's most fashionable shopping street, often compared to Beverly Hills' posh Rodeo Drive. Glance away from the opulence of the shops as you saunter along Robson and you will see why; at the end of a side street lap the peaceful waters of Burrard Inlet. Beyond, the mountains on the north shore glitter with snow for half the year. Vancouver, its residents are fond of saying, is one of the few cities in the world where you can go skiing and sailing on the same day. How remarkable, then, that it should also be one of the few where, sitting ouside a Neapolitan cafe, you can eavesdrop on an impassioned argument in Hungarian and see graffiti in Khmer.

Amtrak offers daily round-trip excursions to Vancouver, BC, on its cushy Spanish Talgo train, leaving Seattle's King Street Station at 7:45am; for reservations, call (800)872-7245.

Visual Arts. Vancouver is a festive city, and art is everywhere. Visitors who fly into Vancouver and enter through the new international terminal building are greeted by an astounding display of the rich culture of the Musqueum people, the Coast Salish inhabitants of the lands around the airport. The focal point of the new terminal is preeminent Northwest Coast Native artist Bill Reid's magnificent bronze sculpture *The Spirit of Haida Gwaii, the Jade Canoe*, displayed on a bed of polished jade-colored marble. Downtown, Francis Rattenbury's elegant old courthouse is now the Vancouver Art Gallery, which holds more than 20 major exhibitions a year and whose permanent collection includes works by Goya, Emily Carr, Gainsborough, and Picasso; 750 Hornby Street, (604)662-4719. Across the street from the VAG, tucked behind the impressive facade of Cathedral Place, is the Canadian Craft Museum, Canada's first national museum devoted to crafts; 639 Hornby Street, (604)687-8266. Many of the city's commercial galleries are located on the dozen blocks just south of the Granville Bridge; and Granville Island, site of the Emily Carr Institute of Art and Design, has a number of potteries and craft studios. The avant-garde is most often at spaces such as the Helen Pitt Gallery, 882 Homer Street, (604)681-6740. The Museum of Anthropology at the University of British Columbia, 6393 NW Marine Drive, (604)822-3825, has an extensive collection of artifacts from Native American cultures of coastal British Columbia (including an impressive display of totem poles), as well as artifacts from Africa and the Orient.

Music. Over the last decade, the city has witnessed a renaissance in the proliferation of classical, jazz, and world music. The Vancouver Symphony Orchestra has reached new heights of artistic splendor under the leadership of maestro Sergiu Comissiona. The main season starts in October at the Orpheum, an old vaudeville theater (884 Granville, (604)876-3434). The Vancouver Opera puts on five productions a year at the Queen Elizabeth Theatre (Hamilton at W Georgia, (604)683-0222); the program is a balance of contemporary and traditional. The sets are spectacular and the artists are of international caliber. The du Maurier International Jazz Festival attracts crowds of more than 250,000 jazz lovers (held in June, call (888)GET-JAZZ for details), and the annual Vancouver Folk Music Festival is extremely popular as well; (604)602-9798. For information about any musical event, call Ticketmaster, (604)280-4444.

Theater. The Vancouver Playhouse Theatre Company explores contemporary and classical theater, offering six plays each season, October to May, in the Vancouver Playhouse; Hamilton and Dunsmuir, (604)873-3311. The Arts Club is a commercial theater with two locations and, usually, less production panache than the Playhouse; Granville Island, (604)687-1644. Contemporary theater in Vancouver is largely centered in the Vancouver

East Cultural Center (known to locals as The Cultch); 1895 E Venables Street, (604)254-9578. Vancouver's new home of the megamusical is the Ford Centre for the Performing Arts (777 Hornby Street, (604)602-0616); its two most striking features are the intimacy of the 1,824-seat auditorium and the visual power of the seven-story, mirrored-wall grand staircase that unites all levels.

OTHER THINGS TO DO

Parks and Gardens. The city is blessed with a climate—very similar to Britain's—that is well suited for flowers and greenery. Take a walk through the quiet rainforest in the heart of Stanley Park. At Queen Elizabeth Park, dramatic winding paths, sunken gardens, and waterfalls skirt the Bloedel Conservatory; Cambie Street and 33rd Avenue, (604)872-5513. The University of British Columbia campus boasts several superb gardens—the Botanical Garden, Nitobe Memorial Gardens, and Totem Park—along with the Physick Garden, which re-creates a 16th-century monastic herb garden, and the Food Garden, an amazing example of efficient gardening; UBC, SW Marine Drive; (604)822-9666. The Chinese Classical Garden within Dr. Sun Yat-Sen Park is a spectacular reconstruction of a Chinese scholar's garden, complete with pavilions and water-walkways; 578 Carrall Street, (604)662-3207. Near Queen Elizabeth Park, the VanDusen Botanical Garden stretches over 55 acres; 5251 Oak Street, (604)878-9274.

Shopping. Vancouver has always been bursting with storefronts. In Yaletown, brick warehouses have been transformed into chic shops that have become the destination of choice for exciting and eccentric fashion for oneself and one's home. Robson Street is the meeting place of cultures and couture, as *tout le monde* can be found strolling among its many boutiques and restaurants every day. Downtown is full of outstanding shops. In poor weather, head underground for the Pacific Centre and Vancouver Centre malls, with shops like Holt Renfrew, Eaton's, and The Bay. South Granville, the area from the Granville Bridge in the north to 16th Avenue in the south, is rich with an abundance of specialty shops full of high-end merchandise. At Granville Island Public Market on the south shore of False Creek, you can get everything from just-caught salmon to packages of fresh herbs to a wonderful array of fresh produce. Or visit the lesser-known public market at Lonsdale Quay in North Vancouver, with two levels of shops and produce, right at the North Shore SeaBus terminal. It's a 15-minute SeaBus ride from the terminal near Canada Place across Burrard Inlet. Gastown is a restored 1890s precinct, once touristy, now anchored by some really good shops that are of use to locals as well. Book Alley, the 300 and 400 blocks of West Pender, has bookstores specializing in everything from cookbooks to radical politics to science fiction.

Nightlife. On a warm summer night, the music spilling out from Vancouver's clubs and bars ranges from down-and-dirty R&B

at the suitably raunchy Yale Hotel (1300 Granville, (604)681-9253) and the rollicking Blarney Stone Olde Irish pub (216 Carrall Street, (604)687-4322), where you see entire families partying together, through local alternative bands at the Town Pump (66 Water, (604)683-6695) and disco thump at Richard's on Richards, the yuppie meat market (1036 Richards, (604)687-6794). The Railway Club (579 Dunsmuir, (604)681-1625) has a remarkably varied membership and presents consistently good music, whether pop or rock. To find out who's playing where, pick up a copy of the *Georgia Straight* or Thursday's *Vancouver Sun*. Another fun option is to get out of town on the Pacific Starlight Dinner Train, which passes along part of the famous Sea-to-Sky Route beside Howe Sound (June through October); (604)984-5500 or (800)363-3373.

Sports. The Canucks, Vancouver's hockey team, haven't managed to win the Stanley Cup yet, but they've come close a few times (GM Place, (604)899-4625). The Vancouver 86ers, the local soccer team, has a devoted following (Swangard Stadium, in Burnaby; (604)273-0086). Canada's own brand of football may become the farm league for the NFL, and that may be the only way Vancouver will manage to keep the BC Lions (BC Place, (604)589-7627). Visiting baseball enthusiasts should try to catch the minor-league Vancouver triple-A Canadians game at the Nat Bailey Stadium, (604)872-5232, a venue New York Yankee stalwart Roger Maris once called "the prettiest ballpark I've ever played in." But most Vancouverites would rather play than watch. Golf, sailing, hefting weights, exploring the local creeks and inlets by any kind of boat you can name—the city has first-rate facilities for these activities and many more. For information, contact Sport, BC (1367 W Broadway, (604)737-3000).

Ethnic Vancouver. The oldest and biggest of Vancouver's ethnic communities is Chinatown. The 200 block of E Pender is the main market area; to get started, try Yuen Fong for teas or the Dollar Market for barbecued pork or duck. Many Asians have moved into Richmond, as evidenced by the increasing number of outstanding Chinese restaurants and the New Aberdeen Centre, where you can get ginseng in bulk or durian from Thailand, and eat home-style Chinese food while you bowl. Italian commercial and cultural life thrives in the distinctive neighborhood around Commercial Drive, east of downtown. A second, less discovered Italian district is on Little Italy's northern border—the 2300 to 2500 blocks of E Hastings. Vancouver's 60,000 East Indian immigrants have established their own shopping area, called the Punjabi Market, in south Vancouver at 49th and Main Streets, where you can bargain for spices, chutney, and sweets. One of Vancouver's longest-established groups of ethnic inhabitants, the Greeks, live and shop west of the intersection of MacDonald and W Broadway; and a large Iranian population has settled in North Vancouver, as the many Iranian markets and saffron-scented restaurants attest.

Bishop's ★★★★ No restaurant is as personal as this minimalist Kitsilano space, where master host John Bishop reigns. Bishop has cooked for Presidents Clinton and Yeltsin (he now has a standing invitation to the White House). Hollywood knows about Bishop's as well—Glenn Close, Robin Williams, Richard Gere, Robert De Niro, and others have been spotted here. Bishop warmly greets his guests (celebrity and otherwise) and, assisted by the most professionally polished young waitstaff in the city, proceeds to demonstrate that he understands the true art of hospitality. Chef Dennis Green's entrees are uncomplicated. The rack of venison with goat cheese fritters and the ginger-steamed halibut (in season) are standouts. So are the pan-seared scallops scented with lemongrass and topped with a crisp potato pancake. Everything bears the Bishop trademark of light, subtly complex flavors and bright, graphic color. Desserts like the moist ginger cake, pooled in toffee sauce with homemade vanilla ice cream, and the Death by Chocolate are legendary. ■ *2183 W 4th Ave (between Arbutus and Yew Sts), Vancouver; (604) 738-2025; bishops@settingsun.com; www.settingsun. com/bishops; $$$; full bar; AE, DC, MC, V; no checks; dinner every day (closed for two weeks in Jan).*

Chartwell (The Four Seasons) ★★★★ Chartwell remains in the bold forefront of excellent hotel dining. It evokes an upper-class English men's-club atmosphere. Executive chef Marc Miron, former executive chef of the award-winning Four Seasons resort in Nevis, produces food of the highest quality that is generous both in proportion and in inspiration. Begin with his house-smoked salmon with onion and dill biscotti and lemon crème fraîche, and move on to Dungeness crab cakes with Fraser Valley greens. The rosy calf's liver with double-smoked bacon and garlic roasted onion confit with buttermilk herb mashed potatoes is world class. Master host Angelo Cecconi and his talented staff give Chartwell its distinctive stamp of personal service—warm, discreet, and attentive. A pre-theater dinner menu with valet parking is an outstanding value. The wine list is an award winner, and the winemaker dinners are the most popular in the city. ■ *791 W Georgia St (at Howe), Vancouver; (604) 689-9333; www.fshr.com; $$$; full bar; AE, DC, JCB, MC, V; no checks; breakfast every day, lunch Sun–Fri, dinner every day.* &

Le Crocodile ★★★★ France without a passport—that's Le Crocodile. Chef and owner Michel Jacob named his bistro after his favorite restaurant in his hometown of Strasbourg, and his Franco-German culinary heritage is obvious. He accompanies a wonderfully savory onion tart with chilled Alsatian wine in green-stemmed glasses. Salmon tartare and sautéed scallops in an herb sauce are both showstoppers. Luscious Dover sole,

duck (crisp outside, moist inside) accompanied by a light orange sauce, calf's liver with spinach butter—it's agony to
choose. The best desserts are the traditional ones. The well-
thought-out wine list and European atmosphere make a dinner
at Le Crocodile an affair to remember. ■ *100-909 Burrard St (at
Smithe), Vancouver; (604) 669-4298; $$$; full bar; AE, DC, MC,
V; no checks; lunch Mon–Fri, dinner Mon–Sat.* ⅙

Tojo's ★★★★ Tojo Hidekazu is Tojo's. One of the best-known
sushi maestros in Vancouver, this beaming Japanese chef has
a loyal clientele that regularly fills his spacious upstairs restau-
rant, though most people want to sit at the 10-seat sushi bar—
not big enough for all his devoted patrons. He's endlessly
innovative, surgically precise, and committed to fresh ingredi-
ents. Show an interest in the food, and he might offer you a bit
of this and that from the kitchen: Tojo tuna or perhaps special
beef (very thin beef wrapped around asparagus and shrimp) or
shrimp dumplings with hot mustard sauce. Getting to be a reg-
ular is not difficult, and it's highly recommended. The dining
room has a view of the stunning North Shore mountains and
plenty of table seating. Japanese menu standards like tempura
and teriyaki are always reliable, and daily specials are usually

superb: pine mushroom soup in the fall, steamed monkfish liver
from October to May, and cherry blossoms with scallops and
sautéed halibut cheeks with shiitake in the spring. Plum wine
and fresh orange pieces complete the meal. ■ *202-777 W Broad-
way (between Heather and Willow), Vancouver; (604) 872-8050;
$$$; full bar; AE, DC, JCB, MC, V; no checks; dinner Mon–Sat.* ⅙

Allegro Cafe ★★★ If a restaurant can be called a flirt, this is it.
Tucked away in the courtyard of a businesslike office tower
across from the Law Courts, Allegro beckons with a warm, intimate appeal. All decked out in curvy, dark green velvet banquettes, warm lighting, and red, green, and gold draperies, this
restaurant has become a hot spot for the young urban set.
Partly it's the great '60s modern decor, but mostly it's the excellent food at more-than-reasonable prices. Mike Mitton from
Il Barino has hooked up with chef Barbara Reese (of the Reese
peanut butter cup family) to offer Mediterranean dishes with a
West Coast panache: flavorful soups (try the roasted garlic), creative pastas (capelli with grilled scallops, leeks, Roma tomatoes,
and tarragon in a mascarpone cream sauce with salmon caviar),
and seafood and meat cooked to perfection. Reese knows when
to go all out with flavor—and when to approach a dish with fi-
nesse. For instance, a charbroiled veal chop with Gorgonzola
and grainy mustard cream sauce could have been a disastrous
cacophony of flavors but instead was a symphony of subtlety.
The only drawback is that the place is so popular you may wait
quite a while for your table. Pull up a stool at the bar, order an

excellent martini, and settle in for some serious people-watching. Yes, there's a peanut butter pie for dessert. ■ *1G-888 Nelson St (between Hornby and Howe), Vancouver; (604) 683-8485; $$; full bar; AE, DC, MC, V; no checks; lunch Mon–Fri, dinner Mon–Sat.*

Bacchus Ristorante (The Wedgewood Hotel) ★★★ Dedicated hotelier Eleni Skalbania and executive chef Alan Groom have put Bacchus on the culinary map, and Groom's superb cooking is just what people want now: Northern Italian with an emphasis on fresh and simple, using the bounty of BC's local products. At lunchtime, Bacchus attracts the "legal beagles" from the neighboring courthouse for penne with Gorgonzola, pizza rustica, or Il Taitano (a holdout from Skalbania's previous property, the Georgia Hotel, Il Taitano is a comforting trio of shrimp, avocado, and tomato on an English muffin with grilled fontina cheese). Afternoon tea (2 until 4pm) in front of the fireplace hits the spot, with finger sandwiches followed by freshly baked scones with dollops of Devon clotted cream, and tea pastries swished down by your favorite blend. The changing dinner menu might include grilled halibut with horseradish mashed potatoes, tiger prawns with lemongrass, or olive-crusted rack of lamb. Hope that the homey bread-and-butter pudding with sun-dried cranberries happens to be on the menu, or surrender to the Chocolate Seduction for two. There's a rich new look, featuring a wraparound bar, cozy banquettes, and a cigar room. Nightly, except Sunday, a pianist tickles the ivories. ■ *845 Hornby St (at Robson), Vancouver; (604) 689-7777; www.travel.bc.ca/ w/wedgewood/; $$; full bar; AE, DC, MC, V; no checks; breakfast, lunch, dinner every day, brunch Sat–Sun.* ᠔

Beetnix Pasta Bar and Grill ★★★ You could walk by Beetnix umpteen times without noticing it in its slightly subterranean location on a busy intersection. That would be a mistake. Once you enter this elegant little eatery, you'll discover an oasis of cool and calm in the busy city. Pale green walls, white-and-blue table settings, and fabulous art nouveau light fixtures provide the setting for some very fine food. Co-owners Kim Boyson and Adrienne Woolfries seem to specialize in the freshest of foods that pay homage both to local cuisine and to the flavors of the Pacific Rim. Start with one of the big, pungent salads before embarking on a pasta adventure (the warm-bread-and-tomato salad with greens and feta, olives, and balsamic vinegar is the best in town). Or try something from the grill, or the crisp duck breast, redolent of intense flavors, or whatever the daily special is. A fillet of sea bass arrived at our table, bringing with it a whimsical sense of the tropics—coconut crust, a whiff of curry, and a marvelously sunny fruit sauce. A selection of fresh sorbets and ice creams finish the meal—mix and match to suit your taste. ▪ *2459 Cambie St (at Broadway), Vancouver; (604)874-7133; $$; full bar; AE, MC, V; no checks; lunch Mon–Fri, dinner Mon–Sat.*

Caffe de Medici ★★★ As you enter Caffe de Medici, you are immediately made to feel like a favored guest. The high molded ceilings, serene portraits of members of the 15th-century Medici family, chairs and drapery in Renaissance green against crisp white table linen, and walls the color of zabaglione create a slightly palatial feeling that is businesslike by day, romantic by night. Skip the soups and order the beautiful antipasto: a bright collage of marinated eggplant, artichoke hearts, peppers, olives, squid, and Italian meats. Pasta dishes are flat-out magnifico: a slightly chewy plateful of tortellini alla panna comes so rich with cheese you'll never order any of the others. Although it's mostly a Florentine restaurant (with a knockout version of beefsteak marinated in red wine and olive oil), we've also sampled a fine Roman-style rack of lamb. ▪ *1025 Robson St (between Burrard and Thurlow), Vancouver; (604)669-9322; medici@settingsun.com; www.settingsun.com/medici; $$$; full bar; AE, DC, MC, V; no checks; lunch Mon–Fri, dinner every day.* ♿

CinCin ★★★ CinCin is a hearty Italian toast, a wish of health and good cheer, all of which is implied in this sunny Mediterranean space. The scent from wood-burning ovens, the warm surroundings—what more could one need? Best seats are in the northeast corner by the window. CinCin's breadsticks and flatbreads (rosemary and oatmeal) are irresistible. Launch your meal with a carpaccio or a saffron-scented cioppino. Noodles are made fresh daily. Rigatoni is tossed with house-made sausage, clams, and fennel; linguine ribbons are laced with beef tenderloin and tomatoes; and penne is dotted with juicy morsels of roast chicken and capers. Another bonus: the wine list is not only one of the best in town but, because of a reduced markup on wines, economical. Desserts are all homemade in the best sense of the word. This is a great place to sip wine with the gang in the lounge (food's served until 11:30pm). ▪ *1154 Robson St (between Bute and Robson), Vancouver; (604)688-7338; www.araxi.com; $$$; full bar; AE, DC, MC, V; no checks; lunch Mon–Fri, dinner every day.*

Diva at the Met (Metropolitan Hotel) ★★★ An airy multi-tiered space with an exhibition kitchen has set the stage for imaginative, well-executed cooking at what's sure to become one of the finest hotel restaurants in the city. Thanks to some restaurant raiding, Michael Noble of the Four Seasons, David Griffiths of Alabaster, and Ray Henry of Waterfront Centre all have their spoons in the soup here. Whatever is served, it ranks with the best, but it's sometimes slow getting to you. It's worth a wait, however, for the unique starter—a chilled tomato martini—and the entrees—the grilled prawns, the avocado and Dungeness crab risotto, or a lamb rack with kalamata olive butter. Brunchers swoon over the smoked Alaskan black cod hash topped with poached eggs. All the desserts are winners, but the Stilton cheesecake is a must-order. No maître d' abuse here: ex-Crocodile manager John Blakeley strives for the highest standard of service. And the wine list is sure to win awards. ■ *645 Howe St (between Dunsmuir and Georgia Sts), Vancouver; (604) 602-7788; reservations@divamet.com; www.metropolitan. com/; $$; full bar; AE, DC, MC, V; no checks; breakfast, lunch, dinner every day.*

The Fish House at Stanley Park ★★★ Ever since high-profile restaurateur Bud Kanke put chef Karen Barnaby in the Fish House kitchen, he's been winning accolades from critics and diners alike. Here, seafood rules (salmon, sea bass, shellfish of all kinds)—everything you'd expect and some things you wouldn't. As an appy, try the deep-fried cornmeal oysters with a chipotle-flavored tartare sauce. It's the whole plate that impresses. Barnaby's vegetables aren't an afterthought; each is a discovery in itself: red cabbage with fennel, spaghetti squash with poppy seeds, and buttermilk mashed potatoes. Ahi tuna comes as "two-fisted" loins (a pair), barely grilled through and fork-tender in a green pepper sauce, with buttermilk mashed potatoes. Barnaby's chocolate lava cake is lethal. ■ *2099 Beach Ave (entrance to Stanley Park), Vancouver; (604) 681-7275; $$; full bar; AE, DC, E, MC, V; no checks; lunch Mon–Sat, dinner every day, brunch Sun.* &

Five Sails (Pan Pacific Hotel) ★★★ The drop-dead gorgeous harbor view at the Five Sails may lure diners here for the first time, but it's chef Cheryle Michio's imaginative ways with fresh fish, soups, duck, and more that bring them back. Don't even think of not ordering the smoked Alaska black cod chowder. Second choice would be the seared scallops on wasabi mashed potatoes. Winning entrees include crisp sea bass with sweet lemon and sour orange sauce, seared sesame salmon with hot-and-sour carrot butter sauce, and medallions of veal in a bacon wrap. Set sail on an individual baked Alaska. The eager-to-please service is icing on the cake. Become a member here of La Confrerie du Sabre d'Or by ordering champagne and sabering the bottle. Free parking. ■ *999 Canada Pl (between Burrard and Howe Sts), Vancouver; (604) 891-2892; preserve@panpacific hotel.com; www.panpac.com; $$$; full bar; AE, DC, MC, V; no checks; dinner every day.* &

Fleuri (Sutton Place Hotel) ★★★ Elegant meals and a very civilized tea await those who venture through Sutton Place Hotel's chandeliered lobby to the newly renamed Fleuri. Hotel guests—corporate types and movie stars (celeb-spotting is a popular sport)—converse over classic English tea or a traditional Japanese tea ceremony with hand-whisked matcha tea

Vancouver

Restaurants

▲

and bean jelly. For $15, you can nibble on finger sandwiches, pastries, and scones and cream. Buffets are a specialty: Friday and Saturday, tables are laden with seafood and fish for the "Taste of Atlantis." The Chocoholic Bar has become a legend on Thursdays, Fridays, and Saturdays, and the Sunday brunch has been rated as the number-one special-occasion place in town. ■ *845 Burrard St (between Robson and Smithe), Vancouver; (604)682-5511; info@suttonplace.com; www.travelweb.com/sutton.html; $$; full bar; AE, DC, MC, V; no checks; breakfast, lunch, dinner every day, brunch Sun.* ♿

Grand King Seafood Restaurant ★★★ Chef Lam Kam Shing and partner Simon Lee, the team behind the brief Camelot-like brilliance of the old Dynasty Restaurant in the Ramada Renaissance Hotel, are now wowing local and visiting lovers of Chinese food in their well-established restaurant located in the Holiday Inn on West Broadway. Granted, the decor here is no match for the elegant Dynasty, but the service, less formal, ever courteous, informative, and helpful, is unmatched. The menu is trademark Lam—a creative assimilation of his diverse experience in Chinese regional cuisines with innovative touches gleaned from Japanese and other Asian cooking styles. Local ingredients become new classics in dishes like pan-fried live spot prawns in chile soya, stewed black cod with garlic, and house-barbecued pork. One of our recent favorites is the Dungeness crab—the body meat steamed in its shell, laced with its rich roe, minced pork, and cellophane noodles, and surrounded by its legs crisp-fried with spicy rock salt. Another is superb double-boiled winter melon soup cooked inside the melon and laden with seafood. The list goes on. One more thing: you'll be happy to know that those addictive complimentary candied walnuts and their dynamite X.O. chile sauce are now bottled to go at the cashier's desk on your way out. ■ *705 W Broadway (in the Holiday Inn, at Heather), Vancouver; (604)876-7855; $$$; full bar; AE, MC, V; no checks; lunch, dinner every day.*

Il Giardino di Umberto ★★★ Stars, stargazers, and movers and shakers come to Umberto Menghi's Il Giardino to mingle amid the Tuscan villa decor: high ceilings, tiled floors, winking candlelight, and a vine-draped terrace for dining alfresco (no better place in summer). The emphasis is on pasta and game, with an Italian nuova elegance: farm-raised pheasant with roasted-pepper stuffing and port wine sauce, tender veal with a mélange of lightly grilled wild mushrooms. Be warned: the prices on the specials are in their own category. For dessert, go for the prize-winning tiramisu—the best version of this pick-me-up in town. ■ *1382 Hornby St (at Pacific), Vancouver; (604)669-2422; inquire@umberto.com; www.umberto.com; $$$; full bar; AE, DC, MC, V; no checks; lunch Mon–Fri, dinner Mon–Sat.*

Imperial Chinese Seafood Restaurant ★★★ The Imperial may lay claim to being the most opulent Chinese dining room around. There's a feeling of being in a grand ballroom of eras past: a central staircase leads to the balustrade-lined mezzanine; diplomatic dignitaries and rock stars dine in luxurious private rooms; and windows two stories high look out onto the panorama of Burrard Inlet and the North Shore mountains. The food can be equally polished—lobster in black bean sauce with fresh egg noodles, pan-fried scallops garnished with coconut-laced deep-fried milk, sautéed spinach with minced pork and Chinese anchovies, a superb pan-smoked black cod, and the addictive beef sauté in chiles with honey walnuts. Dim sum also is consistently good. However, reports of uneven service continue to mar what otherwise might be a perfect restaurant in its class. Reservations are recommended on weekdays. ■ *355 Burrard St (at W Hastings), Vancouver; (604) 688-8191; $$; full bar; AE, MC, V; no checks; lunch, dinner every day.*

Kirin Mandarin Restaurant ■ Kirin Seafood Restaurant ★★★ Kirin's postmodern decor—high ceilings, slate-green walls, black lacquer trim—is oriented around the two-story-high mystical dragonlike creature that is the restaurant's namesake. The menu reads like a trilingual (Chinese, English, and Japanese) opus spanning the culinary capitals of China: Canton, Sichuan, Shanghai, and Beijing (live lobsters and crabs can be ordered in 11 different preparations). Remarkably, most of the vastly different regional cuisines are authentic and well executed, but the Northern Chinese specialties are the best. Peking duck is as good as it gets this side of China, and braised dishes such as sea cucumber with prawn roe sauce are "royal" treats. Atypical of Chinese restaurants, desserts can be excellent—try the red bean pie, a thin crêpe folded around a sweet bean filling and fried to a fluffy crispness. The Western-style service is attentive though sometimes a tad aggressive. Unless you are in the mood to splurge, stay away from the Cognac cart. The second, equally fine outpost is in City Square, with a passable view of the city. Here fresh seasonal seafood choices, such as drunken live spot prawns and whole Alaskan king crab, are often presented with dramatic tableside special effects. It also has great dim sum (including a definitive har gow or shrimp dumpling). ■ *1166 Alberni St (between Bute and Thurlow), Vancouver; (604) 682-8833; $$$; full bar; AE, DC, JCB, V; checks OK; lunch, dinner every day.* ■ *201-555 W 12th Ave (City Square at Cambie), Vancouver; (604) 879-8038; $$$; full bar; AE, DC, JCB, V; checks OK; lunch, dinner every day.* &

Le Gavroche ★★★ Arguably the most romantic restaurant in the city, Le Gavroche is one of the city's leading French kitchens (with a Northwest influence), enhanced by a discreet upstairs room and complete with blazing fire and glimpses of the harbor and mountains. For starters, try the endive, pear, and Stilton cheese salad with port-orange vinaigrette. We loved the previous chef's sea bass cassoulet with white beans, pancetta, spinach, and apple cider sauce, but at this writing, a new chef, Anna Anderson, has taken the reins, so new specialties may be in store. Service is formal but friendly and subtly attentive. For dessert, try the trademark lili cake—a soft almond and hazelnut meringue with an almond crème anglaise—even *Gourmet* magazine requested the recipe. Le Gavroche has one of the city's better wine cellars, with a range of Bordeaux and Burgundies. ■ *1616 Alberni St (at Cardero), Vancouver; (604)685-3924; $$$; full bar; AE, DC, JCB, MC, V; no checks; lunch Mon–Fri, dinner every day.*

Lola's Restaurant ★★★ Lola's is a sexy, glamorous eatery, a ménage of chef Scott Kidd's excellent and adventurous cooking, the over-the-top team from Delilah's, and the antique opulence of the heritage building that houses them. Once the valet has whisked away your vehicle, you'll step into a baroque world that teeters giddily between sophistication and camp. An elegant marble foyer is watched over by a fresco of Renaissance angels. Inside, it's all crystal chandeliers, purple velvet draperies and banquettes, midnight blue ceiling, gilt trim, and a touch of turn-of-the-century art deco. Eclectic tunes set the mood—everything from Cole Porter to Nancy Sinatra—as neosophisticates sip champagne cocktails and martinis. The crowd tends to be young, hip, and urban, or older and moneyed. Kidd, who used to cook at Le Gavroche, prepares French classics with nuances of the West Coast and Pacific Rim. Sweetbreads, for instance, might come with a turnip pancake and Asian-inspired sauces; a crème brûlée is spiked with citrus and served in a lidded porcelain pot. The occasional shortcomings in the menu department are compensated for by the great cocktail and wine list. Lola's has brought the champagne cocktail back into style with more than a dozen varieties that range from the classic sugar cube soaked in bitters to one garnished with a banana. ■ *432 Richards St (between Hastings and Pender), Vancouver; (604)684-5652; $$$; full bar; AE, MC, V, no checks; lunch Mon–Fri, dinner every day.*

Lumière ★★★ The minimalistic elegance of this room on the ever-expanding Broadway corridor showcases both the chef's exquisite creations and the Armani-clad clientele. Although the decor is a tad austere—very pale, very stark—the food is luxurious, flaunting the skills of Robert Feenie's kitchen. In fact, Lumière serves up some of the very best food the city has to offer, a sort of French gone modern. Whether Feenie is preparing a hearty dish like the exquisite stuffed saddle of rabbit on braised leeks or something lighter, he always seems to achieve a perfect balance of flavors and textures. Appetizers at Lumière are especially delicious and make choices especially difficult—for instance, how to decide between the caramelized onion and goat cheese tart with organic cherry tomatoes and the warm mille-feuille with shiitake and oyster mushrooms in a red wine butter reduction? A decent wine list accompanies the food. The palate-cleansing sorbet brought between courses ensures that each meal is a proper celebration of the dining experience. The service is informed, attentive, and helpful. ■ *2551 W Broadway (between Larch and Trafalgar), Vancouver; (604) 739-8185; $$$; full bar; AE, MC, V; no checks; dinner Tues–Sun.*

Mangiamo! ★★★ "Let's eat!" urges this chic eatery in Yaletown, and indeed we're delighted to do so. Mangiamo! is a happy collaboration between gastronomic guru Umberto Menghi and chef Ken Bogas, formerly of Saltimbocca in Kitsilano. At Mangiamo!, Bogas's occasionally wacky creations are beautifully mellowed by Umberto's sometimes staid insistence on quality. This creates a menu and an environment that are elegant and tasteful, yet fun and vibrant. (The cheesy puns on the menu help, too.) No wonder so many celebrities can be spotted at the white-cloth-covered tables. The room itself is gracious, but it's the food that keeps bringing people back. Bogas takes traditional Italian dishes and gives them a bit of West Coast spin. A shellfish soup is served with enoki mushrooms, a seasonal asparagus soup is adorned by a crunchy corn and Dungeness crab fritter. A green salad may come with seared portobello mushrooms and Gorgonzola croutons, all tossed in a tomato chipotle vinaigrette. The menu is extensive, with a focus on creatively prepared seafood—paillard of BC salmon with tequila lime fresca, for instance. ■ *1116 Mainland St (at Helmcken), Vancouver; (604) 687-1116; $$$; full bar; AE, MC, V; no checks; lunch Mon–Fri, dinner Mon–Sat.*

Montri's Thai Restaurant ★★★ Why go anywhere else for Thai food when Montri's is simply the best in town? After a hiatus for a trip to Thailand, Montri Rattanaraj is back, and his food is better than ever. He presents an authentic cuisine, not watered down for Vancouver tastes but with little touches all his own, like the salmon steak in red curry sauce. Thai cuisine is a careful balancing act, based on six interconnecting concepts: bitter, salty, sweet, hot, herbaceous, and fragrant. The heat content is rated on a scale of one to five chile symbols, five being the level for masochists and Thai nationals. What to order? Everything is good. *Tom yum goong* is Thailand's national soup, a lemony prawn broth, and it lives up to its name—yum. The *tod mun* fish cakes blended with prawns and chile curry are excellent, as is the salmon simmered in red curry and coconut sauce. Rattanaraj's *Thai gai-yang*, chicken marinated in coconut milk and broiled, is a close cousin to the chicken sold on the beach at Phuket. Have it with *som-tam*, a green papaya salad served with sticky rice and wedges of raw cabbage; the cabbage and the rice are coolants, and you will need them (Thailand's Singha beer also helps). ■ *3629 W Broadway (between Dunbar and Elma), Vancouver; (604) 738-9888; $$; full bar; MC, V; no checks; dinner every day.* &

900 West (Hotel Vancouver) ★★★

CP Hotels lured California chef Jeremiah Tower to Vancouver with a three-year contract to work with executive chef Robert Le Crom in creating an inspired menu. After a multimillion-dollar renovation, the fusty old Timber Club has been turned into one of the most fashionable rooms in the city. The restaurant is reminiscent of a cruise ship dining room, recalling the era of the great luxury liners. There's a wine bar area (you can order a snack from the lounge menu), an open kitchen, and live entertainment that keeps the action churning. Standouts on the menu include a superb starter of charred rare ahi tuna arranged as a tower with a pasilla chile aioli and a spit-roasted pheasant breast with blueberry-yam pudding. The well-thought-out wine list complements the menu. ■ *900 W Georgia St (at Burrard), Vancouver; (604) 669-9378; lcockburn@hvc.mhs.compuserve.com; $$$; full bar; AE, DC, MC, V; no checks; lunch Mon–Sat, dinner every day.* &

Phnom Penh Restaurant ★★★

Phnom Penh was once a treasure Vancouverites kept to themselves, but this restaurant now wins a steady stream of accolades from sources as diverse as local magazine polls and the *New York Times*. The decor is basic, but the menu ranges from its original rice-and-noodle focus to the cuisines of China, Vietnam, and Cambodia. Pineapple-spiked hot and sour soup, with your choice of chicken, fish, or prawns, is richly flavored and redolent of lemongrass and purple basil. An excellent appetizer of marinated beef sliced carpaccio-thin is seared rare and dressed with *nuoc mam* (a spicy, fishy sauce—the Vietnamese staple). Sautéed baby shrimp in prawn roe and tender slivers of salted pork cover hot, velvety steamed rice cakes—a real masterpiece. Grandma's recipe of garlic chile squid, prawns, or crab with lemon pepper dip has been uniformly declared "unbeatable." The chicken salad with cabbage is a refreshing twist on a pedestrian vegetable, and the oyster omelet is a dream. If it's good enough for Julia Child, it should be good enough for you. Service is knowledgeable and friendly. ■ *244 E Georgia St (at Main St), Vancouver; (604) 682-5777; $; full bar; AE, MC; no checks; lunch, dinner Wed–Mon.* ■ *955 W Broadway (at Oak St), Vancouver; (604) 734-8898; $; full bar; AE, MC; no checks; lunch, dinner Wed–Mon.*

Piccolo Mondo ★★★

Seldom do you meet people with as intense a dedication to fine food as the husband-and-wife team of George Baugh and Michele Geris, proprietors of this exquisite Italian restaurant. Their little world is one of Vancouver's best-kept secrets, a place where the setting is calm and elegant, the food absolutely authentic, the wine list phenomenal, and the service immaculate. The stately European room can seem stiff and formal at first. But just wait. Within minutes, Geris will have you feeling happy and comfortable, and by the time you've taken your first sip of wine, you'll be right at home. The wine list is a marvel that is yearly honored by *Wine Spectator* magazine. As for the food, chef Stephane Meyer oversees a menu that is small but nearly perfect. Each dish is packed with the intense flavors of Northern Italy, and the kitchen is dedicated to using only the best, freshest ingredients. To start, try the saffron-scented fish soup or one of the composed salads. Follow that up with, perhaps, the powerful risotto with duck, red pepper, and Gorgonzola; the veal osso buco with lemon and capers; or the house specialty, a creamy salted cod with pine nuts and raisins. By the time dessert comes around, you'll be convinced: this is the best of all possible worlds. ■ *850 Thurlow St (at Haro), Vancouver; (604) 688-1633; $$$; full bar; AE, DC, MC, V; no checks; lunch Mon–Fri, dinner Mon–Sat.*

Quattro on Fourth ★★★ Antonio Corsi took over the westside space that had been home to Montri's Thai Restaurant and turned it into one of the most comfortable Italian restaurants in the city. There's a high sense of *abbondanza* here. An impressive selection of antipasti includes no less than eight different carpaccio offerings; razor-thin sliced raw swordfish is superb, as are the grilled radicchio bocconcini and portobello mushrooms. Spaghetti Piga ("for Italians only") rewards with a well-spiced sauce of chicken, chiles, black beans, and plenty of garlic. Food is prepared with lots of TLC from son Patrick and staff. Quattro also has a heated patio that seats 35. ■ *2611 W 4th Ave (at Trafalgar), Vancouver; (604) 734-4444; $$; full bar; AE, DC, MC, V; no checks; dinner every day.*

Seasons in the Park ★★★ Considerable attention in the kitchen has contributed to Seasons in the Park's fine reputation. Although the Queen Elizabeth Park setting and the stunning view of downtown and the North Shore mountains guarantee a line of tour buses outside, visitors to Seasons (including visiting presidents Clinton and Yeltsin) come as much for the food as the view. Diners are treated to chef Pierre Delacorte's menu of just-picked produce, succulent seafood, and local wines. Popular dishes include a sun-dried tomato tart baked with Stilton cheese, seared prawns and scallops sauced with Pernod and green peppercorns, and constantly changing wild or farmed Pacific or Atlantic salmon entrees. For dessert, the sunburned lemon pie with fresh fruit coulis ends the meal on a high note. This is also a good place to get hitched—either on the patio or in the 60-seat gazebo. ■ *In Queen Elizabeth Park (Cambie St at W 33rd Ave), Vancouver; (604) 874-8008; seasons@settingsun.com;*

www.settingsun.com/seasons; $$; full bar; AE, MC, V; no checks; lunch Mon–Fri, dinner every day, brunch Sat–Sun. ⑂

Sun Sui Wah Seafood Restaurant ★★★ The splashy Sun Sui Wah in Vancouver, with its sail-like sculpture stretching across the glass-domed roof designed by Bing Thom, is fast becoming the talk of the town. This is the place for dim sum, and being named the best Cantonese restaurant in the Lower Mainland by a Canadian Chinese radio poll only serves to firmly set the jewel in the crown. Simon Chan brought the proven track record and signature dishes of this successful Hong Kong group to Vancouver a decade ago, and his team has been playing to packed houses ever since, both in Vancouver and in Richmond. The reasons are legion: crisp, tender roasted squabs and sculpted Cantonese masterpieces such as the luscious broccoli-skirted steamed chicken interwoven with black mushrooms and Chinese ham; deftly steamed scallops on silky bean curd topped with creamy-crunchy tobiko (flying-fish roe) sauce; live Alaskan king crab dressed in wine and garlic; lobster hot pot with egg noodles; giant beach oysters steamed to perfection in black bean sauce; and lightly sautéed geoduck paired with deep-fried "milk"—fragrant with sweet coconut in a fluffy crust. Reserve early, as this is now the hot spot in town for weddings. ■ *3888 Main St (at 23rd St), Vancouver; (604) 872-8822; $$; full bar; AE, MC, V; no checks; lunch, dinner every day.* ■ *4940 No 3 Rd (Alderbridge Plaza), Richmond; (604) 273-8208; $$; full bar; AE, MC, V; no checks; lunch, dinner every day.* ⑂

Villa del Lupo ★★★ Owners Julio Gonzalez Perini and Vince Piccolo boast culinary pedigrees, and it shows. The "house of the wolf" is a simple, elegant space warmed with a sunny Tuscan palette that balances heritage with contemporary. Prices tend to be high, but portions are generous. Almost everything is wonderful: a simply broiled lamb chop with a carrot-and-basil reduction is accompanied by herbed mashed potatoes to soak up the juices; fresh salmon and shrimp cakes are served with a piquant saffron and lime mayonnaise. The osso buco is a constant and for serious appetites only. The wine list offers table wines from France as well as Italy, and grappa and eaux-de-vie are available as well. Service is always correct. ■ *869 Hamilton St (between Robson and Smithe), Vancouver; (604) 688-7436; vpiccolo@portal.ca; $$$; full bar; AE, DC, MC, V; no checks; dinner every day.*

The William Tell (The Georgian Court Hotel) ★★★ This is special-occasion dining at its very best, thanks to owner Erwin Doebeli. The consummate restaurateur, Doebeli is possibly the most charming man in Vancouver and will personally ensure that you have a wonderful meal. His restaurant reflects his Old World dedication to excellent food and service. The old-fashioned

darkness of the room has been lightened and it's now a bright, elegant spot for dining, drinks before the theater, late-night dessert, or any special celebration. Proximity to the Queen Elizabeth and Ford Theatres makes this a perfect place for a big night out: have an early dinner and then come back after the show for dessert and a spectacular flaming caffé diablo. A revitalized menu ranges from the traditional (chateaubriand for two) to Swiss-inspired dishes (veal scaloppine with morel mushrooms in cream sauce) to the light and flavorful, such as the fish braid of salmon, arctic char, and sea bass. The desserts are pure decadence: meringue glace au chocolat, hot fruit soufflés, and opulently rich crêpes Suzette prepared at your table. The sommelier reigns over one of the best wine cellars in the city (aficionados should ask to see the reserve wine menu). Sunday night is family dining, with a Swiss farmer's buffet (no à la carte menu). ■ *765 Beatty St (between Robson and Georgia), Vancouver; (604)688-3504; erwin@smart.com; www.webcouver.com/dining/williamtell/; $$$; full bar; AE, DC, MC, V; no checks; breakfast every day, lunch Mon–Fri, dinner every day.* ⅄

Bridges ★★ One of the city's most popular hangouts has a superb setting on Granville Island. Seats on the outdoor deck, with sweeping views of downtown and the mountains, are at a premium on warm days. Bridges is actually three separate entities: a casual bistro, a pub, and a more formal upstairs dining room. The bistro's casual offerings are the best bet. Upstairs, the kitchen takes its seafood seriously, but expect to pay for more than what you get. The move, however, of chef Andrew Skorzewski from Raintree at the Landing has had a positive effect. ■ *1696 Duranleau St (Granville Island, on the waterfront), Vancouver; (604)687-4400; $$; full bar; AE, MC, V; no checks; lunch, dinner every day, brunch Sun.* ⅄

Cafe de Paris ★★ Lace curtains at the window, paper covers on the tables, a mirrored bar, and Piaf or Aznavour on the sound system: this is the bistro that takes you back to the Left Bank. Cafe de Paris's heart-of-the-West-End location draws locals and Francophiles alike. The frites—genuine french fries—have become a Vancouver legend; crisp and light, they accompany all entrees and have regulars begging for more. As in France, you can opt for the three-course table d'hôte menu or pick and choose from à la carte offerings. Among the latter: a savory bouillabaisse dense with prawns, scallops, mussels, and monkfish, its broth infused with saffron and Pernod, and a deeply comforting cassoulet. Chef André Bernier also creates his own contemporary French cuisine: orange-glazed salmon slices perfumed with tarragon and flashed under a salamander; smoked rack of lamb. Table d'hôte offerings may include the leek and duck confit tarte, a satiny hot chicken parfait, or meltingly tender roast pork in a garlic cream sauce. Try this bistro for lunch or dinner, *naturellement*, and be sure to glance at the commendable wine list, with several surprises in store. Check out the couscous festival held in September. ■ *751 Denman St (at Robson), Vancouver; (604) 687-1418; $$$; full bar; AE, MC, V; no checks; lunch Mon–Fri, dinner every day.*

The Cannery Seafood House ★★ Frederic Couton is the new chef, and he makes the trek out to this relatively remote east end dockside location unquestionably worthwhile. Serving "salmon by the sea" for 25 years, The Cannery resides in a building that has been cleverly refurbished to look and feel even older than that. On any given day, you'll find a baker's dozen of honestly prepared, high-quality seafood choices on the fresh sheet, including a delicate arctic char, a juicy grilled swordfish, and a meaty tuna (you can order a trio of for $21.95). Salmon Wellington has been a signature since 1971; recently rematched with a pinot noir sauce, it's still a winner. Our favorite, though, is the buttery steamed Alaska black cod. The non-fish-lover is catered to with herb-crusted rack of lamb, a free-range chicken breast, or a simple grilled beef tenderloin. Wine enthusiast Michael Mameli presides over the solid cellar, and his award-winning list is one of the city's best. Service is friendly. ■ *2205 Commissioner St (near Victoria Dr), Vancouver; (604) 254-9606; cannery@ uniserve.com; $$$; full bar; AE, DC, MC, V; no checks; lunch Mon–Fri, dinner every day.*

Century Grill ★★ Whether you're checking out the action at the bar or slicing into the best beef in town, this urban, upscale steak house is great fun. Loud, friendly, and boisterous, it's a great place to hang with your friends—or to make some new ones. Typical of the trendy new Yaletown eateries, the Century Grill is built in an old warehouse, and much of the room's charm comes from the exposed wooden beams and industrial fittings. The kitchen opens onto the dining area, giving diners a great view of the cooks doing their pyrotechnics behind the counter. The pepper steak is a meat-lover's dream, all spicy crust gentled with a creamy sauce and served with a mound of fluffy garlic mashed potatoes. Although the steak is the star here, salads and pastas are perfectly respectable, and there is a good selection of appetizers and side dishes to tempt as well. Servings are hearty and the food well prepared. Don't, however, expect adventurous dining—or a cozy, romantic evening with your beloved. This place is very noisy and popular with the trendy set, whom you'll see sipping martinis and smoking cigars at what's shaping up to be the city's hottest bar scene. ■ *1095 Hamilton St (at Helmcken St), Vancouver; (604) 688-8088; $$$; full bar; AE, MC, V; no checks; lunch, dinner every day, brunch Sun.*

Chili Club Thai Restaurant ★★ Despite the name, with a few noteworthy exceptions Chili Club's fare is not particularly hot. The staff members, however, are well informed and helpful, and if you want it spicy, they'll gladly oblige. We've enjoyed pork satay and Tom Yum Kung soup (prawns and mushrooms married in a good broth with hot spice and deep-scented lemongrass. When giant smoked New Zealand mussels stuffed with a mild thick curry paste are available, order them; the same goes for solidly spiced chicken curry, made with coconut milk and bite-size Thai eggplant. There's plenty to choose from. Popular wines and beers are available at realistic prices. For the best view of False Creek, try the holding bar upstairs with ceiling-to-floor windows on all sides. Even when the food is fiery, the decor is rather cold. Chili Club is located close to the water, under the Burrard Street Bridge. ■ *1000 Beach Ave (between Thurlow and Hornby), Vancouver; (604)681-6000; $$; full bar; AE, DC, MC, V; checks OK; lunch, dinner every day.* ⅊

Cipriano's Ristorante & Pizzeria ★★ This compact pasta-pizza house is an institution of basic and most plentiful portions. Strains of Tony Bennett and Frank Sinatra fill the air as straightforward Italian home cooking arrives at your table, preceded by fabulous garlic bread, dripping with butter and deluged with Parmesan. The giant caesar salad (made to share), an exercise in excess, is garlic-laden and crammed with croutons. Deepdish pizza, pasta puttanesca, and chicken cacciatore are all worth your attention, though some sauces can be remarkably similar. Short routines from owner and onetime standup comedian Frank Cipriano punctuate the meal that wife Christina prepares. For atmosphere and value, few places compare: reservations are a must. ■ *3995 Main St (at 24th), Vancouver; (604)879-0020; $$; full bar; V; no checks; dinner Tues–Sat.*

Farrago ★★ Farrago is, as the name suggests, a medley of lovely things: a modern restaurant in an antique building with rough brick walls, contemporary artworks, and delicate fixtures highlighted in purple, bronze, and gold. This Yaletown restaurant also has a patio in a former carriage turnaround that is possibly the most beautiful outdoor eating spot in town. The menu is an eclectic mix of flavors and ideas. Some dishes are exquisite, tantalizing all the senses while they please the palate. A squid-ink fettuccine with shrimp, orange, and poppyseed dressing is a marvel of design and delicate flavors, and the baby lettuces are just lightly bathed in a perfect, almost sweet, lemon-honey vinaigrette. Unfortunately, some of the dishes are better as concepts than as realities, being overflavored and served with sides that don't readily balance them. The caesar salad, for instance, is overwhelmed by the oceanful of anchovies in the dressing; the slow-roasted duck needs a lighter, sharper partner than the rich stuffed red onion and pools of syrupy, sweet sauce. On the other hand, the room is so pretty and the wine list so reasonable that it becomes easy to ignore a few flaws. At press time, Farrago has turned its bar area into a bistro serving tapas, pizzas, and reasonably priced entrees. ▪ *1138 Homer St (between Davie and Helmcken), Vancouver; (604) 684-4044; $$$; full bar; AE, DC, MC, V; no checks; lunch Mon–Fri, dinner Mon–Sat.*

Griffins (Hotel Vancouver) ★★

The eminently respectable Hotel Vancouver (one of the historic Canadian Pacific châteaus that dot Canada) houses a bright and lively bistro. With taxicab-yellow walls, griffin-motif carpet, and a feeling of urban action, the place has energy to burn. Three meals a day are served à la carte, but the buffet meals are the way to go. The breakfast buffet lets you veer toward the healthy (muesli, fresh fruit compote, and such) or the hedonistic (carved Pepsi Cola–glazed ham). An Asian corner supplies early birds with a fix of grilled salmon and toasted nori. Make a dinner of smoked salmon or roasted peppers with basil at the appetizer bar, or work your way through entrees of silver-dollar scallops in garlic sauce, an exemplary steak, or a pasta dish, and then take a run or three at the pastry bar. ▪ *900 W Georgia St (between Hornby and Burrard), Vancouver; (604) 662-1900; www.cphotels.com; $$; full bar; AE, DC, MC, V; no checks; breakfast, lunch, dinner every day.* ᕒ

Herons (Waterfront Centre Hotel) ★★

In the Waterfront Centre, Herons' high-ceilinged dining room is a multipurpose bistro and restaurant with an open kitchen. Daryle Ryo Nagata is a rising young chef who's up to the challenge of attracting diners' attention away from the panoramic harbor view and the hustle and bustle of the hotel, both inside and out. His menu changes weekly, and there's a daily fresh sheet of contemporary Canadian cooking with a fusion flair. Start with an appetizer of musk ox carpaccio. It gets a lift from a shaving of Parmesan cheese and a roasted bell pepper aioli. Or share the salmon sampler—generous portions of salmon and Dungeness crab cakes, salmon tartare, warm pan-seared gravlax, alderwood smoked salmon, and salmon-belly tempura. Everyone appreciates Nagata's rooftop herb garden and his emphasis on healthy cuisine. Try the Imperial herbal soup, the citrus-and-gillyflower-peppered salmon pasta, and the Similkameen peach cobbler with bee pollen and stevia crust. Or order a traditional clubhouse. On Sundays, a trio from Vancouver Symphony Orchestra plays during brunch. Service is warm and accommodating despite the room's lack of intimacy. Food and wine promotions are innovative. ▪ *900 Canada Pl (between Howe and Burrard), Vancouver; (604) 691-1991; www.cphotels.com; $$; full bar; AE, DC, E, JCB, MC, V; no checks; breakfast, lunch, dinner every day, brunch Sun.*

Joe Fortes ★★ You might be in New York or Boston: Joe Fortes—named for the city's best-loved lifeguard—has that kind of high-energy, uptown chophouse feel to it. "Joe's" is one of downtown's hippest watering holes, where Vancouver's glossiest young professionals flock after putting in a hard day at the stock exchange or the ad agency. The draw is more than the big U-shaped bar where martinis and single-malt scotch are in equal demand. It's the oyster bar too, with Bob Skinner dispensing faultlessly fresh Quilcenes or Malpeques or any of a dozen other varieties, all sold individually. Service is attentive. ■ *777 Thurlow St (between Robson and Alberni), Vancouver; (604)669-1940; $$; full bar; AE, DC, MC, V; no checks; lunch Mon–Fri, dinner every day, brunch Sat–Sun.*

Kalamata Greek Taverna ★★ Not just your usual souvlakia-and-pita spot, Kalamata serves up excellent Greek classics with a modern touch. The cooks at this bright, lively restaurant take an unusually light hand to a cuisine that can often be over-bearing and predictable. Fluffy zucchini rice and delicious roasted vegetables, including skewers of tart, grilled artichoke hearts, take the edge off the usual meat-heavy menu. The location is a bit unfortunate, right at a busy, loud intersection, and the service can be slow. But the truly good food and excellent prices make it worthwhile. ■ *478 W Broadway (at Cambie), Vancouver; (604)872-7050; $$; full bar; AE, MC, V; no checks; lunch Tues–Fri, dinner Tues–Sun.*

Kamei Sushi ★★ With five locations, Kamei may no longer be the best Japanese restaurant in town, but its simple, Westernized dishes certainly make it one of the most popular. The luxury-class Kamei Royale on West Georgia Street seats more than 300, with open and private tatami rooms. Combination platters contain all the standards, or try the red snapper usu zukuri, thinly sliced and fanned on the plate, accompanied by a citrus sauce. Robata dishes are the special focus at the Broadway Plaza location and can be very good. ■ *1030 W Georgia St (at Hemlock), Vancouver (and branches); (604)687-8588; $$; full bar; AE, DC, MC, V; no checks; lunch Mon–Sat, dinner every day.* &

Koji Japanese Restaurant ★★ In our opinion, Koji has the most beautiful garden of any downtown Vancouver restaurant—an island of pine trees and river rocks on a patio above Hornby Street. The best seats are the ones by the windows looking out on the garden, or at the sushi and robata bars. The rest of the restaurant is crowded and often full of Japanese tourists. The sushi is not the best in town, but selections from the robata grill are dependable: grilled shiitakes, topped with bonito flakes and tiny filaments of dry seaweed, are sublime. The Japanese boxed lunch might contain chicken kara-age, superb smoked black cod, prawn and vegetable tempura, two or three small salads, rice with black sesame seeds, pickled vegetables, miso soup, and fresh fruit—all for around $10. Finish with green tea ice cream. ■ *630 Hornby St (between Georgia and Dunsmuir), Vancouver; (604) 685-7355; $$; full bar; AE, DC, MC, V; no checks; breakfast every day, lunch Mon–Fri, dinner every day.* ♿

Nat's New York Pizzeria ★★ Cousins Nat and Franco Bastone headed to their uncle's pizza parlor in Yonkers, where he taught them how to create Naples-style pizza. Then they opened up Nat's on Broadway's busy retail strip and now serve up some of the best thin-crust pizza around. Have it delivered or ask for it three-quarters baked and cook it crisp at home. Or pull up a chair under the Big Apple memorabilia and watch the world go by while you sink your teeth into some pie loaded with chorizo and mushrooms, or artichokes and pesto, or cappocolla and hot peppers. Or try the 5th Avenue (sweet onion, spinach, tomato, and feta cheese) or the Hot Veg (sun-dried tomatoes, hot peppers, and mushrooms). Top it off with the oven-baked garlic shavings or the selection of other condiments you can sprinkle on top. Avoid Nat's on weekdays between 11:30 and 12:15 (the local Kits high school breaks for lunch and they take over Nat's). If you're there before they leave, you'll notice students squeezing honey on their leftover crust for dessert. ■ *2684 W Broadway (between Stephens and Trafalgar), Vancouver; (604) 737-0707; $; no alcohol; no credit cards; no checks; lunch, dinner Mon–Sat.*

The Pink Pearl ★★ Tanks of fresh fish are your first clue that the Cantonese menu is especially strong on seafood. If you order the crab sautéed with rock salt and chiles, you'll be further convinced. It's a spectacular dish—crisp, chile-hot, salty on the outside, and moist on the inside. A good dim sum is served every day (be sure to arrive early on weekends to avoid the lineups), and the cart jockeys always seem to have time to smile as you choose among sticky rice wrapped in lotus leaf, stuffed dumplings, and fried white turnip cakes. Table clearing is an event in itself. The tablecloth is actually a thick stack of white plastic sheets; when you're finished eating, a waiter grabs the corners of the top sheet and, with a quick flip, scoops everything up, dishes and all, and hauls the lot away. This is a great place for kids. ■ *1132 E Hastings St (at Clark Dr), Vancouver; (604) 253-4316; $$; full bar; AE, DC, MC, V; no checks; breakfast, lunch, dinner every day, brunch Sat–Sun.* ♿

Planet Veg ★★ There's hope for the slender wallet at Planet Veg. This new, mostly Indian fast-food spot is located in the heart of health-conscious Kitsilano and serves the juiciest veggie burger in BC. You can also get roti rolls (a meal in themselves), samosas, and potato salad. It's as inexpensive here as it is tasty. Inside seating is limited, so you may want to perch outdoors during the warmer months, or avail yourself of the popular take-out. ■ *1941 Cornwall Ave (between Cypress and*

Walnut), Vancouver; (604) 734-1001; $; no alcohol; no credit cards; no checks; lunch, dinner every day.

Raincity Grill ★★ Raincity Grill is recognized for its extensive list of Pacific Northwest wines, but that's only one reason to visit this bright, contemporary restaurant. Fantastically situated at the happening intersection of Davie and Denman, Raincity provides diners with excellent views of English Bay all year round: in winter, from its tall windows; in summer, from the outdoor patio. Owner Harry Kambolis has welcomed a new chef, Chris Johnson (from Mayne Island's Oceanwood Country Inn), and at press time they have just instituted Johnson's new menu. Check out Kambolis's latest venture, C, a contemporary fish restaurant located at the foot of Howe Street overlooking Granville Island (which just opened at press time). ■ *1193 Denman St (at Davie St), Vancouver; (604) 685-7337; $$; full bar; AE, DC, MC, V; no checks; lunch, dinner every day, brunch Sat–Sun.* &

Raku Kushiyaki ★★ This almost-too-stark restaurant sports an innovative fusion menu. It offers skewered tidbits and tiny preparations from the Far East, the Middle East, India, Thailand, France, and the Caribbean. There are some delicious surprises here, and some pitfalls as well. Those looking for the unusual find perfectly prepared Indonesian tamarind spiced beans and a combination of Japanese chicken rolls with chiles rellenos. Too many liberties are taken with tuna carpaccio: instead of paper-thin slices, we were presented with a sashimi cut. You can nibble, nosh, and share at Raku, but watch out—it adds up. ■ *4422 W 10th Ave (between Tremble and Sasamat), Vancouver; (604) 222-8188; $$; full bar; DC, MC, V; checks OK; dinner Tues–Sun.*

The Red Onion ★★ Forget drive-ins and head to Kerrisdale for the best double dogs, cheeseburgers, and fries (with a sour cream and dill dip) in town. The menu is designed to please everyone (we like the hot chicken salad; others pick the veggie soup). The wieners are the Onion's own, and so are the buns. At breakfast, the muffins (blueberry, chocolate chip, or banana) and aromatic cinnamon buns are baked on the premises. This is the best of its kind in the city, with take-out, too. ■ *2028 W 41st Ave (between Arbutus and Granville), Vancouver; (604) 263-0833; $; beer and wine; MC, V; no checks; breakfast, lunch, dinner every day.* &

Shijo Japanese Restaurant ★★ Shijo is a pleasant, uncluttered sushi bar serving excellent sushi, sashimi, and robata. Oysters, grilled on the half shell and painted with a light miso sauce, are a good bet, as are butterflied tiger prawns or shiitake foilyaki— mushrooms sprinkled with lemony ponzu sauce and cooked in foil. Meals end in a refreshing manner at this second-floor perch, with orange sherbet served in a hollowed-out orange. ■ *1926 W 4th Ave (at Cypress), Vancouver; (604) 732-4676; $$$; full bar; AE, JCB, MC, V; no checks; lunch, dinner every day.* ⅍

Sophie's Cosmic Cafe ★★ Where "Leave It to Beaver" meets Pee Wee Herman—this funky diner-cum-garage-sale is a fun place to be. Don't worry about the wait—there's plenty to look at, including Sophie's collection of colorful lunch boxes and hats that were once stashed in her attic. People rave about the huge spicy burgers and chocolate shakes, but the best thing here is the stick-to-the-ribs-style breakfast: Mexican eggs (with sausage, peppers, and onions and spiced with hot pepper sauce poured from a wine bottle). ■ *2095 W 4th Ave (at Arbutus), Vancouver; (604) 732-6810; $; beer and wine; MC, V; no checks; breakfast, lunch, dinner every day, brunch Sat–Sun.* ⅍

The Teahouse at Ferguson Point ★★ This stunning location in Stanley Park is a magnet for tourists, with its park setting and spectacular view of English Bay, but a faithful following of locals attests to the consistency of fare. Appetizers run the gamut from Teahouse stuffed mushrooms (crab, shrimp, Emmentaler cheese) to steamed mussels in a saffron-anchovy broth. Salmon is always a good bet, served with seasonal sauces. Executive chef Dino Gazzola's rack of lamb in fresh herb crust is a perennial favorite—even without the view attached. Desserts include a dark and milk chocolate torta milano with mascarpone mousse or the lemon hazelnut parfait with a blackberry coulis. If you're planning a summer wedding, check out the sunset patio overlooking English Bay. ■ *7501 Stanley Park Dr (in Stanley Park), Vancouver; (604) 669-3281; teahouse@settingsun.com; www.settingsun.com/teahouse; $$; full bar; AE, MC, V; no checks; lunch Mon–Fri, dinner every day, brunch Sat–Sun.* ⅍

Victoria Chinese Restaurant ★★ This upmarket, well-maintained, professional restaurant in the Royal Centre adjacent to the Hyatt Regency Hotel is now a downtown favorite. Superb dim sum is made to order from a sizable menu featuring tasty bites such as shrimp salad roll, egg rolls with shrimp and mayonnaise filling, satay calamari, and, on a good day, ostrich pot-stickers. The dinner menu traverses all Chinese culinary regions. Standouts include finger-licking lettuce wrap with minced squab; succulent, perfectly cooked salt-and-chile black cod; creamy braised napa cabbage; and superior pan-fried prawns in soya. The older sister restaurant, East Ocean Seafood Restaurant at 108-777 W Broadway, was among the very first of the new-style Chinese dining rooms to cross the Pacific from Hong Kong and remains one of the most popular. ■ *1088 Melville St (Royal Centre), Vancouver; (604) 669-8383; $$; full bar; AE, MC; no checks; lunch, dinner every day.*

Vij's ★★ A civilized change from ersatz curry houses. Vikram Vij dishes up home-cooked Indian fare that evolves at whim. His seasonal menu changes every three months but almost always includes a mean curry or a killer saag. Courtesy and simplicity rule as Vik waits carefully on all who arrive early enough to get in—first greeting them with a glass of chai before discussing the menu. The prices are civilized too. ■ *1480 W 11th Ave (at Granville), Vancouver; (604) 736-6664; $; beer and wine; AE, MC, V; no checks; dinner Mon–Sat.* &

Vong's Kitchen ★★ At least two generations of Vancouverites cut their teeth on the Vong family's cooking. After inheriting the secrets from Mom and then putting in time in Hong Kong, Tony Vong, the hippest Chinese chef in town, is now manning the giant woks in his tiny kitchen in between filming commercials for Chinese TV. For a unique opener, Tony's fried curried beef wontons are a must-try. Follow that with Jade Chicken, named for its jewel-like garnish of deep-fried spinach surrounding tender morsels of Sichuan peppercorn-spiced chicken. Then garlic chile prawns, honey orange beef, seafood and vegetables in a deep-fried potato nest . . . we never seem able to stop ordering more than we should. But somehow, we always manage to find room for those banana fritters that come with the bill. Note the new location with its cheery canary-yellow paint job (courtesy of number-two son), which matches the ever-sprightly service of number-one daughter—a winning combination that completes the picture of an exemplary family operation. ■ *4298 Fraser St (at 27th), Vancouver; (604) 879-4298; $; no alcohol; no credit cards; no checks; dinner Tues–Sun.*

The Bread Garden ★ The Bread Garden is Vancouver's original bakery/cafe and still its most successful. Opened in 1981 as a croissant bakery, the First Avenue location is still Kitsilano's happening scene for weekend breakfast, but now there are 10 Bread Gardens in the Lower Mainland to choose from. The Bute and Granville Street locations are open 24 hours a day, convenient whether you're looking for a late-night snack after an evening of dancing, a homey midweek dinner, a quick sit-down lunch, or just a muffin to go. As the franchise grows, the deli cases keep expanding, stuffed with salads, sandwiches, and ready-to-nuke fare such as quiches, frittatas, roast vegetable lasagne, and enchiladas. You can have a wholesome muffin or scone, or throw caution to the winds and let the dessert list tempt you with cheesecake or the maple pecan bar. ■ *1880 W 1st Ave (between Burrard and Cypress), Vancouver (and branches); (604) 738-6684; $; beer and wine (except Park & Tilford location); MC, V; no checks; breakfast, lunch, dinner, midnight snacks every day.* &

Delilah's ★ Back in the old days, when was it tucked into the basement of the old Buchan Hotel, Delilah's was one of the city's best secrets. Cozy, romantic, and boisterous all at once, it was a voluptuous dining experience. Diners felt like the fortunate members of a special, in-the-know clique, and the restaurant's potentially annoying quirks—like the rule about no reservations for parties under six—merely added to its charm. But now Delilah's has moved uptown, only a few blocks in distance, but miles away in atmosphere. It still has the cheeky cupids painted on the ceiling, and the plush red velvet banquettes, and the fabulous martini menu—the city's first and still its best. Unfortunately, though, in expanding the room and letting in more light, Delilah's has lost a great deal of what made it so charming. Now the waitstaff seem too rushed to dish with the customers, the hour-long wait at the bar is irritating (why won't they take reservations?), and the multiple-choice menu a tad tiresome. The food itself is fresh and inventive, although the staff occasionally falls short on the preparation side of things. Luckily, though, the wine list is extensive and reasonably priced, and it's worth dropping by just for the martinis, with names like the Blue Dolphin, the Surrealist, the Metropolitan, and nearly 30 others. Reservations are accepted only for groups of six or more. ■ _1739 Comox St (at Denman, in the Coast Plaza at Stanley Park), Vancouver; (604) 687-3424; $$; full bar; AE, DC, MC, V; no checks; dinner every day._ ⅃

Liliget Feast House ★ Architect Arthur Erickson designed this downstairs West End space for Vancouver's only First Nations restaurant (Muckamuck) almost 20 years ago. Today the place continues as a First Nations restaurant. And an unusual but delightful culinary foray it is. The bannock is Native caterer Dolly Watts's signature, and you'll never taste better. You'll also sample dishes you never dreamed of—pan-fried oolichans, toasted seaweed, and wild blackberry pie with whipped soapolallie berries. Another taste thrill is the Hagul Jam soup, a broth of salmon and vegetables. Coupled with the Wild Man Salad and Dolly's bannock, it's a meal in itself. The Liliget Feast platter for two ($39.95) is heaped with alder-grilled salmon, buffalo smokies, rabbit, halibut, and smoked oolichans and easily serves three. The small wine list is well chosen, and there are even a chardonnay and a pinot noir from the Inkameep Reserve (Inniskillin). The only flub: vegetables appear to be an afterthought. But save room for dessert—upside-down blueberry cobbler topped with real whipped cream is a winner. ■ _1724 Davie St (between Denman and Didwell), Vancouver; (604) 681-7044; $$; full bar; AE, MC, V; no checks; dinner every day._

Olympia Seafood Market and Grill ★ The Olympia is now around the corner from its original Robson Street location. It's first and foremost a fish shop, but it purveys some of the best fish and chips in the Lower Mainland. Eleven years ago, fish merchant Carlo Sorace decided that what Robson Street really needed was a good place to get fish and chips. Whatever is on special in the store, which might be halibut cheeks, scallops, catfish, or calamari, is the day's special at the 12-seat counter and is served along with the tried-and-true halibut and cod versions. Soft drinks include Chinotto (Italian herbal and fruit-flavored sparkling water) and root beer. Eat in or take out. ▪ *820 Thurlow St (between Robson and Smithe), Vancouver; (604) 685-0716; $$; no alcohol; V; checks OK; lunch, dinner every day.*

Stepho's Souvlakia ★ This is one of those little restaurants that just keeps on going, regardless of the economy or whether it's a Monday or a Saturday night. This is basic, good Greek fare: lots of pungent tzatziki; megasalads; decent-size hunks of pita—in a nutshell, great value, along with plenty of regulars and a staff that really seems to care. The interior is no-nonsense comfortable, with enough posters of the Parthenon to start a travel agency, bunches of fresh carnations on every table, and plenty of tiles and greenery. Despite the heavy traffic, it's also clean, and the service is prompt and polite. Portions are generous: even a single, sizable brochette fights for space on a plate loaded with rice pilaf, giant buttery roast potatoes, Greek salad with plenty of black olives, parsley, tomato, feta, and peppers, a healthy serving of tzatziki, and hot pita bread on the side for dipping. This is good Greek food, cheap, with a well-priced wine list. Even though Stepho's has doubled its space, fans still have to wait in the rain to get in. ▪ *1124 Davie St (between Thurlow and Bute), Vancouver; (604) 683-2555; $; full bar; AE, MC, V; no checks; lunch, dinner every day.* &

Subeez ★ Subeez has all of the urban edge that Vancouver can muster. Decor is neogothic, postnuclear, and thrown into this postmodern cocktail are massive wax-encrusted medieval candelabra. It's as much a bar and meeting place as it is a restaurant. Almost everything has been recycled (the bathroom sinks are from Oakalla prison) in this 225-seater that you have to see to believe. It's great Vancouver theater, and it also has the best french fries going: they come with garlic mayo (order extra). All that, plus a thoughtful, well-priced wine list. Although it's clearly not the Main Event, the food is imaginative and sometimes quite good—the lamb on focaccia, the chicken-and-Brie sandwich, and the veggie burger, for example. There's an ominous 30-speaker sound system with appropriately manic music. Keep earplugs handy. The kitchen's open till 1am. ▪ *891 Homer St (at Smithe), Vancouver; (604) 687-6107; $; full bar; MC, V; no checks; lunch, dinner, midnight snacks every day, brunch Sat–Sun.* &

Tomato Fresh Food Cafe ★ Chef-on-the-run Diane Clement and daughter Jennifer have a real neighborhood joint here. But when you slip into a wooden booth, you're in for some serious eating. For years, this was a greasy spoon; now it has an overlay of young, retro energy, most lucidly expressed in the big, chunky, wildly colored bowls used for serving specialties such as "teapuccino"—cappuccino made with tea. Young waitstaff serve a variation of mom food: vegetarian chile with really good corn bread, a whacking slab of turkey in the turkey sandwich, and real milk shakes. There's also great take-out from Tomato To Go (open Monday–Saturday) with the best scones and muffins in the city. Diane has just taken over the barber shop next door, which has doubled the seating. She's also hired a talented new chef, Lisa Rowson. Look for more stars here next time. ■ *3305 Cambie St (at 17th St), Vancouver; (604) 874-6020; $; beer and wine; MC, V; no checks; breakfast, lunch, dinner Mon–Fri, brunch Sat–Sun.*

Ezogiku Noodle Cafe Ramen dishes are the order of the day at this 70-seater cafe. Ramen comes in regular (pork), miso, or soy broth; there's a fried noodle dish, a curried dish, and gyozas—and that's it. Ezogiku's focus is the secret to the large bowls of perfectly cooked chewy noodles in rich, steaming broth. Do what the old master in the movie *Tampopo* instructed: study, sniff, and savor. Other branches are in Honolulu and Tokyo. ■ *1329 Robson St (at Cardero), Vancouver; (604) 685-8606; $; no alcohol; no credit cards; no checks; lunch, dinner every day.*

LODGINGS

English Bay Inn ★★★★ Owner Bob Chapin devotes meticulous attention to his romantic five-room English Bay Inn, and he has proven himself to be a top-rated innkeeper, year after year. Down comforters rest atop Louis Philippe sleigh beds beneath alabaster lighting fixtures. The pièce de résistance is a two-level suite on the top floor with a fireplace in the bedroom. Extras include terrycloth robes, evening port or sherry, and phones in each guest room. All rooms have private baths, and two back rooms open onto a small garden. A fabulous breakfast is served in a formal dining room complete with gothic dining suite, crackling (albeit gas) fire, and ticking grandfather clock. Stanley Park and English Bay are just minutes away by foot. ■ *1968 Comox St (a few blocks off English Bay), Vancouver, BC V6G 1R4; (604) 683-8002; $$$; AE, MC, V; checks OK.*

The Four Seasons ★★★★ The upscale chain of Four Seasons hotels is well known for pampering guests, and the Vancouver hotel only enhances that reputation. Arrival is awkward, since guests must enter from a small driveway wedged between concrete pillars and then go up a floor to the lobby, which is also connected to the Pacific Centre shopping mall. Once the hurdle of check in has been overcome, however, guests wallow in luxury. Although the hotel is located smack-dab in the center of high-rise downtown, many of the guest rooms offer surprising views of the city. Amenities include bathrobes, hair dryers, VCRs, a complimentary shoeshine, 24-hour valet and room service, a year-round indoor-outdoor pool, complimentary use of health club facilities, and a rooftop garden. Kids are welcomed with complimentary milk and cookie on arrival. Business travelers appreciate phones with voice mail in English, French, or Japanese, and modular phones are available for computer hookup. Chartwell (see review) is one of the best dining rooms in the city. The Garden Terrace, just off the lobby, is a place to see and be seen. ■ *791 W Georgia St (at Howe), Vancouver, BC V6E 2T4; (604) 689-9333 or (800) 332-3442 (from the US only); www.fshr.com; $$$; AE, DC, JCB, MC, V; no checks.* &

The Sutton Place Hotel ★★★★ Vancouver's most elegant hotel would rank as a top lodging in any European capital. All 397 soundproofed rooms in this sumptuous residential-style hotel look and feel like part of a beautiful home. The beds are king-size; the furnishings are reproductions of European antiques. (There are plenty of spectacular original pieces throughout the hotel's public spaces.) Maids faithfully appear twice a day with all the amenities one could wish for—including fresh flowers, umbrellas, and complimentary shoeshines. There are 11 no-smoking floors and the fastest elevators in town. The lobby recalls a European manor and posts a concierge service. Bellhops snap to attention whether you arrive wearing blue jeans in a beat-up truck or in black tie and a limo. Sutton Place's restaurant and lounges have been popular with locals since the day they opened, with the richly paneled Gerard Lounge ranking as one of the best watering holes in the Northwest. Elegant meals and a very civilized tea await those who venture into Fleuri (see review). Le Spa offers a swimming pool, a fitness room, and beauty salons. Sutton Place also provides the best wheelchair-accessible rooms in the city. The best rental condominiums in the city are located in a separate building connected to the hotel. **La Grande Résidence** provides all the amenities of a luxury hotel in 162 spiffy one- and two-bedroom apartments with kitchens and balconies. The minimum stay is seven nights (starting at $185 per night). ■ *845 Burrard St (between Robson and Smithe), Vancouver, BC V6Z 2K6; (604) 682-5111 or (800) 543-4300; info@vcr.suttonplace.com; www.travelweb.com/sutton. html; $$$; AE, DC, DIS, E, JCB, MC, V; no checks.* &

The French Quarter ★★★ *C'est magnifique!* Ginette Bertrand's French country–style home nestled in the historic, exclusive First Shaughnessy district has a delightful, cozy, well-appointed room in the main house or a private poolside cottage with all the amenities: a queen-size bed, large closet and bathroom, fireplace, TV/VCR, refrigerator, and complimentary sherry. The open kitchen, dining room, pool deck, and living room are spacious and offer privacy. A gourmet sweet or savory breakfast menu topped off with fresh fruit is served from 8:30am to 10:30am. Access to a well-equipped fitness room is included. Ideal for a romantic getaway, though families with children 8 and older are welcome. Some small pets are allowed. There's a minimum two-day stay during summer peak season. ■ *2051 W 19th Ave (at Maple), Vancouver, BC V6J 2P5; (604) 737-0973; www.bcbandb.com/vanc/french.html; $$$; MC, V; checks OK.*

Georgian Court Hotel ★★★ Compared with the other pricey hotels in the city, there's good value to be enjoyed at this intimate and luxurious 180-room European-style hotel situated across from BC Place Stadium and the Queen Elizabeth Theatre. All rooms feature desks, minibars, three telephones, nightly turndown service on request, and (at last) good reading lamps. Among Vancouverites, the Georgian Court Hotel is best known as the home of the William Tell Restaurant (see review), where for years flamboyant owner Erwin Doebeli has set the standard for fine dining in Vancouver. The hotel's strong point is value for dollars in a luxury hotel, but a guest—or any visitor to the city—would be remiss not to dine in the William Tell. ■ *773 Beatty St (between Robson and Georgia), Vancouver, BC V6B 2M4; (604) 682-5555 or (800) 663-1155; $$; AE, DC, DIS, E, JCB, MC, V; Canadian checks OK.* &

▼

Hotel Vancouver ★★★ One of the grand French château-style hotels owned by the Canadian Pacific Railway, the Hotel Vancouver dates back to 1887. The original building was destroyed in a fire, however, and was rebuilt in 1939. The green, steeply pitched copper roof dominated the city's skyline for decades but is a less-obvious landmark today. A complete renovation began in 1989, and the final phase, a $12.7 million refit of the main lobby and lower shopping arcade, recently wrapped up. Stone arches, friezes, and other design elements hidden by earlier renovations have been restored or re-created. A new Lobby Bar and the "elegantly casual" 900 West restaurant (see review) replace the main floor lobby and Timber Club, but the Roof Restaurant has being turned into meeting space. The new shopping arcade includes a Canadian Pacific Store, featuring private-label goods reminiscent of the early days of Canadian travel. The 508-room hotel is popular for conventions and tour groups; nonetheless, service remains quite good and includes complimentary coffee and newspapers in the morning. There is a health club with a skylighted lap pool. Try for a room high above the street noise. ■ *900 W Georgia St (between Hornby and Burrard), Vancouver, BC V6C 2W6; (604) 684-3131 or (800) 441-1414; $$$; AE, DC, DIS, E, JCB, MC, V; checks OK.* &

The Johnson House ★★★ To say that owners Ron and Sandy Johnson are quite fond of antiques would be an understatement. They have restored a 1920s Craftsman-style home on a quiet street in the city's Kerrisdale neighborhood and turned it into one of Vancouver's most intriguing bed and breakfasts. Everywhere you turn in the three-story house there are relics from the past: coffee grinders, gramophones, even carousel horses in the largest of the five guest rooms. Above the front door is a genuine old Vancouver street lamp acting as the porch light. The rooms on the top floor and in the basement are cozy; the Carousel Suite, with its adjoining mermaid-themed en suite bath, is the grandest. A separate guest telephone line, plus a guidebook and map to Vancouver in every room, contribute to the friendly atmosphere. Breakfast is served in a bright, airy cottage-style room on the main floor. Suitable for families with children 12 and over. No pets. ■ *2278 W 34th Ave (from Oak St, left to 33rd, left onto Vine, then left onto 34th), Vancouver, BC V6M 1G6; (604)266-4175; $$; no credit cards; checks OK.*

Metropolitan Hotel ★★★ The Met's been a hit since owner Henry Wu began wooing Vancouverites and cosmopolitan travelers. Mandarin International built this richly appointed, 197-room hotel in time for Expo 86. Now, Metropolitan Hotels recently purchased this gem, and is beginning to bring back the Mandarin sparkle, attention to detail, and personal around-the-clock service it offered back during Expo. Located in the heart of downtown's business and financial district, it offers outstanding concierge service, private Jaguar limousine service, nightly turn-down service on request, 24-hour room service, a full-scale business center, and one of the finest hotel health clubs in the city. (You can even watch CNN in the sauna.) There are 18 palatial suites; all other rooms are deluxe, with balconies and peekaboo views of the city, elegant contemporary appointments, European duvets, and Frette bathrobes. Technologically enhanced business guest rooms include laser-quality printers and in-room faxes that deliver the latest breaking news from the *Wall Street Journal* and Japan's *Yomiuri Report.* Diva at the Met is the hotel's newest streetfront bar and 116-seat restaurant; it has some of Vancouver's top chefs rockin' on the pans, a logo inspired by Picasso, and dessert plates inspired by Kandinsky (see review). ■ *645 Howe St (between Dunsmuir and Georgia), Vancouver, BC V6C 2Y9; (604)687-1122 or (800)667-2300; reservations@metropolitan.com; www.metropolitan.com/; $$$; AE, DC, MC, V; no checks.* &

Pacific Palisades ★★★ The internationally celebrated Shangri-La chain purchased the Pacific Palisades in 1991 and promptly began a complete renovation of what was already a good hotel. The 233 rooms, most of which are one-bedroom suites, have long been popular with the many movie production crews that visit Vancouver. Part of the appeal comes from the hotel's personal attention to guests' needs, but the major draw is spacious rooms, all with minikitchens that include a fridge, microwave, and coffee-maker. There's a health club and one of the largest hotel swimming pools in the city. The location on Robson Street is tough to beat if you want to be where the action is. ▪ *1277 Robson St (between Bute and Jervis), Vancouver, BC V6E 1C4; (604)688-0461 or (800)663-1815; $$$; AE, DC, E, JCB, MC, V; no checks.* &

Pan Pacific Hotel ★★★ No hotel in Vancouver has a more stunning location, a better health club, or a more remarkable architectural presence. As part of Canada Place, the Pan Pacific juts out into Vancouver's inner harbor with its five giant white signature sails. The building, which is also the embarkation point for the thriving summertime Alaska cruise ship market, hasn't achieved the fame of Sydney's Opera House, but it was meant to. The first four floors of the building make up the World Trade Centre Vancouver, but up on the eighth, where the guest rooms begin, things become more diminutive. Standard guest rooms are among the smallest in any of Vancouver's luxury hotels, and the decor is all a bit disappointing after such a grand facade. Nonetheless, the spectacular views make up for any shortcomings. The best views face west, but you can't beat a corner room (with views from your tub). A complete range of guest services is offered. The fine-dining restaurant, the Five Sails, has achieved a fair bit of attention for its exquisite Pacific Rim cuisine (see review). The Cascades Lounge, just off the lobby, is a must if you want to watch ships sail into the sunset while seaplanes land beneath you against the backdrop of the North Shore mountains. ▪ *300-999 Canada Pl Way (between Burrard and Howe), Vancouver, BC V6C 3B5; (604)662-8111 or (800)663-1515 from Canada, (800)937-1515 from the US; preserve@panpacific-hotel.com; www.panpac.com; $$$; AE, DC, E, JCB, MC, V; no checks.* &

Waterfront Centre Hotel ★★★ The tasteful rooms in the 23-story Waterfront Centre are among the best in the city. Their size and rich appointments clearly outclass those of the Pan Pacific Hotel, just across the street on Vancouver's inner harbor. Underground passageways connect the Waterfront Centre to Canada Place and the Trade and Convention Centre. Expect wonderful surprises, such as third-floor guest rooms with private terraces and herb gardens that supply Herons restaurant (see review). Two club floors called Entrée Gold cater to every whim, offering a private concierge, continental breakfast, nightly hors d'oeuvres, and private conference room. Of the 489 guest rooms, 29 are suites and one is fit for royalty. Operated by Canadian Pacific, the Waterfront Centre was named one of the world's top 10 business hotels by *Report on Business* magazine, and it has the most Canadian feel of any of the city's hotels. There is an excellent health club, complete with outdoor pool (a view-and-a-half), nightly turn-down service, no-smoking floors, and rooms designed for people with disabilities. All harborside rooms have amenities, such as data ports, for business travelers. The works of Canadian artists are prominently displayed throughout the hotel's public spaces and guest rooms. Sunday brunch at Herons features music by members of the Vancouver Symphony. ■ *900 Canada Pl Way (between Burrard and Howe), Vancouver, BC V6C 3L5; (604)691-1991 or (800)441-1414; www.cphotels.com; $$$; AE, DC, DIS, E, JCB, MC, V; no checks.* &

The Wedgewood Hotel ★★★ Owner and manager Eleni Skalbania takes great pride in the Wedgewood Hotel. And Ms. Skalbania has much to be proud of. This is a hotel you will want to return to time and time again. Ideally located in the heart of Vancouver's finest shopping district, and across the street from the art gallery, the gardens of Robson Square, and the courthouse built of glass, the Wedgewood offers Old World charm and scrupulous attention to every detail of hospitality. From the potted flowers flourishing on the balcony of every room to the renowned Bacchus Ristorante (see review), this 93-room hotel is all that a small urban luxury hotel should be. This is the only luxury hotel in the city where you'll hardly ever find tour buses unloading swarms of visitors. The finely appointed rooms, which are surprisingly large and are decorated with vibrant colors and genuine English antiques, have the feel of a grand home. Nightly turn-down service, a bare-essentials fitness room, and 24-hour room service are offered. This is the place to spend your honeymoon (and many do), but any weekend at the Wedgewood is a weekend to savor. ■ *845 Hornby St (at Robson), Vancouver, BC V6Z 1V1; (604)689-7777 or (800)663-0666; www.travel.bc.ca/w/wedgewood/; $$$; AE, DC, DIS, E, JCB, MC, V; no checks.*

Coast Plaza at Stanley Park ★★ Situated just off the main artery through the vibrant West End, this former apartment tower offers 267 large rooms, including 170 suites, a dozen with two bedrooms. All have balconies, and more than two-thirds of the rooms have complete kitchens, making this a great place for vacationing families and Hollywood film crews working in Vancouver (the stars stay elsewhere). Amenities include 24-hour room service, a minibar, and a small fridge. But the hotel's strongest point is its proximity to Stanley Park. Request a room with a park view. Guests are welcome at the adjoining health club (popular with local singles). ■ *1733 Comox St (at Denman), Vancouver, BC V6G 1P6; (604)688-7711 or (800)663-1144; $$$; AE, DC, E, MC, V; checks OK.* &

Delta Vancouver Airport Hotel and Marina ★★ This is the closest hotel to Vancouver International Airport, and it spreads along the banks of the Fraser River. There are an outdoor pool, a bar, and a barbecue as well as bicycle and running trails. Not a bad place for a layover. Eastside rooms face the river and marina. Downtown is 30 minutes away. The 415 guest rooms and the dozen or so meeting rooms are popular for conventions and with corporate travelers. "Business Zone" rooms are available for an extra $15. There's a small fitness center on the top floor, or guests are welcome to take the shuttle to the more extensive facilities at the Delta Pacific Resort nearby. Kids under 6 eat free in the hotel's dining facilities. ■ *3500 Cessna Dr (at Miller Rd), Vancouver, BC V7B 1C7; (604)278-1241; www.delta hotels.com; $$$; AE, DC, DIS, E, JCB, MC, V; no checks.* &

Hyatt Regency ★★ No surprises here. This is a good Hyatt Regency, like all the others around the world. It's popular with conventions and tour groups yet continues to offer personalized service. Good views of the harbor and mountains are available from north-facing upper floors. Try for a corner room with a balcony. A Regency Club floor, with special keyed access, has its own concierge, complimentary breakfast, midday cookies, and late-afternoon hors d'oeuvres. There's complimentary use of health club and pool for all guests. Standard rooms are among the largest in the city. ■ *655 Burrard St (at W Georgia), Vancouver, BC V6C 2R7; 683-1234 or (800)233-1234; www.hyatt. com; $$$; AE, DC, DIS, E, JCB, MC, V; checks OK.* &

Kingston Hotel ★★ Guests often comment that this centrally located inn reminds them of a European bed and breakfast, especially its facade of cut granite and heavy wood and its Tudor-style windows. Rooms with private baths have color TVs; other rooms share bath and TV facilities. All rooms have phones. A continental breakfast is served in the small lounge downstairs. Facilities include a sauna and a coin-op laundry. A neighborhood pub, the Rose and Thorn, is on the main floor. This three-story bed and breakfast continues to be a great downtown value, and it even offers seniors' discounts. ■ *757 Richards St (W Georgia), Vancouver, BC V6B 3A6; (604)684-9024; $; AE, MC, V; no checks.*

Penny Farthing Inn ★★ This 1912 Edwardian home is a historic treasure in Vancouver's trendy westside Kitsilano district. Try for the attic room overlooking the pretty English garden backdropped by the North Shore mountains. Owner Lyn Hainstock is a professional innkeeper with a wealth of information about Vancouver. Breakfast, served on the brick patio, is a gourmet's feast. All the rooms now have fridges and phones, and frolicking cats entertain. ■ *2855 W 6th Ave (between Bayswater and Macdonald Sts), Vancouver, BC V7R 1B4; (604)739-9002; far thing@uniserve.com; $$; no credit cards; checks OK.*

Sheraton Wall Centre Hotel ★★ This stunning 35-story glass tower houses a wonderful addition to Vancouver's already rich luxury lodging scene. What distinguishes this hotel from the competition is its very stylish decor. The lobby area features furnishings in playful primary colors and dramatic marble. Standard double rooms are small, although expansive views from the higher floors make them feel larger. Check into a one-bedroom corner suite with a two-vista view; floor-to-ceiling windows face north up Burrard Street, with Grouse Mountain in the distance, and west to English Bay and the Coast Mountains beyond. Most suites feature a deep soaking tub in the marble bathroom along with a wet bar and a microwave. There's a full health club with a 15-meter (50-foot) lap pool and a beauty salon in the complex. Complimentary morning newspapers and turn-down service are also offered. All in all, this is a wonderful place to stay. ■ *1088 Burrard (at Helmcken), Vancouver, BC V6Z 2R9; (604)331-1000 or (800)663-9255; $$$; AE, DC, JCB, MC, V; no checks.* ₺

Two Cedars Bed and Breakfast Suite ★★ Tourism and hospitality industry veterans Tracy Lott and Peter Burrow have a bright, airy suite for bed-and-breakfast guests in their renovated 1911 Kits Point district home. Two Cedars' prime location, only 2½ blocks from the recreation amenities of Kitsilano Beach, is also within walking distance of downtown and Granville Island. The guest suite has its own terraced garden entrance at the rear and a reserved parking spot to boot. The suite accommodates up to four adults. Kids are welcome. Special treats include continental breakfast served in bed and afternoon wine-tastings. ■ *1423 Walnut St (near Cornwall and Cypress), Vancouver, BC V6J 3R2; (604)731-0785; $$; V; checks OK.*

West End Guest House ★★ Don't be put off by the blazing pink exterior of this early-1900s Victorian home, which is located on a residential street close to Stanley Park and just a block off Robson Street. Owner Evan Penner runs a fine eight-room inn (each room with private bath), and during summer a vacancy is rare. Rooms are generally small but nicely furnished, and there are antiques throughout the house. The staff members have all worked in major hotels and know what hospitality is. Sherry or iced tea is served in the afternoons. Nightly turn-down service, feather beds and lambskin mattress covers, robes, and telephones are provided in every room. Breakfast is a bountiful cooked meal served family style or delivered to your room. There is guest parking (a rarity in the West End). Families with children are accepted, but just be careful with the antiques. ■ *1362 Haro St (at Broughton), Vancouver, BC V6E 1G2; (604)681-2889; wegh@idmail.ca; www.bcbandb.com; $$$; AE, DIS, MC, V; checks OK.*

Westin Bayshore Hotel ★★ The Bayshore sits on the southern shore of Coal Harbour next to the main entrance to Stanley Park. Set back from busy Georgia Street, this is the only downtown hotel that resembles a resort (children love it here). Rooms look out over a large outdoor pool, with Coal Harbour's colorful marina as a backdrop and the North Shore mountains beyond. At a kiosk near the indoor pool you can rent bicycles, and if you're up for a one-hour ride, you can't beat the scenery along the connecting Stanley Park seawall. The marina has moorage for visiting boaters and charter vessels for those who want to get even closer to the water. Amenities include all that you'd expect from a Westin. Guest rooms in the tower all have balconies and have been totally renovated. There's also a full, newly upgraded health club. A currency exchange is on site, and the major business and shopping areas of downtown are a pleasant 15-minute walk away. ■ *1601 W Georgia St (at Cardero), Vancouver, BC V6G 2V4; (604) 682-3377 or (800) 228-3000; www.westin.com; $$$; AE, DC, DIS, E, JCB, MC, V; checks OK.*

Hotel Georgia ★ This attractive 12-story stone hotel, built in 1927, offers old-fashioned charm with its small oak-paneled lobby, elaborate brass elevators, and comfortable rooms furnished with contemporary oak furniture. Yet it has the feel of a hotel for traveling salespeople and bus tours. The rooms with the best views face south to the Vancouver Art Gallery, but they are on a busy, noisy street. Executive rooms have a seating area that is useful for conducting business. The hotel's location couldn't be more central. The Georgia has two bars that are popular with locals. At press time, a major renovation is planned, and the Georgia will become a Crowne Plaza by March 1998. ■ *801 W Georgia St (between Howe and Hornby), Vancouver, BC V6C 2W6; (604) 682-5566 or (800) 663-1111; $$$; AE, DC, JCB, MC, V; no checks.* &

Sylvia Hotel A favorite for price and location, this ivy-covered eight-story historic brick hotel is a landmark adjacent to English Bay, Vancouver's most popular beach and strutting grounds. Try for a south-facing room. A low-rise addition was built to compensate for the busy summer season, when you might just need to settle for any room. Doubles begin at $65, and reservations are required well in advance. All 119 rooms (some quite small) have baths. Families or small groups should request the one-bedroom suites, which can sleep four and which come equipped with kitchen and living room. Covered parking is extra. The hotel also offers room service, a restaurant, and a lounge—reportedly the first cocktail bar in Vancouver (opened in 1954), and on some winter afternoons it looks as though the original clientele is still there. ■ *1154 Gilford St (at Beach Ave), Vancouver, BC V6G 2P6; (604) 681-9321; $; AE, DC, MC, V; checks OK.*

BURNABY

RESTAURANTS

Horizons on Burnaby Mountain ★★ A drive to the top of Burnaby Mountain leads right to this spacious room, whose numerous windows command a spectacular view of the city, snug in Burrard Inlet far below. A continuing emphasis on local fare in the hands of new chef John Garrett has produced a menu with specialties such as alder-grilled BC salmon, a scallop and prawn risotto, and seafood bouillabaisse. Many BC wines are featured on the restaurant's extensive list. Watch for seasonal food and wine promotions. ■ *100 Centennial Way (in Burnaby Mountain Park), Burnaby; (604)299-1155; www.horizonsrestaurant. com; $$; full bar; AE, E, MC, V; no checks; lunch, dinner every day, brunch Sun.*

RICHMOND

RESTAURANTS

Floata Seafood Restaurant ★★ Vancouver's historical Chinatown begins its facelift as we speed forward into the new millennium, and the Floata Restaurant Group leads the pack with its opening of the largest restaurant in Vancouver to date. The cavernous, sparsely postmodern room seats 1,000 (yes, 1,000). The room is equipped with wall-to-ceiling partitions that can carve up the impressive space, to order, into restaurant-size private dining rooms, each equipped with its very own karaoke sound system. An already brisk dim sum trade ensures fresh and very good nibbles for those who are there to enjoy this popular Chinese roving lunch-hour feast. Unfortunately, dinner experiences at the Vancouver branch have fallen short of the high quality one comes to expect at the group's other location here in Richmond, where the succulent crisp-skinned chicken, the tender lobster in cream sauce, the velvety braised Chinese mushrooms with mustard greens, and other Cantonese favorites are local standard-bearers of the cuisine. We hope that, given time, the latest Chinatown landmark will come to deserve the vote of confidence its suburban elder sister received from a recent polling of Chinese diners, who voted it one of the top 10 fine dining Chinese restaurants in the Lower Mainland. ■ *1425-4380 No. 3 Rd (Parker Place Shopping Centre), Richmond; (604)270-8889; $$; full bar; AE, V; no checks; lunch, dinner every day.* ⅙ ■ *400-180 Keefer St (at Columbia), Vancouver; (604)602-0368; $$; full bar; AE, DC, MC, V; no checks; lunch (dim sum), dinner every day.*

Top Gun Chinese Seafood Restaurant ★★ A visit to Top Gun is never just a culinary experience, it's also a crash course on Pacific Rim cultural immersion. The Hong Kong–style Aberdeen

Shopping Centre in which it's located, together with the adjacent Yaohan Centre and nearby Parker Place, is part of an area nicknamed "Little Asia." In these few square blocks are an education center, a Buddhist temple, bookstores, barbecue shops, bakeries, video arcades, herbalist clinics, and even a bonsai studio. All this makes weekend dim sum here seem more like an excursion than a meal. Expect a lineup and sometimes indifferent service. The dinner menu is generic Cantonese, but specials can be quite interesting. Try sautéed spiced frogs' legs with fagara, baby abalone on mustard greens, or sea scallops with jackfruit and fresh pears in a potato nest. For dessert, amble across the mall to Rhino's Cafe (next to the bowling alley) and try some of the unusual Eurasian cakes and pastries that are featured there. ■ *2110-4151 Hazelbridge Way (Aberdeen Shopping Centre), Richmond; (604)273-2883; $$; full bar; V; no checks; lunch, dinner every day.* &

LODGINGS

Delta Pacific Resort ★★ Formerly called the Delta Airport Inn, this is one of two Delta hotels in the vicinity of Vancouver International Airport. Both are well run and offer a wealth of recreational facilities. This 10-acre resort includes three swimming pools (one indoor), an indoor waterslide, year-round tennis courts under a bubble, a play center with spring-break and summer camp for kids (ages 5 to 12), exercise classes, volleyball nets, and a golf practice net. There are meeting rooms and a restaurant, cafe, and bar. Special rooms for business travelers, with amenities like private faxes, are available for $15 over the normal rate. The free shuttle service goes to and from the airport as well as to major nearby shopping centers. If you're driving, ask for directions from the freeway. ■ *10251 St Edwards Dr (at Cambie), Richmond, BC V6X 2M9; (604)278-9611 or (800)268-1133; www.deltahotels.com; $$$; AE, DC, DIS, E, JCB, MC, V; no checks.* &

Radisson President Hotel and Suites ★★ We knew we were in for a treat at Richmond's President Hotel and Suites when we received impeccable directions to the hotel over the phone and gracious assistance with some rather unusual park-and-fly arrangements. This new airport hotel is a class act, offering everything from Cantonese cuisine in the President Chinese Restaurant, to meeting and conference room space, to shopping at the adjoining President Plaza. Staff handled even the most abstruse requests with ease: customer service here is prompt and friendly. Rooms are spacious and well appointed (you can actually open the windows), and business-class accommodations cover small needs and large—from a free morning newspaper to data port hookups for your laptop. Complimentary shuttle service to the airport is available every half hour. The atmosphere in Gustos' Bistro is bright and funky (we liked the color scheme and the cheery round coffeepots), but breakfast prices are expense-account high. The appealing Mediterranean-style lunch and dinner menu created for the Bistro by executive chef Rod Klockow offers a much better value. ■ *8181 Cambie Rd (from Hwy 99 S, take No. 4 Rd south to exit 39A, turn west on Cambie Rd), Richmond, BC V6X 3X9; (604)276-8181 or (800)333-3333; $$$; AE, DC, DIS, E, JCB, MC, V; no checks.* &

WEST VANCOUVER

RESTAURANTS

The Beach House at Dundarave Pier ★★★ On sunny days, this waterside favorite, only meters away from Dundarave beach, offers unequaled Kodak moments on its year-round heated patio. Misty nights, when dining is accompanied by the basso profundo of distant foghorns, are equally appealing. First opened as a teahouse in 1912, this heritage building has been recently restored by designer Robin Ratcliffe. Wooden floors, creamy walls (check out the art by Jade Ratcliffe), and plenty of glass lend a warm neighborhood feel. Chef Sonny Mendoza consistently puts out fine West Coast dishes: superb cornmeal-crusted Fanny Bay oysters, grilled salmon on a raft of asparagus in a sea of red chile. If you're offered the crème brûlée with toasted hazelnuts and an orange shortbread cookie, don't pass it up. And, by all means, take advantage of the tremendous wine list chosen by managing partner Ken Brooks. It features many good wines by the glass, the best of British Columbia estate wineries, an impressive mix of U.S. West Coast varietals, and a sizable number of bottles from around the world. ■ *150-25th St (waterfront at Dundarave Pier), West Vancouver; (604)922-1414; $$; full bar; AE, DC, MC, V; no checks; lunch, dinner every day, brunch Sat–Sun.* &

Beach Side Cafe ★★★ The Beach Side just keeps getting better and better. With their creative and varied approach to regional cuisine, owner Janet McGuire and chef Carol Chow have turned this little Ambleside haunt into the area's most serious kitchen. The summertime deck rates among the city's best, with views of Stanley Park and Kitsilano across the water. Choices are plentiful, with emphasis on daily specials as well as a cutting-edge list of better West Coast wines. Start with the warm Cambozola with hazelnuts, roasted garlic, and toast points, or the grilled Fanny Bay oysters with a lemon-basil aioli. Definitely order pan-seared scallops with an Oriental noodle pancake and a tomato black bean butter. Dessert lovers swear by the lemon meringue pie. Take advantage of the view, during a leisurely Sunday brunch, with a woodsy oyster mushroom omelet and freshly baked banana bread. This is a great place to do lunch too. ■ *1362 Marine Dr (between 13th and 14th), West*

Vancouver; (604) 925-1945; $$; full bar; AE, MC, V; no checks; lunch Mon–Fri, dinner every day, brunch Sat–Sun. ♿

La Toque Blanche ★★ This cozy, '70s retro-woodsy retreat tucked behind the Cypress Park Mohawk gas station is still a well-kept culinary secret. Owner John-Carlo Felicella has a passion for detail, manifest in appetizers such as the smoked duck carpaccio and the wickedly rich lobster bisque. His entrees are no slouches either, as proved by salmon and crab cakes with seared scallops and red pepper butter, and rack of lamb crusted with figs, cooked perfectly pink. A moderately priced wine list complements the menu. Prices are almost a bargain by today's standards—especially considering the quality, detail, and presentation. At press time, renovations are in the works to update the front of the house. ▪ *4368 Marine Dr (at Erwin Dr), West Vancouver; (604) 926-1006; $$; full bar; AE, MC, V; checks OK; dinner Tues–Sun.* ♿

The Salmon House on the Hill ★★ Northwest Coast Native artifacts reflect the origins of chef Dan Atkinson's Salmon House menu. The hallmark dish at Salmon House is BC salmon cooked over green alder wood, which delivers a distinctive, delicate, and smoky flavor—certainly worth the drive halfway to Horseshoe Bay (but only 10 minutes from downtown). There's a fresh sheet every day. Try the alder-grilled oysters with a jalapeño and bacon vinaigrette; they're perfectly prepared. The wine list favors good BC, Oregon, and Washington wines. There's a striking entrance area, but the lounge is smoky and somewhat uninviting despite the incredible view. Service is friendly and correct, and parking is free. Check out the annual salmon festival in October. ▪ *2229 Folkestone Way (21st St exit off Hwy 1), West Vancouver; (604) 926-3212; $$$; full bar; AE, DC, MC, V; no checks; lunch, dinner every day, brunch Sun.*

LODGINGS

Park Royal Hotel ★★ The Park Royal Hotel is a study in contradictions. It's nestled into its own little forest of mature greenery just yards away from one of Vancouver's busiest freeways, but traffic noise never seems to intrude into your surroundings. Some of the rooms are beautifully appointed with custom woodwork and bathrooms full of marble and brass, but a few are still stuck in the '70s. A complete renovation, however, is slated for 1997. The coziness and romantic setting make it a popular place for weddings. We've seen the human ingredient at work here in some really touching ways. If you arrive at the right time of day, you just might catch the crack kitchen team of toqued and tender-hearted chefs feeding their loyal coterie of alley cats! (People are fed well too, from the revitalized menus in the lounge and dining room.) We like the genuinely friendly housekeeping staff, and the legendary hospitality of owner Mario Corsi is, well, legendary. When he's around, things and people get looked after in a special way. ■ *540 Clyde Ave (just off Marine Dr at Taylor Way, then Clyde Ave on right), West Vancouver, BC V7T 2J7; (604) 926-5511; $$; AE, DC, E, MC, V; no checks.* ঙ

NORTH VANCOUVER

RESTAURANTS

Café Norté Mexican Restaurant ★★ Tucked away in Edgemont Village, this friendly spot is just minutes away from the north end of the Lions Gate Bridge. Peruse the menu while sampling the house salsa and tortilla chips. There's a full range of serious nachos: warm black bean guacamole, chile con queso topped with chorizo, sweet pineapple with jalapeño, and more. Smooth, rich cream of crab soup comes with a garnish of finely chopped red peppers and parsley. Fajitas arrive with tender pieces of still-sizzling chicken nudged up against onions and green peppers. For diehard traditionalists, the refried beans are great and the margaritas perfectly slushy. Of the too few Mexican restaurants in Vancouver, Café Norté reigns supreme. Check out Norté's sibling Cafe Centro in Kits; (604) 734-5422. ■ *3108 Edgemont Blvd (at Highland Blvd), North Vancouver; (604) 990-4600; $$; full bar; AE, MC, V; no checks; lunch Mon–Sat, dinner every day.*

Corsi Trattoria ★★ This little family-run trattoria makes a great excuse for a mini-cruise via the SeaBus. The Corsi family was here on the North Shore before the SeaBus terminal and Lonsdale Quay Public Market existed. The family ran a trattoria in Italy, and the old-country touches still show. Twenty-odd home-made pastas include the house specialty, rotolo—pasta tubes stuffed with veal, spinach, and ricotta and topped with cream and tomato sauces. Or try *trenette al salmone affumicata*—pasta with smoked salmon, cream, olives, and tomatoes. Adventurous eaters might try the (huge) Roman food orgy: four pastas, mixed salad, a platter of lamb, veal, and prawns, followed by coffee and dessert. ■ *1 Lonsdale Ave (across from Lonsdale Market), North Vancouver; (604) 987-9910; $$; full bar; AE, DC, MC, V; no checks; lunch Mon–Fri, dinner Mon–Sat.* ঙ

La Cucina Italiana ★★ Stuck rather incongruously in the middle of North Vancouver's strip of car dealerships and video shops, La Cucina has a rustic character that overcomes its surroundings. The attractive dining room has Italian opera playing at just the right volume. When it's available, try bresaola—air-dried beef imported from Switzerland—as an appetizer, or the cold antipasto. Pastas range from traditional spaghetti with tomato and meat sauce to fettuccine with squid and sweet red peppers. Fish specials are usually good. Don't leave without sampling the homemade ice cream. ■ *1509 Marine Dr (between MacGowan and Tatlow), North Vancouver; (604) 986-1334; $$; full bar; AE, MC, V; no checks; lunch Mon–Fri, dinner Mon–Sat.* ঙ

Vivace! ★★ Bring your appetite if you're headed to Vivace! This fun and lively spot is a good place to take the family or a group of friends for huge servings of excellent pastas, tasty grilled meats, and hearty appetizers. Until recently, this was the location of Cafe Roma, a longtime '70s-style Italian restaurant that has been reworked into a breezy, open room with red-and-gold columns, colorful tiles, and lots of light streaming in through huge windows with a view of the harbor and the city. The menu features reasonable prices for both wine and food, and a fairly creative selection of dishes. Start your meal with the steamed clams or mussels; they nestle in a spicy broth of either saffron or tomato and hot pepper. Or try the appetizer portions of prawns hot off the grill. The grill works overtime at Vivace!, cooking up seafood, chicken, and a beef tenderloin in a reduction of balsamic vinegar. The choice of pastas is extensive as well, so it's a good thing you can have an enormous three-pasta combo that costs about $14 a person. The hot, tomatoey spaghetti vivace is advertised as "for Italians only—hot, hot, hot," and while it doesn't quite live up to its billing, it is very tasty. Meanwhile, the squid-ink fettuccine with scallops in a pesto cream sauce is a delicate and lovely choice. ■ *60 Semisch Way (at Esplanade St), North Vancouver; (604) 984-0274; $$; full bar; AE, DC, MC, V; no checks; lunch Mon–Fri, dinner every day.*

The Tomahawk ★ The Tomahawk must be the original inspiration for all those hokey, totem-pole theme restaurants on highways across North America. In Vancouver, it's a 70-year-plus institution, famous for its hungry-man-size meals. Everyone comes for the eye-opening Yukon Breakfast—five rashers of bacon, two eggs, hashbrowns, and toast—served all day. For lunch, there are several hamburger platters (named after Native American chiefs), sandwiches, fried chicken, fish and chips, and even oysters. Pies (lemon meringue, Dutch apple, banana cream) are baked on the premises, and the staff will gladly wrap one to go. ■ *1550 Philip Ave (at Marine Dr), North Vancouver; (604) 988-2612; $; no alcohol; AE, DC, MC, V; no checks; breakfast, lunch, dinner every day.*

LODGINGS

Laburnum Cottage Bed and Breakfast ★★ This elegant country home is set off by an award-winning English garden that has been tended with care over the past four decades by innkeeper Delphine Masterton, who raised five children here before opening the home to lodgers. The main house, furnished with antiques and collectibles, features four light and airy guest rooms with private baths and garden views. Two of these have a queen bed plus a single. The Summerhouse Cottage—situated in the midst of the garden and accessed by a footbridge that crosses a small creek—is a Rosamund Pilcher novel come to life, perfect for honeymooning couples. A larger cottage, with private entrance, kitchen, fireplace, and children's loft, sleeps five. Delphine's gift for being welcoming, and her ability to weave strangers into friends over the cheerful breakfast table, make a stay here all it should be. Geraldo the cat is still in residence. ■ *1388 Terrace Ave (6 km from downtown, 1 block from Capilano; call for directions), North Vancouver, BC V7R 1B4; (604)988-4877 or (888)686-4877; $$; E, MC, V; checks OK.*

Lonsdale Quay Hotel ★ Few visitors take the time to explore the North Shore, which has what are perhaps the best wilderness areas of any major North American city. The pleasant Lonsdale Quay Hotel, located inside the enjoyable Lonsdale Quay market and across the harbor from downtown Vancouver (yet only 15 minutes away via the SeaBus), gives you a comfortable place to stay (as long as you don't need to be pampered). French doors on south-facing rooms open up to the Vancouver skyline, a dazzling sight at night, when the lights reflect off the water. ■ *123 Carrie Cates Ct (at Lonsdale Quay), North Vancouver, BC V7M 2E4; (604)986-6111 or (800)836-6111; lqh@fleethouse.com; $$$; AE, DC, DIS, E, JCB, MC, V; no checks.* &

LADNER

LODGINGS

River Run Cottages ★★ River Run Cottages is a jewel on the Fraser River. Located in historic Ladner, 30 minutes south of downtown Vancouver and quite near the ferries to Victoria, the cottages are set among a community of houseboats and offer closeness to nature. Ducks, swans, leaping salmon, and bald eagles all put on a show while you look from your deck at the North Shore mountains and Vancouver Island. Bikes and a two-person kayak are available for exploring. The complex features one floating cottage and three on shore, each with deck, private bath, wood-burning stove, wet bar, mini-fridge, and microwave. A hot gourmet breakfast is delivered. No pets. ■ *4551 River Rd W (west on Hwy 10 to Ladner Trunk Rd, which becomes River Rd W), Ladner, BC V4K 1R9; (604)946-7778; riverrun@ direct.ca; $$; MC, V; checks OK.*

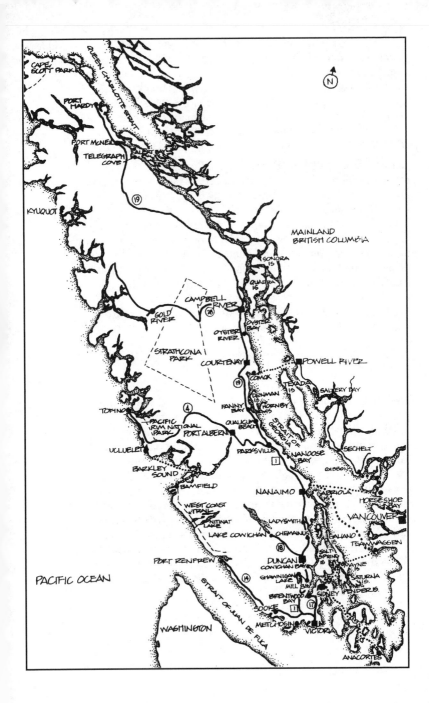

Victoria and Vancouver Island

From Victoria and environs—westward to Sooke, northward to Sidney. From there, the Gulf Islands, then a short jog inland to Port Alberni (and access to west coast towns); then back to Qualicum Beach and north along the east coast to Port Hardy.

VICTORIA

Romantic as Victoria may be, with its delightful natural harbor and the Olympic Mountains of Washington State on the horizon, the provincial capital of British Columbia is less a museum piece nowadays than it is a tourist mecca. Visitors pour in to gawk at vast sculptured gardens and London-style double-decker buses, to shop for Irish linens and Harris tweeds, to sip afternoon tea, and to soak up what they believe is the last light of British imperialism to set on the Western Hemisphere. Raves in the travel press have brought new crops of younger residents to upset Victoria's reputation as a peaceful but dull sanctuary for retiring civil servants from eastern Canada. The quality and variety of restaurants has improved as a result, and no longer are Victoria's streets silent after 10pm.

Ferries. From Seattle, the passenger-only Victoria Clippers, four jet-propelled catamarans, make 2- to 3-hour voyages up and back four times daily in summer (one of which goes via the San Juan Islands) and once or twice daily off-season ($69–109 round trip). The good seats on the upper deck next to windows are quickly taken, so board early; from Vancouver, call (250)382-8100; from Seattle, (206)448-5000; or (800)888-2535 (outside Seattle or outside BC). For those who want to take their cars north, the *Princess Marguerite III* leaves once a day at 1pm ($49 each way for car and driver, $29 each way for each additional passenger). The *Princess* trip takes 4½ hours; (206)448-5000. Other ferry services from Washington to the Victoria area: Washington State Ferries run year-round, **departing Anacortes**, north of Seattle, to Sidney, BC, 27 kilometers (almost 17 miles) north of Victoria, one of the most scenic water routes in the Pacific Northwest; (206)464-6400 or (250)381-1551, $36 round trip in summer or $30 in winter. WSF does accept reservations on the Anacortes-to-Sidney run, but do make sure to call at least a few days in advance. Ferries to Victoria also **leave Port Angeles** on the Olympic Peninsula (via the privately run Black Ball ferry), a 1½-hour voyage (year-round) on which cars are allowed, but for which no reservations are taken

Victoria and Vancouver Island

(call a day in advance to find out how long the wait will be); (360) 457-4491 or (250) 386-2202; $27.25 one way for car and driver, $6.75 for foot passengers. **From Bellingham** the Victoria San Juan Cruises offer one daily sailing (June through October); (206) 738-8099 or (800) 443-4552. Ferries **from British Columbia** mainland depart from Tsawwassen to Swartz Bay, 32 kilometers (20 miles) north of Victoria, every hour from 7am to 10pm in summer, following a scenic route through the Gulf Islands; $26 one way for car and an additional $7 for driver and each passenger; call BC Ferries at (250) 386-3431.

Air Transportation. The fastest link to Victoria (Inner Harbour) is provided by seaplane. There are several airlines from Vancouver (Air BC, (604) 688-5515, or Helijet Airways, (604) 273-1414) or call the local chamber for a complete list. From Seattle, Kenmore Air offers a trip several times daily for about $109 round trip; (800) 543-9595 or (425) 486-1257.

Attractions. First stop should be **Tourism Victoria**, a well-staffed office dispensing useful information on the sights; 812 Wharf Street, (250) 953-2033. The **Royal British Columbia Museum** is one of the finest of its kind in the country, offering dramatic dioramas of natural landscapes and full-scale reconstructions of Victorian storefronts. Of particular interest is the Northwest Coast Indian exhibit, rich with spiritual and cultural artifacts. Watch for special seasonal and touring exhibitions and an intriguing "undersea" show. Open every day, Belleville and Government Streets, (250) 387-3701. The **Art Gallery of Greater Victoria** houses one of the world's finest collections of Oriental art (including the only Shinto shrine in North America), with special historical and contemporary exhibits on display throughout the year. Open every day, 1040 Moss Street, (250) 384-4101. **McPherson Playhouse**, a former Pantages vaudeville house done up with baroque trappings, offers evening entertainment throughout the summer. The box office, (250) 386-6121, also has information about plays and concerts at the Royal Theatre and other sites. The free *Monday Magazine* offers the city's best weekly calendar of events; pick it up at various shops and other locations throughout the city. Spreading out over 184 acres just south of downtown, **Beacon Hill Park** provides splendid views of the water, but the real interest here is in the landscaping (much of it left wild) and the hand-holding couples who stroll the walkways and give retirement a good name. It's a lovely spot to get away from the shopping mania downtown. **Crystal Garden** is a turn-of-the-century swimming-pool building converted into a glass conservatory with a tropical theme (lush greenery, live flamingos and macaws)—a fine place to spend a rainy day; admission is $7. Open every day, 713 Douglas Street, (250) 381-1213. Just across the street is the Victoria Conference Centre, linked to the Empress Hotel by a beautifully restored conservatory and accommodating 1,500 delegates. **Butchart Gardens**, 21 kilometers (13 miles) north of town, shows what can be

▼ **Victoria** ▲

done with reclaimed limestone quarries. The 50 acres of gardens are lovely, beautifully manicured displays in many international styles; they're lighted after dark. Take the time to look beyond the profusion of blooms to the landscape structure and its relationship to the setting of rocky bays and tree-covered mountains. In the summer it's best to go in late afternoon, after the busloads of tourists have left. Concerts, fireworks on Saturday evenings in summer, a surprisingly good afternoon tea, and light meals provide diversions. Open every day, (250)652-5256. **Craigdarroch Castle** puts you back into an era of unfettered wealth and ostentation. Vancouver Island coal tycoon Robert Dunsmuir built this 19th-century mansion to induce a Scottish wife to live in faraway Victoria. Open every day, 1050 Joan Crescent, (250)592-5323. You can visit five of the better-restored **Victoria heritage homes**, (250)387-4697: Helmcken House, behind Thunderbird Park, east of BC Royal Museum; Point Ellice House, at Bay Street and Pleasant Street; Craigflower Manor, 110 Island Highway; Craigflower Schoolhouse at Admirals and Gorge Road W; and Carr House, at Government and Simcoe. Admission to all five is $3.25. The **Esquimalt and Nanaimo (E&N) Railway** leaves early in the morning from a mock-Victorian station near the Johnson Street Bridge and heads up-island to towns with fine resorts. The trip is slow but scenic; there's no food service. Call Via Rail, (250)383-4324 or (800)561-8630.

Specialty Shopping. For British woolens, suits, gifts, and sweets, the downtown area north from the Empress on Government Street is the place to shop. W & J Wilson Clothiers sells English wool suits and women's clothes; Sasquatch Trading Company Ltd. offers some of the best of the Cowichan sweaters; EA Morris Tobacconist Ltd. carries a very proper Victorian mix of fine pipes and tobaccos; Munro's, a monumental 19th-century bank-building-turned-bookstore, has a thoughtful selection; Murchie's Teas and Coffee offers the city's finest selection of specially blended teas and coffees; and don't forget Roger's Chocolates and the English Sweet Shop for chocolates, almond brittle, black-currant pastilles, marzipan bars, Pontefract cakes, and more; and Bernard Callebaut Chocolaterie for picture-perfect chocolates in the Belgian style. **Market Square** is a restored 19th-century courtyard surrounded by a jumble of shops, restaurants, and offices on three floors. A few blocks farther on at Fisgard Street, the entrance to Victoria's small and seemingly shrinking **Chinatown** is marked by the splendid, lion-bedecked Gate of Harmonious Interest. Visit the tiny shops and studios on Fan Tan Alley and check out Morley Co. Ltd., a Chinese grocery. **Antique hunters** should head east of downtown, up Fort Street to Antique Row—block after block of shops, the best of which are the Connoisseurs Shop and David Robinson Ltd., with excellent 18th-century English pieces. Visit **Bastion Square** for sidewalk restaurants, galleries, the Maritime Museum, the alleged location of Victoria's old gallows, and a great gardener's shop called Dig This; and **Windsor Court** for boutique items and gifts.

RESTAURANTS

Chez Daniel ★★★ Unquestionably one of Victoria's finest French restaurants, although off the beaten path in Oak Bay, it's definitely worth a visit. Chef/owner Daniel Rigollet has been wowing locals and tourists alike for 20 years. An award-winning wine list reflects Daniel's membership in the Chaine des Rotisseurs, with bottles running from $20 for a vin de table to $950 for a well-aged Chateau d'Yquem. The pâté maison puts all others in town to shame and succulent escargots were bred to be wed to the garlic butter. Hard to find on the west coast, Dover sole is perfectly cooked and carefully boned. Roast duck with chestnuts is bursting with flavor, and boneless loin of young rabbit with Dijon mustard cream sauce melts in your mouth. Homemade sorbets and handmade chocolate truffles are not to be missed. ■ *2524 Estevan Ave (Estevan and Beach, 10 minutes from downtown), Victoria; (250)592-7424; $$$; full bar; AE, MC, V; checks OK; dinner Tues–Sat.* &

Herald Street Caffe ★★★ Still trendy after all these years and once again with a menu to match, the Caffe now has one of the most successfully innovative menus in town. Dungeness crab cakes with cilantro lime pesto and tomato salsa, and the alder smoked salmon on apple potato latkes with balsamico cream are absolutely delicious, while the caesar salad is probably the best in town. There are a lot of East-meets-West dishes, especially those made with pasta, and the kitchen takes full advantage of the abundance of fresh local seafood: tiger prawns, mussels, scallops, and salmon jostle for attention. Shaker lemon pie is still one of the most popular desserts, but homemade ice creams and sorbets are also definitely worth trying. An excellent wine list has been carefully chosen to match the eclectic menu. Knowledgeable, courteous service makes for an above-average dining experience. Tables may be a little close together, but on busy nights the atmosphere is quite electric. Reservations are highly recommended, and later hours (until midnight) make this an ideal venue for the post-theater crowd. ■ *546 Herald St (at Government, 1 block past Chinatown), Victoria; (250)381-1441; $$; full bar; AE, MC, V; no checks; lunch Wed–Sun, dinner every day, brunch Sun.* &

The Victorian Restaurant (Ocean Pointe Resort) ★★★ Here's an elegant space with an unsurpassed view, located in one of Victoria's finest hotels. Unquestionably one of the best chefs in Victoria, Craig Stoneman has created a menu that adheres to his personal philosophy of lowfat without sacrificing flavor. Everything on this menu (which advises the number of calories, grams of fat, and volume of salt per dish) is superb, from venison carpaccio and cinnamon-smoked quail breast with goat cheese fritters and a walnut and watercress salad, to escargots with wild mushrooms and roasted garlic in a filo pastry cup with a red wine and thyme jus. Sautéed jumbo prawns and Digby scallops in a crisp potato basket with a Pernod-lime cream sauce are magical. Presentation is breathtaking, from soups to salads to main courses and desserts. The massive 250-room waterfront resort stands as a modern counterpoint to the bulk of the Empress and the Parliament Buildings opposite (see review). ■ *45 Songhees Rd (across the Johnson St Bridge from downtown), Victoria; (250)360-2999; $$$; full bar; AE, DC, JCB, MC, V; no checks; dinner Mon–Sat.* &

Camille's ★★ Still Victoria's most romantic basement, with soft lights, music, and wine from a selection of over 200 stored in a huge, walk-in vault. Chefs/owners Paige Robinson and David Mincey have designed their menu based on fresh ingredients from Vancouver Island farmers and growers. Warm duck salad with ginger and sesame-citrus vinaigrette is a divine appetizer, as is the snow crab and avocado salad. Venison with a juniper-berry and rosemary sauce melts in the mouth and breast of pheasant with wild mushrooms is perfectly tender. The Louisiana-style jambalaya is deliciously rich and smoky, with tiger prawns, chorizo sausage, okra, and corn in a spicy tomato sauce. A wicked pear-and-lime granita makes a perfect ending to a perfect meal. Wine-tasting dinners (monthly, Sundays) are highly popular—reserve early. Camille's has a faithful local following. ■ *45 Bastion Square (Fort and Langley), Victoria; (250)381-3433; $$; full bar; MC, V; no checks; dinner every day.* &

Don Mee Seafood Restaurant ★★ Located in Chinatown, Don Mee has the most extensive dim sum offered in Victoria. In business for over 60 years and serving some of the only dim sum in the city that is made on the premises, the restaurant starts filling up early. "Dim sum" means "made from the heart," and a lot of attention goes into the myriad dishes. There is no menu, just a never-ending variety, served from carts that ceaselessly circle the room. Pork fried dumplings with Chinese vinegar, steamed buns filled with chicken, curried pork puffs, rice wrappers stuffed with shrimp and dipped into hot sauce—all are ethereal. Ginger and pork dumplings, shrimp toasts, and shrimp balls stuffed with a crab claw and encrusted with noodles are just a few more of the many memorable choices. Sesame balls stuffed with bean paste are a sweet dim sum not to be missed. Regular menus are available—but we recommend you experience the dim sum. Arrive before 11:30am to be sure of a table. ■ *538 Fisgard St (at Government), Victoria; (250)383-1032; $; full bar; AE, MC, V; no checks; lunch (dim sum only), dinner every day.*

▼

Victoria

Restaurants

▲

Il Terrazzo Ristorante ★★ This is the loveliest terrace in Victoria for dining alfresco. Surrounded by five outdoor fireplaces and an abundance of plants and flowers, Il Terrazzo offers a haven of privacy in busy downtown. Eclectic charm and chic ambience provide the interior decor, and wood-burning ovens provide the homemade focaccia and designer thin-crust pizzas. Topped with grilled chicken, sun-dried tomatoes, smoked mozzarella cheese, roasted peppers, and pesto, Pollo Pizza is a happy choice—as is crabmeat, spinach, and ricotta cheese baked in filo pastry and served with a green salad. Salads are wonderful in summer, but pasta dishes tend to be a little uneven. ■ *555 Johnson St (near the Wharf), Victoria; (250) 361-0028; $$; full bar; AE, MC, V; no checks; lunch Mon–Sat, dinner every day.* ₲

Millos Restaurant ★★ Its cool blue tiles and its saganaki flambé—sharp salty goat cheese sautéed in oil and flamed in brandy at the table—evoke the Aegean influence which has helped make this restaurant a favorite for visitors and residents alike. But to taste a sampling of what this restaurant really can do, try the appetizer platter: it offers something for everyone, from spanakopita to calamari, dolmathes, taramasalata, and more (it also makes a delightful lunch for two). Lots of lamb, from roast to racks; souvlakia made with halibut, chicken, lamb, or beef; and slowly simmered chicken in herbed tomato sauce match the outstanding service. Belly dancers perform on occasion. ■ *716 Burdett St (at Douglas), Victoria; (250) 382-4422; $$; full bar; AE, MC, V; no checks; lunch Mon–Sat, dinner every day.* ₲

Panda Szechuan ★★ Originally opened by the government of the Province of Sichuan, Panda is now in private hands. The magnificent decor remains a tribute to the workmanship of the people of Sichuan Province. English-speaking servers are a boon for those who might want an explanation of certain dishes, but everything is good. A buffet lunch offers a choice of three soups, appetizers, salad fixings, fruit, six stir-fries, steamed rice, fried rice, and chow mein noodles. Honeybuns constitute dessert. From the regular menu, dumplings, spicy pork ribs, onion cakes, and deep-fried wontons are good choices to start. Hot and spicy prawns with black bean and garlic and stir-fried scallops are part of a large array of seafood. Kung pao chicken, moo shu pork, and mushroom royale offer different aspects of a menu that features Mongolian and Mandarin as well as Sichuan. ■ *818 Douglas St (between Courteney and Humboldt), Victoria; (250) 388-0080; $; full bar; AE, MC, V; no checks; lunch, dinner every day.* ₲

Sam's Deli ★★ As so many downtown office workers can attest, this 20-year-old restaurant offers the most bang for your buck in the city. Famous for its shrimp and avocado sandwiches (you'll be thrilled with the generous portion of fresh shrimp), Sam's is generous on everything, from large tureens of a daily soup to a ploughman's lunch with a choice of meat or vegetable pâté, two different cheeses, dill pickle, fresh fruit, and sourdough bread (enough for a meal and a half). Specially cured ham, roast beef, and pastrami on lovely dark rye, or an enormous bowl of spinach salad with an excellent dressing, can be eaten in, munched on the curbside terrace, or taken out for a picnic down by the Inner Harbour, a stone's throw away. ■ *805 Government St (between Humboldt and Courteney), Victoria; (250)382-8424; $; full bar; no credit cards; no checks; breakfast, lunch, dinner every day.* ௫

Siam ★★ One of two very good Thai restaurants in Victoria, Siam is a large restaurant, but delicate details give it an intimate Oriental ambience. The food is star rated, from one-star mild to four-star raging. The yum talay salad of mixed seafood, cooked with onions, cilantro, and mint leaves in lime juice and full of prawns, scallops, and squid, has an attitude—it talks back. Siam Curry, with a subtle blend of bamboo shoots, peppers, basil, and coconut milk in a red curry sauce, should not be missed. *Pho peah*, deep-fried spring rolls, are light and crisp, with a sensational dipping sauce. Share a tureen of *tom yum koong*, hot and sour soup with prawns and Thai spices—it's Thai magic! ■ *512 Fort St (near the foot of Fort St), Victoria; (250)383-9911; $$; full bar; AE, MC, V; no checks; lunch Mon–Sat, dinner every day.* ௫

Spice Jammer Restaurant ★★ This pretty little East Indian restaurant, with very atypically Western decor, is overseen with an effervescent charm and good humor by the manager, Amin Essa. His wife, Billie, is the chef, and with her excellent curries and his good service you just can't go wrong. The menu is standard curry house, but the preparation is a cut above average. Appetizers like samosas, pakoras, and stuffed naan are menu regulars, but crisp fried cassava with chutney is different. Pride of place on the menu goes to the tandoori dishes, but every dish, from vindaloo to marsala, is a jewel in the crown. Prawns, butter chicken, and veggie curries all deliver Promethean virtue: your choice of mild, medium, hot, or extra hot. Bhunna beef, palak lamb, and aloo gobi not only sound exotic but taste exotic, and rice pilau cooked with cardamom, cumin, saffron, and cinnamon wakes up the senses. There are token alternatives for those who don't like curries, but don't give them a second glance. You're here for the curries or you're not. ■ *852 Fort St (at Quadra), Victoria; (250)480-1055; $$; full bar; AE, MC, V; no checks; lunch, dinner Tues–Sun, brunch Sun.* ௫

Tomoe Japanese Restaurant ★★ Very fresh sushi is the order of the day in this above-average Japanese restaurant, but sashimi is the star of the show—eye-catching and mouthwatering, with delicate little morsels of the freshest fish, including salmon, tuna, shrimps, scallops, halibut, and mackerel. Tomoe Soba, buckwheat noodles with tempura shrimp, has a very delicate broth and oodles of noodles. Tempura is probably the best in town, with bountiful prawns and a large selection of veggies, done in the lightest of batters. The sushi bar provides the opportunity to watch the artistry of talented chefs as they swing into action; or try one of the tatami rooms for more privacy. ■ *726 Johnson St (at Douglas St), Victoria; (250) 381-0223; $$; full bar; AE, MC, V; no checks; lunch Mon–Fri, dinner every day.* &

Vin Santo Urban Bistro ★★ Located in quaint Trounce Alley, Vin Santo assaults your senses with a wonderful aroma of herbs and garlic. Tomatoes marinated with basil and olive oil on crunchy toasted bread spread with roasted garlic and topped with Parmesan cheese constitutes a heavenly version of bruschetta. The spinach salad with bocconcini of mozzarella cheese and roasted hazelnuts is heavenly too (although you may need to beg for more of the charred tomato dressing). Menus change regularly, so what's on this month may not be on next. Marinated lamb sirloin with a minted yogurt and herb sauce is truly inspired. Pizzas possess great potential, with a selection of very interesting toppings, but fall short in execution. A very smooth and creamy vanilla cheesecake, exquisitely presented, is certainly worth a try. ■ *620 Trounce Alley (at Government), Victoria; (250) 480-5560; $$$; full bar; AE, MC, V; no checks; lunch, dinner every day.* &

The Windsor House Tea Room ★★ This joyful restaurant tucked away in Oak Bay is quintessentially English and oozes Victorian charm: lead-pane windows, lace tablecloths, and teapots with tea cozies. Soups are sensational, and so are the wonderful homemade steak and kidney pie (by far the best in town) and chicken potpie (laden with chicken and veggies simmered in a white wine sauce and topped with a flaky crust). A small kitchen makes for a small menu (and the reason the dessert pies are not homemade), but sandwiches couldn't be fresher. If an English tea is what you're looking for, homemade scones and buttered crumpets with jam and clotted cream are sure to appeal. ■ *2540 Windsor Ave (at Newport), Victoria; (250) 595-3135; $; full bar; MC, V; no checks; lunch, tea Tues–Sat, dinner Fri.* &

Demitasse ★ Coffee is hot all over the Pacific Northwest, and tea-infused Victoria is no exception. Demitasse is one of the first coffeehouses to offer upscale food to match their roasted beans. All-day breakfasts are very popular here, as are the homemade croisssants piled high with a variety of fillings. Although the place is not strictly vegetarian, its bent is toward nonmeat fillings for the enormous sandwiches. Homemade soups change daily, as do specials, and desserts offer a nice variety. After the morning office-crowd rush, the tempo slackens until lunch, when the pace picks up again. This is a trendy spot, too, for a post-movie snack or coffee and dessert. ■ *1320 Blanshard St* *(corner of Johnson), Victoria; (250) 386-4442; $; beer and wine; AE, MC, V; checks OK; breakfast, lunch, dinner every day.* &

John's Place ★ John's Place is a haven for the younger set, for breakfast and lunch in particular, but its reasonable prices make it appealing to any age. Exceedingly large portions match exceedingly long lineups on weekends for the brunch trade. (Laserlike service usually has the line moving fairly quickly, but expect a 10- to 15-minute wait.) The eggs Benedict and the Belgian waffles are justifiably famous, but the Mediterranean Combo (with falafel, hummus, and a Greek salad) and the Thai spring rolls vie for attention. Jukeboxes on the wall are reminiscent of '50s dating booths, but the decor befits this Heritage building. ■ *723 Pandora Ave (at Douglas), Victoria; (250) 389-0711; $; full bar; MC, V; no checks; breakfast Mon–Sat, lunch, dinner every day, brunch Sun.* &

Pagliacci's ★ Still as popular as ever, Pag's appeals to all ages, but be prepared to queue. Large portions, reasonable prices, and overall pretty good food are responsible. Pack 'em in is the style, but the decor and menu reflect owner Howie Siegel's passion for movies. Marco Polo grilled chicken salad with artichoke hearts, black olives, red onions, tomatoes, and Romano cheese zapped with a pesto vinaigrette is one of the best in town. The Roman Holiday, the restaurant's version of linguine carbonara, has an excellent sauce but slightly overcooked pasta. Rustica Country Pie is a rustic quiche in pastry; Last Chicken in Paris, with a Marsala wine cream sauce and tricolored fettuccine, would benefit from more of the vino. Sunday brunches are legendary. ■ *1011 Broad St (between Fort and Broughton, near Eaton Centre), Victoria; (250) 386-1662; $$; full bar; MC, V; checks OK; lunch Mon–Sat, dinner every day, brunch Sun.* &

Re-bar ★ Victoria's original vegetarian health-food and smoke-free restaurant is as popular as ever. Lunchtime crowds pack the dining room, and lineups are common. Delicious pizzas with oyster mushrooms, Anaheim chiles, tomatillo salsa, and Asiago and Jack cheeses are specialties, along with pastas, Oriental salads, and black bean chili. Breads are all homemade; honey-cornmeal and rosemary-walnut are filled with an exotic assortment of tastes and textures. Lemon tahini dressing and basil vinaigrette are delicious salad-toppers. Freshly squeezed fruit juices, as well as wheat-grass and spirulina-based drinks, are all good for what ails you, the latter two offering healthy alternatives to a cup of java. Friendly, helpful service exemplifies the Re-bar's philosophy. ■ *50 Bastion Square (at Langley), Victoria; (250) 361-9223; $; beer and wine; AE, MC, V; local checks only; breakfast, lunch, dinner Mon–Sat, brunch Sun.* &

Spinnakers Brew Pub ★ One of the first brewpubs on the Island, Spinnakers, situated right on Inner Harbour, also has the best view of any pub in Victoria. In the Tap Room upstairs, traditional pub fare is the order of the day with rather ho-hum fish and chips, burgers, pastas, and curries, but good salads. (You'll also find pub games here.) Downstairs in the dining room (where you can bring minors) you'll find a very similar menu, with the addition of potpies, stir-fries, and the inevitable ploughman's lunch. ■ *308 Catherine St (travel west over the Johnson St Bridge to Catherine, or take a water taxi from the Inner Harbour), Victoria; (604) 386-2739; $; full bar; AE, MC, V; no checks; breakfast, lunch, dinner every day.* &

Yoshi Sushi ★ Although it's a little off the beaten track, a trip to Yoshi Sushi is definitely warranted. Sushi is carefully formed by one of the best sushi chefs in town. Long a local favorite, owner Yoshi Shimizu delights in demonstrating his expertise. Sushi selections vary depending on what is the freshest fish available that day, and you can't go wrong with a magnificent boat laden with a superb selection and presentation of sashimi. Bento boxes offer a choice of sushi, yakitori (Japanese barbecue), and sunomono. For those not partial to raw fish, there is kara age chicken, teriyaki beef, tonkatsu donburi (pork cutlet with rice), and a good selection of vegetarian and noodle dishes. All meals are preceded by a delightful miso soup garnished with fine dice of tofu. Friendly and helpful service complement very good food. You can choose to sit at the sushi bar, at the robata bar, or in a tatami room. ■ *602-771 Vernon Ave (in Gateway Village Mall, just outside of town on Hwy 17), Victoria; (250) 475-3900; $$; full bar; AE, MC, V; no checks; lunch Mon–Sat, dinner every day.* &

Barb's Place It's truly spartan alfresco dining, with only a couple of picnic tables, but the fish doesn't get any fresher than this. Located down at Fisherman's Wharf, this place is as popular with locals as it is with tourists. Terrific fish (halibut or cod in a light, crisp batter) and homemade chips heads the menu, but burgers have been added in recent years. If the tables are taken, there's a small park nearby where you can sit on the grass and enjoy your lunch. A perfect place for families with boisterous (but hungry) kids. ■ *310 St. Lawrence St (Fisherman's Wharf), Victoria; (604) 384-6515; $; no alcohol; no credit cards; no checks; breakfast, lunch, dinner every day.* &

LODGINGS

Abigail's Hotel ★★★ The Tudor-style Abigail's is all gables and gardens and crystal chandeliers, with three floors of odd-shaped rooms. The third-floor "Celebration Rooms" are grandest. Not a lavish detail is missed: crystal goblets, down duvets, and fresh flowers grace each room. Our favorite rooms have a double-sided wood-burning fireplace, so you can enjoy the fire whether you're in bed or in the deep, comfortable soaking tub. Practicalities, too, are all well in place—a light shines in the shower, the walls are well soundproofed (light sleepers, however, may want to request a room as far from noisy Quadra Street as possible). In short, Abigail's combines the beauty of the Old World with the comforts of the New. The guest library is inviting, especially with a glass of sherry after a day spent exploring Victoria. Guests have a choice of entrees from the breakfast menu, which changes daily. Although children over 10 are accepted, this is a romantic-getaway type of establishment that's more suitable for adults. Abigail's also manages a two-bedroom beach house 10 minutes from downtown Victoria that's perfect for families. ■ *906 McClure St (at Vancouver), Victoria, BC V8V 3E7; (250) 388-5363 or (800) 561-6565; innkeeper@abigailshotel. com; www.abigailshotel.com; $$$; AE, MC, V; no checks.*

The Beaconsfield ★★★ Of all the imitation-England spots, this is the best. Tree-lined Humboldt Street is closer to the hub of downtown than its quiet demeanor would suggest, so the Beaconsfield's location just two blocks from Beacon Hill Park is prime. It's meant to convey a sense of romance and hideaway and does, with nine antique-filled bedrooms, all with private baths and down comforters. The Attic Room, Jacuzzi and all, is exceedingly private. The Duchess Room has a half-canopied queen-size bed, with inlaid-mahogany pieces and an unusual wood-enclosed period bathtub. The antiques are offset by rediscovered "modernities" such as steam-heated towel racks. There is so much dark, gleaming mahogany in this 1905 Edwardian home that one can feel a bit cloistered on a sunny day, but this is easily remedied in the conservatory (where breakfast is often served). The Beaconsfield also offers a cozy beach cottage for two located near the University of Victoria. ■ *998 Humboldt St (at Vancouver), Victoria, BC V8V 2Z8; (250) 384-4044; beaconsfield@islandnet.com; www.islandnet.com/beacons field; $$$; MC, V; checks OK.* &

Laurel Point Inn ★★★ Laurel Point's angular construction means that all of the 200 rooms and suites offer views of the harbor or the ship channel. We much prefer the junior suites in the newer south wing; all are beautifully appointed, with graceful Japanese accents and private decks. Spacious marble bathrooms are fitted with deep-soak tubs and sexy, peekaboo stall showers. The channel-side rooms offer the best view of the comings and goings of boats and seaplanes, the Olympic Mountains, and the serene Japanese garden at channel's edge. Rooms in the older north wing are rather average, although some have a nice view of the Inner Harbour. The dining room, Cafe Laurel, is a wicker-and-fern affair with better-than-adequate food. ■ *680 Montreal St (at Belleville), Victoria, BC V8V 1Z8;*

(250)386-8721 or (800)663-7667; laurelpoint@ampsc.com; www. islandnet.com/~cvcprod/laurel.html; $$$; AE, DC, JCB, MC, V; no checks. &

Andersen House ★★ Andersen House combines some of the best features of a traditional Victorian B&B with modern creature comforts such as telephones and CD players in each room. The house, built in 1891, is beautifully kept, and features 12-foot ceilings, stained-glass windows, and hardwood floors. We especially like the sparely elegant decor, an eclectic mélange of antiques, original modern art, and Persian rugs; it doesn't have that froufrou, overdecorated feeling of so many B&Bs. Each of the rooms has a private entrance, so you can come and go without feeling that you're disturbing anyone. The upstairs Casablanca Room has a sun deck with a view of the Olympic Mountains, while the Garden Studio looks out onto the lovely garden and has a whirlpool tub. For an especially romantic, unusual stay, opt for the *Mamita*, a 1927 motor yacht moored in the harbor just a few blocks from Andersen House. ■ *301 Kingston St (at Pendray), Victoria, BC V8V 1V5; (250)388-4565; andersen@islandnet.com; www.islandnet.com/~andersen/; $$$; MC, V; checks OK.*

▼
Victoria

Lodgings

▲

The Coast Victoria Harbourside Hotel ★★ The Coast Victoria features Victoria's only indoor/outdoor pool, plus views of the Olympic Mountains, the Strait of Juan de Fuca, or the Inner Harbour. We like the location: on the water near Fisherman's Wharf, yet in a quiet residential neighborhood removed from the hustle and bustle of downtown. It's a quick 10-minute walk to the Parliament Buildings, or you can take the little Victoria Harbour Ferry. The penthouse suites offer much in the way of comfort (sleeping quarters adjoin cushy sitting rooms), though the decor—bold, dark colors, expensive, high-gloss furnishings, and gigantic wide-screen TVs—may strike some as seriously overblown. The standard guest rooms are on the small side, though the view helps them feel larger. Other features are underground parking, air conditioning, whirlpool, sauna, exercise rooms, and a 42-slip marina. ■ *146 Kingston St (between Laurel Point and Fisherman's Wharf), Victoria, BC V8V 1V4; (250)360-1211 or (800)663-1144; $$$; AE, DC, JCB, MC, V; checks OK.* &

The Empress ★★ The hotel that once stood as the quiet, ivy-clad dowager of the Inner Harbour had a $45 million facelift in 1989. In the years since then, that lovely facade has proven to be a facelift that only the Queen Mother could love. First the good news: a separate guest entrance pavilion was added, the Palm Court and the Crystal Ballroom were polished up, and 50 new rooms brought the total to 482. The grounds were landscaped, and a restored conservatory at the rear of the hotel now connects it to the Victoria Conference Centre. And now for the bad: many of the rooms received little or no attention, and the rates in high season are astonishing, especially for rooms with a view (off-season prices, although still high, offer a much better value). Keep in mind that this old hotel isn't air-conditioned, although there are ceiling fans. If money is no object, the Entree Gold rooms have the nicest furnishings and the best views, as well as private check-in and concierge. For these prices, one expects perfection or pretty darn close to it. But because the hotel is so big, service is hard-pressed to live up to expectations: lines for checking in and out are lengthy, and we were dismayed in the morning to see room-service trays still in the hallways from dinner the night before. Nevertheless, the Empress is the most notable landmark in town and is worth a stroll (take the excellent historical tour offered each morning at 10am). High tea is served daily by reservation, and while it may be overpriced, it's still the best value at the Empress.

The Empress dining room is certainly the most visually impressive restaurant in Victoria. The grand space retains the originally carved beams in the ceiling, spacious tables, and comfortable chairs. Entrees, such as the smoked duck with a sour cherry sauce and rosemary biscotti, or the sensational seared tuna with a wasabi-ginger sauce and grilled veggies, are original and well executed. Desserts don't disappoint either; make your selection from the roving trolley or try one of the hotel's signature desserts, such as the crème brûlée with a subtle hint of ginger or the lemon flan, lightly glazed and dusted with powdered sugar. ■ *721 Government St (between Humboldt and Belleville), Victoria, BC V8W 1W5; (250) 384-8111 or (800) 441-1414; cdick@emp.mhs.compuserve.com; www.vvv.com/empress; $$$; full bar; AE, DC, MC, V; checks OK; dinner Tues–Sun.* &

The Haterleigh ★★ The Haterleigh House was built in 1901 by Thomas Hooper, an architect who designed many of Victoria's Victorian homes. The house has been well preserved and well restored. Fine, curved stained-glass windows grace the parlor. Geared toward romance, the rooms are generously sized and charmingly decorated. We especially like the Secret Garden Room, which has a lovely view of the Olympic Mountains. Breakfast might include eggs goldenrod (a variation of eggs Benedict), a fruit plate, and homemade baked goods. Upon arrival, guests enjoy a glass of sherry and samples of rich Rogers chocolates, made in Victoria. ■ *243 Kingston St (at Pendray), Victoria, BC V8V 1V5; (250) 384-9995; paulk@tnet.net; www.vvv.com/~paulk; $$$; MC, V; no checks.*

Holland House Inn ★★ The inn is housed in a modestly attractive gray stucco structure (just the antidote to the endless Olde England theme so prevalent in Victoria), decked with rose trellises and a picket fence. Inside, there are 10 rooms stylishly decorated with a mixture of bold prints and some unusual antiques. Rooms 20 and 30 have fireplaces, and all but one have their own balcony or patio. The location, in a residential neighborhood just a few short blocks from the Inner Harbour, is prime, although light sleepers may be irritated by traffic noise from Government Street. A full breakfast is served, either in the dining room or in the solarium depending on the season. ■ *595 Michigan St (at Government), Victoria, BC V8V 1S7; (250)384-6644 or (800)335-3466; stay@hollandhouse.victoria.bc.ca; www.island net.com/~holndhus/; $$$; AE, DC, MC, V; checks OK.*

Joan Brown's B&B ★★ Joan Brown may monopolize the conversation at the breakfast table, but most visitors enjoy listening to her tales. This lovely house draped with wisteria is in the renowned Rockland neighborhood, a short drive from downtown. The spacious rooms (a few are ballroom-size) and Joan's quirky ways of running an inn (and eccentric sense of humor) make this stately bed and breakfast a very comfortable stay for those who prefer a traditional B&B with lots of personality. Our choice of room is the one with a Second Empire flavor, furnished with a king-size bed, fireplace, bath, and bay window. Nothing could be better for a rainy afternoon than the well-stocked library. ■ *729 Pemberton Rd (off Fort St), Victoria, BC V8S 3R3; (250)592-5929; $$; no credit cards; checks OK.*

Oak Bay Beach Hotel ★★ Presiding over the Haro Strait, this Tudor-style hotel is in the loveliest part of Victoria, a nice place to stay if you want to be removed from downtown. Even so, it's a very busy spot—especially its bar. Still, it evokes another world: handsome antiques dot the comfortable rooms full of nooks and gables. The best rooms are those with private balconies and a water view. Some of the rooms seem a little down at the heels. The dining room, Bentley's on the Bay, is prettily done but isn't up to the rest of the place. Opt for libations in the inviting, English pub–style snug, where you can sit before the fire with your pint. Across the street is the private Victoria Golf Club, dramatically bordered by the sea. And do enjoy the hotel's afternoon tea—a proper affair that deserves (but doesn't require) proper attire. ■ *1175 Beach Dr (near Oak Bay Ave), Victoria, BC V8S 2N2; (250)598-4556 or (800)668-7758; $$$; AE, DC, MC, V; checks OK.*

Ocean Pointe Resort ★★ You can't miss Ocean Pointe as you enter the Inner Harbour from the sea. The massive 250-room waterfront resort stands as a modern counterpoint to the bulk of the Empress and the Parliament Buildings opposite. The lobby is elegant, with lots of marble and dramatic flower arrangements. Unfortunately, the guest rooms themselves are rather average (with the notable exception of the suites), but the ones facing the harbor do have a great view. Stay at Ocean Pointe to enjoy its facilities, especially the pool and the luxurious spa. There's a choice of restaurants (see The Victorian Restaurant review), fine dining or informal. It's a short walk over the Johnson Street Bridge to the heart of downtown, or you can hop on a harbor ferry. ■ *45 Songhees Rd (at Esquimault), Victoria, BC V9A 6T3; (250)360-2999 or (800)667-4677; ocean_pointe@pinc.com; www.oprhotel.com; $$$; AE, DC, JCB, MC, V; no checks.* &

The Prior House ★★ No imitation here: this grand B&B occupies an English mansion built during the Edwardian period for the King's representative in British Columbia. It is in the quiet Rockland neighborhood, about 1½ kilometers (1 mile) from downtown. Many of the rooms have fireplaces and views of water; the Lieutenant Governor's Suite has an extravagant bath with a whirlpool tub, gold fixtures, and crystal chandeliers. Innkeeper Candis Cooperrider prepares a full breakfast that may be taken in the dining room or in the privacy of your room. Afternoon tea is served at 4pm. Families with children older than 9 may stay in one of the lower-level Garden Suites, which have private entrances and full kitchens. ■ *620 St. Charles (at Rockland), Victoria, BC V8S 3N7; (250)592-8847; innkeeper@priorhouse.com; www.priorhouse.com; $$$; MC, V; checks OK.*

Victoria Regent Hotel ★★ For those with a taste for very luxurious condo living, the modern Victoria Regent is a posh apartment hotel in the heart of downtown Victoria, with grandstand views of the Inner Harbour. Don't let the unadorned exterior put you off. Inside, you'll find huge, nicely decorated one- and two-bedroom suites. Each apartment has a living room, dining room, balcony, and kitchen; most have views of city and harbor. Full room service from the Water's Edge Cafe is available. ■ *1234 Wharf St (near Yates), Victoria, BC V8W 3H9; (250)386-2211 or (800)663-7472; regent@pinc.com; $$$; AE, DC, JCB, MC, V; no checks.* &

The Bedford Regency Hotel ★ The liveried doorman is gone, and so is afternoon tea. In fact, we've been hearing reports that much has gone downhill at what used to be our favorite small hotel in Victoria: understaffing at the front desk and lack of attention to detail have been the general themes. However, the thick and pillowy quilts on the beds, the private Jacuzzis, and the dozen rooms with fireplaces are still here. Most of the 40 rooms are pricey and lack a view, but the hotel's central downtown location is hard to beat for shoppers (although it can also be noisy, especially in summer, as the hotel is not air-conditioned). ■ *1140 Government St (between Fort and Yates), Victoria, BC V8W 1Y2; (250)384-6835 or (800)665-6500; $$$; AE, MC, V; no checks.* &

Craigmyle Guest House ★ Built as a guest house early in the century, the Craigmyle stands next to Craigdarroch Castle (a grand, well-preserved mansion) and close to the Art Gallery of Greater Victoria, in the Rockland district, about 1½ kilometers (1 mile) from the city center. Best rooms are those with views of the neighboring castle. A large breakfast with homemade preserves and good coffee is served, and the main lounge features traditional wainscoting, lofty ceilings, an enormous fireplace, and annoying easy-listening music. Reasonably priced, the Craigmyle is one of the few guest houses in Victoria that allows children. ▪ *1037 Craigdarroch Rd (off Fort), Victoria, BC V8S 2A5; (250)595-5411 or (888)595-5411; craigmyle@vicsurf. com; www.bctravel.com/craigmyle.html; $; AE, MC, V; no checks.*

Heritage House ★ This 1910 beauty is 5 kilometers (3 miles) from the center of town. The four rooms (which share three baths) have been redecorated to the original Craftsman style of the house, and are enchanting, as is the Garden Room, a reading room with three walls of windows. Downstairs, the fireplace parlor is a cozy place; a wraparound porch provides ample seating for garden appreciators (the garden is splendid). Gourmet breakfasts consist of several courses and—if you're lucky—a much-praised salmon quiche. Two-day minimum stay. ▪ *3808 Heritage Lane (off McKenzie), Victoria, BC V8Z 7A7; (250)479-0892; www.victoriabc.com/accom/heritage.html; $; MC, V; no checks.*

Ramada Huntingdon Manor ★ Don't be misled by the Ramada name: this is no typical chain motel. A comfortable antique-furnished parlor with a blazing log fireplace and an indoor whirlpool and sauna make for a pleasant stay at the Huntingdon. Rooms are nicely furnished, some with four-poster beds, and the spacious two-story gallery suites have bedroom lofts (a good choice for families; kids under 18 stay free). This is a full-service hotel with a reliable restaurant, but some rooms have kitchen facilities. The location, a block from the Victoria Clipper terminal, is convenient yet fairly quiet. ▪ *330 Quebec St (at Oswego), Victoria, BC V8V 1W3; (250)381-3456 or (800)663-7557; huntingdon@visual.net; www.visual.net/storefront/hunt ingdon; $$; AE, DC, MC, V; no checks.* ⅙

Swans Hotel ★ Behind the traditional facade of this 1913 building hide 29 modern suites, complete with kitchen facilities and living areas. The two-bedroom suites are an especially good deal for families, as they don't cost much more than a studio and can sleep up to six (although there is an additional charge for more than two people in a room). The decor is rather bland, but you get plenty of room to spread out. Especially in summer, be sure to ask for a room away from the pub; like most hotels in Victoria, Swans is not air-conditioned. The downstairs cafe and pub (which serves beer brewed on the premises) are lively gathering spots. In the pub, the menu matches in quality and preparation the ales, lagers, and stouts from the on-site brewery. A glassed-in terrace allows diners to watch the action without being blown to bits on a windy day. ▪ *506 Pandora Ave (at Store), Victoria, BC V8W 1N6; (250)361-3310 or (800)668-7926;*

swans@islandnet.com; www.islandnet.com/~swans; $$; full bar; AE, DC, JCB, MC, V; no checks; breakfast, lunch, dinner every day.

SOOKE

This relatively undiscovered area, a half hour west of Victoria, offers spectacular beach scenery and seclusion. The road continues to Port Renfrew, where it peters out into the famous **West Coast Trail**, one of the greatest (and most demanding) hikes in the Northwest (see Bamfield).

Royal Roads University, on the road to Sooke, is a Dunsmuir family castle turned Provincial university; the beautiful grounds are open to the public each day 10am to 4pm; (250)391-2511.

East Sooke Park, a wilderness park, offers hiking trails in the forest, spectacular views, and good swimming beaches.

Sooke Region Museum mounts some interesting displays of logging and pioneer equipment, Indian artifacts, and a fully restored historic cottage showing turn-of-the-century lifestyles. The museum also sponsors BC's largest juried fine-arts show, held every August in the Sooke Arena. Open Tuesday–Sunday; call (250)642-6351 for more information.

For local crafts, organic vegetables, and children's activities, stop by the **Sooke Country Market**, every Saturday May through September, at the Sooke Elementary School .

The entire coast between Sooke and Port Renfrew has excellent parks, with trails down to ocean beaches—all of which offer fine beachcombing possibilities and good waves for surfers—or into the forest. Mirror Creek is a favorite; ask at the Sooke Region Museum for details. **Botanical Beach**, just west of Port Renfrew, has exceptionally low tides in the early summer that expose miles of sea life and sculpted sandstone.

RESTAURANTS

Country Cupboard Cafe ★★ Jennie Vivian, waitress turned chief cook and restaurateur, had her eye on this roadside A-frame for years before getting her hands on it. Her small cafe's "country" theme (Raggedy Ann dolls and toddler-sized tea sets, potbelly stove and dried flowers, heart-shaped stencils and garage sale knickknacks) might be a bit much for some. But it doesn't keep the local logging contingent from showing up with muddy boots, lured here by Jennie's fabulous mile-high, liqueur-infused cheesecakes and her daughter Ginger's crumble-topped pies. The menu is a simple, welcome, herb- and garlic-laced anomaly out here in Deep-Fried Country. Pastas and stir-fries shine at dinner, tweaked with generous helpings of carefully cooked prawns, moist chicken breast, and bright vegetables. Lunch offerings include steamed Sooke clams and locally smoked salmon as well as creatively composed sandwiches (read: pesto mayo, smoked chicken, herbed sourdough). Patio dining helps make room for summer crowds. Wine lovers should stick to the BC beers. ■ *402 Sheringham Point Rd (at West Coast Rd), Sooke; (250)646-2323; $$; beer and wine; MC, V; no checks; lunch, dinner every day.*

Good Life Bookstore and Cafe ★ The good life is, indeed, good food served among books. This is a funky establishment with a mishmash of furnishings in an old house where the former living room is now the dining room and a couple of the bedrooms a bookstore. Locals will tell you the food is not anything fancy but it's quite good and well priced. Breakfast is just coffee and muffins (and occasionally eggs). Lunches usually entail two soups served with homemade soda bread and a number of vegetarian entrees (lots of seafood too). Seafood and chicken star at dinner (which off-season is limited to only two days a week). ■ *2113 Otter Point Rd (downtown), Sooke; (250)642-6821; $$; beer and wine; MC, V; checks OK; lunch Tues–Sun, dinner Fri–Sat (call for summer hours).* ♿

LODGINGS

Sooke Harbour House ★★★★ This white clapboard farmhouse, perched waterside at the end of the road in a modest Sooke neighborhood, is one of British Columbia's finest inns. The original 1931 building features three spectacularly angular upstairs suites (the Blue Heron Room has the best view, a Jacuzzi, and a fireplace) and sits adjacent to another house with 10 rooms. Each room is lovingly, singularly decorated. Views, decks (or patios), and artful extras—such as bouquets of fresh flowers in every room, a decanter of fine port, and terrycloth bathrobes—are givens. A lavish breakfast platter (delivered to your room) and a light lunch are included in the cost of a night's stay. The country-cozy **Sooke Harbour House dining room** with a central stone hearth and candlelit tables offers a stunning view of the Strait of Juan de Fuca. For more than a dozen years, owners Sinclair and Frederica Philip, along with their team of chefs, have gained international attention for their rare dedication to the freshest local ingredients blended with a good deal of energy and flashes of searing innovation. You'll pay dearly for all this attention to detail (some say nothing is worth these prices, others disagree). We say, go, stay. You'll find no better rooms in British Columbia—and if you enjoy the pricey meal, then you'll be that much happier.

The Sinclairs also lease the Malahat Farm Cottage on a 40-acre "gentleman's farm" that is a perfect escape for any city slickers (and their family or friends) longing for a little taste of the country. ■ *1528 Whiffen Spit Rd, RR 4 (at the very end of Whiffen Spit Rd), Sooke, BC V0S 1N0; (250)642-3421 or (800)889-9688; shh@islandnet.com; www.sookenet.com/shh; $$$; full bar; AE, MC, V; checks OK; dinner every day.* ♿

Hartmann House ★★★ Bed-and-breakfast competition is stiff in Sooke, what with a B&B sign every 500 feet, but if you're going to choose one, this should be it. It doesn't have many rooms (and we usually steer clear of places with three or fewer rooms), but there's an exception to every rule. And here's one. Ray and Ann Hartmann have created an environment that even Martha Stewart might envy. This is a stunning English-style country garden setting (and very, very private) with distant views of the water. Leave the kids behind and spend an entire summer day lounging on the white wicker furniture on the patio just above the trellised garden—full of well-tended vegetables, herbs, and perennials. Although, any time of year, you'll find the inside of this stone house equally inviting (from the sherry in front of the fireplace to the eiderdown quilts, the private baths, the robes, and the whole nine yards). A new 700-square-foot suite (with French doors opening onto the garden) is being added at press time. ■ *5262 Sooke Rd (6 km/3¾ miles east of Sooke), Sooke, BC V0S 1N0; (250) 642-3761; $$$; V; checks OK.*

Fossil Bay Resort ★★ Don't be misled by the name. The only resortlike expectations you should have about these immaculate, modern, ocean-front cottages is that you can "resort" to doing little or nothing here (save fixing a meal, if you're inclined). Expect all the comforts of home (a small, well-equipped kitchen, TV and VCR, king-size bed) and a few luxurious extras (a fireplace, match-ready, facing a comfy sofa; a very private patio hot tub, great for stargazing; daily, unobtrusive maid service). Though they're perhaps a bit subdivision-esque in design (bring slippers, the handsome tile floor can be cold), this clutch of six studio-type dwellings are the perfect answer for those seeking solitude. Kind owners Gerhard and Maria Wild live on-site, though you'll rarely see them. Ditto your neighboring vacationers. You'll have to leave the kids at home (but given the chance at romance, who wouldn't want to?). Housebroken pups are welcome in two of the cottages. ■ *1603 West Coast Rd (24 km/15 miles west of downtown Sooke on Hwy 14), Sooke, BC V0S 1N0; (250) 646-2073; wild@fossilbay.com; www.fossilbay.com; $$$; MC, V; checks OK.*

Richview House ★★ François and Joan Gething's farmhouse is a three-minute walk from its famous neighbor, the Sooke Harbour House—and a pleasant, low-key alternative to the often-booked inn. Three matching guest rooms, each with private entrance, sitting area, fireplace, and deck—with a Jacuzzi and a view of the strait—are nestled upstairs in the farmhouse's B&B addition, with its handsome fir floors, hardwood furnishings, and tasteful, simple appointments. Joan's three-course breakfast can be delivered to your room. ■ *7031 Richview Dr, RR 4 (take Whiffen Spit Rd to Richview Rd, turn right), Sooke,*

BC V0S 1N0; (250)642-5520; rvh@islandnet.com; www.island
net.com/~rvh; $$$; MC, V; local checks only.

Ocean Wilderness ★ This log cabin (with a nine-room wing for
guests) is a good choice if you want to leave pretensions be-
hind. The rooms are big and filled with an odd assortment of
nice furnishings. Best rooms for the view are those on the top
floor. The place swarms with honeymooners who come pri-
marily for the location, set back in a cove with a nice trail to the
beach. There's a separate Jacuzzi in its own Japanese-style
gazebo (reserved soakings), and three rooms have private soak-
ing tubs. Guests are served a large breakfast and, come evening,
some delight in building a bonfire on the beach and grilling
salmon on the barbecue. ■ _109 W Coast Rd (10 minutes west of
Sooke), Sooke, BC V0S 1N0; (250)646-2116 or (800)323-2116;
ocean@sookenet.com; www.sookenet.com/ocean; $$$; MC, V; checks
OK._ ☐

Point No Point Resort ★ The Soderberg family owns a mile of
beach and 40 acres of wild, undeveloped, quintessentially
Northwest coastline facing the Strait of Juan de Fuca and the
Pacific. They rent 20 reasonably priced rustic cabins among the
trees on or near the cliffside, catering to those who eschew TV
and telephones and seek remote beauty and tranquillity (cabins 3 and 4 allow pets). Four of the pricier cabins have hot tubs;
four hang right over the water. The only distractions here are
the crashing of the rolling swells and the crackle of the fireplace. Firewood is supplied, but stop on the way to Point No
Point and buy your own food. Meals (dinner Wednesday though
Sunday in summer only) and afternoon tea (with mediocre pastries) are served in a convivial but tired dining room. ■ _1505
West Coast Rd, RR 2 (Hwy 14, 24 km/15 miles west of Sooke),
Sooke, BC V0S 1N0; (250)646-2020; $$$; AE, MC, V; checks
OK._ ☐

SIDNEY AND THE SAANICH PENINSULA

RESTAURANTS

Deep Cove Chalet ★★★ Scrupulously manicured lawn rolls
down to the cove. Even in winter the fragrance of an extrava-
gant English flower arrangement greets you at the door. The
service is professional without being stuffy. Pierre Koffel is one
of the most gifted chefs on Vancouver Island—and one of the
most entertaining. He's not above taking on whatever task
needs attention in the Chalet: on any given night he might be
spied clearing a table, ceremoniously decanting a bottle of wine,
or greeting a guest with the warmest of welcomes. As eccentric
as he is, regulars know he's a stickler for freshness and qual-
ity. The wine list touts lots of high-priced California bottlings.
Finish with classic crêpes Suzette, prepared tableside. ■ _11190_

Chalet Rd (40 km/25 miles north of Victoria on the Trans-Canada Hwy), Sidney; (250) 656-3541; $$$; full bar; AE, MC, V; checks OK; lunch, dinner Tues–Sun.

Cafe Mozart ★★ James and Marietta Hamilton have a fascination with Mozart; they even married on the anniversary of his death. So it's not surprising that the couple, with their Austrian ties and Swiss training, named their small European cafe after the maestro. It's stark with lots of shiny black furniture, the walls are covered with musical instruments and framed prints to match, and guess who's playing on the stereo? The food remains quite good, with such outstanding items as smoked goose breast and kiwi salad or prawns and scallops Amoureuse—a brochette marinated with fresh herbs and served with a Cognac-and-lobster-flavored butter sauce. Reservations are essential. ■ *2470 Beacon Ave (downtown, between 2nd and 3rd), Sidney; (250) 655-1554; $$; full bar; MC, V; local checks only; dinner Wed–Sun.*

Carden Street Cafe ★★ Surrounded by flowers and a deck for warm summer dining, an eclectic interior is in harmony with a Pacific Rim menu. Incredible soups in enormous rimmed bowls—spicy prawn redolent of lemongrass, or curried sweet potato—put a Western twist on an Eastern theme. Wonderful curries with fragrant basmati rice hold appeal for meat eaters and vegetarians alike. Sandwiches are both simple and exotic: muffalata with a tapenade of green and black olives, roasted red peppers, garlic, parsley, and Parmesan cheese is a divine culinary entente cordiale. Desserts are a light-as-air Pavlova and a chocolate delight. ■ *1164 Stelly's Cross Rd (corner of W Saanich Rd), Victoria; (250) 544-1475; $$; beer and wine; AE, MC, V; local checks only; lunch, dinner Tues–Sat.* &

Blue Peter Pub and Restaurant The "blue peter" is the international flag yachtsmen use to signal that their ship is about to sail. There are plenty of boats here, but the sailors are often found moored to the deck of this pub. Pub dining is fun, with fare that's a cut above average, including the requisite burgers, club sandwiches, and fish 'n' chips. The more formal dining room doesn't always meet expectations; however, the promise of sunsets in summer fills the restaurant to capacity inside and out. ■ *2270 Harbour Rd (3 km/2 miles north of Sidney), Sidney; (250) 656-4551; $; full bar; MC, V; no checks; lunch, dinner Mon–Sun (Tues–Sun in winter).*

THE GULF ISLANDS

Stretching for 240 kilometers (149 miles) up the broad expanse of the Strait of Georgia are clusters of forested islands, Canada's more remote version of the U.S. San Juans. Development on most is sparse—a shop or two at the ferry terminal, some farms and pastureland, a scattering of lodgings. Well-stocked stores, bank machines, gas stations, and even restaurants are scarce to nonexistent on most of the islands, so plan accordingly. But natural beauty and recreational opportunities abound—all in the rain shadow of Vancouver Island's mountains.

Often collectively referred to as the Gulf Islands, these gems fall into three groups. The best known and most populous are the southern Gulf Islands—Gabriola, Galiano, Mayne, Salt Spring, Saturna, and Pender—tucked along Vancouver Island's shore between Victoria and Nanaimo. Visited several times daily by ferries, the southern Gulfs offer the widest choices of inns, eateries, and enhancements. Farther north, Denman and Hornby are a short hop from the big island. East of Campbell River lies the dense grouping of the Discovery Islands—Quadra, Cortes, and Sonora—fishing and boating meccas.

BC Ferries from Tsawwassen and numerous spots on Vancouver Island service most of the islands. If you're in a car, don't expect simply to arrive at the terminal and drive aboard. The perplexing web of schedules, routes, and fares makes advance planning (and, often, reservations) a must. Or spare yourself the stress and expense by leaving your car at home; most inns and B&Bs will pick you up at the dock (and the islands are great for cycling). Interisland ferries ply the waters of the southern Gulfs, operating on a first-come, first-served basis. For more information, call BC Ferries, (604) 669-1211 or (888) 223-3779 (toll-free only within Canada).

▼

**The Gulf
Islands**

▲

THE GULF ISLANDS: SONORA

LODGINGS

Sonora Resort and Conference Center ★★ Sonora is big and it's posh—a multimillion-dollar resort catering to those who want to fish from the lap of luxury. You'll pay more than $1,000 per night (two-night minimum), but everything (well, except the professional massage) is included: airfare from Vancouver, guided fishing (fly-fishing, too), gourmet meals, drinks, fishing rods, rain gear, and more. Luxurious suites—including Jacuzzis—are grouped in six different lodges; each lodge has a common room with hot tub, steam bath, and complimentary bar. Other amenities include world-class billiard tables, a small convention center, a lap pool, and tennis courts. The kitchen is competent and serves a well-selected variety of fresh fish. Occasionally a special chef is brought in for a fête around the teppan cooker.
■ *On Sonora Island (48 km/30 miles north of Campbell River, accessible by boat or plane only); (250) 287-2869; mail: 625-B 11th Ave, Campbell River, BC V9W 4G5; $$$; full bar; MC, V; checks OK; breakfast, lunch, dinner every day (Nov–Mar).*

THE GULF ISLANDS: QUADRA

Quadra is a 10-minute ferry ride from the salmon-fishing mecca of Campbell River. Resident artists and craftspeople make the island a fine place to sleuth around for pottery and other wares. Ask in Quathiaska Cove, just up the road from the ferry dock, for a detailed map of the island, or pick one up at the **Kwagiulth Museum**, 3 kilometers (almost 2 miles) south of the ferry dock on Green Road; (250)285-3733. Their outstanding collection of Native American masks, blankets, and carvings rivals displays in the finest international museums.

LODGINGS

April Point Lodge ★★★ Between April and October this famous resort draws serious fisherfolk and celebrities from all over the world for the salmon fishing—bluebacks in April and May, chinook from April through early September, coho throughout the summer. The staff expertly pairs guides with guests. Fishing is the primary activity (although the cost of it is not included in the room rate), but April Point also offers more family-oriented activities, with bicycle and kayak rentals and opportunities for horseback riding, golf, and tennis on Quadra or in Campbell River. Lovely beach walks are accessible for about 8 kilometers (5 miles) in either direction: the lighthouse to the south, Rebecca Spit Provincial Marine Park to the east. The resort's accommodations—spacious and beautifully appointed—range from large guest houses to lodge rooms or suites to comfortable cabins; some have fireplaces, hot tubs or Jacuzzis, sun decks, kitchens, separate sitting/living areas, and water views. Reserve a month or two in advance, earlier if you want a specific accommodation. The main lodge is sunny and cheerful; the food is always very good, many of the vegetables, herbs, and edible flowers coming from the lodge's own island farm. If you're lucky, your visit will coincide with a Kwagiulth-inspired feast: staked salmon barbecued over an open fire pit and bentwood-box cooking. ■ *April Point Rd (10 minutes north of the ferry dock; follow signs), Quadra Island; (250)285-2222 or (888)334-3474; PO Box 1, Campbell River, BC V9W 4Z9; aprilpt@vquest. com; $$$; AE, DC, MC, V; checks OK (full service Apr–Oct; cabins available in off season).* ය

Tsa-Kwa-Luten Lodge ★★ The Cape Mudge band of the Kwagiulth built this contemporary lodge on 110 acres of land in the spirit of a longhouse, something immediately apparent when you walk into the great room at the lodge entrance. Huge cedar beams reflect the monumental nature of Native architecture, and Native arts are showcased. The 35 units (including three fully equipped beach cabins) all overlook Discovery Passage; some have fireplaces, some have lofts. Guests can fish for salmon in season, explore the beach with its ancient petroglyphs, hike to nearby Cape Mudge Lighthouse, or visit the Kwagiulth Museum. Mountain bikes are available for rent, and the staff can arrange boat cruises, scuba diving, kayaking, or transportation for exploring other parts of the island. Local seafood—steamed clams, three styles of smoked salmon, oysters, mussels, prawns, halibut—is the catch in the dining room. In summer, the lodge offers a weekly buffet of regional foods, with Kwagiulth dances following; breakfast is included in the off season. ■ *Lighthouse Rd (about 10 minutes south of the ferry dock; look for signs), Quadra Island; (250) 285-2042 or (800) 665-7745; PO Box 460, Quathiaska Cove, BC V0P 1N0; $$–$$$; full bar; AE, DC, MC, V; checks OK; breakfast, lunch, dinner every day (lodge open mid-Apr to Oct).*

THE GULF ISLANDS: DENMAN AND HORNBY

Tranquil and bucolic, the sister islands of Denman and Hornby sit just off the east coast of Vancouver Island. Denman, the larger of the two (10 minutes by ferry from Buckley Bay, south of Courtenay), is known for its pastoral farmlands and its population of talented artisans. The relatively flat landscape and untraveled roads make it a natural for cyclists. Hornby (10 minutes by ferry from Denman) boasts Helliwell Park, with dramatic seaside cliffs and forest trails, as well as a lovely long beach at Tribune Bay. Especially in summer, reserve Hornby accommodation before venturing onto the ferry.

LODGINGS

Sea Breeze Lodge Catch the ferry from Denman before 6pm (10pm Fridays) and stay in one of these 13 beachside cottages. Owned for more than 25 years by the Bishop family, Sea Breeze has evolved into a comfortable family retreat. Maintenance seems to be getting a little tired these days, but the resort still boasts a loyal following. From June to the end of September, cabin rates include three home-cooked meals. The rest of the year, the rustic dining room is open only on weekends, so reserve a cabin with a kitchen. Soak in the hot tub (glass-enclosed in winter, open in summer) and enjoy the view. ■ *Tralee Point, Hornby Island; (250) 335-2321; mail: Big Tree 3-2, Hornby Island, BC V0R 1Z0; $$; MC, V; checks OK.*

THE GULF ISLANDS: GABRIOLA

Although this most accessible island has become a bedroom community for nearby Nanaimo (20 minutes by ferry), it manages to remain fairly rustic and beachy. Highlight of the fine beach walks along the west shore is the **Malaspina Gallery**, weird rock formations and caves carved by the sea. You'll have to look elsewhere, however, for recommended accommodations.

THE GULF ISLANDS: GALIANO

Despite being the first stop off the Tsawwassen ferry, Galiano retains an undeveloped, secluded character. Dedicated residents have worked hard to protect the natural features that extend along the island's narrow, 30-kilometer (19-mile) length: densely forested hillsides, towering bluffs, wildflower meadows, and sheltered harbors. Pick up a map onboard the ferry (check the brochure rack) or ask at the island ferry dock.

On **Bodega Ridge**, trails wind through old-growth forests and skirt fields of often rare wildflowers; views extend as far as the Olympic Mountains in Washington. From **Bluffs Park** and **Mount Galiano**, you can watch eagles, ferries, and sweeping tides on Active Pass, and walk or cycle forested roads and trails. Most Galiano roads (and in particular the partially paved eastern route) allow you to pedal untroubled by traffic, but be aware that most roads are steep, curving, and narrow. Or explore the islands by water: contact Gulf Islands Kayaking, (250)539-2442, or Sutil Lodge, (250)539-2930, a restored 1928 fishing lodge where owners Tom and Anne Hennessy offer kayak lessons and rentals or a four-hour nature sail with gourmet picnic aboard a 46-foot catamaran. **Montague Harbour** is a lovely, sheltered bay with beaches, picnic and camping areas, boat launch, and stunning sunset views. At the northern tip of Galiano is ruggedly beautiful **Dionisio Point Provincial Park**, which offers more primitive camping.

With barely 1,200 permanent residents, Galiano has one gas station, no bank, and a few stores, including some interesting craft galleries, all clustered at the southern end. Eateries are scarce, although you'll find hearty pub food and local color at the popular Hummingbird Inn (junction of Sturdies Bay and Georgeson Bay Roads, (250)539-5472). Drop by the Trincomali Bakery and Deli, just up the hill from the ferry dock, for coffee and a bun while you peruse the latest real estate listings and dream about your island hideaway.

RESTAURANTS

La Berengerie ★ Popular with locals and visitors alike, this quaint 40-seat restaurant occupies the main floor of a two-story, wood-sided house, set back from the road amid huge cedars. Owner/chef/hotelier Huguette Benger, who learned the trade running a small hotel in Paris, offers a four-course menu that might include local venison with raisin sauce, and crisp Galiano-grown vegetables. The service and atmosphere are casual (Berger is often your server as well as your chef). Reservations are a must. In July and August, there's a vegetarian-only outdoor dining cafe on the deck out back for lazy afternoons. There are four modest guest rooms, two with private baths and all with paper-thin walls. The hot tub on the deck up at Benger's house and the good breakfast make up for any flaws. ■ *Montague Harbour*

Rd (corner of Clanton Rd), Galiano Island, BC V0N 1P0; (250)539-5392; $$; full bar; V; checks OK; lunch, dinner every day (Thurs–Sun off season; closed Nov–Mar).

LODGINGS

Woodstone Country Inn ★★★ Host and co-owner Andrew Nielsen-Pich is anxious to indulge guests, and the reasonable prices make this inn one of the best values in upper-end accommodation on the Gulf Islands. It's not on the water, but the setting, overlooking field and forest, is still perfectly relaxing. Business retreats are encouraged (one of the rooms can be converted to a small conference room); children are not. Each of the 12 rooms is spacious and bright, with tall windows, sitting areas, private baths (some with Jacuzzis or soaker tubs), and such touches as hand-stenciled wallpaper or original artwork. All but two have fireplaces. In the comfortable common room are a piano and well-stocked bookshelves. For breakfast (included in the rate), expect something rich and delicious; in the afternoon, guests regroup for tea.

The dining room here ranks high: chef and co-owner Gail Nielsen-Pich tempts with a reasonably priced table d'hôte dinner, which can include such specialties as a savory cheese and tomato strudel, breast of duck with red wine and rhubarb sauce, swordfish with caperberry butter, or vegetarian dishes such as artichoke and mushroom pie with Italian caponata. Desserts are outstanding; Galiano residents would stage a full-scale rebellion if the bread pudding with rum sauce disappeared from the menu. ■ *Georgeson Bay Rd, RR 1 (bear left off Sturdies Bay Rd, follow signs to turnoff), Galiano Island, BC V0N 1P0; (250)539-2022; $$$; full bar; AE, MC, V; checks OK; dinner every day (closed Jan).* &

The Bellhouse Inn ★★ This turn-of-the-century farmhouse, run as an inn from the 1920s to the 1960s, has been renovated by Andrea Porter and David Birchall and is an inn once again. Its 6 acres look out on Active Pass; you can watch the ferries and the whales from one of Galiano's rare sand beaches, lie in a hammock under the plum tree, or feed apples to the small flock of sheep—their wool used for the duvets at Bellhouse. Just around the corner is Bellhouse Park, an ideal location for a slow walk. The Kingfisher is the best of the rooms, with a fine view out over the pass and a Jacuzzi for overcycled muscles. Also on the property is a duplex cabin; each side has two bedrooms, a kitchen, living space, and a patio with a view. Breakfast specialty of the house is Eggs Bellhouse, eggs Benedict with salmon and shrimp standing in for ham. Arrive in style: David can pick you up from the ferry in a 1935 Bentley. You can continue the mood by playing croquet on the lawn, sipping a sherry, and sampling Andrea's tart and very English lemon curd. ■ *Farmhouse Rd (from the ferry terminal, up the hill, left on Burrill, left on Jack),*

*Galiano Island; (250)539-5667 or (800)970-7464; PO Box 16,
Site 4, Galiano Island, BC V0N 1P0; bellhouse@gulfislands.com;
www.monday.com/bellhouse; $$$; MC, V; checks OK.*

Mount Galiano Eagle's Nest ★★ Just about the time you think
you must have turned onto a logging road by mistake, you fi-
nally come upon Francine Renaud and Bernard Mignault's un-
usual home, nestled in its roost at the foot of Mount Galiano
with an eagle's-eye view of Trincomali Channel. Built from a
combination of slash wood and salvaged architectural elements,
the house sits on 75 acres of land and a whole kilometer of wa-
terfront—all abutting the Galiano Mountain Wilderness Park.
Renaud and Mignault's garden is a work of art (and a prolific
producer). And the breakfasts: melon and grapefruit served
with nasturtium blossoms, followed by waffles accompanied by
all manner of toppings. Our favorite of the three rooms is the
romantic, peach-colored upstairs chamber, now with an adjoin-
ing room that makes a suite suitable for a family. A new room
with glassed-in front looks out over the gardens and the water;
the third room has a loft. This place is an absolute treat unless
you have something against shared bathrooms or friendly cats.
■ *2-720 Active Pass Dr (call for directions), Galiano Island, BC
V0N 1P0; (250)539-2567; www.victoriabc.com/accom/mgaliano.
htm; $$; V; checks OK.*

Bodega Resort ★ On a high, westward-facing bluff in the
center of Galiano is a Western-style resort, ideal for families or
large, casual groups. There are seven two-story log chalets,
with fir and cedar paneling and touches such as lace country
curtains, custom cherrywood cabinets, and cast-iron stoves.
Each has three bedrooms, 1½ baths, a fully equipped kitchen,
and two view decks; the ranch-style unit has one bath and a
large sun deck surrounded by a rose garden. The lodge has a
conference room and a few additional rooms. For fun, there's
horseback riding, a trout pond, hiking trails, and Bodega Ridge
and Dionisio Point nearby. Turn your back on the recently
logged hillside and soak up the unobstructed views to the west.
■ *120 Monasty Rd (follow Porlier Pass Rd 22½ km/14 miles
north of Sturdies Bay to Cook Rd then to Monasty Rd), Galiano
Island; (250)539-2677; PO Box 115, Galiano Island, BC V0N
1P0; $$; MC, V; checks OK.*

THE GULF ISLANDS: SALT SPRING

Named for the cold and briny springs on the north end of the
island, Salt Spring is the largest, most populated, and most
visited of the Gulf chain. It's serviced by three ferry routes:
Tsawwassen–Long Harbour, Crofton–Vesuvius, and Swartz
Bay–Fulford. The island is known for its sheep-raising; be sure to
tour the rolling pastures on the north end (visit in the spring, and

you'll never order rack of lamb again). Salt Spring is also known as a center for arts and crafts; pick up a map of the studios from the tourist bureau, (250) 537-5252.

All roads lead to **Ganges**, the biggest and most bustling town in the Gulfs. There are more stores, services, restaurants, and galleries (not to mention tourists and cars) crammed into Ganges than exist on any other island. Even nonshoppers, however, enjoy historic **Mouat's Mall**, a rickety white-and-green building where you can browse a fine art collection at **Pegasus Gallery**; (250) 537-2421. Walk down to the water for lunch at **Alfresco's**, where you'll find marvelous bread and up to five different soupes du jour (if you're lucky, they'll have the roasted garlic and Spanish sausage); then stop next door at the **Naikai Gallery** for more art and crafts; (250) 537-4400. On Saturday mornings in the summer, wander the farmers market in the park; head any summer day to the **crafts market** at Mahon Hall on Lower Ganges Road. For local ambience, harbor views, and great pub food, visit **Moby's Marine Pub** (at the head of the harbor, (250) 537-5559).

Fulford, at the island's southern end, consists mostly of a few crafts shops, a Mexican cafe, the ferry terminal, and a decidedly laid-back atmosphere. Next to the ferry dock at the island's northern end is **Vesuvius Inn**, (250) 537-2312. The food ranges from good to so-so, but the view from the veranda fully compensates: this is one of the few ferry docks where you can park your car in line, then wander over and quaff a beer while you wait for your ship to come in.

Good camping facilities are available at St. Mary Lake, the waterfront Ruckle Provincial Park, and Mouat Provincial Park on the southeastern tip of the island, where you'll find a spectacular mixture of virgin forest, rock-and-clamshell beach, and rugged headlands. Or drive Cranberry Road up to the top of Mount **Maxwell** for a panorama of the archipelago from Salt Spring to the U.S. mainland.

RESTAURANTS

House Piccolo ★★ Some of the best food in Ganges can be had at this cozy house/restaurant right in the middle of things. The menu is European with a decidedly Scandinavian slant— Swedish meatballs and wiener schnitzel at lunch; seafood and other specialties for dinner. Try the pan-roasted breast of duckling with rosemary and cherry jus, or the roast venison with juniper and mountain-ash berries. Do not miss dessert, especially the traditional Finnish preparation of frozen cranberries with caramel sauce. ■ *108 Hereford Ave (heading north, it's at second main intersection in town, near Thrifty Foods), Ganges; (250) 537-1844; $$; full bar; AE, MC, V; local checks only; dinner Wed–Mon.*

Pomodori ★ "Eclectic" describes just about everything at this restaurant at the old Booth Bay Resort. Mirjana Vukman has converted the 1911 heritage house—the old cabins are gone and much of the land is being strata-titled—into a highly individualistic restaurant serving Mediterranean farmhouse cuisine. In two rooms are old whitewashed tables, twig chairs, wooden benches, overstuffed couches, regular dining-room chairs with woven seats, thick glass eggcups for wine glasses, well-used silver cutlery, wrought-iron ceiling fixtures, plaster busts, oyster-shell decorations: a conglomeration that shouldn't work but does. The daily menu is on a blackboard: roast tomatoes with peppers and feta in balsamic vinegar; homemade goat's cheese gnocchi, perhaps; rack of lamb with leek strudel and caramelized shallots; or rock prawns smothered in Roma tomatoes and a salsa of chiles, garlic, and lemon, with polenta. For dessert, try the baked Brie in filo with berry compote. Vukman has a colorful vocabulary, and no hesitation in using it on customers who prove insufficiently discerning. But that's part of the fun of the place: everyone has a story about their visit to Pomodori. And the view out over Booth Bay is enchanting. Vukman also rents out two upstairs rooms: linen sheets, ocean view, hardwood floors with kilim rugs, ample breakfast. ■ *375 Baker Rd (take Vesuvius Bay Rd north from Ganges and watch for Booth Bay/Pomodori sign), Salt Spring Island; (250)537-2247; $$$; full bar; MC; local checks only; dinner every day.*

LODGINGS

Hastings House ★★★★ Standing in all its gentrified splendor and imbued with an almost formidable air of genteel hospitality, Hastings House aspires to being the ultimate country retreat. It very nearly achieves that goal. The setting is postcard-perfect, the accommodations both luxurious and distinctive, and, under the watchful eye of manager Mark Gottaas, the service impeccable. It's also less snooty than it used to be under the previous owners: visitors report less of a sense that they have to live up to their surroundings. Four restored farm buildings and a cottage, surrounded by meadows, gardens, gnarled fruit trees, and rolling lawns, overlook a peaceful cove. The 12 suites are all beautifully furnished, each with fireplace or wood-burning stove, wet bar, sitting area, and touches such as down comforters and artwork. We like the Post—a charming garden cottage with antique wicker furniture. In the reconstructed barn, we prefer the Hayloft, with its bay window seat, Franklin stove, and quaint folk art. Perfect for two couples is the two-story, two-suite, stucco-and-half-timbered Farmhouse. In the Tudor-style Manor House, the two upstairs rooms have prime water views through leaded casement windows; the only drawback is that the kitchen and dining room are directly below. Included in the stiff tariff—this is the most expensive place in the Gulf Islands—are wake-up coffee and muffins delivered to your room, a delectable breakfast, and afternoon tea seated around the huge stone hearth in the Manor House. No children under 16.

Whether you stay at Hastings House or not, you should reserve a place at Marcel Kauer's table d'hôte dinner. Traditionally served in the handsome Tudor dining room, it is now also available in a less formal dining area (gentlemen, jacket and tie not required) and at a table for two right in the kitchen, where fascinated diners can watch food preparation—all part of the attempt to make Hastings House a little less formal. Dinner begins with cocktails on the lawn or in the parlor, and progresses through five expertly prepared and beautifully presented courses, all served by a knowledgeable and gracious staff. An appetizer might be junipered venison carpaccio with asparagus and sunflower oil, followed by a carrot and orange bisque, then marinated grilled sea bass with spinach and a tomato coulis. You have five choices of entree: usually a Salt Spring lamb dish, perhaps Fraser Valley duck breast with braised onions and cranberries; other entrees are dependent on the season and the mood of chef Kauer. The ingredients are local, and the fruit, vegetables, and herbs are often from the inn's own gardens. ■ *160 Upper Ganges Rd (just north of Ganges), Salt Spring Island, BC V8K 2S2; (250)537-2362; hasthouse@saltspring.com; www. hastingshouse.com; $$$; full bar; AE, MC, V; local checks only; dinner every day, brunch Sun (July–Oct).* &

The Old Farmhouse ★★★ On this island boasting nearly a hundred bed and breakfasts, the Old Farmhouse stands out. German-born hosts Gertie and Karl Fuss have turned their heritage farmhouse into an inn worthy of *House Beautiful*. Four guest rooms, each with a private bath and a patio or balcony, are charmingly decorated: brilliant whitewashed wainscoting, crisp floral wallpaper, stained-glass and leaded windows, French doors, polished pine floors, feather beds and starched duvets, a bouquet of fresh roses. It's all here, and scrupulously maintained by very professional hosts (who know everything about the island, down to all the ferry times). A gazebo, a hammock, and a couple of porch swings abet the appearance and reality of near-perfect relaxation.

Morning coffee is delivered to your room, followed by an elegant and copious breakfast at the country dining room table. There's not a detail these hosts miss: they even supply doggie bags (so you can take the inevitable extras with you for an afternoon picnic), then suggest the best picnic spot. ■ *1077 North End Rd, RR 4 (4 km/2½ miles north of Ganges), Salt Spring Island, BC V8K 1L9; (250)537-4113; $$$; MC, V; checks OK.*

The Beach House on Sunset Drive ★★ This extraordinary property a few kilometers north of Vesuvius is in a league of its own. Jon De West, an affable, gregarious expatriate from the

Vancouver rat race, and his wife, Maureen, a former instructor from the Cordon Bleu, were born to be B&B hosts. Coffee is delivered to each room in the morning. Maureen's four-course breakfasts, served around the big table in the view dining room, are legendary. The sprawling home lies right on the ocean, enjoying warm currents sweeping up from the south that heat the surf to bathtub temperature in spring and summer. Two large guest rooms are in a private wing of the main house, but best is the namesake Beach Cottage, a cozy refurbished boathouse with a wraparound deck, kitchenette, bedroom, and breathtaking sunset vista. This one has honeymoon written all over it. ■ *930 Sunset Dr, RR 1 (up Sunset Dr from Vesuvius Bay), Salt Spring Island, BC V8K 1E6; (250)537-2879; beachhouse@saltspring. com; www.saltspring.com/beachhouse; $$$; MC, V; checks OK.*

Bold Bluff Retreat ★★ Accessible only by boat (Tamar Griggs picks you up at Burgoyne Bay), Bold Bluff Retreat is the perfect antidote to even the most stress-filled day: 100 acres of rock, trees, and moss and a mile of waterfront with eagles, seals, and serenity for company. The Garden Cottage, behind the main house on a cove facing Samsun Narrows and Vancouver Island, has two bedrooms, a claw-footed tub, a kitchen, a big dining and living area, duvets, and a wood stove. Salty's Cabin, which is available from April through November, is a five-minute walk through the forest, completely private on an even tinier cove, where the tide rushes in under the deck and the cabin. You can swim here (in August); clamber along the rocks and investigate the tide pools the rest of the year. There's no power at the cabin: instead, a wood stove, a composting toilet, and an outdoor shower under the trees. Climb up the bluff and sit on a level with the eagles, looking out over the narrows to see the tide surge through. Bring your canoe or kayak and explore the shoreline. Bring your own food, and settle in for a stay completely removed from anywhere. Two-night minimum. ■ *1 Bold Bluff (accessible by boat from Burgoyne Bay), Salt Spring Island, BC V8K 2A6; (250)653-4377; $$$; no credit cards; checks OK.*

Green Rose Farm and Guest House ★★ Hosts Ron Aird and Tom Hoff have restored this 1916 farmhouse on 17 acres of orchard, meadow, and woods, and the result is classic and inviting. The decor serves as welcome antidote to the chintz-and-Laura-Ashley style of so many other B&Bs. Here, it's sort of farmhouse-nautical, sure-handedly decorated with yachting accoutrements, painted pine floors, crisp white duvets on the beds, and handsome pinstriped wallpaper. All three guest rooms have private baths. In the guests' living room are comfortable couches and a beautiful renovated fireplace. Hoff, who attended culinary school, makes a full breakfast each morning. ■ *346 Robinson Rd*

**Victoria and
Vancouver
Island**

▼

**The Gulf
Islands:
Salt Spring**

Lodgings

▲

*(take Upper Ganges Rd, stay right until Robinson), Salt Spring
Island, BC V8K 1P7; (250) 537-9927; $$$; MC, V; local checks only.*

Weston Lake Inn ★★ The owners of this contemporary farm-
house just above Weston lake—Susan Evans, Ted Harrison,
and Cass (their new sheepdog)—have become experts at fad-
ing into the background and letting their guests enjoy the com-
fortable space. Their touches are everywhere: in Harrison's
petit-point embroideries, framed and hanging in the three guest
rooms; in Evans's excellent, hearty breakfasts (with vegetables
from their organic garden); and in the blooming results of their
gardening efforts. Paintings by local artists, including Evans's
mother, hang on the walls. Outside are a series of lovingly de-
veloped gardens for guests to walk through or sit in. The cou-
ple tries to grow as much of the produce they use as possible,
and breakfast can include homemade jams, home-laid eggs,
herbs, asparagus, berries, and—in a good year—apple juice.
Evans knows and loves her island and is a fount of local knowl-
edge. Guests have access to two living rooms, one a comfort-
able lounge with fireplace, library, TV, and VCR (including a
decent collection of videos), and to the hot tub out on the deck.
Ted offers charters aboard the 36-foot sailing sloop *Malaika*. ■
*813 Beaver Point Rd (3½ km/2⅕ miles east of Fulford Harbour
ferry dock), Salt Spring Island, BC V8K 1X9; (250) 653-4311;
$$–$$$; MC, V; checks OK.*

Beddis House Bed and Breakfast ★ With all the bed and break-
fasts on Salt Spring, it should be easy to find one on the water.
It isn't, and that makes Beddis House special, since the charm-
ing white shingled-and-clapboard farmhouse—built in 1900—
and the next-door coach house—modern, but in harmonizing
style—are close to a private beach on Ganges Harbour. Hidden
away at the end of a country road, far enough from town that
you can see the stars at night and the seals and otters in the day-
time, the Coach House contains three very private rooms with
claw-footed tubs, country-style furniture, wood stoves, and
decks or balconies that look out toward the water. Breakfast
and afternoon tea are served in the old house, where you will
also find a guest lounge. ■ *131 Miles Ave (follow Beddis Rd from
the Fulford-Ganges Road, turn left onto Miles Rd), Salt Spring Is-
land, BC V8K 2E1; (250) 537-1028; beddis@saltspring.com; www.
saltspring.com/beddishouse; $$$; MC, V; no checks.*

Pauper's Perch ★ Short of the top of Mount Maxwell, this place
has one of the best views you'll find on Salt Spring: 1,000 feet
above the sea, looking out over the Gulf Islands and the Strait
of Georgia, taking in the Canadian and American mainland
mountains. This is almost sybaritic comfort: recline in the double Roman soaker tub in the Parker Suite while you watch
the flames dance in the double-sided fireplace, and look
through the wide glass windows to the misty straits far below.

The old-fashioned wedding dress on the wall above the four-poster bed leaves no doubt that this suite is intended for honeymooners. Though the magenta tones throughout are a little startling, all three rooms are comfortable and luxurious. Host Libby Jutras sometimes presents Mexican dishes for breakfast (don't worry; she'll ask first); if you're lucky, her commercial-fisherman husband will have brought something home from the sea. ■ *225 Armand Way (Fulford-Ganges Rd to Dukes Rd, up the hill to Seymour Heights, then onto Armand Way—don't give up), Salt Spring Island, BC V8K 2B6; (250)653-2030; ljutras@ saltspring.com; www.saltspring.com/paupersperch; $$$; MC, V; no checks (open Mar–Nov).*

Spindrift ★ Spindrift is that most precious of commodities in island resorts: a place on the ocean, private, secluded, quiet, with forest walks outside your door. The six ocean-front cottages on 6 acres of the Welbury Point Peninsula all have ocean views, wood fireplaces, and full kitchens. Each is named for a woman who fought for women's rights. We like Charlotte, with its ocean-front deck, and Henrietta's Rose—the most private and spacious of the cottages—but others prefer the studio duplexes Amelia and Rose, for their decks on both ocean and land side, for daylong sunshine. No telephones, no televisions, no hot tubs; just the long private stroll around the peninsula, the quiet coves ideal for watching seals and eagles, the deer and rabbits that poke curious noses toward you, and the resident dog menagerie. Adults only; quiet leashed pets are allowed by prior arrangement. ■ *255 Welbury Dr (on Welbury Point, near Long Harbour ferry terminal), Salt Spring Island, BC V8K 2L7; (250)537-5311; $$–$$$; no credit cards; checks OK.*

THE GULF ISLANDS: MAYNE

Rolling orchards and warm rock-strewn beaches abound on this rustic 13-square-kilometer (5-square-mile) island. It's small enough for a day trip, but pretty enough for a lifetime. Sink your teeth into a steak or some seafood or hoist a pint at the comfortably dilapidated **Springwater Lodge** (400 Fernhill Drive, (250)539-5521), drop by the lighthouse, watch the frantic activity as fishermen wait till the last minute to get out of the ferry's way in Active Pass, or stroll up to the top of Mayne's mountain for a view of the Strait of Georgia—and you'll begin to discover what Mayne is all about. Rent a boat from Mayne Island Kayak and Canoe Rentals, (250)539-2667. By ferry, the island's usually the second stop from Tsawwassen (1½ hours) and the fourth or second from Swartz Bay (1½ hours). Check the brochure rack on the ferry for a map of the island, in the general Mayne brochure.

Oceanwood Country Inn ★★★ This fine island inn continues to garner rave reviews for its facilities, its location, its cuisine—but most of all for the hospitality of its owners, Jonathan and Marilyn Chilvers. Truly innkeepers' innkeepers, they seem as accustomed as ever to meeting the needs of their guests, thinking of everything, right down to a written list of nearby scenic walks. Oceanwood underwent major renovations in 1995, increasing the square footage (there are now 12 rooms) and moving the dining room to face the water. The best of the accommodations is the Wisteria Suite, with a soaking tub on one of two private decks overlooking Navy Channel. Rooms have some combination of fireplaces, a soaking tub or whirlpool, decks or balconies, and views of either the water or the garden—an Oceanwood feature, with herbs, spring bulbs, roses, lavender, dahlias, and other showy seasonal performers.

The setting, with tree-webbed views of Navy Channel and distant islands, is lovely. Breakfasts are innovative and hearty, with breads baked by chef Ed Sodke and features such as homemade sausage or orange French toast with raspberry purée. At teatime, you can munch on cookies and watch the eagles, or chat with fellow guests. Sodke and the Chilverses emphasize fresh local products in their dining room: you might find steelhead on the menu, or get to taste bread baked with four kinds of wild mushrooms. Dinner is a set four-course menu, with two choices of main course. The wine list is carefully chosen, and the dining room suitably intimate. Coffee (or something off the admirable list of ports and single-malt Scotches) by the fire in the library is the perfect finale. ■ *630 Dinner Bay Rd (right on Dalton Dr, right on Mariners, immediate left onto Dinner Bay Rd; look for sign), Mayne Island, BC V0N 2J0; (250) 539-5074; oceanwood@gulfislands.com; www.gulf islands.com/mayne/oceanwood; $$$; full bar; MC, V; Canadian checks only; dinner every day. &. (limited)*

A Coach House on Oyster Bay ★ When you're lounging in the hot tub inches from the high tide line at Heather and Brian Johnston's bed and breakfast, it's difficult even to remember what stress is. These relative newcomers to Mayne seem to have grasped right away what it's all about: watching the seals and otters and eagles, strolling to the lighthouse around the corner at low tide, gazing across the Strait of Georgia at the mainland mountains. Brian, an architect by trade, has designed three fine and spacious rooms. The Landau upstairs is the best, with a private deck and a good view of the sea. The Hansom and Cabriolet Rooms are downstairs; the Cabriolet has an expansive view. Breakfast is four courses, and includes fruit, cereal, fresh-baked muffins, and a hot dish such as eggs Benedict or strawberry crêpes; coffee and tea come to your door a half hour before breakfast. Certified scuba divers, the Johnstons can advise on dive sites; they'll also arrange for kayak rentals— delivered to the door—and charter boat cruises. ■ *511 Bayview Dr (call for directions), Mayne Island, BC V0N 2J0; (250)539-3368 or (888)629-6322; $$$; MC, V; checks OK.*

THE GULF ISLANDS: NORTH AND SOUTH PENDER

North and South Pender islands are separated by a canal and united by a bridge. Much of the islands is green and rural, but a massive subdivision on North Pender was one of the catalysts for the creation of the watchdog Islands Trust in the 1970s, as Gulf Islanders worried that similar development could spell an end to the islands' charm. The population is decidedly residential; don't expect many restaurants, lodgings, or shops. Beaches, however, abound, including **Mortimer Spit** and **Gowlland Point Beach**, both on South Pender. Hike up **Mount Norman**, one of three provincial parks, for spectacular views. During the summer, you can ogle the hundreds of cruising boats that pass through **Bedwell Harbor**, location of Canadian customs. South Pender's gentle topography is especially inviting to bikers. Rent bikes at Otter Bay Marina, (250)629-6659, on North Pender, or a kayak from Mouat Point Kayaks, (250)629-6767, next door. The ferry lands at the dock in Otter Bay, where the **Stand**, (250)629-3292—an unprepossessing trailer—grills the best burgers (try the venison or the oyster burgers) around.

If you can get a group of 10 to 30 people together, **Clam Bay Country Estate**, (800)626-5955, is well worth checking out. This 100-acre farm estate with cabins and cottages in the woods and on the beach is getting excellent reviews as the location for a company or group retreat, but they accept only groups.

LODGINGS

Corbett House B&B ★ Owners John Eckfeldt and Linda Wolfe run a fine B&B in a beautiful pastoral setting. The Yellow, Red, and Blue Rooms are all equally cozy. The Yellow Room is the only one with a full bath (though water pressure is minimal) and a private balcony. The parlor is open to guests, who often gather around the fireplace for evening coffee or quiet reading. The hosts provide an ample breakfast of fresh-baked goods, fruit, coffee, and varying entrees, all generally from local sources. Long country walks fit in well here. ■ *4309 Corbett Rd, RR 1 (½ km/⅓ mile from the ferry on Corbett Rd, call ahead for directions), Pender Island, BC V0N 2M0; (250)629-6305; $$; MC; checks OK.*

Bedwell Harbour Island Resort This sprawling resort complex, in operation for decades, includes a marina, rooms, cabins, villas in a condo building, a pub, and a restaurant. And there may be more in the works: the owners and the Islands Trust have finally worked out just how much expansion will be allowed.

The resort is in an ideal South Pender location: a perfectly shel-tered cove and marina, backed by a gentle, wooded hillside, with stunning sunset views. The rooms and cabins (long a part of the resort) have wood stoves, balconies or decks, kitchens or kitch-enettes, and sweeping views. Newer, more luxurious accom-modations are available in the condominiums—two-bedroom villas done in broad pine, with fully equipped kitchens, fire-places, and decks. A breakfast package (served in the dining room) is available with the rooms that lack kitchens. Restaurant chef Nora Brulotte loves to experiment with spice—prawns in coconut curry, halibut with ginger-lime sauce—and appetizers and desserts are specialties. The waterfront pub offers typical pub fare. ■ *9801 Spalding Rd (follow Canal Rd from the bridge to Spalding, Spalding to Bedwell Harbour), South Pender Island, BC V0N 2M3; (250)629-3212 or (800)663-2899; bedwell@ islandnet.com; www.islandnet.com/~bedwell/; $$; full bar; AE, MC, V; no checks; breakfast, lunch (in pub), dinner every day (closed Oct–Mar).*

THE GULF ISLANDS: SATURNA

Rural, sparsely populated, and difficult to reach, Saturna is easily the least spoiled of the Gulf Islands. **Winter Cove Marine Park** is a naturalist's paradise—an inviting place to beachcomb, mean-der deep into forests, or picnic above the Strait of Georgia (but no camping, here or anywhere else on Saturna). A hike up **Mount Warburton** rewards you with dazzling views. Or drive remote East Point Road out to the tidal pools and sculpted sandstone of **East Point**. Saturna's big social event is the annual lamb barbe-cue, held on Canada Day (July 1).

RESTAURANTS

Saturna Lodge ★★ This resort (formerly Boot Cove) has changed names, owners, managers, and chefs in the last few years and has finally regained a reputation for reliability and good food. Jean Luc Bertrand moved over from Le Gavroche in Vancouver to fashion an elegant but casual country inn, and is now in charge of the new vineyard planted beside the lodge: watch for wine tastings once the vines begin to produce. The lovely frame lodge itself sits high on a hill overlooking an inlet and an oyster farm. Windows wrap around the simple, com-forting dining room; a crackling fire makes it even more invit-ing on a cool evening. Chef Denis Scipion entices diners to boat in from other islands to take advantage of the prix-fixe menu— one of the best deals on the islands, at $20 for three courses, three choices with each course—and the limited but well-chosen wine list. On a given evening, you might choose from prawns, salad, or soup; halibut in mustard sauce, chicken breast stuffed with spinach, or three-cheese pasta; hazelnut chocolate cake, crêpes Chantilly, or fresh herbed goat cheese.

The seven bright and sunny B&B rooms upstairs are contemporary in feel, with pleasant sitting areas and serene views. All have private baths; the honeymoon suite ($140) has a soaker tub and private balcony. Reservations for meals and accommodation are essential. There's pickup and delivery of guests from Winter Cove anchorage and the Saturna ferry dock. ■ *130 Payne Rd (follow signs from ferry), Saturna Island; (250)539-2254; PO Box 54, Saturna Island, BC V0N 2Y0; www.gulf islands.com/saturna/satlodge/; $$–$$$; full bar; MC, V; checks OK; lunch, dinner every day.*

LODGINGS

Stone House Farm Resort ★★ Derrick and Pip Woodcock have brought a touch of ye olde England to Saturna. Their white stone farmhouse on its perch above Narvaez Bay, with gardens and arbors (and most decidedly not-in-Olde-England kiwi fruit vines), Tudor construction, low ceilings, warm wood paneling, plaster walls, and period furniture transport you to a 17th-century English inn. Every window opens onto peaceful views of the bay and distant Mount Baker; a comfortable sitting room with a soapstone fireplace invites quiet contemplation. The three B&B rooms upstairs, with private baths and balconies, are pleasant and simply adorned. A cottage on the property sleeps up to eight. In the games room, you can curl up in front of the VCR or play billiards. Bring a big appetite to Pip's hearty English breakfast, wander the Woodcocks' 25 acres in search of eagles and deer, venture onto the briny deep in a rowboat, or say hello to the cow and the sheep. ■ *Narvaez Bay Rd (from ferry, take East Point Rd to Narvaez Bay Rd, follow nearly to end), Saturna Island; (250)539-2683; Box 10, 207 Narvaez Bay Rd, Saturna Island, BC V0N 2Y0; $$$; MC, V; checks OK.*

MALAHAT

LODGINGS

The Aerie ★★★ The Aerie is the successful expression of an unlikely dream: to build a European-style luxury resort on an arbutus-and-fir mountainside. Opened in the early 1990s by Maria and Leo Schuster (and expanded twice since), the resort looks as if it had been transplanted from Monte Carlo. The view over Finlayson Arm far below is magnificent on a fine day; in mist and cloud, you feel insulated from the cares of the world. The Aerie has 23 spacious rooms and suites in three buildings; some have Jacuzzis and fireplaces and most have balconies or sun decks. Look for Persian and Chinese carpets, furniture from Asia and Europe, four-poster king-size beds, and prices that soar up to $375 a night. There's an indoor pool, an outdoor tennis court, and a spa that offers services such as facials, massage, and manicures.

Though the resort has grown, the dining room still feels intimate, divided into a number of smaller rooms. Leo is the executive chef, Chris Jones the chef here; the meal is a seven-course prix-fixe affair. Guests receive a complimentary breakfast of pastries, juices, fresh fruit, cereal, and eggs with something—perhaps smoked salmon. ■ *600 Ebedora Lane (take Spectacle Lake turnoff from Trans-Canada Hwy), Malahat; (250) 743-7115; PO Box 108, Malahat, BC V0R 2L0; aerie@relaischateaux.fr; www.integra.fr/relaischateaux/aerie; $$$; full bar; AE, MC, V; no checks; breakfast, dinner every day.*

THE COWICHAN VALLEY

The Cowichan Valley is a gentle stretch of farmland and forest from Shawnigan Lake in the south to Chemainus in the north. On the way north through the valley, stop at one of the pullouts along the Malahat section of the highway for stunning views of the Saanich Peninsula and Salt Spring Island. Five wineries and a cider-maker grow grapes and apples and make their products south of Duncan; visit the **Cherry Point Vineyards** (840 Cherry Point Road, Cobble Hill, (250)743-1272), **Vigneti Zanatta** (5039 Marshall Road, Glenora, (250)748-2338), **La Vinoteca** in Duncan, which at press time was temporarily closed, **Blue Grouse Vineyards** (Blue Grouse Road, off Lakeside Road, (250)743-3834), or **Merridale Cider Works** (1230 Merridale Road, Cobble Hill, (250)743-4293) for tastings.

Wander through **Cowichan Bay**, a laid-back seaside community with restaurants (try the seafood chowder or the pie and coffee at The Bluenose, or the seafood quesadilla at The Inn at the Water), craft stores, and marinas. The Wooden Boat Society display and the hands-on exhibits at the Maritime Centre are well worth a visit.

DUNCAN

The **Native Heritage Centre** is a must-see for admirers of Native arts and crafts. In summer you can watch the creation of the famous Cowichan sweaters as they are hand-knit in one piece, their unique patterns reflecting the knitter's family designs (some even spin their own wool). The Centre also features an open-air carving shed, where Native carvers with handmade tools craft traditional 12- to 20-foot totem poles, each pole representing the carver's interpretation of a tribal design. An excellent art gallery/gift shop has many Native carvings and prints for sale. There are 66 totem poles in Duncan, both downtown and along a half-kilometer section of the Trans-Canada Highway. The Native Heritage Centre is at 200 Cowichan Way, (250)746-8119; call for schedule.

RESTAURANTS

The Quamichan Inn ★★ Set amid several acres of lawn and garden, this comfortable turn-of-the-century home has been nicely transformed into a bed-and-breakfast-cum-dinner-house. You may stay in one of three guest rooms and start your morning with an English hunt breakfast. Dinner might include escargots bourguignon, Indian curry, or roast prime rib with Yorkshire pudding. There are Fanny Bay oysters, locally produced clams, and imported wines (from a list far less sophisticated than the menu). Take your after-dinner coffee in the garden among fragrant wisteria, blooming fuchsias, and colorful dahlias. If you're staying on your boat at one of the nearby marinas, the proprietors will pick you up at Maple Bay or Genoa Bay and drop you off again when dinner's over. ■ *1478 Maple Bay Rd, RR 5 (just east of Duncan), Duncan; (250) 746-7028; $$$; full bar; AE, MC, V; checks OK; dinner every day.*

The Inglenook ★ Some things seem hauntingly familiar when you enter this pleasant house just north of Duncan: a name or two on the menu, the atmosphere, the style of cooking. And so they should, if you have been dining in these regions for a few decades. Inglenook owners Eberhard and Jeanette Hahn opened the Jaeger House in Shawnigan Lake in the mid-1970s; they've been running the Inglenook since 1990, and are as attentive and helpful as ever. You'll still see a jaeger schnitzel—venison with hunter sauce—on the menu (*jaeger*, in Germany, can mean "gamekeeper" as well as "hunter"). You'll also find medallion of ostrich from the farm next door, but since ostrich itself doesn't have a lot of flavor, why not instead try the breast of duck roasted with red currants and shiitake mushrooms, with passion torte for dessert (smaller portions available for those of lesser, um, appetites). While you're waiting for your meal, browse the paintings on the walls: they are Eberhard's work. ■ *7621 Trans-Canada Hwy (a few km north of Duncan, east of the hwy), Duncan; (250) 746-4031; $$–$$$; full bar; AE, MC, V; local checks only; dinner Tues–Sun.*

LODGINGS

Fairburn Farm Country Manor ★★ Originally an Irish millionaire's country estate, it's now a 130-acre organic sheep farm and country inn overlooking a vista reminiscent of southern England. The working-farm orientation is the charm of the place, especially for families. Six large guest rooms feature Jacuzzi tubs and comfortable furniture. There's also a six-person cottage available in summer. Guests are welcome to use two downstairs parlors (family reunions often book Fairburn) and to roam the grounds, where a sheepdog minds the lambs and a creek flows idly by. The hearty breakfast always begins with porridge. Arrange ahead for other meals. In this modern-day Eden you can witness a stunning example of how it is still possible to live off the land: almost everything you eat is organ-ically homegrown. There's a two-night minimum stay. ■ *3310 Jackson Rd (11 km/7 miles south of Duncan), Duncan; (250) 746-4637; RR 7, Duncan, BC V9L 4W4; $$–$$$; MC, V; checks OK (open Easter to mid-Oct).*

Grove Hall Estate ★★ This place is tough for the curious to find, but an undisturbed retreat for guests. Seventeen wooded acres surround this 1912 Tudor manse near Lake Quamichan. Host Judy Oliver has made spacious rooms even more so, reducing them to two and incorporating a private bath for each. The Singapore Room centers on a 400-year-old Chinese wedding bed. The Indonesian Room, decorated with pieces from Djakarta and Bali, expands into a sitting area and then onto a balcony overlooking the lake. There's also a one-bedroom cottage—originally the caretaker's cottage—decorated with antiques and in vibrant art deco colors (two-night minimum stay). Play tennis on the private court or games in the billiards room, or stroll along the quiet lakefront. A full breakfast is included in the room rates, an add-on for the cottage; Oliver serves afternoon tea or wine and hors d'oeuvres. ■ *6159 Lakes Rd (call for directions), Duncan, BC V9L 4J6; (250) 746-6152; $$$; no credit cards; checks OK.*

CHEMAINUS

Faced with the shutdown of its mill, this logging town bucked up and hired artists to paint murals telling the story of the town—all over everything. Chemainus is now a tourist attraction, and with each passing year it takes on more class and less tackiness, managing to project an air of old-fashioned small-town charm. Check out the **Dinner Theatre**—(250) 246-9820 or (800) 565-7738—with a classy buffet before a theater presentation.

RESTAURANTS

The Waterford Inn & Restaurant Ltd. ★★ You might take it for a tearoom in this town of tearooms and funky cafes, but the Waterford offers the finest dining for the thinnest dollar in this neck of the woods. Linda Maslen runs the front of house and her husband, Dwayne, is the chef. Service is personal and prompt, while the food more than lives up to its billing. You can expect to pay no more here for a lunch of delicate sole amandine, New York steak, or seafood crêpes than you'd pay elsewhere for a burger and fries. Dinner, a tad more formal, includes such specialties as seafood jambalaya, frogs' legs Provençal, ostrich steak charbroiled with an apricot and pine nut glaze, and rabbit cassis, with a black-currant and cream sauce. ■ *9875 Maple St (a few blocks from downtown), Chemainus; (250) 246-1046; $$; full bar; AE, MC, V; local checks only; lunch, dinner Tues–Sun (closed Mon–Tues in winter).* ಈ

Bird Song Cottage ★ Once you start dressing up in the Victorian hats and costumes in this cottage a block from the water, you may decide to stick around and try out for a Chemainus Theatre production. Virginia and Larry Blatchford have created an unashamedly dramatic air at their bed and breakfast, from the new veranda that looks as though it had always adorned the turn-of-the-century gingerbread house to the piano and harp music they play while guests breakfast. The downstairs room looks out on the fishpond; the low-ceilinged Hummingbird Room upstairs has an ocean view. Both of these rooms as well as the Bluebird Room have window seats and private baths. The walls are hung with paintings by Virginia's sister, one of the Chemainus mural artists. There's a four-seater swing and an arbor in the gardens outside. Virginia takes pride in her artistic and often vegetarian breakfasts; she'll get you theater tickets, too. ■ *9909 Maple St (from Chemainus Rd, go down the hill on Oak St to Maple, turn left, and look for the white cottage), Chemainus; (250) 246-9910 or (250) 246-2909; PO Box 1432, Chemainus, BC V0R 1K0; $$; MC, V; checks OK.*

LADYSMITH

RESTAURANTS

Crow and Gate Neighbourhood Pub ★ The Crow and Gate was one of the first neighborhood pubs in British Columbia. It set the standard for those that followed: modeled after a Sussex pub, it succeeds where many an imitation fails. The fireplace is big enough to roast an ox in, patrons are expected to share the long plank tables, and there's a good variety of draft beers. But the real attraction is the food: the steak and kidney pie is the very best of its kind, rich and meaty, and the pan-fried oysters are perfect: plump, greaseless, flavorful. If it's warm, take a table in the garden, and laze away the afternoon waiting for your substantial dinner. ■ *2313 Yellow Point Rd (about 13 km/8 miles south of Nanaimo), Ladysmith; (250) 722-3731; $; full bar; MC, V; no checks; lunch, dinner every day.*

LODGINGS

Yellow Point Lodge ★★★ It's said that the only way to get a Christmas reservation at Yellow Point Lodge, on a forested promontory overlooking Stuart Channel, is to wait for one of the regulars to die. And regulars there are: many visitors have been spending their vacations, their special occasions, and their getaway weekends here since their first honeymoon trip. The lodge, which replaced the original building destroyed by fire in 1985, is every bit as charming as the original. Many of the lodge rooms have private baths and two have private balconies. Most sought after, however, are the rustic beach cabins, which are available May to October (no heat). The best are the self-contained White Beach cabins overlooking the strait. Of the cabins on the beach, the Cliff Cabin is most remote, and the nicest; Eve's is the most private of the cabins in the woods. And there are the very popular beach barracks, ramshackle quarters with thin walls, built right on the shoreline rocks, with a "tree shower." Food, eaten family style at shared round tables that seat 10 or so (with no kids under 16 to detract from the mood), is good and wholesome, not fancy, with a set menu each night: roast beef on Sunday, chicken one night, salmon another. Breads and desserts are homemade. Best of all is the site: two good tennis courts, a huge seawater pool, 130 acres of meadow and forest for strolling, a hot tub, a sauna, a classic 32-foot boat for picnic cruising, and big slabs of rock jutting into the sea for sunbathing. ■ *Yellow Point Rd, RR 3 (14½ km/9 miles east of Ladysmith), Ladysmith, BC V0R 2E0; (250)245-7422; $$–$$$; MC, V; checks OK.*

Inn of the Sea Inn of the Sea's nicest feature is the scenery, especially the long stretch of beach along Stuart Channel. Deluxe suites have fireplaces, kitchens, and balconies; large parties can request rooms that connect vertically via a spiral staircase. (Many of the rooms are smaller than standard, though.) There is a pleasant dining room with a touch of formality. The owners offer a range of beach and boating activities, and you might play tennis or swim in the large heated pool at the water's edge. A pier out front allows for boat moorage, with water and power hookup. ■ *3600 Yellow Point Rd, RR 3 (14½ km/9 miles east of Ladysmith), Ladysmith, BC V0R 2E0; (250)245-2211 or (800)663-7327; $$; full bar; AE, MC, V; no checks; dinner every day.* ♿

NANAIMO

This former coal-mining town has evolved into something very different, with a clean, accessible waterfront, cultural festivals in the summer, a university campus with a marvelous view, and vastly improved dining. Nanaimo claims itself as the home of North America's first (and only) bridge built specifically for **bungee jumpers**. You can watch or jump ($95) from this 140-foot bridge above the Nanaimo River; contact Bungy Zone, (250)753-5867. Or, for $4.50, ferry over to the **Dinghy Dock Pub**, a very nautical floating bar off Protection Island. At **The Bastion**, built in 1853 and one of the few Hudson's Bay Company bastions still standing, there's a cannon-firing every day at noon in the summer. **The Nanaimo District Museum**, 100 Cameron Road, (250)753-1821, has a replica of a Chinatown street, among other displays.

Wandering. The waterfront promenade extends from the downtown harbor, past the modern seaplane terminal, through Swy-a-lana Lagoon Park (Canada's only man-made tidal lagoon), over the new pedestrian bridge, by the Nanaimo Yacht Club, and as far as the BC Ferry Terminal. The **Bastion Street Bookstore**, 76 Bastion Street, (250)753-3011, houses an impressive collection of children's books, natural history texts, guidebooks, and books by Canadian authors. On nearby Commercial Street, the Scotch Bakery concocts the namesake Nanaimo bar. Head up the hill to Heritage Mews, off Bastion Street, to sample coffee bars, restaurants, clothing shops (new and used), and home decorating emporia.

Several companies offer **wildlife and harbor tours**; Bastion City Wildlife Cruises, (250)754-8474, provides informative commentary, and fresh fruit and baked goodies too.

Parks. Pipers Lagoon, northeast of downtown, includes a spit that extends into the Strait of Georgia, backed by sheer bluffs that are great for bird-watching. Newcastle Island is an autoless wilderness island reached by ferries that leave frequently in summer and weekends year-round from behind the civic arena; it has a long shoreline trail, a trail that accommodates wheelchairs, and some fine old-growth timber.

Golf. Nanaimo and the area to the north have seen the proliferation of golf courses with a view. Most noteworthy is the **Nanaimo Golf Club**, 5 kilometers (3 miles) north of the city, a demanding 18-hole course with beautiful views of the water; (250)758-6332. Others include Pryde Vista Golf Club in Nanaimo, (250)753-6188; FairWinds at Nanoose, (250)468-7766; and Morning Star, (250)248-2244, and EagleCrest, (250)752-9744, near Parksville/Qualicum.

RESTAURANTS

The Mahle House ★★ This 1904 orange-ice house in Cedar is off the beaten track, but once discovered, it impresses guests who come back again and again. Three elegant, airy rooms are done in a country motif. The affable owners, Delbert Horrocks and his sister, Maureen Loucks, emphasize fresh, locally produced ingredients: their rabbit, venison, and free-range chicken, for example, all come from just down the road. A dozen daily specials make you salivate: thick, savory squash-and-garlic soup is a favorite, as are porcupine prawns with wasabi mayonnaise. The regular menu competes, with fresh rack of lamb with cassis or braised local rabbit with bacon, apple, onion, sage, and thyme. End the meal with one of a battery of homemade desserts—the chef dare not remove the peanut butter pie from the menu, and the homemade white chocolate/dark chocolate ice cream has many fans. Delbert is a wine connoisseur who is delighted to discuss the more than 200 varieties in his cellar. ■ *RR 4 (corner of Cedar at Hemer Rd), Nanaimo; (250)722-3621; www.island. net/~mahle/; $$–$$$; full bar; MC, V; local checks only; dinner Wed–Sun.* ⅋

The Wesley Street Cafe ★★ Jennifer Rollison prefers to do exactly what she feels like in her Wesley Street Cafe, and that's just fine with us. If you simply want a taster dessert, she'll cut the standard portion in half; she may steer you to a cheaper wine that she feels is a better choice to accompany the food you have selected. The menu is imaginative: try the trio of Fanny Bay oysters—house-smoked, peppercorn-crusted, cornmeal-crusted—or the exotic mushroom strudel with rosemary and wine cream for an appetizer, then go on to the rack of lamb with a thyme and mustard reduction, or sample one of the specials: veal chops with a port wine sauce, perhaps. Rollison has garnered a loyal local following with her emphasis on fresh local ingredients and the relaxed atmosphere—brown butcher paper over the tablecloths, muted light, gentle jazz music (live on Saturdays). ■ *321 Wesley St (from downtown, head up the hill on Bastion St, then turn left on Wesley), Nanaimo; (250) 753-4004; $$–$$$; full bar; AE, MC, V; local checks only; lunch, dinner every day.*

Delicado's ★ Don't try to keep your fingers clean at Delicado's; you can always lick off the chipotle sauce and black bean and corn salsa after you finish one of the handheld roll-ups. (These people were into wraps before they became the latest cooking rage.) The cafe/deli in an old machine shop near Heritage Mews attracts a mixed Birkenstock, yuppie, and student crowd, who savor good, solid, spicy soups or burritos and enchiladas and who can finish up with a wildberry chocolate square before they head off with a parcel of take-out. ■ *358 Wesley St (on the hill west of the hwy), Nanaimo; (250) 753-6524; $; beer and wine; V; no checks; lunch, early dinner Mon–Sat.*

La Fontana If you can't make it away for a Mediterranean cruise this year, try out Simone and J. J. Aaron's restaurant instead. These refugees from the nightclub and restaurant scene at Whistler have created a cozy Mediterranean bistro in downtown Nanaimo, with dishes from all around that sea: Italian, French, Spanish, Greek, Moroccan. Pizza and pastas are popular; try the radiatore, with chorizo and stir-fried vegetables in a light tomato cream sauce. Or you could do what the locals often do and share appetizers with a group of friends before heading off to a play or an author's reading. We like the warm Moroccan olives, the goat cheese salad, and the corn chips with crab, spinach, and feta dip. Service can be slow. ■ *99 Chapel St (off Church St, downtown), Nanaimo; (250) 755-1922; $$; full bar; AE, DC, MC, V; checks OK; lunch Tues–Fri, dinner Tues–Sun.*

LODGINGS

Best Western Dorchester Hotel ★★ Though it was built in the late 1880s on the site of an opera house and the residence of a coal baron, there's little hint of the past at this refurbished

Nanaimo landmark. That's partly because the original third
floor, with its archways and detailing, was removed after a fire
in the 1950s and replaced with utilitarian block architecture.
The rooms are tastefully decorated; many have lovely views of
the harbor and the Bastion. There have been some suggestions
that the hotel service can be abrupt. The restaurant, Café
Casablanca, offers good food at surprisingly reasonable rates
(and a view too). It is popular with locals, who venture in for the
Brie and apricot chutney in filo pastry, the braised lamb shank,
and the tresse of salmon and halibut. Service is prompt and attentive; the wine list is touted even in Vancouver. ■ *70 Church
St (at Front St), Nanaimo, BC V9R 5H4; (250) 754-6835 or
(800) 661-2449; $$; full bar; AE, DC, MC, V; no checks; break-
fast, lunch, dinner every day.*

Coast Bastion Inn ★★ All 179 rooms of this popular hotel have
views of the restored Hudson's Bay Bastion and the harbor; all
are tastefully styled in postmodern hues. There's a formal meet-
ing room, and there are a trio of formula eateries: the family-
style Cutters Cafe, the Offshore Lounge, and Sgt. O'Flaherty,
a New York–style deli. A sauna, a hot tub, and a cool tub make
the Bastion a self-sustaining entity. It's right in the middle of
things downtown. ■ *11 Bastion St (at Front St), Nanaimo, BC
V9R 2Z9; (250) 753-6601 or (800) 663-1144; $$$; AE, DC, MC,
V; no checks.*

PARKSVILLE

Parksville and the surrounding area offer good sandy beaches;
the annual Brant Wildlife Festival (early April; (250) 248-4117) and
the annual Sandcastle Competition (July); lovely picnic sites on
Cameron Lake, Englishman River Falls, and Little Qualicum Falls;
and fine fresh- and saltwater fishing. **MacMillan Provincial
Park**, 32 kilometers (20 miles) west of Parksville on Route 4 heading for Port Alberni, contains Cathedral Grove, a haunting old-
growth forest of Douglas firs and cedars that range up to 200 feet
high and up to 800 years old. Note that the new highway bypasses
the town: watch for signs indicating Parksville exits.

RESTAURANTS

Kalvas Seafood ★ Restaurants come and go in Parksville, but
Kalvas still brings them in: tourists taking a break from self-
catering, locals celebrating a birthday or taking their prairie visitors out for seafood that isn't too daunting. The big log building
by the main street of town can be noisy; avoid tables near the
kitchen, or risk feeling like you're on an airport runway. But the
food is substantial and appetizing. The shellfish platter combines a lobster tail, prawns, scallops, and oysters; oysters are a
feature here, available raw, Rockefeller, poached, smoked, or
fried. Meat-eaters can go for pheasant, or stick with the hunter

schnitzel, prepared with mushrooms, onions, cream, and brandy. With most dishes you have a choice of potato, rice, or spaetzle, a German dumpling-like noodle. ■ *180 Moillet St (at Island Hwy N), Parksville; (250) 248-6933; $$–$$$; full bar; MC, V; no checks; dinner every day.*

LODGINGS

Tigh-Na-Mara Hotel ★ Owners Jackie and Joe Hirsch's complex of log cottages, and beachfront condominiums (all with fireplaces and views of the Strait of Georgia, some with Jacuzzis) are the pick of the pack of the half-dozen resorts that sprawl along Rathtrevor Beach, with its warm water and acres of gently sloping sands at low tide. The 40 or so log cabins are spread among 22 acres of natural arbutus and fir. Twelve viewless suites and bachelor units in the lodge are surprisingly cozy, with a fireplace, fridge, full bath, and kitchenette. Oceanside condominium units range from bachelors with Jacuzzis to suites with or without. With the indoor pool and Jacuzzi, outdoor tennis courts, volleyball, and 700 feet of beachfront, you'll have no problem working up an appetite you can satisfy by dining in the resort restaurant, a comfortable log building where the menu is increasingly adventurous. For lunch, try the tempura oysters with chipotle mayonnaise and cornbread or the smoked salmon sandwich. At dinner, you may find seafood pie or buffalo with mushrooms and brandy on the specials list. Or content yourself with salmon Wellington or Asian-style tiger prawns with black bean, garlic, ginger, peppers, and roasted cashews from the regular menu. ■ *1095 E Island Hwy (2 km/1¼ miles south of Parksville on the old Island Hwy), Parksville, BC V9P 2E5; (250) 248-2072 or (800) 663-7373; tnm@island.net; www.island.net/~tnm; $$; AE, DC, MC, V; local checks only.*

▼
Parksville

Restaurants

▲

PORT ALBERNI

Head for **Alberni Harbour Quay** at the foot of Argyle Street in Port Alberni, a friendly conglomeration of restaurants, galleries, and tour operators. Drop by the **Blue Door Cafe** for a coffee and cholesterol breakfast (served 5am to 3:30pm) and a friendly slanging match with the waitresses, or see if watercolorist Penny Cote is painting at the Argyle Gallery (5304 Argyle, (250) 723-9993). In summer, the steam locomotive **Two Spot** departs from the station at the head of the quay for a tourist tour along the waterfront.

The *Lady Rose* or the *Frances Barkley* departs from the quay for Bamfield on Tuesdays, Thursdays, and Saturdays year-round, with Friday and Sunday trips during July and August. Round-trip fare is $38; (250) 723-8313 or (800) 663-7192. Early June to late September, one of the ships sails for Ucluelet and the Broken Islands Group on Mondays, Wednesdays, and Fridays. Round-trip fare is $40–44. The 5-hour cruise down Alberni Inlet and through the Broken Islands Group is breathtaking, though the quarters are a little claustrophobic if the rain is pelting down. Breakfast and lunch are served. Or take along a loaf of cheese bread from the **Flour Shop**, (250)723-1105.

RESTAURANTS

Swale Rock Cafe This bright and busy eatery at the entrance to the Alberni Harbor Quay caters to office workers on their lunch hours, boat crews ashore for a break, and tourists on the quay. At lunch seats fill quickly, but few people linger, so you won't have long to wait. Try the halibut fish and chips, or the seafood salad with crab and shrimp. Evening meals here are less rushed; specialties are the charbroiled salmon or halibut, and the mammoth seafood platter for two—seafood salad, crab, prawns, oysters, halibut, cod, and scallops. Lesser appetites are satisfied by the seafood crêpes. ■ *5328 Argyle St (near the harbor quay), Port Alberni; (250)723-0777; $$; full bar; MC, V; no checks; lunch, dinner every day.*

BAMFIELD

Bamfield is a tiny fishing village heavily populated by marine biologists. The *Lady Rose* from Port Alberni comes on Tuesdays, Thursdays, and Saturdays (and Fridays and Sundays in summer); see Port Alberni introduction. The gravel logging road in takes about two hours, and it's heavily used by logging trucks during the week, so those unused to industrial traffic might prefer to take the boat. For hikers, it's the end (or the start) of a beach-and-forest trek along the **West Coast Trail** from Port Renfrew. This rugged 77-kilometer (48-mile) stretch that was once a lifesaving trail for shipwrecked sailors can be traveled only on foot, a strenuous but spectacular five- to six-day hike for hardy and experienced backpackers. The number of hikers is now limited in order to protect against overuse and preserve the fragile ecology of the area. Reservations are by telephone: call (250)728-1282 after March 1 for the season May 1 to September 30. You can sample the trail on a day hike from the Bamfield area, where you can camp within sight and sound of the surf.

LODGINGS

Wood's End Landing Cottages ★ When Terry Giddens arrived at Bamfield a decade ago, he knew he had found his metier: building from driftwood and recycled timber salvaged from decaying Bamfield buildings. The result is Wood's End Landing in West Bamfield overlooking Bamfield Inlet, with four cottages and two suites set in 2 acres of 50-year-old perennial gardens where climbing roses twine through the salal. Each cabin has a spacious living/dining/cooking area on the ground floor and two loft-style bedrooms above. Silvery driftwood forms the stair bannister, the balcony rails, and the bed frames in the

Beachcomber Cabin; the sturdy table is made from boards salvaged from a tumbledown house. The Woodsman, high on the hill, and the Angler, the front half of the old house on the property, have the best views. The Berry Patch, a one-bedroom suite that occupies the other half of the house, is the least expensive. Bring your own food—the small store up the boardwalk has limited selection, and the cafe uncertain hours—and be prepared to entertain yourself. A rowboat is available for guests. Terry also runs nature adventure tours and fishing expeditions in his aluminum boat. No pets. ■ *168 Wild Duck Rd (across the inlet from the government dock), Bamfield, BC V0R 1B0; (250)728-3383; $$; MC, V; no checks.*

UCLUELET

Pacific Rim National Park, the first National Marine Park in Canada, comprises three separate areas—Long Beach, the Broken Islands Group, and the West Coast Trail (see Bamfield introduction)—each conceived as a platform from which visitors can experience the power of the Pacific Ocean. Long Beach, a 30-kilometer (19-mile) expanse of deep sandy beaches and rocky outcrops, backed by forest and mountains, can be reached by car from Port Alberni over a winding (take care if you're driving) mountain highway. You can hike along the beaches and across the headlands on the 19-kilometer (12-mile) stretch from Schooner Cove to Half-Moon Bay. The Broken Islands Group—more than 100 in all, at the entrance to Barkley Sound—is accessible only by boat. This area is famous for sea lions, seals, and whales, and is very popular with fishermen, scuba divers, and kayakers. For more information on the park, go to the information center at the park entrance on Highway 4 or call (250)726-4212; Pacific Rim National Park, Box 280, Ucluelet, BC V0R 3A0. Though there are no accommodations within the park, resorts and bed and breakfasts are clustered at the north end, as well as in Tofino and Ucluelet.

The Wickaninnish Interpretive Center has interesting oceanic exhibits and an expansive view; (250)726-7333, 10 kilometers (6 miles) north of Ucluelet off Highway 4. The same building houses the **Wickaninnish Restaurant**, with its spectacular setting overlooking the surf: slow service, often crowded, good food, closed in winter (not to be confused with the Wickaninnish Inn in Tofino; see review).

Whale watching. During March and April, all of the gray whales in the world—about 19,000—migrate past the West Coast. The **Pacific Rim Whale Festival** takes place between mid-March and early April; call Whalefest, (250)726-4641 or (250)725-3414, or write Box 428, Ucluelet, BC V0R 3A0 or Box 476, Tofino, BC V0R 2Z0, for information packages and festival schedule. A dozen companies run whale-watching tours from Ucluelet or Tofino.

In **Ucluelet**, pick up a sandwich at the **Grey Whale Ice Cream and Deli** (1950 Peninsula Road) and picnic on the rocks at **Amphitrite Point lighthouse**.

LODGINGS

A Snug Harbour Inn ★★   From the street at the far end of Ucluelet, Skip and Denise Rowland's Snug Harbour Inn looks like a nice, but not extraordinary, cedar-and-glass house on a suburban street. Inside, the image changes. This bed-and-breakfast inn is built atop a headland overlooking a small cove and Barkley Sound, but the view is just the icing on the cake. The living room centers on a giant wood-burning fireplace and looks out onto a deck that contains a hot tub under the stars. Powerful binoculars allow you to track Pacific marine traffic; weather-monitoring instruments let you play captain. Steep wooden steps lead to the private cove below.

Each of the four rooms follows a theme: favorites are the Sawadee Room (Thai for "welcome"—the Rowlands lived in Thailand for five years), where fabric and Thai carving create a mood reinforced by the teal Jacuzzi with its rock surround and the fireplace visible from both bedroom and bathroom; and the Atlantis, billed as a fantasy room and popular with honeymooning couples, featuring a canopy bed, Jacuzzi with cascading water, sitting room, and private deck. A continental breakfast is served, and guests can use the kitchen in the common area. And just in case you want to tour the area in style, the Rowlands will arrange for heli-tours (there's a heli-pad on premises). ▪ *460 Marine Dr (through the village and right on Marine Dr), Ucluelet, BC V0R 3A0; (250) 726-2686 or (888) 936-5222; asnughbr@island.net; www.innplace.com/inns/ A002177. html; $$$; MC, V; no checks.*

Canadian Princess Fishing Resort ★   A retired 235-foot survey ship in the Ucluelet boat basin has been converted to 30 cabins and a below-decks dining room. Unless you're nostalgic for your previous life as a salty sea dog, you would be better off bypassing the cramped cabins (one to six berths, shared washrooms) for one of the 46 much roomier, newer shoreside units. The onboard galley serves reasonable food and opens at 4:30am for breakfast during the fishing season. The *Canadian Princess*, with 10 charter boats, serves as a base for fishermen. ▪ *1948 Peninsula Rd (in the boat basin), Ucluelet; (250) 726-777; PO Box 939, Ucluelet, BC V0R 3A0; $–$$; full bar; AE, MC, V; no checks; breakfast, lunch, dinner every day (closed Oct–Feb).*

TOFINO

Literally at the end of the road, Tofino, once a timber and fishing town, has become a favored destination for Northwest and European travelers alike. Local environmentalists and artists have banded together to suspend destruction of one of the last virgin timberlands on the west coast of Vancouver Island and halt the rapid development for which the area is prime. It boasts miles of sandy beaches to the south, islands of old-growth cedar, migrating gray whales (March through April, September through October), natural hot springs, colonies of sea lions, and a temperate climate.

Tofino Sea-Kayaking Company offers guided day trips with an experienced boater and naturalist, (250)725-4222; or explore the wilds of the west coast with one of the eight charter **water taxi companies** (which are as available as their four-wheeled counterparts in New York City); or contact the seaplane company **Tofino Air Lines**, (250)725-4454, to venture out to the sea lion caves or other remote places on the west coast of Vancouver Island. **Remote Passages** offers half-day or daylong Zodiac tours in Clayoquot Sound; (250)725-3330 or (800)666-9833. The **Nuu-chah-nulth Booking & Info Centre** in the Himwitsa Building is operated by knowledgeable First Nations members and offers water taxi service, Meares Island interpretive tours, Pacific Rim National Park Eco Tours, and wilderness adventures; call (250)725-2888 or (800)665-WHALE. A number of companies offer boat or float-plane day trips to Hot Springs Cove, an oasis north of Tofino where you walk through rain forest to the mineral springs and natural rock pools—or stay overnight at **Hot Springs Lodge**, a six-room lodge operated by the Hesquiaht First Nation; (250)724-8570.

Galleries. There are two excellent Native-run galleries in town: the hand-hewn longhouse, Eagle Aerie Gallery, (250)725-3235, which displays Tsimshian artist Roy Henry Vickers's work, and the House of Himwitsa (which includes a gallery, restaurant, and lodging facilities); (250)725-2017 or (800)899-1947.

RESTAURANTS

The Pointe Restaurant (Wickaninnish Inn) ★★★★ It's hard to think of another inn that has occasioned such positive response so rapidly. The McDiarmid family opened this handsome lodging and The Pointe restaurant in 1996, and almost every restaurant critic in the Pacific Northwest has made the trek to sample chef Rodney Butters's wares. With good reason, too: Butters has set a new standard on the island's west coast, both for his food and for elegant presentation. But there's no need to bring your best bib and tucker: the staff are skilled at creating the sort of relaxed atmosphere that goes with west coast wind and waves, and there's no snootiness here. The three-course prix-fixe menu is reasonably priced at $35: it might include warm Ucluelet goat cheese and eggplant torte with oven-dried-tomato sauce; oat-crusted Arctic char and smoked bacon and spinach flan with browned maple butter; and the chef's signature dessert, a light and magnificent double chocolate mashed potato brioche with almond-caramel and raspberry sauces. Visitors are raving over the Wickaninnish potlatch, fish and shellfish in a stewed tomato broth—but it's hard to go wrong no matter what you choose. Eighty percent of the wines are from BC. The restaurant and bar command a 240-degree view over Chesterman Beach, with big cedar beams and a warm copper-topped fireplace in the center (but, frankly, most eyes are on the food).

The 46 guest rooms each have ocean views through floor-to-ceiling windows, fireplaces, private balconies, refrigerators, microwaves, and down duvets; some have Jacuzzis. Furnishings are of recycled pine, cedar, and driftwood; handmade soaps come from Salt Spring Island. ■ *Osprey Lane at Chesterman's Beach (off Hwy 4 north of Long Beach), Tofino; (250) 725-3100 or (800) 333-4604; PO Box 250, Tofino, BC V0R 2Z0; wick@ island.net; www.island.net/~wick; $$$; full bar; AE, MC, V; checks OK; breakfast, lunch, dinner every day.*

Himwitsa Lodge and the Sea Shanty Restaurant ★★
The House of Himwitsa, the First Nations–run enterprise of Lewis and Cathy George, takes in the Sea Shanty Restaurant, Himwitsa Lodge, and a Native art gallery, all in a log building in one of the best locations in town, on the waterfront right near the government dock. This is a great place to watch seaplanes take off and land (or maybe spot an occasional whale), whether you're devouring Tofino's most outstanding steamed crab on the patio of the Sea Shanty or drinking in the sunset from your private deck above. The menu is Northwest Coast with a French twist, and the crab is so good and so fresh, if this is your first time here, just order it. Upstairs there are five rooms, three with kitchens. We recommend you reserve one of the three with a harbor view; but of those, the one with a hot tub on the deck is hands-down the best (especially after a rain-soaked day on the beach). ■ *300 Main St (across from the main dock), Tofino; (250) 725-2902 (restaurant), (250) 725-3319 (lodge) or (800) 899-1947; PO Box 176, Tofino, BC V0R 2Z0; Himwitsa@Vancouver-Island-BC.Com; $$ (lodging $$$); full bar; MC, V; no checks; breakfast, lunch, dinner every day. ⅄ (restaurant only)*

Common Loaf Bake Shop ★
A perennial town meeting place to which visitors are referred long before they set foot in Tofino, this is the place to discover what's happening on the environmental front; you can pick up save-the-trees newsletters and eavesdrop—or join in—on the latest strategy. Wonderful cinnamon buns and healthful peasant bread are tempting year-round; come summer, pizza's the thing and the Common Loaf is the busiest nook in town. A fabulous seafood combo pizza is topped with smoked salmon, shrimp, and mushrooms; a European version has beer sausage and cheese. Line up at the counter for your food and drink; carry it upstairs to the log tables and benches, and get into the relax-and-crusade mood this place

inspires. ■ *180 1st St (just behind the bank), Tofino; (250) 725-
3915; $; beer and wine; no credit cards; no checks; breakfast,
lunch every day (dinner in summer only).* &

Surfside Pizza/Clayoquot Catering There you are at the seaside,
paying a small fortune for your magnificent view and wonderful room. But you're out all day at the beach; come evening, you
don't feel like cooking or, in fact, even moving. Or, say, you're
filming a movie way out in Clayoquot Sound, and you're hungry. In comes Surfside Pizza: delivered to you (by car, boat, or
plane if they must). Try the superb Sicilian-style pizza, with
tomato or pesto sauce, or maybe smoked salmon on a bagel, or
chicken Sichuan stir-fry, or salad and focaccia bread; or ask
what's good tonight (they're open until midnight) and let the
owners steer you to a decision. The pesto pizza with everything
is a local favorite. Look for the menu almost anywhere in Tofino
(but you might want to grab a menu *before* you paddle out to an
island, just in case). ■ *Delivery only; (250) 725-2882; $; beer and
wine pickup; no credit cards; checks OK; dinner Tues–Sun.*

LODGINGS

Middle Beach Lodge ★★★ Those who thought they knew the
Middle Beach should look again: there's a whole new lodge
called The Headlands, with bright, spacious rooms on the second floor and a variety of cottages built along the headland
south of the original Middle Beach lodge (now called The
Beach). This place is special: the rooms are big enough that you
can spend all your time lounging there—especially if you choose
a room or suite with a balcony—but you can also choose to be
more social in the big common room that overlooks the Pacific.
The best room at The Headlands is the front room, with a 270-
degree view; you can also choose from suites in single, double,
triplex, or sixplex cabins. Children are welcome here, but not
at The Beach—the original resort, with smaller rooms, half of
which face the forest, half the beach. From The Headlands, you
can hear the waves crashing on the rocks below, look out on a
full moon reflected on the water, or snuggle up beside the big
fireplace in the common room or the small one in your room.
At The Beach lodge, you can take a midnight stroll along the
cove. Breakfast is continental style, with lots of granola, fresh
croissants, home-baked muffins, and a good choice of fruit and
juice. In the summer, the resort serves dinner several nights a
week. ■ *400 MacKenzie Beach Rd (south of Tofino off Rt 4, look
for signs), Tofino; (250) 725-2900; PO Box 413, Tofino, BC V0R
2Z0; $$; MC, V; no checks.*

Wilp Gybuu (Wolf House) Bed & Breakfast ★★ A spotlessly
clean and shining west coast contemporary home, Wilp Gybuu
has comfortable beds and absolutely all the amenities (slippers,
candies, magazines, and thoughtful toiletries in the en suite

bathroom). And every room has its own private entrance. Hosts Wendy and Ralph Burgess have much more to offer than delicious breakfasts—sparkling conversation, for one thing. An early-morning tray of coffee is left outside your door. Wendy makes every guest feel as though he or she is the first and only guest she's ever had. Thanks. ■ *311 Leighton Way (Hwy 4 turns into Campbell, turn left onto 1st, right on Arnet Rd, left onto Leighton Way), Tofino; (250) 725-2330; PO Box 396, Tofino, BC V0R 2Z0; $$; no credit cards; no checks.*

Cable Cove Inn ★ The Cable Cove Inn is tucked away at the end of Main Street, at the north end of Tofino. Each of the six spacious, nicely appointed rooms has a tree-screened view of the cove and the ocean, a fireplace, and a private deck facing the water; five have private Jacuzzis. The Hot Tub Suite, over two floors, has a four-poster queen-size bed, a fireplace, and a hot tub on the deck outside downstairs, and a comfortable observation room upstairs. Juice and coffee come to your room in the morning; breakfast is continental style in the common area. A shared kitchen is available. ■ *201 Main St (follow Main St north to its end), Tofino; (250) 725-4236 or (800) 663-6449; PO Box 339, Tofino, BC V0R 2Z0; Cablecin@island.net; www.bbcanada.com/1138.html; $$–$$$; AE, MC, V; checks OK.*

Chesterman's Beach Bed and Breakfast ★ With its location on Chesterman's Beach, you can't go wrong: kilometers of beach stretch out at low tide to nearby islands with ever-changing tide pools. Joan Dublanko designed her home around driftwood and travelers. Each space is different and very much your own: a romantic nook for two, a separate one-bedroom cabin (no view, sleeps up to four), or the main floor of the house with its own entrance (two bedrooms, kitchen, and sauna). Showers should be quick; the hot water sometimes runs low. In the evening, you can have beach bonfires long into the night. ■ *1345 Chesterman's Beach Rd (first left after Pacific Sands Resort), Tofino; (250) 725-3726; PO Box 72, Tofino, BC, V0R 2Z0; $$$; MC, V; checks OK.*

Paddler's Inn Bed and Breakfast ★ The bookstore and espresso bar that Dorothy Baert runs downstairs in her bed-and-breakfast-cum-sea-kayaking company headquarters on the Tofino waterfront make a good place even better. The five rooms in Tofino's original hotel are as basic and lovely as Tofino itself: no phones, no TVS, white cotton sheets, down comforters, clean-lined Scandinavian furniture, shared bath. You can serve yourself from a continental breakfast bar in the kitchen, or opt for the Paddlers' Suite, where you can cook your own. Baert is a fund of information on the area; check the guidebooks in the bookstore for more info. ■ *320 Main St (just above the 1st St dock), Tofino; (250) 725-4222; PO Box 620, Tofino, BC V0R 2Z0; paddlers@island.net; $; MC, V; no checks.*

▼

Tofino

Lodgings

▲

Ocean Village Beach Resort It's too bad this motel, like the other large motels on the Esowista Peninsula, doesn't live up to its setting (could any motel?): a kilometer and a half of marvelous beach with a tiny island reached by sandbar at low tide, secluded rocky coves a short walk away where you can gather mussels. Just north of Pacific Rim National Park, Ocean Village is the best value of the on-the-beach motels. It has three rows of odd-shaped cedar-shake housekeeping units for families of four; all units face the beach. The heated indoor pool and hot tub are very welcome should you be enjoying a winter getaway vacation. In summer, minimum stay is two days and the indoor pool and hot tub are often full of children. ■ *555 Hellesen Dr (4 km/2½ miles south of Tofino, look for signs), Tofino; (250) 725-3755; PO Box 490, Tofino, BC V0R 2Z0; $$; MC, V; no checks.*

Vargas Island Inn Where else can you find an inn on an island all to itself? You're a couple of hours by kayak or a half hour by skiff from Tofino, so you should expect a few sacrifices: there aren't any refrigerators or chefs (though owner Marilyn Buckle is an expert on cookies and crab). But that's a small price to pay to be so far from civilization and so close to the warmth of a living-room fireplace, sipping tea in the wood stove–heated kitchen, steaming in the beach sauna, or sleeping in absolute silence. Upstairs there are five modest rooms. What more? There's a hobbitlike A-frame nearby (great, and cheap—for groups of six or so), not to mention all the crab or cod you (and the Buckles) happen to catch. ■ *Accessible only by water taxi or private boat from Tofino; (250) 725-3309, or call the Village Gallery, (250) 725-4229; PO Box 267, Tofino, BC V0R 2Z0; $; MC, V; checks OK.*

QUALICUM BEACH

RESTAURANTS

Old Dutch Inn It's a funny place—a motel and dining room done in a Dutch motif with a spectacular view of expansive Qualicum Bay. The 34 rooms that make up the hotel portion of the inn are comfortable enough; some feature views, and there's less traffic on the road between the motel and the beach now that the main highway bypasses these seashore communities. But the real draw is the Dutch cuisine. The chef is something of a celebrity, having cooked for Her Majesty Queen Elizabeth on two occasions when she stayed in private homes nearby. So join the other travelers, and the many retired people who lunch at the inn, for the *uitsmyter* (an open-faced sandwich topped with Dutch smoked ham and Gouda cheese), the Indonesian *loempia* (a 10-spice spring roll with pork and roast peanuts), or one of the daily specials. Be sure to save room for dessert: the traditional

Dutch apple cake with fresh whipped cream is delicious. ■ *2690 West Island Hwy (on the old Island Hwy, center of town), Qualicum Beach, BC V9K 1G8; (250)752-6914 or (800)661-0199 (from Canada only); $$; full bar; MC, V; no checks; breakfast, lunch, dinner every day.*

FANNY BAY

RESTAURANTS

The Fanny Bay Inn Ever wonder what a real roadhouse looks like? Come to the FBI, an unassuming haunt with local clientele, a fine fireplace, the obligatory collection of tankards, a dart board, and hearty pub fare (great hamburgers). Fanny Bay oysters are known up and down the coast, so what else would you eat here, this close to their home? Try them plain and pan-fried, or Cajun-style (bartender, another pint, please!). This is a low-key, convenient stop on the trek north from Parksville. Stop in for a game of darts at this classic slice of Canadiana whose blue roof is a local landmark. If you're lucky, the window table in the back will be free, and you can look out over the flats to the sea. ■ *7480 Island Hwy (south end of town), Fanny Bay; (250)335-2323; $; full bar; MC, V; no checks; lunch, dinner every day.* ⅄

LODGINGS

Ships Point Beach House ★★ Dave and Lorinda Rawlings's seaside retreat is located right on the water, with views out over Baynes Sound and the Vancouver Island mountains; the Executive Suite downstairs can be converted to a conference or special-occasion (e.g., wedding) space. Upstairs, the Periwinkle and Tequila Sunrise Rooms front the ocean, while the Teddy Bear and Captain Vancouver Rooms have a less extensive view. The Rose Garden Room looks over the—yes—rose garden. Lorinda likes to cook up a storm for breakfast: orange soufflé pancakes or a hangtown fry (oyster omelet), perhaps, with homemade breads and muffins. Evening meals, usually beef tenderloin, salmon, or other seafood on the barbecue, can be arranged in advance. Guests can go oyster-picking or clam digging on the beach, and salmon fishing and sea kayaking can be arranged. ■ *7584 Ships Point Rd (follow signs from the old Island Hwy toward the water, 8 km/5 miles north of Deep Bay), Fanny Bay; (250)335-2200 or (800)925-1595; mail: Site 39, Comp 76, Fanny Bay, BC V0R 1W0; ships@comox.island.net; www.ships point.com; $$$; AE, DC, MC, V; checks OK.*

COURTENAY/COMOX

The Comox Valley has skiing in winter, water sports in summer, some of the best restaurants around, and scenic access to Powell

River on the Sunshine Coast via the ferry *Queen of Sidney*, which leaves four times daily from Comox; (250)339-3310. Cross-country and downhill skiers flock to a pair of surprisingly decent hills: **Mount Washington**, where four chairlifts operate over 140 days of the year and there are 29 kilometers of cross-country tracks, (250)338-1386; and **Forbidden Plateau**, named for an Indian tale, a half hour from downtown Courtenay, (250)334-4744.

RESTAURANTS

La Crémaillère ★★ Locals suggest that this restaurant has become the best place in town. La Crémaillère, a two-story Tudor with a Puntledge River view, relies on the culinary skills of Michel Hubert, a menu that transforms the region's delicacies into fine French cuisine, and an ambience that offers more intimacy than the Old House down the road. Start your meal with huîtres Rockefeller (using local oysters) or an extraordinarily delicate pheasant pâté, and follow up with salmon en papillote. Opt for the plush private dining room for two if you like. The emphasis on regional products stops at the wine cellar—La Crémaillère features an excellent selection of French wines. ■ *975 Comox Rd (cross the river on the 17th St Bridge, turn left toward Campbell River, then left onto Comox Rd), Courtenay; (250)338-8131; $$$; full bar; AE, DC, MC, V; no checks; lunch Wed–Fri, dinner Wed–Sun.*

The Old House Restaurant ★★ This carefully restored pioneer-style home is set amid lovely trees and colorful flower gardens. Cedar shakes cover the outside; inside, the exposed heavy ceiling beams, large stone fireplace, copperware, and old porcelain combine to create an air of simple, rough-hewn charm. The Old House is actually two restaurants in one: a formal upstairs dining room and the more casual downstairs restaurant with latticed deck; the same menu is served in both. There's some suggestion that the Old House has been content to rest on its laurels a little and that the menu is less interesting, the food not quite as good, as it used to be. But it's still a popular place, especially at lunchtime, when you'll find a heavily female crowd sampling seafood chowder or smoked chicken and roasted cashew salad. At night, the menu goes upscale, with dishes such as a salmon fillet baked on a cedar plank with strawberry, shallot, and black peppercorn sauce, or roasted pork loin with smoked oyster stuffing—though you can also opt for barbecued ribs and a baked potato. ■ *1760 Riverside Lane (turn right toward the 17th St Bridge to Comox/Campbell River, then take the first right, just before the bridge), Courtenay; (250)338-5406; $$; full bar; AE, DC, MC, V; checks OK; lunch, dinner every day, brunch Sun.* ⅊

Greystone Manor ★ Conveniently close to the booming ski scene at Mount Washington and Forbidden Plateau, midway between the boaters' havens of Nanaimo and Campbell River, this elegant three-room B&B (each room now with private bath) is a welcome alternative to a night in a featureless Island Highway hotel. There are authentic Victoriana and other splendid period furnishings, and an English flower garden that's the envy of the island. ■ *4014 Haas Rd (5 km/3 miles south of Courtenay on Island Hwy, watch for signs), Courtenay; (250) 338-1422; mail: 4014 Haas Rd, Site 684, Comp 2, Courtenay, BC V9N 8H9; $$; MC, V; no checks.*

Quality Inn and Suites—Kingfisher Set off the highway among a grove of trees, five minutes south of Courtenay, this motel with its clean lines, cedar-shake roof, and white stucco walls is pleasing to the eye after the dozens of run-of-the-mill places that line the route. The lobby invites with a large fireplace, skylight, and hanging plants; and the rooms are spacious with striking, simple furnishings, refrigerators, and decks overlooking the pool and the Strait of Georgia. Diversions include an outdoor pool, a tennis court, and a whirlpool. Plans are afoot for a big new development here: beachfront condominium suites with fireplaces and jetted tubs, an indoor pool, and a spa. ■ *4330 S Island Hwy (8 km/5 miles south of Courtenay), Courtenay; (250) 338-1323 or (800) 663-7929; RR 6, Site 672, C-1, Courtenay, BC V9N 8H9; kingfshr@mars.ark.com; $$; AE, DC, MC, V; no checks.* &

▼

Oyster Bay

Restaurants

▲

OYSTER BAY

RESTAURANTS

Gourmet-by-the-Sea ★ The good food, reasonable prices, and oceanside location here have been attracting diners for years. Chef Michel Rabu's clientele is mostly local and loyal, sprinkled with a few newcomers who hear of his fresh leeks wrapped in prosciutto and cheese sauce, the simple watercress salad sprinkled with a lovely raspberry vinaigrette, and the mousseline of scallops in a sauce of puréed lobster reduced in whipping cream and accented with Cognac. Two lamb dishes—lamb Provençal and boneless lamb loin marinated in olive oil and herbs and then roasted—are top choices, as is the Thai prawn soup. Seafood specialties are utterly fresh: don't miss the bouillabaisse. All the tables look out to a magnificent view. The bistro menu, served in a separate dining area, offers lighter fare. ■ *4378 S Island Hwy (14½ km/9 miles south of Campbell River on Discovery Bay), Campbell River; (250) 923-5234; $$; full bar; AE, MC, V; no checks; dinner Wed–Sun.*

A town of over 20,000 people, Campbell River is big as Island cities go. It's completely ringed with shopping malls, yet the city center still looks and feels as it undoubtedly did in the '50s. Here you'll find some of the best fishing outfitters on the island; during the Salmon Festival in July, the town is abuzz with famous and ordinary sportsfisherfolk. An excellent museum is worth a visit, and you can rent a rod and reel and try your luck on the town's 600-foot-long fishing pier. For information on the region's wealth of trails and dive sites, call the Chamber of Commerce, (250)287-4636. The Museum at Campbell River, housed on the highway south of the town center, is well worth a visit for its collection of Northwest Coast Native masks and other art (470 Island Highway, (250)287-3103).

Strathcona Provincial Park, to the west, is a park of superlatives. It has Canada's highest waterfall as well as Vancouver Island's highest mountain, and offers a wide variety of landscapes to explore, including a glacier, alpine meadows and lakes, and large stands of virgin cedar and Douglas fir. Easily accessible by road (take Highway 28 from Campbell River), the park has campgrounds and boat-launching facilities at Buttle Lake, and a good lakeside accommodation, **Strathcona Park Lodge** (see review). The park also has fine trout lakes and an extensive trail system for backpacking; (250)337-5121.

▼
Campbell
River

▲

RESTAURANTS

Koto ★★ It makes sense: a very fresh sushi bar smack in the middle of fishing country. Still, it's tough to find essential Japanese ingredients in a place where most people opt for loggers' cuisine. In his pleasant Campbell River restaurant, Takeo (Tony) Maeda has single-handedly turned that around. Locals are now familiar with (and fond of) his sushi specialties and other Japanese fare from teriyaki to sukiyaki. It's a nice meal, especially if you pull into town late. There's only one sushi chef, so when it's busy (especially in summer) the service can be slow. ■ *80 10th Ave (behind the Bank of BC building), Campbell River; (250)286-1422, $$; full bar; AE, MC, V; no checks; lunch Tues–Fri, dinner Tues–Sat.*

Vincenti's ★ Michele and Rossana Vincenti have created a simple Italian family restaurant on Campbell River's main street. It isn't fancy—regulation red-checked tablecloths and minimal decor—but with Michele creating satisfying pastas and main courses in the kitchen and Rossana charming the customers out front, they seem set for a long run. Try the pasta arrabiata, with tomato, garlic, and chiles, or the beefsteak with garlic. Add a salad caprese—tomato, toasted bread, bocconcini, olive oil, and oregano—and a carafe of red wine, and you'll forget all about the rain outside. Small portions are available. When the sun is shining, you can sit on the patio and watch the wharf traffic. ▪ *702 Island Hwy (opposite Discovery Pier), Campbell River; (250) 287-3737; $–$$; full bar; DIS, MC, V; no checks; dinner every day.* ♿

LODGINGS

Painter's Lodge ★ You'd never know this was a 60-year-old fishing lodge. Burned out in 1985, the place is as modern as any in town. Old photos of big-name types and their award-winning fish line the plush lobby, the lounge, and the dark Tyee Pub, where salty fishermen seem almost out of place, but aren't. Pandemonium breaks out at 4am as the seaplanes and 50 Boston whalers zoom in to pick up the anglers and shatter any non-fisherman's sleep. Packages that include eight hours of fishing are available. Painter's includes four buildings (in addition to the main lodge) totaling 94 rooms, plus a scattering of woodland cottages. Best are rooms in the main lodge (no longer for anglers only), with two steps down into the bedroom and a porch overlooking Discovery Passage and Quadra Island. In the evening, appetizers in the lounge are our choice. Dinners may be inconsistent and service less than competent. ▪ *1625 McDonald Rd (at Island Hwy, 4 km/2½ miles north of Campbell River), Campbell River; (250) 286-1102 or (800) 663-7090; Box 460, Dept 2, Campbell River, BC V9W 5C1; obmg@pinc.com; www.obmg.com/; $$–$$$; full bar; AE, MC, V; no checks; breakfast, lunch, dinner every day (open Apr–Oct).*

Strathcona Park Lodge A week-in-the-woods experience on lovely Upper Campbell Lake: canoeing, day hikes, lake play. Amenities are simple but certainly adequate. Stay in one of the camper-style cabins with kitchens or one of the modest lodge units (a bit overpriced for what you get, but you couldn't ask for a better location). Service can be a little absent-minded, as staff are sometimes more interested in their own outdoor activities than in what you want indoors, but they are always happy to talk about recreation opportunities in the area. There are lots of outdoor programs (including rock climbing and rope courses) perfect for families seeking fresh-air fun. Paddle your own canoe or rent theirs. Family-style buffet meals at strictly regulated hours feature healthful food. Don't be late for meals—other guests have extremely hearty appetites. ▪ *At the edge of Strathcona Park, 45 km/28 miles west of Campbell River; (250) 286-8206 or (250) 286-3122; PO Box 2160, Campbell River, BC V9W 5C9; $$; full bar; MC, V; checks OK; breakfast, lunch, dinner every day (limited facilities Dec–Feb).*

GOLD RIVER

The *Uchuck III* takes you for a magnificent 10-hour chug from Gold River along Vancouver Island's broken western coastline to

the remote settlement of Kyuquot, calling at logging camps, fish
farms, and settlers' cabins en route. You spend the night at a bed
and breakfast and return the next day ($280 couple, $165 single,
all-inclusive); PO Box 57, Gold River, BC V0P 1G0; (250)283-2325.
Book these tours well in advance. Gold River also offers fine cav-
ing for spelunkers.

PORT McNEILL

The major asset of this remote spot is proximity to all things wild
and wonderful—great boating, diving, whale watching, salmon
fishing, and tide pooling.

The **U'mista Cultural Centre** in Alert Bay, an inspiring
Kwakwaka'wakw museum, is a short ferry ride from Port McNeill
and examines cultural origins and potlatch traditions. Seasonal
hours: (250)974-5403.

Whale watching is superior (July through October only)
from Telegraph Cove, 16 kilometers (10 miles) south of Port Mc-
Neill. Stubbs Island Charters, (250)928-3185, takes groups out for
morning and afternoon cruises to view the cetaceans on their mi-
gration down Johnstone Strait, and can accommodate groups of
five or more in a cluster of modest harborfront cabins. Old homes
at Telegraph Cove have been refurbished and gaily painted and
are also available for overnight stays. Kayak outfitters operate out
of Port McNeill and Telegraph Cove.

▼

Gold River

▲

LODGINGS

Hidden Cove Lodge ★★ This place is a spacious log retreat just
north of Telegraph Cove in its very own secluded cove on 9½
acres: no TVS, no phones, no fancy amenities—just acres of
woodsy, waterfront property, with nature trails for walking.
Hosts Dan and Sandra Kirby key you in to the best of what to
do in the area. Or ask them to plan something for you and they
might sign you up for a whale-watching trip, saltwater fishing,
or a no-holds-barred heli-venture (like flying out to a salmon
stream where they have exclusive fishing rights). The nine
rooms (with private baths) are simply furnished in pine, and accommodations can include continental breakfast or three meals,
all prepared by Sandy. A wraparound, window-lined lounge invites convivial gatherings, quiet reading, and frequent sightings
of herons, eagles, whales, and even bears. ■ *From Hwy 19, take
Beaver Cove/Telegraph Cove cutoff and watch for sign; (250)956-
3916; PO Box 258, Port McNeill, BC V0N 2R0; $$$; V; checks
OK (closed Oct–Apr).*

PORT HARDY

You'll feel as though you're on the edge of the world in Port
Hardy—to venture any farther north, you'll need a boat or a plane.
It's a town of loggers, fishermen, and miners—as well as travelers

stopping long enough to catch the 15-hour ferry to Prince Rupert or to travel on the newly introduced midcoast ferry to Bella Coola. The Prince Rupert boat leaves every other day in summer and once a week in winter; the Bella Coola boat comes and goes on alternate days. For information, call BC Ferries, (250)949-6722 or (888)223-3779; reservations are required. Reserve accommodation in Port Hardy ahead in summer; motels are usually packed the night before the Prince Rupert boat leaves and the night after it arrives.

The famous Edward S. Curtis film *In the Land of the War Canoes* was filmed in nearby **Fort Rupert**, a good place to purchase authentic Native American art.

Cape Scott Park. A drive of 1½ hours on a gravel road west of Port Hardy and then a 20-minute hike on a boardwalk through old-growth forest bring you to spectacular San Josef Bay. A longer and more grueling hike leads to the island's northern tip. (Don't leave valuables in the car.) For exact directions or information on hikes at the northernmost tip of the Island, contact the Chamber of Commerce, (250)949-7622.

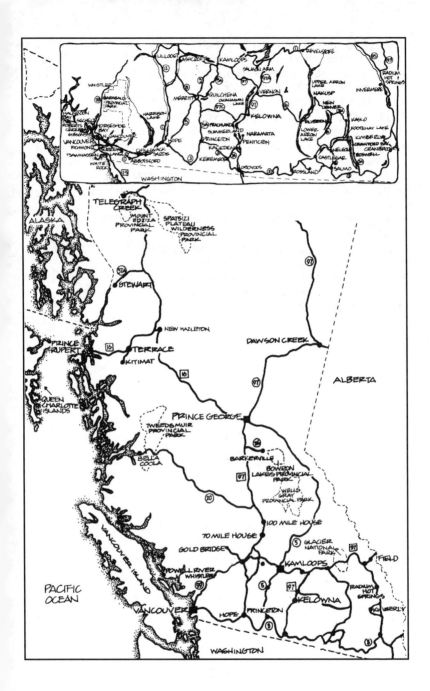

Mainland
British Columbia

*First, north from the U.S./Canada border
(skipping Vancouver) along the Sunshine Coast to
Powell River, then inland to Whistler, Lillooet, and Gold
Bridge. North to Prince George, then west to Prince Rupert
and the Queen Charlotte Islands. Then the eastward route out
of Vancouver from Fort Langley, through Harrison Hot Springs
and Hope, turning northward at Manning Provincial Park,
through Kamloops and Ashcroft. The Okanagan Valley at
Osoyoos, then north along Lake Okanagan, east to
the Rocky Mountains, turning south, then westward
again along the southern rim of the province.*

WHITE ROCK

RESTAURANTS

Giraffe ★★ This delightful, elegant neighborhood restaurant with a view of Semiahmoo Bay strongly believes in the three G's of California-style cooking—garlic, goat cheese, and grilling. As you peruse the menu, a basket of crisp pappadams is delivered to the table. Nobody will rush you through luxurious appetizers of wonton skins filled with fresh crab, or a layered torta basilica of cream cheese, pesto, pine nuts, and sun-dried tomatoes with garlic crostini. The lamb loin in mustard-herb sauce with caramelized onions is outstanding—ditto the boneless chicken breast with mixed berries. Be sure to graze the dessert menu. A heated patio opens in spring. ■ *15053 Marine Dr (across from the pier), White Rock; (604)538-6878; $$; full bar; AE, MC, V; local checks only; lunch Mon–Fri, dinner every day, brunch Sun.* &

THE SUNSHINE COAST

The southernmost end of the Sunshine Coast is only about 32 kilometers (20 miles) from downtown Vancouver, but the glittering waters of Howe Sound set the two places a world apart. It's part of the mainland, but the reliance upon two ferries makes it feel more like an island. Once a logging and fishing center, the Sunshine Coast (a bit of a misnomer) has long been a magnet for artists and writers as well as retired people. It has always been a place to relax—but relaxing, we suppose, is beginning to catch on.

Lack of direct road access has probably saved this beautiful peninsula from rapid development. Still, each year lineups are longer for the 40-minute ferry ride from Horseshoe Bay to Langdale and the even more spectacular 55-minute ride through the fjordlike waters of Jervis Inlet between Earls Cove and Saltery Bay. This northern ferry ride brings you to the final stretch of Highway 101, which continues from the ferry landing at Saltery Bay, through Powell River, to the village of Lund and the end of Highway 101.

Getting There. If you can, travel midweek to avoid lines, or at least leave Vancouver early Friday afternoon or late Saturday morning and return early on Monday. Those traveling up the entire coast or returning via Vancouver Island should ask at the Horseshoe Bay terminal about special fares (which can save you up to 30 percent) for the **circle tour** (four ferry rides). For information about getting to the Sunshine Coast, call BC Ferries, (604)669-1211, or visit their website at www.bcferries.bc.ca/ferries.

GIBSONS

Gibsons, just west of Langdale, became widely known years ago as the setting for "The Beachcombers," a once-popular TV series, and has not been slow to cash in on its fame. Seventeen kilometers (10½ miles) farther up Highway 101 is **Sechelt**, one of the fastest-growing towns in Canada. It's also home to the Sechelt Nation's cultural center, the **House of Hewhiwus**, which houses an art center and the Raven's Cry theater; (604)885-4597.

Turn off the main highway and you discover a scattering of small coastal communities where life still unfolds at a leisurely pace. **Roberts Creek**, between Gibsons and Sechelt, is a favorite haunt of painters and craftspeople.

RESTAURANTS

Chez Philippe ★★ Prior to taking over the Bonniebrook Lodge and opening Chez Philippe, chef Philippe Lacoste worked at Vancouver's Le Crocodile and Le Gavroche. The menu is French-inspired, with Northwest influences. Appetizers include traditional French offerings such as escargots. The best choices on the menu, though, are the seafood entrees: the sweet, delicate flavors of grilled prawns and scallops are enhanced by a light saffron cream sauce. Let a dessert of profiteroles, filled with ice cream rather than custard, and topped with a delicious hot chocolate sauce, finish the meal. The dining room is elegant, with a crackling fireplace and views toward the water. ■ *1532 Ocean Beach Esplanade (outside Gibsons, at Gower Point), Gibsons; (604)886-2188; $$; full bar; AE, DC, MC, V; no checks; dinner every day in summer, Fri–Mon in winter (closed Jan).*

Howl at the Moon If you find yourself aboard the ferry hungry enough to howl, forgo the notoriously bad ferry food and hold your appetite till you get to Gibsons. Howl at the Moon frightens away those hunger pains with Tex-Mex staples augmented by steaks, burgers, and six imaginative chicken dishes. We suggest you stick with the Tex-Mex (especially the spicy marinated steak or the fajita caesar). Service is prompt and friendly, portions are generous, and the water view is almost as expansive as if you were back on that ferry (balcony tables, too). ■ *450 Marine Dr (on the 1st block of Marine Dr going toward Langdale), Gibsons; (604)886-8881; $; full bar; AE, MC, V; no checks; lunch, dinner every day (closed Mon in winter).* &

LODGINGS

Rosewood Bed & Breakfast ★★ Owner Frank Tonne felled and milled the timber growing on his steep slope overlooking the Strait of Georgia and combined it with classic doors and windows rescued from older Vancouver houses. The result harks back to the spacious elegance of earlier times: an Edwardian-style mansion, but filled with light. White walls and blond wood give the house a warm, honeyed glow and provide a perfect setting for the Oriental rugs and period furniture. Of the two rooms, the suite with the bay-window bath looking out to the sea is the better. Wake up to champagne and orange juice in the airy sun room. Breakfast can be pretty much whatever the guests would like and, like dinner, is provided after prior discussion. ■ *575 Pine Rd (Pine Rd starts at Lower Rd turnoff from Hwy 101, about 6½ km/4 miles west of Gibsons), Gibsons; (604)886-4714; mail: S46 C21, RR2, Gibsons, BC V0N 1V0; www.idirect.com/~dneff/ rose.htm; $$; no credit cards; checks OK; dinner available if booked in advance.* &

Bonniebrook Lodge This simple yellow clapboard house on the water has been a guest house since 1922. Its combination of inn with campground and RV sites is not for everyone, but the owners have made extensive renovations and redecorated it from top to bottom. Of the four rooms in the inn, we prefer either of the two rooms facing the Strait of Georgia, even though they are among the three rooms that share a bath. If you prefer, there are a few campsites behind the lodge and on the water. Breakfast is served in Chez Philippe restaurant (for guests only). ■ *1532 Ocean Beach Esplanade (outside Gibsons, at Gower Point), Gibsons; (604)886-2887; mail: S10 C34, RR4, Gibsons, BC V0N 1V0; $$; AE, MC, V; no checks (closed Jan).*

ROBERTS CREEK

RESTAURANTS

The Creek House ★★ Situated in a house with a view of a tree-filled garden, Yvan Citerneschi's restaurant (he's the former chef at Vancouver's Le Bistro) is decorated simply with white walls, light wood floors, flowers on the tables, and original contemporary art. On a given night, you may choose from 10 entrees that change seasonally, such as wild boar, rack of lamb Provençal, sautéed prawns, or locally caught rabbit. Mango mousse lightens up the evening. ■ *1041 Roberts Creek Rd (at Beach Ave), Roberts Creek; (604)885-9321; $$; full bar; MC, V; local checks only; dinner Wed–Sun.* ♿

Gumboot Garden Just around the corner from the Creek House is an old maroon house with a simple sign: Cafe. Inside, a terracotta sun on the yellow-painted wall radiates warmth, and the menu shines with a strong Mexican influence. Try the Huevos Gumboot, a hearty breakfast dish that's actually available all day: eggs and black beans on a tortilla with Monterey Jack, green onions, and homemade salsa. Breads and cheesecakes are baked daily, and organic produce is used when possible. Locals come to hang out and listen to music on Friday nights as well as to eat. In keeping with the community and the clientele, service is laid back. ■ *1057 Roberts Creek Rd (junction of Lower Rd), Roberts Creek; (604)885-4216; $; beer and wine; no credit cards; checks OK; breakfast, lunch every day, dinner Thurs–Sat.* ♿

LODGINGS

Country Cottage Bed and Breakfast ★ Philip and Loragene Gaulin's charming butterscotch farmhouse is surrounded by a cherry orchard, over 100 rosebushes, and a field of grazing sheep that Loragene raises for wool. There are two lodging options here. You can stay in a pretty one-room cottage or, better, in the supremely comfortable Adirondack-style cedar lodge (sleeps six), complete with a huge river-rock fireplace and an adjacent wood-fired sauna. Two of the three queen-size beds are in lofts, so the less-dexterous will want to sleep in the adjoining cabin that is rented with the lodge. Your uncommonly genial hostess will prepare you a breakfast from what's in season, such as garden-fresh asparagus crêpes with cheese and fresh fruit, or a vegetable frittata prepared with fresh eggs from the hens-in-residence. Later on, Loragene serves afternoon tea. You're a pleasant five-minute stroll from a sandbar beach. ■ *1183 Roberts Creek Rd (14½ km/9 miles from the ferry, off Hwy 101), Roberts Creek, BC V0N 2W0; (604)885-7448; $$; no credit cards; checks OK.*

SECHELT

Pender Harbour, north of Sechelt, was once the winter head-quarters of the Sechelt Nation, and on nearby **Mount Daniel** you can see the remains of moon rings (stone circles built by Sechelt girls as they entered womanhood); Sechelt pictographs mark the cliffs above Sakinaw Lake. Garden Bay is a scenic small village on the north side of Pender Harbour; the deck of the pub at the Garden Bay Hotel is a fine place to while away a summer afternoon.

If you want to get away from the highway and explore the attractions of the Sunshine Coast in more intimate detail, there are plenty of hiking trails, from pleasant strolls to all-day tramps and longer. The really adventurous might launch an overnight expedition to climb 6,200-foot **Mount Drew**, known locally as Red Top.

A visit to **Princess Louisa Inlet** and **Chatterbox Falls** is considered by many to be the loveliest trip in British Columbia. You can take a day trip via boat (contact Sunshine Coast Tours, care of Lowe's Resort in Pender Harbour; (604) 883-2456 or (800) 870-9055), or you can drop in via floatplane (contact Coast Western Airlines at (604) 684-8768 in Vancouver or (604) 885-4711 in Sechelt).

RESTAURANTS

Blue Heron Inn ★★ One of the nicest places to dine on the Sunshine Coast is the Blue Heron. Partly for the waterfront view (and the blue herons, of course), partly for the food (fresh clams, a carpaccio-style roast loin of veal, grilled salmon with fennel, smoked black cod), and partly for the relaxed vacation-like atmosphere (fresh flowers, local art). Gail Medeiros makes sure you're comfortable and well fed. What more could you want on the Sunshine Coast? (Reservations are highly recommended.) ■ *Porpoise Bay Rd (turn right at lights at Wharf St and right at Porpoise Bay Rd), Sechelt; (604) 885-3847 or (800) 818-8977; $$; full bar; AE, DC, MC, V; no checks; dinner Wed–Sun.*

HALFMOON BAY

The scenery gets wilder as you proceed north, and one great side trip (and a good excuse to stretch your legs) is a 2-kilometer (1¼-mile) round-trip hike to **Smugglers Cove Marine Park**, just west of Halfmoon Bay. It's an easy (even for toddlers) and wonderful way to experience the coastal wilderness firsthand.

LODGINGS

Halfmoon Bay Cabin ★★ This rustic yet luxurious 120-square-meter (1,300-square-foot) waterfront cabin is the place you want to be. Forever, if possible. For a weekend, if nothing else. It's a private retreat that has everything you might want, from a massive stone fireplace to an outdoor shower on the deck. Surrounded by an English country garden, it sits on a hill overlooking its own beach, complete with private cabana. It's a one-of-a-kind place, for a one-of-a-kind weekend for you or yourself and a few friends. Midweek off-season rates are a bargain for such a stay. ■ *8617 Redroofs Rd (6 km/3¾ miles north of Sechelt), Halfmoon Bay; (604) 688-5058; mail: No. 502 - 1290 Burnaby St, Vancouver, BC V6E 1P5; perbus@portal.ca; www2. portal.ca/~perbus/; $$$; MC, V; checks OK.* &

Lord Jim's Resort Hotel ★ Operated by Coast Hotels, Lord Jim's aspires to be *the* resort on the Sunshine Coast (although new finds have recently leaped ahead of it). In some respects, it succeeds: the location, on a quiet, lovely cove, is prime, and the facilities include a restaurant, an outdoor pool, and a picnic area. The resort can also arrange for activities like fishing, scuba diving, and kayaking. Most of the rooms have been recently redecorated and are attractive, with handsome furnishings and colorful bedspreads (no phones or TVs); the rooms that have not been updated are definitely in need of attention. Unfortunately, though, the overall impression is still closer to utilitarian motel than sumptuous resort. The cabins are plain and simple, but they do have sun decks with views of the water. Food at the restaurant is only average, although we've heard good things about their treatment of fresh fish in season. And the restaurant, with its bird's-eye view of Thormanby Island, is a great place for an afternoon or evening drink. ■ *Turn left on Mercer Road off Hwy 101 north of Sechelt, Halfmoon Bay; (604) 885-7038 or (888) 757-FISH; mail: RR2 Ole's Cove Site, C-1, Halfmoon Bay, BC V0N 1Y0; $$; AE, MC, V; no checks.*

MADEIRA PARK

LODGINGS

Ruby Lake Resort ★ The Sunshine Coast is dotted with a surprising number of freshwater lakes. One of the most scenic is Ruby Lake, toward the north end of the Sechelt Peninsula. Here you'll find the Ruby Lake Resort, a collection of 10 units facing a private lagoon just across Highway 101 from the lake. An engaging family from Milan, Italy, bought the resort and rebuilt the cottages, which are now nicely furnished and have full kitchens and TVs. It's a great place to bring the kids. Paddleboats are available, and you can rent canoes to take out onto the lake. The resort's restaurant has been drawing accolades for its Northern Italian cuisine and fresh seafood. Plan to come in time for the eagle feeding at 6pm each evening. ■ *Hwy 101 north of Madeira Park; (604) 883-2269 or (800) 717-6611; mail: C65 S15, RR1, Madeira Park, BC V0N 2H0; rubylake@spinn.com; www. triumphsystems.com/rubylake/local.html; $$; full bar; MC, V; no checks; breakfast, lunch, dinner every day (summers), dinner Thurs–Sun (winters; closed Jan).*

EGMONT

One of British Columbia's greatest natural sites, **Skookumchuck Rapids** near Egmont, lies at the northern tip of the peninsula. Here onlookers (and kayakers) time their visit with the incoming tide to see (and surf) the largest saltwater rapids on the West Coast. Tide changes trigger huge iridescent turquoise waves in this bottleneck, resulting in whirlpools that can be 18 meters (59 feet) across and 2½ meters (8 feet) high. Getting there requires a relatively easy 8-kilometer (5-mile) round-trip hike (2 kilometers or 1¼ miles off Highway 101 toward Egmont), but it's not recommended for kids. Timing your visit with the tides is everything; locals know how to calculate the best viewing time, so call Bathgate's Store and Marina, (604) 883-2222, or the Sechelt Visitor Infocentre, (604) 885-3100.

From here, take the quaint 50-minute ferry trip from Earls Cove through the fjords of Jervis Inlet to Saltery Bay and eventually Powell River.

POWELL RIVER

Powell River is two boat rides from Vancouver, or one from Comox on Vancouver Island; for ferry information, call (604) 485-2943 in Powell River, or the general BC Ferries number at (604) 669-1211. Powell River, home to about 18,000 people, has traditionally been dependent on the logging industry for its survival. Tourism is developing quickly, thanks in part to an abundance of sun and clear water. The clarity of the water makes this a diver's paradise, while the nearby mountains have plenty of uncrowded trails. For hikers, the 13-kilometer (8-mile) **Inland Lake Trail** is fully accessible by wheelchair; for details, contact the Powell River Visitor Infocentre at (604) 485-4701.

RESTAURANTS

jitterbug cafe ★ Walk through Haida-born landscape artist April White's Wind Spirit Gallery and you'll find Powell River's best bet for eats: the jitterbug cafe. It's a stylish little place that's open only during the high season, but it's a fine stop for a simple meal based on local ingredients (and some wonderful homemade breads). At lunch, try the chicken sandwich on their warm cheese bread, or the smoked salmon pasta. Dinners are a little more involved: sautéed chicken breast with an Asiago cheese sauce, or a delightful and delicious lemon linguine. On a warm afternoon, sit out on the deck that looks over the Strait of Georgia, Texada Island, and Vancouver Island beyond—a true lift to the spirits. ■ *4643 Marine Ave (in the Wind Spirit Gallery, on the west side of Hwy 101), Powell River; (604) 485-7797; www.windspirit.com; $$; MC, V; no checks; lunch, dinner Tues–Sat in summer (call ahead for hours during shoulder season; closed Oct–Apr).*

LODGINGS

Beach Gardens Resort ★ Sitting on a protected section of the Strait of Georgia, the Beach Gardens Resort is a mecca for scuba enthusiasts, who come for the near-tropical clarity of the water and the abundant marine life (there's a dive shop on the premises). Off-season, the resort is often booked with conventions and seminars. There are tennis courts and a fitness center with an indoor swimming pool. A marina accommodates boaters. The rooms are comfortable—nothing sensational, except the views of all that water. Divers prefer the less expensive cabins without views. The dining room offers reliable seafood entrees—and a fantastic caesar salad. The popular pub upstairs has a great view. ■ *7074 Westminster Ave (½ hour north of Saltery Bay ferry on Hwy 101), Powell River, BC V8A 1C5; (604) 485-6267 or (800) 663-7070; bgardens@www.coc.powell-river.bc.ca; $$; full bar; AE, DC, MC, V; no checks; breakfast, lunch, dinner every day.* ᬗ

LUND

The pristine waters of **Desolation Sound** are surrounded by steep evergreen mountains—all teeming with the wildest of wildlife. The Sound sits at the end of British Columbia's Sunshine Coast, the northernmost terminus of Highway 101 (which begins 24,000 kilometers or 14,880 miles south in Chile). The tiny hamlet of Lund is only 153 kilometers (95 miles) north of Vancouver, but it takes a good five hours (including two BC ferry rides) to get there. Lund is the jumping-off point for boat trips to Desolation Sound and **Copeland Islands Marine Park**. You can also rent scuba gear and kayaks here, at Good Diving and Kayaking; (604) 483-3223. This is pretty rugged terrain, home to martens, bobcats, and black bears. As well as excellent hiking, this last stretch of the coast has some fine lakes for canoeing—but it's worth the drive from Powell River just to sample the blackberry cinnamon rolls at **Nancy's Bakery** on the town pier; (604) 483-4180.

LODGINGS

Desolation Resort *[unrated]* Early reports suggest that this northernmost resort on the Sunshine Coast is also bound to become the most desirable. Bernd and Josephine Scheifele's stunning waterfront cabins on Okeover Inlet are unlike any others on the Sunshine Coast. In fact, they're unlike anything. An absence of building codes in this remote land has allowed the Scheifeles to create five whimsical houses (five more are planned for 1998). Inspired by cartoons on napkins, these hobbitlike towers were built from scratch out of local yellow cedar, red cedar, alder, and fir—resulting in tree-house-like efficiency on a high-end budget. Everything is class, right down to bed frames of old-growth fir, the deep-green duvets, the plum-colored couches, and the techy glass and hammered-iron dining tables. But all of this is only the beginning. The rest is beyond, in Desolation Sound Marine Park, and accessible only by boat, four-wheel drive, or on foot (with a guide and a gun—for grizzlies). Sea kayaks and canoes are available, and there are plenty of local guides for other adventures. Three-night minimum in high season. ▪ *Take Malaspina Road off Hwy 101 south of Lund; (604)483-3592; mail: C-36, Malaspina Rd, RR2, Powell River, BC V8A 4Z3; $$$; MC, V; checks OK (winter closures possible).*

SQUAMISH

Forty-five minutes north of Vancouver, you'll find the logging town of Squamish, where the granite cliffs, stiff winds, challenging golf courses, and exciting white water are now playgrounds for outdoor adventurers. The mammoth granite **Stawamus Chief** is one of the top 10 climbs in North America. And rock climbers on Smoke Bluffs outside Squamish are lobbying for these walls to be the first Canadian national park designated for climbers. Windsurfers set sail at Squamish Spit. Golfers tee up at the **Furry Creek Golf and Country Club**; (604)922-9461. Nearby is **Shannon Falls**, the fifth-largest waterfall in the world, which plummets 335 meters (1,100 feet) past granite and air. For more outdoor information (especially for rafting and kayaking expeditions), call the Sunwolf Outdoor Centre; (604)898-1537.

LODGINGS

Howe Sound Inn and Brewing Company ★ This perfect stop on the way up (or down) from Whistler gives you a close-up view of Stawamus Chief—and a peek at the revitalization of Squamish. Owners Dave Fenn and Stephen Shard have a one-of-a-kind inn (and what we like to call the roadhouse for the 21st century). Where else but in Squamish would you find an inn with a granite climbing wall, a brewpub, and a high-tech conference room (which doubles as the town's Friday-night movie house)? Moreover, this casual place (which often houses the crews of the many films produced in the Vancouver area) features an eatery that could hold its own almost anywhere, with beyond-brewpub fixings such as crab and cod cakes with Asian noodles, or a roasted pork tenderloin with garlic mashed potatoes. The 20 rooms are simple, warmed by the use of wood and window seats. What else? Homemade baked goods (thanks to the spent wheat from the brewery), lockers for your gear, and a reading lounge (with maps) to plan your next outing. ▪ *37801 Cleveland Ave (at the south end of town), Squamish; (604)892-2603 or (800)919-ALES; PO Box 978, Squamish, BC V0N 3G0; hsibrew@ mountain-inter.net; www.mountain-inter.net/hsibrew; $$; full bar; AE, MC, V; checks OK; breakfast, lunch, dinner every day.*

Whistler Resort, nestled at the base of two mountains in British Columbia's Coast Range, two hours from Vancouver and 32 kilometers (20 miles) from the Pacific, has been ranked the number-one ski resort in North America year after year, the number-one snowboarding mountain in the world, and the favorite international destination of Japanese skiers. And no wonder. Whistler/Blackcomb now logs 7,000 skiable acres (with hopes to double that in the near future) and has the greatest vertical drop in North America (5,280 feet). But that's only winter sports; Whistler is now a great four-season getaway—although May and October still have a definite off-season feel.

Reservations. Advance reservations are recommended for all lodging and restaurants in Whistler Resort. Call **Central Reservations**, (604) 932-4222; from Vancouver, (604) 685-3650; from the US and Canada (except BC), (800) WHISTLER. Many of the rooms in the area, as well as condos, are owned by different management companies. All 18 management companies can be reached through the (800) WHISTLER number. A few of the bigger companies include Whiski Jack Resorts, 4227-14 Village Stroll, (604) 932-6500 or (800) 944-7545; Whistler Chalets, 45211 Sunshine Place, (604) 932-6699 or (800) 663-7711; and Powder Resort Properties, (800) 777-0185. For a simpler, less expensive stay, ask about the hotels, pensions, and "budget" (remember, it's all relative in Whistler) accommodations outside the Village. Come summer, prices are drastically reduced. Ask Central Reservations about cancellations and special deals; they change daily.

Surrounded by 10,000-foot peaks of the **Garibaldi Provincial Park**, Whistler offers some of the finest skiing in the world. Canada's first resort municipality is actually four cheek-by-jowl communities (and two mountains): **Whistler Village** (the main hub); **Blackcomb Resort** (often called the Upper Village); **Creekside** (the southernmost community, at the original base of the mountain); and **Village North** (the northernmost development, which consists of MarketPlace and TownPlaza). Walking in the pedestrian-only villages used to have a faintly European feel, with sociable plazas, broad boulevards, and unexpected alleyways. With continuous expansion, though, the resort now buzzes with the sound of multimillion-dollar condo and retail construction, including fine-art galleries and designer stores. Fortunately, it's all being designed with access to the mountain in mind, making it almost easier to get around the resort on foot than by car. Free shuttle buses link each village, and local buses connect outlying residential areas to each village.

Friendly rivalry between Whistler and Blackcomb Mountains has always paid off for the skier, with high-speed lifts and gondolas added regularly. Now, with North America's premier four-season resort developer, Intrawest, owning both mountains,

▼

Whistler

▲

the competition's gone, but the the expectation is that the two will work in harmony. The whole idea is to create a village-to-village ski resort similar to some of the larger European resorts.

For **cross-country skiers**, 30 kilometers of cross-country trails begin just outside Whistler. **Adventure activities** include snowboarding (rentals and lessons are available) and paragliding (lessons with or without skis), dogsledding, snowshoeing, snow-mobiling, ice-skating, and sleigh rides. Call the **Whistler Activity and Information Centre**, (604)932-2394, for info on all of the above.

Meadow Park Sports Centre, (604)938-PARK, is Whistler's outstanding aquatic, ice, and fitness facility (6 km/3¾ miles north of the village). Call ahead for public sessions and available court times. Racquet rentals available.

Although diehards can ski Horstman Glacier until mid-August, come **summer**, do what the locals do. Turn your back on the Village square and head for the hills (many consider the area to be the best mountain-biking terrain in the world), the lakes (this is where board-sailing started in Canada), or the rivers (by raft, canoe, or kayak). Whistler Outdoor Experience Co., (604)932-3389, is a broker for guided hikes, mountain horseback riding, river rafting, and fly-in fishing.

Golfers can try the scenic Arnold Palmer–designed Whistler Golf Club, (604)932-3280, rated one of the best courses in the world by *Golf* magazine, or the Robert Trent Jones Jr. link-course at Chateau Whistler (open to the public); (604)938-2092. Another possibility is Nicklaus North, a Jack Nicklaus–designed course in the Green Lake area; (604)938-9898. Beyond Whistler, there is Pemberton's Big Sky (north of Whistler; a *Golf Digest* favorite); (604)894-6106.

The good times roll year-round in Whistler, with daily street entertainment, and many festivals from June to September (call (800)WHISTLER).

RESTAURANTS

La Rua (Le Chamois) ★★★ Mario Enero runs a stylish but comfortable restaurant in Le Chamois Hotel that prides itself on snap-of-the-finger service and a great wine list. The food, *nuova* Mediterranean with Asian tweaks, is some of the best in Whistler. No one makes better lamb (Washington State rack with mint pesto, or a shank set atop root vegetables and lentils). There's always an unforgettable vegetarian dish, plus inspired pastas, including butternut squash agnolotti with smoked duck in a curry cream sauce. Save room for homemade biscotti and chocolate truffles. When the weather warms up, cigar aficionados hit the deck for ice wine or port with their stogies. ■
4557 Blackcomb Way (Upper Village on Blackcomb), Whistler; (604)932-5011; $$$; full bar; AE, DC, MC, V; no checks; lunch (summer only), dinner every day. &

Quattro at the Pinnacle ★★★ Right from the start everyone loved Antonio Corsi's cornerstone restaurant in the Pinnacle Hotel. It's upbeat, it's vibrant, and it's innovative. Fireplaces and fish tanks add a flicker to the room. Corsi is passionate about food the way any good Italian should be; and here is where you'll see that passion, simple and uncomplicated, come through (Antonio especially loves to make a fuss about Valentine's Day). The hefty antipasto plate lets you nibble through an array of appetizers, the best of which are the mozzarella wrapped with prosciutto and radicchio and the prawns with saffron and Cognac. His deboned, somewhat spicy Cornish game hen is sensational, as is the roasted rack of lamb in a mustard-and-herb crust. The staff is knowledgeable, friendly, and attentive. Desserts are stunning. The Pinnacle Hotel (relatively small by Whistler standards) looks pretty, but the 80 or so rooms (all with kitchen, Jacuzzi, and fireplace) are unremarkable ■ *4319 Main St (in Village North Town Plaza), Whistler, BC V0N 1B4; (604) 905-4844; $$$; full bar; MC, V; no checks; dinner Wed–Sun.* &

Rim Rock Cafe and Oyster Bar ★★★ Filled to the rafters with a hip local crowd, this cozy cafe with a stone fireplace has been dishing out great food for years. Split into two levels (smokers in the downstairs bistro), the Rim Rock is housed in an unprepossessing hotel near Creekside. Bob Dawson and Rolf Gunther's restaurant is remarkable proof that fresh seafood and wondrous cuisine are not anomalies in the mountains. The freshest seafood appears on the specials sheet in all sorts of lovely incarnations. Begin with opulent oysters (raw, of course) with vodka, crème fraîche, and caviar. For the main event, choose a delicacy such as herb-infused salmon, or pan-fried mahi-mahi in an almond-ginger crust. The Death by Chocolate can make grown men cry. Service is top-drawer—knowledgeable without the airs. Reservations are a must in high season. ■ *2101 Whistler Rd (just north of Creekside, in the Highland Lodge), Whistler; (604) 932-5565; $$$; full bar; AE, MC, V; no checks; dinner every day.*

Val d'Isère ★★★ Whether you want to impress or be impressed, you can't go wrong in this sophisticated dining room while superchef Roland Pfaff presides over the kitchen. Reserve a window seat and start with a slice of onion pie, a dense, smoky specialty, or warm smoked salmon in a horseradish cream. For entrees it's difficult to decide between the artful baked sea bass (topped with layers of potato slices arranged like the scales of a fish) served with a pinot noir sauce, and Pfaff's classic loin of venison with sautéed chanterelles. An extravagant chocolate gâteau with a peppermint sauce towers over the dessert plate. ■ *4433 Sundial Pl (upstairs in St. Andrews House in Whistler Village), Whistler; (604) 932-4666; $$$;*

full bar; AE, DC, MC, V; no checks; dinner every day (closed after Canadian Thanksgiving and open before American Thanksgiving). 点

Caramba ★★ For great food, upbeat atmosphere, and value in Whistler, you really can't beat this fun, boisterous, Mediterranean-influenced restaurant. Owned by Mario Enero (La Rua), Caramba reflects his ability to wow even those on a modest budget. He has combined high-energy service with big, soul-satisfying portions of spaghetti and meatballs, roasted rosemary chicken, and pesto pizza. The open kitchen, Mediterranean tones, and alderwood-burning pizza ovens lend a warm, casual tone. Can't stay? They'll whip up a take-out meal in 15 minutes. Kids and adults both love the platter of three-cheese macaroni after a strenuous day on the slopes. ■ *12-4314 Main St (in Village North), Whistler; (604) 938-1879; $$; full bar; AE, MC, V; no checks; lunch, dinner every day.* 点

Il Caminetto di Umberto ★★ The ubiquitous Umberto Menghi is at Whistler, too. Not surprisingly, this is a great place to go in the Village. Few things can top fresh pasta and a bottle of red wine after a day on the mountains—even though the tables at this perennial favorite are too tightly packed together, and noise from the bar and cabaret interferes with table talk. Aside from pasta, aim for the specials such as the roasted rack of lamb with rosemary and garlic crust. Leave room for the mascarpone cheesecake. The less expensive **Trattoria di Umberto** in the Mountainside Lodge, (604) 932-5858, appeals to the more informal crowd for pasta and rotisserie items. ■ *4242 Village Stroll (across from the Crystal Lodge), Whistler; (604) 932-4442; $$; full bar; AE, DC, MC, V; no checks; dinner every day.* 点

Joel's Restaurant at Nicklaus North ★★ Joel Thibault is a well-known name around Whistler: he used to own Chez Joel, and he was one of the promoters behind the famous moonlight cross-country ski and fondue dinners. Joel's is Joel's most recent venture and, as far as we've been able to ascertain, one of his best yet. Located in the grand Nicklaus North Clubhouse at the Nicklaus North Golf Course on the edge of Green Lake, Joel's is quickly becoming *the* restaurant to escape to. For indeed, it's here (a few miles from the Village) where you can probably still get a last-minute reservation and a buttery beef tenderloin so good that you'll find yourself forgiving the few flaws in the appetizers. Any night will feel like a special night here, and you'll probably leave on a first-name basis with Joel himself. Ask about the special golf-and-dine package. ■ *8080 Nicklaus North Blvd (5 km/3 miles north of the Village at the Nicklaus North Clubhouse), Whistler; (604) 932-1240; $$-$$$; full bar; AE, MC, V; no checks; breakfast, lunch, dinner every day.* 点

▼

Whistler

Restaurants

▲

Ristorante Araxi ★★ A cousin to Vancouver's top-rated CinCin, Araxi is one of the long-standing culinary cornerstones of Whistler. And in a town with more restaurants per square foot than probably any other in the country, sticking around that long has got to say something for consistency. Not to mention that it's located right in the middle of all the action in Whistler Village Square; few vantage points can compare with Araxi's summer patio. Other showy establishments have nudged Araxi off the A-list (and service, at times, seems off). Still, the Italian menu speaks with a decidedly West Coast accent (and chef Martin Pearsall does an excellent job with fresh fish, free-range fowl, and house-made pastas), the wine list (awarded several Vancouver International Wine Festival medals) is impressive (though pricey), and the ever-entertaining scenery makes Araxi a Whistler experience worth sliding into. ■ *4222 Village Square (central Whistler Village), Whistler; (604) 932-4540; araxi@ whistler.net; $$$; full bar; AE, DC, MC, V; no checks; lunch, dinner every day May–Oct, dinner only Dec–April (closed in Nov some years).* &

Sushi Village ★★ Sushi Village is a welcome reprieve from the boundless activity that Whistler offers. A civilized hush hovers over this refreshingly modest Japanese eatery, where the staff is knowledgeable, gracious—and familiar year after year. Consistently delicious sushi and sashimi plates are prepared by animated experts at the counter. It's straightforward and dependable. Reservations accepted only for parties of four or more. Tatami rooms available. ■ *4272 Mountain Square (2nd floor of the Westbrook Hotel), Whistler; (604) 932-3330; $$; full bar; AE, DC, MC, V; no checks; lunch Wed–Sun, dinner every day (lunch weekends only in the off-season).* &

Wildflower Restaurant (Chateau Whistler Resort) ★★ Splashy Chateau Whistler's restaurant melds a big, formal space with folk-arty touches, and likewise combines a seriousness about food with personable service. The menu uses local Northwest products—free-range chicken and lamb, wild salmon, and organic beef and produce—to create inspired dishes. Unfortunately, ever since Bernard Casavant's departure to open his own restaurant we've heard conflicting reports on preparation. We know this place is capable of much more consistency, and we're withholding a third star until the consistency returns. Dip into the Bailey's chocolate fondue for dessert. Brunch on Sunday is as popular as ever. ■ *4599 Chateau Blvd (at the base of Blackcomb Mountain, in the Chateau Whistler), Whistler; (604) 938-8000; $$$; full bar; AE, DC, DIS, JCB, MC, V; no checks; breakfast, lunch, dinner every day, brunch Sun.* &

Chateau Whistler Resort ★★★ This is the place to see and be seen on Whistler—where a valet parks even your ski gear. The Paul Bunyan–sized country mansion has 342 rooms (would Canadian Pacific construct anything small?). And by the time this book is published, there will be another 221 rooms, additional conference space and a ballroom, a spa for all, and a much-anticipated rooftop garden. The lobby, appropriately termed the Great Hall, sets you amid a floor of giant slate slabs covered with oversize hooked rugs, walls decorated with huge hand-painted stencils of maple leaves, two mammoth limestone fireplaces, and a 40-foot-high beamed ceiling. The funky collection of folk-art birdhouses and the weathered antique furnishings warm up the grandeur. The health spa is especially swank: a heated pool flowing both indoors and out, allowing swimmers to splash away under the chairlifts or soak in the Jacuzzi under the stars. Other services include a multilingual staff, baby-sitting, room service, and a dozen or so shops. The rooms themselves are a bit disappointing (if only because your expectations are set so high in the grand entrance); nonsuite rooms are surprisingly small and undistinguished. Do it right and ask for a "ski-view" room. On-site eateries include a market-style deli scheduled to open soon (at press time) and the Wildflower Restaurant, of course (see review). ■ *4599 Chateau Blvd (at the base of Blackcomb Mountain), Whistler, BC V0N 1B4; (604) 938-8000 or (800) 606-8244; $$$; www.cphotels.ca; full bar; AE, DC, MC, V; no checks.* &

▼

Whistler

Lodgings

▲

Durlacher Hof ★★★ Erika and Peter Durlacher's reputation as Whistler's most welcoming and generous innkeepers is legendary. Their Austrian pension, complete with edelweiss, is a short ride from the base of Whistler-Blackcomb. Erika's painstaking attention to detail is evident in the cozy après-ski area and the immaculate rooms (some suites) with hand-carved pine furniture and comfortable beds with goose-down duvets. Part Mother Teresa who just can't do enough for her guests and part sergeant-major with a relentless drive for perfection, Erika never stops. Her lavish breakfasts are a new reason to smile when the sun comes up—a groaning sideboard holds a feast. And then come the special dishes she prepares for each guest—perhaps *Kaiserschmarren* (pancakes with stewed plums) or *Apfelschmarren* (fresh apple pancakes). From the moment the Durlachers get up before daybreak to bake the day's bread, to the last cup of *Glühwein* late at night, sharing the Hof with them is a joy. Want to be closer to the skiing action? Ask about the studio in Whistler. ■ *7055 Nesters Rd (call for directions), Whistler; (604) 932-1924; PO Box 1125, Whistler, BC V0N 1B0; $$$; MC, V; checks OK.* &

Brew Creek Lodge ★★ This quiet, welcome retreat is a few kilometers south of Whistler. The lodge and two guest houses are decorated in a rustic style with post-and-beam timber frames, a huge stone fireplace, and nostalgic touches of Westernalia here and there. The lodge rooms, with sumptuous beds covered with folksy spreads, are spacious (room 1 is best; room 6 is over the kitchen). Still, Brew Creek is best suited for groups— a wedding party, a family reunion, or a corporate retreat—who reserve the entire place or at least a portion of it. Our favorite is the guest house (sleeps 13), which comes with a tiny tree house (a romantic little loft). The Brew House is a bit smaller and more whimsical. A separate conference room is built right over trout-filled Brew Creek. Food is prepared with advance notice (and they're often catering dinner here); the breakfasts we've sampled have been satisfying, if a tad ordinary. Affable hosts Peter and Susan Vera are hard at work keeping the lodge a comfortable, attractive place to stay, and Cinders the cat is hard at work finding a warm lap in which to lie. ■ *1 Brew Creek Rd (off Hwy 99 just before Brandywine Falls, south of Whistler Village), Whistler, BC V0N 1B1; (604)932-7210; $$$; MC, V; checks OK.*

Edelweiss ★★ Ursula and Jacques Morel's nonsmoking Bavarian-style guest house, run in a European fashion, is one of our favorites of its kind (there are many around Whistler). The eight rooms are simple and spotlessly clean, with down comforters and private baths. Extras include the shared sauna, Jacuzzi, and massage on request. Jacques (a former competitive skier) and Ursula cook a variety of ample breakfasts with an international flair in their sunny breakfast room. Twice a week, the Morels prepare a *raclette* (a fonduelike treat made by wrapping melted cheese over ham, baby potatoes, bread, or vegetables) and serve it with French or German wine and espresso drinks. Regardless of how brisk, friendly, and accommodating the hosts are, if you're in a room downstairs, you may be awakened by guests clomping around in their ski boots. If your legs are strong, Edelweiss is within walking distance of the Village; otherwise hop the free bus (it's easier than parking in the Village). ■ *7162 Nancy Greene Dr (1½ km/1 mile north of Whistler Village in White Gold Estates), Whistler; (604)932-3641; PO Box 850, Whistler, BC V0N 1B0; $$; AE, MC, V; checks OK.*

Le Chamois ★★ The inviting six-story condo/hotel, though somewhat dwarfed by its gargantuan neighbor, the Chateau Whistler, has a sleek, refined air. Rooms are large and aesthetically pleasing. Light, airy, and clean, they feature simple Euro-style furnishings and smart color schemes. Single bedrooms are built to accommodate four; each includes a living area with either a fold-out sofa bed or a Murphy bed (and every room has a view, though views of the mountain cost more). During high season the hotel requires a minimum stay of two nights. All rooms are privately owned—this is a condo, after all—and some have special touches (one three-bedroom corner suite is furnished with a piano). The compact kitchens feature all the things you need for preparing quick meals—microwave, refrigerator, and all utensils—and some larger suites offer full kitchens (with dishwasher and oven). Downstairs, the elegant La Rua (see review) specializes in Mediterranean cooking with a continental flair, while more casual dining can be found at the new Thai One On. Other amenities include a small conference area, a very small fitness room with an outdoor pool, and a Jacuzzi. Children under 12 stay free. ■ *4557 Blackcomb Way (at the base of Blackcomb Mountain), Upper Village; (604) 932-8700 or (800) 777-0185; PO Box 1044, Whistler, BC V0N 1B0; powder@ whistler.net; www.whistler.net/resort/accommodation/powder; $$$; AE, DIS, MC, V; no checks.* &

Delta Whistler Resort ★ It may not be as grand as Chateau Whistler nor as chic as Le Chamois, but the Delta Whistler Resort, one of the oldest and largest hotels in the area, offers nearly 300 rooms, restaurant and bar, exercise room, swimming pool, and dome-covered year-round tennis courts. It's a good spot for hosting business meetings, with a conference area that holds 400. The rooms are plain; the better ones offer kitchen, fireplace, balcony, Jacuzzi, minibar, and view of the mountains. A snazzy restaurant, Evergreens, has some innovative items on its menu. Delta sits just 45 meters (50 yards) from Whistler's base lift. Dogs allowed. ■ *4050 Whistler Way (Whistler Village), Whistler; (604) 932-1982 or (800) 515-4050; PO Box 550, Whistler, BC V0N 1B0; www.deltahotels.com; $$$; AE, DC, MC, V; checks OK; breakfast, lunch, dinner every day, brunch Sun.* &

Edgewater ★ While many Whistler accommodations make the most of every priceless square foot of space, the 12-room Edgewater sits in solitude on its own 45-acre Green Lake estate. It's an incredible piece of real estate—especially for a place with so few rooms. And it's probably the only hotel in Whistler where you see more wildlife than life that is wild. For all its potential, the personally run place is actually quite low-key and impersonal. There's no lobby; the rooms (though they're serviceable, and each has its own outside entrance) are small and unimpressive; and aside from the lakeside Jacuzzi, there's a noticeable lack of fireplaces and common areas. That said, those who come to Whistler for its natural beauty will want to stay here. The small lakefront restaurant, with its odd assortment of furnishings, serves surprisingly excellent food, especially the venison (fresh from a herd of reindeer in Lillooet). Outstanding service. Desserts are an afterthought. ■ *8841 Hwy 99 (6 km/ 3¾ miles north of the Village, across the street from the Meadow Park Sports Centre), Whistler; (604) 932-0688; Box 369, Whistler,*

*BC V0N 1B0; jays@whistler.net; www.whistler.net/accomadate/
edgewater/; $$$; full bar; MC, V; checks OK; dinner every day.* &

Timberline Lodge ★ The enormous moose head that greets you
in the lobby tells you this place has more of a sense of humor
than the other big-name hotels. It's the kind of spot where you
feel at home clomping into the lobby in your ski boots to warm
your toes by the enormous fireplace. Timberline's 42 rooms are
simple and rustic, with four-poster beds of rough-hewn wood;
some rooms have fireplaces, others have balconies, and a few
have both. A heated pool and Jacuzzi are also available. Full
breakfast included during ski season. ■ *4122 Village Green (ad-
jacent to Conference Center in Whistler Village), Whistler, BC
V0N 1B4; (604) 932-5211 or (800) 777-0185; powder@whistler.
net; www.whistler.net/resort/accommodation/powder; $$$; AE,
MC, V; no checks.* &

Delta Whistler Village Suites [*unrated*] Big is in here, and big
this place will be, with 207 suites and mini-condos at the edge
of Village North (which, if Delta Whistler has a say in the matter, will no longer be on the edge of town). Plans for plenty of
shops, three restaurants (ranging from an upscale steakhouse
to a breakfast-all-day spot), and perhaps Whistler's biggest nightclub (Garfinkels, open at press time) should persuade many
guests that they don't need the main village for an evening of
entertainment. ■ *4308 Main St (in Village North), Whistler, BC
V0N 1B4; (800) 268-1133; www.deltahotels.com; $$$.*

Pan Pacific [*unrated*] The Pan Pacific's first resort lodge has
nabbed one of the most desirable locations in Whistler/Black-
comb, just a few paces from the gondolas at the base of each
world-class mountain. Scheduled to open in December 1997,
each of the 121 suites will have fireplace, kitchenette, and all the
amenities we've come to expect in a top-rated hotel chain. In ad-
dition, the eight-story Pan Pacific, designed by Intrawest, the
continent's premier four-season resort developer, plans to dis-
tinguish itself with a year-round outdoor pool and spa, slope-
side dining, and an on-premises laundry facility. ■ *4320 Sundial
Crescent (at the base of Whistler and Blackcomb gondolas),
Whistler, BC V0N1B4; (604) 905-2999 or (800) 327-8585; $$$;
AE, MC, V; checks OK.* &

LILLOOET

Two hours north of Whistler, you'll happen upon Lillooet—mile
0 of the Cariboo Gold Rush Trail. The best thing about Lillooet is
getting there (via either car or train). The BC Rail line between
Lillooet and Vancouver is a vital link to the outside world for the
loggers, miners, and farmers who live in remote areas of the
Coastal Range. It's also one of the most scenic stretches in British

Columbia, along pretty Howe Sound and into the jagged mountains. The route links Vancouver with Whistler, Lillooet, and Prince George; call BC Rail at (604)984-5246.

FRASER RIVER

The **Fraser River** and the **Thompson River** descend from Lillooet and Ashcroft, respectively, to converge in Lytton, where they squeeze through the narrow walls of the **Fraser River Canyon**. British Columbia's mightiest river rushes through the canyon for 85 kilometers (53 miles). While you can get a good sense of the river's whirling rapids from the many roadside pullouts, it's far more fun to pick a hot summer day, call a raft company, and buy some wet thrills. The Thompson River (from Spences Bridge to Lytton) throws the most whitewater rapids. The biggest fleet on the river is Kumsheen Raft Adventures Ltd. (Main Street, Lytton; (250)455-2296). Other companies located in Spences Bridge include Ryan's Rapid Rafting, (250)458-2479, and River Rogues, (250)458-2252.

Downriver the popular **Hell's Gate Airtram** (Boston Bar; (604)867-9277) takes you (from May to mid-October) across the boiling waters of the Fraser at the narrowest part of the gorge to a good restaurant with salmon chowder. The river turns sharply west and calms at Hope, 140 kilometers (87 miles) east of Vancouver.

GOLD BRIDGE

LODGINGS

Tyax Mountain Lake Resort ★ In the wilderness of the Chilcotin Range about 160 kilometers (100 miles) north of Vancouver, floatplanes are seen dropping incoming guests off at Tyaughton Lake's dock and taking fishermen up to Trophy Lakes; a helicopter out back lifts thrill-seekers to enjoy heli-anything (heli-skiing, heli-hiking, and even heli-fossil hunting). But it's not all a high-tech adventure: you can be just as happy canoeing, gold panning, ice-skating, or horseback riding. There are 29 suites (with beamed ceilings, balconies, and down-filled quilts) in the freshly hewn spruce-log lodge. We prefer one of the large chalets (each with kitchen, loft, and a balcony overlooking Tyaughton Lake and the mountains), especially for longer stays. Unless you're in a chalet, you take all your meals in the dining room (where the undistinguished food is overpriced). Other amenities include a sauna, an outdoor Jacuzzi, a game room, aerobics classes, and workout rooms. The only thing an active person might run out of in this paradise is energy (or money). ■ *If you're without a floatplane, take the train from Vancouver to Lillooet—the resort will pick you up; (250)238-2221;*

mail: General Delivery, Gold Bridge, BC V0K 1P0; $$$; AE, MC, V; no checks.

70 MILE HOUSE

LODGINGS

Flying U Guest Ranch ★ It's a working ranch, ideal for families who like to ride horses. There are 25,000 acres to explore, and cattle to round up if you wish. Back at the lodge, you can stay in log cabins and canoe on the nearby lake, and you'll dine at the over-140-years-old main building. Movies, bonfires, hayrides, or square dancing often follow the meal. A saloon features a full bar and snacks. Rates are all-inclusive (three meals a day, all you can chow). ■ *20 km (12 miles) east of 70 Mile House on N Greenlake Rd; (604) 456-7717; Box 69, 70 Mile House, BC V0K 2K0; $$; MC, V; checks OK.*

100 MILE HOUSE

LODGINGS

Best Western 108 Resort ★ At what seems like the edge of civilization (8 miles north of 100 Mile House, hence its name), this full-scale Best Western–owned resort covers thousands of acres of rangeland. Among its offerings are horseback riding, a large pool, tennis courts, mountain biking, canoeing, and a topflight 18-hole golf course. In winter, the cross-country skiing is some of the best in the Northwest, with over 200 kilometers of well-maintained trails. The restaurant has a fine view of the golf course and of two lakes, but the menu is limited to the expected. ■ *Hwy 97, 13 km (8 miles) north of 100 Mile House; (250) 791-5211; Box 2, 108 Mile Ranch, BC V0K 2Z0; $$; AE, DC, MC, V; no checks.*

BARKERVILLE

Billy Barker found lots of gold here in 1862, whereupon the town became the largest city north of San Francisco; then it became a ghost town; and now it's a place revived for the tourist trade. It's not bad, really: restored old buildings and a general store full of 5-cent jawbreakers and lots of retro '60s (that's 1860s) goods. The whole place shuts down after the summer season (May to September).

Canoe Trips. Six lakes form an amazingly regular rectangle in **Bowron Lake Provincial Park**, a scenic and challenging setting for a 120-kilometer (75-mile) canoe trip (with a number of portages in between). Plan on spending a week to 10 days. For outfitting, a couple of lodges just outside of Barkerville offer canoe, paddle, and life-belt rentals. Becker's Lodge has campsites, cabins, and a dining room; call (250) 992-8864 or (800) 808-4761 for reservations. For more information call Visitors Information in

Quesnel, (250)992-8716, or Bowron Lake canoe registration at (250)992-3111.

RESTAURANTS

Wake Up Jake's There's nothing about this old-time saloon that isn't 1870s authentic: they don't serve french fries (which hadn't been invented yet), and they don't use processed anything. Instead, it's all real: soups, caribou stew, sourdough-bread sandwiches, steaks, flaky-crusted fruit pies, and even the specials— pheasant, or perhaps cheese and potato pie—amid saloon decor. ■ *In the center of town, Barkerville; (604)994-3259; $; beer and wine; MC, V; no checks; breakfast, lunch, dinner every day (closed Oct–Apr).*

PRINCE GEORGE

Prince George, the fourth-largest city in the province, is the hub of north and central British Columbia, and the jump-off point for brave souls heading up the Alaska Highway. The city sits between two mountain ranges on a dry plateau at the confluence of the Nechako and Fraser Rivers, on the traditional trading route of the Carrier Sekani tribe. Forestry is the main industry here, and loads of logging roads take hunters and fishermen back into remote and bountiful spots. Hundreds of lakes are located within easy driving distance, and in summer folks who like to fish for native rainbow trout, as well as outdoor enthusiasts who canoe, hike, and watch birds, head for this city deep in the boreal forest. The **Stellako River**, west of Prince George near Fraser Lake, is famous for its record trout. The **Cottonwood Island Nature Park**, along the Nechako River, has an extensive trail system suitable for hiking in the summer and cross-country skiing in the winter. Adjacent to the park is the **Prince George Railway Museum**; (250)563-7351. Two city galleries are of interest: **Prince George Art Gallery**, (250)563-6447, features regional and national exhibits monthly; **Native Art Gallery**, (250)562-7385, exhibits local Native American art and crafts.

   Railroads. BC Rail will roll you through 744 kilometers (462 miles) of some of the most beautiful scenery in BC, from Vancouver to Prince George, via Rail Canada in 13 hours; (250)984-5246. Transfer to the passenger run to Prince Rupert, where ferries to the Queen Charlotte Islands, Vancouver Island, and Alaska depart regularly; (250)669-1211 for ferries within BC, (800)642-0066 for Alaska Marine Highway information.

LODGINGS

Esther's Inn Bring your swimsuit to Prince George, even in the middle of winter, and pretend you're in the tropics. This Polynesian-style hotel brings the tropics to the North, with palm trees, philodendrons, and waterfalls that cascade around the warm indoor swimming pool. There are also three Jacuzzis, two indoor water slides that spiral into a separate pool, and a sauna. Rates are reasonable—so what if they lay it on a little thick? ■ *1151 Commercial Dr (off Hwy 97 at 10th Ave), Prince George, BC V2M 6W6; (250)562-4131; $$; AE, DC, DIS, MC, V; no checks.*

The Inn on Ferry Breakfasts at The Inn on Ferry are legendary, at least in northern British Columbia, thanks to the fact that Manfred Zumbrunn is a former baker. He serves up generous breakfasts heavily flavored by his German heritage. Zumbrunn and his wife, Jutta, run the bed and breakfast, so German is also spoken here. The inn is a favorite with business travelers. There's plenty of room to spread out in this 5,000-square-foot house; guests can use the lounge and library. Request the large (700 square feet) suite that looks out on the Fraser River. ■ *1506 Ferry Ave (just off the Hwy 97 bridge across the Fraser River), Prince George, BC V2L 5H2; (250)562-4450; $$-$$$; MC, V; checks OK.*

Westhaven Cottage-By-The-Lake B&B Guests can stay in a rustic cottage that has a small kitchen, a living area with a fireplace, and a bedroom. Or there is one guest room in the adjacent house. Both are on the shores of West Lake, a small lake that's more popular among canoers than with fishermen. There are rainbow trout in the lake, but there's better fishing at many of the hundreds of other lakes in the region. The loons arrive in May and stay into October, so bird-watchers flock to the lake, too. Guests can rent canoes at the bed and breakfast, or innkeeper Ray Giffin will arrange and lead custom wilderness canoe and hiking excursions. ■ *23357 Fyfe Rd (19 km/12 miles west of Prince George on Hwy 16), Prince George, BC V2N 2S7; (250)964-0180; $$; no credit cards; checks OK.*

PRINCE RUPERT

Prince Rupert began as a dream. Founder Charles Melville Hays saw this island as the perfect terminus for rail as well as sea travel and trade. Unfortunately, on a trip back from Europe, where he was rustling up money to help finance his vision, he met with an untimely death aboard the *Titanic*. Seventy-five years later, a number of local folks rekindled Hays's dream, and by the mid-1980s Prince Rupert had two major export terminals and a booming economy. With this newfound prosperity have come culture and tourism. The **Museum of Northern British Columbia** has one of the finest collections of Northwest Coast Indian art you're likely to find anywhere: First Avenue E and McBride; (250)624-3207.

Ferries. Prince Rupert is called the gateway to the north, but it's also a place where ferries can take you west (to the remote Queen Charlotte Islands—see listing, below) or south (through the Inside Passage to Vancouver Island—see Port Hardy). The

Alaska ferry winds north through the panhandle to Skagway. Call (250)669-1211 for ferries within BC (or visit their website at www.bcferries.bc.ca/ferries), or (800)642-0066 for Alaska Marine Highway information.

RESTAURANTS

Smile's Seafood Cafe ★ Since 1922, Smile's Cafe has been tucked unobtrusively among the fish-processing plants beside the railroad. Favorites still include the fresh Dungeness crab, halibut, and black cod; the french fries are a perfect nongreasy, brown-skinned complement to the fish. Service is small-town friendly. ▪ *131 Cow Bay Rd (follow 3rd Ave into George Hills Way), Prince Rupert; (250)624-3072; $$; full bar; MC, V; no checks; breakfast, lunch, dinner every day.*

QUEEN CHARLOTTE ISLANDS

A microcosm of the British Columbia coast, the Galápagos of the Northwest, these sparsely populated, beautiful islands (150 in all) offer an escape to a rough-edged (and often rainy) paradise. There are countless beaches, streams, fishing holes, coves, and abandoned Indian villages to explore. Many unique subspecies of flora and fauna share these islands with the 6,000 residents.

This 180-mile-long string of islands is the ancestral home of the **Haida**, a nation legendary for its art. Many visitors come to the islands to see the abandoned villages on Moresby Island, accessible only by boat, and reservations are necessary (check with the Canadian park service before you visit any of the protected sites). The Haida quarry and carve rare black argillite, found only on these islands, into miniature totem poles, jewelry, and boxes. A few artist's studios may be open for you to visit (ask around upon your arrival), or purchase the art at one of several gift shops, including the one at the **Haida Gwaii Museum**; (250)559-4643.

Transportation. There are only 120 kilometers (75 miles) of paved roads in the Queen Charlotte Islands and the cost of transporting your car on the ferry is prohibitive, so we suggest leaving your car behind and letting boats, foot, or taxi be your mode of transport. Take the six- to eight-hour ferry crossing from Prince Rupert (BC Ferries; (604)381-1401), fly in to the small airstrip on Moresby Island, or take a seaplane. Food and lodging are available, mainly on Graham Island, but most people who come camp. For information, call the local Chamber of Commerce, (250)559-8188, or call Kallahin Expeditions (out of Queen Charlotte City) for island-related excursions—everything from a bus-tour package to a pickup for you and your kayak, (250)559-8070. Pacific Synergies offers sailing excursions in the area; (604)932-3107. Or explore the island via kayak or sailboat with the help of Ecosummer; (604)669-7741.

QUEEN CHARLOTTE ISLANDS: MASSET

LODGINGS

Copper Beech House ★★★ The garden's a bit tangled, and so are all the memorabilia and rare collectibles inside this turn-of-the-century home. But come spring the garden smells wonderful, and come morning so does breakfast. David Philips cans his summer fruits for year-round breakfasts and smokes his own seafood. Upstairs are three guest rooms with Mission-style oak furniture; one has its own living room. But most visitors prefer to spend time at Philips's table (dinner for guests upon request). On an island where fresh food is nearly impossible to obtain, Philips's bounty might include halibut from the local fishermen and tomatoes from the garden. An unusual soup (such as a buttery peach and tomato) proves Philips is inspired, not limited, by local ingredients. His culinary improvisations and unparalleled hospitality would be appreciated anywhere. In the Queen Charlottes, they're a godsend. ■ *1590 Delkatlah (right by the fishing boat docks, at Collison), Masset; (250)626-5441; Box 97, Masset, BC V0T 1M0; $; MC, V; checks OK.*

QUEEN CHARLOTTE ISLANDS: QUEEN CHARLOTTE CITY

LODGINGS

Spruce Point Lodge What started as just a lawn and a shower offered to the occasional kayaker who needed a place to stay is now a cedar-clad building wrapped with a balcony. The lodge, on Skidegate Inlet, attracts families and couples alike—and still, most often, kayakers. There are seven clean rooms—each with a full bath, cable TV, and locally made pine furnishings. Reasonable rates include a continental breakfast and an occasional impromptu seafood barbecue. Mary Kellie and Nancy Hett's lawn is not available anymore, but adventurers on a budget will appreciate the hostel rooms (sheets and pillowcases provided). There's use of the kitchen and laundry. Kayaks for rent. Pets and kids welcome. ■ *609 6th Ave (5½ km/3½ miles west of ferry, left after Chevron station, then 2nd left), Queen Charlotte City; (250)559-8234; PO Box 735, Queen Charlotte City, BC V0T 1S0; $; MC, V; checks OK.*

FORT LANGLEY

RESTAURANTS

Bedford House ★ A lovely place with a picturesque view of the Fraser River, this restored 1904 house is furnished with English antiques and has a pleasant, countrified elegance. The menu is rich with fancy continental cuisine: roast duckling with a fruit sauce, broiled fillet of salmon with hollandaise, or scallops and

prawns served on puff pastry with a creamy champagne sauce.
■ *9272 Glover Rd (on the bank of the Fraser River, downtown),*
Fort Langley; (604) 888-2333; $$; full bar; AE, MC, V; no checks;
dinner every day, brunch Sun.

CHILLIWACK

The name's not the only thing that's curious about this prosper-
ous farming and dairy center: speakers set in downtown blare
easy-listening music, and antique cars seem plentiful. Local land-
marks include an offbeat military museum at the **Canadian
Forces Base**, open Sundays all year, midweek during the sum-
mer, (604) 858-1011; **Minter Gardens**, 10 large theme gardens, 14
kilometers (8⅗ miles) east at the Highway 9 junction, (604) 794-
7191; and **Bridal Falls Provincial Park**, 15 kilometers (9 miles)
east on Highway 1.

RESTAURANTS

La Mansione Ristorante ★ There's a menu of mixed delights in
this handsome mock-Tudor mansion with leaded-glass win-
dows and a warm fireplace for winter evenings. (Beware the air
conditioner in summer; sitting near it can easily ruin the meal.)
Sample the delicious seafood chowder, brimming with shrimp,
crab, and clams, or the veal, pan-fried in butter with lemon and
capers. Specialties include chateaubriand, rack of lamb, and
veal scaloppine Sergio (the legacy of the former owner). Owner
Peter Graham carries an extensive selection of wines by the
glass. ■ *46290 Yale Rd E (near Williams St), Chilliwack;*
(604) 792-8910; $$; full bar; AE, DC, MC, V; no checks; lunch
Mon–Fri, dinner every day.

HARRISON HOT SPRINGS

Situated at the southern end of Harrison Lake, the town is a
small, quiet row of low buildings facing the sandy beach and lagoon. The hot springs themselves are in a strangely enclosed
temple with sulfur steam billowing out and an occasional Coke
can strewn along the bottom of the pool. But don't be dismayed;
the public soaking pool (which has cooled hot-spring water
pumped into it) is large and wonderfully warm (100°F average).
In addition, there are sailboards and bikes to rent, hiking trails
nearby, helicopters to ride, and a pub or two. In winter, skiers
use Harrison as their spa after a day on the slopes at Hemlock
Valley (a 40-minute drive).

RESTAURANTS

Black Forest ★ Bavarian food seems a staple in BC, and here's
an authentic restaurant serving more than just schnitzel. This
is also the place for goulash soup, and beef *rouladen*—sirloin

**Mainland
British
Columbia**

▼

**Harrison
Hot Springs**

Restaurants

▲

stuffed with onions, pickles, mustard, and bacon; braised in red wine; and served with red cabbage and spaetzle. Be sure to make a reservation. ■ *180 Esplanade Ave (1 block west of Hwy 9), Harrison Hot Springs; (604) 796-9343; $$; full bar; AE, MC, V; no checks; dinner every day.*

LODGINGS

The Harrison Hotel Located on the southern shore of long and beautiful Harrison Lake, this legendary hotel is really a better place to view than to visit. The first hotel was built here in 1885 to take advantage of the hot springs; it burned down, and the present "old" building dates back to 1926. Since then the additions have changed the hotel into a sprawling mishmash of unrelated architecture. Grounds are pretty and spacious, with tennis courts and exercise circuit, but the best part about the place is definitely the hot spring water: two indoor pools (103°F and 90°F) and one outdoor (90°F)—open only to hotel guests. A scenic golf course is 3 kilometers (almost 2 miles) away. Staying here is expensive (there are extra charges for almost everything). Most of the rooms in the old wing still have 1950s decor. And since the hotel won't guarantee lake views, a safer bet is to book a room in the newer tower (on the east side). Our advice would be to use the place for a short stay, arrive in time to enjoy the excellent pools and a poolside drink, and then promenade down the street to eat. ■ *100 Esplanade Ave (west end of Esplanade Ave), Harrison Hot Springs, BC V0M 1K0; (604) 796-2244; $$$; AE, MC, V; checks OK.* &

MANNING PROVINCIAL PARK

LODGINGS

Manning Park Resort Situated within the boundaries of pretty Manning Provincial Park, this simple lodge gives you easy access to both gentle and arduous hiking trails. With a short drive, you can also be paddling a rented canoe on Lightning Lake or riding a horse through the surrounding country. Besides the 41 motel rooms, the low-key resort includes a restaurant, coffee shop, cabins, and triplexes—all in the same plain, functional style. If you have 49 friends, however, book the Last Resort a few yards down the highway, a real old-fashioned '40s charmer that sleeps 50. In winter (two-day minimum then) the park turns into cross-country and downhill ski heaven: Gibsons Ski Area is just out the back door. ■ *Just off Hwy 3 in Manning Provincial Park; (250) 840-8822; Box 1480, Manning Provincial Park, BC V0X 1R0; $$; AE, MC, V; no checks.*

QUILCHENA

LODGINGS

Quilchena Hotel ★★ Remote Quilchena Hotel captures the ambience of southwestern BC's cattle country. It attracts a motley assortment: moneyed urbanites who fly over (the Quilchena has its own landing strip) in search of relaxation; cattle barons who come to buy livestock; gentlemanly senior citizens in search of the perfect golf course; and cowboys, Canada-style. It's a delightful stew, and meant to be that way: there are no phones or TVs in the 16 rooms; guests share bathrooms and dine together in the parlor. It's not elegant, but guests happily gather around the piano for an impromptu recital. Daytime finds you riding horses, playing tennis, golfing on the adjacent course, or searching the nearby fossil beds. For extended stays, there's a three-bedroom ranch house on the grounds. Expect lots of beef on the restaurant's menu. ■ *Take the 2nd Merritt exit off the Coquihalla Hwy; (250)378-2611; Box 1, Hwy 5A, Quilchena, BC V0E 2R0; $$; MC, V; no checks (closed mid-Oct to mid-Apr).*

MERRITT

LODGINGS

Corbett Lake Country Inn ★ French-trained owner and chef Peter McVey first came from England to British Columbia on a fishing trip. Today McVey's country inn caters to lovers of fly-fishing in the summer and cross-country skiers in the winter. There are three nondescript rooms in the lodge, but most guests choose to stay in one of the 10 simple cabins, each with its own kitchen. The two duplexes have fireplaces, and one has a separate bedroom/living room. Aside from the outdoor activities, the food's the thing here. Dinner (by reservation only) is something different every night. McVey creates wonderful four-course evenings, starting with soup (perhaps fresh mushroom), a salad (caesar, hot German, or cucumber), and continuing to an entree that could be anything from loin of pork with Dijon mustard to beef Wellington with Yorkshire pudding. Corbett Lake holds plenty of fish, but an extra fee gains you the privilege of angling in two privately stocked lakes. ■ *12 km/7½ miles south of Merritt on Hwy 5A; (250)378-4334; Box 327, Merritt, BC V0K 2B0; $$; V; checks OK; breakfast, dinner every day (dinner by reservation only); open May–Oct and first week in Jan.*

KAMLOOPS

A sprawling city of nearly 75,000 residents, Kamloops is the midway point between Vancouver (four hours west) and Banff National Park in Alberta (just three hours east on the Trans-Canada 1 Highway). With the forest industry waning, Kamloops is turning its attention to tourism and to enticing outdoor enthusiasts, who will find enough activities here to keep them busy. Named after a Shuswap Indian word meaning "meeting place," Kamloops is at the confluence of the **North** and **South Thompson Rivers**. Fishermen dip their lines into the rivers or flock to Paul Lake to catch trophy-sized Kamloops trout year-round (be prepared to cut through ice up to 3 feet thick to ice-fish in winter). **Fly-in fishing lodges** are located on some of the 700 lakes in the area; flights depart and return to the Kamloops Airport. For a list of lodges, contact the Kamloops Visitor Info Centre, (800)662-1994, or the BC Fishing Resorts & Outfitters Association, (250)374-8646. **Golfers** can tee off at any of the five 18-hole courses, (800)662-1994, within a 15-minute drive of Kamloops, including the Sun Peaks Resort Golf Course, (250)578-7222, and the Kamloops Golf Club, (250)376-3231. And, because Kamloops is known as "the Tournament Capital," there's always a game in town. The Western Hockey League Kamloops Blazers, (250)828-3339, play in the Riverside Coliseum. **Wells Gray Provincial Park**, 128 kilometers (80 miles) north of Kamloops, has five major lakes, two river systems, and plenty of smaller backcountry alpine lakes. The largest freshwater lake in North America, **Murtle Lake**, is a one-hour portage from the parking lot, but the trail is wide enough for wheeled boat carriers. Casual paddlers use the park's Clearwater and Azure Lakes, linked by a river with challenging rapids; in summer Clearwater Lake Tours, (250)674-2121, operates daily cruises on both lakes. Wells Gray Park also has cinder cones, lava flows, and basalt cliffs, remnants of ancient volcanic activity; (250)587-6150.

Skiers head for a family area, Harper Mountain, (250)573-5115, which has 12 runs and only one chair but is just a 20-minute drive east. Those with more ambition head for Sun Peaks Resort, (250)578-7222, with 63 runs and a high-speed quad chair, about an hour's drive northeast of Kamloops. **Cross-country ski trails** are groomed at Lac Le Jeune, (250)372-2722; Roche Lake Resort, (250)828-2007; Walloper Lake Resort, (250)372-9843; Stake Lake, (270)372-5514; and Sun Peaks, (250)372-8077.

RESTAURANTS

Minos ★ Minos had a tradition of being a family-owned operation, and owner Gus Krokos maintains the successful enterprise begun by a previous owner. Service is exceptionally friendly, prompt, and well informed, helping to create a warm atmosphere. The menu still leans heavily toward Greek fare—souvlaki of lamb, chicken, and seafood. Try a piece of honey-sweet baklava with a strong cup of Greek coffee for dessert. ■ *262 Tranquille Rd (1 km/½ mile north of Overlander Bridge), Kamloops; (250)376-2010; $; beer and wine; AE, MC, V; checks OK; lunch Mon–Sat, dinner every day.*

Peter's Pasta ★ What Peter's Pasta lacks in ambience, it makes up for in the sauces. It's easy to overlook this narrow cafe in downtown Kamloops, but the locals rave about the homemade pasta that Peter puts on your plate. It's so popular you may run into a short wait for a table—even this far north. Diners choose from four pastas and a generous range of sauces, clam to tomato to alfredo. Small and large portions are available; all come with toasted garlic bread. Salads are extra, but you may find your heaping portion of pasta enough without one. The dessert menu includes several Italian ices, but look for the chocolate mousse. The wine and beer list falls short in selections, especially considering the plethora of wineries to the south in Kelowna and the growing number of microbreweries in the region. ■ *149 Victoria St (downtown), Kamloops; (250) 372-8514; $; beer and wine; MC, V; no checks; lunch Tues–Fri, dinner Tues–Sat.*

LODGINGS

Lac Le Jeune Resort ★ Well equipped and pleasant, this lodge puts you right on the lake for fishing and at the edge of the wilderness for hiking. You can stay in the lodge, in a self-contained cabin (perfect for families), or in a chalet. The resort includes an indoor whirlpool and sauna, and meeting rooms for up to 200. Breakfast and dinner buffets are served for guests only. Adjacent is a downhill ski area; more than 100 kilometers of cross-country skiing trails wind through the property. Boats and canoes are available for rent (the famous Kamloops trout are great to catch—and eat). Large tour groups tend to book the place en masse during the summer months, so reserve early or take a chance on a last-minute cancellation. ■ *650 Victoria St (off Coquihalla Hwy, Lac Le Jeune exit, 29 km/18 miles southwest of Kamloops), Kamloops, BC V2C 2B4; (250) 372-2722; $$; full bar; AE, DC, MC, V; checks OK (open mid-Apr to late Oct).*

Sevinth Heaven B&B ★ With Paul Lake—the site of the 1993 World Flyfishing Championships—just outside the front door, Sevinth Heaven is in a gem of a location. So no wonder fly fishermen flock to the area in search of the giant Kamloops. In the winter Paul Lake freezes, offering a perfect surface for cross-country skiing, snowmobiling, and ice fishing. (And Harper Mountain ski area is five minutes up the road). Anne Sevin runs a small, one-guest-room operation, but she does a wonderful job, and the setting could not be more serene. Look for the loons in May. Don't plan on going to bed early, since the warm but creaking living room and kitchen are above your room. The road along the lake to the B&B is one lane, which can be a challenge during snowfalls. ■ *7007 Paul Lake Rd (east of town), Kamloops; (250) 573-7533; mail: Site 1, Comp 42, RR5, Kamloops, BC V2C 6C2; $; no credit cards; checks OK.*

The Thompson ★ Many references are made in this area to the 19th-century explorer David Thompson, and the naming of this hotel is just one; however, there's nothing adventuresome about the lodging here. It's standard hotel fare, but the best you'll find at the moment in Kamloops—nice rooms and suites with broad windows, minifridges, hair dryers, and coffee-makers. Some rooms have a view of the Thompson River, although the railroad tracks run between the hotel and the river. Amenities include an indoor basketball court, indoor pool and hot tub, fitness room, laundry facilities, and a restaurant and sports bar (the Memorial Arena, where the local hockey team plays, is just a block away). Downtown is a two-block walk away. ■ *650 Victoria St (downtown), Kamloops, BC V2C 2B4; (250)374-1999 or (800)561-5253; $-$$; AE, DC, MC, V; checks OK.*

Sun Peaks Resort [*unrated*] A major investment is transforming what was a family ski area into a destination resort 53 kilometers (33 miles) northeast of Kamloops. Improvements to the ski area include two high-speed quad chairs and new runs. The chairlift runs summers, too, for hikers and sightseers, and there's a nine-hole golf course that's rated as challenging. On-mountain lodging is in the 100-room Nancy Greene's Cahilty Lodge and the 44-room European-style Sun Peaks Lodge, both of which will have restaurants. Look for full reviews and ratings next edition. ■ *Northeast of Kamloops; (800)807-3257; PO Box 869, Kamloops, BC V2C 5M8; $$$.*

ASHCROFT

LODGINGS

Sundance Ranch ★★ Here's a dude ranch set in high plateau country, with the Thompson River cutting a deep gorge just to the west. Low buildings of dark-stained wood contain handsome pine-paneled rooms. Children can stay in their own wing or with their parents. The pool is quite grand, and there's now a tennis court. But the real attraction is the corral, where 100 good horses await you for the two daily rides, morning and late afternoon (it can get very hot here during midday). More than a dozen buffalo live in the adjacent fields. Excellent evening meals are often served on the barbecue patio; Saturday nights there's a dance. Rustic public rooms set the scene for drinks, parties, and games. You'll sleep well, breathing the cool, sage-scented air. ■ *Off Kirkland Ranch Rd (8 km/5 miles south of town), Ashcroft; (250)453-2422; PO Box 489, Ashcroft, BC V0K 1A0; sundance@mail.netshop.net; $$; MC, V; no checks (open Mar–Oct).*

KEREMEOS

LODGINGS

Cathedral Lakes Resort ★★ To say this resort is remote is more than an understatement. First you have to get to base camp, which is a 21-kilometer (13-mile) gravel-road journey off Highway 3 along the Ashnola River. Once you're there, a four-wheel-drive vehicle from the resort picks you up and takes you on a one-hour, 14½-kilometer (9-mile) journey to the lodge. The resort is heavy on recreation (hiking, canoeing, fishing), light on modern conveniences (such as phones and TVs). All rooms have hot water and views of the lakes and peaks that surround the resort. Choose a cabin (which can accommodate up to eight) or a room in the chalet or the lodge. Showers and toilets are shared. Three big meals are served (box lunches available upon request). Make your reservations early, since the season is short and space is limited. The resort is located inside the Cathedral Lake Provincial Park; the entire area is a protected wildlife refuge and a unique geological region. At 6,000 to 8,000 feet, the air is cool and dry, the views of surrounding Cascade mountains spectacular. Mount Baker, Mount Rainier, the Coast Range, and the Kootenays are all visible from Lakeview Mountain, a day hike from the lodge. ■ *Call ahead for directions; (250)226-7560 or (888)255-4453; mail: RR1, Cawston, BC V0X 1C0; $$$; no credit cards; checks OK (open June–Oct).*

THE OKANAGAN VALLEY

The Canadian Okanagans, stretching from Osoyoos at the U.S. border to Vernon to the north, are a summer playground. The valley is laden with **orchards**, making it especially appealing in spring when the fruit trees are in full bloom. The best time to pick up some of the valley's bounty is mid-August through early September; however, beginning as early as late June the fruit starts ripening: cherries (late June through mid-July), peaches (mid-July through September), pears (August through September), apricots (mid-July through mid-August), plums (September), apples (August through October), and grapes (September through mid-October).

Wineries. Fruit aside, winemaking is the hot ticket in the Okanagan. British Columbians have long taken inordinate pride in their wines—even when those mostly came from a few largish factories like Kelowna's Calona, on Richter Street; (250)762-3332. However, ever since British Columbia authorized estate and smaller farmgate wineries, many excellent small wineries have popped up. Nearly three dozen wineries operate in the Okanagan Valley from Vernon to Osoyoos; some have tasting rooms, Most are open summers and through the wine crush in September. Maps for self-guided tours of the wineries are available from the British Columbia

Wine Institute, 1855 Kirschner Rd, Kelowna, BC V1Y 4N7; (250) 762-4887.

Kelowna is the center of the burgeoning wine industry. The biggest and best known of the Okanagan wineries is Summerhill, 4870 Chute Lake Road, (800) 667-3538. Other notable Kelowna wineries include St. Hubertus Estate Winery, 5225 Lakeshore Road, (800) 989-9463, which specializes in dry Swiss-style wines, and the excellent Quails' Gate Estate Winery, 3303 Boucherie Road, (800) 420-9463, where the tasting room is in a historic pioneer log cabin. Some of the best estate offerings come out of Gray Monk, 8 kilometers (5 miles) west of Winfield off Highway 97, (250) 766-3168; CedarCreek, 14 kilometers (9 miles) south of Kelowna, (250) 764-8866; Sumac Ridge, off Highway 97, just north of Summerland, (250) 494-0451; and Hainle Vineyards in Peachland, (250) 767-2525. A farmgate vineyard to keep an eye on is Wild Goose Vineyards just south of Okanagan Falls; (250) 497-8919. Other notable wineries to visit: Mission Hill, south of Kelowna in Westbank off Boucherie Road, (250) 768-5125; Gehringer Brothers, 4 kilometers (2½ miles) south of Oliver off Highway 97 on Road 8, (250) 498-3537; Vincor Okanagan Cellars, between Oliver and Vaseaux Lake on Highway 97, (250) 498-4981; Okanagan Vineyards, 5 kilometers (3 miles) south of Oliver off Highway 97, (250) 498-6663; and Lang Vineyards, south of Naramata on Gammon Road, (250) 496-5987.

Skiing. The local climate is a powdery happy medium between the chill of the Rockies and the slush of the Coast Range, and the slopes are distributed along the valley. Silver Star, east of Vernon, has full resort facilities; (250) 542-0224. Crystal Mountain is the nearest stop from Kelowna for day schussing, (250) 768-5189; but Big White, (250) 765-3101, to the east has many more runs (44, and up to 1,850 vertical feet), full facilities, and even cross-country trails, and claims the greatest altitude of all the ski areas in the province. Apex Alpine, Penticton's full-facility resort known for its challenging terrain, has added a number of "family" runs to complement its harder stuff; (250) 292-8222. Southwest of Penticton on Highway 3A, the Twin Lakes Golf Club doubles as a cross-country course in winter; (250) 497-5359. There's more downhill at Mount Baldy Ski Area west of Osoyoos, (250) 498-4086—one of the first mountains in the area to have snow.

Houseboating. From April to October, you and your family can explore the 1,600 kilometers (1,000 miles) or so of the Shuswap Lake shoreline at the northern end of the Okanagan Valley on a houseboat—stocked with everything from a microwave oven to a water slide. Seven-day trips run you between $1,500 and $4,000 depending on your boat choice, not including gas. Call Twin Anchors Houseboat Rentals, (800) 663-4026, fax (250) 836-4824; or Waterway Houseboat Vacations, (800) 663-4022.

Osoyoos bills itself as "the Spanish capital of Canada," but not because of any pioneer ethnic roots. It's purely a gimmicky town theme selected by city fathers. The climate is Canada's driest, with 10 inches of rain a year, and Osoyoos Lake is reportedly Canada's warmest freshwater lake. A good short hike is up **Mount Kobau**, just west of Osoyoos off Kobau Road. Take the Kobau Lookout trail (2 kilometers or 1¼ miles) to the fire lookout, or the Testalinden Trail (5 kilometers or 3 miles), a loop trail with views of the Similkameen Valley.

RESTAURANTS

Diamond Steak & Seafood House ★ Just about everyone in Osoyoos likes this casual steak, seafood, and pizza house on the main street of town. The decor carries out the town's ersatz Spanish theme better than most, and the pizzas are quite good, if you like crust that's crisp enough to snap. The Greek salad is the best in town (no wonder—the owner is Greek). The wine list shows a collection of labels (literally) from several valley wineries, and there are refreshing Okanagan apple and pear ciders, too. ■ *Main St (near 89th), Osoyoos; (250)495-6223; $$; full bar; MC, V; checks OK; dinner every day.* ঙ

LODGINGS

Reflections Guesthouse ★ Apple orchards crawl up the hill behind this new bed and breakfast, built by owner Gary Fox. Out front there's a small private lake (surrounded by homes). Four suites are complete with kitchens and balconies. The setting is quiet; the accommodations are contemporary. Guests can stroll through the orchard, sit in the garden, or soak in the hot tub. Breakfast is continental-style. ■ *From Osoyoos, take Hwy 97 south to 74th Ave, turn west at 103rd St, follow signs; (250)495-5229; RR 2, Site 82, Comp 7, Osoyoos, BC V0H 1V0; $; no credit cards; checks OK.*

Inkaneep Point Resort Down a steep, winding road, on a little peninsula in Osoyoos Lake, is this unassuming resort. The best thing about it is location: all 10 of the beach-level rooms face directly south for maximum sun (although the two dark cabins face north) and open only feet away from the water's edge. Families (some in their third generation of vacationing here) don't mind the fact the accommodations are a bit campish, because they really come for the sun. Don and Esme Hellyer book rooms by the week in summer (July and August get booked up early in the year), love kids, and eschew loud boats and pets. ■ *3 km (almost 2 miles) north of Osoyoos off Hwy 97; (250)495-6353; RR 2, Osoyoos, BC V0H 1V0; $; no credit cards; checks OK (open mid-May through mid-Oct).*

KALEDEN

LODGINGS

Ponderosa Point Resort ★★ Ponderosa Point's compound of 26 individually owned rental cabins on a peninsula extending out into Skaha Lake is an ideal spot to take a thick book. The most attractive units are the one- and two-bedroom Pan Abodes set on a ponderosa pine–covered bluff above the lake. There's a 600-foot sandy beach, boat rentals, tennis courts, a playground, and a big grassy central common. The cabins, individually furnished by the owners, are not plush or contemporary, but they're universally comfortable and clean. Greasewood Cabin, for two, has furniture with a hand-hewn look—perfect for the setting. Minimum stay for any of the cabins is three days in the off-season or a week in the summer. ■ *319 Ponderosa Ave (7 km/4 miles south of Penticton on Hwy 97), Kalenden; (250) 497-5354; Box 106, Kalenden, BC V0H 1K0; $$$; no credit cards; checks OK (open May–Oct).*

PENTICTON

Penticton takes full advantage of its dual lakefronts. The south end of town (with its go-cart tracks, amusement centers, miniature golf courses, water slides, and RV parks) touches the north shore of **Skaha Lake**. The north end of town sidles along the southern tip of 113-kilometer-long (70-mile-long) **Lake Okanagan**.

RESTAURANTS

Granny Bogner's ★★ One of the province's best restaurants is also one of the most consistent, and it has just about everything—great food, great location, great building, and desserts that alone make the trip here worthwhile. The restaurant is located in a big Arts and Crafts–style house. Diners relax in wing chairs in front of the fireplace with a glass of wine or after-dinner coffee. The menu covers a broad spectrum from halibut to prime rib, but it's the presentation of the food that sets this place apart. Entrees arrive garnished with an eye for color and shape; vegetables are artfully arranged. The dessert specials, often using fresh local fruit, are the best choices. Enjoy dessert or brandy in the inviting bar, with its comfy chintz chairs. The wine list does a grand job of representing the best local estate wineries. ■ *302 Eckhardt Ave W (2 blocks south of Main), Penticton; (250) 493-2711; $$$; full bar; AE, MC, V; no checks; dinner Tues–Sat.*

Theo's ★ The ever-popular Theo's sports a series of sun-dappled interior patios, roofed with heavy rough-sawn beams, floored with red tile, walled in white stucco. Patrons say Theo's cooks an excellent rabbit (from nearby Summerland) and swear by the octopus. We agree, but we wish the accompaniments (white rice, carrots, overcooked potatoes) were a little more in-spired. That said, by all means go in the late afternoon for an aperitif and a plate of excellent fried squid, or late at night to eat moussaka. ■ *687 Main St (near corner of Eckhardt), Penticton; (250) 492-4019; $$; full bar; AE, DC, MC, V; local checks only; lunch Mon–Sat, dinner every day.* &

LODGINGS

Castle Rock B&B ★ This is the place to stay in Penticton—that is, if you can find a time when they've got a place for you to stay. The owners run the local microbrewery and don't advertise the place, which makes it all the more attractive. It's a massive 7,500-square-foot hand-hewn log lodge located high above Okanagan and Skaha Lakes, with a knockout view of both. Stay in any of the four rooms, play on any of the 20 hilltop acres. It makes a great base to enjoy numerous Okanagan adventures, or simply borrow the owners' mountain bikes for the morning and return here for an afternoon of sunning beside the heated outdoor pool. ■ *2050 Sutherland Rd (just north of downtown, off Naramata Rd), Penticton; (250) 492-4429; mail: C22, S200, RR1, Penticton, BC V2A 6J6; $$; MC, V; checks OK.*

Coast Lakeside Resort The Coast Lakeside (formerly the Delta Lakeside), the flagship of the Lake Okanagan shore, is looking a little forgotten these days (it needs paint and some new land-scaping)—strange for the most expensive place in town. It's the only resort here with its own beachfront. There are 204 rooms with balconies; the north-facing rooms have lake views. There are outdoor tennis courts, an indoor pool, and two restaurants (one with outdoor seating). ■ *21 Lakeshore Dr W (at Main), Pen-ticton, BC V2A 7M5; (250) 493-8221; $$$; full bar; AE, DC, MC, V; checks OK; breakfast, lunch, dinner every day.*

NARAMATA

RESTAURANTS

The Country Squire ★★★ Every meal becomes an event at this clubby old house. Dinner might take up to four hours. However long it is, the table's yours for the night—you can even take a walk between courses if you'd like (a good idea if you want a view of the lake). Master of ceremonies is Ron Dyck, who owns and operates this shrine of Okanagan cookery with his wife, Patt. Some think the flourishes are simply too much; others like all of Ron's personal touches. The opening act takes place when you call for reservations, at which time you are asked to choose from among several seasonal entrees. Upon arrival you find a formal card detailing the courses to come: perhaps a coarse duck pâté surrounded with Cumberland sauce to begin; a soup; your entree; a platter of well-selected cheeses and fruit; and dessert, such as the chocolate ginger pear, poached in sauvignon blanc. The food is good, if rococo, with only the occasional in-explicable lapse. The price is a flat $39.50—and Ron is at your side throughout the meal, decanting one his 350 wines, flam-béeing the steak Diane, or carving the beef Wellington. He's also a splendid resource on local wines, many of which reside in his own deep cellar. ■ *3950 1st St (take Naramata Rd, left on Robinson, right on 1st), Naramata; (250) 496-5416; $$; full bar; MC, V; local checks only; dinner Wed–Sun.* &

LODGINGS

Sandy Beach Lodge ★★ Here is the archetypal summer lodge on the lake, where the same families have signed up for the same two weeks in the same cabin for as long as anyone can re-member. The setting is just about perfect: a wide, green lawn (perfect for horseshoes, croquet, or shuffleboard), breezy with stately pines and shady maples, sloping down to a quiet cove with a sandy beach. The log duplexes are tastefully decorated and furnished; request one of the five closest to the lake (they all have decks and outdoor barbecues). There are also six small rooms in the pine-log lodge. Tennis courts, a small swimming pool, rental boats, and wooden lawn chairs provide ample di-versions. During peak summer season, reservations may be necessary up to a year in advance (and priority is given to re-turning guests). ■ *4275 Mill Rd (off Robson), Naramata; (250) 496-5765; PO Box 8, Naramata, BC V0H 1N0; $$; MC, V; checks OK.* &

SUMMERLAND

A theme town done in the same spirit as Osoyoos, only this time they chose to do it Tudor-style. Old Summerland is down on the water, but most of the town's business now thrives up on the hill.

RESTAURANTS

Shaughnessy's Cove Shaughnessy's strong suits are its dra-matic view of Lake Okanagan (it's built as close to the water as the law allows) and its airy atmosphere. The restaurant is tiered into four levels, with two outdoor decks, 20-foot ceilings, an old oak bar, skylights, three fireplaces, and pleasant decor. The menu ranges from fish 'n' chips to chimichangas to a filling stew served in a hollowed-out loaf of bread. The caesars are so powerful you'll also get a stick of chewing gum for later. Own-ers go way out of their way to make it easy for you to dine here: the Shaughnessy Shuttle will pick customers up at their home or inn and return them at the end of the evening, at no charge. ■ *12817 Lakeshore Dr (in Old Summerland), Summerland; (250) 494-1212; $; full bar; AE, DC, MC, V; no checks; lunch, dinner every day.* &

KELOWNA

On the east side of Lake Okanagan, Kelowna is the largest and liveliest of the Okanagan cities, with some noisy nightlife, a bit of culture (an art museum and summer theater), a range of continental and ethnic restaurants, a big regatta in July, and an interesting historical preserve at Father Pandosy's Mission, (250)860-8369. Kelowna even has its own version of the Loch Ness monster: Ogopogo. Keep a lookout for him (her?) while supping on the gaily decked-out paddle wheeler *Fintry Queen* or touring aboard the *Okanagan Princess*; (250)861-1515 for information on both tours.

Fruit is big in the region and there are even free Tree Fruit Tours; (800)665-5254. Kelowna is the center of the burgeoning wine industry. The biggest and best known of the Okanagan wineries is Summerhill, 4870 Chute Lake Road, (800)667-3538 (see the Okanagan Valley introduction for more information on local vineyards).

Golf. Of the 37 golf courses scattered from Osoyoos to Vernon, Kelowna boasts 15. Most courses open in March and golfers play into November some years. Fruit trees and water hazards challenge golfers on many courses. Kelowna Springs Golf Course, (250)765-4653, has seven natural spring-fed lakes; more than a thousand apple trees grow on the fairways of Harvest Golf Club, (250)862-3103; Gallagher's Canyon Golf & Country Club, (250)861-4240, straddles Gallagher's Canyon, through which a river runs. Predator Ridge Golf Course, (250)542-3436, has undulating greens and dozens of bunkers set on the drier and hilly terrain near Vernon. The T Times Central Booking Service, (800)689-4653 or (250)762-7844, will book tee-times at most of the courses in the area.

RESTAURANTS

De Montreuil ★★★ Dinners here are ordered by the course—two, three, four, or five—but the fare, called Cascadian Cuisine (which favors organic, locally grown ingredients), leans more toward rustic than pretentious. Everything on the menu bursts with just the right combination of flavors and seasonings. Roasted free-range chicken infused with tarragon and lime might be served atop a bed of a quartered potato, whole carrots, and snow peas. Or penne might be paired with Bartlett pears, cinnamon/chipotle butter, and grilled rare tuna. Spend the extra time and money on the five-course option: you'll be a happier person for it (especially when dessert arrives). ■ *368 Bernard Ave (corner of Pandosy), Kelowna; (250)860-5508; $$$; beer and wine; AE, MC, V; no checks; lunch Tues–Fri, dinner every day.*

Kitchen Cowboy ★★ A graceful mixture of Santa Fe style and the real Old West, Kitchen Cowboy serves up food to match. Breakfast here is great—whether it's the French toast with real maple syrup, the huevos rancheros, or the traditional (and cowboy-sized) eggs, bacon or ham, and toast (the bread is fresh from a nearby bakery). Kitchen Cowboy roasts its own coffee beans, so the coffee here is stout. The dinner menu is a bit more adventuresome. Despite the restaurant's name, it leans on Italian fare, but it does best with such things as cornbreaded breast of chicken with spicy corn salsa, or the Kitchen Cowboy hamburger. Desserts include Italian ice cream and cheesecake, but when the local fruit harvest is under way, go for the pie. ■ *353 Bernard Ave (near Pandosy), Kelowna; (250)868-8288; $$; beer and wine; AE, MC, V; no checks; breakfast, lunch, dinner every day (summer), dinner Tues–Sat (winter, but dinner schedule can vary—call ahead).*

Vintage Room (Capri Hotel) ★★

Nobody really wants to like this elegant, pricey restaurant on the ground floor of the Capri Hotel because it's tucked back in a dark, unappealing corner of the main floor of the hotel. Maybe that's what makes the Vintage Room try so hard—and most often succeed. The service is impeccable, and the restaurant bends over backward to accommodate your whims. It offers some of the most sophisticated food in the Okanagan, with such classic fare as escargots, chateaubriand, and lobster tail. Avoid the mediocre desserts, and watch out for the tour groups that can slow service. ■ *1171 Harvey Ave (at Gordon), Kelowna; (250)860-6060; $$; full bar; AE, DC, MC, V; no checks; lunch Mon–Fri, dinner every day, brunch Sun.*

Joey Tomato's Kitchen ★

Kelowna's version of Joey Tomato's follows the formula of this chain of family eateries: plenty of tables and booths crowded into a new warehouse-style building, decorated in a mixture of tomato motif and sports bar. The ceiling-mounted TVs throughout the restaurant all are tuned to sporting events—preferably hockey. Generally the atmosphere is chaotic, with loud pop music in the air. Servers are relentlessly cheerful and entrees consistent (albeit mainstream). Pizzas may be the main event at Joey Tomato's (and they are the most interesting), but there are other choices—such as BC salmon baked in maple syrup or burgers. We favor the themed pizzas such as the Santa Fe, with a guacamole and refried bean sauce topped with bacon, plump shrimp, green onions, and mozzarella. Summers, the patio tables afford a clear view of, well, the traffic on Highway 97. ■ *300-2475 Hwy 97 N (in north Kelowna), Kelowna; (250)860-8999; beer and wine; $-$$; AE, MC, V; no checks; lunch, dinner every day.* ৬

Schroth Wood Fire Bakery ★

The best pizza in Kelowna comes out of the wood-fired ovens of this bakery. The toppings (Black Forest ham or basil-tomato sauce, for instance) change daily, but the crust is always thick, with a crunchy edge. Those not inclined to pizza will find roast beef on kaiser rolls, and a few soups and salads—but the scent of the wood-fired oven in the air reminds you of this place's real strength. The pastries—chocolate-topped Florentines, tortes, and tarts, for example—and the fresh-baked breads even outshine the pizza. Service is cafeteria style. Ambience is nil, unless the weather permits seating outside on the broad, covered veranda. And the yodeling that occasionally breaks out behind the counter is entertaining. ■ *2041 Harvey (on Hwy 97 in north Kelowna), Kelowna; (250) 762-2626; $; no alcohol; no credit cards; checks OK; lunch Mon–Sat.*

LODGINGS

The Grand Okanagan Lakefront Resort ★★ This posh resort dominates the eastern shoreline just west of downtown Kelowna with a 10-story tower of 205 guest rooms. It's not right on the water, but with a waterfront park right in front of the hotel, consider it so. It's a great place in the summer, with floatplane tours and jet-ski rentals. And winter times are fun too, especially with the year-round use of the heated outdoor pool. Best rooms are the lakeside rooms, but they're all full of fairly typical hotel decor. Other facilities include a fitness room and a restaurant call Dolphin's. Downtown Kelowna is a five-minute walk. ■ *1310 Water St (almost 1 km/½ mile west of Harvey St), Kelowna, BC V1Y 9P3; (250) 763-4500 or (800) 465-4651; www.grandokanagan. com; $$$; AE, MC, V; no checks.*

Hotel Eldorado ★★ Hands down, this is the best place to stay on Lake Okanagan—that is, if a boardwalk along the shore will do instead of a sandy beach. (Rotary Beach is just a short walk away.) Originally built for a countess of Scottish descent, in 1989 it caught fire and burned almost to the ground. Consequently, the rebuilt manse feels very new, yet has the grandeur of a bygone era. Each of the 19 rooms has an antique armoire, most have balconies, and some have Jacuzzis. Best are the lakeside or corner rooms. The boardroom, with a large patio, is an excellent meeting place for 10 to 60 people. The Round House nearby can hold up to 85 for banquets. There's not much of a lobby, as the restaurant and lounge take up most of the first floor. The restaurant has been consistently excellent. The wine selection is primarily British Columbian. Breakfast in the sun room is an extremely pleasant way to wake up. ■ *500 Cook Rd (follow Pandosy, which becomes Lakeshore, for 6½ km/4 miles south of the Okanagan Floating Bridge), Kelowna, BC V1W 3G9; (250) 763-7500; $$$; full bar; AE, DC, MC, V; no checks; breakfast, lunch Mon–Sat, dinner every day, brunch Sun.*

Crawford View Bed and Breakfast ★ When Fred and Gaby Geismayr moved to Kelowna from Ontario and opened this bed and breakfast, it consisted of two extra bedrooms in the spacious house set amid the vineyards and apple orchards. Soon, though, they built a second story above the three-car garage and created two additional spacious rooms plus a smaller room with twin beds appropriate for children. The rooms, separated from the house by a breezeway, all have private entrances, so it's easy to find solitude here. The Geismayrs farm a small apple orchard, which guests enjoy along with the tennis court and the outdoor swimming pool. The latter has an outstanding view of the city of Kelowna and the lake that is downright stunning at night, although only one of the rooms affords this view, and that's the breakfast nook. ■ *810 Crawford Rd (off Lakeshore Dr), Kelowna, BC V1W 4N3; (250) 764-1140; $-$$; MC, V; checks OK.*

Lake Okanagan Resort ★ You reach the 300-acre resort via a pine-clad winding road on the west side of Lake Okanagan. The appointments are not first-class (in fact, they're time-share units that also rent by the night). Open year-round, it offers sailing, swimming, golf (nine holes), tennis (seven courts), and horseback riding to keep you busy. You can stay in a large condominium or a smaller chalet (both with wood-burning fireplaces), or any of four different inns. Because the resort is located on a very steep hillside, many of the rooms are a good climb from the activities, but a resort shuttle makes a quick job of it. The evening restaurant, Chateau, serves unremarkable resort fare. A poolside lounge makes for an interesting social setting. ■ *2751 Westside Rd (17 km/10½ miles north of Kelowna), Kelowna, BC V1Y 8B2; (250) 769-3511; $$$; full bar; AE, MC, V; checks OK; breakfast, lunch, dinner every day.* &

Capri Hotel The best of the 185 rooms here look out to the courtyard (with its outdoor hot tub and pool), but privacy is lacking on the ground floor. There are two dining options: the informal Garden Cafe and the outstanding Vintage Room (see review). For relaxation there's an outdoor hot tub and pool, men's and ladies' saunas, and for a taste of nightlife, there's Angie's Pub. ■ *1171 Harvey Ave (at Gordon), Kelowna, BC V1Y 6E8; (250) 860-6060; $$$; AE, DC, MC, V; checks OK.*

REVELSTOKE

Revelstoke's history is tied to the building of the Canadian Pacific Railway, which you can delve into at the **Revelstoke Railway Museum**, 719 Track Street; (250) 837-6060. Towering mountains rise all around Revelstoke, and it's clear the town is trying to build a tourist industry that appeals to hikers and skiers. The four-block-long downtown on MacKenzie Avenue makes a nice stroll; a map for a self-guided heritage **walking tour** is available at the Revelstoke Museum, 315 W First Street, (250) 837-3067. Free tours of the Revelstoke Dam, five minutes north of Revelstoke, are offered from mid-March to late October; call (250) 837-6515 for hours. The Canyon Hotsprings, (250) 837-2420, are 34 kilometers (21 miles) east of Revelstoke on Trans-Canada 1, with a mineral-water hot pool and a mineral-water swimming pool, but are open summers only.

Heli-skiing. For the serious skier, Revelstoke serves as a base camp to some amazing runs in and around the Albert Icefields. The catch: you need a helicopter to get there. The answer: Selkirk Tangiers Helicopter Skiing Ltd.; (250)837-5378. For a few grand, Canadian Mountain Holidays will take you out, for a week at a time, to one of their fully staffed lodges in remote hideaways for some great skiing and hiking; (800)662-0252 or (250)837-9344. Skiers of expert ability can sign on to ski 25 scenic peaks and 14 glaciers with Selkirk Mountain Experience, (250)837-2381, or Selkirk Lodge, (800)663-7080.

RESTAURANTS

Black Forest Inn Inside this A-frame you'll find a bit of Bavaria, with cute cuckoo clocks and German souvenirs cluttering every spare inch of space. Fondue Provençal, British Columbia salmon fillets, and a variety of beef tenderloins round out a rather extensive menu; we recommend one of the Bavarian dishes such as sauerbraten or schnitzel. Swiss-born chef Kurt Amsler's specialty is rainbow trout from a local hatchery; the servings grow larger as summer and trout progress. ■ *3251 Weirdwood Rd (5 km/3 miles west of Revelstoke on the Trans-Canada Hwy), Revelstoke; (250)837-3495; $$; full bar; AE, MC, V; local checks only; dinner Wed–Mon (closed Nov).*

The 112 Located in the Regent Inn downtown, The 112 is a unanimous favorite among locals. The masculine decor of dark cedar paneling, the historical photographs of the Revelstoke region in the 19th century, and the soft lighting blend well with the continental cuisine. Chef Peter Mueller specializes in veal dishes, but the cioppino and the lamb Provençal also come with high recommendations. The wine list has been expanded to include some French and Australian labels but still emphasizes British Columbia's own vintners. A variety of after-dinner flaming coffees are good for show but little else. ■ *112 E 1st St (at McKenzie), Revelstoke; (250)837-2107; $$; full bar; AE, DC, MC, V; no checks; lunch Mon–Fri, dinner Mon–Sat.* &

LODGINGS

3 Valley Gap Motor Inn The biggest plus about the 3 Valley Gap is that guests can stroll out the front door right onto the beach of Shuswap Lake, or into the inn's formal gardens. The season here is short, since the motel is located where deep winter snows pile up. The Trans-Canada Highway 1 flanks the motel, so ask for a room away from the road and facing the lake. Revelstoke is 19 kilometers (12 miles) west, but there's a family restaurant on-site. ■ *On Trans-Canada Hwy 1, east of Revelstoke; (250)837-2109; Box 860, Revelstoke, BC V0E 2S0; $$; AE, DIS, MC, V; no checks (closed mid-Oct to mid-Apr).* &

FIELD

LODGINGS

Emerald Lake Lodge ★★★★ In the heart of Yoho National Park, surrounded by the Rocky Mountains and stunning views, is the Emerald Lake Lodge. And a jewel it is—any time of year, you'll be well taken care of here. The complex includes 24 buildings as well as the main lodge. The lakeside buildings (12 to 15, 24 to 26, 32 and 33) have the best views; 32 and 33 offer the most privacy. The big lodge retains the feel of an old parks lodge, with wood beams and plenty of couches and chairs cozied up to big stone fireplaces. The bellmen won't let you lift a finger (except to light the match to the readied fire). Winter here is nearly as popular as summer; every room has a fireplace and twig chairs for curling up with a book on snowy days. In the clubhouse building, there's a hot tub, sauna, and exercise facility; upstairs in the main lodge is a billiards room. The dining room menu boasts plenty of wild game—medallions of venison, caribou, and buffalo—and barley soup for dinner, Alberta lake trout for breakfast. Hikers can order a sack lunch from the dining room. You're miles from anywhere, but no corners are cut.

Most people opt for horseback riding, trout fishing, canoeing, or hiking (there's a nice trail around the alpine lake as well as more serious hikes to Takakkaw Falls, one of Canada's highest waterfalls, with a free fall of more than 1,200 feet). Come winter, there's cross-country skiing. The kids will never miss the TV. ■ *In Yoho National Park, 8 km/5 miles north of the Trans-Canada Hwy (no parking at the lodge; leave the car at parking lot and call the bellhop for transport); (250) 343-6321 or (800) 663-6336; PO Box 10, Field, BC V0A 1G0; emeraldl@agt. net; $$$; full bar; AE, DC, MC, V; checks OK; breakfast, lunch, dinner every day.* &

RADIUM

The town of Radium is little more than a support system for area vacation developments—gas stations, a couple of cafes, and a string of motels that grow denser as they near Radium Hot Springs. But people don't come here for the town. Winters, two ski areas—Fairmont and Panorama—are within easy driving distance. Summers, golfing and soaking in Radium Hot Springs are the activities of choice. The town is within the boundaries of **Kootenay National Park**, which has the same mountain peaks and glaciers as Alberta's more famous Banff National Park. Kootenay is thick with hiking trails, accessible from Radium. Highway 93 through the park is closed in winter, but cross-country skiers and snowshoers can enter from the south and find plenty of ungroomed terrain.

Radium Hot Springs, on Highway 93, 3 kilometers (not quite 2 miles) from Radium Junction, (250)347-9485, makes an ideal soaking stop at the base of the Kootenay mountain range. The hot springs, open to the public year-round, are equipped with two pools: one heated, the other cooler for more athletic swimming. Unlike some hot springs, these waters are free of odorous sulphur. The water temperature varies with the season; in spring, the snowmelt cools the thermally heated springs. Those staying in Kootenay or Banff National Parks overnight need to stop at the park entrance and pay a use fee. (Bring the receipt into the hot springs resort; a $1 use fee is charged at the hot springs in addition to the entrance fees for those not staying in the park.) If you didn't pack your bathing suit, don't worry; they'll rent you one for a buck and a half. Nearby you'll find golfing, lodging, tennis, and camping; information is available from Kootenay National Park; (250)347-9615.

LODGINGS

Springs at Radium Golf Resort ★★ It's clear that golf is the show at this resort on the opposite end of town from the hot springs: nearly all the rooms look out onto fairways or greens of the two 18-hole courses. Nongolfers can play tennis, squash, or racquetball—or simply relax on their balcony or on the patio just outside the indoor swimming pool. The resort has 118 guest rooms, some of which are two-bedroom condominiums. The best lodgings of the lot, the condos and the "villas," are a vigorous walk from the dining room. The standard rooms are in separate buildings connected with covered walkways. The resort has a full-service dining room. Summers, there are places to eat (but nothing particularly recommended) in Radium, which is a 10-minute drive north. Many of the restaurants close in winter, but the resort has a bed-and-breakfast package. Golf and ski packages also available. ■ *South of Radium on Hwy 93; (250)347-9311 or (800)665-3585; Box 310, Radium Hot Springs, BC V0A 1M0; $$$; AE, DC, E, JCB, MC, V; no checks.*

Storm Mountain Lodge ★★ Although it's technically located in Banff National Park, this is the place to stay near Radium (it's owned by the people who own the Post Hotel in Lake Louise). Located on Vermilion Pass at an elevation of 5,600 feet, the lodge was built in 1922 by the Canadian Pacific Railway. It's rustic, but loaded with alpine lodge ambience. Each of the 12 single-room log cabins has a wood-burning fireplace, and bathrooms with showers were added in a remodel. In the cool main lodge, the fire's often kept blazing throughout the summer. The dining room, which serves up appropriately hearty fare, will pack a hiker's lunch, and also serves afternoon tea to those who are done for the day. Eighty kilometers (50 miles) of hiking trails originate near the lodge. True to the name, the winds howl across Storm Mountain (and Vermilion Pass) late into the spring and early in the fall, so the beds come with down comforters. No wonder this remote place is open only from late May to early September. (We've heard that the lodge plans to winterize, though, so stay tuned.) ■ *At Vermilion Pass on Hwy 93; (403) 762-4155; PO Box 670, Banff, AB T0L 0C0; $$$; AE, MC, V; no checks.*

INVERMERE

RESTAURANTS

Strand's Old House ★★ Built in 1912 by pioneer Alexander Ritchie, this house has been converted to an idyllic setting for some of the finest dining in eastern British Columbia. Beyond the yard lined with beech trees are gardens with views to the mountains. Chef Tony Wood makes everything from scratch, right down to the mayonnaise served with the steamed artichokes. The elaborate leather-bound menu features page after page of outstanding appetizers and entrees. A cold, spicy avocado soup is a fresh starter; follow it with a well-prepared veal steak with a morel mushroom sauce or an exceptional creamy chicken Oscar, stuffed with crab. Regional wines and beers add gusto to occasional evenings of live music. Be sure to make reservations. ■ *818 12th St (in the middle of town), Invermere; (250) 342-6344; $$; full bar; AE, DC, MC, V; no checks; dinner every day (closed Sun–Mon in Nov some years—call ahead).*

LODGINGS

Panorama Resort ★ More than a resort, Panorama is its own village—a sprawling establishment in the Purcell Mountains that contains a seven-lift ski area, condos, a hotel (even kennels for your dog), lots of restaurants and nightspots, and outdoor recreation aplenty. Eight well-maintained tennis courts, horses, hiking trails, and river rafting on Toby Creek relieve the resort from dependence on the winter ski trade. But ski season is still the time to go. The snow is deep, white powder (World Cup competitions have been held here), and if nature doesn't dispense the white stuff, machines will. We recommend the condos rather than the hotel units: they're more expensive, but they all have kitchens. Wherever you stay, you're never more than a five-minute walk from the chairlifts. ■ *18 km (11 miles) west of Invermere on Toby Creek Rd; (250) 342-6941 or (800) 663-2929; PO Box 7000, Invermere, BC V0A 1T0; www.panorama resort.com; $$; AE, DC, MC, V; checks OK.*

KIMBERLEY

Like many foundering mining towns in the early 1970s, Kimberley looked to tourism (and chose a Bavarian theme) to bolster a faltering economy. At 4,000 feet, Kimberley is the highest incorporated city in Canada. Views of the snowcapped Rocky Mountains are stunning, especially from the Kimberley Ski Resort, with more than 30 downhill runs. There are 26 kilometers of Nordic trails; 3 kilometers are lighted at night.

The town was named in 1896 after Kimberley, South Africa, because of a rich outcrop of minerals at the Sullivan Mine. Now owned by Cominco Ltd., **Sullivan Mine** is one of the largest lead, zinc, and silver mines in the world. It once employed 1,200; now half that many work there (the town's population is 6,700). The mountainside was initially mined as an open pit, and even though the pit has been filled in, it remains as an ugly scar. Ore is now mined 2 miles deep into the mountain and carried by railcar to the Cominco smelter in Trail, BC.

Gardeners shouldn't miss the teahouse, greenhouse, and immaculately kept gardens, once maintained by Cominco and now under the care of the city, on the grounds of the Kimberly District Hospital.

The Heritage Museum, 105 Spokane Street, (250) 427-7510, has an excellent display of the town's mining history and memorabilia, such as hockey equipment from the town team that won the World Senior Amateur Hockey Championships in 1937. Accordion music is played on loudspeakers at the center of the **Bavarian Platzl** (the town's three-block walking street). For a quarter, a yodeling puppet pops out of the upper window of Canada's largest cuckoo clock. For a nice selection of regional books, try **Bookends,** 100 Deer Park Avenue, (250) 427-2500. The **Bauerhaus Restaurant,** 280 Norton Avenue, (250) 427-5133, has an outstanding view of the mountains; however, the well-regarded restaurant, dismantled in Austria and reconstructed here, is open only during ski season and in the height of summer.

RESTAURANTS

Chef Bernard's Kitchen ★ Originally a fresh-pasta eatery, Chef Bernard's also dishes up Lousiana specialties such as blackened catfish fillet and Gulf shrimp étouffée. The steaks are named for celebrities: the Paul Newman steak is served with Atlantic scallops in cream and brandy, the Chi Chi Rodriguez steak is served with smoked salmon in cream and Chablis. Nice tries; but the fresh pasta's the thing here. Try it with gingered chicken or the rainbow trout. An impressive German and Austrian wine list. ■ *170 Spokane St (on the Bavarian Platzl), Kimberley; (250) 427-4820; $$; full bar; AE, DC, MC, V; checks OK; lunch Mon–Sat, dinner every day (breakfast, lunch, dinner every day in summer).*

The Snowdrift Cafe The local hangout for the young sporting crowd, this small eatery located in a 100-year-old converted house boasts plenty of healthful foods: homemade whole-wheat bread and muffins, vegetarian chili, spinach and caesar salads, a good carbo-loading lasagne for avid skiers and cyclers. The

Hungarian mushroom soup, flavored with dill and filled with mushrooms, comes with thick slices of the whole-wheat bread. Locals claim this cafe has the best coffee and cheesecake in the Kootenays. ■ *110 Spokane St (on the Bavarian Platzl), Kimberley; (250) 427-2001; $; beer and wine; no credit cards; checks OK; lunch, dinner every day.*

LODGINGS

Inn West/Kirkwood Inn ★ Five kilometers (3 miles) from Kimberley, adjacent to the ski and summer resort, is the Inn West/Kirkwood Inn. There are hotel rooms (Inn West), but we suggest opting for a condo instead. The condos (Kirkwood Inn) have kitchens and fireplaces; they also have access to laundry facilities and sauna, hot tub, and swimming pool (seasonal), and the balconies have views of the Rockies (although the views are through the trees in front of some). The trailhead of the Nordic ski-trail system is across the parking lot, and the ski lift at the downhill area is only a block away. ■ *840 North Star Dr (at the top of the hill at Kimberley Ski Resort); (250) 427-7616 or (800) 663-4755; PO Box 247, Kimberley, BC V1A 2Y6; $$$; AE, DIS, MC, V; checks OK.* &

BOSWELL

LODGINGS

Destiny Bay Resort ★★ German-born Rolf and Hanna Langerfeld brought a bit of Europe to the little town of Boswell on Kootenay Lake. You stay in one of the five sod-roofed cabins or in one of the suites in the lodge. Tall pines screen the lake view from the decks, and the road is a tad too close for such a remote place, but we don't mind the absence of TVs or phones. The reasonably priced restaurant offers some of the best food for miles. On sunny days the wraparound deck on the second floor is the spot—for seafood to schnitzels to herring salads, and for the view. ■ *11935 Hwy 3A (40 minutes from Creston), Box 6, Boswell, BC V0B 1A0; (250) 223-8455 or (800) 818-6633; $$; beer and wine; MC, V; no checks; breakfast, dinner every day (closed Nov–Mar).*

CRAWFORD BAY

The tiny community of Crawford Bay, accessible via an hour's ferry ride from Balfour (32 kilometers or 19 miles east of Nelson), happens to be the home of one of British Columbia's finest golf courses, **Kokanee Springs Golf Course**; (250) 227-9226. Just up from the ferry dock is **La Chance Swiss Restaurant**, (250) 227-9477, a local hangout with a menu that leans toward Swiss and German fare; it's open April through October.

Wedgwood Manor ★★ On 50 acres that tilt westward toward the Purcell Mountains, this lovely 1910 board-and-batten-style house is one of the finest lodgings in southeastern British Columbia. Downstairs there's a dining room and a parlor with a fireplace (where afternoon tea is served). There are six rooms (all with baths en suite). The four spacious upstairs rooms open onto a quiet, comfortable reading room; the Charles Darwin Room and the Commander's Room get most of the afternoon sun. The room off the parlor is too tiny, but it has a big view of the garden from the double bed. In summer the large front porch is a very pleasant spot from which to gaze out over the big lawn and flower gardens to the Kokanee Glacier across the lake. The owners have taken over the former servants' quarters next door, so the house is entirely yours, so to speak. ■ *16002 Crawford Creek Rd (east of Nelson on Hwy 3A, take Balfour ferry to Kootenay Bay and head south), Crawford Bay; (250) 227-9233 or (800) 862-0022; PO Box 135, Crawford Bay, BC V0B 1E0; $$; MC, V; checks OK (open Apr to mid-Oct).*

SILVERTON

LODGINGS

Silverton Resort ★ You'll be pleased with this little resort in the heart of Hidden Valley. Bill and Lorraine Landers's cabins on the shores of Slocan Lake are a great place if you like water play; bring your own canoe, windsurfer, or rowboat, or rent theirs. There are a couple of mountain bikes available too. You stay in one of the five hemlock-log cabins—all spotlessly clean and simple and each named after a mythological hero. Some have sleeping lofts; all have kitchens and south-facing decks. They're all at the water's edge (though not far from the road), but Thor 4 is our favorite. A lakefront resort backed by a glacier in Valhalla Provincial Park—ahhh. ■ *Lake Ave (on the lakeshore), Silverton; (250) 358-7157; Box 107, Silverton, BC V0G 2B0; $$; MC, V; checks OK.*

NELSON

Nestled in a valley on the shore of Kootenay Lake, Nelson sprang up with the silver and gold mining boom back in the late 1890s and has retained its Victorian character. Its main street has changed little in a century, luring more than one filmmaker to use its downtown as a set. More than 350 heritage sites are listed in this picturesque city of about 10,000 people. For the best overall view of Nelson, stroll to the vista point through **Gyro Park**, on the hillside just north of the town center. The park has picturesque gardens and a nice wading pool for children. An interesting pictorial exhibit of the region's history can be seen at the **Nelson Museum,**

402 Anderson St, (250)352-9813, which is open year-round. The mountains surrounding Nelson are a mecca for hikers, backcountry skiers, and sightseers; a popular destination is **Kokanee Glacier Provincial Park**, 29 kilometers (18 miles) northeast of Nelson (Ministry of Parks, RR 3, Nelson, BC V1L 5P6; (250)825-3500).

Shopping. Nelson has raised afternoon browsing to a fine art. In addition to the many galleries, there are a plethora of other interesting shops in the downtown area. Outdoor enthusiasts should stop in at Snowpack, 333 Baker Street; (250)352-6411. For art and crafts by some of the many regionally based artists, visit the Craft Connection, 441 Baker Street; (250)352-3006. The Kootenay Baker, 295 Baker Street, (250)352-2274, boasts one of the best selections of health foods in the region, including organic baked goods.

Art. The art shows and theater brought into Nelson by the town's arts council are well selected. From theatrical productions to wildlife lectures to classical guitarists to nationally known folk-rock groups, there's almost always something going on at the Capitol Theatre; (250)352-6363. From June through August the entire town turns into an art gallery, with artists' work exhibited in almost 20 shops, restaurants, and galleries. Pick up a map of Artwalk Gallery Tours at the Tourist Information Bureau (225 Hall Street, (250)352-3433), or contact Artwalk (Box 422, Nelson, BC V1L 5R2; (250)352-2402). For a calendar of weekly events, pick up a free copy of the *Kootenay Weekly Express*, distributed at local businesses around town.

Skiing. The small local ski area, Whitewater, provides some of the best (and deepest) powder in the lower Kootenays. There are only three chairs, with a high percentage of expert runs; call (250)354-4944 for information or (250)352-7669 for the 24-hour snow report. Good cross-country ski trails begin at the base of Mount Ymir, where the road to Whitewater leaves the highway.

A scenic day trip through sleepy villages follows Highways 31, 31A, and 6, then loops back into Nelson. On the way, take the two-hour (round-trip) **Balfour ferry** across Kootenay Lake to Crawford Bay. It's a pretty trip and happens to be the world's longest free ferry ride. Don't miss **Ainsworth Hot Springs**, (250)229-4212, where for $6 you can explore caves of piping-hot (112°F), waist-deep water, or swim in the slightly cooler pool (open 365 days a year). The restaurant here offers a stunning view of Kootenay Lake. Tour the SS *Moyie*, (250)353-2525, a stern-wheeler that plied the waters of Kootenay Lake from 1898 until 1957; open summers only, hours vary.

RESTAURANTS

Fiddler's Green ★★ Summer dining is best. But regardless of the season, this is Nelson's favorite spot for a special-occasion dinner. Locals quibble over whether the food is really the best in town, but they agree unanimously that this old estate house has the best atmosphere—and the only garden dining. There are three intimate dining rooms and one larger area (if the season calls for inside dining, ask to sit next to the fireplace). The focus is definitely not on the food—but sometimes, when you're seated next to the fireplace (or at Sunday brunch in the summer garden), the conversation flows, regardless of occasionally inconsistent food preparation. ■ *Lower 6 Mile Rd (on the north lakeshore, 9½ km/6 miles north of town), Nelson; (250)825-4466; $$; full bar; MC, V; local checks only; dinner every day (July–Dec), Fri–Sun (Jan–June), brunch Sun.*

Book Garden Cafe Cafe fare and books just seem to go together naturally, and this bookstore-eatery combination is no exception. You can always get a fresh salad here; on hot summer days, we recommend the caesar, fresh lemonade, and dessert. The northside parking lot has become an outdoor eating area, where containers filled with blooms help soften the concrete look. Inside during winter, the cafe's a perfect place to while away the hours with a good book. The number of books about the Kootenays available here is impressive. ■ *556 Josephine St (1 block up the hill from Baker St), Nelson; (250)352-1812; $; beer and wine; MC, V; checks OK; breakfast, lunch every day, brunch Sun.*

LODGINGS

Willow Point Lodge ★★ You'll feel quite welcome in Anni Muhlegg and Florent Barille's large, rambling 1922 Victorian perched on a hill amid 3½ spacious acres. The living room has a large stone fireplace. Of the six guest rooms, the spacious Green Room is our favorite: it sports a large, private, covered balcony looking out toward the Selkirk Mountains and Kootenay Lake. Breakfast is up whenever you are. ■ *Taylor Dr (4 km/2½ miles north of Nelson on Hwy 3A over Nelson Bridge to Taylor); (250)825-9411 or (800)949-2211; mail: RR1, S-21, C-31, Nelson, BC V1L 5P4; $$; MC, V; local checks only.*

Emory House ★ A pretty Arts and Crafts–style cottage at the north edge of downtown, the Emory House is perfectly situated for those who want to explore Nelson on foot. Fans of the Arts and Crafts style will appreciate the beautifully preseved hardwood floors, woodwork, and built-in dining buffet. Opt for the rooms that overlook the lake rather than the busy street— the home is adjacent to the Civic Centre. (Two rooms have private baths; two share a bath.) Because owner Mark Giffin (who shares responsibilities with co-owner Janeen Mather) is a former chef, breakfast is an event that might include a banana-walnut Belgian waffle, or an omelet with Gouda, sun-dried tomatoes, and herbs and edible flowers fresh from the garden (in season, of course). ■ *811 Vernon St (at the north end of Vernon St, downtown), Nelson, BC V1L 4G3; (250)352-7007; $$; MC, V; checks OK.*

Inn the Garden ★ Toronto expatriates Lynda Stevens and Jerry Van Veen bought this Victorian (only a couple of blocks from downtown) and decorated it in a garden theme. In Toronto she was a genetics teacher, he was a graphic artist. Of the six guest rooms, three have views of the lake; the Tamarack Suite is a two-bedroom suite. The garden itself is the place for relaxing over afternoon tea, and perhaps for breakfast. ■ *408 Victoria St (1 block south of Baker St between Stanley and Ward), Nelson, BC V1L 4K5; (250)352-3226; $$$; AE, MC, V; checks OK.*

KASLO

RESTAURANTS

The Rosewood Cafe The Rosewood draws clientele from as far away as New Denver (a 40-minute drive) and Spokane, Washington. Decor is casual and prices reasonable, but the menu is ambitious, especially for the eastern reaches of British Columbia. Appetizers include calamari, Camembert fondue, and French onion soup with three cheeses; entrees range from blackened redfish to tortellini in curry sauce. Everything is homemade, including breads and great desserts. There's a nice kids menu, too. ■ *1435 Kaslo (at the end of the main street), Kaslo; (250)353-7673; $; full bar; MC, V; local checks only; lunch, dinner every day, brunch Sun (closed Mon in winter).* ♿

NEW DENVER

This former mining town is now noted mainly for its spectacular location on Slocan Lake, with the peaks of the Valhalla Mountains rising more than 7,000 feet on the opposite shore. During World War II, New Denver was the site of an internment camp that housed some 2,000 Japanese-Canadians displaced from their West Coast homes. This shameful period of history has been commemorated with the **Nikkei Internment Memorial Centre**, on Josephine Street off Third Avenue, (250)358-2663; the center is open during the summer only, off-season by appointment. For such a small town, New Denver has a fine bookstore: **The Motherlode**, 317 Sixth Avenue; (250)358-7274.

LODGINGS

Sweet Dreams Guesthouse The old Craftsman-style former municipal building across the street from Slocan Lake has been renovated and transformed into a delightful B&B comfortably decorated with pine wainscoting and wicker furniture. All five rooms share the four bathrooms; room 4 upstairs has the best view of the lake and the breathtaking peaks of the Valhallas beyond. Breakfast is so big it's served in the former courtroom.

Lunch is served summers on the patio, and dinner is served year-round. All three meals are open to the public by reservation. ■ *702 Eldorado Ave (1 block off the main street, across from the lake), New Denver; (250)358-2415; PO Box 177, New Denver, BC V0G 1S0; $-$$; beer and wine; MC, V; checks OK.*

ROSSLAND

This 1890s Gold Rush town has experienced a second boom recently. This time the gold is not in Red Mountain, but on it. **Red Mountain Ski Area**, 5½ kilometers (3 miles) southwest of town, is one of the more challenging ski areas in British Columbia, with runs steep enough to keep even the most adventurous skiers alert; (250)362-7700 or (800)663-0105, or call (250)362-5500 for snow conditions. There are over 40 kilometers of cross-country ski trails (about half are groomed); for information, call Black Jack Cross-Country Ski Club, (250)362-5811.

In the summer, the colorful turn-of-the-century main street of tiny Rossland bustles with hikers bound for alpine lakes, mountain bikers en route to explore the numerous trails, or visitors seeking scenery. **Gold Rush Books and Espresso**, 2063 Washington Street, (250)362-5333, is a good place to linger over a latte and a good book. For something a little stiffer, stop by the **Flying Steamshovel Inn and Onlywell Pub**, 2003 Second Avenue, (250)362-7323, a favorite local watering hole named after the unfortunate fellow who piloted—and then crashed—the first helicopter in North America.

Tour the fascinating **Le Roi Gold Mine**, Canada's only hard-rock gold mine open to the public. It's not just another roadside attraction (open May through September); (250)362-7722.

RESTAURANTS

Elmer's Corner The namesake of its elderly landlord, Elmer's Corner is run by two women from Quebec City, who missed the cafes there. Since opening , Elmer's has won over locals with its funky atmosphere, homemade breads, and mostly (but not all) vegetarian entrees. The thin-crust pizzas are excellent; the desserts are not. ■ *1999 2nd Ave (2 blocks up from Columbia, on Washington), Rossland; (250)362-5266; $; MC, V; local checks only; lunch, dinner every day (dinner only every day in winter).*

Sunshine Cafe Virtually anybody will feel a bit of shine in Rossland's favorite little cafe, which features a range of internationally inspired foods. Sit in the front of the restaurant or walk past the kitchen to the back room. The food doesn't try to be fancy, just good, and there's lots of it. You'll do well to start with the Malaysian egg rolls (ground beef, coconut, and spices) dipped in a plum sauce, and then go on to one of the Mexican dishes, the Budgie Burger (boneless breast of chicken with ham and Swiss), or a simple entree such as the curried chicken. Huevos rancheros are a favorite of the breakfast crowd. Mealtimes are crowded, and during ski season, weekend reservations are recommended. No smoking. ■ *2116 Columbia Ave (in the middle of town on the main street), Rossland; (250) 362-7630; $; beer and wine; MC, V; local checks only; breakfast, lunch, dinner every day.*

LODGINGS

Ram's Head Inn ★★ Second-generation owners Tauna and Greg Butler run this comfortable nonsmoking inn, which is the choice place to stay in this mountainous part of the province: it's just a few hundred yards' walk to the Red Mountain ski area. Of 12 rooms, the 4 in the addition are the plushest. Still, it's the comfortable public room that's best, with a lofty ceiling, a stone fireplace, and big windows looking out to the wooded backyard. Package deals combine lift tickets with a bed and a full breakfast, not to mention the hot tub and sauna. ■ *Red Mountain Rd (at the base of Red Mountain, 3 km/2 miles north of town), Rossland; (250) 362-9577; Box 636, Rossland, BC V0G 1Y0; $$-$$$; AE, DIS, MC, V; checks OK.*

Angela's Place British transplant Angela Wright "guarantees" her accommodations. They're casual and fun, as they should be in this ski town. If you stay downstairs in the apartment with the fireplace, Wright will serve up a delicious skier's breakfast in her breakfast nook, meanwhile entertaining you with her British humor. If she likes you and isn't rushing out to the slopes herself, she might make you breakfast even if you stay in the upstairs suite, which has its own kitchen. The outdoor tub is for all guests. Prices are also flexible; she uses an honor-system sliding scale. This is a ski season–only place; Wright heads for the coast in the summers. ■ *1520 Spokane St (4 blocks down the hill from the Uplander Hotel), Rossland; (250) 362-7790; Box 944, Rossland, BC V0G 1Y0; $-$$; no credit cards; checks OK (closed summers).*

Index

We Stand By Our Reviews

Sasquatch Books is proud of *Northwest Best Places*. Our editors and contributors go to great lengths and expense to see that all of the reviews are as accurate, up-to-date, and honest as possible. If we have disappointed you, please accept our apologies; however, if a recommendation in this 12th edition of *Northwest Best Places* has seriously misled you, Sasquatch Books would like to refund your purchase price. To receive your refund:

1) Tell us where you purchased your book and return the book and the book-purchase receipt to the address below.

2) Enclose the original hotel or restaurant receipt from the establishment in question, including date of visit.

3) Write a full explanation of your stay or meal and how *Northwest Best Places* specifically misled you.

4) Include your name, address, and phone number.

Refund is valid only while the 12th edition of *Northwest Best Places* is in print. If the ownership, management, or chef has changed since publication, Sasquatch Books cannot be held responsible. Postage and tax on the returned book is your responsibility. Please allow six to eight weeks for processing.

Please address to Satisfaction Guaranteed, *Northwest Best Places*, and send to:

Sasquatch Books
615 Second Avenue, Suite 260
Seattle, WA 98104

Northwest Best Places
REPORT FORM

Based on my personal experience, I wish to nominate the following restaurant or place of lodging as a "Best Place"; or confirm/correct/disagree with the current review.

_____

_____

_____

_____

_____

(Please include address and telephone number of establishment, if convenient.)

REPORT:

(Please describe food, service, style, comfort, value, date of visit, and other aspects of your experience; continue on the other side if necessary.)

_____

_____

_____

_____

_____

_____

_____

I am not concerned, directly or indirectly, with the management or ownership of this establishment.

Signed _____

Address _____

_____

Phone Number _____

Date _____

Please address to _Northwest Best Places_ and send to:
Sasquatch Books
615 Second Avenue, Suite 260
Seattle, WA 98104
Feel free to email feedback as well: books@sasquatchbooks.com